D1027805

Changing Their Minds?

Changing Their Minds?

Donald Trump and Presidential Leadership

GEORGE C. EDWARDS III

UNIVERSITY OF CHICAGO PRESS   CHICAGO AND LONDON

The University of Chicago Press, Chicago 60637
The University of Chicago Press, Ltd., London
© 2021 by The University of Chicago
All rights reserved. No part of this book may be used or reproduced in any manner
whatsoever without written permission, except in the case of brief quotations in critical
articles and reviews. For more information, contact the University of Chicago Press,
1427 E. 60th St., Chicago, IL 60637.
Published 2021
Printed in the United States of America

30 29 28 27 26 25 24 23 22 21   1 2 3 4 5

ISBN-13: 978-0-226-77550-0 (cloth)
ISBN-13: 978-0-226-77581-4 (paper)
ISBN-13: 978-0-226-77564-7 (e-book)
doi: https://doi.org/10.7208/chicago/9780226775647.001.0001

Library of Congress Cataloging-in-Publication Data

Names: Edwards, George C., author.
Title: Changing their minds? : Donald Trump and presidential leadership /
    George C. Edwards III.
Description: Chicago : University of Chicago Press, 2021. | Includes bibliographical
    references and index.
Identifiers: LCCN 2020043067 | ISBN 9780226775500 (cloth) | ISBN 9780226775814
    (paperback) | ISBN 9780226775647 (ebook)
Subjects: LCSH: Trump, Donald, 1946– | Presidents—United States. |
    Political leadership—United States. | Executive power—United States. |
    Executive-legislative relations—United States.
Classification: LCC E913 .E39 2021 | DDC 973.933092—dc23
LC record available at https://lccn.loc.gov/2020043067

∞ This paper meets the requirements of ANSI/NISO Z39.48-1992 (Permanence of Paper).

TO CARMELLA —
WHOM I ADORE

Contents

Preface

In December 2016, a month before Donald Trump took office, I wrote a piece for the *Washington Post* predicting that despite his talent for self-promotion, the new president would not succeed in persuading the public to support his policies. His base, approximately 40 percent of the public, would stand by him, but those less inclined to agree with him would not.[1] In other venues, I also predicted the president would not succeed in winning support for his legislative program despite his extensive experience as a negotiator.

Why did I reach these conclusions, even before Trump's inauguration? My predictions were based on two pillars. First, an analysis of the president's strategic position revealed that there was little potential for creating opportunities for policy change. Neither the public nor Congress was open to persuasion. Second, presidents, no matter how politically skilled, cannot overcome their strategic positions. They cannot create opportunities for change. Instead, they are dependent on the opportunities already present in their environments.

I have fleshed out this argument in a series of books, articles, and essays.[2] Donald Trump provides a fascinating test of my theory of presidential leadership, one I could not pass up. In this volume, I seek to explain the president's level of leadership success, first by focusing on the possibilities of success in his environment and, second by carefully examining his performance in office. I find that Trump, like all other presidents, well illustrates the impact of the context in which he is attempting to govern and the limitations of attempts at persuasion. I also conclude that the president was ineffective as a leader and failed to take advantage of the opportunities he did have.

Special thanks go to Chuck Myers, one of the best editors in the business with whom it is a pleasure to work. Mary Tong did a fine job as copy editor and Mary Corrado efficiently guided the book through the production process. Alicia Sparrow did an excellent job on manuscript preparation. I am grateful to them all. I am also indebted to Nuffield College at Oxford and the Department of Political Science at Texas A&M University for providing supportive research environments. For parts of this book, I relied heavily on data from the Roper Center for Public Opinion Research at Cornell, a great national resource. My greatest debt, as always, is to my wife, Carmella, who creates the conditions conducive to writing and who makes all the effort worthwhile.

CHAPTER ONE

Trump as a Test

Much to the surprise of most political commentators and even the candidate himself, Donald Trump was elected president of the United States. The New York real estate mogul ran an unusual campaign and possessed a unique background for a chief executive. He was a true *nonpareil*. No one has ever arrived at the presidency with so little experience in politics, government, or the military. He never served in any public office and was poorly informed about issues. Nevertheless, he took the oath of office as president on January 20, 2017.

Trump provides an intriguing case for the study of presidential leadership. Despite his lack of conventional credentials for the presidency, he came to the White House with two sets of skills that seemed relevant to leading the people and their government. First, he possessed well-honed promotional talents, abilities sharpened over a lifetime of marketing himself and his brand, including a stint as a successful reality television star. Second, Trump boasted of being an able negotiator. Announcing his candidacy for the presidency on June 16, 2015, he proclaimed, "If you can't make a good deal with a politician, then there's something wrong with you. You're certainly not very good. And that's what we have representing us. They will never make America great again. They don't even have a chance . . . our country needs a truly great leader now. We need a leader that wrote *The Art of the Deal*."[1] Thus, the future president claimed that he was uniquely qualified to lead the country, unite the public, and overcome gridlock in Congress.

To accomplish these goals would require successful persuasion. Was this talented self-promoter able to win public support for his initiatives? Was this experienced negotiator able to overcome polarization in Congress and obtain agreement on his proposals? Was Donald Trump an effective leader?

Answering these questions is the focus of this book. First, however, we need to clarify some key concepts.

Leadership

Leadership may be the most commonly employed idea in politics. Yet it is an elusive concept. According to James MacGregor Burns, "Leadership is one of the most observed and least understood phenomena on earth."[2] Writers and commentators employ the term "leadership" to mean just about everything a person who occupies what we often refer to as "a position of leadership" does—or should do.

When we define a term so broadly, however, it loses its utility. The Constitution and federal laws invest significant discretionary authority in the president. Making decisions, issuing commands, and implementing policy are important, and doing them well requires courage, wisdom, and skill. At times, the exercise of unilateral authority may result in historic changes in the politics and policy of the country.

In the extreme case, the president can launch a nuclear attack at his discretion. The consequences would be vast. Most people would not view such an act as one of leadership, however. In exercising discretionary authority, the president, in effect, acts alone. It is not necessary for him to *lead* anyone to do something. At its core, decision-making represents a different dimension of the job of the chief executive than obtaining the support of others.

An important element of a chief executive's job may be creating the organizational and personal conditions that promote innovative thinking, the frank and open presentation and analysis of alternatives, and effective implementation of decisions by advisors and members of the bureaucracy. We may reasonably view such actions as a form of leadership, and there is no doubt that the processes of decision-making and policy implementation are critical to governing. In this volume, however, I focus on the leadership of those who are not directly on the president's team—the public and Congress—and who are thus less obligated to support his initiatives. Presidents invest a substantial portion of their time working on these tasks, and the success of their efforts has significant consequences for public policy.

It is important for all of us to understand how successful presidents actually lead. What are the essential presidential leadership skills? Under what conditions are they most effective? How can these skills contribute to engendering change? The answers to these questions should influence presidents' efforts to govern, the focus of scholarly research and journalistic coverage, and the expectations and evaluations of citizens. Thus, we seek a better understanding of presidential leadership in order to think sensibly about the role of the chief executive in the nation's political system.

Persuasion and Presidential Power

A second key concept is persuasion. In broad terms, persuasion refers to causing others to do something by reasoning, urging, or inducement. Influencing others is central to the conception of leadership of most political scientists. Scholars of the presidency want to know whether the chief executive can affect the output of government by influencing the actions and attitudes of others. In a democracy, we are particularly attuned to efforts to persuade, especially when most potentially significant policy changes require the assent of multiple power holders.

The best-known dictum regarding the American presidency is that "presidential power is the power to persuade,"[3] the felicitous phrase that captures the essence of Richard Neustadt's argument in *Presidential Power*. For three generations, scholars and students—and many presidents—have viewed the presidency through the lens of Richard Neustadt's core premise. Unfortunately, they have frequently misunderstood his argument.

Neustadt's first point was that presidents are week and thus have no choice but to rely on persuasion. The subtitle of *Presidential Power* is *The Politics of Leadership*. In essence, presidential leadership is the power to persuade. As he put it, "'powers' are no guarantee of power"[4] and *"the probabilities of power do not derive from the literary theory of the Constitution."*[5] Presidents would have to struggle to get their way. Indeed, it was the inherent weakness of the presidency that made it necessary for presidents to understand how to use their resources most effectively.

What did Neustadt mean by "persuasion"? "The essence of a President's persuasive task, with congressmen and everybody else," he argued, "is to induce them to believe that what he wants of them is what their own appraisal of their own responsibilities requires them to do in their interest, not his. . . . Persuasion deals in the coin of self-interest with men who have some freedom to reject what they find counterfeit."[6] Thus, "The power to persuade is the power to bargain."[7]

In other words, the president is not likely to change many minds among those who disagree with him on substance or have little incentive to help him succeed. Although Neustadt did not focus extensively on public opinion, we can generalize beyond public officials to their constituents. His endorsement of the findings in *On Deaf Ears*[8] that presidents rarely move the public in their direction reflects his skepticism about changing public opinion.

Missing the Point

Neustadt argued, then, that presidents need to persuade—*not* that they will succeed in doing so. Many commentators—and presidents—miss this point. They suggest that all presidents have to do to obtain the support of the public or members of Congress is to reach into their inventory of leadership skills and employ the appropriate means of persuasion. Most presidents, at least at the beginning of their tenures, seem to believe they can *create* opportunities for change.

For example, public support is a key political resource, and modern presidents have typically sought it for themselves and their policies. Their goal has been to leverage public opinion to obtain backing for their proposals in Congress and, in their first term, to win reelection. It is natural for new presidents, basking in the glow of an electoral victory, to focus on creating, rather than exploiting, opportunities for change. It may seem quite reasonable for leaders who have just won the biggest prize in American politics by convincing voters and party leaders to support their candidacies to conclude that they should be able to convince members of the public and the US Congress to support their policies. Why focus on evaluating existing possibilities when you can fashion new ones?

Campaigning is different than governing, however. Campaigns focus on short-term victory, and candidates wage them in either/or terms. To win an election, a candidate need only convince voters that he or she is a better choice than the few available alternatives. In addition, someone always wins whether or not voters support the victor's policy positions.

Governing, on the other hand, involves deliberation, negotiation, and often compromise over an extended period. Moreover, in governing, the president's policy is just one of a wide range of alternatives. Furthermore, delay is a common objective—and a common outcome—in matters of public policy. Neither the public nor elected officials have to choose.

Although stalemate may sometimes be the president's goal, the White House usually wishes to convince people to support a positive action.

In sum, one should not infer from success in winning elections that the White House can persuade members of the public and Congress to change their minds and support policies they would otherwise oppose. The American political system is not a fertile field for the exercise of presidential leadership. Most political actors, from the average citizen to members of Congress, are free to choose whether to follow the chief executive's lead; the president cannot force them to act. At the same time, the sharing of powers established by the Constitution's checks and balances not only prevents the president from acting unilaterally on most important matters but also gives other power holders different perspectives on issues and policy proposals.

Thus, it is a mistake for presidents to assume they can change public opinion. There is nothing in the historical record to support such a belief, and there are long-term forces that work against presidential leadership of the public.[9] Adopting strategies for governing that are prone to failure waste rather than create opportunities,[10] so it is critically important for presidents to assess accurately the potential for obtaining public support.

Nevertheless, even experienced and successful politicians overestimate their persuasive powers. Bill Clinton's aides reported that he exhibited an "unbelievable arrogance" regarding his ability to change public opinion and felt he could "create new political capital all the time" by going public.[11] Similarly, Barack Obama believed in the power of rhetoric to rally the public on behalf of policy change. As he proclaimed while running for president in 2008,

> Don't tell me words don't matter. "I have a dream"—just words. "We hold these truths to be self-evident that all men are created equal"—just words. "We have nothing to fear but fear itself"—just words, just speeches. It's true that speeches don't solve all problems, but what is also true is that if we can't inspire our country to believe again, then it doesn't matter how many policies and plans we have, and that is why I'm running for president of the United States of America, . . . because the American people want to believe in change again. Don't tell me words don't matter![12]

It is not surprising that the president dismissed the advice of his top assistants and pursued health care reform in his first year, confident that he could win the public's support.[13]

Donald Trump wasted no time in conducting a permanent campaign for public support. Two days before his inauguration, he announced his reelection campaign slogan ("Keep America Great"). Two days later, on the day of his inauguration, Trump filed for reelection with the Federal Election Commission. Less than a month later, on February 18, 2017, he held the first of what were to be dozens of political rallies around the country.

The president's own staff may also buy into the myth of presidential persuasiveness. One White House aide recalled how a few of his colleagues considered highlighting some pages of Robert Caro's book about Lyndon Johnson as Senate majority leader and leaving it on Obama's desk. "Sometimes a president just needs to knock heads," the aide declared. As he saw it, Johnson "twisted their arm, they had no choice—he was going [to] defund them, ruin 'em, support their opponent . . . and the deal was cut."[14] The absence of evidence for this misremembered history[15] seemed to be irrelevant.

Challenging the Conventional Wisdom

Writers have long debated the "great man" interpretation of history. The two sides of this issue assumed their best-known forms in the nineteenth century. In *Heroes and Hero-Worship and the Heroic in History*, published in 1841, Thomas Carlyle argued that great men alone were responsible for the direction of history. To Carlyle, the environment of the hero was generally malleable and thus receptive to leadership.

Adopting a polar perspective, various schools of social determinists, including the Spencerians, Hegelians, and Marxists, viewed history as an inexorable and unidirectional march, with change occurring only when the culture was ripe for it. They concluded that great men could not have acted differently from the way they did. Leo Tolstoy's portrayal of Napoleon in *War and Peace* is perhaps the most memorable depiction of this interpretation.

It is common to maintain that it makes a difference who the president is. For example, commentators often offer the example of the attempted assassination of president-elect Franklin D. Roosevelt on February 15, 1933, to make the point. If anarchist Giuseppe Zangara had succeeded in assassinating Roosevelt instead of Chicago mayor Anton Cermak, they contend, the history of the United States would have been different. No doubt.

It does not follow, however, that the difference Roosevelt made lay in his ability to build supportive coalitions through persuasive leadership. The question is not whether presidents matter. Of course they do. The question is *how* they matter—how do they bring about change? To understand the nature of presidential leadership and the potential of persuasion, we must not conflate persuasion with other dimensions of the presidency, such as discretionary decision-making.[16]

In recent decades, scholars have been hard at work studying the power to persuade. They have found that institutional fundamentals, the nature of public opinion, and broader historical forces constrain presidential leadership in important arenas such as the public and Congress. An extensive body of research in political science has shown that even the most skilled presidents have great difficulty in persuading the public or members of Congress to support them.[17] Lyndon Johnson, for example, was much more constrained as president than he was as Senate majority leader.[18] Ronald Reagan was not able to lead the public to support his policies.[19] When presidents and their aides exaggerate the potential of persuasion, they are prone to overreaching, sometimes resulting in political disaster.[20]

In his important work on the *Politics Presidents Make*, Stephen Skowronek maintains that the presidency's capacity to transform American government and politics results from its blunt and disruptive effects. Andrew Jackson forced the submission of the nullifiers and undermined the Bank of the United States, Franklin Pierce deployed the resources of his office on behalf of the Kansas-Nebraska Act, and Lincoln bludgeoned the South into submission. All were transformative acts that changed the landscape of American government and politics, yet he shows that persuasion was not central to any of these actions.[21] Bruce Miroff has similarly emphasized that the context of a presidency dominates what the president can accomplish.[22]

Thus, the thrust of contemporary scholarship is that presidential leadership is *not* the power to persuade. Furthermore, I argue, because presidents are not in strong positions to create opportunities for success by persuading members of Congress or the public to change their minds about supporting White House initiatives, successful leadership is the result of recognizing and exploiting opportunities present in their political environment.[23]

Donald Trump, with his considerable public relations and negotiating skills, poses an intriguing and challenging test for my theory of presidential leadership. If he succeeded in leading the public and Congress to support his policies, it would be appropriate to revise our conclusions about the effectiveness of persuasion as a tool of leadership. Conversely, a failure to persuade will provide strong support for the view that presidential power is not the power to persuade. Moreover, analyzing his performance as a leader operating in a particular political environment provides the basis for a dispassionate evaluation of his presidency.

A Distinctive Character

Any analysis of the presidency must cope with the person occupying the office. Only forty-four individuals have served as president, and each has been a distinctive personality. From the wise and magisterial George Washington and the reflective and humble Abraham Lincoln to those marginally fit for the job, such as James Buchanan and Warren G. Harding, each president has been unique. The forty-fifth president is no exception.

Donald Trump has a distinctive personality and style and an unusual background for a chief executive. In addition to his extensive experience at self-promotion and negotiation, his many distinctive—and frequently disturbing—characteristics include his

- lack of job preparation
- routine use of hyperbole, distortion, and fabrication
- intellectual incoherence and disarray
- ignorance of policy and the functioning of government
- uninformed, impulsive, and capricious approach to decision-making
- rejection of inconvenient information
- narcissistic certitude
- belligerency and temperamental unsuitability for the presidency
- vengefulness and crude trashing of critics
- incapacity for moral and intellectual embarrassment

Much of the commentary on the Trump presidency revolves around the president's personal style and behavior. No president in modern times has adopted a decision-making style less reliant on information and more dependent on instinct. None has engaged in such coarse public discourse, had such an uneasy relationship with accuracy and the truth, and gone to such great lengths to delegitimize the opposition. By all appearances, the president's personal needs drove much of his public behavior and his approach to governing.

President Trump dramatically changed the direction of federal policy toward the environment, energy industries, immigration, health care, education, civil rights, taxation, trade, the federal workforce, and the federal court system. The president also upended agreements on climate change, arms control, and Iranian nuclear development, and he weakened long-standing international alliances. In each case, he exercised unilateral power. The question for us is whether he persuaded the public and Congress to support his initiatives.

Neustadt encourages us to focus on the strategic level of power when we examined presidential persuasion. To think strategically about power, we must search for generalizations. According to Neustadt:

> There are two ways to study "presidential power." One way is to focus on the tactics . . . of influencing certain men in given situations. . . . The other way is to step back from tactics . . . and to deal with influence in more strategic terms: what is its nature and what are its sources? . . . Strategically, [for example,] the question is not how he masters Congress in a peculiar instance, but what he does to boost his chance for mastery in any instance.[24]

An emphasis on the personal in politics, based on the assumption of the potential success of persuasion, has led some to overlook the importance of the context in which the president operates as well as his institutional setting. Doing so encourages ad hoc explanations and discourages generalizations about the strategic level of power. Reaching such generalizations should be central to our enterprise, however.

Can we reach generalizations about presidential leadership while analyzing the behavior and success of a unique personality?[25] As political scientists, can we enhance the often-insightful journalistic critiques of a particular president?

Plan of the Book

I believe we can. In chapters that follow, I engage in two analytic thrusts. First, I employ my theory of presidential leadership—that in essence the president's opportunity structure is the key to understanding it—to generate expectations of the president's success in leading the public and

Congress to support his initiatives. Moving beyond the president as an individual, the analysis of the president's strategic position, his opportunity structure, is guided by the framework I presented in *Predicting the Presidency*. I also evaluate the president's success in persuading the public and Congress and compare it to my predictions. If my hypothesizing proves to be correct, the Trump presidency will provide further evidence that presidential power is not the power to persuade and is highly dependent on an opportunity structure that is largely beyond the president's control. If Trump overcame the constraints of his strategic position, it will be appropriate to reexamine the theory.

I have also argued that because presidents are not in strong positions to create opportunities for success by persuading members of Congress or the public to change their minds about supporting White House initiatives, successful leadership is the result of recognizing and exploiting opportunities present in their political environment.[26] Here is where we can focus on the president as an individual. Thus, the second analytical thrust closely examines the president's efforts to lead. I offer a detailed investigation of the president's taking his case to the public and the nature and consequences of his public discourse. I also provide an in-depth treatment of Trump's relations with Congress.

Part 1 examines Trump's leadership of the public. In chapter 2, I analyze his strategic position to determine his opportunity structure and predict the likely outcome of his attempts to sway opinion. Chapter 3 explores some of the distinctive elements of the president's public outreach. In chapter 4, I examine the public's responses to the president, focusing on the key issues of the president's tenure. Finally, in chapter 5, I discuss the most prominent characteristics of the president's public discourse and their consequences for both the president's attempts at leadership and the polity as a whole.

Part 2 focuses on the president's leadership of Congress. I begin with an analysis of the president's strategic position in chapter 6. In chapter 7, I focus on the president as negotiator with the legislature, what he touted as one of his signal skills. Chapter 8 continues the analysis of his leadership style, highlighting his efforts at bipartisanship, his party leadership, and his success in winning support.

The focus of this volume is both the nature of presidential leadership and Donald Trump's performance as president. Chapter 9 sums up my findings regarding his leadership and puts them in the perspective of broader theorizing about presidential leadership.

PART I

The Promoter? Leading the Public

CHAPTER TWO

Strategic Position with the Public

Throughout his career, Donald Trump has displayed a distinctive approach to his relations with the public. As a business entrepreneur and a reality television star, he honed skills in promoting himself and his brand. He brought this proficiency to the White House, providing an excellent test of the theory of presidential leadership outlined in chapter 1. In the chapters that follow, I examine Trump's approach to leading the public and evaluate his level of success. First, however, I analyze his strategic position with the public. This analysis provides the basis for predictions for his success in obtaining public support and the fundamental explanation for it.

What was the president's opportunity structure regarding the public? What were the contours of opinion when the president took office, and what was the potential for attracting support? Ascertaining the president's strategic position with the public requires answering four key questions:

- Does the president have an electoral mandate from the voters for his policies?
- Does the public support the general direction of the president's policies?
- How polarized is public opinion?
- How malleable is public opinion?

Mandate

New presidents traditionally claim a mandate from the people, because the most effective means of setting the terms of debate and overcoming opposition is the perception of an electoral mandate, an impression that the voters want to see the winner's programs implemented. Donald Trump did not hesitate to claim his own mandate to govern.

Despite the claims of Trump and his aides, however, he did not receive a mandate. To begin, he received only 46 percent of the vote, hardly a landslide. Moreover, he did not win even a plurality of the votes, receiving nearly three million fewer votes than Hillary Clinton. Trump's party also lost six seats in the House and two in the Senate. The public was not clamoring to give him power.

In addition, preelection polls found that no candidate since 1980 had a lower percentage of voters saying they planned to cast a vote *for* their candidate. In late October, most Trump voters were voting *against* Hillary Clinton rather than for him.[1] He had the lowest feeling thermometer rating of any major party candidate in the history of the American National Election Study.[2] Immediately after the election, 43 percent of the public had a positive response, but 52 percent were upset or dissatisfied.[3]

Further undercutting any claim to a mandate was the fact that Trump did not emphasize many specific policies during the 2016 campaign—building a wall along the Mexican border and slashing corporate tax rates being the prime exceptions. Instead, he stressed general aspirations, such as making America great again or providing better and less expensive health care. Therefore, there is little evidence to support claims of a mandate for many specific policies, and his election sent no signals to members of Congress that would encourage them to achieve a consensus.

The public seemed to agree. After the election, just 29 percent said Trump had a mandate to carry out the agenda he presented during the campaign, while 59 percent thought he should compromise with Democrats when they strongly disagreed with the specifics of his policy proposals.[4] The first Gallup report on his approval found his initial rating was lower than that of any previous president. Moreover, his approval was the most polarized: 90 percent for Republicans but only 14 percent among Democrats.[5]

Support for the Direction of the President's Program

To bring about change, presidents generally require broad public support for the general direction of their initiatives. Donald Trump was highly critical of Barack Obama's policies and wished to transform them. Despite his eccentric style, Trump governed as a conservative Republican on most social and economic issues (international trade being the principal exception). From restricting funding for abortions and ending regulations

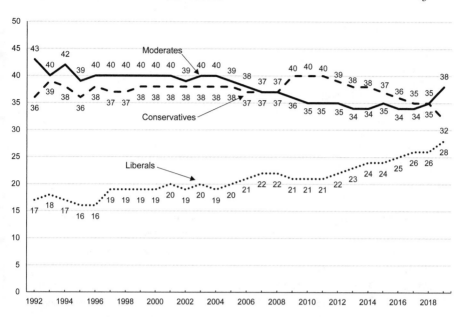

FIGURE 2.1 Self-reporting ideology of the public, as percentage. Respondents answered the following questions: "How would you describe your political views—very conservative, conservative, moderate, liberal, or very liberal?" (Gallup poll) and "How would you describe your political views—very conservative, somewhat conservative, moderate, somewhat liberal, very liberal?" (Kaiser Family Foundation poll).

Sources: Gallup polls, 1992–2018; Kaiser Family Foundation poll, 2019.

designed to protect the environment to slashing the budgets for social programs and reducing taxes, Trump was on the right.

Had the country shifted in the same direction? Not really. Although Americans have self-identified as conservative since the Gallup Poll began asking the question, the public has been moving in a more liberal direction (figure 2.1). Conservatives had a 19-point advantage over liberals in 1992, 15 points in 2008, 11 in 2016, and only 9 in 2017 and 2018. In 2017, net conservative scores had declined in all but four states over the previous decade, with eight states showing declines of 10 points or more.[6] In short, the country was trending left while the president was attempting to move policy in the opposite direction.

Although more people identified as conservative than liberal, 65 percent of the public did not. If we disaggregate the results into party groups (table 2.1), we find that only among Republicans did conservatism dominate. A clear plurality of Independents saw themselves as moderates, and

TABLE 2.1. **Ideological self-identification of party groups**

Party ID	Conservative (%)		Moderate (%)		Liberal (%)	
	2017	2018	2017	2018	2017	2018
Republican	69	73	25	22	5	4
Independent	29	28	43	45	24	22
Democrat	13	13	35	34	50	51

Note: The table shows the 2017 and 2018 averages of the answer to the question, "How would you describe your political views—very conservative, conservative, moderate, liberal, or very liberal?"
Source: Gallup polls, 2017, 2018.

fewer than 30 percent said they were conservative. We also find for the first time that half of Democrats declared themselves liberals.

The Gallup Poll also found that on social issues, 34 percent of the public identified as conservative, but 30 percent responded that they were liberal, with 34 percent reporting they were moderate. These figures reflect a notable shift to the left over the past two decades. Americans also held record liberal views on moral issues.[7] On economic issues, both Democrats and Republicans had become less conservative since the beginning of the Obama administration.[8]

Ideological identification is not determinative, of course, and there is a well-known paradox of the incongruity between ideological identification and issue attitudes.[9] Scholars have long known that only a fraction of the public exhibits the requisite traits of an "ideologue."[10] Nevertheless, many more Americans are able to choose an ideological label and use it to guide their political judgments than in previous decades.[11] Scholars have found that ideological self-placements are influential determinants of vote choice,[12] issue attitudes,[13] and views toward government spending.[14]

We can drill more deeply into general political attitudes and ask whether the public wishes to have an active or a less-active government. In most issue areas, conservatives such as Donald Trump prefer smaller, less-active government, fewer regulations, and less spending. Conservatives, of course, do seek additional restraints on some people, such as potential immigrants and those seeking abortions.

In April 2017, 57 percent of Americans said they wanted to see "government do more to solve problems and help meet the needs of people"—up seven points from 2015 and the highest percentage since the question was first asked in 1995.[15] Throughout Trump's tenure, when asked whether government should do more to solve problems or was doing too many things that should be left to others, the public clearly preferred a more activist government. Moreover, support for an activist government did not decline during Trump's tenure in office.[16]

From 2008 through 2015, a majority of the public favored smaller government providing fewer services, compared with larger government providing more services (table 2.2). When Donald Trump took office, however, opinion had changed, and slight pluralities now favored larger government (opinion evened out in 2019). There was also broad support for maintaining or increasing federal spending across a wide range of programs,[17] contrary to the president's budget proposals. Clear majorities of the public saw it as the federal government's responsibility to make sure all Americans had health care coverage.[18] Similarly, in 2018, 62 percent of the people thought the national government was doing too little to protect

TABLE 2.2. **Public support for larger government**

Date of poll	Smaller government (%)	Larger government (%)	Unsure (%)
June 12–15, 2008[a]	50	45	5
Jan. 13–16, 2009[a]	53	43	4
June 18–21, 2009[a]	54	41	4
Jan. 12–15, 2010[a]	58	38	4
Apr. 22–25, 2010[a]	56	40	4
Aug. 29–Sept. 1, 2011[a]	56	38	6
Aug. 22–25, 2012[a]	54	41	5
Sept. 4–8, 2013[b]	51	40	9
June 4–Sept. 30, 2014[b]	51	42	7
July 29–Aug. 4, 2014[c]	56	35	9
Aug. 6–10, 2014[d]	54	42	5
Sept. 2–9, 2014[b]	50	42	8
Oct. 1–6, 2014[d]	52	41	7
Feb. 6–Apr. 6, 2015[b]	52	45	3
Oct. 6–11, 2016[c]	46	42	12
Apr. 5–11, 2017[b]	45	48	6
June 27–July 9, 2017[b]	45	48	6
Apr. 25–May 1, 2018[b]	45	46	9
Mar. 20–25, 2019[b]	47	47	6
Sept. 5–16, 2019[b]	48	46	6

[a]"Generally speaking, would you say you favor smaller government with fewer services, or larger government with more services?" (ABC News poll).
[b]"If you had to choose, would you rather have a smaller government providing fewer services, or a bigger government providing more services?" (Pew Research Center poll. The question asked of half the sample of 1,501 for the April 5–11, 2017, poll).
[c]"If you had to choose, would you rather have a smaller government providing fewer services, or a bigger government providing more services?" (CBS News poll; Pew Research Center/*USA Today* poll).
[d]"If you had to choose, would you rather have a smaller government providing fewer services, or a bigger government providing more services?" (Reason Foundation, Arthur N. Rupe Foundation poll).

TABLE 2.3. **Is the government doing too much or too little?**

Category of respondent	All parties		
	Not enough (%)	Right amount (%)	Too much (%)
Older	65	27	5
Younger	51	29	13
Poor	62	19	15
Middle class	61	30	4
Wealthy	5	25	64

	Democrats		
	Not enough (%)	About right amount (%)	Too much (%)
Older	73	24	1
Younger	69	23	4
Poor	82	12	4
Middle class	70	24	2
Wealthy	4	14	77

	Republicans		
	Not enough (%)	About right amount (%)	Too much (%)
Older	58	32	8
Younger	29	36	27
Poor	36	27	33
Middle class	51	39	7
Wealthy	6	42	46

Note: Respondents answered the question, "How much help does the federal government provide to each group?"
Source: Pew Research Center poll, Jan. 10–15, 2018.

the environment, the highest percentage since 2000 (the figure was 61 percent in 2019).[19] Sixty-nine percent of the public thought the federal government was doing too little to protect water quality, 64 percent air quality, 63 percent animals and their habitats, and 57 percent national parks and nature preserves. In addition, 67 percent felt the federal government was doing too little to reduce the effects of global climate change.[20]

One year into Trump's tenure as president, the Pew Research Center asked a national sample whether government was doing too much or too little for various groups of people in society. Overall, majorities felt government was doing too little for all but the wealthy (table 2.3). Unsurprisingly, large majorities of Democrats supported government doing more for every category except the wealthy. What is more interesting is that majorities of Republicans wanted government to do more for older people and the middle class, and a plurality wanted to do more for the poor. Only one-third of Republicans thought government was doing too much for the poor, and only about one-quarter of them thought it was doing too much for the young.[21]

The public's resistance to Trump's attempts to move to the right should not be surprising, because it has a tendency to move in opposition to the ideology of the party in power. In their sweeping "macro" view of public opinion, Robert Erikson, Michael MacKuen, and James Stimson show that opinion always moves contrary to the president's position. They argue that a moderate public always gets too much liberalism from Democrats and too much conservatism from Republicans. Because public officials have policy beliefs as well as an interest in reelection, they are not likely to calibrate their policy stances exactly to match those of the public. Therefore, opinion movement is typically contrary to the ideological persuasion of presidents. Liberal presidents produce movement in the conservative direction and conservatives generate public support for more liberal policies.[22]

The public continuously adjusts its views of current policy in the direction of a long-run equilibrium path as it compares its preferences for ideal policy with its views of current policy.[23] Thus, the conservative policy period of the 1950s produced a liberal mood that resulted in the liberal policy changes of the mid-1960s. These policies in turn helped elect conservative Richard Nixon. In the late 1970s, Jimmy Carter's liberal policies paved the way for Ronald Reagan's conservative tenure, which in turn laid the foundation for Bill Clinton's more liberal stances. Negative reaction to the conservatism of George W. Bush encouraged the election of the more liberal Barack Obama. Stuart Soroka and Christopher Wlezien have reached similar conclusions with their thermostatic model of public opinion.[24]

In sum, President Trump did not take office with public opinion at his back. The country had not shifted to the right. Indeed, it had moved in the opposite direction. Similarly, people wanted government to do more to solve problems and provide services, not less. The public's views would not ease the president's burden in obtaining its support for his policies.

Partisan Polarization of the Public

Presidents rarely enjoy consensual public support, and opinion is naturally divided when the White House advocates controversial policies. In the absence of large majorities in both houses of Congress, however, enacting major changes in public policy usually requires expanding public support beyond those who identify with the president's party. The degree of partisan polarization will strongly influence the prospects of doing so.

If there is overlap between identifiers of the two parties, there may be potential for the president to reach out to the center and add to his coalition those who might be sympathetic to his policies. If adherents to the parties have distinctive views and animosity to the other party, the White House will have a much more difficult time convincing opposition party identifiers to support its initiatives.

In recent decades, there has been an increase in partisan-ideological polarization. As Americans increasingly base their party loyalties on their ideological beliefs,[25] they are less likely to hold a mix of liberal and conservative views,[26] and they align their policy preferences more closely with their core political predispositions.[27] Partisans are more likely to apply ideological labels to themselves; a declining number of them call themselves moderate (figure 2.1), and the differences in the ideological self-placements of Republicans and Democrats have grown dramatically since the 1980s. This polarization has contributed to much more ideological voting behavior.[28] Moreover, the most ideologically oriented Americans make their voices heard through greater participation in every stage of the political process.[29] They are the likeliest to vote, contribute to political campaigns, and discuss politics with others. They are also less likely to support compromise.

The Policy Divide

The policy divide between the Democratic and Republican electoral coalitions now encompasses a wide variety of issues, including both economic and social concerns.[30] The divisions between Republicans and Democrats on fundamental political values—government, race and gender, immigration, helping the needy, national security, environmental protection, and other areas—reached record levels during Barack Obama's presidency. In Donald Trump's first year as president, these gaps grew even larger. Moreover, the magnitude of these differences dwarfs other divisions in society, along such lines as gender, race and ethnicity, religious observance, or education. Pew found parties further apart than ever on most key issues (table 2.4).[31]

Since 1994, the Pew Research Center has surveyed the public on ten questions from those listed in table 2.4. In 2017, the gap between the political views of Democrats and Republicans was greater than at any point in

TABLE 2.4. **The partisan policy divide in public opinion**

	Those who agree with the issue (%)			
	2017		2019	
Issue	Democrats/ leaners	Republicans/ Leaners	Democrats/ leaners	Republicans/ leaners
The government is almost always wasteful and inefficient.	45	69	47	68

Helping the needy

The government should do more to help needy Americans even if it means going deeper into debt.	71	24	59	17
The government today cannot afford to do much more to help needy.	24	69	10	46
Poor people have hard lives because government benefits don't go far enough to help them live decently.	76	25	72	24
Poor people have it easy because they can get government benefits without doing anything in return.	18	65	74	25

Racial discrimination

The country needs to continue to make changes to give blacks equal rights with whites.	81	36	N/A	N/A
Racial discrimination is the main reason why many black people can't get ahead these days.	64	14	68	13
Blacks who cannot get ahead in this country are mostly responsible for their own condition.	28	75	N/A	N/A

continues

TABLE 2.4. (*continued*)

	Those who agree with the issue (%)			
	2017		2019	
Racial discrimination				
Affirmative action programs designed to increase the number of black and minority students on college campuses are a good thing.	84	52	N/A	N/A
Affirmative action programs designed to increase the number of black and minority students on college campuses are a bad thing.	10	39	N/A	N/A
Gender discrimination				
Obstacles that once made it harder for women to get ahead are largely gone.	25	63	23	66
Significant obstacles still make it harder for women to get ahead.	73	34	77	33
Immigration				
Immigrants strengthen the country with their work and talents.	84	42	79	39
Immigrants are a burden on our country because they take our jobs, housing, and health care.	12	44	19	58
Regulation				
Government regulation of business is necessary to protect the public interest.	66	31	75	38
Government regulation of business usually does more harm than good.	30	63	61	23
Homosexuality				
Homosexuality should be accepted by society.	83	54	81	48

TABLE 2.4. (*continued*)

	Those who agree with the issue (%)		
	2017		2019

Economy

	2017		2019	
The economic system in this country is generally fair to most Americans.	17	50	12	50
The economic system in this country unfairly favors powerful interests.	82	46	86	50
Most people can make it if they are willing to work hard.	49	77	45	78
Hard work and determination is no guarantee of success for most people.	49	20	54	22
Most corporations make a fair and reasonable profit.	24	52	18	50
Most corporations make too much profit.	73	43	80	48

Environment

	2017		2019	
There is solid evidence that the average temperature on Earth has been getting warmer.	92	52	89	45
There is solid evidence of global warming caused by human activity.	78	24	77	23
Stricter environmental laws and regulations are worth the cost.	77	36	85	43
Stricter environmental laws and regulations cost too many jobs and hurt the economy.	20	58	55	14

International trade

	2017		2019	
US involvement in the global economy is a good thing.	70	60	76	71

continues

TABLE 2.4. (*continued*)

	Those who agree with the issue (%)			
	2017		2019	
Foreign affairs				
It is best for the future of our country to be active in world affairs.	56	39	62	45
We should pay less attention to problems overseas and concentrate on problems here at home.	39	54	54	38
The US should follow its own national interests.	22	54	15	48
The US should take into account the interests of its allies.	74	41	83	48
National security				
The best way to ensure peace is through military strength.	13	53	9	46
Good diplomacy is the best way to achieve peace.	83	33	90	53

Source: Pew Research Center polls, June 8–18, 2017, June 27–July 9, 2017, and Sept. 3–15, 2019.

the time series. On average, there was a difference of 36 percentage points between Democrats and Republicans across these questions. Overall, the median Republican was more conservative than 97 percent of Democrats, and the median Democrat was more liberal than 95 percent of Republicans.[32] By 2019, the partisan gap had increased to 39 percentage points.[33]

Larry Bartels has also found that Democrats and Republicans sharply disagree about what politics is about, with Democrats mostly focused on role of government and Republicans mostly focused on cultural concerns. He suggests that it may be even more difficult to bridge this disagreement than differences over specific issues or values.[34]

Affective Polarization

An important component of partisan polarization is the intense animosity party identifiers feel toward members of the other party. Scholars term this hostility "affective polarization." In 2018, large majorities of both parties thought that the members of the opposing party rarely or never had the best interests of the country at heart and constituted a least a somewhat serious threat to the country and its people.[35] It is not surprising that partisan loyalty and dislike of the opposing party and its candidates were more important than policies in determining voters' choices in that year's midterm elections.[36]

Significant percentages of the public view members of the opposition party in a negative light,[37] including being close-minded, immoral, lazy, dishonest, unpatriotic, and even unintelligent (table 2.5). People are less likely to defer to the leader of a party whose members they view as dishonest and immoral. Demeaning and delegitimizing partisan opponents by attributing the worst characteristics and motivations to them encourages resistance to that party's overtures and helps partisans rationalize nearly any transgression by leaders of their own party.

Members of each party also tend to see the other party as ideologically extreme,[38] and people tend to overestimate considerably the extent to which party supporters belong to party-stereotypical groups. For instance, Republicans thought that 38 percent of Democrats were LGBT (versus 6 percent in reality), and Democrats thought 44 percent of Republicans earned over $250,000 per year (versus 2 percent in reality).[39]

A related element of affective polarization is antipathy toward the other party. Substantial percentages of both Democrats and Republicans say the other party stirs in them feelings of frustration, anger, and fear (table 2.6). More than half of Democrats (55 percent) said the Republican Party makes them "afraid," while 49 percent of Republicans reacted the same way to the Democratic Party. Among those highly engaged in politics—those who say they vote regularly and either volunteer for or

TABLE 2.5. **Partisan views of the other party**

Characteristic	Republicans' view of Democrats (%)		Democrats' view of Republicans (%)	
	2016	2019	2016	2019
Close-minded	52	64	70	75
Immoral	47	44	35	47
Lazy	46	46	18	20
Dishonest	45	—	42	—
Unintelligent	32	36	33	38
Unpatriotic	—	63	—	23

Source: Pew Research Center polls, Mar. 2–28, 2016, Apr. 5–May 2, 2016, and Sept. 3–5, 2019.

TABLE 2.6. **Fear, anger, and frustration among partisans**

	Emotions evoked by the other party			
Emotion	Democrats (%)	Highly engaged* Democrats (%)	Republicans (%)	Highly engaged* Republicans (%)
Afraid	55	70	49	62
Angry	47	58	46	58
Frustrated	58	60	57	58

Source: Pew Research Center polls, Mar. 2–28, 2016, and Apr. 5–May 2, 2016.
*Engagement scale based on voting frequency, campaign volunteerism, and/or contributions.

donate to campaigns—fully 70 percent of Democrats and 62 percent of Republicans said they were afraid of the other party.

As Donald Trump was sewing up the Republican nomination for president, the Pew Research Center found that 45 percent of Republicans said that Democratic policies were not only wrong but also "threaten the nation's well-being." Forty-one percent of Democrats viewed Republican policies in equally stark terms.[40] In June 2017, Pew found that 81 percent of both Democrats and Republicans had unfavorable views of the other party, and 44 percent of Democrats and 45 percent of Republicans had *very* unfavorable views.[41] The following March, 86 percent of Democrats and 84 percent of Republicans had unfavorable views of the other party. Forty-three percent of Democrats and 45 percent of Republicans had *very* unfavorable views of the other party.[42]

More broadly, there is an increasing partisan polarization of worldviews among ordinary Americans.[43] Indeed, partisan polarization is so strong that it bleeds into other areas of social life, including the economy, marriage, and even inanimate objects linked to the opposing party.[44] In addition, affective polarization is a driver of the growing elite polarization in American politics.[45]

When parties view one another as mortal enemies, the stakes of losing heighten dramatically, leading to less civil competition that may reinforce beliefs that the other party poses a dangerous threat.[46] The growing lack of trust in the other party creates a barrier to supporting that party's initiatives or reaching a compromise.[47]

CAUSES OF AFFECTIVE POLARIZATION. There is not agreement about the causes of affective polarization. Some argue that it is the result of increased confluence of voters' partisan, ideological, and policy preferences resulting from partisan sorting,[48] reinforcing individuals' partisan identities.[49] Others deemphasize the role of sorting and stress the social identity nature of party affiliation.[50] A number of social and economic cleavages, including ethnicity, urban-rural residence, gender, and religion have aligned with the party divide, reinforcing a visceral identity with one's party and encouraging party affiliates to see less in common with the other side.[51] Partisans' feelings toward the social groups linked to their party have grown more positive, and feelings toward the groups associated with the other party have become more negative over time.[52] People increasingly view members of the other party as "others" and rely on stereotypes, which exacerbates affective polarization.[53]

SOCIAL ISOLATION. Social isolation further reinforces affective polarization. Sixty-three percent of consistent conservatives and 49 percent of consistent liberals say most of their close friends share their political views, compared with just 35 percent among the public as a whole.[54] Most Democrats and Republicans report that they have just a few or no friends in other party, and they rate such people "coldly" on a 0–100 thermometer scale. Moreover, this rating got colder once Trump took office.[55] Geographic separation also plays a contributing role.[56] Family socialization also exacerbates party polarization. Political correspondence between married couples and parent-offspring agreement have both increased substantially because of increased mate selection based on politics. Spousal agreement in turn creates an "echo chamber" that facilitates intergenerational continuity.[57]

RACE. Race was a polarizing factor in opinion about Barack Obama's policies, starting with the 2008 election.[58] There is evidence that predispositions to opposing the president, combined with the salience of race, contributed to the acceptance of smearing labels such as that Obama was Muslim or a socialist.[59] There is also reason to believe that negative stereotypes about blacks significantly eroded white support for the president,[60] as did racial resentment.[61] The race of the president (and thus racism) influenced partisan preferences[62] and support for health care reform.[63]

The polarizing role of race (and religion[64]) continued in the Trump presidency. One reason may well be the president's racially tinged claims regarding immigration, voter fraud, crime, and protests. This racial priming may explain why, although white racial resentment has remained stable over time, it became much more highly correlated with partisan-ship, ideological self-identification, voting behavior, and attitudes about issues such as government spending and health care policy.[65]

White evangelicals are at the heart of the Trump coalition, and their declining proportion of the population seems to be fueling racial and religious anxieties among them. Of all US religious groups, they have the most negative attitudes toward immigrants. More importantly, their conservatism correlates strongly with their perceptions of anti-white dis-crimination. Fully 50 percent of white evangelical respondents in 2016 reported feeling they face discrimination that is comparable to, or even higher than, the discrimination they believe Muslim Americans face. Those who believe they are discriminated against are more likely to hold con-servative attitudes on issues as wide ranging as climate change, tax policy, and health care reform.[66] Similarly, Diana Mutz found that the primary reason for white evangelicals' support for Trump was fear of losing racial status as the dominant racial group and their perceptions that they are targets of discrimination.[67]

WORLDVIEWS. According to Marc Hetherington and Jonathan Weiler, the dividing line between the parties is no longer a philosophy about governing (a political ideology—more or less government). Instead, it is differences in worldviews separate Democrats and Republicans. The "fixed" worldview describes people who are more wary of social and cul-tural change and hence more set in their ways, more suspicious of out-siders, and more comfortable with the familiar and predictable. People with a "fluid" worldview, by contrast, support changing social and cultural norms, are excited by things that are new and novel, and are open to—and welcoming of—people who look and sound different.[68] With partisan affiliations and worldviews so closely aligned, it is difficult to compromise.

THE MEDIA. The fragmented nature of the news media also contributes to polarization. Cable news channels provide the opportunity for parti-sans to obtain news from compatible sources, and people often choose to do so.[69] Forty percent of those who said they voted for Donald Trump in 2016 also reported relying on Fox News, which is known for its con-servative reporting and commentators and support for Donald Trump, as their main source of election news, as opposed to 3 percent of Hillary Clinton voters.[70] Among consistent conservatives, 47 percent relied on Fox News as their main source for news about government and politics.

In addition, 31 percent of those with mostly conservative views relied on Fox. No other news source came close. Liberals, on the other hand, used a more diverse range of news sources, but tended to rely on CNN, NPR, MSNBC, and the *New York Times*.[71] There is evidence that this insulation and reinforcement contributes to political polarization.[72]

The Internet provides an extraordinarily wide range of news choices, greatly facilitating partisans' ability to obtain political information and commentary consistent with their leanings, and people take advantage of the opportunity.[73] In addition, vast social networks allow extensive recirculation of news reports and commentary, increasing the intensity of partisans' echo chambers.[74] Partisans are more likely to skip online ads from the other party and watch ads from their own.[75] Unsurprisingly, access to the Internet increases partisan hostility.[76]

Also significant is the growth of an "outrage industry," especially in talk radio, characterized by vitriol, distortion, falsehoods, character assassination, hysterical assertions, conspiracy theories, and incendiary charges.[77] Jamieson and Cappella argue that these outlets create an enclave for conservatives, shielding them from other information sources and promoting strongly negative associations with political opponents.[78] Given the one-sidedness of the discussions, they can only aggravate partisan animosity.

THE PRESIDENT.   The president himself contributes to polarization. According to Gary Jacobson, in the increasing nationalization of politics, the public's assessment of the president strongly affects how his party is evaluated, perceived, and adopted as an object of identification. The Trump presidency was no exception.[79] Donald Trump is a highly polarizing figure who often focused on emotionally laden issues, such as those dealing with ethnicity, race, and gender. It is not surprising, then, that the differences in approval of the president's performance between partisans reached record levels in the Trump administration. He had the most polarized ratings of any elected first-year president in the history of the Gallup Poll (table 2.7).

Trump's second-year ratings were even more polarized, the most polarized in the history of the Gallup Poll for any president in any year: 79 percentage points. Eighty-seven percent of Republicans approved of his job performance but only 8 percent of Democrats did.[80] Similarly, the 2018 midterm electorate featured the most polarized views of a president ever documented.[81] The Gallup poll taken during and right after the elections reported the widest partisan gap in presidential approval

TABLE 2.7. **Partisan job approval ratings for first-year elected presidents**

President	Republicans (%)	Independents (%)	Democrats (%)	Party gap (percentage points)
Trump	83	34	8	75
Obama	23	54	88	65
Clinton	23	45	75	52
G. W. Bush	92	64	47	45
Reagan	85	59	39	46
Nixon	82	61	49	33
G. H. W. Bush	83	61	51	32
Eisenhower	87	69	56	31
Kennedy	58	72	87	29
Carter	46	59	72	26

Note: Respondents answered the question, "Do you approve or disapprove of the job ____ is doing as president"?
Source: Gallup polls.

ever recorded in the time series stretching back to Harry Truman, with 91 percent of Republicans but only 5 percent of Democrats approving of Trump's job performance.[82]

The president's third year in office witnessed yet another polarization record. Eighty-nine percent of Republicans approved of his handling of his job, but only 7 percent of Democrats agreed.[83] By June 2020, 91 percent of Republicans but only 2 percent of Democrats approved of Trump's performance in office, creating an 89-point gap between identifiers with the two parties.[84] There is not much potential to reach out to other-party identifiers when your approval among them is in the single digits.

Other data make the same point. The Gallup poll of October 2–5, 2017, asked respondents how supportive they were of Donald Trump on a 100-point scale where 0 meant one did not support anything he was doing as president and 100 meant one supported everything he was doing. Seventy-three percent of Democrats placed themselves in the 0–20 category while 53 percent of Republicans put themselves in the 81–100 group. Only 12 percent of Democrats choose anything above 40, and only 9 percent of Republicans placed themselves below 40. In June 2018, 77 percent of Democrats supported impeaching the president. Only 9 percent of Republicans felt the same way.[85]

Even if people do not approve of a president's performance, they may have some degree of respect for him as a person, offering some potential for following his lead. Table 2.8 shows evaluations of the president as a person. Only 7 percent of Democrats rated Trump positively, while 73 per-

TABLE 2.8. **Partisan views of Donald Trump as a person**

Group	Positive (%)	Negative (%)	Unsure (%)
All	36	55	10
Republicans	73	20	7
Independents	31	55	13
Democrats	7	88	5

Note: Respondents answered the question, "Thinking about Donald Trump as a person, do you have a positive or negative opinion of him?"
Source: Gallup poll, June 11–17, 2018.

cent of Republicans did. Once again, we see little potential for the president to win support among Democrats.

Motivated Reasoning

The broad policy disagreements between the parties and the hostility of partisans to the other party and its members mean that any president takes office with the cards stacked against him in his efforts to expand his public support. Is there much prospect of changing people's minds? There is not.

Motivated reasoning is a central concept in the study of political behavior. Sources of it include the confirmation bias (seeking out information that confirms prior beliefs), a prior attitude effect (viewing evidence consistent with prior opinions as more compelling than evidence that is inconsistent with them), and the disconfirmation bias (challenging and dismissing evidence inconsistent with prior opinions, regardless of their objective accuracy).

Motivated reasoning may distort a person's exposure to and perception of new information and the conclusions she reaches about it. Most people seek out information confirming their preexisting opinions and ignore or reject arguments contrary to their predispositions. When exposed to competing arguments, they typically accept the confirming ones and dismiss or argue against the opposing ones.[86]

Partisan identification is a primary anchor of political behavior and the basis for much motivated reasoning.[87] Partisan leanings significantly influence perceptions of conditions and policies, as well as interpretations of and responses to politics. Partisans display a selective pattern of learning in which they have higher levels of knowledge for facts that confirm their worldview and lower levels of knowledge for facts that challenge them.[88]

The more intensely people identify with their party and denigrate the other, the more incentive there is to engage in partisan motivated reasoning. Such rationalization allows partisans to protect their sense of identity from threats such as criticism of their party regarding policies or the behavior of party leaders.[89]

Although some work deemphasizes partisan bias or argues that individuals can overcome it,[90] the bulk of scholarship finds that party identification has strong independent effects on perceptions and thinking about politics.[91] Moreover, these consequences occur over a wide range of policies and political phenomena, including the presence of weapons of mass destruction in Iraq,[92] assessments of the economy,[93] energy policy,[94] presidential approval,[95] performance in presidential debates,[96] belief in political conspiracies,[97] and the Watergate and Lewinsky scandals.[98]

Partisans tend to discount or reject uncongenial information. Even the most basic facts are often in contention between adherents of the parties,[99] such as whether inflation, tax rates, or the budget deficit has risen or fallen; whether there were weapons of mass destruction in Iraq; or whether the number of people with health insurance increased under Obamacare.[100] In June 2017, 42 percent of Republicans—but 76 percent of Democrats—accepted the widely reported consensus judgment within the intelligence community that Russia interfered in the 2016 election.[101] In July 2020, Republicans were far less likely than Democrats to view COVID-19 as a major threat to public health.[102] Similarly, partisans frequently credit a president of their own political party for perceived policy successes and blame a president of the opposite party for perceived failures.[103]

As Adam Berinsky puts it, "In the battle between facts and partisanship, partisanship always wins."[104] Partisan bias and the misperceptions it causes are often most prevalent among those who are generally well informed about politics.[105] Political knowledge neither corrects nor mitigates partisan bias in perception of objective conditions. Instead, it enhances it.

Impact on Presidential Leadership

Partisan polarization and motivated reasoning should increase the prospects of presidents obtaining the support of their copartisans, as the latter bring their policy views in line with their partisan and ideological predispositions. Such change is most likely to occur on views that are not strongly held. People can resolve dissonance by shifting their own view on issues that are not central to them. Crystallized opinions on matters such as abortion or racial and ethnic attitudes, however, are not as likely to change.[106]

When the president and opposition party leaders speak, they clarify where their parties stand. Members of the public use the cues of elites to align their partisanship and ideology, usually bringing their issue attitudes in line with the stances of their party's elites.[107] Thus, "when partisan elites debate an issue and the news media cover it, partisan predispositions are activated in the minds of citizens and subsequently constrain their policy preferences."[108] In times of highly polarized politics, the incentive to be loyal to one's own group and maximize differences with the opposition group is likely to be especially strong.[109]

It is not surprising that research has found that party cues influence opinion.[110] Polarized environments intensify the impact of party endorsements on opinions, decrease the impact of substantive information, and, ironically, stimulate greater confidence in those—less substantively grounded— opinions. Under conditions of high polarization and when presented with opposing frames, partisans' opinions move in the direction of the frame endorsed by their party, regardless of strength of the frames.[111] Moreover, increased confidence in their opinions makes people less likely to consider alternative positions and more likely to take action based on their opinions, such as attempting to persuade others.[112]

The impact of party cues are especially evident in elections. Christopher Achen and Larry Bartels conclude, "unlike particular social identities tied to the special interests of groups, the reach of partisanship is very broad. For the voters who identify with a party, partisanship pulls together conceptually nearly every aspect of electoral politics."[113] Issues take a back seat to partisan attachments and group loyalty.[114] Voters are so locked in to supporting party leaders that the best estimate of the effects of campaign contact and advertising on Americans' candidates choices in general elections is zero.[115]

Elite signaling does not encourage people to change their minds by reasoning about an issue. Instead, signaling provides cues to people that serve to short-circuit their reasoning processes, trigger motivated reasoning, and thus shape how they process information provided by different sides, including largely ignoring arguments from the opposition.[116] Thus, when a party leader voices a strong opinion on an issue, many people will just accept that view. In effect, people replace a difficult question such as "How do I feel about corporate taxation?" with an easy question, "How does my party answer this question?" Some work has found that party cues encourage motivated reasoning to produce arguments supporting the correctness of their party's position.[117] Either way, the signaler is showing supporters where their predispositions should take them on a particular matter. Persuasion begins *after* people have expressed their predispositions.

Individuals interpret a policy, ranging from war to the budget deficit, in light of their opinions concerning the policy's sponsor.[118] The president typically enjoys high levels of approval from his copartisans and much lower levels from identifiers with the opposition party. Those who approve of the president likely should be influenced by White House cues.[119] Because the president's credibility mediates his impact as a cue giver,[120] the chief executive is likely to be more credible to those predisposed to support him than to adherents of the opposition party.[121]

Motivated reasoning, then, may provide an opportunity for the president as leader of his party. When the president signals his views on issues, identifiers with his party should be responsive to those signals. These cues help his copartisans cut through the complexity of policy debates and reach a conclusion. Of course, the strength of a person's partisanship should moderate partisan-motivated reasoning.[122] In addition, those who lack information or knowledge of the parties' traditional issue positions are likely to be less constrained in following a president of their party, because political knowledge is highly correlated with the levels of ideological constraint and issue consistency.[123]

At a campaign rally in January 2016, Donald Trump boasted "I could stand in the middle of 5th Avenue and shoot somebody and I wouldn't lose voters."[124] There is some truth to his claim. Republican senator Bob Corker described Trump's support in stark terms: "It's more than strong, it's tribal in nature. . . . People don't ask about issues anymore. They don't care about issues. They want to know if you're with Trump or not."[125] Similarly, Corry Bliss, head of the Congressional Leadership Fund, the super PAC charged with protecting the House's Republican majority in 2020, asked, "Are you with Trump or not?" "It's not about ideology anymore. It's only about Trump. Are you with him or are you against him? That's the only thing that matters to voters in the Republican base."[126] In December 2019, a poll found that a majority of Republicans chose Trump over Lincoln as the better president.[127] At the height of the coronavirus pandemic in April 2020, when 65 percent of the public thought Trump was too slow to take major steps to address the threat of the outbreak,

52 percent of Republicans said it was unacceptable for officials to fault the administration's response.[128]

It is not surprising, then, that by the end of 2018, White House aides had adopted what one official termed a "shrugged shoulders" strategy for the findings of special counsel Robert Mueller's investigation, calculating that most of Trump's base would believe whatever the president told them to believe.[129] They were probably correct. On May 29, 2019, Mueller declined to say that the president had not committed a crime. Seventy-four percent of Trump voters who said they heard or read Mueller's statement still said they believed that Mueller's report cleared the president of any wrongdoing, making them actually *more* likely than those who had not seen or heard the quote to believe that Trump had been fully vindicated. By contrast, 90 percent of Hillary Clinton voters who saw or heard Mueller believed the report did not clear Trump, as did about half of the Clinton voters who had not seen or heard Mueller's quote or were not sure if they had. Nonvoters were the least likely of any group to say they had seen the quote. Those who did mostly said that Mueller's report was not an exoneration, while those who had not were mostly unsure.[130]

Using a novel survey experiment in January 2017, Michael Barber and Jeremy Pope found that when told that President Trump supported a liberal policy, Republicans were substantially more likely also to endorse this policy, compared with the response when the same question was asked with no mention of Trump's position. The same was true, to a smaller extent, when Republicans were informed that Trump supported a conservative policy. Low-knowledge respondents, strong Republicans, those who approved of Trump, and self-described ideological conservatives were the most likely to respond to the treatment condition in *both* a liberal and a conservative direction. These results paint a picture of partisans who emphasize group attachment over issue positions.[131]

Other experiments have found that citizens did not change their attitudes toward Trump significantly, even when the subjects were told explicitly that the president had reversed his foreign policy stances. Partisan-motivated reasoning and preexisting attitudes toward Trump overwhelmed the impact of policy reversals on most matters of foreign policy.[132] Such findings are consistent with other work that finds that elites can persuade some citizens (primarily their supporters) to update their attitudes so that they agree with the elite's new stance and also mold beliefs about their motives by offering a satisfactory justification for their change.[133]

Motivated reasoning provides a solid base of presidential support. In July 2016, YouGov asked respondents to rate Trump as "intelligent," "a strong leader," "knowledgeable," "inspiring" and "moral." This poll was taken at a positive point for Trump: it was before the release of the *Access Hollywood* tape; before we learned of hush-money payments to silence stories about his affairs; before we learned of Russian interference in the presidential election and his firing of FBI director James Comey; before he told countless falsehoods about both his critics and public policy; and before his poorly informed and impulsive behavior in the Oval Office. The results of a second poll taken in November 2017 were barely distinguishable from responses to the same questions from the same two thousand people. None of the average trait ratings changed by as much as five points on a hundred-point scale, and the overall erosion in impressions of Trump's character amounted to less than two points.[134]

Motivated reasoning cuts two ways, however. Just as it may aid presidents' leadership of their copartisans, it should encourage identifiers with the out party to *oppose* the administration's policies. Their predispositions are likely to be a difficult barrier to overcome. In an environment of high partisan polarization, there is little potential for the president to increase support for his initiatives, even if he switches to positions with which they agree.[135] Thus, although the president has a potential to sway opinions among his base, he also is likely to create a backlash among his detractors. We will explore this point in detail in chapter 4.

In the end, motivated reasoning solidifies public opinion. Panel studies of the public over the first two years of Trump's tenure found that 85 percent of Americans consistently held the same views about the president. Almost half (48 percent) of Americans had a consistently unfavorable view. By contrast, 36 percent had a consistently favorable opinion. Only 15 percent of Americans changed their views at some point—having some combination of favorable or unfavorable views, or saying they didn't know over this time period.[136]

Enduring Constraints on Opinion Change

The contexts of individual presidencies vary, but there are some features of the political landscape that every president faces. Just how malleable is public opinion? What obstacles do all presidents have to overcome in their attempts to move the public to support their policies?[137]

Lack of Attention

The first step in the president's efforts to lead the public is focusing its attention, and reaching the public typically requires frequent repetition of the president's views.[138] Moreover, the impact of communications tends to decay rapidly, and people tend to rely on the most recent message (and the most recent events) when forming their attitudes.[139]

Given the protracted nature of the legislative process and the president's need for public support at all stages of it, sustaining a message can be equally as important as sending it in the first place. Nevertheless, despite the enormous total volume of presidential public statements, they are dispersed over a broad range of policies, and wide audiences hear only a small portion of the president's remarks. The president rarely concentrates a televised address on an issue before Congress and actually makes few statements on even significant legislation. In addition, the president faces strong competition for the public's attention from previous commitments of government, congressional initiatives, opposing elites, and mass media. Of equal consequence, the president often provides competition for himself as he addresses other issues, some of which are on his own agenda and others that events and people force upon him.

Reception and Understanding of Messages

If the president is going to lead the public successfully, the public must *receive* and *understand* his messages. Yet the White House finds it increasingly difficult to obtain an audience for its views—or even airtime on television to express them. Those who are unaware of a message are unlikely to know the president's positions. Moreover, many people who do pay attention miss the president's points. Because the president rarely speaks directly to the American people as a whole, the White House is dependent on the press to transmit its messages. The media are unlikely to adopt consistently either the White House's priorities or its framing of issues.

Presidents make a substantial effort to frame issues in ways that will favor their preferred policy options and place their own performance in a favorable light. However, as we will see, there are many limitations on successful framing, including the presence of competing frames and the fact that different people perceive the same message differently. With all his personal, ideological, and partisan baggage, no president can assume that all citizens hear the same thing when he speaks.

Predispositions

Perhaps the most difficult task for the president in leading people to change their minds about his policies or his performance is overcoming their predispositions. A series of related psychological mechanisms often biases peoples' perceptions of both facts and their evaluations of them. As we have seen, most people seek out information that confirms their preexisting opinions and ignore or reject arguments contrary to their predispositions. When exposed to competing arguments, they typically uncritically accept the confirming ones and dismiss or argue against the opposing ones. Partisanship is especially likely to bias processing perceptions, interpretations, and responses to the political world.

Those who pay close attention to politics and policy, the very people who might be attentive to the president, are likely to have well-developed views and strong partisan attachments and thus be less susceptible to persuasion. Better-informed citizens possess the information and sophistication necessary to identify the implications of messages. They are best able to construct ostensibly reasonable counterarguments and rebuttals to evidence that they are emotionally inclined to resist and thus reject communications inconsistent with their values. In the typical situation of competing frames offered by elites, reinforcement and polarization of views are more likely than conversion among attentive citizens.[140]

It may seem that those with less interest and knowledge present the most potential for presidential persuasion. Such people cannot resist arguments if they do not possess information about the implications of those arguments for their values, interests, and other predispositions. However, these people are also less likely to be aware of the president's messages, limiting the president's influence.[141] To the extent that they do receive the messages, they will also hear from the opposition how the president's views are inconsistent with their predispositions.

Even if their predispositions make them sympathetic to the president's arguments, people may lack the understanding to make the connection between the president's arguments and their own underlying values. Moreover, the more abstract the link between message and value, the fewer the number of people who will make the connection.[142]

Misinformation

In addition, people are frequently *misinformed* (as opposed to uninformed) about policy, and the less they know, the more confidence they have in their beliefs. Thus, they resist correct information. Even when others present them with factual information, they resist changing their opinions.[143] The increasing array of media choices means that individuals are less likely to encounter information that would correct misperceptions. Moreover, the tendency to process information with a bias toward their preexisting views means that those who are most susceptible to misinformation may reject the corrections that they receive.[144] Interestingly, as we have seen, misperceptions are often most prevalent among those who are generally well informed about politics.[145]

Other psychological factors also increase the likelihood that corrections will fail to undo the effects of misperceptions. Negations (i.e., "I am not a crook") often reinforce the perception they are intended to counter.[146] In addition, even if people initially accept corrections debunking a false statement, they may eventually fall victim to an "illusion of truth" effect, in which people misremember false statements as true over time.[147] When information is retracted or refuted, it often exerts the opposite of the intended effect.[148] Finally, misleading statements about politics continue to influence subjects' beliefs even after these statements have been discredited.[149]

In the contemporary environment, there is no reliable external check on misinformation. The public lacks trust in experts, at least partly because the experts seem so often to contradict one another.[150] Moreover, the rise of social media has undermined the ability of central gatekeepers to vet the information that reaches the public.

Loss Aversion

Research in psychology has found that people have a broad predisposition to avoid loss and place more emphasis on avoiding potential losses than on obtaining potential gains.[151] In their decision-making, they place more weight on information that has negative, as opposed to positive, implications for their interests. Similarly, when individuals form impressions of situations or other people, they weigh negative information more heavily than positive. Impressions based on negative information, moreover, tend to be more lasting and more resistant to change.[152]

Risk and loss aversion and distrust of government make people wary of policy initiatives, especially when they are complex and their consequences are uncertain. Since uncertainty accompanies virtually every proposal for a major shift in public policy, it is not surprising that people are naturally inclined against change.[153] Further encouraging this predisposition is the media's focus on political conflict and strategy, which elevates the prominence of political wheeling and dealing in individuals' evaluations of political leaders and policy proposals. The resulting increase in public cynicism highlights the risk of altering the status quo.

The predisposition for loss aversion is an obstacle for presidential leadership of the public. Most presidents want to leave some substantial change at the core of their legacies. Yet those proposing new directions in policy—and Donald Trump was about change—encounter a more formidable task than do advocates of the status quo. Those opposing change have the more modest task of emphasizing the negative to increase the public's uncertainty and anxiety to avoid risk.[154]

Michael Cobb and James Kuklinski found in an experimental study of opinion change on the North American Free Trade Agreement (NAFTA) and health care that arguments against both worked especially well. They found people to be averse to both risk and loss, and arguments against change, which accentuate the unpleasant consequences of a proposed policy, easily resonated with the average person. In addition, they suggested that fear and anger, which negative arguments presumably evoke, are among the strongest emotions and serve as readily available shortcuts for decision-making when people evaluate an impending policy initiative.[155] Kevin Arceneaux found a similar bias toward loss aversion.[156]

Conclusion

Donald Trump's strategic position with public opinion was not strong and provided him little in the way of opportunity for passing major legislation. The public did not provide him with a mandate for governing and was less than enthusiastic about a conservative turn to public policy. Equally important, the public was highly polarized, offering little potential for bipartisan support. Finally, long-term factors put significant constraints on the movement of opinion. Many in the public always were inclined to support the president's policies, of course, but the prospects of expanding his coalition and sending a strong signal to Congress were dim.

Under these circumstances, the reasonable prediction is that public opinion would not respond positively to Trump's persuasive efforts. Instead, it would resist the president's messages offered in his tweets, remarks, speeches, and rallies. The public was also likely to be unresponsive to the president's supporters in Congress, the media, and online. Instead, we should expect the public to oppose the president's policies, presenting an obstacle to obtaining support from members of Congress not already inclined to support him. As we will see, this prediction accurately describes the battles to come.

CHAPTER THREE

Going Public

A t the core of Donald Trump's political success were his public relations skills. Before entering the Oval Office, he had spent a lifetime
promoting himself and his real estate ventures and had gained fame as
a reality television star. In his campaign for the Republican presidential
nomination, he dominated the media and gained widespread—and free—
coverage to advance his cause. It is no surprise, then, that once in office
Trump followed the standard orientation of modern presidents of going
public to seek public support for themselves and their policies.[1]

President Trump began his tenure from a weak strategic position; he
lacked a mandate and broad support for his orientation toward policy. He
also faced a highly polarized public. Moreover, the public is typically resistant
to changing their minds. Nevertheless, his White House, like every other, expended substantial amounts of time and energy attempting to lead the public.

There are three possible goals for these efforts. First, presidents wish
to expand their coalitions by persuading those not in their base to support
their initiatives. If more people favor the administration's programs, the
theory goes, the more likely Congress is to vote for them. Presidents virtually always fail in their efforts to move public opinion, however.[2]

There are two other reasons to go public. The president may want to
rally those already in support of his programs to bolster his own ego and
those of his fellow party members in Congress. In addition, when either
the president or a proposal is popular in an area of the county, the president may be able to demonstrate this support to the members of Congress
from that area through visits to those sections and through attempts to
mobilize supporters to communicate with Congress.

In this chapter, I examine the Trump White House's efforts to lead the
public, concentrating on the classic challenges that every administration

faces in reaching the public with its messages, focusing the public's attention, and framing issues to its advantage, devoting special attention to the
president's unique approach to public relations.

Reaching the Public

All presidents need to attract the public's attention as a first step to getting their messages through. Reaching the public likely requires frequent
repetition of the president's views. According to George W. Bush, "In my
line of work you got to keep repeating things over and over and over again
for the truth to sink in, to kind of catapult the propaganda."[3] Given the
protracted nature of the legislative process and the president's need for
public support at all stages of it, sustaining a message can be equally important as sending it in the first place. As former White House public relations counselor David Gergen put it, "History teaches that almost nothing
a leader says is heard if spoken only once." Administrations attempt to
establish a "line of the day" so that many voices echo the same point.[4]

The lack of interest in politics shown by most Americans, as evidenced
by the low turnouts in elections, compounds the challenge of reaching
the public. Policymaking is a complex enterprise, and most voters do not
have the time, expertise, or inclination to think extensively about most issues. In fact, people generally have only a few issues that are particularly
important to them and to which they pay attention.[5] The importance of
specific issues to the public varies over time and is closely tied to objective
conditions such as unemployment, inflation, international tensions, and
racial conflict. In addition, different issues are likely to be salient to different groups in the population at any given time. For example, some groups
may be concerned about inflation, others about unemployment, and yet
others about a particular aspect of foreign policy or race relations.

A hallmark of the contemporary presidency is the White House's failure to draw impressive audiences for nationally televised speeches. Although wide viewership was common during the early decades of television, when presidential speeches routinely attracted more than 8o percent
of those watching television, recent presidents have seen their audiences
decline to the point where less than half of the public—often substantially less—watch their televised addresses.[6] Paradoxically, developments
in technology have allowed the president to reach mass audiences, yet
further developments have made it easier to for these same audiences to

avoid listening to the White House. Cable television[7] and news networks provide alternatives that make it easy to tune out the president. The average home now receives about two hundred channels.[8]

Table 3.1 lists Donald Trump's nationally televised speeches and their viewership. Two points stand out. The president rarely addressed the nation on a specific issue. When he did so, as in his discussion of a trip to Asia in 2017, his announcement of bombing of Syria in 2018, or his statement on protests and riots in 2020, his presentation typically was short or not in prime time. The only time the president addressed the nation about a matter before Congress in prime time was on his nominations of Neil Gorsuch and Brett Kavanaugh to the Supreme Court. Several of the president's talks to the nation were not in prime time.

TABLE 3.1. **Viewership of Donald Trump's nationally televised speeches**

Date	Venue	Topic	Prime time	Audience size (million)
Jan. 20, 2017	Capitol	Inaugural Address	Yes	30.6
Jan. 31, 2017	White House	Nomination of Neil Gorsuch to Supreme Court	Yes	32.4
Feb. 28, 2017	Joint Session of Congress	Overview of administration	Yes	47.7
Aug. 21, 2017	Ft. Myer, VA	Afghanistan	Yes	27.6
Nov. 15, 2017	White House	Asia trip	No	N/A
Jan. 30, 2018	Joint Session of Congress	State of the Union message	Yes	45.6
Apr. 13, 2018[a]	White House	Bombing of Syria	No	N/A
July 9, 2018	White House	Nomination of Brett Kavanaugh to Supreme Court	Yes	25.6
Jan. 8, 2019	White House	Immigration	Yes	39.6
Jan. 19, 2019	White House	Immigration/shutdown		N/A
Feb. 5, 2019	Joint Session of Congress	State of the Union message	Yes	46.8
Oct. 27, 2019	White House	Death of Abu Bakr al-Baghdadi	No	N/A
Jan. 8, 2020	White House	Iranian attack on US Bases	No	N/A
Feb. 4, 2020	Joint Session of Congress	State of the Union message	Yes	37.2
Feb. 6, 2020	White House	Impeachment acquittal	No	N/A
Mar. 11, 2020	White House	Coronavirus	Yes	N/A
Sept. 26, 2020	White House	Nomination of Amy Coney Barrett to Supreme Court	No	N/A

Source: Nielsen Company viewership data.
[a]Short statement.

When the president did speak, he reached only a small percentage of the nation's 330 million people. Although many people chose to watch the president speak, the great majority of people did not—even for major addresses. Moreover, as the novelty of the new president wore off, the audiences for his prime-time televised addresses declined. The audience size dropped by about 20 percent (nearly 10 million viewers) between his 2019 and 2020 State of the Union messages.

Commentary cascades from the White House. One official estimated that the White House produces as many as five million words a year in the president's name in outlets such as speeches, written statements, and proclamations.[9] Wide audiences hear only a small proportion of the president's statements, however. Comments about policy proposals at news conferences and question-and-answer sessions and in most interviews are also usually brief and made in the context of a discussion of many other policies. Written statements and remarks to individual groups may be focused, but the audience for these communications is modest. In addition, as David Gergen puts it, nearly all of the president's statements "wash over the public. They are dull, gray prose, eminently forgettable."[10]

The public can miss the point of even the most pointed rhetoric. Nine months after the president signed the 2017 tax bill, 60 percent of Americans underestimated the size of personal tax cuts, which Trump had touted as a great Christmas gift to the public.[11] Similarly, only 40 percent of the public knew the stock market had risen substantially in 2017, despite the president's frequent references to it. Partisan filters were at play here. Although 67 percent of Trump voters correctly said that the stock market has risen, just 35 percent of Hillary Clinton voters agreed.[12] Similarly, in March 2018, despite Trump's frequent boasts about the strength of the economy, many people did not agree. Democrats in particular thought the economy was in worse shape than before the president took office.[13]

Trump's Travels

One of the most surprising aspects of the early Trump presidency was the president's reluctance to take his case to the public. The issue of health care dominated his relations with Congress during this period, but he barely mentioned the topic on his few stops outside Washington and at his golf properties in Florida and New Jersey. Neither the Republican bills nor the president were widely popular,[14] but there were pockets of support the president could have tried to exploit.

But he did not. At a rally in Cedar Rapids, Iowa, on June 21, 2017, for example, he made only a few scattered references to the issue. During Trump's travels to Ohio and Wisconsin, also in June, he staged only secondary events meant to highlight "victims of Obamacare."[15] The president's rallies seemed to be focused on the president's personal needs, more on vanity than on governing.

He made no effort to encourage his supporters to communicate their support of the House or Senate bills to their representatives in Congress. Given the durability of Trump's support among his base, many lawmakers were disappointed that he had not done more to give them political cover in their home states, especially as they prepared to meet constituents in the summer recesses.[16] According to Republican representative Charlie Dent, health care "was outsourced to Congress."[17]

The president traveled west of the Mississippi only once—to Iowa—in his first six months in office. White House director of legislative affairs Marc Short acknowledged that the president's travel schedule had not reflected a significant drive on health care, as officials had said it would.[18]

Trump did tweet to rally his base in support of the various Republican plans, but a count in mid-July 2017 found only five occasions when he tweeted anything resembling a specific comment about the policies he favored. Moreover, all of the tweets were misleading, incorrect, or false. He was really asking people to trust him rather than trying to convince them. Unfortunately for the White House, most people were skeptical of the plans and did not trust the president.[19]

In sum, although the president frequently mentioned what he viewed as the "disaster" of Obamacare, he rarely made the case for the Republican proposals. Perhaps the explanation is that he did not fully understand them and had no fixed convictions on what should replace the Affordable Care Act.

Nevertheless, congressional Republicans still wanted Trump to take their case to the public. Representative Tom Rooney, a deputy House Republican whip, noted that the president was "extremely popular" in conservative districts. Thus, said Rooney, "He needs to whip these votes, not just to members of Congress but to their constituents."[20]

Key Republicans said that passing their massive tax plan would be nearly impossible without the president playing a vital role in selling the plan. "At the end of the day, President Trump will be incredibly crucial to the success of this," declared Kevin Brady, chair of the House Ways and Means Committee.[21]

Trump seemed to have gotten the point. He made a number of trips to hold rallies on behalf of tax cuts, including visits to Missouri, North Dakota, and Indiana. The president also went to Pennsylvania. He won each of these states in 2016 and each had a Democratic senator whose support could be crucial to the fate of tax cuts. He held his normal campaign-style rallies, but he also made a pitch for bipartisan support for tax cuts. In Indiana, Trump made a rare direct appeal to voters during his speech, imploring them to call their representatives and senators and demand action on the tax proposal. "Let them know you're watching," Trump entreated. "Let them know you're waiting."[22]

Nevertheless, in his first two years year in office, Trump traveled far less frequently in pursuit of his agenda than his immediate predecessors had. Moreover, he overwhelmingly used that travel to preach to the converted in campaign-style rallies in states he won in 2016 or to support Republican candidates in the 2018 midterm elections.[23]

Tweeting

President Trump had another tool for reaching the public aside from travel: the tweet. Trump was the first president to rely on social media as a primary means of communicating with the public. He sent thousands of tweets, and he carefully crafted his messages. Former White House director of message strategy Cliff Sims explained that the president was "meticulous with not just the words that he wants to use but the punctuation."[24]

According to one journalist, "His musings in bursts of 280 characters or less—often littered with misleading material, nods to conspiracy theories or downright falsehoods—have become a fixture of American life, driving cable news coverage and punctuating the political discourse."[25] The president deployed Twitter to fire cabinet members, belittle his rivals, rally his base, befuddle world leaders, announce impulsive decisions, and vent his grievances. More than half of the president's posts were attacks. His targets included the Federal Reserve Board, previous administrations, entire cities led by Democrats, and adversaries from outspoken athletes to chief executives who displeased him. The most frequent targets of Trump's ire were Democrats, news organizations, and investigations, particularly the Russia and impeachment inquiries.[26]

Trump was firm in his belief that Twitter was essential to his success. On June 6, 2017, he tweeted, "if I would have relied on the Fake News of CNN, NBC, ABC, CBS, washpost or nytimes, I would have had ZERO chance winning WH." "I doubt I would be here if it weren't for social media," he told interviewer Maria Bartiromo on the Fox Business Network's *Mornings with Maria* on October 21, 2017. "When somebody says something about me, I am able to go bing, bing, bing, and I take care of it," Trump added. Earlier in the year, he told Fox News, "let me tell you about Twitter. I think that maybe I wouldn't be here if it wasn't for Twitter, because I get such a fake press, such a dishonest press." "Twitter is a wonderful thing for me, because I get the word out."[27]

Trump did indeed spread his message. His account, @realDonaldTrump, had seventy-six million followers in April 2020; and the @potus account had twenty-nine million. He also had twenty-seven million likes on Facebook and nineteen million followers on Instagram. Many of these followers were duplicates, of course. Nevertheless, the president had the potential to directly reach tens of millions Americans completely on his terms.

Most people did not encounter the president's messages on their Twitter feed, however. In a Gallup poll in May 2018, only 8 percent of the sample—30 percent of Twitter users—followed Trump on Twitter. Of that 8 percent, 55 percent reported reading all or most of his tweets. That represents about 4 percent of the population. Another 2 percent said they read some of his tweets.[28] Over the next year, the Pew Research Center found that 19 percent of adult Twitter users with public accounts, including 31 percent of Republicans, followed Trump.[29] A *New York Times* analysis of the Pew data found that about 4 percent of American adults, or about 11 million people, followed the president. Mostly the president was preaching to the converted. His followers tended to be disproportionately older, white, and male, fitting the profile of his core supporters.[30] Another poll found that just 14 percent of Trump voters and 11 percent of Americans as a whole said they learned about something Trump posted on Twitter because they saw it on the website.[31]

Nevertheless, half the public reported seeing, reading, or hearing "a lot" about the president's tweets, and another quarter say they encountered "a fair amount" of information about them.[32] Two-thirds of his voters and 64 percent of all Americans said they were more likely to come across them in a news story.[33] Thus, despite the use of the technology of social media, the president was actually still dependent on the media to convey his case to the public.

The most important question is how people responded to the president's tweets. Despite Trump's affection for tweeting, the public was less appreciative. A Fox News poll in March 2017 found that 50 percent of registered voters disapproved of his tweeting, while only 16 percent approved. Even 51 percent of Trump voters thought he should be more cautious.[34] Later polls found about two-thirds of the public to be disapproving of the president's use of Twitter.[35]

By large margins, the public found the president's tweets "misleading."[36] A series of polls taken in 2017 concluded that only one-fifth of the public thought Trump's tweeting was "effective and informative." More than two-thirds felt it was "reckless and distracting." Even Trump voters had mixed reactions.[37] Similar percentages saw Trump's use of Twitter as a "risky" way to communicate.[38] Indeed, they were. For example, his efforts to have his travel bans upheld were undermined by his repeated tweets suggesting that the measures were intended to block Muslims from entering the country. On May 26, 2020, Twitter for the first time added labels to two Trump tweets that included misinformation about voter fraud, directing the president's followers to "Get the facts" about the president's false claims.[39]

Moreover, the public opposed personal assaults in tweets, such as the president's attack on the hosts of MSNBC's *Morning Joe*, Joe Scarborough and Mika Brzezinski.[40] On June 29, 2017, Trump tweeted, "I heard poorly rated @Morning_Joe speaks badly of me (don't watch anymore). Then how come low I.Q. Crazy Mika, along with Psycho Joe, came to Mar-a-Lago 3 nights in a row around New Year's Eve, and insisted on joining me. She was bleeding badly from a face-lift. I said no!"[41] The public was not amused by the president's imputations. Trump was not deterred, however. In May 2020, he sent several tweets pushing a conspiracy theory that falsely accused Scarborough of the murder of Lori Klausutis.[42] Trump persisted even in the face of pleas from the deceased woman's husband to desist. Twitter apologized to the woman's family but left the tweets online.

Trump fired secretary of state Rex Tillerson by tweet on March 13, 2018. When Tillerson made critical comments about him the following December, Trump tweeted incongruously that his former chief diplomat and the former chief executive of Exxon was "dumb as a rock and I couldn't get rid of him fast enough. He was lazy as hell."[43]

Significantly, there is evidence that the president's tweets have little influence on public opinion[44] or even have the unintended consequence of driving the public away from the president's position on an issue.[45]

It is not surprising, then, that the public overwhelmingly thought the president should stop tweeting (table 3.2).[46] A January 2018 poll found that only 11 percent of the public felt Trump's use of Twitter was helping his presidency. Sixty-six percent thought it was hurting it. Only 21 percent

TABLE 3.2. **Should President Trump continue to tweet?**

Date of poll	Yes (%)	No (%)	No opinion (%)
Jan. 5–9, 2017	32	64	5
Jan. 20–25, 2017	33	62	5
Mar. 16–21, 2017	35	59	5
Apr. 12–18, 2017	28	68	4
May 4–9, 2017	33	61	6
June 22–27, 2017	32	61	7
July 17–Aug. 1, 2017	27	69	4
Aug. 9–15, 2017	31	66	3
Aug. 17–21, 2017	28	69	4
Sept. 21–26, 2017	26	69	4
Oct. 5–10, 2017	27	70	3
Nov. 7–13, 2017	33	63	5
Nov. 29–Dec. 4, 2017	28	66	5
Jan. 5–8, 2018	26	69	5
Apr. 6–9, 2018	27	67	6
Aug. 9–13, 2018	26	66	8
Mar. 21–25, 2019	28	63	9

Note: Respondents answered the question, "As president, do you think Donald Trump should continue tweeting from his personal Twitter account, or not?" (asked of registered voters).
Source: Quinnipiac University polls.

of Republicans said his tweets were helping, while twice as many, 43 percent, thought they were hurting.[47] Moreover, there is some evidence that the president's tweets had the unintended consequence of driving the public away from the president's position on an issue.[48]

Dominating the News

In *The Art of the Deal*, Donald Trump wrote, "Even a critical story, which may be hurtful personally, can be very valuable to your business."[49] He seemed to believe that attention creates value[50] and to place more importance on receiving coverage at all than on the nature of the coverage. From one perspective he was correct. If you are the story, you are on people's minds and you are crowding out competitors.

In the president's view, then, it is important to dominate the news—and he did. He captured more media attention than his rivals in the Republican primaries and caucuses in 2016 as well as in the general election.[51] Once president, he was the number-one story nearly every day. In a review of the news 2017, Echelon Insights examined nearly 3 billion tweets in the US covering 250 topics. It found that

2017 was primarily a story about one man: President Donald Trump. He was tweeted about an estimated 901.8 million times in the United States, a doubling of last year's figure and nearly ten times Barack Obama's total of 91 million in his last year in office. There were only 17 days in 2017 where Donald Trump was NOT the top topic of conversation, and he was the #1 story every week for every audience.[52]

In the spring of 2019, Trump was the subject of more Google searches and social media interactions and received more mentions on cable television news than all of the two dozen candidates for the Democratic nomination for president combined.[53] A year later the president's presence dwarfed Joe Biden's across nearly every media channel, including television, social media, Google searches, and internet stories.[54]

The president also knew that it is easier to get bad press than good. As the saying goes, the press does not report on planes that land safely. Thus, the media covered what he said or tweeted because his communications were outrageous, incendiary, crude, unseemly, and appalling. In the end, the president set the national agenda and also the terms and tone of the debate.[55]

There are downsides to this ascendency, however. Trump's view about news coverage may have been correct about real estate development, but it did not necessarily translate to politics. If you set the terms of debate through dissensus and division, you are weakly positioned to attract broad support. If you react to criticism by demeaning others, you are likely to end up demeaning yourself. If you spend your time defending unpresidential behavior, you inevitably focus attention on that behavior.

We will see that most people did not like the president nor did they support his policies. Roughly two-thirds of the tweets studied by Echelon Insights were sent by liberals,[56] no doubt in opposition to Trump. Many people seemed to tune the president out. As George Will put it, "For most Americans, President Trump's expostulations are audible wallpaper, always there but not really noticed."[57] Dominating the news is not an end in itself in politics.

Focusing Attention

The White House not only wishes to have the public receive its messages, it also wants to focus the public's attention on its priorities.[58] The president is unlikely to influence people who are not attentive to the issues on which he wishes to lead. If the president's messages are to meet his coalition-building needs, the public must sort through the profusion of communications in its environment, overcome its limited interest in government and politics, and concentrate on the president's priority concerns. Even within the domain of politics, political communications (many of which originate in the White House) bombard Americans every day. The sheer volume of these communications far exceeds the attentive capacity of any individual.

Despite the enormous total volume of presidential public statements, they are dispersed over a broad range of policies, and wide audiences hear only a small portion of the president's remarks. The president rarely concentrates a televised address on an issue before Congress and actually makes few statements on most significant legislation.

In addition, the president faces strong competition for the public's attention from previous commitments of government, congressional initiatives, opposing elites, and mass media.[59] Moreover, every administration must respond to unanticipated or simply overlooked problems, including international crises. These issues simultaneously affect the attention of the public and the priorities of Congress and thus the White House's success in focusing attention on its priority issues.[60]

Administration officials also cannot ignore events, as campaigns often do. Campaigns are tightly focused on one goal: winning elections. Governing requires attention to multiple goals, many of which are thrust upon the White House. Thus, the president must speak on many issues and to many audiences simultaneously. As Obama White House senior advisor David Axelrod put it, the challenge of managing and controlling messages in a campaign and in the White House is "the difference between tick-tack-toe and three-dimensional tick-tack-toe. It's vastly more complicated."[61] Thus, the sheer volume of crises often overwhelms the message.[62]

Obama communications director Daniel Pfeiffer agreed: "In the White House, you have the myriad of challenges on any given day and are generally being forced to communicate on a number of complex subjects at the same time."[63] Every day the White House had a communications plan on what message it was trying to tell country, but most of time it had had to rip it up in the first morning meeting in order to deal with an unexpected crisis that had popped up overnight.[64]

Of equal consequence, the president often provides competition for himself as he addresses other issues, some of which are on his own agenda and some that events and others force upon him. Donald Trump's late-night tweeting often dominated the headlines and created distractions from his priority initiatives.

Distractions

There were many challenges to the Trump White House focusing on its priorities. One was the distraction of peripheral issues. Sometimes, these distractions were beyond the president's control, and sometimes they were of his own making. One of the president's signature campaign issues, infrastructure development, illustrates both these points.

In June 2017, the administration sought to put a week-long spotlight on the president's plans for infrastructure renewal, highlighting the need for privatization of air-traffic control. The effort was quickly eclipsed by former FBI Director James Comey's dramatic testimony before Congress and the president's criticisms of his own Department of Justice. In August, the administration launched its second "infrastructure week," focusing on reforms to the federal permitting process. This time it was derailed by Trump blaming "both sides" for violence at a rally of white nationalists in Charlottesville, Virginia, that left one woman dead.

In February 2018, the White House prepared its biggest push on infrastructure yet with the rollout of an actual plan for roads, bridges, and waterways. The president debuted his plan at a White House discussion with state and local leaders. At the meeting, he told officials, "And if you don't want it, that's okay with me, too." Although he expressed hope that the initiative would draw support from members of Congress, he added, "If for any reason, they don't want to support to it, hey, that's going to be up to them."[65] Unsurprisingly, these remarks left observers questioning how committed he was to seeing legislation pass.[66]

The White House chose to roll out its infrastructure initiative on the same day it released its budget for the coming year. Most media outlets viewed the budget as the bigger story, and it contained cuts to several existing infrastructure programs, handing Democrats ammunition to question Trump's commitment.

More important still, the effort was overshadowed by the furor over allegations of spousal abuse against senior Trump aide Rob Porter, the White House's changing answers to questions about the matter, and the president's days-long silence on domestic violence. At the same time, there was a horrific mass shooting in a school in Florida, focusing the nation's attention and forcing Trump to cancel a trip to Orlando to pitch his infrastructure plan. Moreover, the president himself bungled his response to the shooting by laying some blame on the gunman's classmates.

Another major distraction occurred when Trump's longtime lawyer, Michael Cohen, acknowledged that he paid an adult film star known as Stormy Daniels $130,000 a month before the 2016 presidential election to prevent her from publicly claiming she had had an affair with the candidate.

At the end of the week, the White House press office sent a release to reporters with the essentials of the president's infrastructure initiative. It landed in reporters' inboxes just as deputy attorney general Rod J. Rosenstein stepped to a lectern to discuss an indictment of thirteen Russians for interfering in the 2016 election—yet another story that would eclipse Trump's infrastructure effort.[67]

On April 30, 2019, the president met with Democratic leaders Nancy Pelosi and Charles Schumer. They announced an agreement to pursue a $2 trillion infrastructure initiative. Within minutes of the meeting, however, Trump was tweeting about other matters, including criticism of the Federal Reserve Board and European allies, threats against Cuba, and encouragement of an uprising against Juan Guaidó's Venezuelan government. Further undermining any legislative success, acting White House chief of staff Mick Mulvaney immediately announced that such a plan had little chance of passing. Moreover, it soon became clear that the White House had no plan. It is not surprising that Urban Dictionary defined "infrastructure week" as "a repeatedly failed attempt to stay on-task endlessly derailed by high-profile distractions caused by one's own ineptitude."[68]

On October 26, 2018, shortly before the midterm elections, the president made an announcement of a plan to reduce the cost of prescription drugs offered through Medicare. He lamented that it did not receive as much news coverage as he would have liked. Even worse, he asserted, the lack of media attention to politics was slowing Republican momentum ahead of the elections. The media, he complained, were devoting their attention to " 'Bomb' stuff,' " the bombs sent to leading Democrats around the country.[69] More broadly, Trump's focus on a caravan of migrants in Mexico overshadowed the positive story his supporters wanted him to tell about the economy.

On December 20, 2018, the president signed a huge farm bill. The next day, he signed an important reform of federal criminal justice laws. Once again, Trump stepped on his own success. Instead of extoling the bipartisanship responsible for passing the bills, the president used the ceremonies as opportunities to castigate Democrats for their opposition to his border wall. A few hours after the criminal justice bill signing, the government shut down over wall funding. In addition, secretary of defense James Mattis resigned over the president's decision to withdraw all US troops from Syria. Both matters eclipsed his signing of the criminal justice overhaul.

Donald Trump was not a focused communicator. He rarely stuck to a script, whether for a theme week in the White House, an address to a rally or organization, or a discussion with congressional leaders. The president often veered off subject and undermined the messages he intended to send. While negotiating with congressional leaders on an immigration bill in January 2018, he rejected protecting immigrants from Haiti, El Salvador, and African countries. "Why are we having all these people from shithole countries come here?"[70] Trump asked. It is not surprising that Trump's insulting language regarding black immigrants caused a firestorm of criticism and set back efforts to reach an agreement on immigration.

In June 2017, the White House announced Infrastructure Week, followed by Workforce Development Week, Technology Week, and Energy Week. Of the president's 163 tweets on Monday through Friday of each of those four weeks, only twelve—7 percent—addressed the subject that the White House was focusing on that week, including two Twitter ads about infrastructure that ran on his account. During Technology Week, he did not once tweet about technology—except to deny that he had personally taped any conversations in the Oval Office.[71]

The president's propensity to create diversions and follow tangents kept him from focusing fully on his legislative agenda and sometimes forced lawmakers who might have been natural allies on key policies into the uncomfortable position of having to answer for his behavior and outbursts. For instance, Trump's news conference with Senate Majority Leader Mitch McConnell on October 23, 2017, was orchestrated to project GOP unity on taxes. However, the president falsely accused his predecessors of not calling the families of fallen soldiers, which set the White House on the defensive and dominated the national media for several days.[72]

On September 7, 2018, the Department of Labor released a positive report about jobs and wages. The president made no statement or tweet about the jobs report, but he did tweet about Bob Woodward's new book about his presidency, *Fear*, and an anonymous op-ed in the *New York Times* that described a nonliberal "resistance" to him inside the administration.

He held a session with reporters on the way to a fundraiser in Fargo, North Dakota. When one of the reporters asked him if Attorney General Jeff Sessions should investigate the writer's identity, he replied, "I think so. It's national security." One of the reporters also asked whether any action should be taken against the *Times*. "I'm looking at that right now," Trump replied. "It only happened yesterday." By the time he reached the fundraiser, the homepages of the *Times* and the *Washington Post* websites were both featuring his remarks about Sessions, and those stories had bumped down ones about the economic news.[73]

The coronavirus pandemic of 2020 offered the president an opportunity to position himself as a clear-eyed leader above the political fray who understood the crisis and had a firm grip on circumstances and policy responses. Instead, the president made highly visible and contradictory claims about the following:

- the seriousness of the virus
- how rapidly it would dissipate
- the availability and importance of tests for the disease
- whether he told Vice President Mike Pence not to call governors who were critical of the federal response to the pandemic
- whether individual states or the federal government were responsible for testing
- how soon a vaccine would be available
- the utility of a malaria treatment for curing people of the infection
- whether he would put a hold on funds for the World Health Organization
- China's handling of the pandemic
- whether he had invoked the Defense Production Act to require companies to reduce medical supplies
- how well governors were performing
- whether he would leave it to governors to open their states or encourage protests against them
- how many ventilators New York required
- whether he was disbanding the White House coronavirus task force

The self-described wartime president also claimed he was merely a backup for the states. It is not surprising that in April 2020, 55 percent of the public felt Trump had been "largely inconsistent in his coronavirus press briefings.[74]

Trump contradicted both himself as well as statements from government officials sharing the same White House podium. Sometimes he even denied making statements he had made in front of a wide television audience. As two reporters put it, he was

> a president who governs as if producing and starring in a reality television show, with each day a new episode and each news cycle his own creation, a successive installment to be conquered. Facing a global pandemic, Trump still seems to lurch from moment to moment, with his methods and messages each day disconnected from—and in some cases contradictory to—the ones just prior.[75]

Often the president's contractions became stories themselves, distracting from his purpose and muddling his points. Even the conservative *Wall Street Journal* editorial board chastised the president for his behavior at the briefings.[76] Trump "sometimes drowns out his own message," said Republican senator Lindsey Graham.[77] "People are confused about whether this is really serious. People are confused about how long this may last," complained Steve Adler, mayor of Austin, Texas. "We're trying to get as much containment as we can by limiting the number of physical interactions taking place, but they're hearing it's not a big deal, it's going to be over soon, and getting community buy-in becomes a harder thing to achieve." "He at times just says whatever comes to mind, or tweets, then someone on TV is saying the opposite," Maryland governor Larry Hogan added. "It's critically important that the message is straightforward and fact-based for the public." In Dayton, Ohio, Mayor Nan Whaley described the challenges of keeping people informed as their lives were uprooted. "I have people in my city texting me what the president said, and they go, 'Well, what you're saying isn't true because the president says the opposite.' Every day is a different message from the federal government and there is no consistency."[78]

Creating Distractions

Twitter is an impulsive medium that requires neither reflection nor nuance. When the president was angry, he frequently expressed it in tweets. These impulses did not help his standing with the public, but they may have served as a diversion from news he did not like. On September 24, 2017, amidst his stalled congressional agenda and the devastation from Hurricane Maria in Puerto Rico and the inadequate federal response to it, Trump lashed out at NFL players, mostly black, who kneeled during the national anthem to protest racially inspired police brutality. The president tweeted, "Sports fans should never condone players that do not stand proud for their National Anthem or their Country. NFL should change policy!"[79] Later, he sent Vice President Pence to an NFL game with instructions to walk out if the players kneeled—which was exactly what happened.

This issue had no policy stakes, but it succeeded in creating a weeks-long firestorm, distracting attention from presidential failures. It dominated both the political and sports media. By igniting a racialized controversy, the president also drove a deep wedge into our cultural divisions. As Ezra Klein put it, "Trump's opponents were angry—the president was a racist, he was dismissing police brutality, he was turning us against each other. His supporters were indignant—the president was a patriot, he was defending the flag and the country." "Telling the mostly white attendees at his rallies that 'people like yourselves' should not have to see 'those people' kneeling during the anthem was a transparent effort to distract us, to inflame our divisions, to lure us to have the fight Trump wanted to have rather than continue discussing his flailing governance."[80]

In the 2018 midterm elections, Republicans found that the issues such as the 2017 tax cut and strong economy were not playing as strongly with voters as they had hoped. President Trump campaigned vigorously for Republican candidates and changed the policy focus of the election by emphasizing the "threat" from a group of unarmed asylum seekers, mostly women and children, slowly moving through Mexico toward the United States; he even sent troops to the border. Democrats claimed the president was trying to manufacture a crisis to distract from his poor position in the polls. In the end, Republicans lost forty seats, and thus their majority, in the House, but they did retain their majority in the Senate.

In May 2020, facing an enemy in the coronavirus he could not tweet into submission, Trump suffered poor ratings for his handling of the pandemic and was eager to the change the subject. What followed were baseless charges of a conspiracy by former president Barack Obama and others to sabotage his presidency, unproven allegations of widespread voter fraud from mail-in ballots, and even the revival of debunked accusations about the death of a former staffer to then congressman Joe Scarborough. Later in the month, the president stoked racial tensions over the George Floyd's death in police custody in Minneapolis by tweeting comments so incendiary that Twitter flagged them as violating the platform's rule against glorifying violence.[81] Anthony Scaramucci, a former senior administration official who became a Trump critic, explained, "What are his political instincts here? I want to distract you from what's going on. I want to deflect away from the reality. And oh, by the way, I want to remind you that the pandemic is not my fault, and it's us against them."[82]

Framing the Message

Presidents are interested in not only what conclusions the public reaches about a policy but also *how* they are thinking about it. Policy issues are usually complex and subject to alternative interpretations. The sheer complexity of most issues, combined with the competing values that are relevant to evaluating them, creates cognitive burdens for most people. They cope by acting as cognitive misers and simplify their decisions by employing short cuts,[83] focusing on the dimensions they deem to be most important for their evaluations. In this decisional process, people are likely to weigh most heavily the information and values that are most easily accessible. Recent discussion by political leaders is one factor that determines their accessibility.[84]

The cognitive challenges of citizens are an opportunity for the White House. Although a president will have little impact on the values people hold, people use cues from elites as to the ideological or partisan implications of messages[85] (the source of a message is itself an important cue[86]). By defining and simplifying a complex issue through *framing*, presidents attempt to define what a public policy issue is about.[87] They hope to influence which attitudes and information people incorporate into their judgments of his policies and performance,[88] setting the terms of the debate on their proposals and thus the premises on which the public evaluates them. In the process, presidents attempt to show the public that their positions are consistent with their values. As one leading advisor to Ronald Reagan put it, "I've always believed that 80 percent of any legislative or political matter is how you frame the debate."[89]

It is not clear whether an issue frame interacts with an individual's memory so as to *prime* certain considerations, making some more accessible than others and therefore more likely to be used in formulating a political preference, or whether framing works by encouraging individuals to think deliberately about the importance of considerations suggested by a frame.[90] In either case, the frame raises the priority and weight that individuals assign to particular attitudes already stored in their memories.[91]

Instead of trying to persuade the public directly on the merits of a proposal, then, the White House often uses public statements and the press coverage they generate to articulate relatively simple themes. Public opinion research may have identified these themes as favoring the president's positions.[92] The president may also attempt to prime perceptions of objective circumstances such as the level of economic prosperity. Similarly, presidents try to prime people to view them in terms of positive characteristics such as strength, competence, and empathy.[93] An additional potential advantage for the president is that framing and priming—because they are relatively simple—are less susceptible to distortion by journalists and opponents than direct persuasion on the merits of a policy proposal.[94]

Attempts to frame issues are as old as the Republic.[95] Each side of a political contest usually attempts to frame the debate to its own advantage. Byron Shafer and William Claggett argue that public opinion is organized around two clusters of issues, both of which are favored by a majority of voters: social welfare, social insurance, and civil rights (associated with Democrats); and cultural values, civil liberties, and foreign relations (associated with Republicans). Each party's best strategy is to frame the choice for voters by focusing attention on the party's most successful cluster of issues.[96] John Petrocik has found that candidates tend to campaign on issues that favor them in order to prime the salience of these issues in voters' decision-making.[97] Similarly, an important aspect of campaigning is activating the latent predispositions of partisans by priming party identification as a crucial consideration in deciding for whom to vote.[98]

Despite its potential advantages, framing issues successfully is a challenge for the White House. When there is elite consensus, and thus only one set of cues offered to the public, the potential for opinion leadership may be substantial. Occasions in which elite commentary is one-sided are rare, however. Consensual issues tend to be new, with few people having committed themselves to a view about them. Most issues that generate consensual elite discourse arise from external events, for example, surprise attacks on the United States such as the terrorist assaults on September 11, 2001, or from its allies, such as the invasion of Kuwait in 1990. Thus, the president's greatest chance of influencing public opinion is in a crisis (which attracts the public's attention) in which elites articulate a unified message. At other times, most people are too inattentive or too committed to views to be strongly influenced by elite efforts at persuasion.[99]

Usually, the president faces committed, well-organized, and well-funded opponents who provide competing frames. When elite discourse is divided, generating conflicting messages, people respond to issues according to their predispositions, especially their core partisan and ideological views, and discount the frames from the opposition party.[100] Similarly, when people can choose their sources of information, as almost everyone can, they are unresponsive to opinion leadership.[101]

Many factors condition the impact of framing,[102] and most systematic studies of real world conditions have found that the public is not very responsive to elite frames.[103] Even what appears to be successful framing may not be,[104] and issue frames seem to have modest effects on how the public later evaluates politicians.[105]

We know very little about the terms in which the public thinks about issues. Although frames may evolve over decades,[106] presidents do not have the luxury of such a leisurely perspective. Chief executives need public support during their tenures, usually in their first terms when they are more likely to have majorities in Congress. In addition, the White House must advocate the passage of many proposals at roughly the same time, further complicating its efforts to structure choice on any single issue.

A fundamental limitation on presidential framing and priming is the public's lack of attention to politics, which restricts its susceptibility to taking cues from political elites. There are widely varying levels of interest in and information about politics and public policy.[107] Even if their predispositions make them sympathetic to the president's arguments, less interested and less informed citizens may lack the understanding to make the connection between the president's arguments and their own underlying values. Moreover, the more abstract the link between message and value, the fewer people who will make the connection.[108]

In addition, for the president to frame issues for the public, people must perceive accurately the frame offered by the White House. There is reason to believe, however, that different people perceive the same message differently. The media are of little help, as they are unlikely to adopt uniformly or reliably the White House's framing of issues. Moreover, with all his personal, ideological, and partisan baggage, no president can assume that all citizens hear the same thing when he speaks. Partisanship is especially likely to bias processing perceptions, interpretations, and responses to the political world.[109]

Despite vigorous efforts to frame issues in ways that would win widespread support for himself and his policies, Donald Trump was not able to establish a positive narrative for his administration.[110] There were always counter-frames that many people found more compelling than those offered by the White House. The president's seems to have impacted those already inclined to agree with him.[111]

He promoted taxes as agents of economic growth but more people saw them as giveaways to the wealthy and a cause of exploding deficits. He advocated restricting immigration in terms of protecting the country from gangs and terrorists, job losses to "illegal aliens," amnesty for lawbreakers, and assaults of American values. Opponents, however, saw unfairness to Dreamers and other undocumented immigrants, a loss of needed workers, a barrier to uniting families, religious discrimination, and racism.

According to the president, he needed to renegotiate international trade agreements to protect American jobs and lower the trade deficit. Others saw the same policy as limiting the sale of US services, manufactured goods, and agricultural products abroad and raising the cost of living for nearly everyone. When US intelligence agencies concluded that the Saudi Arabian crown prince Mohammed bin Salman ordered the murder of journalist Jamal Ahmad Khashoggi, Trump argued that the United States should take no action such as limiting arms sales because of the loss of jobs, the need to keep the price of oil low, and Saudi Arabia's cooperation in resisting Iran. Opponents, including some Republicans, argued that the president had made outlandish claims regarding new jobs and that the Saudi-led OPEC raised the price of oil shortly after the incident.

When in early 2019 President Trump declared a national emergency to bypass Congress and obtain funds to build a border wall, most Americans and most members of Congress opposed the move. They argued that the president was violating the Constitution, which grants Congress— not the president—control over government spending, thereby setting a potentially dangerous precedent. Preceding the Senate vote to overturn his declaration, Trump explicitly sought to frame the debate in terms of immigration, not the Constitution. On March 6, he tweeted, "Senate Republicans are not voting on constitutionality or precedent, they are voting on desperately needed Border Security & the Wall. Our Country is being invaded with Drugs, Human Traffickers, & Criminals of all shapes and sizes. That's what this vote is all about." A week later he sent another tweet, "Republican Senators are overthinking tomorrow's vote on National Emergency. It is very simply Border Security/No Crime—Should not be thought of any other way."[112] Nevertheless, twelve Republican senators opposed the president as the Senate voted 59–41 to nullify his declaration of emergency.

On June 1, 2020, amid the nationwide protests over the death of George Floyd in the custody of Minneapolis police, Trump made a statement in the White House Rose Garden condemning violence. National

Guard military police and other law enforcement officers then used tear gas and flash grenades to clear a large crowd of peaceful demonstrators from Lafayette Square, which is located between the White House and St. John's Church. The basement of the church parish house had been set afire the previous night. Without commentary the president stood in front of the boarded up church posing for photographs with a Bible. After a few minutes, he walked back to the White House.

Trump wanted to frame the issue as one of backing for law and order and also show he was not cowed by the protests. Others saw the issue differently. Some saw hypocrisy in the president's claim that he supported peaceful protests while forcibly moving nonviolent protestors to clear the path for a photo op. Critics also thought the president was contributing to the nation's discord. The Right Reverend Mariann Budde, the Episcopal bishop of Washington, D.C., was "outraged" by Trump's appropriating one of her churches for public relations purposes and for inflaming violence with his divisiveness.[113]

Conclusion

There can be little question that Donald Trump was skilled at attracting attention. His actions, statements, and tweets dominated the news. Nevertheless, he faced the same challenges that bedevil all presidents in obtaining and focusing the public's attention and framing the terms of debate. Moreover, sometimes his inflammatory rhetoric and lack of message discipline created distractions from his priorities and alienated voters. In the next chapter we examine the end result of the president's public relations efforts: his level of success in obtaining the public's support.

On Deaf Ears

Shortly before his inauguration, Donald Trump warned congressional Republicans that if the party faltered, he was ready to use the power of the presidency—and Twitter—to usher his legislation to passage. "The Congress can't get cold feet because the people will not let that happen,"[1] he declared. The implication was that he could mobilize opinion behind his policies and leverage that opinion to move Congress. Trump's orientation to governing was standard for modern presidents.[2] Nevertheless, presidents almost always fail to succeed in leading the public.[3] Was Trump an exception?

In this chapter, I examine three issues that dominated the Trump legislative agenda in his first two years in office: health care, taxes, and immigration. I also investigate his policies regarding international trade, a key issue in his third year in office. My focus is on the president's success in obtaining the public's backing for his policies. All presidents start with a core of supporters, centered among those who share his party affiliation. Yet this base is typically too small to represent a majority of the public. Thus, the question is whether the president can persuade those outside his base to change their minds and support his initiatives.

The four issues provide a best test case of the potential for opinion leadership. The health care policy the president sought to replace, the Affordable Care Act, had been unpopular since Congress passed it in 2010. Giving people a tax cut is hardly a politician's nightmare. There is a broad consensus on the importance of securing our borders and obeying immigration laws. Finally, the president's argument that he was protecting American workers and businesses from unfair foreign competition is unlikely on its face to alienate many people. If the president, with all his finely honed public relations skills, could not move the public to support his policies in these four areas, his failure provides yet further evidence that persuading the public is not at the core of presidential leadership. We saw in chapter 2 that President Trump's strategic position with the public provided limited opportunity for him to move opinion. That context and its centrality to the impact of presidential leadership leads me to predict that he would not be successful in leading the public.[4] Yet Donald Trump was no ordinary president. Did his undoubted skills at attracting attention and labeling opponents and thus dominating the media and political discourse enable him to expand his base to win majority support for his policies, support he could then leverage to move Congress to back them?

Health Care

The Affordable Care Act (ACA), otherwise known as Obamacare, was a signature achievement of Barack Obama and the Democrat-controlled Congress of 2009–2010. During the 2016 presidential campaign, Donald Trump identified repealing and replacing the ACA as a top priority and promised to act on it immediately after taking office. Republican leaders put repeal of the ACA atop their legislative agenda and employed the budgetary reconciliation process to avoid a Democratic filibuster in the Senate.

From one perspective, repealing and replacing the ACA should not have been a difficult task. It was unpopular when it passed and remained so until Trump took office.[5] If presidents can move public opinion in their direction, Trump was well positioned to obtain the public's support for the alternatives he championed. On the other hand, the public's aversion to loss, its resistance to being led, and Trump's unpopularity and lack of competence in communicating beyond his base should make us reluctant to anticipate success.

The Affordable Care Act

If our theorizing about the prospects for presidential leadership of the public is correct, we should expect to see the public resist the Republicans' initiative. That is exactly what happened. In the face of the president's criticism of the ACA, first pluralities and then majorities responded that they had favorable views of Obamacare (table 4.1). In other words, once Trump tried to repeal the law, it became more popular than it had ever been.

TABLE 4.1. **Public opinion of the Affordable Care Act**

Date of poll	Favorable (%)	Unfavorable (%)	Unsure (%)
Dec. 13–19, 2016	43	46	11
Feb. 13–19, 2017	48	42	10
Mar. 6–12, 2017	49	44	6
Apr. 17–23, 2017	48	41	12
May 16–22, 2017	49	42	9
June 14–19, 2017	51	41	8
July 5–10, 2017	50	44	6
Aug. 1–6, 2017	52	39	8
Sept. 13–18, 2017	46	44	10
Oct. 5–10, 2017	51	40	9
Nov. 8–13, 2017	50	46	5
Jan. 16–21, 2018	50	42	8
Feb. 15–20, 2018	54	42	5
Mar. 8–13, 2018	50	43	7
Apr. 20–30, 2018	49	43	9
June 11–20, 2018	50	41	8
July 17–22, 2018	48	40	11
Aug. 23–28, 2018	50	40	10
Sept. 19–Oct. 2, 2018	49	42	9
Nov. 14–19, 2018	53	44	8
Jan. 9–14, 2019	51	40	10
Feb. 14–24, 2019	50	37	13
Mar. 13–18, 2019	50	39	12
Apr. 11–16, 2019	50	38	13
May 30–June 4, 2019	46	40	12
July 18–23, 2019	48	41	12
Sept. 3–8, 2019	53	41	7
Oct. 3–8, 2019	51	40	8
Nov. 7–12, 2019	52	41	7
Jan. 16–22, 2020	53	37	10
Feb. 13–28, 2020	55	37	9
Mar. 25–30, 2020	50	39	12
May 13–18, 2020	51	41	8
July 14–19, 2020	51	36	13

Note: Respondents answered the question, "As you may know, a health reform bill was signed into law in 2010. Given what you know about the health reform law, do you have a generally favorable or generally unfavorable opinion of it?"
Source: Kaiser Health Tracking polls.

The data in table 4.1 come from the Kaiser Family Foundation's Health Tracking Poll. The Gallup Poll had similar findings (table 4.2). In November 2016, it found that 42 percent approved of the ACA while 53 percent disapproved. By early April 2017, opinion had changed to 55 percent approval and only 41 percent disapproval.[6] Notable change occurred among all party groups, including Republicans.

TABLE 4.2. **Changes in partisan approval of the Affordable Care Act**

	Approval (%)		
Group	Nov. 2016	Apr. 2017	Change in Approval (percentage points)
All	42	55	+13
Democrats	76	86	+10
Independents	40	57	+17
Republicans	7	17	+10
Democrats + leaners	71	87	+16
Republicans + leaners	11	19	+8

Note: Respondents answered the question, "Do you generally approve or disapprove of the 2010 Affordable Care Act, signed into law by President Obama that restructured the US health care system?"
Source: Gallup polls, Nov. 9–13, 2016, and Apr. 1–2, 2017.

TABLE 4.3. **Public approval of the Affordable Care Act**

Date of poll	Approve (%)	Disapprove (%)	Unsure (%)
Oct. 20–25, 2016	46	51	4
Nov. 30–Dec. 5, 2016	48	47	5
Feb. 7–12, 2017	54	43	3
Nov. 29–Dec. 4, 2017	56	38	6

Note: Respondents answered the question, "Do you approve or disapprove of the health care law passed by Barack Obama and Congress in 2010?"
Source: Pew Research Center polls.

The data in table 4.3, from the Pew Research Center, show just how swift the opinion turnaround was. A majority of the public disapproved of the ACA just before the 2016 presidential election. By February 2017, a majority approved it, approval that continued through the end of the year.

Republican Health Care Proposals

Nevertheless, the White House and congressional Republicans persisted in attempting to repeal and replace the ACA. Congressional leaders proposed a number of alternatives, and the president supported all of them. The House passed the American Health Care Act (ACHA) on May 4, 2017. The public's reaction was overwhelmingly negative (table 4.4), both during its consideration by the House and after it passed. At no point did even a third of the public, much less a plurality, support the bill. Most

TABLE 4.4. **Support for House Republican health care bills, 2017**

Date of poll	Support (%)	Oppose (%)	Unsure (%)
Mar. 13–14[a]	32	43	26
Mar. 15–17[b]	12	41	47
Mar. 16–17[c]	24	45	31
Mar. 16–21[d]	17	56	26
Mar. 19–21[a]	31	45	25
Mar. 25[c]	22	52	27
Mar. 25–28[e]	29	63	10
May 4–9[f]	21	56	22
May 6[g]	31	44	25
May 11–13[h]	23	48	29
May 13, 15–17[i]	32	55	13
May 16–22[j]	31	55	13
May 17–23[d]	20	57	23
May 31–June 5[k]	33	57	8
May 31–June 6[d]	17	62	21
June 14–19[j]	30	55	15
June 15–18[e]	32	59	10
June 17–20[h]	16	48	36
June 22–27[l]	16	58	26
July 5–10[j]	28	61	11
July 10–13[m]	24	50	26

[a]YouGov/*The Economist* poll: "Overall, given what you know about them, do you support or oppose the proposed changes to the health care system being developed by Congress and the Trump [a]dministration?"
[b]YouGov/CBS News poll: "Do you support or oppose the new health care bill from House Republicans?"
[c]*HuffPost*/YouGov poll: "As you may know, Republican leaders in the House of Representatives recently released a new health care bill. Do you generally favor or oppose this bill?"
[d]Quinnipiac University poll: "There is a Republican health care plan to replace Obamacare, known as the American Health Care Act. Do you approve or disapprove of this Republican health care plan?" (asked of registered voters).
[e]CBS News poll: "As you may know, Republicans in Congress passed a bill in the House of Representatives to repeal and replace the 2010 health care law. From what you have heard or read, do you approve or disapprove this plan?"
[f]Quinnipiac University poll: "There is a revised Republican health care plan to replace Obamacare, known as the American Health Care Act. Do you approve or disapprove of this revised Republican health care plan?" (asked of registered voters).
[g]*HuffPost*/YouGov poll: "As you may know, Republican leaders in the House of Representatives recently passed a new health care bill. Do you generally favor or oppose this bill?"
[h]NBC News/*Wall Street Journal* poll: "Now as you may know, health care legislation was recently passed by the House of Representatives and supported by Donald Trump. From what you have heard about this health care legislation, do you think it is [ROTATE]—a good idea or a bad idea? If you do not have an opinion either way, please just say so.
[i]Monmouth University poll: "Earlier this month, the House of Representatives passed the American Health Care Act. This new bill repeals or replaces certain provisions of the 2010 Affordable Care Act, sometimes called Obamacare. Do you approve or disapprove of this new bill?"
[j]Kaiser Family Foundation Tracking poll: "As you may know, Congress is currently discussing a health care plan that would repeal and replace the Affordable Care Act. Given what you know about this proposed new health care plan, do you have a generally favorable or generally unfavorable opinion of it?"
[k]Democracy Corps poll: "From what you know, do you approve or disapprove the health care bill that House Republicans passed earlier this month to replace Obamacare, known as the American Health Care Act?"
[l]Quinnipiac University poll: "There is a Republican health care plan to replace Obamacare. Do you approve or disapprove of this Republican health care plan?" (asked of registered voters).
[m]*Washington Post*/ABC News poll: "What do you prefer: the current federal health care law, known as Obamacare, or the Republican plan to replace it?"

polls showed majorities in opposition. Indeed, the ACHA did not garner majority support in a single state.[7]

After the House passed the ACHA, the legislative focus moved to the Senate. The Republican proposals in the upper chamber were no more popular than were proposals in the House. They had very little support and typically met with opposition from a majority of the public (table 4.5).

Approval of Trump's Handling of Health Care

Presidents want not only support for their policies but also approval of their performance. Did Donald Trump win the public's approval of his handling of health care? The answer is clear: majorities of the public always disapproved of the president's performance on health care (table 4.6). Approval was typically below 40 percent. The public did not like the president's performance any more than it cared for the policies he backed.[8]

TABLE 4.5. **Support for Senate Republican version of health care reform, 2017**

Date of poll	Support (%)	Oppose (%)	Unsure (%)
June 21–25[a]	17	55	27
June 24–27[b]	12	45	43
July 13–16[c]	27	56	17
July 17–Aug. 1[d]	25	64	11
Sept. 18–21[e]	33	56	11
Sept. 21–24[f]	20	52	28
Sept. 21–26[g]	19	59	22

[a]NPR/PBS *NewsHour* poll: "From what you have read or heard, do you approve or disapprove of the health care plan Senate Republicans have proposed?"
[b]Suffolk University/*USA Today* poll: "Senate Republicans have unveiled their proposed health care plan to replace Obamacare. Do you support or oppose the GOP plan, or don't you know enough to have an opinion?"
[c]Monmouth University poll: "Do you approve or disapprove of this Senate Bill (to repeal or replace certain provisions of the 2010 Affordable Care Act)?"
[d]Quinnipiac University poll: "Do you approve or disapprove of the Republican ideas to replace Obamacare?" (asked of registered voters).
[e]*Washington Post*/ABC News poll: "There's a new Republican proposal to replace the current federal health care law, known as Obamacare. It would end the national requirement for nearly all Americans to have health insurance, phase out the use of federal funds to help lower- and moderate-income people buy health insurance, and let states replace federal rules on health care coverage with their own rules. What do you prefer: the current federal health care law, or this Republican plan to replace it?"
[f]CBS News poll: "As you may know, Republicans in the Senate recently put forward a new plan, called Graham-Cassidy, that would repeal and replace the Affordable Care Act of 2010. From what you have heard or read, do you approve or disapprove of Graham-Cassidy, the new Republican plan?
[g]Quinnipiac University poll: "There is a Republican health care plan to replace Obamacare. Do you approve or disapprove of this Republican health care plan?" (asked of registered voters).

TABLE 4.6. **Public approval of Trump's handling health care**

Date of poll	Approve (%)	Disapprove (%)	Unsure (%)
Jan. 31–Feb. 2, 2017[a]	42	50	9
Mar. 1–4, 2017[a]	43	53	4
Mar. 12–14, 2017[b]	35	55	10
Mar. 16–21, 2017[c]	29	61	10
Mar. 23–27, 2017[d]	37	62	1
Mar. 25–28, 2017[e]	32	59	9
Mar. 30–Apr. 4, 2017[c]	28	64	9
Apr. 12–18, 2017[c]	29	65	6
Apr. 22–25, 2017[a]	36	61	4
Apr. 23–25, 2017[b]	35	56	9
May 4–9, 2017[c]	28	66	6
May 17–23, 2017[c]	32	62	6
May 31–June 6, 2017[c]	28	66	6
June 7–11, 2017[f]	28	67	5
June 8–11, 2017[d]	32	66	1
June 22–27, 2017[c]	29	63	8
June 25–27, 2017[b]	36	55	9
July 16–18, 2017[b]	32	59	9
July 27–Aug. 1, 2017[c]	28	65	7
Aug. 3–6, 2017[a]	31	62	7
Aug. 3–6, 2017[e]	32	59	9
Aug. 9–15, 2017[c]	33	63	5
Aug. 17–22, 2017[c]	30	65	5
Aug. 27–29, 2017[b]	34	60	6
Sept. 14–18, 2017[g]	27	53	10
Sept. 17–20, 2017[a]	31	59	10
Sept. 21–24, 2017[e]	29	62	9
Sept. 21–26, 2017[c]	34	60	6
Sept. 24–26, 2017[b]	35	58	7
Sept. 28–Oct. 2, 2017[d]	31	68	1
Oct. 12–15, 2017[a]	34	60	7
Oct. 22–24, 2017[b]	33	60	7
Oct. 23–26, 2017[g]	27	57	16
Nov. 2–5, 2017[a]	33	59	8
November 2–8, 2017[f]	31	64	5
Dec. 4–7, 2017[h]	35	58	7
Dec. 6–11, 2017[c]	29	64	7
Dec. 7–11, 2017[d]	29	70	0
Jan. 12–16, 2018[c]	33	60	6
Jan. 2–23, 2018[b]	40	51	8
June 14–17, 2018[a]	33	54	13
June 27–July 1, 2018[c]	37	55	8
Aug. 16–20, 2018[d]	36	63	0
Aug. 19–21, 2018[b]	36	55	9
Sept. 16–19, 2018[b]	38	52	10
Oct. 11–14, 2018[d]	38	62	2
Oct. 13–16, 2018[b]	37	53	9
Dec. 9–11, 2018[b]	33	56	11
Jan. 16–20, 2019[d]	35	62	3
Jan. 18–21, 2019[e]	35	54	12
May 11–14, 2019[b]	36	55	9

TABLE 4.6. (*continued*)

Date of poll	Approve (%)	Disapprove (%)	Unsure (%)
June 13–17, 2019[d]	35	62	2
June 28–July 1, 2019[i]	38	54	8
July 9–Aug. 5, 2019[j]	36	61	2
July 21–23, 2019[b]	38	51	11
Aug. 15–18, 2019[d]	37	61	3
Aug. 16–20, 2019[k]	37	61	3
Sept. 15–17, 2019[b]	34	56	10
Oct. 24–28, 2019[d]	43	55	2
Oct. 27–30, 2019[b]	35	53	12
Jan. 16–21, 2020[d]	38	61	14
Jan. 16–19, 2020[a]	38	53	9
Jan. 19–22, 2020[b]	38	54	7
Feb. 23–26, 2020[b]	38	53	9
Mar. 26–29, 2020[d]	42	57	1
Apr. 2–6, 2020[c]	39	54	6
Apr. 3–6, 2020[a]	42	52	6
Apr. 16–20, 2020[d]	39	60	2
May 7–10, 2020[a]	42	53	6
May 13–18, 2020[i]	45	51	5
May 14–18, 2020[c]	41	54	5
May 14–18, 2020[d]	42	56	2
June 11–15, 2020[d]	40	59	2
June 11–15, 2020[c]	39	56	5
June 13–16, 2020[b]	39	53	8
July 9–13, 2020[c]	39	59	7
July 14–19, 2020[i]	36	55	8
July 16–20, 2020[d]	36	63	0

[a]CNN poll: "Do you approve or disapprove of the way Donald Trump is handling health care policy?"
[b]Fox News poll: "Do you approve or disapprove of the way Donald Trump is handling health care?" (asked of registered voters).
[c]Quinnipiac University poll: "Do you approve or disapprove of the way Donald Trump is handling health care?" (asked of registered voters).
[d]Associated Press poll: "Overall, do you approve or disapprove of the way Donald Trump is handling health care?"
[e]CBS News poll: "Do you approve or disapprove of the way Donald Trump is handling health care?"
[f]Gallup poll: "Do you approve or disapprove of the way Donald Trump is handling health care policy?"
[g]NBC News/*Wall Street Journal* poll: "Please tell me if you approve or disapprove of President (Donald) Trump's handling [of] health care."
[h]NPR/PBS *NewsHour* poll: "Thinking about President Donald Trump's first year in office, do you approve or disapprove of his handling of health care?"
[i]ABC News/*Washington Post* poll: "Do you approve or disapprove of the way Trump is handling health care?" (asked of half the sample).
[j]*Washington Post*/Kaiser Family Foundation poll: "Do you approve or disapprove of the way President Trump is handling health care?"
[k]Monmouth University poll: "Overall, do you approve or disapprove of the way Donald Trump is handling health care?"
[l]Kaiser Family Foundation poll: "Do you approve or disapprove of the way President Donald Trump is handling health care?"

Government Responsibility for Health Care

At the heart of the Republican proposals for health care insurance was limiting the numbers covered by government programs by restricting Medicaid, cutting insurance subsidies, or abolishing the mandate for individuals to have health insurance. Trump wanted to persuade the public to support such moves. I have argued that he was likely to fail (other than on the unpopular individual mandate) because the public's preference for increased government action tends to move in opposition to the ideology of the party in power.

That is exactly what happened. Data from Gallup and the American Enterprise Institute (table 4.7) show that over the previous few years there had been a gradual increase in the view that government has responsibility to ensure health care coverage for everyone. Those holding

TABLE 4.7. **Government responsibility to ensure health care**

Date of poll	Believe it is (%)	Believe it is not (%)	Unsure (%)
Jan. 13–16, 2000	59	38	3
Sept. 11–13, 2000	64	31	5
Nov. 8–11, 2001*	62	34	4
Nov. 11–14, 2002*	62	35	3
Nov. 3–5, 2003*	59	39	2
Nov. 7–10, 2004*	64	34	2
Nov. 7–10, 2005*	58	38	4
Nov. 9–12, 2006*	69	28	3
Nov. 11–14, 2007*	64	33	3
Nov. 13–16, 2008*	54	41	5
Nov. 5–8, 2009	47	50	3
Nov. 4–7, 2010	47	50	3
Nov. 3–6, 2011	50	46	4
Nov. 15–18, 2012	44	54	2
Nov. 7–10, 2013	42	56	2
Nov. 6–9, 2014	45	52	3
Nov. 4–8, 2015	51	47	2
Nov. 9–13, 2016	52	45	3
Nov. 2–8, 2017	56	42	2
Nov. 1–11, 2018	57	40	3
Nov. 1–14, 2019	54	45	1
May 21–June 5, 2020	63	35	2

Note: Respondents answered the question, "Do you think it is the responsibility of the federal government to make sure all Americans have health care coverage, or is that not the responsibility of the federal government?"
Source: Gallup polls except for May 21–June 5, 2020, which is an American Enterprise Institute poll.
*Asked of half the sample.

TABLE 4.8. **Is the government responsible for ensuring health care coverage?**

Date of poll	Believe it is (%)	Believe it is not (%)	Unsure (%)
Jan. 23–Feb. 9, 2014	47	50	3
Mar. 17–27, 2016	51	46	2
Jan. 4–9, 2017	60	38	2
June 8–18, 2017	60	39	2
Sept. 18–24, 2018	60	37	3
July 22–Aug. 4, 2019	60	37	2
Sept. 3–15, 2019	59	41	1

Note: Respondents answered the question, "Do you think it is the responsibility of the federal government to make sure all Americans have health care coverage, or is that not the responsibility of the federal government?"
Source: Pew Research Center polls.

this belief increased to 63 percent in 2020, no doubt influenced by the coronavirus pandemic.

The Pew Research Center also found a significant increase in the view that government has responsibility for health care, increasing 9 percentage points between 2016 and 2017 (table 4.8). The view that the government has a responsibility to ensure health coverage increased across many groups over 2016, but the rise was particularly striking among lower- and middle-income Republicans, a key Trump constituency and a group that benefitted substantially from the Affordable Care Act. In early 2017, 52 percent of Republicans with family incomes below $30,000 said the federal government had a responsibility to ensure health coverage for all, up from just 31 percent in 2016. There was also a 20 percentage-point increase among Republicans with incomes of $30,000–$74,999 (from 14 percent to 34 percent).

The unpopularity of the Republicans' efforts to change health care policy came back to haunt them in the 2018 midterm elections. A plurality of 41 percent of the public identified health care as the issue most important to their vote. Unsurprisingly, Democrats made health care the centerpiece of their campaign in races throughout the country. Asked which party would better address Americans with preexisting conditions, 58 percent said Democrats, compared with 34 percent who said Republicans.[9]

Tax Cuts

Tax cuts typically are not difficult sells. People naturally prefer having more money in their pockets. Moreover, many people feel they pay more than their fair share of taxes and that their taxes are too high.[10] The president tried to capitalize on the public's inclinations and tweeted and spoke frequently about the benefits of cutting taxes for individuals and businesses.

Did the public respond to the president's arguments? It did not. The data in table 4.9 show that at no time did the Republican tax proposals obtain the support of a majority—or even a plurality—of the public. Moreover, as Congress began focusing on tax legislation in earnest following the 2017 August recess and as the president held tax reform rallies around the country, support for the bills did not increase. There was a short period in January through March 2018, after the tax cut bill passed, when support ticked up. Nevertheless, opponents still outnumbered supporters, and support dropped to low levels as spring set in.

Table 4.10 provides data on registered voters and tells a similar story. Majorities of registered voters typically opposed the tax cuts, and there

TABLE 4.9. **Public approval of Republican tax proposals**

Date of poll	Support (%)	Oppose (%)	Unsure (%)
Sept. 18–21, 2017[a]	28	44	28
Oct. 12–15, 2017[b]	34	52	14
Oct. 23–26, 2017[c]	25	35	40
Oct. 29–Nov. 1, 2017[a]	33	50	17
Nov. 2–5, 2017[d]	31	45	24
Nov. 19–2, 2017[e]	30	41	29
Nov. 28–29, 2017[f]	30	39	30
Dec. 1–2, 2017[g]	29	56	16
Dec. 3–5, 2017[h]	35	53	12
Dec. 3–5, 2017[e]	31	42	27
Dec. 5–7, 2017[i]	28	43	29
Dec. 10–12, 2017[j]	26	47	27
Dec. 10–13, 2017[k]	26	38	36
Dec. 13–15, 2017[c]	24	41	35
Dec. 14–17, 2017[d]	33	55	12
Dec. 17–19, 2017[e]	32	41	26
Jan. 2–7, 2018[l]	33	55	12
Jan. 10–15, 2018[m]	37	46	17
Jan. 13–16, 2018[n]	40	48	12
Jan. 28–30, 2018[o]	44	44	13
Feb. 26–Mar. 4, 2018[l]	39	48	13
Mar. 2–5, 2018[o]	41	42	17
Mar. 8–11, 2018[p]	38	47	15
Mar. 22–25, 2018[q]	34	36	30
Apr. 2–11, 2018[l]	39	52	8
Apr. 5–May 14, 2018[r]	35	44	20
Apr. 8–11, 2018[c]	27	36	37

TABLE 4.9. (*continued*)

Date of poll	Support (%)	Oppose (%)	Unsure (%)
May 3–6, 2018[p]	43	46	11
May 14–30, 2018[s]	39	48	12
June 12–13, 2018[t]	34	41	24
July 23–Aug. 9, 2018[s]	41	48	12
Aug. 19–21, 2018[u]	31	35	34
Sept. 18–24, 2018[v]	36	46	18
Sept. 24–30, 2018[j]	39	46	15
Oct. 14–17, 2018[p]	35	44	20
Mar. 20–25, 2019[w]	37	48	15
Apr. 1–9, 2019[x]	40	49	11
Apr. 11–15, 2019[t]	34	43	23
Apr. 28–May 1, 2019[c]	27	36	37

[a]ABC News/*Washington Post* poll: "Given what you've heard or read about it, do you support or oppose Trump's tax plan?"

[b]CNN poll: "Overall, do you favor or oppose the tax reform proposals made by the Trump administration?"

[c]*Wall Street Journal*/NBC News poll: "Is the Republican tax law a good idea or bad idea?"

[d]CNN poll: "Overall, do you favor or oppose the tax reform proposals made by Republicans in Congress?"

[e]*The Economist*/YouGov poll: "From what you know about it now, do you support or oppose the Republican tax plan being debated in Congress?"

[f]*HuffPost*/YouGov poll: "As you know, Republican leaders in Congress are working to pass a new tax reform bill. Do you generally favor or oppose their proposals?"

[g]Gallup poll: "From what you've heard or read about them, would you say you approve or disapprove of these proposed changes to the tax code?"

[h]CBS News poll: "From what you have heard or read, do you approve or disapprove of the Republican tax plan?"

[i]*HuffPost* / YouGov poll: "As you may know, Senate Republicans recently passed a new tax reform bill. Do you generally favor or oppose the bill?"

[j]Monmouth University poll: "Have you heard that the Senate and the House have passed tax reform bills and are now working on a final version, or haven't you heard about this?" "Do you approve or disapprove of this tax reform plan?"

[k]CNBC All-America Economic Survey. "From what you have heard, do you favor or oppose the approach that President Trump and the Republicans in Congress are taking to change and reform the tax system? If you do not know enough to say, please just say so."

[l]Gallup poll: "Do you approve or disapprove of the tax bill passed by Congress and signed into law by the president last December?"

[m]Pew Research Center poll: "Do you approve or disapprove of the tax law passed by Donald Trump and Congress last month?"

[n]CBS News poll: "From what you have heard or read, do you approve or disapprove of the tax law that was passed by Congress and signed by Donald Trump in December?"

[o]Monmouth University poll: "Do you approve or disapprove of the tax reform plan passed by Congress in December?"

[p]CBS News poll: "From what you have heard or read, do you approve or disapprove of the tax law that was passed by Congress and signed by Donald Trump?"

[q]*HuffPost*/YouGov poll: "Do you generally favor or oppose the tax reform law recently passed by Congress?"

[r]Democracy Fund Voter Study Group poll: "Do you favor or oppose the tax plan that was passed by Congress and signed into law by President Trump?"

[s]GW Politics poll: "Do you favor or oppose the tax plan that was passed by Congress and signed into law by President Trump?" (asked of registered voters).

[t]Monmouth University poll: "Do you approve or disapprove of the tax reform passed by Congress in December 2017?"

[u]*The Economist*/YouGov poll: "From what you know about it now, do you support or oppose the new tax reform law?"

[v]Pew Research Center poll: "Do you approve or disapprove of the tax law passed by Donald Trump and Congress last year?"

[w]Pew Research Center poll: "Do you approve or disapprove of the tax law passed by Donald Trump and Congress in 2017?"

[x]Gallup poll: "Do you approve or disapprove of the tax bill passed by Congress and signed into law by the president (Donald Trump) in December 2017?"

TABLE 4.10. **Registered voters' approval of Republican tax plans**

Date of poll	Favor (%)	Oppose (%)	Unsure (%)
Nov. 7–13, 2017	25	52	23
Nov. 29–Dec. 4, 2017	29	53	18
Dec. 6–11, 2017	26	55	18
Jan. 5–9, 2018	32	52	16
Feb. 2–5, 2018	39	47	14
Mar. 3–5, 2018	36	50	14
Mar. 16–20, 2018	38	47	16
June 14–17, 2018*	39	46	15

Note: Respondents answered the question, "Do you approve or disapprove of the Republican tax plan?"
Source: Quinnipiac University polls.
*"Do you approve or disapprove of the 2017 tax law passed by Congress and signed by President Trump?"

was always a substantial gap between the percentages of supporters and opponents. The president never obtained even 40 percent approval of his policy. Thus, he could take no solace in support from those who were most likely to vote in the 2018 midterm elections.

Why did the public not support tax cuts? It is clear that most people did not accept the president's narrative. People thought the tax cuts would benefit the wealthy and large corporations. Table 4.11 shows the responses of the public regarding the income groups it expected to benefit from the tax cuts.[11] There was little change in opinion throughout Congress's consideration of the bill. Most people opposed such reductions,[12] because they felt the wealthy and large businesses were already not paying their fair share. Indeed, the public wanted to *increase* taxes on them.[13] People typically did not expect the tax bill to reduce their taxes, and many expected their taxes to increase rather than decrease.[14] By January 2019, 65 percent of the public supported increasing tax rates on families earning over $1 million a year.[15] In September 2019, 58 percent supported raising the taxes of households earning more than $250,000 a year.[16]

The president argued that tax cuts to businesses, especially, would stimulate the economy and create jobs. The public was skeptical.[17] At the end of October 2017, CBS News found that 57 percent of the public thought that corporations would use tax reductions to increase dividends for shareholders rather than to expand hiring. Although the White House and congressional Republicans argued vigorously that businesses would use their tax savings to expand employment, the percentage of the public expecting corporations instead to spend their augmented revenue on

TABLE 4.11. **Who benefits from tax cuts?**

Date of poll	Low income (%)	Middle class (%)	Wealthy (%)	Unsure (%)
May 4–9, 2017[a]	4	27	63	7
Aug. 30–Sept. 3, 2017[b]	10	29	52	9
Nov. 7–13, 2017[c]	6	24	61	9
Nov. 29–Dec. 4, 2017[c]	5	24	64	8
Dec. 6–11, 2017[c]	4	21	65	9
Dec. 14–17, 2017[d]	—	27	66	7
Jan. 5–9, 2018[c]	4	22	66	8
Feb. 2–5, 2018[c]	5	26	62	7

[a]Quinnipiac University poll: "Who do you think will benefit the most from this (President Donald Trump's tax) plan: low-income Americans, middle-class Americans, or wealthy Americans?" (asked of registered voters).
[b]*Politico*/Harvard Public Health poll: "Who do you think will benefit the most from President Donald Trump's tax plan? Low-income households, middle-income households, high-income households?"
[c]Quinnipiac University poll: "Who do you think will benefit the most from this Republican tax plan: low-income Americans, middle-class Americans, or wealthy Americans?" (asked of registered voters).
[d]CNN poll: "Overall, do you think the tax reform proposals made by the Republicans in Congress will do more to benefit the middle class or do more to benefit the wealthy?"

dividends rose to 64 percent in early December, shortly before the tax bill became law.[18]

America First Policies, a pro-Trump nonprofit group, commissioned a poll over February 16–20, 2018, which asked: "When talking about the bonuses that companies like AT&T, Wells Fargo and Visa have recently given their employees due to tax reform, Nancy Pelosi said, 'In terms of the bonus that corporate America received versus the crumbs that they are giving workers to kind of put the schmooze on is so pathetic.' Do you agree or disagree with Nancy Pelosi's statement?" We can assume that the commissioners were expecting a rejection of the Democratic leader's comments. Instead, the poll found that 49 percent of respondents "totally agreed" with her statement, while 43 percent disagreed.

The administration also claimed that the tax cuts would stimulate the economy, producing so much tax revenue that they would actually shrink yearly deficits.[19] Once again, the public was not buying the argument. Polls repeatedly found that people expected the tax cuts to increase the size of annual deficits rather than to pay for themselves.[20]

It is not surprising, then, that the public not only failed to support the Republican tax bills, but they also found the president wanting on tax policy (table 4.12). Despite the president's efforts to portray himself as giving Americans a great Christmas present in the form of reduced taxes and to provide a vigorous stimulus to the economy, majorities or large pluralities

TABLE 4.12. **Public approval of Trump's handling of taxes**

Date of poll	Approve (%)	Disapprove (%)	Unsure (%)
Mar. 1–4, 2017[a]	43	48	9
Mar. 23–27, 2017[b]	44	54	3
Apr. 23–25, 2017[c]	40	44	17
May 4–9, 2017[d]	34	54	13
June 7–11, 2017[e]	35	57	7
Aug. 3–6, 2017[a]	34	48	18
Aug. 27–29, 2017[c]	37	45	18
Sept. 17–20, 2017[a]	34	47	19
Oct. 5–10, 2017[d]	37	49	14
Oct. 12–15, 2017[a]	36	50	14
Oct. 12–16, 2017[b]	39	59	2
Oct. 22–24, 2017[c]	37	51	13
Nov. 2–5, 2017[a]	35	51	14
Nov. 2–8, 2017[e]	37	55	8
Nov. 7–13, 2017[d]	34	55	11
Dec. 3–5, 2017[f]	38	47	15
Dec. 6–11, 2017[d]	35	58	7
Dec. 7–11, 2017[b]	32	66	1
Dec. 14–17, 2017[a]	34	57	9
Dec. 17–19, 2017[f]	37	47	15
Jan. 4–18, 2018[a]	42	46	12
Jan. 5–9, 2018[d]	42	51	7
Feb. 1–10, 2018[e]	46	52	2
Feb. 2–5, 2018[d]	45	47	7
Mar. 4–8, 2018[g]	47	48	5
Mar. 14–19, 2018[b]	46	53	1
Mar. 18–21, 2018[c]	48	46	7
Apr. 6–9, 2018[d]	46	47	7
June 27–July1, 2018[d]	43	51	6
Aug. 9–12, 2018[a]	45	46	9
Aug. 16–20, 2018[b]	44	54	1
Nov. 1–3, 2018[a]	43	49	8
Jan. 16–20, 2019[b]	40	57	3
Feb. 12–28, 2019[e]	45	52	3
Mar. 14–17, 2019[a]	42	49	9
Mar. 17–20, 2019[c]	42	48	9
May 11–14, 2019[c]	41	52	6
June 13–17, 2019[b]	42	55	3
June 28–July 1, 2019[h]	42	49	9
Oct. 6–10, 2019[i]	47	49	4

[a]CNN poll: "Do you approve or disapprove of the way Donald Trump is handling taxes?" (asked of half the sample of 1,025 in the March 1–4, 2017 poll; asked of half the sample of 1,018 in the August 3–6 2017 poll).
[b]Associated Press poll: "Overall, do you approve or disapprove of the way Donald Trump is handling taxes?"
[c]Fox News poll: "Do you approve or disapprove of the way Donald Trump is handling taxes?" (asked of registered voters).
[d]Quinnipiac University poll: "Do you approve or disapprove of the way Donald Trump is handling taxes?" (asked of registered voters).
[e]Gallup poll: "Do you approve or disapprove of the way Donald Trump is handling taxes?"
[f]*Economist*/ YouGov poll: "Do you approve or disapprove of the way Donald Trump is handling taxes?"
[g]George Washington University Battleground poll: "And, thinking about how Donald Trump has been doing on some issues, I am going to read you a list of issues. For each one, please tell me if you approve or disapprove of the job that Donald Trump has been doing on this issue. . . . Taxes."
[h]ABC News/*Washington Post* poll: "Do you approve or disapprove of the way Trump is handling taxes?" (asked of half the sample).
[i]Georgetown Institute of Politics and Public Service poll: "Please tell me if you approve or disapprove of the job that Donald Trump has been doing on taxes."

of the public consistently disapproved of his handling of taxes throughout Congress's consideration of tax cuts in 2017. Once Congress passed the tax cuts in December, approval of the president's handling of taxes ticked up, but only one poll (a Fox News poll of registered voters in March 2018) ever found a plurality approving. No poll found majority approval.

Immigration

Immigration was perhaps the defining issue of Donald Trump's 2016 campaign. It was the center of his June 2015 announcement speech, and his positions were prominently placed on his campaign website. He campaigned for president on a platform of blocking undocumented immigrants from entering the country and deporting those already living in the United States. Once president, Trump made tough border security and strict enforcement of immigration laws a focal point of his presidency and of his campaigning for Republicans in the 2018 midterm elections.

Debate over immigrants, legal and illegal, came to the fore of the national discourse at the start of Trump's campaign and intensified as he has moved to deliver on his pledges as president. No policy energized the president as much as immigration, and he spoke and tweeted frequently about his plans and strongly criticized those who opposed them. Few Americans could be unaware of the thrust of Trump's views. The question is whether the public followed the president's lead.

Illegal Immigration: The Wall

The iconic image of the Trump presidency is a wall along the border with Mexico. Building the wall was central to Trump's promises to his base and to his identity as a candidate. The president promised to build it—and to make Mexico pay for it—throughout his campaign, and crowds greeted him chanting, "Build that wall! Build that wall!" Once in office, he wasted no time in issuing an executive order to do just that. On January 25, 2017, the president declared that it was his policy to "secure the southern border of the United States through the immediate construction of a physical wall on the southern border, monitored and supported by adequate personnel so as to prevent illegal immigration, drug and human trafficking, and acts of terrorism." Trump also directed the Department of Homeland Security to "immediately construct, operate, control, or establish contracts to construct, operate, or control facilities to detain aliens at or near the land border with Mexico."[21]

From one perspective, building a wall should not have been a tough sell to the public. In a review days before the 2016 election, the Gallup Poll reported, "Most Americans agree that keeping people from entering the country illegally is a good thing. As a rule, if it is illegal, Americans want it stopped." Gallup found that 77 percent of Americans said that "controlling US borders to halt the flow of illegal immigrants into the US" was extremely or very important. Moreover, 83 percent favored "tightening security at US borders."[22]

Despite broad backing for the principle of controlling our borders, Trump was not able to convince the American people to support his signature policy of building a wall. The data in table 4.13 show that the public consistently disagreed with the president. No matter how pollsters worded the question, clear majorities opposed the wall. Typically, less than 40 percent of the people supported it. Thus, despite widespread agreement on stopping illegal entry into the United States, the president was not able to obtain the public's support for his policy to operationalize that objective.

Table 4.14 shows the results of repeatedly asking the same question to a national sample of registered voters. The results are just as lopsided against the president as are those in the previous table. Both tables 4.13 and 4.14 show a very slight increase in support for a wall in January 2019. This change, primarily among Republicans, may have been the result of party loyalty strengthening during the government shutdown, or it may have been the result of the changing definition of what constitutes a "wall." In any case, the data do not indicate Trump's efforts at persuasion had much impact.

Illegal Immigration: Separating Children from Their Parents

On April 6, 2018, Attorney General Jeff Sessions announced a "zero-tolerance" policy in which the federal government would prosecute all immigrants who illegally cross the border, including those with young children. When the Border Patrol apprehended families or individuals, they went into Department of Homeland Security (DHS) custody. DHS officials referred any adult believed to have committed any crime, including illegal entry, to the Justice Department for prosecution. A conviction would trigger deportation proceedings. The policy included those who were seeking asylum but arrived illegally.

TABLE 4.13. **Public support for building a wall between the United States and Mexico**

Date of poll	Support (%)	Oppose (%)	Unsure (%)
Jan. 12–15, 2017[a]	37	60	3
Jan. 13–17, 2017[b]	37	59	3
Jan. 30–31, 2017[c]	38	60	2
Jan. 31–Feb. 2, 2017[d]	38	60	1
Feb. 7–12, 2017[e]	35	62	3
Feb. 17–21, 2017[b]	39	58	3
Feb. 28–Mar. 12, 2017[e]	40	59	1
Mar. 9–29, 2017[f]	36	56	7
Apr. 21–24, 2017[g]	37	61	3
Aug. 3–6, 2017[g]	36	61	3
Aug. 27–29, 2017[h]	39	56	5
Sept. 15–19, 2017[i]	35	60	5
Sept. 17–20, 2017[d]	33	63	3
Sept. 18–21, 2017[a]	37	62	1
Sept. 28–Oct. 2, 2017[j]	33	50	18
Oct. 18–30, 2017[k]	36	63	2
Dec. 3–5, 2017[g]	36	61	3
Jan. 10–15, 2018[l]	37	60	3
Jan. 13–16, 2018[g]	35	61	4
Jan. 14–18, 2018[d]	35	62	3
Jan. 15–18, 2018[a]	34	63	3
Jan. 21–23, 2018[h]	40	53	7
Jan. 28–30, 2018[i]	40	57	3
Feb. 21–25, 2018[m]	41	55	4
Mar. 8–11, 2018[g]	38	60	2
May 3–6, 2018[g]	38	59	3
June 5–12, 2018[l]	40	56	4
June 20–24, 2018[k]	31	63	5
June 27–July 2, 2018[n]	42	55	3
Sept. 16–19, 2018[h]	39	51	10
Sept. 17–Oct. 1, 2018[k]	41	58	1
Oct. 1–16, 2018[o]	39	59	2
Oct. 14–17, 2018[g]	37	60	3
Nov. 15–18, 2018[g]	38	59	2
Dec. 6–9, 2018[d]	38	57	4
Dec. 31–Jan. 1, 2018[p]	43	43	12
Jan. 8–11, 2019[q]	42	54	4
Jan. 9–11, 2019[e]	45	55	0
Jan. 9–14, 2019[l]	40	58	2
Jan. 10–11, 2019[d]	39	56	5
Jan. 12–15, 2019[p]	39	48	13
Jan. 16–20, 2019[q]	36	49	15
Jan. 20–22, 2019[h]	43	51	6
Jan. 21–24, 2019[a]	42	54	4
Jan. 25–27, 2019[i]	44	52	4
Feb. 10–12, 2019[h]	46	50	4
Feb. 14–15, 2019[r]	45	49	6
Mar. 1–4, 2019[i]	44	51	4

continues

TABLE 4.13. (*continued*)

Date of poll	Support (%)	Oppose (%)	Unsure (%)
Mar. 17–20, 2019[h]	44	51	5
Apr. 11–15, 2019[i]	42	56	3
Apr. 14–16, 2019[h]	45	53	2
May 11–14, 2019[h]	43	51	6
June 9–12, 2019[h]	42	55	2
Sept. 13–16, 2019[s]	43	56	1
Sept. 20–23, 2019[j]	38	46	15
Dec. 8–11, 2019[h]	44	52	4
July 16–20, 2020[j]	34	47	18

[a]ABC News/*Washington Post* poll: "Do you support or oppose building a wall along the US border with Mexico?"

[b]CBS News poll: "Would you favor or oppose building a wall along the US-Mexico border to try to stop illegal immigration?"

[c]Gallup poll: "Thinking now about some of the specific actions Donald Trump has taken since he has been in office, would you say you approve or disapprove of each of the following? How about ordering construction of a wall along the southern border with Mexico?"

[d]CNN poll: "Would you favor or oppose building a wall along the entire border with Mexico?"

[e]Pew Research Center poll: "All in all, would you favor or oppose building a wall along the entire border with Mexico?"

[f]Gallup poll: "Now, I am going to read several actions either taken or proposed by President Trump. For each one, tell me if you agree or disagree with it, or if you don't know enough to have an opinion. How about begin the construction of a wall between the US and Mexico?" (asked of half the sample of 1,526).

[g]CBS News poll: "Do you favor or oppose building a wall along the US-Mexico border to try to stop illegal immigration?"

[h]Fox News poll: "Do you favor or oppose building a wall along the US-Mexico border?" (asked of registered voters).

[i]Monmouth University poll: "Do you favor or oppose building a wall along the US border with Mexico?"

[j]Associated Press poll: "Do you favor, oppose, or neither favor nor oppose building a wall along the Mexican border to help stop illegal immigration into the United States?"

[k]PRRI American Values survey: "Do you strongly favor, favor, oppose or strongly oppose building a wall along the US border with Mexico"

[l]Pew Research Center poll: "As you may know, there is a proposal to substantially expand the wall along the US border with Mexico. In general, do you favor or oppose this proposal?"

[m]*Politico*/Harvard Public Health poll: "Do you favor or oppose building a wall along most of the US-Mexico border to try to stop illegal immigration?"

[n]*Washington Post*–Schar School poll: "Would you support or oppose building a wall along the US border with Mexico?"

[o]Program for Public Consultation poll: "Do you favor or oppose the government spending $25 billion to build a stronger barrier along the US southern border with Mexico, primarily by building a wall?" (asked of registered voters).

[p]*The Economist*/YouGov poll: "Do you favor or oppose building a wall along the US-Mexico border to try to stop illegal immigration?"

[q]Associated Press poll: "Do you favor, oppose, or neither favor nor oppose building a wall along the US-Mexican border?"

[r]*HuffPost*/YouGov poll: "Do you approve or disapprove of President Trump's plan to build a wall along the US border with Mexico?"

[s]NBC News/*Wall Street Journal* poll: "Do you strongly support, somewhat support, somewhat oppose, or strongly oppose building a wall or barrier of more than 200 miles along the United States-Mexico border?"

TABLE 4.14. **Registered voters' support for building a wall between the United States and Mexico**

Date of poll	Support (%)	Oppose (%)	Unsure (%)
Nov. 17–20, 2016	42	55	3
Feb. 2–6, 2017	38	59	3
Feb. 16–21, 2017	37	60	3
Mar. 30–Apr. 3, 2017	33	64	3
Apr. 12–18, 2017	33	64	3
May 4–9, 2017	33	64	3
Sept. 21–26, 2017	37	60	3
Dec. 6–11, 2017	36	62	2
Jan. 5–9, 2018	34	63	3
Feb. 2–5, 2018	37	59	4
Apr. 6–9, 2018	40	57	3
June 14–17, 2018	39	58	4
Aug. 9–13, 2018	38	58	4
Dec. 12–17, 2018	43	54	2
Jan. 9–13, 2019	43	55	2
Jan. 25–28, 2019	41	55	4
Mar. 1–4, 2019	41	55	5

Note: Respondents answered the question, "Do you support or oppose building a wall along the border with Mexico?"
Source: Quinnipiac University polls.

Illegal entry is a misdemeanor for first-time offenders, and a conviction is grounds for deportation. Under the zero-tolerance policy, the DHS could deport people for misdemeanors more easily, because the government would no longer prioritize the removal of dangerous criminals, gang members, or threats to national security. While parents were held in detention, the children were placed in immigrant shelters. The DHS then tried to place them with relatives or sponsors. Parents could be deported without their children, against their will. Between May 5, 2018, and June 9, 2018, more than 2,342 children were taken from their parents.

The president argued that he had no choice but to separate the immigrants from their children and blamed existing law—and the Democrats—for the separation. Trump also claimed that the parents illegally crossing the US-Mexico border with their children "could be murderers and thieves and so much else"[23] and warned they could increase gang crime and usher in cultural changes. Other administration officials maintained that the separation of children from their parents would deter future immigrants and that the policy would serve as a bargaining tool for negotiating with congressional Democrats over immigration policy.

The president's claims about his lack of discretion—and the culpability of the Democrats—were inaccurate. No law or court order required that families be separated at the border. A 1997 federal consent decree, known as the Flores settlement, requires the government to release all children apprehended crossing the border within twenty days. No part of the decree requires that families be *separated* after twenty days. Courts have ruled that the government must release children from detention facilities within twenty days under the Flores consent decree, but none of these legal developments prevented the government from releasing parents along with children.

In 2008, Congress passed a law meant to curb human trafficking called the Trafficking Victims Protection Reauthorization Act (TVPRA). This law covers children of all nationalities except Canadians and Mexicans and specifies that children who are apprehended trying to enter the United States must be released rather than detained and are exempt from prompt return to their home countries. The law passed unanimously in both chambers of Congress and was signed by Republican president George W. Bush. No part of the TVPRA requires family separations.

Both the George W. Bush and Barack Obama administrations chose to release parents who arrived with children, pending judicial proceedings. The Trump administration followed the same policy during its first fifteen months. The legal landscape did not change in the fifteen months preceding the zero-tolerance policy. What changed was the administration's handling of detainees.

The president's policy was roundly condemned. Critics included all four living former first ladies; the US Conference of Catholic Bishops and the Southern Baptist Convention; the US Chamber of Commerce; the entire Republican Senate conference and many Republican House members, including Speaker Paul Ryan; and the entire Democratic membership of Congress.

Despite the president's many public statements and vigorous use of social media, average citizens were no more pleased than his more visible critics. Two-thirds of the public found the policy of separating children from parents detained after entering the United States to be unacceptable.[24]

On June 20, 2018, the president signed an executive order ending his policy of separating children from parents apprehended for illegally crossing the Mexican border. The zero-tolerance policy remained in place, but the White House envisioned a system in which families would be housed together in detention centers. It was also asking the courts to modify the Flores settlement and allow the detention of children for longer than twenty days. Soon it became clear that there was a lack of facilities to house families, so border security personnel stopped handing over immigrant families for prosecution.

Legal Immigration: Travel Bans

The president was concerned about legal as well as illegal immigration. On January 27, 2017, a week after his inauguration and two days after he ordered the building of a wall, Trump signed an executive order banning entry to the United States for 90 days by citizens from seven majority Muslim countries: Iraq, Syria, Iran, Libya, Somalia, Sudan, and Yemen. He also suspended all refugees from entering the United States for 120 days. At the same time, he ordered the departments of State, Defense, and Homeland Security to review the vetting procedures for all immigration and refugee admissions. Once refugee admissions resumed, it called for the State Department to prioritize religious minorities like Christians in the Middle East and indefinitely ban all Syrian refugees. The president's policy set off a round of protests and created chaos in airports across the country. A number of judges found his order to be in violation of constitutional guarantees against religious discrimination.

On March 6, 2017, the president issued a new executive order that excluded Iraq from the list of Muslim-majority countries whose citizens he had temporarily blocked in the first order. The ban, which was set to take effect on March 16, barred foreign nationals from Iran, Libya, Somalia, Sudan, Syria, and Yemen from entering the United States for 90 days. It excised the permanent ban on Syrian refugees but maintained a 120-day ban on all refugees, and it exempted legal permanent residents and anyone who already had a valid visa.

Trump referred to the second ban as a "watered-down version of the first one," but a number of federal courts found it unconstitutional anyway. The president complained of "unprecedented judicial overreach," and in June, the Supreme Court allowed a limited travel ban to go into effect until there was a full hearing, scheduled for the fall. The Court ruled that the 90-day ban on citizens from Iran, Libya, Somalia, Sudan, Syria, and Yemen, and the 120-day ban on all refugees could begin, except for those who could prove a "bona fide" relationship to a person or entity in the United States. The ban went into effect on June 29, 2017. In response to a lawsuit filed by the state of Hawaii, the Supreme Court on July 19 expanded the definition of "bona fide relationships" to include grandparents and grandchildren, aunts and uncles, and cousins. In September, the Ninth Circuit Court of Appeals ruled that refugees with a formal assurance from a resettlement organization in the United States counted as a bona fide relationship, but on September 12, the Supreme Court overruled the lower court and allowed the stricter ban on refugees to remain in place.

The second ban expired on September 24, and the Supreme Court dismissed the case it was set to hear later in the fall because it no longer represented a case or controversy. The refugee ban remained in place until its October 24 expiration date.

On September 24, the administration issued a presidential proclamation barring travel indefinitely from seven countries that it determined lacked sufficient systems for sharing information about potential immigrants. These nations included Iran, Syria, Somalia, Yemen, and Libya from the original list plus Chad, North Korea, and Venezuela (targeting its leaders and their family members). These new conditions-based restrictions meant the administration could add or remove countries, depending on whether they complied with the new US standards. (Chad was later removed from the list.) In addition, the order allowed case-by-case waivers for individuals, and the rules varied by country. These provisions were meant to inoculate the administration from legal challenges. The Supreme Court allowed the ban to take effect temporarily and formally upheld it on June 26, 2018.

Trump couched his travel bans in terms of keeping terrorists out of the country. Protecting the nation from terrorism is a consensual policy, so one might expect that the public would be inclined to support the president. However, the figures in table 4.15 show that the travel bans were never popular with the American public. None obtained majority support. Within a week of the first ban, majorities or clear pluralities always opposed them. Moreover, support for the bans did not increase over time. Indeed, support typically decreased after the first few days. Even wording questions specifically to mention suspending immigration from "terror-prone" regions, a core argument of the Trump administration, did not win the president majority support (table 4.16). Moreover, rather than increasing its support for the president's policy, the public moved against it over time.

Why was public opposition to the travel bans so strong, and why did it increase some after the president announced the first ban? One reason may be that opponents succeeded in framing the ban as inconsistent with

TABLE 4.15. **Public support for Trump travel Ban**

Date of poll	Support (%)	Oppose (%)	Unsure (%)
First travel ban			
Jan. 30–31, 2017[a]	42	55	3
Jan. 30–31, 2017[b]	48	41	10
Jan. 30–31, 2017[c]	47	49	4
Jan. 31–Feb. 1, 2017[d]	48	44	8
Jan. 31–Feb. 2, 2017[e]	47	53	0
Feb. 1–2, 2017[f]	45	51	4
Feb. 2–6, 2017[g]	46	51	3
Feb. 7–12, 2017[h]	38	59	3
Feb. 11–13, 2017[d]	45	45	10
Feb. 16–21, 2017[g]	45	53	2
Feb. 16–Mar. 15, 2017[i]	47	52	1
Mar. 2–5, 2017[j]	39	49	12
Second travel ban			
Mar. 8, 2017[k]	39	50	11
Mar. 9–29, 2017[l]	40	47	13
Mar. 16–21, 2017[m]	43	53	2
Mar. 22–26, 2017[n]	46	50	4
Mar. 22–27, 2017[o]	43	52	5
Apr. 21–24, 2017[p]	43	53	4
Third travel ban			
Sept. 28–Oct. 2, 2017[q]	44	37	19
Oct. 18–30, 2017[r]	40	55	5

[a]Gallup poll: "Thinking now about some of the specific actions Donald Trump has taken since he has been in office, would you say you approve or disapprove of ordering a temporary ban on entry into the US for most people from seven predominately Muslim countries?"

[b]Reuters/Ipsos poll: "Do you agree or disagree with the [e]xecutive [o]rder that President Trump signed blocking refugees and banning people from seven Muslim majority countries from entering the US?"

[c]Public Policy polling: "Do you support or oppose Donald Trump's executive order banning refugees and citizens of certain countries from entering the US?" (asked of registered voters).

[d]*HuffPost*/YouGov poll: "President Trump recently signed an executive order banning travel for people from seven Muslim-majority countries—Iran, Iraq, Syria, Sudan, Libya, Yemen and Somalia—for 90 days, and suspending admission of refugees for 120 days. Do you approve of this ban?"

[e]CNN poll: "As you may know, Donald Trump signed an executive order which prohibits travel to the US for the next three months by citizens of seven majority-Muslim countries, and suspends the US refugee program for four months while reducing the total number of refugees the US will accept this year. Overall, do you favor or oppose this executive order?"

[f]CBS News poll: "As you may know, Donald Trump has issued an executive order that temporarily bans people from entering the US who are from the countries of Iraq, Iran, Libya, Somalia, Sudan, Syria, and Yemen. Do you approve or disapprove of this action?"

[g]Quinnipiac University poll: "Do you support or oppose suspending all travel by citizens of Iraq, Syria, Libya, Somalia, Sudan, and Yemen to the US for 90 days?" (asked of registered voters).

[h]Pew Research Center poll: "Overall, would you say you approve or disapprove of this policy (the executive order signed by Donald Trump to stop refugees from entering the US for 120 days and prevent people from seven Muslim-majority countries from entering the US on a visa for 90 days)?"

[i]Pew Research Center American Trends Panel poll and Pew Global Attitudes Project poll: "As you may know, Donald Trump recently issued an executive order that would temporarily prevent people from entering the US from (February 28–March 2, ask:) seven/(March 2–12, ask:) a number of majority-Muslim countries. Do you approve or disapprove of this action?"

[j]Monmouth University poll: "Have you heard about the Trump administration's travel ban that affected people from certain countries in the Middle East and Africa, or not? Do you think the original travel ban was a good idea or bad idea?"
[k]YouGov poll: "Do you support or oppose President Trump's revised travel ban, which prevents citizens of six Muslim-majority nations from entering the US?"
[l]Gallup poll: "Now, I am going to read several actions either taken or proposed by President Donald Trump. For each one, tell me if you agree or disagree with it, or if you don't know enough to have an opinion. How about . . . impose a 90-day ban on issuing new US travel visas for citizens of six Muslim-majority nations?"
[m]Quinnipiac University poll: "As you may know, Donald Trump has issued a revised executive order that temporarily bans people from entering the US who are from the countries of Iran, Libya, Somalia, Sudan, Syria, and Yemen. Do you support or oppose this action?" (asked of registered voters).
[n]*Politico*/Harvard Public Health poll: "Talking about this same executive order, President Donald Trump ordered a stop to all immigration and travel, with very few exceptions, from six Middle Eastern countries to the US for a period of 90 days. Do you support or oppose this policy?" (asked of half the sample of 1,019).
[o]McClatchy poll: "Do you favor or oppose Donald Trump's executive order to limit entrance to the United States of non-American citizens from six majority-Muslim countries?"
[p]CBS News poll: "Do you favor or oppose temporarily preventing people entering the US from some majority Muslim countries?"
[q]Associated Press/NORC Immigration survey: "Do you favor, oppose, or neither favor nor oppose Donald Trump's new policy indefinitely restricting travel to the US for citizens of Chad, Iran, Libya, Somalia, Syria, Yemen and North Korea, as well as Venezuelan government officials and their family members?"
[r]PRRI American Values survey: "Do you strongly favor, favor, oppose or strongly oppose temporarily preventing people from some majority Muslim countries from entering the US?"

TABLE 4.16. **Public support for suspending immigration from terror-prone regions**

Date of poll	Support (%)	Oppose (%)	Unsure (%)
Nov. 17–20, 2016	50	44	6
Jan. 5–9, 2017	48	42	10
Feb. 2–6, 2017[a]	44	50	6
Feb. 16–21, 2017[a]	43	49	8
Mar. 2–6, 2017[a]	42	51	7
Mar. 16–21, 2017[b]	42	52	6

Note: Respondents answered the question, "Do you support or oppose suspending immigration from 'terror prone' regions, even if it means turning away refugees from these regions?" (asked of registered voters).
Source: Quinnipiac University polls.
[a]First travel ban.
[b]Second travel ban.

American values,[25] especially the nation's egalitarian principles and commitment to religious liberty. Most importantly, they argued that the ban represented discrimination against Muslims. There is some evidence that a majority of people agreed.[26] Fifty-seven percent of the public viewed the ban as contrary to the nation's founding principles.[27] In addition, a plurality of people felt the initial ban did more to harm values than to protect Americans.[28]

Researchers surveyed Americans right before the executive order, and then they surveyed *the same* people just after the order. Their results mirror the national polls. In January 2017, 44 percent of respondents opposed the ban, but just a couple of weeks later, 51 percent of the same respondents opposed it. Interestingly, the more people identified strongly as American, the more they came to oppose the travel ban.[29]

A second major provision of Trump's executive orders was to temporarily prohibit refugees from entering the United States. In theory, the public supports helping those in need. In the face of a specific crisis, however, views often turn less welcoming. The only time Gallup has ever found majority support for accepting refugees was in 1999, when the question specified "hundreds" (rather than thousands) of Albanian refugees from Kosovo.[30]

In 1939, only 9 percent of the public was willing to increase the number of European refuges admitted to the United States.[31] About one-fourth of the public supported accepting 10,000 refugee children from Germany.[32] In 1946, a similar percentage favored a plan to require each nation to take in a given number of Jewish and other European refugees.[33] The next year, a majority opposed taking in displaced Europeans.[34] In May 1953, 47 percent approved President Eisenhower's request to admit 24,000 refugees from Communist countries, but 48 percent opposed.[35] In July 1953, only 36 percent supported the president's later request to allow 200,000 such refugees to enter the United States.[36] Similarly, in 1957 and 1958, the public opposed accepting Hungarian refugees from the 1956 uprising against the Communist government.[37]

In 1975, only 37 percent of the public favored allowing 130,000 Vietnamese refugees to come to the United States.[38] Four years later, only modest percentages favored President Carter's increase in the number of Indo-Chinese asylum seekers, sometimes known as "boat people," admitted to the country.[39] The public was no more willing to allow Cuban refugees to settle in the United States.[40] In 1984, amid growing prosperity, the public still supported *lowering* the number of refugees and immigrants admitted to the United States.[41] Nine years later, the public overwhelmingly opposed granting political asylum to refugees from Haiti.[42] In 2014, as thousands of unaccompanied Central American children illegally entered the United States to avoid violence in their countries, most Americans favored making it easier to *deport* them.[43]

In sum, for decades the public has opposed opening the nation's doors to refugees under a wide range of conditions and from a variety of geographic locations and ethnic and religious backgrounds. President Trump's limits on refugees were consistent with decades of public opinion. The

TABLE 4.17. **Support for Trump refugee ban**

Date of poll	Approve (%)	Disapprove (%)	Unsure (%)
First travel ban			
Jan. 27–Feb. 2, 2017[a]	51	49	1
Jan. 30–31, 2017[b]	43	48	9
Feb. 1–2, 2017, 2017[c]	45	51	5
Feb. 2–6, 2017[d]	37	60	3
Feb. 16–21, 2017[d]	37	60	3
Second travel ban			
Mar. 16–21, 2017[e]	35	61	4
Mar. 22–26, 2017[f]	42	55	3

[a]TIPP/Investor's *Business Daily* poll: "Do you support or oppose a plan by the current administration to stop the entry of refugees into the US temporarily?"
[b]Public Policy polling: "Do you support or oppose the United States indefinitely suspending accepting Syrian refugees?" (asked of registered voters).
[c]CBS News poll: "As you may know, Donald Trump's executive order also temporarily bans any refugees, those forced to leave their country due to violence or persecution, from entering the United States. Do you approve or disapprove of temporarily banning refugees from entering the US?" (numbers reversed to match the table columns).
[d]Quinnipiac University poll: "Do you support or oppose suspending the immigration of all refugees to the US regardless of where they are coming from, for 120 days?" (asked of registered voters).
[e]Quinnipiac University poll: "As you may know, Donald Trump has issued a revised executive order that temporarily bans the immigration of all refugees to the US, regardless of where they are coming from. Do you support or oppose this action?" (asked of registered voters).
[f]*Politico*/Harvard Public Health poll: "The same executive order also stops all refugees, from anywhere in the world, from coming to the US for 120 days. Do you support or oppose this policy?" (asked of half the sample of 1,019).

president could not make the sale, however. In general, majorities of the public in both 2017 and 2018 said the United States had a responsibility to accept refugees in the country.[44] The data in table 4.17 show that the public opposed his bans on refugees. Moreover, opposition grew after the first week of the first ban.

It is interesting that when pollsters asked specifically about the ban on Syrian refugees (table 4.18), opposition to the travel ban *increased*. Clear majorities of the public opposed the president's policy, exactly the opposite of what we would expect from historical experience. Once again, the president was not able to exploit a favorable context, Americans' traditional reluctance to accept refugees, and to win the support of the American people for a signature policy initiative.

Legal Immigration

On August 2, 2017, President Trump embraced a bill sponsored by Republican senators Tom Cotton and David Perdue to institute a merit-based

TABLE 4.18. **Public support for Syrian refugee ban**

Date of poll	Support (%)	Oppose (%)	Unsure (%)
First travel ban			
Jan. 30–31, 2017[a]	36	58	6
Jan. 31–Feb. 2, 2017[b]	45	54	2
Feb. 2–6, 2017[c]	26	70	4
Feb. 16–21, 2017[c]	27	68	4
Second travel ban			
Apr. 12–18, 2017[d]	38	57	5

[a]Gallup poll: "Thinking now about some of the specific actions Donald Trump has taken since he has been in office, would you say you approve or disapprove of indefinitely suspending the United States' Syrian refugee program."
[b]CNN poll: "Do you favor or oppose allowing refugees from Syria to seek asylum in the United States?" (numbers reversed to match table columns).
[c]Quinnipiac University poll: "Do you support or oppose suspending all immigration of Syrian refugees to the US indefinitely?" (asked of registered voters).
[d]Quinnipiac University poll: "Do you support or oppose accepting Syrian refugees into the US?" (asked of registered voters; figures reversed to match the table columns).

system to determine whom the government admits to the country and grants legal residency green cards, favoring applicants based on skills, education, and language ability rather than relations with people already here. The proposal would slash legal immigration to the United States in half within a decade by sharply curtailing the ability of American citizens and legal residents to bring family members into the country.

The public was not impressed. Before the president's statement, Gallup found that 35 percent of the public wanted to decrease immigration. Sixty-two percent favored increasing it or keeping it the same.[45] Immediately after the president's decision, polls found between 30 and 35 percent of the public favored decreasing legal immigration.[46] By September 2017, 39 percent favored decreasing the number of legal immigrants.[47] However, in February 2018, only 17 percent wanted to decrease legal immigration,[48] a figure that had not changed by June in the Quinnipiac poll.[49] In the same month, Gallup found 29 percent wanted to decrease immigration, down from 35 percent the previous year and the lowest level since it began asking the question in 2000.[50]

Similarly, in mid-2018, Pew found that 24 percent of the public wished to decrease immigration, but 32 percent wanted to increase it, the highest percentage in the question's eighteen-year history.[51] The GW Politics poll also found only a quarter of the public favored decreasing immigration throughout the summer and fall of 2018.[52] *The Economist*/YouGov polls in December 2018 and January 2019 found about a fourth of the public supported a decrease in legal immigration.[53] Opinion had moved, but in the *opposite* direction of the president's policy.

By 2019, Gallup found that support for decreasing legal immigration had risen from 31 percent in January to 35 percent in June, the same as it was two years earlier. Nevertheless, the public overwhelmingly wished to increase immigration or keep it at the present level.[54] By mid-2020, support for increasing immigration has risen to 34 percent, the highest in its fifty-five-year time series. Support for decreasing immigration had fallen to 28 percent, a new low for the same period. Another 36 percent of the public wanted to keep immigration at its current level.[55]

Asylum for Central Americans

Related to legal immigration was the issue of offering asylum to Central American refugees, thousands of whom appeared at the southern border. The Trump administration did everything it could to discourage asylum seekers and proclaimed they constituted an "invasion" of the United States. Nevertheless, Gallup found that support for accepting these refugees increased from 51 percent to 57 percent in the period between December 2018 and July 2019. The primary cause of the increase was a 10 percentage point increase in support from Republicans.[56] Other polls found that those who favored allowing Central American refugees to seek asylum clearly outnumbered those who opposed it.[57] Another poll found that even among Republicans, fewer than half supported making it harder for undocumented immigrants to request asylum.[58]

Handling Immigration

Given the public's lack of enthusiasm for the president's specific policies, it is not surprising that it also found him wanting in handling immigration issues in general (table 4.19). Despite the president's highly visible emphasis on immigration and his claims of protecting the country with his policies, clear majorities of the public consistently disapproved of Trump's performance. Moreover, the public's satisfaction did not increase over time. In late 2018, only 36 percent of the public approved of the president's handling of reuniting children separated from their parents at the border, 39 percent approved of his handling the caravan of asylum seekers from Central America, and 36 percent approved of his handling of undocumented immigrants already in the United States. The only bright

TABLE 4.19. **Public approval of Trump's handling of immigration**

Date of poll	Approve (%)	Disapprove (%)	Unsure (%)
Jan. 31–Feb. 2, 2017[a]	42	56	2
Feb. 1–5, 2017[b]	42	57	1
Feb. 2–6, 2017[c]	41	56	3
Feb. 7–12, 2017[d]	36	62	2
Feb. 16–21, 2017[c]	40	58	2
Feb. 17–21, 2017[e]	39	55	5
Mar. 1–4, 2017[a]	44	55	1
Mar. 2–6, 2017[c]	41	56	3
Mar. 12–14, 2017[f]	41	56	3
Mar. 16–21, 2017[c]	38	60	3
Mar. 23–27, 2017[g]	45	54	1
Mar. 25–28, 2017[e]	39	56	5
Mar. 30–Apr. 3, 2017[c]	39	57	4
Apr. 12–18, 2017[c]	39	58	2
Apr. 22–25, 2017[a]	41	57	2
Apr. 23–25, 2017[f]	44	54	3
May 4–9, 2017[c]	35	62	3
May 17–23, 2017[c]	41	57	3
May 31–June 6, 2017[c]	37	60	3
June 7–11, 2017[b]	40	59	2
June 8–11, 2017[g]	39	60	0
June 22–27, 2017[c]	42	56	3
July 16–18, 2017[f]	42	53	6
July 17–Aug. 1, 2017[d]	38	59	3
Aug. 3–6, 2017[a]	40	55	5
Aug. 3–6, 2017[e]	37	57	7
Aug. 9–15, 2017[c]	43	56	2
Aug. 17–22, 2017[c]	40	58	2
Aug. 27–29, 2017[f]	43	54	3
Sept. 6–10, 2017[b]	39	57	2
Sept. 14–18, 2017[h]	39	47	14
Sept. 17–20, 2017[a]	36	60	4
Sept. 18–21, 2017[i]	35	62	3
Sept. 21–24, 2017[e]	35	60	5
Sept. 21–26, 2017[c]	38	59	3
Sept. 24–26, 2017[f]	39	57	4
Sept. 28–Oct. 2, 2017[e]	35	64	1
Oct. 5–10, 2017[c]	39	56	4
Oct. 12–15, 2017[a]	37	59	5
Oct. 12–16, 2017[g]	38	61	1
Nov. 2–5, 2017[a]	37	57	6
Nov. 7–13, 2017[c]	39	57	4
Dec. 4–7, 2017[j]	38	58	5
Dec. 6–11, 2017[c]	37	60	3
Jan. 12–16, 2018[c]	38	60	2
Jan. 13–16, 2018[e]	34	61	5
Jan. 14–18, 2018[a]	38	57	5
Jan. 21–23, 2018[f]	40	54	6
Feb. 1–10, 2018[b]	41	58	2
Feb. 2–5, 2018[c]	39	58	3
Feb. 15–19, 2018[g]	37	62	0

continues

TABLE 4.19. (*continued*)

Date of poll	Approve (%)	Disapprove (%)	Unsure (%)
Feb. 20–23, 2018[a]	36	60	5
Mar. 18–21, 2018[f]	41	55	4
Apr. 22–24, 2018[f]	43	52	5
May 2–5, 2018[a]	40	55	5
May 3–6, 2018[c]	40	57	3
May 31–June 5, 2018[c]	38	58	4
June 3–6, 2018[f]	43	52	5
June 14–17, 2018[a]	35	59	6
June 14–17, 2018[e]	35	62	4
June 27–July 1, 2018[c]	38	58	4
June 27–July 2, 2018[k]	39	59	2
Aug. 1–12, 2018[b]	38	61	1
Aug. 19–21, 2018[f]	39	57	4
Sept. 6–9, 2018[a]	35	59	6
Oct. 4–7, 2018[a]	39	56	5
Oct. 11–14, 2018[g]	41	58	1
Oct. 13–16, 2018[f]	41	55	4
Oct. 14–17, 2018[e]	36	59	5
Nov. 1–3, 2018[a]	37	59	4
Nov. 1–11, 2018[b]	40	57	2
Nov. 14–19, 2018[c]	41	56	4
Nov. 15–18, 2018[e]	37	59	3
Nov. 28–Dec. 4, 2018[l]	44	52	4
Dec. 6–9, 2018[a]	39	54	7
Dec. 9–11, 2018[f]	43	53	4
Jan. 9–13, 2019[c]	42	56	2
Jan. 16–20, 2019[g]	36	62	1
Jan. 18–21, 2019[e]	38	60	2
Jan. 20–22, 2019[f]	42	54	3
Jan. 25–28, 2019[c]	38	59	2
Jan. 30–Feb. 2, 2019[a]	41	54	5
Feb. 12–28, 2019[b]	42	57	1
Mar. 1–4, 2019[c]	40	58	2
Mar. 14–17, 2019[a]	39	58	3
Mar. 17–20, 2019[f]	41	54	5
Apr. 22–25, 2019[i]	39	57	4
May 11–14, 2019[f]	41	54	4
May 17–20, 2019[e]	38	60	3
May 28–31, 2019[a]	41	54	5
June 13–17, 2019[g]	39	59	2
June 28–30, 2019[a]	40	57	3
June 28–July 1, 2019[i]	40	57	2
July 9–Aug. 5, 2019[m]	37	62	1
July 21–23, 2019[f]	41	54	5
Aug. 15–18, 2019[a]	37	58	5
Aug. 15–18, 2019[g]	38	60	2
Aug. 16–20, 2019[n]	38	60	2
Aug. 21–26, 2019[c]	38	59	4
Sept. 3–11, 2019[o]	42	57	1
Sept. 5–9, 2019[a]	37	59	4
Sept. 15–17, 2019[f]	42	54	4

TABLE 4.19. (*continued*)

Date of poll	Approve (%)	Disapprove (%)	Unsure (%)
Sept. 20–23, 2019[g]	40	59	2
Oct. 17–20, 2019[a]	40	58	2
Oct. 27–30, 2019[f]	40	57	3
Nov. 21–24, 2019[a]	39	58	3
Jan. 16–19, 2020[a]	42	56	2
Jan. 19–22, 2020[f]	41	56	3
Jan. 26–29, 2020[e]	40	55	5
Mar. 27–30, 2020[p]	41	51	8

[a]CNN poll: "Do you approve or disapprove of the way Donald Trump is handling immigration?"

[b]Gallup poll: "Do you approve or disapprove of the way Donald Trump is handling immigration?"

[c]Quinnipiac University poll: "Do you approve or disapprove of the way Donald Trump is handling immigration issues?" (asked of registered voters).

[d]Pew Research Center poll: "Do you approve or disapprove of the way Donald Trump is handling the nation's immigration policy?"

[e]CBS News poll: "Do you approve or disapprove of the way Donald Trump is handling the issue of immigration?"

[f]Fox News poll: "Do you approve or disapprove of the way Donald Trump is handling immigration?" (asked of registered voters).

[g]Associated Press/NORC poll: "Overall, do you approve or disapprove of the way Donald Trump is handling immigration?"

[h]NBC News/*Wall Street Journal* poll: "Please tell me if you approve or disapprove of President (Donald) Trump's handling of border security and immigration."

[i]ABC News/*Washington Post* poll: "Do you approve or disapprove of the way Donald Trump is handling immigration?" (2019 question asked of half the sample).

[j]NPR/PBS *NewsHour* poll: "Thinking about President Donald Trump's first year in office, do you approve or disapprove of his handling of immigration?"

[k]*Washington Post*–Schar School poll: "Do you approve or disapprove of the way Donald Trump is handling immigration?"

[l]NPR/PBS *NewsHour* poll: "Do you approve or disapprove of how President Donald Trump is handling immigration policy?"

[m]*Washington Post*–Kaiser Family Foundation poll: "Do you approve or disapprove of the way President Trump is handling immigration?"

[n]Monmouth University poll: "Overall, do you approve or disapprove of the way Donald Trump is handling immigration?"

[o]Marquette Law School poll: "How much do you approve or disapprove of the way Donald Trump is handling immigration?"

[p]Grinnell College poll: "Do you approve or disapprove of the job Donald Trump is doing with immigration?"

spot for the president was 53 percent approval for his handling of the protection of the US borders.[59]

Views of Immigrants

In addition to examining support for specific policies or the president's handling of policies, we can also investigate the public's general views toward immigration and immigrants in the face of the president's strong criticism of both. Have Americans soured on immigrants in response to the president's antagonism?

The answer is "no." In general, Americans saw immigrants in a positive light. The Gallup Poll asked employed adults what effect immigration had on their jobs or the company, business, or organization for which they worked. The findings, shown in table 4.20, are striking. Most workers felt immigration had no impact. Among those who saw an impact, those who saw it as positive greatly outnumbered those who thought it was negative. One of the central features of Donald Trump's rhetoric about immigration was his claims about its effect on jobs, especially immigrants' displacement of American workers, and the burden it placed on taxpayers. The public did not agree. The figures in table 4.21 show that over the period the president sought the 2016 Republican nomination and during his tenure in office, the public was much more likely to view immigrants as a strength of American society than as a burden. Moreover, support for immigration was static and did not decline in response to his hardline approach.[60] A large majority of the public felt that immigrants took jobs Americans did not want.[61] Thus, in late 2018, majorities of each party

TABLE 4.20. **Workers' views on the impact of immigration**

Impact	Positive (%)	No effect (%)	Negative (%)
Your job	27	60	11
Company, business or organization you work for	33	54	12

Note: Respondents answered the question, "Would you say immigration has had a positive effect, a negative effect, or no effect on—A. Your job? B. The company, business, or organization you work for?" (asked of employed adults; sample, 504).
Source: Gallup poll, June 7–11, 2017.

TABLE 4.21. **Are immigrants a strength or a burden?**

Date of poll	Strength (%)	Burden (%)	Other (%)
Mar. 17–26, 2016	59	33	8
Nov. 30–Dec. 5, 2016	63	27	10
June 8–July 9, 2017	65	26	9
Jan. 9–14, 2019	62	28	10
Sept. 3–15, 2019	61	36	3

Note: Respondents answered the question, "As I read each pair, tell me whether the first statement or the second statement comes closer to your own views—even if neither is exactly right. . . . Immigrants today strengthen our country because of their hard work and talents; immigrants today are a burden on our country because they take our jobs, housing, and health care."
Source: Pew Research Center polls.

TABLE 4.22. **Public opinion on the impact of immigrants**

Area of impact	Better (%)	Not much effect	Worse (%)
Food, music, and the arts	57	29	10
Economy in general	45	22	30
Social and moral values	31	38	28
Taxes	23	33	41
Job opportunities	20	51	28
Crime situation	9	43	45

Note: Respondents answered the question, "For each of the following areas, please say whether immigrants to the United States are making the situation in the country better or worse, or not having much effect. How about— [RANDOM ORDER]?" (asked of half the sample).
Source: Gallup poll, June 7–11, 2017.

supported keeping or increasing the number of green cards and temporary work visas.[62]

We can also view immigration more broadly. In the spring of 2018, 58 percent of the public said that having an increasing number of people of different races, ethnic groups, and nationalities in the United States made the country a better place to live; just 9 percent said it made the country a worse place.[63] In June 2017, in the context of months of conflict over the president's travel bans, a clear majority of Americans said immigrants had a positive effect on food, music, and the arts (table 4.22). Nearly half the public said immigration benefited the economy in general—with both of these measures up 17 percentage points from 2007, the last time Gallup asked the question. (In October 2019, 61 percent of the public said immigrants have a mostly positive effect on the economy.[64]) Americans' views that immigrants had a positive effect on social and moral values and taxes were both up by 12 percentage points. Meanwhile, smaller but statistically significant increases occurred among those who said immigrants positively affected job opportunities and the crime situation. Across four measures—the economy, social and moral values, taxes, and job opportunities—Americans were the most positive they had been since Gallup began asking the questions in 2001.[65]

Although more people thought immigrants negatively impacted crime and taxes (though impacts in these two areas might be difficult to identify), those who viewed immigrants as having either a neutral or positive impact on crime and taxes outnumbered those with critical opinions. Polls have found that only small percentages of the public think immigrants commit more violent crimes[66] or more crimes in general than native-born Americans.[67] Most people say immigrants are as honest and hardworking as American citizens.[68] Other polls also had positive findings about the value of immigrants.[69] In June 2018, the Gallup Poll found the highest percentage ever—75 percent, including majorities of all party groups—of the public viewing immigration as good for the country.[70]

Given the generally positive view of immigrants, it is not surprising that Americans have not been eager to deport most illegal immigrants or to decrease legal immigration. In December 2019, only 25 percent of the public felt the United States had accepted too many immigrants recently.[71] Fifty-six percent of the public did not think it was an important goal to deport immigrants in the country illegally.[72]

In March 2017, amid the furor over the president's travel bans, 60 percent of the public responded that the nation's top immigration priority should be to develop a plan to allow those in the United States illegally who have jobs to gain legal status. This number was *up* from 53 percent in the fall of 2016. Ninety percent of the public agreed that illegal immigrants who have been in this country for a number of years, hold a job, speak English, and are willing to pay any back taxes that they owe should be allowed to stay in the country—and eventually be allowed to apply for US citizenship—rather than being deported.[73] Equally important, support for legalizing illegal immigrants *increased* during the president's tenure (table 4.23).[74]

President Trump often focused his rhetoric on removing illegal immigrants who were criminals. Nevertheless, 58 percent of the public were more concerned that deportation efforts would be overzealous, deporting people who had not committed serious crimes. Only 40 percent were more concerned that deportation efforts would not go far enough, leaving dangerous criminals in the country.[75]

The president tried to end the program known as DACA (Deferred Action for Childhood Arrivals) that allowed some individuals (known as "Dreamers") who were brought to the United States illegally as children to receive a renewable two-year period of deferred action from deportation and become eligible for a work permit in the United States. Trump said he would agree to protect the Dreamers in return for stricter border controls and tighter restrictions on legal immigration, but he expended little energy in advocating for a program similar to DACA. It was left to Democrats to promote protections for the Dreamers. The president may have been hesitant, but the public overwhelmingly supported granting permanent legal status to the Dreamers.[76] By December 2019, 86 percent of the public wanted to pass a law to protect them.[77]

TABLE 4.23. **Public support for legalization of illegal immigrants**

Date of poll	Stay, apply for citizenship (%)	Stay, don't apply for citizenship (%)	Be required to leave (%)	Unsure (%)
Jan. 5–9, 2017[a]	59	9	25	6
Jan. 13–16, 2017[b]	61	13	22	4
Feb. 17–21, 2017[b]	60	13	23	4
Mar. 2–6, 2017[a]	63	11	23	4
Aug. 9–15, 2017[a]	63	10	22	4
Sept. 21–26, 2017[a]	68	9	19	4
Sept. 21–26, 2017[c]	82	6	10	2
Dec. 6–11, 2017[c]	77	7	12	3
Jan. 5–9, 2018[c]	79	7	11	3
June 14–17, 2018[a]	67	8	19	8

[a]Quinnipiac University poll: "Which comes closest to your view about illegal immigrants who are currently living in the United States? (A) They should be allowed to stay in the United States and to eventually apply for US citizenship. (B) They should be allowed to remain in the United States, but not be allowed to apply for US citizenship. (C) They should be required to leave the US" (asked of registered voters).
[b]CBS News poll: "Which comes closest to your view about illegal immigrants who are living in the US? They should be allowed to stay in the US and eventually apply for citizenship. They should be allowed to stay in the US legally, but not be allowed to apply for citizenship. OR, They should be required to leave the US" (options rotated).
[c]Quinnipiac University poll: "Which comes closest to your view about undocumented immigrants who were brought to the US as children? A) They should be allowed to stay in the United States and to eventually apply for US citizenship. B) They should be allowed to remain in the United States, but not be allowed to apply for US citizenship. C) They should be required to leave the US" (asked of registered voters).

Government Shutdown, 2018–2019

Perhaps the most dramatic aspect of Trump's immigration policy was the five-week-long shutdown of the federal government during December 2018–January 2019. The president stayed in Washington and communicated continuously with the public, including making two national addresses. He was not successful in winning the public's support. They thought the shutdown was a serious problem for the nation,[78] and they blamed Trump for it (table 4.24).[79] They also disapproved of Trump's handling of the episode.[80]

Trump's most significant effort to convince Americans that it was more important to build a wall on the border with Mexico than fund the government without wall funding was his speech from the Oval Office on January 8, 2019. It did not work. Only 2 percent of the public said the president changed their minds. Forty-nine percent said the address was mostly misleading, compared with the 32 percent who thought it was mostly accurate. By contrast, 39 percent thought the response by Speaker Nancy Pelosi and Senate Minority Leader Charles Schumer was mostly misleading, and 38 percent thought it was mostly accurate.[81]

TABLE 4.24. **Who is to blame for the government shutdown?**

Date of poll	Trump (%)	Congressional Democrats (%)	Congressional Republicans (%)
Dec. 21–23, 2018[a]	43	31	7
Dec. 21–25, 2018[b]	47	33	7
Dec. 30, 2018–Jan. 1, 2019[c]	48	35	4
Jan. 1–7, 2019[b]	51	32	7
Jan. 4–6, 2019[a]	47	33	5
Jan. 8–11, 2019[d]	53*	29	—
Jan. 8–14, 2019[b]	51	34	6
Jan. 9–11, 2019[e]	47	30	3
Jan. 9–13, 2019[f]	56*	36	—
Jan. 10–11, 2019[g]	55*	32	—
Jan. 12–15, 2019[c]	50	32	5
Jan. 20–22, 2019[h]	51	34	3
Jan. 21–24, 2019[d]	53*	34	—
Jan. 25–27, 2019[i]	50	35	10
Jan. 25–28, 2019[f]	56*	34	—

*Options combined Trump and congressional Republicans.
[a]Morning Consult poll: "Who would you say is mostly to blame for the government shutdown?"
[b]Reuters "Who would you say most deserves blame for a deal not being reach[ed], causing the federal government to shut down?"
[c]*The Economist*/ YouGov poll: "Who do you think is MOST to blame for the shutdown of the federal government?"
[d]ABC News/*Washington Post* poll: "Who do you think is mainly responsible for this situation?
[e]CBS News poll: "Who do you blame the most for the partial shutdown of the federal government?"
[f]Quinnipiac University poll: "Who do you think is responsible for this shut down: President Trump and the Republicans in Congress, or the Democrats in Congress?" (asked of registered voters).
[g]CNN poll: "Who do you think is more responsible for the government shutdown?"
[h]Fox News poll: "Who do you think is mostly responsible for the partial shutdown of the federal government— President Trump, Republicans in Congress or Democrats in Congress?" (asked of registered voters).
[i]Monmouth University poll: "Who is most responsible for the length of this shutdown—President Trump, the Democrats in Congress, or the Republicans in Congress?"

Once again, the public did not buy the president's narrative. They continued to oppose a border wall (table 4.13), concluding it was not necessary to protect the border, that it would not make the country safer, that it would not be effective in keeping the border secure, and it would significantly decrease neither illegal immigrants nor illegal drugs.[82] Similarly, the public did not agree that there was a humanitarian and security crisis at the border because of illegal immigration.[83] Only 28 percent of the public thought funding a border wall was worth shutting down the government, and 61 percent of the public thought the border could be secured without the wall.[84] Large majorities opposed Trump using emergency powers to build the wall.[85] Most people saw his declaration of an emergency as an abuse of power[86] and did not agree that there was a crisis on the Mexican border.[87] Moreover, more people trusted the congressional Democrats on border security than the president, a switch from the long-term trend.[88]

International Trade

Foreign trade was a major theme of the 2016 presidential election, with Donald Trump and Bernie Sanders denouncing trade agreements such as NAFTA and the Trans-Pacific Partnership. Trump repeatedly voiced his antagonism to free trade, arguing that it has hurt American workers. Bob Woodward reports the president scribbling "Trade Is Bad" on the text of a speech.[89] What has been the public's views about the benefits of free trade?

Over time, Americans' views of trade have varied, with the public tending to be wary of trade at times when the economy is weaker. Since 2013, however, the public has been more positive about trade (table 4.25). It has rejected the view that free trade is a threat to the economy—a view articulated by candidate Trump. Right after his election, support for free trade climbed even higher. By mid-2019, views of free trade agreements were more positive than at any point in the previous decade.

It is possible that some Americans felt the new president would win better deals for the United States, making free trade more attractive. However, in 2017, Democrats—who were certainly not responding to confidence in the president—increased their support for free trade by 17 percentage points (to 80 percent) while Republican support increased 16 percentage points (to 66 percent). Independents fell in between with

TABLE 4.25. **General views of foreign trade**

Date of poll	Opportunity for growth (%)	Threat from foreign imports (%)	Both, neither, or no opinion (%)
Feb. 7–10, 2013	57	35	7
Feb. 6–9, 2014	54	38	7
Feb. 8–11, 2015	58	33	8
Feb. 3–7, 2016	58	34	7
Feb. 1–5, 2017	72	23	4
Feb. 1–10, 2018	70	25	6
Mar. 10–14, 2018[a]	66	20	14
Oct. 4–7, 2018[b]	71	18	11
Dec. 6–9, 2018[b]	68	20	13
Feb. 1–12, 2019	74	21	5
Dec. 12–15, 2019[b]	71	16	13
Feb. 3–16, 2020	79	18	4

Note: "Respondents answered the question, "Do you see foreign trade more as an opportunity for economic growth through increased US exports or a threat to the economy from foreign imports?"
Source: Gallup polls.
[a]NBC News/*Wall Street Journal* poll (same question wording as Gallup poll).
[b]CNN poll (same question wording as Gallup poll).

TABLE 4.26. **Does international trade create jobs?**

Date of poll	Yes (%)	No (%)	No effect (%)	Unsure (%)
July 8–12, 2016[a]	19	60	14	7
Sept. 28–Oct. 2, 2016	30	45	14	11
Dec. 9–13, 2016	29	48	15	7

Note: Respondents answered the question, "Overall, would you say US trade with other countries creates more jobs for the US, loses more jobs for the US, or does US trade with other countries have no effect on US jobs?"
Source: CBS News polls.
[a]Asked of registered voters.

TABLE 4.27. **Public support for free trade**

Date of poll	Good thing (%)	Bad thing (%)	No opinion (%)
Mar. 31–Apr. 21, 2009[a]	52	34	14
Feb. 22–Mar. 14, 2011[a]	48	41	12
Feb. 27–Mar. 16, 2014[a*]	59	30	10
May 12–18, 2015[a]	58	33	9
Mar. 17–26, 2016[a]	51	39	10
Aug. 9–16, 2016[a]	50	42	8
Oct. 20–25, 2016[a]	45	43	11
Apr. 5–11, 2017[a]	52	40	8
Apr. 25–May 1, 2018[a]	56	30	14
June 12–13, 2018[b]	52	14	35
May 16–20, 2019[b]	51	14	35
July 10–15, 2019[a]	65	22	12
Aug. 10–14, 2019[c]	64	27	9[**]
Jan. 16–20, 2020[b]	57	10	32

[a]Pew Research Center poll: "In general, do you think that free trade agreements between the US and other countries have been a good thing or a bad thing for the United States?"
[b]Monmouth University poll: "In general, do you think that free trade agreements with other countries are good or bad for the United States, or are you not sure?"
[c]NBC News/*Wall Street Journal* poll: "Which of the following statements comes closer to what you think? . . . Statement A: I think free trade with foreign countries is good for America because it opens up new markets and we cannot avoid the fact that it is a global economy. Statement B: I think free trade with foreign countries is bad for America because it has hurt manufacturing and other key industries and there is no proof more trade creates better jobs."
[*]In the February 27–March 2, 2014, survey, the question was worded: "As you may know, the United States is negotiating a free trade agreement with eleven countries in Asia and Latin America called the Trans-Pacific Partnership. Do you think this trade agreement will be a good thing for our country or a bad thing?"
[**]Includes responses that were mixed.

71 percent support (up 8 percentage points over 2016). In 2018, Republican support was up to 68 percent, Independents remained at 71 percent, and Democrats support decreased to 71 percent.

Evaluations of the nation's experience with free trade turned more negative during the 2016 campaign (tables 4.26 and 4.27), perhaps in response to the pounding it took from candidates on the left and the right. Even Hillary Clinton said she was not satisfied with the TPP. Following the 2016 election and during the first two years of the Trump presidency, however, positive views of free trade rebounded.[90]

Equally interesting, *both* Republicans and Democrats *increased* their support for free trade agreements in the face of the president's criticism. In October 2016, only 29 percent of Republicans and Republican-leaning Independents said free trade agreements have been good for the United States, down from 56 percent just a year and -a half earlier. By 2018, however, 43 percent of Republicans responded that trade agreements had been good for the country. Democrats and Democratic-leaning Independents were far more supportive of free trade agreements than Republicans throughout the presidential campaign, but they increased their positive evaluations by 8 percentage points from 59 percent in 2016 to 67 percent in 2018.[91] By mid-2019, 59 percent of Republicans said free trade agreements were good for the United States—roughly double the share who said this in October 2016.[92]

Taking a somewhat longer view, support for international trade increased across several dimensions between 2014 and 2018 (table 4.28). Moreover, Republicans increased their belief that trade is good for the country from 69 percent to 81 percent. Democrats stayed the same at 71 percent.[93]

Similarly, asking about *past* experience, the NBC News/*Wall Street Journal* poll found that the view that free trade had helped the United States increased by 61 percent from 2016 to 2018, while the view that it had hurt the country dropped by 41 percent.[94] The Pew Research Center found that in July 2019, 53 percent of the public thought increased tariffs between the United States and its trading partners had been bad for the country. Only 37 percent thought they had good consequences.[95]

On March 8, 2018, President Trump ordered tariffs on steel and aluminum imports from every country except Canada and Mexico. On May 31,

TABLE 4.28. **Evaluations of free trade**

Trade with other countries:	Agree (%)		
	2014	2018	Change
Is good for the US	68	74	+6
Creates jobs	20	36	+16
Increases wages	17	31	+14
Decreases prices	35	37	+2

Source: Pew Research Center Global Attitudes surveys, Apr. 22–May 11, 2014, and May 14–June 15, 2018.

TABLE 4.29. **Public support for tariffs on steel and aluminum imports**

Date of poll	Support (%)	Oppose (%)	No opinion (%)
Mar. 3–5, 2018[a]	31	50	19
Mar. 8–11, 2018[b]	33	50	17
Mar. 14–19, 2018[c]	38	29	33
Mar. 18–21, 2018[d]	37	48	15
Apr. 25–May 1, 2018[e]	37	45	17
May 3–6, 2018[b]	36	50	14
May 31–June 5, 2018[a]	31	50	19
June 13–18, 2018[f]	35	50	16
June 14–17, 2018[b]	36	48	15
July 23–Aug. 9, 2018[f]	38	49	12

[a]Quinnipiac University poll: "Do you support or oppose imposing a 25% tariff on steel imports and a 10% tariff on aluminum imports?" (asked of registered voters).
[b]CBS News poll: "Do you approve or disapprove of Donald Trump's decision to impose new tariffs on steel and aluminum imports?"
[c]Associated Press/NORC poll: "Do you favor, oppose or neither favor nor oppose placing a tariff, that is an import tax, on steel and aluminum that is brought into the United States from other countries?"
[d]Fox News poll: "Do you think imposing new tariffs or fees on imports of steel and aluminum is a good idea or a bad idea?" (asked of registered voters).
[e]Pew Research Center poll: "Raising tariffs on steel and aluminum would be a good thing for the US"
[f]USA Today poll: "The Trump [a]dministration has imposed tariffs on Mexican steel and aluminum and forced the re-negotiation of NAFTA (North American Free Trade Agreement). Do you think this is the correct approach to US trade relations with Mexico?"
[g]GW Politics poll: "Do you support or oppose Donald Trump's decision to impose new tariffs on steel and aluminum imports?" (asked of registered voters).

he ordered the tariffs to be applied to the two US neighbors. The public did not follow the president's lead. In general, Americans opposed tariffs and felt they were harmful to the country.[96] Similarly, large pluralities opposed tariffs on steel and aluminum (table 4.29). (The one exception in table 4.29, the Associated Press/NORC poll of March 14–19, 2018, had an unusually large percentage of undecided respondents.)

As we would expect, partisanship was pronounced in views about these tariffs. Republicans generally had a positive view of increases in tariffs on steel and aluminum imports, while Democrats held the opposite view. In a poll during April 25–May 1, 2018, the Pew Research Center found that 58 percent of Republicans and Republican-leaning Independents supported the tariffs, while only 22 percent of Democrats and Democratic-leaning Independents agreed. Still, it is striking that Republican support was not higher. The CBS News poll in June found that 71 percent of Republicans supported the tariffs in contrast to only 10 percent of Democrats and 36 percent of Independents.[97] Again, there was slippage in support for the president's policy in the Republican ranks. One explanation for this slippage is that Republicans support both free trade agreements *and* tariffs.[98]

Trump obtained more support for his tariffs on Chinese imports (table 4.30) in 2018. The nation hardly rallied around him, but he garnered stronger support among Republicans than he had for tariffs on aluminum and steel and thus won the support of a majority of the public. Was this a case of effective presidential leadership?

Republicans have been reliable supporters of free trade for many years, providing critical support for NAFTA in 1993 and the extension of permanent normal trade relations to China in 2000. China's entry into the World Trade Organization in 2001 helped boost trade and benefited the US economy in the aggregate, but it also resulted in import competition that hit certain US industries and workers hard, the "China shock."[99]

John Seungmin Kuk, Deborah Seligsohn, and Jiakun Zhang found that Republican attitudes on trade had been evolving long before Donald Trump began criticizing China as a trading partner. Import competition did not affect congressional discourse about free trade, but it did have a significant effect on the discussion of China. Representatives from districts hit by competition, especially Republicans, strategically adjusted their political messaging about China, focusing on Chinese cheating. Scapegoating China for the negative externalities of trade was convenient

TABLE 4.30. **Public support for tariffs on Chinese imports**

Date of poll	Support/good (%)	Oppose/bad (%)	No opinion (%)
Apr. 6–9, 2018[a]	44	45	11
May 31–June 5, 2018[a]	52	36	12
June 7–12, 2018[a]	55	34	11
June 21–29, 2018[b]	51	41	8
May 11–14, 2019[c]	34	45	20
May 16–20, 2019[d]	32	39	32
May 17–20, 2019[e]	24	47	29
Aug. 22–30, 2019[f]	23	53	24

[a]Quinnipiac University poll: "Do you support or oppose raising tariffs on products imported from China? (asked of registered voters).

[b]*Investor's Business Daily* poll: "The US recently imposed a 25 percent tariff on $50 billion of Chinese imports in retaliation of intellectual property theft. After China's threat to retaliate, the US called for an additional 10 percent tariff on $200 billion of Chinese-made goods. Do you support or oppose the decision by the US to place tariffs on Chinese imports?"

[c]Fox News poll: "Recently, the United States increased tariffs or fees on imports from China. In the long run, do you think this strategy will help the US economy, hurt the economy, or not make much of a difference either way?"

[d]Monmouth University poll: "In general, do you think that imposing tariffs on products imported from other countries is good or bad for the United States, or are you not sure?"

[e]CBS News poll: "In the short term, do you think the United States' decision to raise tariffs on Chinese imports will make the economy better, make the economy worse, or will it not have much of an effect?"

[f]*Investor's Business Daily* poll: "Generally speaking, do you think that the tariffs on Chinese goods are helping the US economy, hurting the US economy, or having no significant impact on the economy?"

and let Republican legislators respond to voter concerns while continuing to support their party's position on free trade. Thus, rank-and-file
congressional representatives already had sowed the seeds of economic
nationalism among their constituents, allowing Trump to inherit Republicans' anti-China economic nationalism.[100] It is not surprising that Republicans took their cues about trade with China from the president—but
Democrats had the opposite response. Attitudes about Trump subsumed
opinion about trade policy.[101]

Although many Republicans supported the president's tariffs on Chinese imports, the public was not happy with the president's policies in
general (and support for tariffs on Chinese imports dissipated by 2019). In
only one poll through his entire tenure did the president obtain a majority or even a plurality of public approval of his handling of foreign trade
(table 4.31). In January 2020, a Fox News poll of registered voters found
that while 44 percent of the public thought Trump had been successful in
revising trade deals with other countries to make them more favorable
to the United States, 45 percent replied that he was unsuccessful.[102] Even
after the new United States-Mexico-Canada Agreement (USMCA) was
passed in Congress, opinion was evenly split on the public's confidence in
the president's success in negotiating trade deals.[103]

By May 2019, 48 percent of registered voters felt Trump's trade policies were bad for the economy, whereas 40 percent thought they were
good.[104] The public was also much more likely to think imposing tariffs on
goods from other countries would hurt rather than help the economy and
would be paid for by US consumers.[105]

Party Leadership

In chapter 2, I noted that presidents are much more likely to win the support of their copartisans for their policies than they are to obtain backing
from the opposition party. Much of this support is the result of long-term
partisan and ideological commitments. Unsurprisingly, this pattern has
been exhibited on every issue we have analyzed. Did the president move
Republicans further in the direction of his policies?

Overall, public opinion was unusually stable during the Trump presidency. The GW Politics poll tracked the same group of registered voters
over 2018, interviewing them in May, August, October, and December.
Despite the president's constant drumbeat about immigration and the

TABLE 4.31. **Opinions on Trump's handling of foreign trade**

Date of poll	Approve (%)	Disapprove (%)	No opinion (%)
Feb. 1–5, 2017[a]	45	51	4
May 4–9, 2017[b]	38	49	13
July 8–12, 2017[c]	36	46	18
Dec. 4–7, 2017[d]	43	44	13
Feb. 1–10, 2018[a]	46	49	5
Mar. 3–5, 2018[b]	34	54	13
Mar. 14–19, 2018[e]	40	57	1
Mar. 18–21, 2018[f]	42	49	9
Mar. 22–25, 2018[g]	38	50	12
Apr. 6–9, 2018[b]	40	52	8
May 2–5, 2018[g]	43	46	11
May 3–6, 2018[h]	40	48	11
May 31–June 5, 2018[b]	40	51	9
June 3–6, 2018[f]	41	49	10
June 13–18, 2018[e]	43	55	2
June 14–17, 2018[g]	39	50	11
June 27–July 1, 2018[b]	38	55	7
June 27–July 2, 2018[i]	41	58	2
July 9–11, 2018[f]	41	53	6
July 15–18, 2018[j]	38	45	17
Aug. 1–12, 2018[a]	39	56	5
Aug. 9–12, 2018[g]	38	50	12
Aug. 19–21, 2018[f]	39	53	8
Sept. 6–9, 2018[g]	35	53	12
Oct. 11–14, 2018[e]	40	58	1
Oct. 13–16, 2018[f]	42	49	9
Oct. 14–17, 2018[h]	43	48	9
Nov. 1–3, 2018[g]	40	53	8
Dec. 6–9, 2018[g]	39	50	11
Jan. 9–13, 2019[b]	42	50	8
Jan. 16–20, 2019[e]	39	59	2
Feb. 1–12, 2019[a]	45	50	4
May 16–20, 2019[b]	39	53	8
May 17–20, 2019[h]	41	50	9
May 28–31, 2019[g]	41	47	12
June 13–17, 2019[e]	39	59	3
July 21–23, 2019[k]	40	49	12
Aug. 21–26, 2019[b]	38	54	8
Sept. 5–9, 2019[g]	39	54	7
Oct. 17–20, 2019[g]	43	53	4
Nov. 1–14, 2019[a]	44	54	2
Nov. 21–24, 2019[g]	42	52	7
Jan. 16–19, 2020[g]	45	46	9
Jan. 16–21, 2020[e]	46	53	1
Jan. 16–29, 2020[a]	50	47	2
Jan. 26–29, 2020[h]	45	46	9

[a]Gallup poll: "Do you approve or disapprove of the way Donald Trump is handling foreign trade?"
[b]Quinnipiac University poll: "Do you approve or disapprove of the way Donald Trump is handling trade?" (asked of registered voters).
[c]Bloomberg poll: "Do you approve or disapprove of the job Donald Trump is doing with trade agreements?"
[d]NPR/PBS *NewsHour* poll: "Thinking about President (Donald) Trump's first year in office, do you approve or disapprove of his handling of trade?"

ᵉAssociated Press/NORC poll: "Overall, do you approve or disapprove of the way Donald Trump is handling . . . trade negotiations with other countries?"

ᶠFox News poll: "Do you approve or disapprove of the way Donald Trump is handling international trade?" (asked of registered voters).

ᵍCNN poll: "Do you approve or disapprove of the way Donald Trump is handling foreign trade?"

ʰCBS News poll: "Do you approve or disapprove of the way Donald Trump is handling trade with other countries?"

ⁱ*Washington Post*–Schar School poll: "Do you approve or disapprove of the way Donald Trump is handling international trade?"

ʲNBC News/*Wall Street Journal* poll: "Do you approve or disapprove of President Trump's handling of trade between the United States and foreign countries?"

ᵏFox News oll: "Do you approve or disapprove of the way Donald Trump is handling international trade?" (asked of registered voters).

Mueller investigation (discussed in detail in chapter 5), opinion about him and these issues stayed in a remarkably narrow range (table 4.32). Adherents of both parties did not move their opinions very much.

A report from the Gallup Poll nicely sums up the stability of opinion about the president:

> His job approval ratings in his first two years have been much more stable than those of prior presidents. U.S. successes like record stock market values and low unemployment, Trump accomplishments like federal income tax cuts, and Trump shortcomings like unsuccessful attempts to repeal Obamacare and the government shutdown over the U.S.-Mexico border wall have not done much to move the needle on Trump's approval.[106]

Donald Trump may have campaigned as a populist, but he governed largely as a conservative. Deregulation, lower taxes, opposition to Obamacare, weakened environmental protection, and the nomination of conservative judges were hallmarks of his presidency and core Republican policy stances. Republicans always opposed Obamacare, favored only modest health care reform, and supported low taxes, and they continued to do so with Trump in the White House. Nevertheless, we have seen that there was considerable slippage among Republicans in their support for Trump's policies in both areas. The president's leadership of his party on these issues was not impressive.

What about international trade and immigration? Did Trump convince Republicans to become more nationalist and ethnocentric and less tolerant of globalization and immigration? Republicans were split on international trade. The president had an easy sale on sanctions on China, as Republicans were primed to favor them before he took office. They were more supportive of increases in tariffs than they would have been

TABLE 4.32. **Stability of public opinion**

	Favorable opinion//agree (%)			
Issue	May	July–Aug.	Oct.	Dec.
Donald Trump	43	44	44	43
Pathway to citizenship for illegal immigrants	63	59	60	58
Protecting Dreamers	64	62	63	61
Separating children from parents at border	NA	34	33	33
Decreasing legal immigration	NA	23	25	25
Mueller conducting fair investigation	46	47	50	49

Source: GW Politics polls, May 14–30, 2018, July 23–Aug. 9, 2018, Oct. 17–25, 2018, Dec. 11–19, 2018 (all polls of registered voters).

with Hillary Clinton in the White House, but they hardly followed the president in lockstep on trade, tariffs, or international trade agreements.

Immigration became the signature issue of the Trump presidency. Republicans were clearly more likely than Democrats to support measures to limit both legal and illegal immigration (tables 4.33 and 4.34) and less likely to favor pathways to citizenship for illegal immigrants living in the United States, including Dreamers (table 4.35). Were these stances due to the president's persuasion?

Not really. Republicans supported building the wall even before Trump took office. It is true that their support for it did spike somewhat following the 2018 midterm elections in which the president focused on immigration and amid the partisan wrangling regarding the government shutdown beginning on December 22, 2018.[107] The Pew Research Center found that Republican and Republican leaner support increased from 72 percent in 2018 to 82 percent a year later. (Conversely, Democratic and Democratic leaner support decreased from 13 percent to 6 percent over the same period).[108] It also found a 13 percentage point increase, to 57 percent, in the number of Republicans who responded that America risked losing its identity as a nation if it was too open to foreigners. This was an increase of 13 percentage points over 2018 and 46 percentage points higher than the Democrats.[109] Interestingly, substantial percentages of Republicans always backed a pathway to citizenship for illegal immigrants already living in the country, especially the Dreamers, and they actually *increased* their support for legalization over time.

The basic point remains that Republicans held their conservative views on immigration before Trump occupied the White House.[110] Concern

TABLE 4.33. **Partisan support for building a wall between the United States and Mexico**

· Date of poll	Democrats (%)	Independents (%)	Republicans (%)
Nov. 17–20, 2016	11	43	76
Feb. 2–6, 2017	4	32	81
Feb. 16–21, 2017	8	35	79
Mar. 30–Apr. 3, 2017	6	33	72
Apr. 12–18, 2017	3	30	77
May 4–9, 2017	6	28	74
Sept. 21–26, 2017	7	33	77
Dec. 6–11, 2017	4	30	83
Jan. 5–9, 2018	8	30	78
Feb. 2–5, 2018	9	35	75
Apr. 6–9, 2018	4	39	81
June 14–17, 2018	9	35	77
Aug. 9–13, 2018	7	32	78
Dec. 12–17, 2018	8	45	86
Jan. 9–13, 2019	6	39	88
Jan. 25–28, 2019	7	36	85
Mar. 1–4, 2019	8	36	85

Note: Respondents were asked, "Do you support or oppose building a wall along the border with Mexico?" (asked of registered voters).
Source: Quinnipiac University polls.

TABLE 4.34. **Partisan support for suspending immigration from terror-prone regions**

Date of poll	Democrats (%)	Independents (%)	Republicans (%)
Nov. 17–20, 2016	23	48	78
Jan. 5–9, 2017	24	49	72
Feb. 2–6, 2017*	10	40	84
Feb. 16–21, 2017*	16	43	80
Mar. 2–6, 2017*	13	41	80
Mar. 16–21, 2017**	13	37	81

Note: Respondents were asked, "Do you support or oppose suspending immigrants from 'terror prone' regions, even if it means turning away refugees from these regions?" (asked of registered voters).
Source: Quinnipiac University polls.
*First travel ban.
**Second travel ban.

about immigration was central to Tea Party ideology.[111] Larry Bartels concludes that Republicans were "united and energized by cultural conservatism" and not divided by Trump's "hard-edge nationalism" and "gut-level cultural appeals."[112] Alan Abramowitz finds that white racial resentment was pervasive among Republicans by the end of the Obama presidency, smoothing the path for a candidate whose message focused on it. Trump's

TABLE 4.35. **Partisan support for legalization of illegal Immigrants**

	Those who support staying, applying for citizenship (%)		
Date of poll	Democrats	Independents	Republicans
Jan. 5–9, 2017[a]	80	62	38
Jan. 13–17, 2017[b]	74	61	44
Feb. 17–21, 2017[b]	79	40	36
Mar. 2–6, 2017[a]	84	64	36
Aug. 9–15, 2017[a]	86	62	36
Sept. 21–26, 2017[a]	86	66	49
Sept. 21–26, 2017[c]	95	69	82
Dec. 6–11, 2017[c]	91	81	57
Jan. 5–9, 2018[c]	92	77	64
June 14–17, 2018[a]	88	65	48

[a]Quinnipiac University poll: "Which comes closest to your view about illegal immigrants who are currently living in the United States? (A) They should be allowed to stay in the United States and to eventually apply for US citizenship. (B) They should be allowed to remain in the United States, but not be allowed to apply for US citizenship. (C) They should be required to leave the US" (asked of registered voters).
[b]CBS News poll: "Which comes closest to your view about illegal immigrants who are living in the US? They should be allowed to stay in the US and eventually apply for citizenship. They should be allowed to stay in the US legally, but not be allowed to apply for citizenship. OR, They should be required to leave the US" (options rotated).
[c]Quinnipiac University poll: "Which comes closest to your view about undocumented immigrants who were brought to the US as children? A) They should be allowed to stay in the United States and to eventually apply for US citizenship. B) They should be allowed to remain in the United States, but not be allowed to apply for US citizenship. C) They should be required to leave the US" (asked of registered voters).

appeals to racial resentment and xenophobia resonated especially with less-educated voters uneasy with the increasing diversity of American society. Eighty-one percent of them believed life for people like them had gotten worse in the past fifty years.[113]

Others agree that Trump rose to power by understanding where the party's base already was and channeling those existing worries and desires. As John Sides notes, "The party coalitions were already changing" before Trump came along. Working class whites' movement to the Republican Party mainly occurred from 2009 to 2015 and was not a consequence of the 2016 campaign. Trump's candidacy mostly served to bring to the fore "attitudes about migration, feelings toward black people, and feelings toward Muslims" that were widely shared among Republicans.[114] Similarly, Barry Bennett, a former Trump campaign advisor, concludes, "I would argue that Trump is more a reflection of where the voters are today. I don't think he persuaded them into these stances. That's where they were. He's merely being a mirror to them. . . . He heard what the voters were talking about, what they feared, the pain that they had, and he immediately championed it."[115]

Conclusion

Donald Trump came to office with more experience as a self-promoter and public personality than any previous chief executive. He was undeniably skilled at dominating the news. If such skills were critical for leading the public, we should have found him successfully doing so, especially on policies that should not have been difficult sells to the American people.

What we found, instead, was a president who consistently failed to gain the public's backing for either his policies or his own handling of them. Indeed, he seemed to turn the public in the opposite direction. He made an unpopular health care policy popular and the health care policies he backed unpopular. Similarly, in the face of a general desire to control our borders and protect the country from terrorists, Trump managed to alienate the public from his immigration policies. At the same time, he made a tax cut for nearly all taxpayers and businesses unpopular. In addition, the public remained supportive of free trade and critical of his handling of trade policy. After three years in office, the Pew Research Center found that 58 percent of the public agreed with him on few or almost none of the top issues facing the country.[116]

Trump maintained the support of his base, those who agreed with him before he took office. But what about leading others less inclined to offer their support? Here the president faltered. He made three trips to Louisiana in the month before the 2018 midterm elections, urging voters "to send a message to the corrupt Democrats in Washington" by electing Republican gubernatorial nominee Eddie Rispone.[117] The president put his political capital on the line—and lost. Some of Trump's problems may have been the result of lack of competence in the art of governing, as we discussed in chapter 3. Yet it seems clear that the Trump presidency is one more example of a president not being able to move the American people to support his priority policies, providing further evidence that presidential power is not the power to persuade.

CHAPTER FIVE

The Bully in the Pulpit

Two RAND researchers contend that national political and civil discourse in this century has been characterized by "truth decay": an increasing disagreement about facts and analytical interpretations of facts and data; a blurring of the line between opinion and fact; an increase in the relative volume, and resulting influence, of opinion and personal experience over fact; and lowered trust in formerly respected sources of factual information.[1] Donald Trump has contributed to each of these trends. Indeed, no president in modern times has been so willfully uninformed, so willing to rely on his instincts rather than careful analysis, so unconcerned with the accuracy of his statements, so critical of alternative sources of information, and so ready to violate the norms of civil discourse.

Both the tone and substance of Trump's public rhetoric are far beyond the norms of the presidency. His willingness to demean his opponents; mislead the public about the nature of threats; prevaricate about people, issues, nations, and his policies and accomplishments; employ racially charged language; and challenge the rule of law added a unique—and disturbing—element to American political life. In this chapter, I discuss the most prominent characteristics of the president's public discourse and their consequences for both the president's attempts at leadership and the polity as a whole.

Branding and Delegitimizing

Before taking office, Trump directed his aides "to think of each presidential day as an episode in a television show in which he vanquishes rivals."[2] He followed his own advice. The president's reflexive response to any opposition or criticism is *ad hominem* counterattacks.[3] Unable to divorce disagreement from disrespect and recognize the difference between opponents and enemies, Trump was, in the words of conservative commentator George Will, "incessantly splenetic."[4] Rather than focusing on promoting policies, the president emphasized labeling his opponents, attacking their character or motives and peppering them with puerile taunts.[5]

Moreover, he is skilled at branding, choosing memorable words and repeating them constantly, offering his followers simplicity and consistency. Prime examples include

- "Crooked Hillary"
- "Lyin'" Ted Cruz
- "Pocahontas" (Elizabeth Warren)
- "Fake News"
- The "failing" *New York Times*
- "Cryin'" Chuck Schumer
- "Sleepy Joe" Biden

In the process, he "essentialized" his opponents.[6] Hillary Clinton did not just commit a crime (in Trump's telling); she's crooked to the core. It was not merely that Cruz tells lies; rather, lying is essential to who Ted Cruz is. Elizabeth Warren does not simply espouse foolish ideas; people should not take her seriously at all. Similarly, it is not that the media made a mistake in reporting a story; rather, falsehoods are endemic to what the media are. Even institutions such as the FBI and Justice Department, which he claimed were corrupt and have engaged in "witch hunts," should not be taken seriously.

Trump often invoked the "how-dare-you" argument against his critics. When San Juan Mayor Carmen Yulín Cruz criticized the federal disaster relief efforts in the wake of Hurricane Maria, Trump wondered how she dare complain considering all that the federal government was doing for Puerto Rico. When NFL players responded to his criticism of their kneeling during the playing of the national anthem, he reminded them of their "privilege of making millions" playing football.

The president's goal was to delegitimize his opponents—and he was open and explicit about his strategy. When asked by veteran *60 Minutes* reporter Lesley Stahl why he kept attacking the press, he responded, "You know why I do it? I do it to discredit you all and demean you all, so when you write negative stories about me no one will believe you."[7]

Trump is a prolific insulter.[8] Although the main goal of his criticizing his opponents was to weaken them, it also allowed him to highlight for his base that he was keeping his promise to be an irritant to people in power, calling out the sacred cows in Washington. The president also seemed to think his criticism made him look tough, a quality he valued highly. On July 2, 2017, he posted a doctored video clip showing him bashing the head of a figure representing CNN. It is hardly surprising that the media gave substantial attention to such posts, which are so clearly outside the norms of civility—let alone the norms for a president.

There were no bounds to the president's insults. At a rally in Detroit on December 18, 2019, he turned his attention to Representative Debbie Dingell, the widow of longtime congressman John Dingell. Trump suggested that rather than looking down from heaven, as Debbie had previously told him, perhaps John was "looking up" from hell. At the same event, Trump urged security to handle a female protester a bit more roughly—"You got to get a little bit stronger than that, folks"—and derided her appearance: "There's a slob. There's a real slob."[9] He even found time to ridicule sixteen-year-old climate activist Greta Thunberg, who had been named *Time* magazine's person of the year. In contrast to Lincoln, Trump appealed to the darkest angels of our nature.

In addition, Trump, like Richard Nixon, has bottomless reserves of self-pity. He claimed to be lashing out at critics of his performance because he was the victim of unfair persecution by the nation's elites, Democrats, the media, and law enforcement agencies. According to him—and he is almost completely ignorant of history—no president had ever faced such an onslaught of unfair opposition. "There has been no President in the history of our Country who has been treated so badly as I have," he tweeted.[10]

When the House opened an impeachment inquiry over his alleged efforts to recruit foreign help for his reelection campaign, it was "treason." Speaking to staff members at the United States Mission to the United Nations, Trump called the whistleblower who first raised the issue "almost a spy." He added, "You know what we used to do in the old days when we were smart? Right? With spies and treason, right? We used to handle them a little differently than we do now."[11] When members of his own administration testified before Congress, the president disparaged them.[12]

This posture of vilification inspired sympathy from and solidarity with his aggrieved supporters, particularly because the president suggested that when critics assault him, his base is under attack as well. Moreover, it justifies his criticism of the press, intelligence agencies, the FBI, and other institutions with investigatory capabilities.

If Trump was petty and vindictive, he was so to people whom his base dislikes; and his followers appeared to embrace his incivility. E. J. Dionne, Norman Ornstein, and Thomas Mann have argued that Trump's rhetoric built on longer-term trends that have shaped the modern Republican Party, including a war on the "liberal media," the delegitimization of political opponents, appeals to racism and xenophobia, and hostility to democratic norms. "This history helps explain why so many Republican leaders are reluctant to call out Trump's excesses and to acknowledge the risks he poses to our political system."[13]

Yet his base was a minority of the public and not monolithic. When asked whether it was appropriate for the president to tweet personal attacks on individuals, such as attacking their personal appearance or characteristics, 56 percent of female Trump voters and 36 percent of male Trump voters responded that it was not. Only 32 percent of all Trump voters thought it was appropriate for him to levy personal attacks.[14] Similarly, three-quarters of the public said it bothered them when Trump insulted people,[15] and two-thirds said insulting political opponents was never appropriate.[16]

We do not know the impact of Trump's branding on public opinion. He may well have diminished support for Hillary Clinton by a small amount in 2016, but Republicans did not need him to convince them that they did not care for her. The same is true for Republicans' views of other leading Democrats during the president's tenure. It does not appear that calling Joe Biden "Sleepy Joe" resonated with the public.[17] In addition, as we saw in chapter 4 and as we will see further later in this chapter, Trump did not seem to influence Democrats with his rhetoric, at least not in the direction he intended.

We do know that Trump was much better at branding enemies than policies. Despite his skill at mocking people, it did not help him increase public support for his policies, as we have seen. This lack of impact is not surprising, because it is much more difficult to condense the case for complex policies in a hashtag than it is to ridicule individuals.[18]

The president tried to delegitimize the House's impeachment inquiry in the fall of 2019, with his White House counsel arguing that "this purported 'impeachment inquiry'" was not valid. In addition, the White House continued to hurl insults at Adam Schiff, who was leading the inquiry.[19] At a rally in Minneapolis on October 10, 2019, the president called Democrats "very sick and deranged people" who were trying to undo the 2016 election. Joe Biden, according to Trump, "was only a good vice president because he knew how to kiss Barack Obama's ass."[20] Nevertheless, support for impeaching the president increased during the early weeks of the inquiry and exceeded support for acquittal to the very end of the process.[21]

Moreover, disparaging opponents is hardly conducive to attracting broad support or encouraging people—such as members of Congress—to work with him in the future. The president may have reinforced the views of his followers with his branding, but he seems to have persuaded few people—and may have also alienated many others in the process. He also ended up demeaning himself.

Even during the crisis of the coronavirus pandemic of 2020, the president could not resist ad hominem attacks. Rather than demonstrating above-the-fray unity, he turned on Democratic governors, Mitt Romney, and anyone else who criticized his performance. This behavior may partially explain why he, unlike many governors, received such a small—and transient—boost in his approval ratings.

Trump's greatest influence may have been on the civility of public discourse. There is a difference between attacking a person or a person's motivations and critiquing an idea.[22] Uncivil discourse trivializes serious issues, as commentary on them descends into name-calling and disregards the truth. Demonizing advocates and their ideas eliminates the need for sound counter-reasoning and fact-based argument. "Today the goal is linguistic," said Frank Luntz, a Republican strategist who specializes in the words and messages that candidates employ. "We are no longer rewarding policy; we are rewarding rhetoric." "On a personal level," Luntz added, "it sickens me."[23]

In July 2019, Trump hosted a White House conference on social media. Although he declined to provide a full list of attendees, there is no question that he afforded a stage to people who had a track record of sending inflammatory tweets and videos and posting other troubling content. "They're advocating for a particular kind of social media system where they are allowed to harass, defame [and] post indecent content, and not be censured for it, and not be moderated in any way," said Joan Donovan, the director of the Technology and Social Change Research Project at Harvard University. "They want the benefits of social media with none of the civility."[24]

Trump and his supporters' coarse rhetoric drove some of those who oppose him to extremes of their own. Comedian Kathy Griffin was fired after posing for a picture in which she seemed to be holding the president's decapitated head. Samantha Bee, another comic, apologized for using a crude term to describe Ivanka Trump. Actor Peter Fonda wrote on Twitter, "WE SHOULD RIP BARRON TRUMP FROM HIS MOTHER'S ARMS AND PUT HIM IN A CAGE WITH PEDOPHILES." He also used a vulgar term to describe the president. Fonda later deleted the tweet and apologized: "I went way too far. It was wrong and I should not have done it." Most prominently, Robert De Niro appeared on the nationally televised 2018 Tony Awards show and declared, "I just want to say one thing: F— Trump. It's no longer down with Trump. It's f— Trump."[25] Given the polarized views of the president, it is not surprising that the actor's outburst earned him a sustained standing ovation, but it did little to foster civil discourse.

The share of the public saying Trump was too critical of Hillary Clinton during the 2016 election was substantially higher than voters' assessments of the criticism of any other candidate—of either party—in elections going back more than two decades.[26] In both 2018 and 2019, about 90 percent of the public thought the lack of civility in politics was a serious problem, and a plurality blamed the president.[27]

At the time of the 2018 midterm elections, 74 percent of the public, including 63 percent of Republicans, thought the overall tone and level of civility between Republicans and Democrats in Washington, D.C., had gotten worse since Trump's election. Forty percent felt Trump was most to blame for the negative tone and lack of civility in Washington, while 20 percent faulted the media, 17 percent blamed Democrats in Congress, and 7 percent accused Republicans in Congress. Equally important, 79 percent of the public were concerned that the negative tone and lack of civility in public discourse would lead to violence or acts of terror.[28] In the spring of 2019, majorities of the public concluded that political debate in the United States had become less respectful, less fact-based, and less focused on issues, and 55 percent said Trump had changed the tone and nature of political debate for the worse.[29]

More broadly, incivility inherent in governing by grievance poses challenges for the polity. Seventy-nine percent of the public thought the 2016 presidential election was uncivil. Fifty-nine percent of those who did not vote for the president in that election said incivility played a role in their decisions. The same percentage said they quit paying attention to politics because of incivility. Ninety-seven percent thought it was important for the president to be civil.[30] It is difficult to mobilize voters when they are tuning you out.

Media

The media have been the president's number one irritant, and he criticized them often and harshly. He frequently dismissed unfavorable coverage as "fake news," and after less than a month in office he tweeted, "The FAKE NEWS media (failing @nytimes, @NBCNews, @ABC, @CBS, @CNN) is not my enemy, it is the enemy of the American People!"[31] When discussing the impact of his trade war on Americans, Trump told the Veterans of Foreign Wars on July 24, 2019, "Just remember, what you're seeing and what you are reading is not what's happening."[32]

When challenged that his rhetoric encouraged uncivil and even violent behavior, the president placed responsibility on the press. "The media also has a responsibility to set a civil tone and to stop the endless hostility and constant negative—and oftentimes, false—attacks and stories," Trump explained. With no hint of irony, he declared that those in the political arena should "stop treating their opponents as morally defective."[33]

Sometimes, the president's criticism of the press descended into the absurd. On January 29, 2019, the nation's top intelligence officials testified in open congressional hearings, televised by C-Span, and the director of national intelligence submitted a forty-two-page public statement regarding threats to US national security. Their testimony generated stories about their contradicting what the president had said about Iran, the Islamic State (also known as ISIS), and North Korea. Trump predictably lashed out at his own appointees the next day, tweeting that they were "wrong" and "extremely passive and naïve." He also suggested that they might need to "go back to school." Still, he needed to defuse embarrassing stories, so he accused the media of fabricating a conflict, claiming the officials later told him they were "totally misquoted"[34]—even though their testimony was available for anyone to see in its entirety.

Similarly, the director of the Centers for Disease Control and Prevention, Robert Redfield, gave an interview to the *Washington Post* on April 21, 2020, in which he explained, "There's a possibility that the assault of the virus on our nation next winter will actually be even more difficult than the one we just went through," because we would have a flu epidemic and the coronavirus epidemic at the same time.[35] The next day, Trump tweeted, alleging that Redfield had been misquoted. He accused CNN of having done so, even though CNN merely relayed the comments published by *Post*. The president also said Redfield would be issuing a statement to correct the record. Instead, in a White House briefing the next day, the director said he had been quoted accurately in the article.[36] It is most likely that Trump simply did not like the pessimistic tone of the story and fell back on his routine behavior of blaming the press.

Equally telling was his interchange with a reporter at a coronavirus pandemic briefing on April 13, 2020. During the briefing, the president played a video praising his handling of the crisis. The video had a gap for the critical month of February. When a reporter asked Trump what he had done during that period, the president was flustered and grew angry. Finally, he exclaimed, "Look. Look, you know you're a fake. You know that. Your whole network—the way you cover it—is fake."[37]

The Quinnipiac University Poll regularly asked registered voters who they trust more to tell them the truth about important issues, President Trump or the news media. The news media always won majority support on this question, with little variance over time (table 5.1). We find similar responses when pollsters asked whether people trusted Trump or their "favorite news source" more. People overwhelmingly chose their favorite news source (table 5.2).[38]

However, there is a strong partisan tilt to the responses. For example, in an April 26–29, 2019, poll, 82 percent of Republicans put their trust in Trump while 92 percent of Democrats selected the media, as did 54 percent of Independents.[39] In the same poll, respondents were asked which came closer to their view: "the news media is the enemy of the people, or the news media is an important part of democracy?" Republicans were

TABLE 5.1. **Public trust in Trump vs. trust in media**

Date of poll	Trust Trump (%)	Trust media (%)	No opinion (%)
Feb. 16–21, 2017	37	52	10
Mar. 2–6, 2017	37	53	10
May 4–9, 2017	31	57	12
May 17–23, 2017	34	53	13
Aug. 9–15, 2017	37	55	9
Aug. 17–22, 2017	36	54	10
Oct. 5–10, 2017	37	52	11
Nov. 7–13, 2017	34	54	12
Apr. 20–24, 2018	37	53	10
June 14–17, 2018	36	53	11
July 18–23, 2018	34	54	12
Sept. 6–9, 2018	30	54	16
Nov. 14–19, 2018	34	54	12
Apr. 26–29, 2019	35	52	13

Note: Respondents were asked, "Who do you trust more to tell you the truth about important issues: President Donald Trump or the news media?" (asked of registered voters).
Source: Quinnipiac University polls.

TABLE 5.2. **Public trust in Trump vs. trust in favorite news source**

Date of poll	Favorite news source (%)	Trump (%)	No opinion (%)
Feb. 15–19, 2017	67	28	5
Mar. 22–27, 2017	70	23	7
Oct. 15–17, 2017	65	26	9
Jan. 8–10, 2018	58	29	14
July 19–22, 2018	62	28	10

Note: Respondents were asked, "Who do you trust more? Your favorite news source or Donald Trump?"
Sources: McClatchy polls for Feb. and Mar. 2017; Marist College polls for Oct. 2017; NPR/PBS *NewsHour* polls for 2018.

split, with 49 percent choosing "enemy of the people" and 36 percent selecting "an important part of democracy." Democrats and Independents were not similarly torn. Ninety-two percent of the former and 70 percent of the latter said the news media were "an important part of democracy."

Fueling Fear

Presidents often identify problems facing the country and offer their solutions to solving or at least ameliorating them. They also make decisions that certain matters do *not* require attention. If the president intentionally or unintentionally misleads the country about the extent or nature of a problem or chooses to ignore problems, the public's evaluations of possible solutions are likely to be distorted, undermining rational discourse about the way forward.

Identifying Threats

President Trump tended to see problems that he believed required attention as *threats* to the nation, and his public rhetoric reflected this mindset. In the fourth sentence of his speech accepting the Republican nomination in 2016, Trump declared, "Our convention occurs at a moment of crisis for our nation. The attacks on our police, and the terrorism in our cities, threaten our very way of life." He continued by cataloging the dangers of crime, uncontrolled immigration, the national debt, Iran, ISIS, and other challenges.[40] In his Inaugural Address, he spoke of ending "the American carnage."[41]

According to the president, there were threats to personal safety from violent crime, Islamic terrorism, and immigrants. Then there were threats to people's personal economic status from foreign trade, regulations designed to combat global warming and environmental degradation, the Affordable Care Act, and immigrant labor. There were also threats to group status from immigrants, both legal and illegal. Finally, abortion, Muslims, the LGBTQ community, and others posed threats to American values. Critics of the president's policies were also threats, of course. In his campaigning during the 2018 midterm elections, for example, Trump claimed that Democrats were too dangerous to govern. The president even found threats in a "war" against Christmas and a mysterious effort to change the name of Thanksgiving.[42]

Trump lacked evidence for many of his claims of threats, and many were contrary to the best evidence. During the presidential campaign, he maintained that unemployment was much higher than it was—although he had a change of heart once he took office and could claim credit for low unemployment. Similarly, he claimed health care had deteriorated under President Obama, again without offering evidence.

From shortly after his election and throughout his presidency, Trump asserted that there were millions of illegal voters in the 2016 election. If that were true, there clearly would be need for reform of the administration of our election system. During recounts of some races in the 2018 midterm elections, the president charged that there was fraud in counting the votes. He offered no evidence for either allegation. Many people seemed to believe the president about the prevalence of election fraud,[43] although there is simply no systematic evidence to support such a claim.[44]

Trump warned at the 2016 Republican National Convention that "decades of progress made in bringing down crime are now being reversed."[45] At election time, the Pew Research Center asked voters if crime has worsened since 2008. Fifty-seven percent of voters, including 78 percent of Trump supporters, responded that crime had gotten worse.[46] In reality, the FBI reported that violent and property crimes had decreased by 19 percent and 23 percent, respectively. The Justice Department's Bureau of Justice Statistics found violent crime had fallen by 26 percent and property crime by 22 percent. People typically overestimate the incidence of crime,[47] but in this case the fact that more than twice as many Republicans as Democrats thought crime was increasing indicates that Republicans were likely influenced by their standard bearer's charges. In 2019, the president was still at it, telling a police organization that violent crime was "going down for the first time in a long while."[48] This assertion was false.

Advocating tax cuts, the president tweeted on September 6, 2017, "We are the highest taxed nation in the world." If Trump were correct, he would be providing a strong motivation for policy change, which no doubt was his goal. His assertion was false, however. In fact, the United States has one of the lowest effective tax rates in the developed world.[49] Nevertheless, majorities of registered voters thought their taxes were too high.[50]

In an address to a joint session of Congress on February 28, 2017, the president defended his travel ban by asserting, "According to data provided by the Department of Justice, the vast majority of individuals convicted of terrorism and terrorism-related offenses since 9/11 came here from outside of our country." This statement grossly distorted the facts.[51] In response to a Freedom of Information Action request for data supporting Trump's assertion, the Justice Department responded that "no responsive records were located." There was no report and no support for the president's claim.[52]

Trump campaigned vigorously in the 2018 midterm elections, emphasizing threats to the nation. He characterized a caravan of asylum seekers slowly traveling through Mexico as a potential "invasion" of the United States and sent several thousand troops to help secure the southern border. The president made a number of unsubstantiated claims about the criminals and Middle Eastern terrorists among the travelers, and even charged that the Democrats were paying migrants to enter the United States so that they could vote for Democratic candidates. When a reporter asked him for evidence, he dismissed her question with, "Oh, please, please, don't be a baby."[53] Back in the White House, journalists persisted in asking for evidence of the caravan threat. At that point, he admitted that he had "no proof of anything"—but added that his charges could be true.[54]

More generally, the president lacked perspective on immigration. When he took office, the number of illegal immigrants was at its lowest level in a decade, as was the percentage of undocumented immigrants in the workforce. Moreover, there was a net outflow of undocumented Mexicans back to Mexico.[55] Nevertheless, the president persisted in presenting immigration in apocalyptic terms, as when he declared, "The southern border is a dangerous horrible disaster."[56]

The president also regularly distilled complicated issues into easily understood me-versus-them fights and presented himself as the protector of his base against the threats. He told the Republican National Convention in 2016, "I have joined the political arena so that the powerful can no longer beat up on people that cannot defend themselves. Nobody knows the system better than me, which is why I alone can fix it." "I am your voice," he declared, "I will fight for you, and I will win for you."[57]

By the summer of 2020, running well behind Democrat Joe Biden in the polls, the president resorted to a searing tone and apocalyptic language to describe new threats to the country. Standing in front of Mount Rushmore on July 3, 2020, the president railed against "angry mobs" seeking to "unleash a wave of violent crime in our cities" and pursuing "far-left fascism" and a "left-wing cultural revolution" whose goal was "the end of America."[58] The next day on the South Lawn of the White House, he offered an ominous depiction of the recent protest over racial justice with his promise of "defeating the radical left—the Marxists, the anarchists, the agitators, the looters."[59]

The style of his rhetoric was absolutist, emphasizing nonnegotiable principles and moral outrage at their violation.[60] It was also paranoid, describing how malign forces were working behind the scenes against the interests of the people.[61] This mode of expression has some advantages for the speaker. William Davies argues that an emphasis of fear over facts creates an audience for whom it does not matter what is said, but rather how it makes them feel.[62] Perceived threats increase the likelihood of obtaining the public's attention and evoke emotional responses.[63] Moreover, these threats affect some people's policy views[64] and also may increase in-group identification, political participation,[65] and preference for strong leadership.[66] Perceived threats also bolster views of the competence of the one describing the threats,[67] and absolutist rhetoric boosts impressions of positive character traits of the speaker.[68] Moreover, fear increases the public's tolerance for norm-busting policies to deal with perceived threats.

Offering Reassurance

Leaders not only identify problems; they also reassure the public. Franklin D. Roosevelt famously told the country at the nadir of the Great Depression that "the only thing we have to fear is fear itself—nameless, unreasoning, unjustified terror which paralyzes needed efforts to convert retreat into advance." He did not pretend that conditions were not bad. Instead, he summoned the nation to defy what it feared rather than succumb to it. George W. Bush, standing on a pile of rubble of the World Trade Center in 2001, assured the country that the terrorists responsible for the attack would be punished and the United States would move ahead.

Trump certainly assured the public that his policies would solve the problems he identified. However, he also tried to reassure the public that some problems many people saw were not concerns at all and thus they did not need to worry about them. If the president can convince the public that problems do not exist, there is no need for fashion solutions to them. Moreover, it is not necessary to make trade-offs such as those between economic growth and environmental protection.

CLIMATE CHANGE. In an interview on CBS's *60 Minutes* on October 14, 2018, Trump expressed the view that climate science was nothing more than political opinion and that the scientists who have documented human's impact on the climate had "a very big political agenda."[69] He has never offered any evidence for this view, however, apparently believing it unnecessary.

The next month, on November 23, the federal government released the second volume of the *Fourth National Climate Assessment*, a major scientific report mandated by Congress and issued by thirteen federal agencies. The report presented the starkest warnings to date of the consequences of climate change for the United States, predicting that the failure to rein in global warming posed serious threats to the nation's health, water supply, and economy. The report's findings were directly at odds with Trump's agenda of environmental deregulation, which he asserted would spur economic growth. Trump had taken aggressive steps to allow more planet-warming pollution from automobiles, power plants, and oil wells. Aside from releasing the report on Black Friday, when the White House hoped people would have shopping on their minds, the president largely ignored the study. His primary response was simply, "I don't believe it."[70] A few days later he added, "a lot of people like myself—we have very high levels of intelligence, but we're not necessarily such believers."[71]

The public did not follow the president's lead. Table 5.3 shows responses to questions about how serious a threat climate changed posed to the United States. Most people saw climate change as a "major threat." By January 2018, 46 percent of the public thought dealing with global climate change should be a top priority for the US government, and another 24 percent thought it should be an "important" priority. Only 9 percent agreed with the president's view that no response was necessary.[72] By the last half of 2018, more than 70 percent of the public saw climate change as a "big" problem. Again, only 9 percent saw it as not a problem at all.[73]

In November 2018, 48 percent of the public found evidence of climate change more convincing over the previous five years, while only 13 percent viewed it through the president's eyes and found it less convincing.[74]

TABLE 5.3. **Is climate change a threat?**

Date of poll	Major threat (%)	Minor threat (%)	Not a threat (%)	No opinion (%)
Jan. 4–9, 2017	52	32	14	2
Feb. 16–Mar. 15, 2017	56	26	16	2
Oct. 25–30, 2017	59	24	15	1
May 15–June 15, 2018	59	23	16	2
July 10–15, 2019	57	23	18	2
Mar. 3–29, 2020	60	27	12	1

Note: Respondents were asked, "Do you think that global climate change is a major threat, a minor threat, or not a threat to the well-being of the United States?"
Source: Pew Research Center polls.

Ninety-one percent saw climate change as a serious or very serious problem.[75] In March 2019, 54 percent responded that government had a great deal of responsibility for addressing climate change, while only 12 percent said it had none at all.[76] Similarly, in May 2019, 65 percent of the public saw climate change as a major problem that the government should address.[77] In the summer of that year, 79 percent of the public said human activity was causing climate change, 76 percent felt it was a crisis or a major problem, and 67 percent disapproved of Trump's handling of it.[78] In October, clear majorities thought the government was doing too little to reduce the effects of climate change.[79]

Nevertheless, Republicans, already skeptical about climate change, tended to stick with the president. In July 2019, for example, only 27 percent of Republicans and Republican leaners saw global climate change as a major threat to the United States, compared with 84 percent among Democrats and Democratic leaners.[80] However, in October 2019, clear majorities of the public felt the federal government was doing too little to protect the climate and the environment. Even 39 percent of Republicans and Republican leaners thought the government was doing too little to reduce the effects of climate change.[81] Gallup also found in March 2019 that the public's preference for prioritizing environmental protection over the economy was the greatest it had been since 2000.[82]

RUSSIA.   The issue of Russian interference in the 2016 election haunted Trump throughout his presidency. The president downplayed the impact of any such meddling and took no initiative to combat such interference in the future. It appears that he viewed reports of Russian intrusion as a threat to the legitimacy of his electoral victory. Going far beyond any findings, the president declared at a March 6, 2018, news conference, "the Russians had no impact on our votes whatsoever." He did admit that "there was meddling and probably there was meddling from other countries and maybe other individuals."

On February 13, 2018, top US intelligence officials testified that Russia was already meddling in the midterm elections, trying to worsen the country's political and social divisions. Even though evidence of Russian meddling was, in the words of Trump's national security assistant, Lt. Gen. H. R. McMaster, "incontrovertible," the officials reported that Trump had not directed them specifically to combat Russian interference.

On February 16, 2018, Special Counsel Robert Mueller indicted more than a dozen Russians and three companies for interfering in the 2016 elections. President Trump's first reaction was to claim personal vindication: "The Trump campaign did nothing wrong—no collusion!"[83] he wrote on Twitter that day. He voiced no concern that a foreign power had been trying for nearly four years to upend American democracy, much less resolve to stop it from continuing to do so in that year's midterm elections.

More broadly, Trump made little public effort to rally the nation to confront Moscow for its intrusion or to defend democratic institutions against continued disruption. The president did not impose new sanctions called for in a law passed by Congress in July 2017 to retaliate for the attack on America's political system or team up with European leaders to counter a common threat. Nor did he lead a concerted effort to harden election systems in the United States or press lawmakers to pass legislation addressing the situation.

An issue closely related to the Mueller investigation was the president's relationship with Russian president Vladimir Putin. As a candidate, Trump frequently spoke of his admiration for Putin. Yet he went further. On July 27, 2016, while campaigning for president, Trump invited Russian hacking of his opponent, Hillary Clinton. "Russia, if you're listening, I hope you're able to find the 30,000 emails that are missing. I think you will probably be rewarded mightily by our press."[84] Two years later, Special Counsel Robert Mueller indicted Russian intelligence officers, alleging that on the same day as Trump's invitation, they began targeting Clinton's e-mail server. Mueller's team had already obtained indictments against another group of Russians for attempting to influence the election over social media.

In general, the president spoke of Putin in flattering or friendly terms, avoiding direct criticism. On February 5, 2017, Fox News' Bill O'Reilly interviewed the president on *The O'Reilly Factor*. After Trump reiterated his respect for Putin, O'Reilly interjected, "He's a killer, though. Putin's a killer." To which the president responded, "What do you think, our country's so innocent?" It is not surprising, then, that in March 2018 and in the face of international outrage over the poisoning of a former Russian intelligence officer on British soil and over his advisors' objections, Trump congratulated Putin on winning reelection as Russian president.[85]

When the two leaders held a press conference in Helsinki on July 17, 2018, Trump expressed doubts about US intelligence conclusions that the Russian government tried to influence the outcome of the 2016 US presidential election. Instead, he indicated he believed Putin's denials. "My people came to me. Dan Coats [director of National Intelligence] came to me, and some others. They said they think it's Russia. I have President Putin. He just said it's not Russia. I will say this: I don't see any reason why it would be."[86] Although Trump later backtracked somewhat from his statement, it was consistent with many others over the previous two years.

Despite the president's friendly attitude toward Putin, Americans maintained an unfavorable view of the Russian leader (table 5.4). There was little change from 2015, the year after Russia annexed Crimea, through Trump's tenure as president. Clearly, most Americans did not follow Trump's lead.

Nevertheless, some Republicans did. Table 5.5 shows the results of four Gallup polls. Only Republicans shifted to a more positive view of Putin over the period from 2015 to 2018. Even for this group, however, only 27 percent followed the president's lead. Compared to 2015, then, Republicans switched their views in a more supportive direction by 15 percentage points. Yet most Republicans agreed with the rest of the nation in holding unfavorable views of Putin. These results are consistent with other polls, which found modest changes in Republican opinion.[87]

If we focus on the most visible Trump-Putin interaction, the Helsinki summit in July 2018, we find that only 33 percent of the public approved of how Trump handled the meeting, while 50 percent disapproved. Only 29 percent approved of his expressing doubts about US intelligence on the issue of interference in the election, while 56 percent disapproved. Fifty-one percent of Republicans backed the president, but nearly one-half of his own base did not.[88] Similarly, only 27 percent thought the meeting was a success while 52 percent considered it a failure. Interestingly, only

TABLE 5.4. **Public opinion of Vladimir Putin**

Date of poll	Approve/favorable opinion (%)	Disapprove/unfavorable opinion (%)	Neutral/no opinion (%)
Feb. 8–11, 2015[a]	13	72	16
Feb. 18–22, 2015[b]	12	70	18
Oct. 15–18, 2015[c]	7	66	27
May 15–19, 2016[c]	8	59	33
Aug. 5–8, 2016[d]	9	54	26
Sept. 15–19, 2016[e]	10	52	37
Sept. 16–19, 2016[c]	6	65	28
Jan. 4–9, 2017[b]	16	69	13
Jan. 5–9, 2017[f]	9	68	23
Jan. 12–15, 2017[g]	12	71	16
Jan. 12–15, 2017[c]	7	67	27
Jan. 20–25, 2017[f]	9	70	21
Feb. 1–5, 2017[a]	22	72	6
Feb. 16–21, 2017[f]	7	72	21
Feb. 17–21, 2017[h]	6	49	46
Feb. 28–Mar. 12, 2017[b]	15	77	8
June 7–11, 2017[a]	13	74	12
June 27–July 19, 2017[i]	18	79	3
July 8–12, 2017[d]	15	65	21
Jan. 10–15, 2018[b]	16	68	16
Mar. 8–11, 2018[h]	5	56	20
May 2–5, 2018[g]	11	77	12
June 14–17, 2018[g]	11	72	17
July 18–23, 2018[f]	6	72	21
July 15–18, 2018[c]	5	65	30
Aug. 1–12, 2018[a]	13	76	11
Aug. 5–8, 2018[d]	10	64	26
Sept. 17–Oct. 1, 2018[j]	10	80	10
Apr. 14–16, 2019[k]	9	74	16

[a] Gallup poll: "Please say if you have a favorable or unfavorable opinion of Russian president, Vladimir Putin?"
[b] Pew Research Center poll: "Is your overall opinion of Vladimir Putin very favorable, mostly favorable, mostly unfavorable, or very unfavorable?"
[c] NBC News/*Wall Street Journal* poll: "I'd like you to rate your feelings toward each one as very positive, somewhat positive, neutral, somewhat negative, or very negative. Vladimir Putin." (asked of half the sample in Sept. 2016 and Jan. 2017).
[d] Bloomberg poll: "For each, please tell me if your feelings are very favorable, mostly favorable, mostly unfavorable, or very unfavorable. Vladimir Putin, president of the Russian Federation."
[e] Associated Press poll: "Do you have a favorable or unfavorable opinion of Russian President Vladimir Putin?"
[f] Quinnipiac University poll: "Is your opinion of Vladimir Putin favorable, unfavorable, or haven't you heard enough about him?" (asked of registered voters).
[g] CNN poll: "Please say if you have a favorable or unfavorable opinion of Russian President Vladimir Putin."
[h] CBS News poll: "Is your opinion of Russian President Vladimir Putin favorable, not favorable, undecided, or haven't you heard enough about Vladimir Putin yet to have an opinion?"
[i] Chicago Council on Global Affairs poll: "Do you have a very favorable, somewhat favorable, somewhat unfavorable, or very unfavorable view of Russian President Vladimir Putin?"
[j] PPRI poll: "Please say whether your overall opinion of Russian President Vladimir Putin is very favorable, mostly favorable, mostly unfavorable, or very unfavorable."
[k] Fox News poll: "Please tell me whether you have a generally favorable or unfavorable opinion of Vladimir Putin." (asked of registered voters).

TABLE 5.5. **Partisan views of Vladimir Putin**

	Favorable (%)			
	Feb. 2015	Jan. 2017	June 2017	Aug. 2018
All	13	22	13	13
Republicans	12	32	24	27
Independents	12	23	12	9
Democrats	15	10	4	4

Note: Respondents were asked, "Please say if you have a favorable or unfavorable opinion of Russian president, Vladimir Putin."
Source: Gallup polls, Feb. 8–11, 2015, Feb. 1–5, 2017, June 7–11, 2017, and Aug. 1–12, 2018.

60 percent of Republicans followed the president's lead in proclaiming the summit a success.[89]

There was more movement among partisans regarding the broader issue of relations with Russia. For decades, the identifiers with the Republican Party had been more hawkish toward Russia than Democratic identifiers. That changed with President Trump's election. Republicans became more positive than Democrats toward Russia. In fact, on the issue of Russia cyber-meddling in the US elections, Republican public opinion more closely resembled public opinion in Russia than overall opinion in the United States.[90] In December 2018, half of all registered voters, including 78 percent of Democrats and 52 percent of Independents, thought that Russia had "definitely" interfered in the 2016 presidential election to help Trump. However, only 15 percent of Republicans held that view.[91] By July 2019, 65 percent of Democrats and Democratic leaners felt Russia's power and influence was a major threat to the United States, while only 35 percent of Republicans and Republican leaners agreed.[92]

We can compare Chicago Council on Global Affairs polls taken in June 2016 and June–July 2017 to see the impact of the change in party of the president.[93]

- In 2016, Democrats (62 percent) were more inclined toward cooperation with Russia than were Republicans (50 percent). By 2017, with a Republican in the White House, Republicans were more likely to say that the United States should undertake friendly cooperation and engagement with Russia (56 percent versus 28 percent of Democrats), while Democrats were more likely to say that the United States should actively work to limit Russia's power (70 percent versus 40 percent of Republicans).

- While Republicans grew less likely to believe that Russia was working to undermine US influence (64 percent versus 75 percent in 2016), Democrats grew more likely to believe it to be so (82 percent versus 72 percent in 2016).
- Republicans were far less likely than Democrats to describe as critical threats to the United States Russian influence in US elections (65 percent of Democrats; 19 percent of Republicans) and Russia's military power (50 percent of Democrats; 32 percent of Republicans).
- Democrats (51 percent) were far more likely than Republicans (29 percent) to support increasing sanctions against Russia.

We can also compare results of Pew Research Center polls at the time of Trump's election with those during the summer of 2018. In 2016, 60 percent of Democrats felt "cold" toward Russia, and this figure increased to 76 percent in 2018. Interestingly, Republicans increased their feelings of "cold" as well, from 53 percent to 60 percent. Only 8 percent of Democrats and 12 percent of Republicans felt "warm" toward Russia.[94]

CORONAVIRUS. In early 2020, another issue arose that required presidential leadership in identifying a problem and responding appropriately. The novel coronavirus (COVID-19) spread rapidly across the globe, causing hundreds of thousands of deaths and upending economies on all continents. The president, however, contradicted government medical experts and downplayed the danger posed by the virus, claiming that it would "miraculously" disappear when spring arrived, comparing it to ordinary flu—although the new disease's mortality rate was much higher and its economic impact immeasurably greater. At the point when there were fifteen cases in the United States, the president declared "within a couple of days [it is] going to be down to close to zero." He also claimed the country was "rapidly developing a vaccine" that would be available soon,[95] that Google would have a website ready very quickly where Americans could see if they needed to be tested, that anyone who wanted to be tested could be, and that health industry leaders agreed to waive all costs of coronavirus treatments (when in fact they had agreed only to waive copayments). These reassurances were false. The president oversold the ability to deliver masks and ventilators to health care professionals, and he said two hospital ships were being dispatched to help, but we later learned they were weeks away and would not be helping with the coronavirus. Unsurprisingly, he declared himself a medical savant while displaying an astonishing lack of knowledge. His views were parroted by right wing commentators, including Sean Hannity and Rush Limbaugh.

Insisting on treating the crisis as a partisan battle, the president even wore a Keep America Great campaign cap during his tour of the headquarters of the Centers for Disease Control and Prevention in Atlanta. He also admitted that he wanted to leave passengers stranded on a cruise ship rather than see statistics for the number of cases on American soil go up because it would look bad. With a similar motivation, Trump falsely blamed the Obama administration for impeding coronavirus testing. To make his administration's response look more effective, he claimed that the virus was contained in America—when it was actually spreading rapidly—and he stated that the coronavirus first hit the United States later than it actually did. The president accused the media of perpetuating a hoax, arguing that news organizations were drumming up hysteria over the growing public health crisis as a way to hurt his presidency. On March 9, he retweeted a message that featured Trish Regan, a Fox Business commentator, arguing that his opponents were deliberately inducing stock market losses to harm the president politically.[96] Fox considered Regan's comments so irresponsible that it put her show on hiatus.

The issue, of course, did not disappear. As Peter Baker put it, the coronavirus could not be cowed by Twitter posts, shot down by drones, be overcome by party solidarity, or be overpowered by campaign rally chants.[97] Finally, the president had no choice but to take the pandemic more seriously. Nevertheless, he could not discipline himself to offer measured responses. On March 19, 2020, the president spoke of an antimalarial drug that might be a useful antidote to the coronavirus. "There's tremendous promise based on the results and other tests. There's tremendous promise," he declared. "We're going to be able to make that drug available almost immediately. . . . It's been approved."[98] Unfortunately, the drug had not been approved, nor was it about ready to ship out. Minutes after the president spoke, the FDA commissioner, Dr. Stephen Hahn, emphasized that the drug still needed testing to determine whether it could help patients and warned against giving patients "false hope" before drugs are vetted.

The next day, Trump was at it again. He enthusiastically and repeatedly promoted the promise of two long-used malaria drugs that were still unproven against the coronavirus but were being tested in clinical trials. "I'm a smart guy," he said, while acknowledging he could not predict whether the drugs would work. "I feel good about it." In the same press conference, the nation's leading infectious diseases expert, Dr. Anthony

Fauci, explained that there was no evidence that the drug was useful for COVID-19, and hopes for it were based on only anecdotal evidence.[99]

In response to these differing analyses, NBC correspondent Peter Alexander asked Trump whether he was being overly optimistic about the government's ability to deliver drugs to treat the coronavirus. "Is it possible that your impulse to put a positive spin on things, may be giving Americans a false sense of hope?" "No, I don't think so," Trump said. When the reporter asked the president, "What do you say to Americans who are watching you right now who are scared?" Trump erupted. "I say that you're a terrible reporter; that's what I say. I think it's a very nasty question. And I think it's a very bad signal that you're putting out to the American people. The American people are looking for answers, and they're looking for hope. And you're doing sensationalism." Later, when Alexander asked the same question of the vice president, Mike Pence's replied, "I would say do not be afraid; be vigilant."[100]

Later in the same briefing, Yamiche Alcindor of PBS's *NewsHour* asked when everyone who needed a coronavirus test would be able to get one, as the president has asserted two weeks earlier that every person already could. "Nobody is even talking about it except for you, which doesn't surprise me," Trump responded dismissively. How about people with symptoms who could not get a test, he was asked. "I'm not hearing it," he replied. Despite the president's denials and his refusal to establish a national testing program, the lack of testing resources remained an issue throughout the pandemic.

Most important, Trump's optimistic, inaccurate, and overblown rhetoric had consequences. Democrats were much more likely than Republicans to view the coronavirus as a threat and to take precautions against infection. In contrast, in the crucial early weeks of the crisis most Republicans saw the news reports emphasizing the seriousness of the disease as exaggerated,[101] or they were considerably less likely than Democrats to see it as a threat to either their own or the public's health.[102] More generally, at the very moment when it was most important for the nation to trust the White House, most people did not.[103] In April 2020, just 39 percent of the public said Trump was presenting the situation accurately, while 52 percent thought he was making it seem better than it was.[104] By July, as infections surged across the nation, only 34 percent of the public placed a great deal or good amount of trust in what he said about the virus, while 64 percent trusted him not so much or—in the case of nearly half the public—not at all.[105]

Moreover, if the president had focused less on expressing optimism and more on dealing with the looming crisis, the country, including the economy, would probably suffered much less. Dr. Ashish Jha, director of the Harvard Global Health Institute, argued that if the United States had addressed the pandemic two months earlier, it would have had many fewer infected and much less social and economic disruption: "we are in this position today [March 2020] because we wasted two months not getting an infrastructure together for testing Americans who need to be identified with having COVID-19."[106] Fauci, the director of the National Institute of Allergy and Infectious Diseases, put it succinctly when he told CNN on April 12 that the United States "could have saved lives" if the president had acted sooner on warnings about the pandemic.

Prevaricating

Perhaps the most distinctive aspect of Donald Trump's approach to politics is that he seems to be unconcerned with the accuracy of what he says. Fact checkers from a range of organizations have concluded that the president made thousands of false or misleading claims,[107] far more than any of his predecessors. The *Washington Post* reported that Trump averaged 15 false claims a day in 2018[108] and had made 8,158 false or misleading claims in his first two years in office.[109] As of July 13, 2020, the total had risen to more than 20,000.[110] We have seen that the president frequently exaggerated or otherwise distorted the nature of threats facing the American public and chosen to rationalize away the existence of other dangers.

In August 2019, accused sex trafficker Jeffrey Epstein committed suicide. Perhaps to distract from his past relationship with Epstein, on August 10, Trump retweeted a conspiracy theory alleging that Epstein was killed because he had information on Bill Clinton. On May 26, 2020, the president smeared MSNBC host Joe Scarborough from the lectern in the Rose Garden with an unfounded allegation of killing a staff member in 2001, even though he was eight hundred miles away at the time and the police ruled her death an accident. Promoting such unsubstantiated—and untrue—charges was not new for the president,[111] who seemed to find them an effective tool for emotionally connecting with voters and supporters.

Presidents of both parties are typically very sensitive about saying anything that is not true and go to great lengths to avoid it. President Trump was different. Unburdened by shame, unchastened by criticism, and unconcerned with facts, he said whatever was convenient at the moment. He claimed to have built a wall on the border with Mexico at a time when no wall had been built. He claimed the largest tax cut, the best economy, and the highest defense spending in history, although these assertions were clearly untrue. He declared that steel plants had opened in response to his tariff policy, that the United States had the most liberal immigration laws in the world, that the United States paid most of the budget of NATO, and that defense contracts with Saudi Arabia were responsible for tens of thousands of jobs in the United States. All these and many others were untrue.

To put it simply, the president was a brazen and incessant liar. According to Trump's ally and onetime White House communications director Anthony Scaramucci, "People ask me if the president lies. Are you nuts? He's a f—ing total liar. He lies all the time." When Scaramucci asked Trump, "Are you an act?" Trump replied, "I'm a total act and I don't understand why people don't get it."[112]

Conservative political commentator Amanda Carpenter describes a pattern to many of Trump's lies:

Step 1. Stake out political territory no one else will occupy, taking over the news cycle.

Step 2: Put the falsehood into circulation, but do not own it ("people are saying").

Step 3: Create suspense by promising new evidence or revelations, even if they never appear.

Step 4: Discredit opponents with attacks on their motives or characters.

Step 5: Declare victory, no matter what the circumstances.[113]

At the same time, the president has told the public that the press cannot be trusted to deliver the truth on the matter, thus empowering people to privilege beliefs that fit their personal biases.

Trump, unsurprisingly, had a different view. In an interview on ABC News on October 31, 2018, he gave a halfhearted explanation for his proclivity for falsehoods. "Well, I try. I do try . . . and I always want to tell the truth. When I can, I tell the truth. And sometimes it turns out to be where something happens that's different or there's a change, but I always like to be truthful."[114] The next year, he told ABC News, "I like the truth. You know, I'm actually a very honest guy."[115]

Not exactly. To begin, he was a serial embellisher. In *Trump: The Art of the Deal*, he wrote:

> I play to people's fantasies. People may not always think big themselves, but they can still get very excited by those who do. That's why a little hyperbole never hurts. People want to believe that something is the biggest and the greatest and the most spectacular.
>
> I call it truthful hyperbole. It's an innocent form of exaggeration—and a very effective promotion.[116]

Part of the explanation for the president's falsehoods is that he refused to accept some established facts. Perhaps his extensive experience in New York real estate convinced him that all people are prone to shading their views according to their own self-interest. He does not seem be believe that people are capable of objectivity.[117] Moreover, he relied heavily on instinct. As he put it, "I have a gut, and my gut tells me more sometimes than anybody else's brain can ever tell me."[118] Finally, the president did not read—books, studies, or memos—so he was likely to be poorly informed.[119]

Whatever the reason, he persistently rejected clear evidence regarding a wide range of issues. He refused to accept the innocence of the Central Park Five, despite DNA evidence and a detailed confession from another man. He argued that there was a link between vaccines and autism, a claim medical professionals have rejected. He persisted in his conviction that Barack Obama was born in Kenya long after the state of Hawaii produced Obama's official birth certificate. He resisted accepting the unanimous conclusions of intelligence officials that Russia interfered in the 2016 presidential election or that Prince Mohammed bin Salman was responsible for the death of journalist Jamal Khashoggi.

The president also continued to deny human contribution to climate change, contrary to the nearly unanimous view of the scientific community. In 2019, Thomas Bossert, Trump's first Homeland Security advisor, said he was "deeply disturbed" by the president urging the Ukraine to investigate Democrats, especially since he had repeatedly explained to Trump that the conspiracy theory he was pursuing—that it was Ukraine and not Russia that had intervened in the 2016 election and did so on behalf of the Democrats—was "completely debunked."[120]

There often appeared to be a method to his mendacity, as the president seemed to say whatever was expedient. Sometimes the motivation was simply to make himself look good, such as his exaggerations of the size of his electoral victory in 2016 and the crowds at his inauguration, the number of times he has appeared on the cover of *Time* magazine, or the success of his policies. At other times, Trump simply wanted to avoid personal embarrassment, such as the many iterations of what he knew about payoffs to Stormy Daniels.

A few days before the 2018 midterm elections, the president claimed he was moving rapidly to have Congress pass a 10 percent middle-class tax cut (and not one for businesses). Of course, he never proposed such a bill, and Congress was out of session anyway. Equally suspect were his claims that a caravan of asylum seekers traveling across Mexico was an "invasion" posing a looming threat to America. He even promised to sign an executive order ending the constitutional right to citizenship for children born in the United States to undocumented immigrants (which he lacked the power to do). The president dropped all these matters right after the election.[121] Throughout the 2018 campaign, Trump told supporters at his "Make America Great Again" rallies to "pretend I'm on the ballot." Shortly after the election, he told Fox News, "I didn't run. I wasn't running. My name wasn't on the ballot."[122]

Most frequently, however, he prevaricated in his arguments regarding the nature of problems facing the nation, policy options, and the character and competence of political opponents. Typically, he offered no evidence. Often, his assertions and explanations were so convoluted that it was difficult to understand what he meant. Untethered from the burden of objective proof, the president said whatever he thought would help him win. His narratives often had so many layers of unsubstantiated content that it was difficult to address them clearly.

Some Trump supporters tried to rationalize the president's falsehoods. Anthony Scaramucci told his interviewer on CNN, "Yes, the president is speaking mistruths. Yes, the president is lying." However, he went on to explain, the president was "an intentional liar" who uses "a methodology of mistruth" with the aim of unsettling the mainstream media and the political Left and galvanizing his base.[123] Apparently, lying was acceptable if it helped the president politically.

Trump seemed to agree and even bragged about prevaricating. In a meeting with campaign donors in Missouri, the president admitted to intentionally lying to Canadian prime minister Justin Trudeau. The president inaccurately claimed that the United States had a large trade deficit with Canada. When Trudeau disagreed, Trump said, "Wrong, Justin, you do." Later, in recounting his meeting to the donors, he added, "I didn't even know. . . . I had no idea. I just said, 'You're wrong.'"[124] Despite acknowledging that he "had no idea" about the trade balance, he asserted his claim anyway—and to a head of state of America's close ally and largest trading partner—demonstrating his disdain for objective reality and telling the truth.

Whether the president's frequent falsehoods were the result of his general ignorance of public policy, a desire to make himself look good, sloppiness in doing reality checks on his thoughts, or a well-developed cynicism, it did not take long for the public to conclude that he was untrustworthy. After only three months in office, 59 percent of the public felt his administration regularly made false claims. Only 35 percent did not.[125] In September 2018, only 34 percent of the public thought he was trustworthy.[126] By December 2018, 71 percent of the public thought the president regularly made misleading claims. Forty-nine percent thought these claims were "flat-out" false, while 22 percent saw them as exaggerations. Seventy-one percent of the public thought it was never acceptable for a president to say things that are false.[127] In the unkindest cut of all for Trump, in December 2018, 59 percent of registered voters had little or no trust in Trump's denial of collusion with Russia in the 2016 presidential election.[128]

In March 2019, only 30 percent of the public thought he was honest. Sixty-five percent believed he was not,[129] and 61 percent of the public said the president was not trustworthy. Remarkably, even one-quarter of Republicans and Republican leaners did not describe Trump as trustworthy.[130] In January 2020, after the United States killed Iranian general Qasem Soleimani, more Americans said they had little or no trust in what the Trump administration said about the situation in Iran (53 percent) than said they had a great deal or fair amount of trust (45 percent) in the administration's statements.[131] The next month, Pew found that only 15 percent of the public (and only 31 percent of Republicans and Republican leaners) liked the way Trump conducted himself as president; 53 percent did not. Only 36 percent of the public and 71 percent of Republicans thought he was honest. Similarly, less than one-third of the public (32 percent), including just 62 percent of Republicans, felt the president was morally upstanding.[132]

By April 2020, at the height of the coronavirus pandemic, when trust in the chief executive was critical, only 31 percent of the public viewed Trump as honest and trustworthy. Interestingly, researchers asked respondents which source of television news they trusted most. With one exception, no more than 15 percent of the public thought the president was honest and trustworthy. The exception was the group who trusted Fox News, 78 percent of whom thought the president was honest and trustworthy.[133] In general, 52 percent of the public told pollsters they trusted what Trump said less than they trusted what previous presidents had told them. Only 26 percent trusted him more.[134]

The public's evaluations of Trump's truthfulness were a fragile foundation for gaining support. The president was convinced that his base would believe whatever he told them, and he may have been right. Yet for everyone else, he risked losing credibility. Why would you follow someone you cannot believe?

Distorting the Public's Knowledge

During his presidency, Donald Trump was the most important source of misinformation in the country. His millions of followers on Twitter and the audiences at his rallies and for his variety of television appearances received a constant stream of misrepresentations about government, politics, and policy. Sometimes, the president stooped to publicizing even vicious falsehoods. As one analysis put it, "By retweeting suspect accounts, seemingly without regard for their identity or motives, he has lent credibility to white nationalists, anti-Muslim bigots and obscure QAnon adherents like VB Nationalist, an anonymous account that has promoted a hoax about top Democrats worshiping the Devil and engaging in child sex trafficking."[135] Trump was not alone in spreading misinformation, of course, but he had the biggest platform, and thus the widest audience, for his rhetoric.

Given the trends in public discourse to which the president was a major contributor, it is not surprising that people—even those generally well informed about politics[136]—are frequently misinformed about policy, and the less they know, the more confidence they have in their beliefs. Thus, they resist correct information. Even when others present them with factual information, they resist changing their opinions.[137]

The increasing array of media choices means that individuals are less likely to encounter information that would correct misperceptions. Moreover, the internet and social media exacerbate the speed at which misinformation diffuses throughout society, magnifying its negative effects. In addition, in a polarized world people are more likely to accept disinformation as true if it matches their political views. Even stories that are clearly pranks may be believed by willing readers and go viral.[138]

Three scholars at MIT investigated the diffusion of approximately 126,000 verified true and false news stories tweeted by about 3 million people from 2006 to 2017. People were 70 percent more likely to retweet untrue stories than true stories. In essence, falsehoods diffused "significantly farther, faster, deeper, and more broadly" than the truth in all categories of information, and the effects were more pronounced for false political news than for false news about terrorism, natural disasters, science, urban legends, or financial information. One reason for the differential diffusion may be that false news is more novel than true news and people may be more likely to share novel information.[139]

Once misinformation is initially encoded in a person's mind, that is, once it is stored in one's memory and available for later retrieval, it is difficult to change. Research in psychology demonstrates that widespread myths and rumors that originate at the societal level, such as supposed links between vaccines and autism, are often reinforced at the individual level because of cognitive factors. Once such misinformation is accepted, retractions are often ineffective in changing people's minds and may even reinforce the initial errors. Even if people initially accept corrections debunking a false statement, they may eventually misremember false statements as true.[140] Similarly, negations often reinforce the perception they are intended to counter.[141]

Trump was a master at using repetition to reinforce his falsehoods—in tweets, at rallies, and in statements to the press. He made his false claims about taxes, immigrants, trade, and other important matters dozens or even hundreds of times. Researchers have found that repetition of false information increases the likelihood that recipients accept the information, even if there are warnings of the credibility of the source of the information.[142] The impact of repetition of false statements confirms the common observation that "if people are told something often enough, they'll believe it."[143]

Partisanship and ideology enhance these psychological effects. Even real-time corrections do not have a significant effect on those predisposed to believe the false information.[144] For instance, in 2011, 94 percent of the public had heard that Obama was not born in the United States and did not have a valid birth certificate, and 24 percent, mostly Republicans, agreed or strongly agreed with this misinformation.[145] In July 2012, only 49 percent of respondents correctly thought Obama was a Christian. Among Republicans, the percentage of respondents who incorrectly thought Obama was a Muslim nearly doubled in his first term, increasing from 16 percent in October 2008 to 30 percent in July 2012.[146]

Even strong retractions of encoded misinformation can be ineffective in reversing even weak initial encoding, and incorrect information may continue to affect perceptions, even if individuals recall corrections of misinformation.[147] The Iraq Survey Group concluded that Iraq had destroyed its weapons of mass destruction years before the US invasion in 2003. President George W. Bush and other leading administration officials acknowledged the absence of such weapons. Nevertheless, in December 2014, 42 percent of the public thought that American forces found active weapons of mass destruction. Another 10 percent could not say.[148] These faulty conclusions increased from six years earlier, when 37 percent of the public thought Iraq had the weapons and 9 percent could not say.[149]

It is difficult, perhaps impossible, to isolate the influence of Trump's rhetoric on specific aspects of public knowledge. Although he clearly had the loudest megaphone, there were countless commentators, including many who amplified his communications. He was not the only person advocating restrictions on immigration, higher tariffs, or health care plans.

Some of the president's early exaggerations provide a sense of how he may have distorted public knowledge, however. His talk of a historic electoral victory in 2016 and of millions of illegal voters seems to have influenced some people. Nearly nine months after the 2016 presidential election, 28 percent of all voters and 49 percent of Trump voters believed that he won the popular vote, although he lost it by nearly three million votes.[150] In early 2017, nearly 30 percent of registered voters thought that three to five million people voted illegally in the presidential election.[151]

There is room for hope, however. Table 5.6 lists eleven prominent Trump falsehoods. The most widely believed, that military spending was at an all-time high, had only 36 percent of the public sharing the president's view. Interestingly, there were high levels of *disbelief* of Trump's falsehoods regarding central aspects of his presidency, including global warming, immigration, and the role of Russia and fraudulent voting in the 2016 presidential election.

Nevertheless, the president's falsehoods had an impact. More people believed the president than believed otherwise on North Korea, NATO funding, and military spending. Perhaps they paid less attention to national security issues. In addition, for many of the issues, large percentages of the public simply did not know what to believe. On only three of the eleven issues (global warming, the border wall, and Russia's intervention in the 2016 election) did majorities of the public know the correct answer. It is difficult not to believe that the president's prevaricating

TABLE 5.6. **Public belief in Trump's falsehoods**

False statement	Believe false statement (%)	Don't believe false statement (%)	No opinion (%)
New steel plants opening in the US	12	22	65
Russia did not intervene in 2016 US presidential election	15	65	20
Democratic senators support "open borders"	15	39	45
Global warming results from natural, not human, causes	19	65	16
2017 tax cut was largest in history	24	26	50
Millions of fraudulent votes were cast in 2016 election	25	44	31
Construction has begun on a wall on the Mexican border	26	51	24
Separating children at border in 2018 was required by US laws	30	41	28
North Korea has done more to end its nuclear weapons program in the last 6 months than in the previous 25 years	34	39	27
US funds most of NATO budget	35	27	38
US military spending at record high	36	27	36

Source: Washington Post Fact Checker poll, Nov. 29–Dec. 10, 2018.

confused substantial percentages of the public, undermining their ability to assess policy alternatives.

Those most likely to believe the president's falsehoods were those who reported relying on Fox News as one of their main sources of news. Fox News viewers are also highly likely to be Republicans, a majority of whom identified Fox News as one of their two top political news sources.[152]

There is also a warning sign of growing toleration of prevarication. Although 70 percent of Democrats and 66 percent of Independents said it was "extremely important" for presidential candidates to be honest, that view was held by only 49 percent of Republicans.[153]

Corroding Political Discourse

Trump's reliance on falsehoods and his refusal to admit the truth of widely accepted facts corroded political discourse by spreading a culture of suspicion and distrust of facts. Without a common set of facts, and with a blurring of the line between opinion and fact, it becomes nearly impossible to have a meaningful debate about important policies and topics.

Immigration is a good example. Decisions regarding securing the borders, addressing the rights and futures of undocumented immigrants, determining the need for immigrant workers, and balancing the needs and rights of US citizens and legal residents with those of refugees who seek safety in the United States and of people seeking a better future for their families are important questions and deserve informed deliberation. Such discussion is unlikely to occur if there is no agreement on basic facts.

A key premise of democratic governing is that there is some fundamental reality or commonly accepted set of facts that provide the basis for deliberation and choices about governance. James Pfiffner puts it well when he points out that Trump's falsehoods challenge

the fundamental principles of the Enlightenment, which are premised on the belief that there are objective facts which are discoverable through investigation, empirical evidence, rationality, and the scientific method. From these premises, it follows that political discourse involves making logical arguments and adducing evidence in support of those arguments, rather than asserting one's own self-serving version of reality.[154]

The corrosion of public discourse can be an important factor increasing polarization. As each side develops its own "facts," the opposing sides are likely to move further apart in their beliefs about key issues and even in their perceptions of each other. There is also a decreasing willingness to listen to those with policy expertise. For example, Republicans now think scientists' judgments are as subject to bias as anyone else's judgments.[155]

Undermining Democratic Accountability

Donald Trump's false statements about politics and policy strike at the very heart of democratic accountability. If there are no agreed-on facts, then it becomes impossible for people to make judgments about their government or hold it accountable. In *On Tyranny*, Timothy Snyder argues, "To abandon facts is to abandon freedom. If nothing is true, then no one can criticize power, because there is no basis upon which to do so."[156]

Trump is by no means an autocrat, but his public discourse shares some troubling features with the practices of many authoritarian leaders. In *The Origins of Totalitarianism*, Hannah Arendt observed, "Before mass leaders seize the power to fit reality to their lies, their propaganda is marked by its extreme contempt for facts as such, for in their opinion fact depends entirely on the power of a man who can fabricate it."[157]

If people are to hold the White House accountable, and thus make democracy effective, they must have a reasonable idea of the impact of the president on governing and the consequences of the presidents' policies. Attaining such an understanding is difficult under the best of circumstances because of the complexity of both policies and their effects.

Often presidents exaggerate their accomplishments or take credit for developments for which they typically bear only modest responsibility, such as a strong economy. Donald Trump was no exception. It is not surprising that he overstated his success with Congress, the size of the 2017 tax cuts and the 2018 defense budget, relative performance of the economy, the number of times he appeared on the cover of *Time*, the relative size of his electoral college victory, and even the size of the crowd at his inauguration.

Hyperbole is one thing. Grossly misrepresenting reality is something else. If chief executives badly distort depictions of their successes, they increase the information burdens on voters and undermine democratic accountability. On many policies, including the denuclearization of North Korea, an increase in the funds allies contributed to NATO, the payments of tariffs on Chinese goods, the handling of disaster relief in Puerto Rico, and the opening of new steel plants in response to his tariff decisions, the president claimed great success that simply did not occur.

There are plenty of voices pointing out the president's distortions and untruths. However, many, perhaps most, people will never hear them. Information contradicting the president has a difficult time breaking through the psychological barriers of partisanship and motivated reasoning. Moreover, selective exposure to an ever more fragmented and insulated media further lessens the chances of people confronting information that does not reinforce their dispositions.[158]

Stoking Division

One of the least attractive aspects of President Trump's rhetoric was his stoking cultural divisions and racial tensions and cultivating tribalism. He likened some Hispanic immigrants to "vermin" who would "infest" America. The president referred to some African nations as "shithole countries." He posited that "both sides" were to blame for the deadly white supremacist rally in Charlottesville, Virginia, in 2017. He forwarded tweets from white supremacists and accused black football players who kneeled during the playing of the national anthem to protest police discrimination of being un-American. Trump also embraced the birther myth long after it was debunked and claimed massive voter fraud by African Americans and Mexican Americans. He called for a ban on all Muslim immigrants and declared that an American-born judge of Mexican heritage could not be fair to him because of his ethnic background. Midway through his third year in office, the president was still at it. Following his us-against-them political strategy, in a July 14, 2019, Twitter harangue he advised four female Democratic congresswomen of color to "go back" to the country from which they came, even though three of them were born in the United States.[159]

Sometimes Trump insisted that his critical comments about immigrants referred only to terrorists or members of violent gangs. Whatever his true thoughts and intentions, the president echoed the words and images of the white nationalist movement to dehumanize immigrants and inflame racial tensions. Trump's descriptions of those trying to enter the country illegally were so sharp that critics said they dehumanized people and lumped together millions of migrants with the small minority that are violent. There is little doubt that the president directly targeted white racial and ethnic fears and reinforced deep social divisions in America.

In 2020, in the face of the massive protests against entrenched racism and police brutality toward minorities, the president tweeted context-free videos of random incidents involving black people attacking white people,[160] retweeted a doctored video purportedly showing a "racist baby,"[161] baselessly claimed that the nation's first African American president committed "treason,"[162] used the racist phrase "Kung flu" to describe the coronavirus,[163] and bemoaned the removal of statues honoring the Confederacy.[164] He also retweeted a video showing a supporter yelling "white power," demonstrating his willingness use social media to amplify hateful commentary of some of his followers, even at a moment of unrest. (He deleted his tweet a few hours later in the face of broad criticism.) On July 1, he tweeted that Black Lives Matter was a "symbol of hate."[165]

Before Trump, racial and ethnic differences were potent drivers of political division.[166] Under Trump, their impact only strengthened. During the campaign and throughout his presidency, he reinforced and exacerbated these cleavages by making explicit appeals to racial resentment and white identity.[167] This rhetoric was so clear that more than half of

Americans consistently concluded that the term "racist" described him during the 2016 campaign.[168]

Throughout his tenure as president, majorities of the public continued to describe him with the same term.[169] In 2018, 58 percent of voters, including 91 percent of Democrats and 58 percent of Independents—but only 17 percent of Republicans—thought his derogatory comments about immigrants from Africa and the Caribbean were racist.[170] Similarly, substantial percentages of the public felt his immigration policies were motivated by racism,[171] and majorities thought his "go back" language was racist and inappropriate.[172] A Fox News poll in July 2019 found that 57 percent of the public concluded that the president did not respect racial minorities.[173] In January 2020, 83 percent of African Americans told pollsters they thought Trump was a racist.[174] The next month, the Pew Research Center found that a remarkable 59 percent of the public, including 35 percent of Republicans, thought the president was prejudiced.[175] Fifty-six percent of the entire public and 49 percent of whites thought he had made race relations worse.[176] When asked about his public messages regarding the protests over the killing of George Floyd, 60 percent of the public said Trump's were completely or mostly wrong.[177]

Attitudes about racial and ethnic groups helped fuel Trump's capture of the Republican nomination. He performed best among Republicans who held unfavorable views of African Americans, Muslims, immigrants, and minority groups in general. Perceptions that whites were treated unfairly in the United States and that the country's growing diversity was a bad thing were also significantly associated with support for Trump in the primaries.[178]

In the general election, the effects of racial attitudes were greater than their historically strong impact on Obama's two presidential elections. Perceptions that whites were being treated unfairly relative to minorities were an unusually strong predictor of support for Trump. During the Trump presidency there was a stronger partisan divide than ever between racially sympathetic and racially resentful whites.[179]

Equally important, there is evidence that the president's rhetoric ushered in a climate that favored expression of prejudices[180] (substantial percentages of the public feel this way),[181] and perhaps encouraged white Americans more likely to hold prejudicial views.[182] (The findings on this matter are mixed.[183]) A majority of the public thought Trump made race relations worse and that it had become more common for people to express racist or racially insensitive views.[184] The FBI reported that hate crimes jumped 17 percent in 2017,[185] and there was a 226 percent increase in hate crimes in counties in which the president held rallies in 2016.[186] In 2018, hate crimes reached a sixteen-year high.[187] The Anti-Defamation League found that incidents of white supremacist propaganda distributed across the United States increased by more than 120 percent from 2018 to 2019 and reached the highest number the ADL had ever recorded.[188] Many people also had distorted views of the extent of demographic changes. For example, when asked to estimate the percent of the US population composed of Muslims, the public responded with an average answer of 17 percent. The correct percentage was 1 percent.[189]

Tending to the Base

Every president has two roles that are in inherent tension: the head of state representing the entire country and the head of government leading a governing coalition. Donald Trump performed the unifying role poorly. All presidents like to appear before cheering crowds of supporters, and they make policy choices consistent with their base's broad partisan and ideological orientations. Nevertheless, most presidents make at least an effort to be governing on behalf of all Americans. Emphasizing their desire to bridge differences, George W. Bush declared he was "uniter, not a divider,"[190] and Barack Obama proclaimed "There is not a liberal America and a conservative America; There's the United States of America."[191]

Donald Trump was different. He stoked division by explicitly tending to his base and typically paid no rhetorical deference to the notion of the presidency as a national unifier. General James Mattis, his former secretary of defense, wrote, "Donald Trump is the first president in my lifetime who does not try to unite the American people—does not even pretend to try. Instead he tries to divide us."[192]

Trump's narcissism may have encouraged the president to retreat to people who venerated him, but he had pragmatic motivations as well. We saw in chapter 3 that during his first year in office, Trump traveled far less frequently in pursuit of his agenda than did his immediate predecessors. "When Trump did leave Washington, he was far more likely to visit Trump-friendly states in campaign-style rallies than to try to broaden his coalition's reach." He held nine "Make America Great Again" rallies, the first less than a month into his first term. Instead of traveling to competitive states to try to increase his support, Trump largely rallied in states that he won in 2016. His visits into blue states were largely visits to federal institutions—such as the CIA in Virginia or the Secret Service training facility in Maryland—or visits to his nearby homes, as in New York and New Jersey.[193]

In his second year, the president also traveled less than his immediate predecessors. Of his ninety-seven total trips (excluding vacations and fundraisers), about half were for campaigning to rally his base, to support congressional Republicans before the midterm elections, or both. What's more, on 90 percent of these campaign trips, he visited red states.[194] Although Trump campaigned actively in the 2018 midterm elections, he focused heavily on more rural areas in which he was popular and which he won in 2016. He mostly avoided suburban areas where he was less popular and ran the risk of energizing Democrats or hurting Republican candidates who had tried to distance themselves from him.[195] He campaigned in only three states he did not win in 2016.

One analysis found that Trump traveled nearly five times as often to states he won in 2016 as to those that supported Hillary Clinton. He gave several times more interviews to Fox News than to all the other major networks combined. His social media advertising was aimed disproportionately at older Americans who were the superstructure of his victory in the electoral college in 2016.[196] According to Republican pollster Whit Ayres, "Donald Trump got elected with minority support from the American electorate, and most of his efforts thus far are focused on energizing and solidifying the 40 percent of Americans who were with him, primarily by attacking the 60 percent who were not. That is great for his supporters, but it makes it very difficult to accomplish anything in a democracy."[197]

On October 25, 2019, Trump spoke at Benedict College in Columbia, South Carolina, a historically black college. The White House billed the speech as a chance for the president to step outside the friendly confines of his supporter base and pitch his administration's record on criminal justice reform and black employment directly to a black audience. However, fewer than ten students from Benedict were given tickets to the invitation-only event, which had room for about three hundred attendees. More than half of the seats were reserved for guests and allies of the administration, including many black supporters of Trump who came from out of state.[198]

Most presidents seek to expand their coalitions. Although they rarely move public opinion very far, all of Trump's predecessors enjoyed the support of a majority of the public at some point in their tenures. Trump was different. As we have seen, he won the election as the least popular major party candidate in modern history. He never enjoyed the approval of a majority of the public. Thus, he concluded that he would never persuade most of the public to support either him or his policies. His solution was to fire up his base, mobilizing them to pressure Republican members of Congress and support Republicans at the polls. "This president seems to be operating on 'how do I make my smaller supporters more intensified' as opposed to 'how do I get more supporters?'" explained Matthew Dowd, a former top political advisor to George W. Bush. "Instead of trying to overcome division, he is trying to harden the division."[199]

Trump catered assiduously to the coalition that elected him. Traditional small-government economic conservatives received deregulation and lower taxes, weakened environmental protection, and attacks on the Affordable Care Act. Religious conservatives were happy with his nominations to the Supreme Court, his opposition to abortion, and his strong support for Israel. The white working class, especially males, seemed to enjoy Trump's pugnacious style, disdain for conventional norms of civility and respect for the rule of law, hostility to the mainstream news media, racist and misogynistic appeals, anti-immigrant policies, and resistance to free trade.

The most memorable promise Donald Trump made while campaigning for president was to build a wall along the US border with Mexico. The simplicity of the concept—an idea that could be expressed in a single word—made it a powerful sales pitch on the campaign trail. By 2019, he had spent four years—first as a candidate and then as president—whipping his core supporters into a frenzy over the idea of building a wall. Yet in transforming the wall into a powerful symbol of his anti-immigration message, Trump made the proposal politically untouchable for Democrats, even though such leading Democrats as senators Barack Obama, Hillary Clinton, Joe Biden, and Charles Schumer voted for the Secure Fence Act in 2006, which provided for hundreds of miles of fencing along the border.

Thus, the president deliberately amplified public tensions by seizing on divisive topics and articulating them in blunt us-against-them language to energize his base. This discourse helped to undermine the context necessary for negotiation. When political leaders take their cases directly to the public, they must accommodate the limited attention spans of the public and the availability of space on Twitter and television. As a result, the president (and his opponents) often reduced choices to stark black-and-white terms. When leaders frame issues in such terms, they typically frustrate rather than facilitate building coalitions. Such positions are difficult to compromise, which hardens negotiating positions.

Trump's base was loyal, but he became its captive. Because his base was well under 50 percent of the public, he could not afford to lose any portion of it. As I detail in chapter 8, at various points, the president seemed to agree to a bargain with the Democrats on immigration policy. In each case, prominent commentators representing his base ridiculed him in the most disparaging terms. In late 2018, when it appeared he would forgo funding for a wall on the Mexican border in order to keep the government funded, Rush Limbaugh criticized the deal as "Trump gets nothing and the Democrats get everything." Another conservative firebrand, Ann Coulter, published a column titled "Gutless President in Wall-less Country." The president's rhetoric had painted him into a corner.[200]

In response, Trump immediately recanted, ending negotiations, and in December 2018, his action prompted a shutdown of the government. Instead of moving toward the political center after sweeping Democratic gains in the House in the midterm elections, the president focused on reassuring his most ardent supporters of his commitment to his signature pledge to build a wall on the Mexican border, declaring that he would be "proud to shut down the government for border security." He no doubt galvanized his base, but doing so made it difficult to appeal to the rest of the country.

Only 28 percent of the public saw a wall on the Mexican border as an immediate top priority, and 50 percent said it was not a priority at all. Similarly, 57 percent thought Trump should compromise to prevent gridlock. However, only 29 percent of Republicans felt this way.[201] In general, 62 percent of Americans opposed shutting down the government over funding for a border wall, but 59 percent of Republicans disagreed and supported the shutdown. In addition, the public was more likely to blame Trump and Republicans in Congress than congressional Democrats for the shutdown (table 4.24). Nevertheless, the president saw no choice but to shut down the government.

On January 19, 2019, during the shutdown, the president made a national address in which he tried to reach beyond his base of supporters and speak to a broader swath of Americans. He offered temporary protections for about one million immigrants at risk of deportation in exchange for funding for a wall. Yet in seeking to inch toward the center, Trump alienated portions of his hard-right base while not offering Democrats enough for a compromise. In the end, he had to agree to reopen the government and then declared a controversial emergency to obtain the funds he sought, further alienating a majority of the public.

The president was also held hostage to his base's opposition to gun control. After several of the mass shootings during his tenure, the president responded with support for measures such as enhanced background checks for gun owners. In each case he backed away after hearing from the NRA and its supporters in Congress. In a televised meeting in the Cabinet Room on February 28, 2018, Trump embraced a set of gun control measures, including expanding background checks, keeping guns from the mentally ill, securing schools, and restricting gun sales from some young adults.[202] By March 2, Kellyanne Conway was telling the NRA to stop worrying. "He has an A-plus rating from the N.R.A. because he made specific promises." "He understands the overlap between gun owners and those voters who supported him," she insisted.[203]

In the summer of 2019, after the back-to-back mass shootings in El Paso, Texas, and Dayton, Ohio, Trump said he wanted to pass "very meaningful background checks." The president optimistically explained, "I think my base relies very much on common sense. And they rely on me, in terms of telling them what's happening," he told reporters. Trump also said he was hopeful that the NRA, whose members he called "great patriots," could be persuaded.[204] Apparently, they could not, and the president ended up advocating increasing mental health facilities. Ironically, early in his tenure, at the NRA's urging, Trump signed legislation that repealed an Obama-era regulation designed to prevent certain mentally ill people from purchasing firearms.

By September 2019, warnings from gun rights advocates and Republican lawmakers about the political blowback that would result from more rigorous background checks led to White House indecision about what to do. When Attorney General William P. Barr and White House legislative director Eric Ueland met with Republican lawmakers and distributed a plan to expand background checks, White House officials immediately distanced the president from what they described as a "test run" proposal.[205] In the end, the president abandoned offering proposals to combat gun violence. His political advisors had counseled him that gun legislation could splinter his political coalition, which he needed to remain unified for his reelection bid, particularly amid an impeachment battle.[206]

Similarly, the president vowed to ban flavored vaping products. Just days later, however, he seemed to temper his position, focusing on counterfeit products. He told aides that his position changed after Brad Parscale, his campaign manager, warned him that many of his supporters would oppose a ban on all vaping products.[207] After the president settled on a more limited ban, the president called Alex Azar, the secretary of the Department of Health and Human Services during a campaign meeting and complained about being involved in the decision.[208] Trump also nixed plans to host the G7 summit at the Trump National Doral golf club when Republicans told him they could not defend it.[209]

The base also restricted the president's foreign policy. Trump had to back off his impulsive announcement of the complete, immediate withdrawal of US forces from Syria in December 2018 in order to quell the outcry from his hawkish allies in Congress. Ten months later, when he made a similar decision, causing outrage at abandoning our Kurdish allies among many Republicans, he had to make modifications to relocate troops to Iraq and to other areas of Syria.

Appearing too partisan or too narrowly focused on the views of a minority of the public was disadvantageous in other ways. The president approached governing as zero-sum tribal warfare, deepening the threats people felt from each other, and hoped these perceptions would strengthen his supporters' loyalty to him. Perhaps they did. At the same time, his actions exacerbated the anger and bitterness in American politics. The president's approach was to celebrate his base while denigrating blue America. He declared that New York City and New York state were "falling apart," San Francisco was "disgusting," California was a "disgrace to our country," Baltimore was a "disgusting, rat and rodent infested mess," Atlanta was in "horrible shape" and Chicago was "embarrassing to us as a nation."[210] There is some evidence that one reason for the lack of a national strategy for combating the coronavirus pandemic was that the administration originally believed the problem was restricted to blue states.[211]

When presidents aggressively promote their policies and themselves, they invite opponents to challenge them.[212] The effect is to trigger motivated reasoning and thus activate existing attitudes and partisan beliefs among the opposition, which in Trump's case helped to produce and reinforce sharp partisan differences in support for his policies. Another result was the most polarized job approval ratings in history, as we saw in table 2.7. He had strong support from Republicans, little support from Independents, and almost no support from Democrats.

Another problem is straightforward. The president's base was too small for winning the House and for winning reelection himself. There are more Democrats than Republicans (although the concentration of Republicans in rural states give them an advantage in Senate elections). Even Democrats' tendency toward lower turnout did not hurt them in the 2018 midterm elections. Moreover, they won Independent voters by a 12-point margin and voters who voted for a third-party candidate in 2016 by 13 percentage points.[213]

The president could not expand his base. As Gary Jacobson has shown, in the 163 weekly *The Economist/* YouGov polls taken from January 2017 to March 2020, an average of 90 percent of respondents who said they voted for him approved of his performance, 8 percent disapproved. However, in the same surveys, an average of 93 percent of people who said they voted for Hillary Clinton disapproved of his performance; only 5 percent approved.[214]

Challenging the Rule of Law

At the core of every democracy is a commitment to the rule of law, the principle whereby "all members of a society (including those in government) are equally subject to publicly disclosed legal codes and processes."[215] Donald Trump was at war with the rule of law throughout his presidency, vilifying a range of core institutions that were less than responsive to his wishes. Court decisions overturning many of his administrative efforts involving immigration, environmental protection, and other matters; the FBI and Special Counsel Robert Mueller's investigation of the president's 2016 campaign's possible collusion with Russia; and the failure of Attorney General Jeff Sessions to protect him from investigation and to prosecute Trump's political enemies evoked a torrent of criticism from the White House aimed at demeaning the individuals involved and undermining the legitimacy of their work and decisions. Trump denounced the criminal justice system as a "joke" and a "laughing stock," demanded that a suspect in a terrorist attack be executed, and called a court martial decision "a complete and total disgrace."[216]

After the president's inauguration, not a week passed without his connection to Russia making front-page news. He complained bitterly and frequently about the investigation of possible collusion between his campaign and Russia in 2016.[217] Some observers thought the president had gone even further and had been guilty of obstruction of justice and witness tampering. The investigation turned up violations of the law by Trump's onetime campaign manager, advisors, and one of his lawyers. Sometimes, it distracted him from doing his job.[218]

On May 16, 2017, Deputy Attorney General Rod Rosenstein appointed former FBI director Robert Mueller as special counsel to head an investigation of possible ties between Donald Trump's 2016 presidential campaign and the Russian government. The president began complaining immediately. On May 19, he termed the investigation—which had yet to do anything—"the greatest witch hunt in American history." On June 15, the president sent several tweets criticizing the investigation, including "You are witnessing the single greatest WITCH HUNT in American political history—led by some very bad and conflicted people!"[219]

This criticism continued unabated through the remainder of the investigation. For example, on April 26, 2018, Trump called into Fox News's *Fox & Friends* for a long, and at times furious, interview. In it, the president reiterated several of his primary themes regarding the Mueller investigation.

> They have this witch hunt going on, with people in the Justice Department that shouldn't be there, they have a witch hunt against the president of the United States.

> The people that are doing the investigation, you have 13 people that are Democrats, you have Hillary Clinton people, you have people who worked on Hillary Clinton's foundation.[220]

Similarly, on August 20, 2018, the president tweeted that "Bob Mueller and his whole group of Angry Democrat Thugs" were a "National Disgrace!"[221] Trump and his lawyer, Rudolph Giuliani, repeatedly disparaged Mueller and his team on social media and in television interviews, accusing the lawyers of bias and conflicts of interest and claiming that they were trying to frame the president. There is little doubt that the whole effort was aimed at delegitimizing the investigation.

Related to the White House raising questions about the whole Mueller investigation was its fostering skepticism about the institutions supporting it, principally the FBI and the Department of Justice. The president routinely disparaged the leaders of both organization as well as what he viewed as the biases of the FBI agents directly involved with the investigation. He questioned their integrity and mercilessly mocked Jeff Sessions, his own attorney general.

In addition, constant conflicts with the courts characterized the Trump's presidency. Judges struck down or delayed a large number of his actions, including his travel bans, his barring of transgender troops in the military, his cutting funds for sanctuary cities, his ending the DACA program, his approving of the Keystone XL oil pipeline, his holding migrant families in long-term detention, and his plans for blanket detention of asylum seekers and refusal to accept asylum claims from migrants who entered the United States illegally.

Trump, as was his wont, responded pugnaciously, venting his frustration with complaints about the judges making decisions he did not like. As early as February 5, 2017, the president tweeted, "Just cannot believe a judge would put our country in such peril. If something happens blame him and the court system."[222] Six days later, he declared, "Our legal system is broken!"[223] A year and a half later, on November 22, 2018—Thanksgiving Day, he declared the Ninth Circuit Court of Appeals to be "a complete & total disaster" prone to making political decisions and threatened to break it up.[224]

In March 2017, at his confirmation hearings, Neil Gorsuch, the president's first nominee to the Supreme Court, called Trump's attacks on federal judges "disheartening" and "demoralizing."[225] The next year the president's criticism prompted Chief Justice John G. Roberts Jr. to direct a rare and pointed shot at him. "We do not have Obama judges or Trump judges, Bush judges or Clinton judges," Roberts declared. "What we have is an extraordinary group of dedicated judges doing their level best to do equal right to those appearing before them." Roberts added, "That independent judiciary is something we should all be thankful for."[226]

The Trump administration also flouted the rule of law and ran into pushback from the courts in its efforts at deregulation. From his first days in office, Trump's appointees directed federal agencies to draft regulations meant to delay or reverse policies of the Obama administration. Courts overturned or stayed most of these regulations, generally for violating the Administrative Procedure Act. The Supreme Court voided the administration's attempt to end the Deferred Action for Childhood Arrivals (DACA) program because it violated the APA by failing to engage in "reasoned decision-making."[227] One study found that by the beginning of 2019, there were challenges to thirty major regulations, and the courts had found for the challengers twenty-eight times.[228]

In his Farewell Address in 1796, George Washington warned of the "insidious wiles of foreign influence" because "foreign influence is one of the most baneful foes of republican government."[229] Similarly, in *Federalist 68* Alexander Hamilton cautioned about "the desire in foreign powers to gain an improper ascendant in our councils."[230] Donald Trump took another view, however, and declared he would accept help from a foreign government in an election.[231] He added that his own FBI director, Christopher A. Wray, was "wrong" when he said during congressional testimony that campaign aides should always report offers of assistance from foreign entities to the bureau.[232] (Later, he backtracked on this point after facing widespread criticism.[233])

Trump routinely sought the help of foreign nations in support of his re-election.[234] Laws prohibit foreign contributions to American political campaigns, although it is not clear whether information, rather than money, falls under the legal exclusion. What is less ambiguous is that the president's willingness to accept help from a foreign government upended the norm of American politics that such outside assistance is inappropriate. Moreover, not reporting offers of information may harm national security by depriving law enforcement agencies of tips about foreign interference in US affairs.

In June 2019, the Office of Special Counsel recommended that the president dismiss White House counselor Kellyanne Conway for repeated violations of the Hatch Act, which bars federal employees from engaging in political activity in the course of their work. The president simply ignored the law and told Fox News, "It looks to me like they're trying to take away her right to free speech."[235]

On February 11, 2020, Trump learned of the sentencing recommendation that Department of Justice prosecutors were making for his friend Roger Stone, who had been convicted of lying to Congress and witness tampering. The president immediately tweeted, "This is a horrible and very unfair situation. . . . Cannot allow this miscarriage of justice!"[236] Within hours the department announced it would reduce its sentence recommendation. As a result, four prosecutors withdrew from the case, one of whom also resigned from government completely. Trump also criticized Judge Amy Berman Jackson, who was to sentence Stone. Ultimately, the president commuted Stone's sentence. Many agreed with Mitt Romney's July 11 tweet, "Unprecedented, historic corruption: an American president commutes the sentence of a person convicted by a jury of lying to shield that very president."[237]

In an interview on ABC News on February 13, Attorney General William Barr confirmed that he personally made the decision to overrule the sentence recommended for Stone, noting that the did so before Trump tweeted about it. However, in a remarkable public rebuke, he criticized the president for getting involved: "To have public statements and tweets made about the department, about people in the department, about our men and women here, about cases pending in the department, and about judges before whom we have cases make it impossible for me to do my job and to ensure the courts and the prosecutors in the department that we are doing our work with integrity." "I cannot do my job here at the department with a constant background commentary that undercuts me." The attorney general added, "I think it's time to stop the tweeting about Department of Justice criminal cases" and that he had repeatedly urged Trump to do so. "I'm not going to be bullied or influenced by anybody," Barr declared.[238]

Perhaps not. Shortly before Trump's former national security advisor Michael Flynn was to be sentenced for lying to the FBI about his contacts with Russia, the Department of Justice announced it was dropping the case. Legal authorities were hard pressed to find another instance where the department had voluntarily dropped a case in which the defendant had pleaded guilty and was also well represented by legal counsel. Moreover, the judge in the case had already rejected the department's argument that the FBI had no reason to interview Flynn in the first place — and that, accordingly, the subject matter of the interview was not material to an investigation.

In June 2020, the president fired Geoffrey Berman, the US attorney for the Southern District of New York, the most important district in the country. Berman had won convictions against one of Trump's lawyers and was investigating another, Rudolph Giuliani. He was also investigating a Turkish financial institution, Halkbank, that has close ties to Turkey's president, for undermining US sanctions against Iran. Trump repeatedly tried to intervene in the investigation.[239]

Most presidents face negative court decisions, and many suffer through investigations of themselves or their administrations, but no modern chief executive has so openly flouted the norm of upholding the rule of law or been so active in questioning the legitimacy of judicial and executive officials. Did Donald Trump's harsh rhetoric weaken trust in American legal institutions and the public's allegiance to the rule of law?

On one level, it has not. In 2016, 70 percent of the public said it was important to respect the rules, even if it was more difficult to get things done. Two years later, in February 2018, that number had risen to 79 percent, including 79 percent of Democrats and Democratic leaners and 82 percent of Republicans and Republican leaners.[240]

Nevertheless, historian Jon Meacham argues that "the effect on the life of the nation of a president inventing conspiracy theories in order to distract attention from legitimate investigations or other things he dislikes is corrosive." "The diabolical brilliance of the Trump strategy of disinformation is that many people are simply going to hear the charges and countercharges, and decide that there must be something to them because the president of the United States is saying them."[241] Some research supports Meacham's conclusion. Authority figures can have a strong effect on social norms by creating a false impression that a social consensus exists in support of behavior such as expressing prejudice or evading the law.[242]

The Mueller Investigation

Of all the legal irritants to Trump, the one evoking the most frequent and bitter criticism from the White House was the Mueller investigation. Polling organizations did not start asking questions about the investigation until the fall of 2017. In general, approval of the investigation declined starting in mid-December 2017 (table 5.7). Once that decline occurred, however, opinion stabilized throughout the remainder of the period. Moreover, at no time did a plurality of the public disapprove of the investigation. Interestingly, the highest approval ratings were found in the Fox News polls (June and August 2018) that only questioned registered voters.

At the core of Trump's criticism of the Mueller investigation was the assertion that it was unfair, a witch hunt run by partisan Democrats. Most people disagreed (table 5.8). Typically, a majority, and always a substantial plurality, of the public thought the investigation was fair.[243]

Two polling organizations asked the question about the fairness of the Mueller investigation a little differently, focusing on the confidence people had in the fairness. The results show that most people were confident, with little change over time until Mueller announced the results, at which point confidence increased (table 5.9).[244]

What about Republicans—and Trump's leadership of them? From the beginning, approval of Mueller's appointment evoked a partisan response (table 5.10). Within two weeks of the announcement of the probe, only 63 percent of Republicans approved of Mueller's appointment, and after a month, that approval dropped to 49 percent. It is entirely likely that Republicans in the public lacked long-term views on the issue and so turned to the president for guidance on the appropriate view of the investigation.

TABLE 5.7. **Public approval of Mueller investigation**

Date of poll	Approve (%)	Disapprove (%)	No opinion (%)
Oct. 30–Nov. 1, 2017[a]	58	28	14
Nov. 7–13, 2017[b]	60	27	13
Dec. 6–11, 2017[b]	58	29	13
Dec. 14–17, 2017[b]	47	34	19
Jan. 14–18, 2018[b]	47	33	20
Jan. 15–18, 2018[a]	50	31	19
Feb. 20–23, 2018[b]	47	33	21
Mar. 22–25, 2018[b]	48	35	17
May 2–5, 2018[b]	44	38	18
June 3–6, 2018[c]	55	37	8
June 14–17, 2018[b]	41	39	21
June 27–July 2, 2018[d]	49	45	5
July 9–11, 2018[c]	48	40	12
Aug. 9–12, 2018[b]	47	39	13
Aug. 19–21, 2018[c]	59	37	4
Aug. 26–29, 2018[e]	63	29	8
Sept. 6–9, 2018[b]	50	38	12
Sept. 16–19, 2018[c]	55	39	7
Oct. 4–7, 2018[b]	48	36	16
Dec. 6–9, 2018[b]	43	40	16
Dec. 9–11, 2018[c]	56	37	7
Dec. 12–17, 2018[f]	45	38	17
Jan. 20–22, 2019[c]	49	34	17
Jan. 30–Feb. 2, 2019[b]	44	41	15
Feb. 6–10, 2019[g]	51	34	15
Mar. 26–29, 2019[g]	53	30	17
Apr. 24–29, 2019[h]	54	26	20
Apr. 25–28, 2019[b]	59	30	11
May 11–14, 2019[i]	46	32	22

[a] ABC News/*Washington Post* poll: "A special counsel at the US Justice Department, Robert Mueller, has been investigating possible ties between Donald Trump's 2016 presidential campaign and the Russian government. Do you approve or disapprove of the way Mueller is handling this investigation?"

[b] CNN poll: "Do you approve or disapprove of the way Robert Mueller is handling the investigation into Russian interference in the 2016 election?" (April 2019 poll replaced "is handling" with "handled").

[c] Fox News poll: "Do you approve or disapprove of Robert Mueller's investigation of the 2016 Trump presidential campaign's ties with Russia and potential obstruction of justice charges against members of the Trump administration?" (asked of registered voters).

[d] *Washington Post*–Schar School poll: "Do you approve or disapprove of the way US Justice Department special counsel Robert Mueller is handling the investigation into possible ties between Donald Trump's presidential campaign and the Russian government?"

[e] ABC News/*Washington Post* poll: "Do you support or oppose the investigation of (Donald) Trump and his associates by Special Counsel Robert Mueller?"

[f] Quinnipiac University poll: "Do you approve or disapprove of the way that Special Counsel Robert Mueller is handling his job?"

[g] *Washington Post*–Schar School poll: "As you may know, special counsel Robert Mueller is investigating Russia's role in the 2016 election and its possible ties with Donald Trump's presidential campaign. Do you approve or disapprove of the way Mueller is handling this investigation?"

[h] NPR/PBS *NewsHour* poll: "Do you approve or disapprove of the job Robert Mueller did as special counsel investigating possible wrongdoing and Russian interference in the 2016 election?"

[i] Fox News poll: "Do you approve or disapprove of the way Robert Mueller handled the Russia investigation (on interference in the 2016 presidential election)?"

TABLE 5.8. **Public opinion about the fairness of the Mueller investigation**

Date of poll	Fair (%)	Not fair (%)	No opinion (%)
July 17–Aug. 1, 2017[a]	64	25	11
Aug. 3–6, 2017[b]	58	27	15
Nov. 7–13, 2017[a]	60	27	13
Dec. 6–11, 2017[a]	58	29	13
Jan. 5–9, 2018[a]	59	26	15
Jan. 8–10, 2018[c]	48	28	23
Feb. 2–5, 2018[a]	56	28	16
Feb. 5–7, 2018[d]	53	28	20
Mar. 3–5, 2018[a]	58	28	14
Mar. 5–6, 2018[d]	51	26	23
Mar. 19–21, 2018[d]	48	26	27
Apr. 6–9, 2018[a]	52	32	17
Apr. 10–13, 2018[c]	45	30	26
Apr. 20–24, 2018[a]	54	31	15
May 31–June 5, 2018[a]	50	35	15
July 18–23, 2018[a]	55	31	13
July 19–22, 2018[c]	46	32	21
Aug. 9–13, 2018[a]	51	33	16
Sept. 6–9, 2018[a]	55	32	13
Nov. 28–Dec. 4, 2018[e]	54	33	13
Dec. 12–17, 2018[a]	48	38	13
Mar. 1–4, 2019[a]	54	27	19
Mar. 21–25, 2019[a]	55	26	19
Apr. 22–25, 2019[f]	51	21	28
Apr. 24–29, 2019[c]	57	30	14
Apr. 26–29, 2019[a]	72	18	10

[a] Quinnipiac University poll: "As you may know, Special Counsel Robert Mueller was appointed to oversee the criminal investigation into any links or coordination between President Donald Trump's 2016 presidential campaign and the Russian government. Do you think that he is conducting a fair investigation into this matter, or not?" (for April 2019, wording was changed to "conducted" from "is conducting"; asked of registered voters).
[b] CBS News poll: "As you may know, Robert Mueller is the Special Counsel investigating Russia and the 2016 Trump presidential campaign. From what you have seen or heard so far, do you believe Robert Mueller will conduct a fair investigation into the matter, or won't he?"
[c] NPR/*PBS NewsHour* poll: "From what you have heard about Robert Mueller, the special counsel in the Russia investigation of interference in the 2016 presidential election, do you think the investigation is fair or not fair?" (the April 2019 poll replaced "is" with "was").
[d] Marist College poll: "From what you have read or heard about Robert Mueller, the special counsel in the Russia investigation into alleged interference in the 2016 election, do you think the investigation is fair or not fair?"
[e] NPR/*PBS NewsHour* poll: "Which of the following statements comes closer to your opinion about Special Counsel Robert Mueller's investigation into possible wrongdoing and Russian interference in the 2016 elections? (1) It is a "witch hunt"; (2) It's a fair investigation; (3) Unsure.
[f] ABC News/*Washington Post* poll: "As you may know, Special Counsel Robert Mueller has completed his investigation of possible collusion between Trump's 2016 presidential campaign and Russia. Do you feel that Mueller's report is or is not fair and even-handed?"

Similarly, there were large differences between partisans in views of the fairness of the investigation (table 5.11) and confidence in that fairness (table 5.12). Large majorities of Democrats viewed it as fair, as did majorities of Independents. Republicans, however, saw it quite differently. Only small percentages viewed it as impartial until the Mueller report was made public in mid-April 2019. Again, the signals from the White House and many other Republican officials very likely influenced Republicans' views.[245] The increasing skepticism of Republicans after mid-March 2018 may have been in response to Trump mentioning Mueller by name in a tweet for the first time on March 17. After mid-April, however, when the

TABLE 5.9. **Confidence in the fairness of the Mueller investigation**

Date of poll	Confident (%)	Not confident (%)	No opinion (%)
Nov. 29–Dec. 4, 2017[a]	55	36	8
Jan. 10–15, 2018[a]	54	37	8
Mar. 7–14, 2018[a]	61	37	3
Apr. 4–May 14, 2018[b]	48	37	12
May 14–30, 2018[c]	46	41	13
June 5–12, 2018[a]	55	38	5
July 23–Aug. 9, 2018[c]	47	41	13
Sept. 18–23, 2018[a]	56	37	7
Oct. 17–25, 2018[c]	50	39	12
Dec. 11–19, 2018[c]	49	39	12
Dec. 13–16, 2018[d]	57	42	1
Jan. 9–14, 2019[a]	54	41	5
Mar. 11–14, 2019[d]	62	36	2
Apr. 11–14, 2019[d]	70	28	1
July 10–15, 2019[a]	65	31	4

[a] Pew Research Center poll: "How confident, if at all, are you that the Justice Department special counsel Robert Mueller is conducting a fair investigation into Russian involvement in the 2016 election?" (the July 2019 poll changed the wording from "is conducting" to "conducted")
[b] Democracy Fund Voter Study Group 2018 VOTER survey: "How confident are you that the special counsel Robert Mueller is conducting a fair investigation into Russian involvement in the 2016 election?"
[c] GW Politics poll: "How confident are you that the special counsel Robert Mueller is conducting a fair investigation into Russian involvement in the 2016 election?"
[d] AP poll: "How confident are you that the Justice Department's investigation of Donald Trump's ties to Russia led by former FBI (Federal Bureau of Investigation) Director Robert Mueller is fair and impartial?" (the April 2019 poll changed the wording to "was" instead of "is").

TABLE 5.10. **Partisan approval of Mueller appointment**

	Approval (%)	
Group	May 31–June 6, 2017	June 22–27, 2017
All	73	64
Democrats	81	78
Independents	73	64
Republicans	63	49

Note: Respondents were asked, "As you may know, former Director of the FBI Robert Mueller has been appointed as a special counsel to oversee the criminal investigation into any links or coordination between President Trump's campaign and the Russian government. Do you approve or disapprove of this appointment?" (asked of registered voters).
Source: Quinnipiac University polls.

TABLE 5.11. **Partisan views on the fairness of the Mueller investigation**

Date of poll	Fair (%)		
	Democrats	Independents	Republicans
July 17–Aug. 1, 2017	73	64	54
Nov. 7–13, 2017	76	63	41
Dec. 6–11, 2017	79	58	34
Jan. 5–9, 2018	75	61	37
Feb. 2–5, 2018	77	57	35
Mar. 3–5, 2018	80	57	36
Apr. 6–9, 2018	75	50	30
Apr. 20–24, 2018	79	58	26
May 31–June 5, 2018	73	51	25
July 18–23, 2018	80	59	23
Aug. 9–13, 2018	72	53	29
Sept. 6–9, 2018	77	55	30
Dec. 12–17, 2018	73	49	21
Mar. 1–4, 2019	75	56	33
Mar. 21–25, 2019	65	53	47
Apr. 26–29, 2019	77	78	65

Note: Respondents were asked, "As you may know, Special Counsel Robert Mueller was appointed to oversee the criminal investigation into any links or coordination between President Donald Trump's 2016 presidential campaign and the Russian government. Do you think that he is conducting a fair investigation into this matter, or not?" (asked of registered voters).
Source: Quinnipiac University polls.

TABLE 5.12. **Partisan confidence in the fairness of the Mueller investigation**

Date of poll	Confident (%)	
	Democrats/leaners	Republicans/leaners
Nov. 29–Dec. 4, 2017	68	44
Jan. 10–15, 2018	65	45
Mar. 7–14, 2018	75	46
June 5–12, 2018	70	38
Sept. 18–23, 2018	76	33
Jan. 9–14, 2019	72	39
July 10–15, 2019*	71	60

Note: Respondents were asked, "How confident, if at all, are you that the Justice Department special counsel Robert Mueller is conducting a fair investigation into Russian involvement in the 2016 election?"
Source: Pew Research Center polls.
*The July 2019 poll changed the wording of the question from "is conducting" to "conducted."

report did not find evidence that the Trump campaign colluded with the Russians, Republicans dramatically switched their opinions of the fairness of the investigation and became much more positive.

Partisan differences were even starker when people were asked about the legitimacy of the investigation (table 5.13). Democrats overwhelmingly

TABLE 5.13. Partisan opinion on the legitimacy of the Mueller investigation

	Feel it is legitimate (%)		
Date of poll	Democrats	Independents	Republicans
Jan. 12–16, 2018	79	55	12
Feb. 2–5, 2018	78	54	14
Mar. 3–5, 2018	83	54	15
Apr. 20–24, 2018	88	53	14
May 31–June 5, 2018	82	48	12
July 18–23, 2018	85	55	16
Nov. 14–19, 2018	87	47	12
Mar. 21–25, 2019	84	49	11

Note: Respondents were asked, "Do you think that the investigation into any links or coordination between President Trump's 2016 election campaign and the Russian government is a legitimate investigation, or do you think it is a political witch hunt?" (asked of registered voters).
Source: Quinnipiac University polls.

thought it was legitimate, as did a majority of Independents. Very few Republicans agreed, however.

It is possible that the president was able to create some skepticism among the public about the Mueller investigation, but he could not convince people of the correctness of his opposition to it. Despite Trump's torrent of tweets, statements to the press, and declarations at rallies, the public did not approve of Trump's response to the investigation (table 5.14). Opinion was remarkably stable, and it appears that only his Republican base—less than one-third of the public—approved of his handling the issue.[246] In January 2019, 60 percent of the public were not confident Trump was handling the investigation appropriately.[247] When asked in February 2019 whose version of the facts they were most inclined to accept, Trump's or Mueller's, only 32 percent chose Trump. Fifty-six percent were more inclined to believe Mueller.[248] After the results of the investigation were announced, 45 percent of registered voters said they had more trust in Mueller to tell the truth; only 27 percent had more trust in Trump.[249]

By late August 2018, 63 percent of Americans supported Mueller's investigation of Russian interference in the 2016 election, with 52 percent saying they supported it strongly; 29 percent opposed the probe. Unsurprisingly, opinions on Mueller's work broke on partisan lines, with 61 percent of Republicans opposing the inquiry but an even larger 85 percent of Democrats expressing support. A two-thirds majority of Independents backed the investigation.[250]

The public did not change its distrust of Trump after the Mueller report was made public. Most people concluded that the president had committed

TABLE 5.14. Public opinion on Trump's handling of the Mueller investigation

Date of poll	Approve (%)	Disapprove (%)	No opinion (%)
June 25–27, 2017[a]	37	53	9
Aug. 3–6, 2017[b]	31	59	9
Dec. 14–17, 2017[b]	32	56	13
Jan. 14–15, 17–18, 2018[b]	31	54	15
Feb. 10–13, 2018[a]	33	56	11
Feb. 20–23, 2018[b]	30	55	15
Mar. 22–25, 2018[b]	32	56	11
May 2–5, 2018[b]	31	55	14
June 14–17, 2018[b]	29	55	16
July 9–11, 2018[a]	36	54	10
Aug. 9–12, 2018[b*]	34	55	11
Sept. 6–9, 2018[b]	30	58	12
Oct. 4–7, 2018[b]	33	54	13
Dec. 6–9, 2018[b]	29	57	14
Jan. 16–20, 2019[c]	30	66	30
Jan. 30–Feb. 2, 2019[b]	31	59	9
Feb. 6–10, 2019[d]	35	52	13
Apr. 25–28, 2019[e]	41	51	8

[a] CNN poll: "Do you approve or disapprove of the way Donald Trump is handling the investigation into Russian interference in the 2016 election?"
[b] Fox News poll: "Do you approve or disapprove of the way the Trump administration is handling investigations into Russian involvement in the 2016 presidential election?" (asked of registered voters).
[c] Associated Press poll: "Overall, do you approve or disapprove of the way Donald Trump is handling . . . the Russia investigation (into interference in the 2016 election)?"
[d] *Washington Post*–Schar School poll: "Do you approve or disapprove of the way President Trump has responded to the Mueller investigation?"
[e] CNN poll: "Do you approve or disapprove of the way Donald Trump has handled the release of (Robert) Mueller's report on the investigation into Russian interference in the 2016 election?"
[*] Asked of half the sample.

crimes before he became president, and 46 percent thought he had committed crimes while in the White House.[251] Majorities or pluralities concluded that Trump had attempted to obstruct the Mueller investigation, and majorities did not think the special counsel's report exonerated Trump of all wrongdoing.[252] Moreover, people were nearly twice as likely to believe Mueller than Trump on the question of exoneration.[253] A majority thought the president had lied to the public about matters under investigation.[254] Equally important, a majority remained concerned about the amount of contact between Trump's associates and Russians during the 2016 presidential campaign, and nearly half thought the president had committed serious wrongdoing.[255]

The FBI and Department of Justice

Donald Trump's relationship with the FBI was tumultuous. He fired FBI Director James Comey on May 9, 2017, and two days later told NBC News that "this Russia thing" factored into his decision. Since that point, he did his best to belittle and delegitimize the FBI's role in the Mueller investigation. Did the public follow the president's lead?

When asked whether they had a favorable opinion of the FBI, people generally responded in the affirmative (table 5.15). Similarly, they were much more likely to express positive than negative views of the organization (table 5.16). Although there is some variability in the figures in both tables, support for the FBI was resilient and favorable. There is no clear increase in unfavorable opinions over Trump's presidency. There is more variability in the "favorable" ratings. This fluctuation seems to be a product of the question prompting a "have not heard enough" response. Nevertheless, favorable and positive views of the FBI were not overwhelming, reflecting the long-term decline in approval of institutions in the United States. In April 2019, Gallup found that although 57 percent of the public felt the FBI was doing a good or excellent job, 42 percent rated its performance as only fair or poor.[256] A poll a year later found that 65 percent

TABLE 5.15. **Public impression of FBI performance**

Date of poll	Favorable (%)	Unfavorable (%)	No opinion (%)
Aug. 23–Sept. 2, 2016[a]	71	21	8
Jan. 5–8, 2017[a]	69	21	15
July 8–12, 2017[b]	60	19	12
Feb. 5–7, 2018[c]	65	28	7
Feb. 7–11, 2018[a]	66	23	11
Apr. 2–18, 2018[d]	54	24	22
May 31–June 5, 2018[e]	49	29	22
June 21–29, 2018[f]	39	33	32
July 11–15, 2018[a]	65	26	9
July 18–23, 2018[e]	49	25	25
Sept. 17–Oct. 1, 2018[g]	65	29	7
Sept. 5–16, 2019[a]	72	22	7

[a] Pew Research Center poll: "Is your overall opinion of the FBI very favorable, mostly favorable, mostly unfavorable, or very unfavorable?"
[b] Bloomberg poll: "For each of the following, please tell me if your impression is very favorable, mostly favorable, mostly unfavorable, or very unfavorable. If you don't know enough to give your feelings, just say so. . . . The FBI."
[c] Marist College poll: "Overall, do you have a favorable or an unfavorable impression of the FBI (Federal Bureau of Investigation)?"
[d] Suffolk University/*USA Today* poll: "For each, please tell me if your opinion of them is generally favorable or generally unfavorable. (If you are undecided or if you have never heard of someone, just tell me that.) The FBI (Federal Bureau of Investigation)."
[e] Quinnipiac University poll: "Is your opinion of the FBI favorable, unfavorable or haven't you heard enough about it?"
[f] TIPP/*Investor's Business Daily* poll: "Generally speaking, is your opinion of the FBI (Federal Bureau of Investigation) favorable or unfavorable or you are not familiar enough to say one way or the other?"
[g] PRRI poll: "Please say whether your overall opinion of each of the following is very favorable, mostly favorable, mostly unfavorable, or very unfavorable. . . . The FBI (Federal Bureau of Investigation)."

TABLE 5.16. **Public opinion of the FBI**

Date of poll	Positive (%)	Neutral (%)	Negative (%)	No opinion (%)
June 19–23, 2016	48	33	16	3
July 9–13, 2016	40	31	27	2
Dec. 12–15, 2016	37	35	27	1
Apr. 17–20, 2017	47	34	18	1
May 11–13, 2017	52	30	16	2
June 17–20, 2017	55	30	14	2
Dec. 13–17, 2017	47	32	19	2
Jan. 13–17, 2018	53	25	19	3
Mar. 10–14, 2018	48	30	20	2
June 1–4, 2018	50	30	18	2
Oct. 14–17, 2018	52	29	18	1
Dec. 9–12, 2018	51	30	17	2
Oct. 27–30, 2019	49	32	18	2

Note: Respondents were asked, "I'd like you to rate your feelings toward each one as very positive somewhat positive, neutral, somewhat negative, or very negative. (If you don't know the name, please just say so.) The Federal Bureau of Investigation, or FBI." (asked of half the national sample in June 2016, Dec. 2017, Jan. 2018, June 2018, and Oct. 2019).
Source: NBC News/*Wall Street Journal* polls.

of registered voters thought the FBI routinely broke the law and illegally spied on Americans.[257]

We see the same patterns on the issue of confidence in the FBI in table 5.17, which aggregates the two most supportive responses into the "confident" column and less supportive responses into the "not confident" column. Most people expressed at least some confidence in the organization, but, especially in 2018, many did not. Levels of confidence increased in 2019 and 2020. The figures in table 5.18 show that the confidence of Republicans and Trump supporters fell steadily over the first three polls in 2018 and then rebounded substantially for Republicans in October (data for the support of Trump supporters were not available).

Gallup found the percentage of the public (58 percent) who rated the job the FBI was doing as excellent or good in December 2017 was the same as in in November 2014—except that opinion was weighted more heavily on the "excellent" side in 2017. This stability in overall opinion masked significant shifts among partisan groups. Only 49 percent of Republicans said the FBI was doing an excellent or good job, down 13 percentage points from 62 percent in 2014. By contrast, Democrats' favorable assessment of the job the FBI was doing was up nine percentage points, with 69 percent saying the FBI was doing a good or excellent job.[258] The

TABLE 5.17. **Public confidence in the FBI**

Date of poll	Confident (%)	Not confident (%)	No opinion (%)
Jan. 8–10, 2018[a]	57	39	5
Apr. 10–13, 2018[a]	54	41	5
July 19–22, 2018[a]	56	39	6
Oct. 1, 2018[a]	59	36	5
Oct. 6–8, 2019[b]	69	28	3
Dec. 14–18, 2019[c]	73	26	1
Feb. 13–16, 2020[d]	81	18	1

[a] NPR/PBS *NewsHour* poll: "Do you have a great deal of confidence, quite a lot, not very much confidence, or no confidence at all in the FBI (Federal Bureau of Investigation)?"
[b] Fox News poll: "How much confidence do you have in . . . the FBI (Federal Bureau of Investigation)? . . . A great deal, some, not much, none at all?" (asked of registered voters).
[c] NBC News/*Wall Street Journal* poll: "I'd like you to tell me how much confidence you have in the Federal Bureau of Investigation, or FBI—a great deal, quite a bit, some, very little, or none at all?" (an answer of "some" allocated to "confident").
[d] Associated Press poll: "Would you say you have a great deal of confidence, only some confidence, or hardly any confidence at all the Federal Bureau of Investigation or FBI?"

TABLE 5.18. **Partisan confidence in the FBI**

	Confident (%)			
Date of poll	Democrats	Republicans	Independents	Trump supporters
Jan. 8–10, 2018	63	54	55	44
Apr. 10–13, 2018	68	44	51	36
July 19–22, 2018	73	34	56	32
Oct. 1, 2018	71	58	55	NA

Note: Respondents were asked, "Do you have a great deal of confidence, quite a lot, not very much confidence, or no confidence at all in the FBI (Federal Bureau of Investigation)?"
Source: NPR/PBS *NewsHour* polls.

Pew Research Center found a similar decline in Republicans' evaluation of the agency, from 71 percent favorable in January 2017 to 49 percent favorable in July 2018. Democratic opinions were little changed.[259]

When asked whether the FBI was biased against the president, most people responded "no" (table 5.19), but one- third of the country found the nation's premier law enforcement agency acting in a biased manner against the president. As table 5.20 shows, most Republicans, and two-thirds of Trump supporters, saw the FBI as biased.

In February 2018, pollsters asked the public who they were more likely to believe if President Trump and the FBI disagreed. Sixty-six percent of the public choose the latter. Only 24 percent said they would believe the president.[260] In July 2018, NPR/PBS *NewsHour* asked "With regard to

TABLE 5.19. **Public opinion of FBI bias against Trump**

Date of poll	FBI is not biased (%)	FBI is biased (%)	No opinion (%)
Feb. 2–5, 2018[a]	53	34	12
Feb. 5–7, 2018[b]	71	23	6
Apr. 10–13, 2018[c]	61	31	9
July 18–23, 2018[a]	53	34	12
July 19–22, 2018[c]	59	33	8

[a] Quinnipiac University poll: "Do you think that the FBI (Federal Bureau of Investigation) is biased against President (Donald) Trump, or not?" (asked of registered voters; numbers reversed to match Marist college poll and NPR/PBS *NewsHour* poll).
[b] Marist College poll: "Do you think the FBI (Federal Bureau of Investigation) is just trying to do their job, or [is] biased against the Trump [a]dministration?"
[c] NPR/PBS *NewsHour* poll: "Do you think the FBI (Federal Bureau of Investigation) is just trying to do their job, or [is] biased against the Trump [a]dministration?"

TABLE 5.20. **Partisan views on FBI bias against Trump**

Date of poll	Believe the FBI is biased (%)			
	Democrats	Republicans	Independents	Trump Supporters
Feb. 5–7, 2018[a]	10	49	20	51
Apr. 10–13, 2018[b]	12	56	30	63
July 19–22, 2018[b]	10	55	36	65

[a] Marist College poll: "Do you think the FBI (Federal Bureau of Investigation) is just trying to do their job, or [is] biased against the Trump [a]dministration?" (data represent registered voters).
[b] NPR/PBS *NewsHour* poll: "Do you think the FBI (Federal Bureau of Investigation) is just trying to do their job, or [is] biased against the Trump [a]dministration?" (data represent registered voters).

the concern that Russia meddled in the 2016 US election, are you more likely to believe? US intelligence agencies such as the CIA (Central Intelligence Agency) and the FBI (Federal Bureau of Investigation) who say there was Russian interference, or Russian President (Vladimir) Putin who President Donald Trump says strongly denies his government was involved." Seventy-two percent of the public said they would believe US intelligence agencies such as the CIA and FBI, while only 15 percent said they would believe Putin and, by extension, Trump.[261]

The president was unsparing in his criticism of the Department of Justice, even making public and humiliating criticisms of his attorney general, Jeffrey Sessions. Trump was especially angry with Sessions recusing himself from overseeing the investigation of Russian activity in the 2016 election and not overseeing the Mueller investigation. Nevertheless, when polls asked in August 2018 whether the public took Trump's side or Session's, the

TABLE 5.21. **Opinion about the Department of Justice**

Date of poll	Favorable (%)	Unfavorable (%)	No opinion (%)
Aug. 23–Sept. 2, 2017	56	37	7
Jan. 5–8, 2017	61	30	9
Feb. 7–11, 2018	59	32	10
July 11–15, 2018	58	35	7
Sept. 5–16, 2019	54	41	5
Mar. 24–29, 2020	60	34	6

Note: Respondents were asked, "Is your overall opinion of the Justice Department very favorable, mostly favorable, mostly unfavorable, or very unfavorable?"
Source: Pew Research Center polls.

attorney general won 62 percent to 23 percent. Similarly, 65 percent of the public thought Trump should not fire Sessions. Only 19 percent thought he should.[262]

We have much less information about views of the Department of Justice than we do about other components of the Mueller investigation. We do know that the public maintained its favorable view of the department (table 5.21), although substantial percentages evaluated it unfavorably. Over the January 2017 to July 2018 period, Republicans increased their favorability from 47 to 60 percent while Democrats decreased theirs from 74 to 57 percent. Ironically, after more than a year of the president's critical rhetoric, identifiers with the two parties ended up at the same place. In December 2019, 63 percent of the public had at least some confidence in the department, but 36 percent had very little or not at all.[263] Polarization continued to play a role. In March 2020, 76 percent of Republicans, but only 50 percent of Democrats viewed the department favorably.[264]

The Courts

President Trump yearned for a more supportive judiciary and made it a priority to nominate conservative judges and justices. He was much more concerned with loosening constraints on his actions than with populating the federal bench with dispassionate, highly qualified jurists, occasionally nominating judges that even his own party was loath to support.

Most Americans seemed to agree about the importance of an independent judiciary, however. In February 2017, 97 percent of the public thought a fair judicial system and the rule of law were important to the United States' identity as a nation.[265] In March, only 22 percent thought it would be good for a strong leader to be able to make decisions without

TABLE 5.22. **Support for checks on presidential power**

Date of poll	More effective	Too risky (%)	No opinion (%)
Aug. 9–16, 2016	23	72	5
Feb. 17–12, 2017*	17	77	6
Mar. 7–14, 2018*	21	76	3
July 10–15, 2019*	29	66	5

Note: Respondents were asked the question: "Which comes closer to your view, even if neither is exactly right? "Many of the country's problems could be dealt with more effectively if US presidents didn't have to worry so much about Congress or the Supreme Court. [or] It would be too risky to give US presidents more power to deal directly with many of the country['s] problems."
Source: Pew Research Center polls.
*The wording of the question was changed in these polls from "the Supreme Court" to "the courts."

interference from the legislature or courts.[266] Thus, the public approved of the courts blocking Trump's executive order creating travel bans.[267] In June 2017, only 22 percent favored giving the president more power at the expense of Congress and the courts.[268]

Table 5.22 provides additional insights into the public's views of congressional and judicial checks on presidential power over time and Trump's possible impact on them. Between August 2016 and March 2018, there was little change in the view that it was too risky to reduce the constraints of the other branches on the president. Indeed, there was evidence of the public pushing back against the president. In September 2018, only 37 percent of the public thought "respect the rule of law" applied to Trump.[269] Nevertheless, in July 2019, following the Democratic takeover of the House, there was a 16-percentage-point increase in Republicans agreeing that that presidents could address problems more effectively if they did not have separation of powers constraints. This change pushed the overall agreement to 29 percent.

Not all poll findings were so supportive of the courts, however. In June 2017, only 34 percent of the public felt judges were fair and impartial, while 64 percent said they were more likely to try to shape the law to fit their own ideologies.[270] In January 2018, only 51 percent of the public responded that they had confidence in the courts, with 45 percent replying that they did not. Among registered voters there was little variation among party groups (Republicans had the most confidence), although Trump supporters were slightly less likely to express confidence than were any of the party groups.[271] In March and June 2018, at least 60 percent of the public said they trusted the courts (table 5.23). Nevertheless, 37 percent of the public said they did not. In the June poll, 67 percent of

TABLE 5.23. **Public trust in the courts**

Date of poll	Trust (%)	Do not trust (%)	No opinion (%)
Mar. 22–27, 2017[a]	61	37	2
June 21–25, 2017[b]	60	37	3
Oct. 3–8, 2019[b]	58	39	3

[a] McClatchy poll: "How much do you trust the courts: a great deal, a good amount, not very much, not at all?"
[b] NPR/PBS *NewsHour* poll: "How much do you trust the courts: a great deal, a good amount, not very much, not at all?"

Democrats, 58 percent of Republicans, and 55 percent of Independents trusted the courts. Only 49 percent of Trump supporters did, however.[272]

Donald Trump did not convince most people that the Mueller investigation was a politically motivated witch hunt, that the FBI was biased against him, and that the Department of Justice and the courts were not to be trusted. Yet a substantial percentage of the public did not express positive views about these core institutions in the administration of justice. Republicans were especially critical, and the overlapping set of Trump supporters, even more so. These citizens may have responded as they did even without the vituperative rhetoric of the president, simply adopting views consistent with their political preferences. It is reasonable to conclude, however, that Trump's effort to lead opinion reinforced and probably strengthened these proclivities.

The 2020 Election

Historian Jill Lepore maintained that presidents bear a responsibility to foster faith in democracy. "Far from undermining public confidence in the democracy over which he presides, it is the obligation of every president to cultivate that confidence by guaranteeing voting rights, by condemning foreign interference in American political campaigns, by promoting free, safe and secure elections, and by abiding by their outcome."[273] Apparently, Donald Trump disagreed.

When he appeared to be losing to Hillary Clinton in 2016, he repeatedly suggested that the election was being rigged and would not commit to accepting the results—unless he won. Trailing badly in the polls in 2020, the president refused to commit to accepting the election results[274] and challenged the legitimacy of the election—and the credibility of the entire electoral system. "I have never seen such an effort to sow distrust in our elections," said Michael J. Abramowitz, the president of Freedom House, a nonpartisan organization that promotes democracy around the world. "We are used to seeing this kind of behavior from authoritarians around the globe, but it is particularly disturbing coming from the president of the United States."[275]

By the end of July 2020, Trump had made public comments, posted Twitter messages or reposted others suggesting election fraud ninety-one times during the year.[276] For example, on June 22, 2020, he tweeted, "RIGGED 2020 ELECTION: MILLIONS OF MAIL-IN BALLOTS WILL BE PRINTED BY FOREIGN COUNTRIES, AND OTHERS. IT WILL BE THE SCANDAL OF OUR TIMES!"[277] The next month, on July 21, Trump asserted "Mail-In Voting, unless changed by the courts, will lead to the most CORRUPT ELECTION in our Nation's History! #RIGGEDELECTION."[278] On July 30, he finished the thought by tweeting, "With Universal Mail-In Voting (not Absentee Voting, which is good), 2020 will be the most INACCURATE & FRAUDULENT Election in history. It will be a great embarrassment to the USA. Delay the Election until people can properly, securely and safely vote???"[279]

Undermining the legitimacy of elections—and suggesting postponing them—is tantamount to undermining democracy and was reminiscent of authoritarian countries without the rule of law. The president focused criticism on voting by mail, which he thought would hurt Republican candidates.[280] This, despite the fact that there is no evidence of widespread voter fraud in the United States—including in the five states that were conducting all their voting by mail.

How did the public respond to the president's claims? Again, we find mixed results. On the one hand, Trump failed to convince Americans that they should oppose voting by mail. Instead, the public overwhelmingly favored having that option.[281] However, Trump was successful in persuading nearly one-half of the public that voting by mail posed a major threat of election fraud. Such a view was prevalent among Republicans.[282] A July 2020 poll found that only 28 percent of Joseph Biden's supporters saw mail voting as vulnerable to substantial fraud, whereas 78 percent of Mr. Trump's supporters did.[283] Such beliefs provided the foundation for a challenge to the results in November.

Conclusion

Two days before taking the oath as a new US senator, Mitt Romney published an op-ed in which he argued, "A president should demonstrate the essential qualities of honesty and integrity, and elevate the national discourse with comity and mutual respect. . . . it is in this province where the incumbent's shortfall has been most glaring."[284] The former Republican presidential candidate was correct. Donald Trump's public discourse was characterized by making *ad hominem* attacks aimed at branding and delegitimizing critics and opponents, exaggerating threats or offering inappropriate reassurance, blurring the distinction between fact and fiction, stoking cultural divisions and racial and ethnic tensions, and challenging the rule of law. This rhetoric was both consistent with his pre-presidential expressions and a clear deviation from the norms of the presidency.

Rather than having been an asset for the president, his public discourse diminished his ability to govern. His rhetoric did not aid him in expanding his supportive coalition. Incivility did not prove useful in attracting those not predisposed to support him, and he was not able to brand policies effectively. Nor did he convince most people to distrust his critics, including the media, and he did not persuade them with either his exaggerations or minimizing of threats. His prevaricating did not win him additional adherents. Instead, the public found him untrustworthy and not someone to whom they should defer. His public discourse and his playing to his base brought him low and highly polarized approval ratings. Most Americans considered his rhetoric to be divisive and polarizing.[285] In the end, Trump's rhetoric made it even more difficult to govern effectively.

Equally important, there is reason to conclude that Trump's discourse was deleterious for American democracy. His rhetoric encouraged incivility in public discourse, accelerated the use of disinformation, legitimized the expression of prejudice, increased the salience of cultural divisions and racial and ethnic tensions, and undermined democratic accountability. Although most people rejected both the tone and substance of the president's rhetoric, many Republicans did not. Especially for his copartisans, he distorted the public's knowledge about politics and policy, warped their understanding of policy challenges, and chipped away at respect for the rule of law.

PART 2

The Closer? Leading Congress

CHAPTER SIX

Strategic Position with Congress

I have argued that successful leadership is not the result of a dominant chief executive of political folklore who reshapes the contours of the political landscape, altering his strategic position to pave the way for change. The best evidence is that presidential persuasion is at the margins of congressional decision-making. Even presidents who appeared to dominate Congress were actually facilitators rather than directors of change. They understood their own limitations and quite explicitly took advantage of opportunities in their environments. Working at the margins, they successfully guided legislation through Congress. When these resources diminished, they reverted to the more typical stalemate that usually characterizes presidential-congressional relations.[1]

During the 2016 presidential campaign, Donald Trump promoted himself as an experienced and talented dealmaker who could easily win congressional support for his policies. The implication was that his skill as a negotiator—not his strategic position—was the key to success. Once again, Trump provided an excellent test of my theory of presidential leadership. Is the president's skill the key element in success? Can we separate the unique individual characteristics of the president—his distinctive background, unusual public discourse, intellectual disarray, ignorance of policy, and temperamental unsuitability— from the broader pattern of politics? Can we add value as political scientists to the standard—and often insightful—journalistic critiques of the president? In other words, can we separate the *president* from the *presidency*?

In the chapters that follow, I examine Trump's approach to leading Congress and detail his level of support. First, however, I analyze his strategic position with Congress. This assessment provides the basis for predictions for his success with Congress and offers a core explanation for it. Once we understand his opportunity structure, we can turn to the individual in the White House and ask how well he exploited the opportunities in the context in which he governed.

Making strategic assessments about the president's political environment provides us crucial leverage for evaluating a president's likely success in achieving his legislative goals. In *Predicting the Presidency*, I specified six key questions, the answers to which allow us to ascertain the president's strategic position:[2]

1. Is there a perception in Congress that the president received an electoral mandate on behalf of specific policies?
2. Does the president's party enjoy a majority in a chamber? If so, how large is it?
3. What is the degree of ideological polarization in Congress?
4. How cohesive is the president's party in Congress?
5. Are there cross-pressures among the public in constituencies represented by the opposition party that would counter these members' ideological predispositions to oppose the president?
6. Does the structure of a decision facing Congress favor the president?

Mandate

Mandates can be powerful symbols in American politics. They accord added legitimacy and credibility to the newly elected president's legislative proposals. Concerns for representation and political survival encourage members of Congress to support the president if they feel the people have spoken.[3] Major changes in policy, such as in 1933, 1965, and 1981, rarely occur in the absence of such perceptions. Mandates change the premises of decisions. For example, perceptions of a mandate in 1980 placed a stigma on big government and exalted the unregulated marketplace and large defense budgets, providing Ronald Reagan a favorable strategic position for dealing with Congress.

We saw in chapter 2 that Donald Trump did not receive a mandate to govern. He

- lost the popular vote to Hillary Clinton by nearly three million votes;
- won only 46 percent of the vote;
- was personally unpopular with the bulk of the electorate;
- failed to present many specific policy proposals;
- led a party that lost seats in both houses of Congress.

Thus, the 2016 election results did not signal to most members of Congress that the people wished them to defer to the new president.

Unified Government

Presidents can expect to receive high levels of support from their own party (table 6.1). Thus, the presence or absence of unified government is critical to presidential success in Congress. The president's initiatives are much less likely to pass under divided government,[4] and control of the agenda can facilitate or obstruct their progress in the legislative process.

The House is the chamber where majority control is most important, because the rules allow the majority to control the agenda and many of the alternatives on which members vote. Republicans controlled the House in the 115th Congress. Indeed, they enjoyed the largest majority they had had since 1925. The margin of forty-seven seats was reasonably comfortable but not always large enough to accommodate ideological divisions within the party.

A Republican majority in the Senate meant there would be fewer hearings harassing the administration and, more important, that the president's

TABLE 6.1. **Presidential support in Congress, by party**

		Support (%)*			
		House		Senate	
President	Party	Own party	Opposition party	Own party	Opposition party
Eisenhower	R	63	42	69	36
Kennedy	D	73	26	65	33
Johnson	D	71	27	56	44
Nixon/Ford	R	64	39	63	33
Carter	D	63	31	63	37
Reagan	R	70	29	74	31
G. H. W. Bush	R	73	27	75	29
Clinton	D	75	24	83	22
G. W. Bush	R	83	19	86	18
Obama	D	86	13	92	22
Trump**	R	92	9	95	13

*On roll-call votes on which the winning side was supported by fewer than 80 percent of those voting.
**2017–2019.

proposals would arrive on the floor. However, the Republican majority of only 52 to 48—and then 51 to 49 after Democrat Doug Jones won the special election to fill the seat vacated by Jeff Sessions in Alabama—was not large enough to overcome the persistent threat of filibusters and forced the Republicans to rely on the reconciliation process for major legislation such as health care and tax reform. Their leaders had few votes to spare in securing a majority.

As Congress polarized along party lines, members instituted more centralized, leadership-driven legislative procedures that we might expect would facilitate partisan lawmaking.[5] We might also anticipate that majority parties in Congress should have greater capacity to legislate a partisan program. However, James Curry and Frances Lee show that this is not the typical pattern. Majority parties have not gotten better at enacting their legislative programs, and there are only modest differences between the success of unified and divided governments. Most of the time, congressional majorities achieved none of what they wanted to achieve, and it is unusual for them to achieve most of what they set out to accomplish.[6]

Polarization

Because the president cannot depend on a compatible party majority to pass his policies, he typically requires support from the opposition party. Thus, an important aspect of the president's opportunity structure is the ideological division of members of Congress. The degree of polarization will affect the potential for the president to reach across the aisle and obtain support from the opposition party.

This support is typically essential for the passage of legislation. Most legislation that passes, including landmark legislation, does so with a majority of the minority party in support, even under unified government. "Even those majority parties who possess the unusual advantage of unified party control do not pass much landmark legislation on partisan lines."[7] They rarely enact priority agenda items over the opposition of a majority of the minority.

Those most likely to respond to the president are moderates, near the middle of the ideological spectrum. Yet there are relatively few moderates in Congress. Persons with such views are less likely to run for Congress than those at the extremes. The benefits of legislative service are too low for them to do so, as they have become more at odds with the rest of their party delegation. Thus, it is increasingly difficult for moderates to achieve their policy goals and advance within the party or chamber, and they have fewer like-minded colleagues to work and interact with in office.[8]

The ideological distance between the parties in the House reached record highs during the Obama administration, and the 2016 election did nothing to mitigate the ideological differences between the congressional parties.[9] As figures 6.1 and 6.2 show, there was no ideological overlap at all

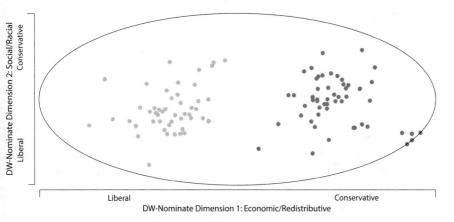

FIGURE 6.1 Senators' ideology in the 115th Congress (2017–2019). Light gray, Democrats; dark gray, Republicans.

Source: voteview.com/congress/senate.

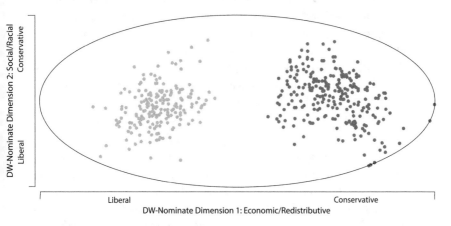

FIGURE 6.2 House members' ideology in the 115th Congress (2017–2019). Light gray, Democrats; dark gray, Republicans.

Source: voteview.com/congress/house.

between the parties in the 115th Congress (2017–2018). Moreover, the distances between the centers of each party were large, especially in the House. Trump inherited the most polarized Congress of any Republican president governing under unified control. Indeed, the differences between the two parties in both the House and Senate were the greatest ever recorded.[10]

The House Republican caucus in 116th Congress was more conservative than in the 115th. Although retiring Republicans were typical of their party colleagues, twenty-three of the thirty Republican incumbents who lost their reelection bids in 2018 were more moderate than the median Republican in the chamber.[11] In the spring of 2018, twenty-three House Republicans signed on to a discharge petition to force an immigration vote. Five of them retired and another nine were defeated in the midterm elections.

The picture of the 2019 Democratic caucus was more complicated, as it gained dozens of new members. On the one hand, some of the new representatives were outspoken representatives of the left wing of the party. By contrast, many moderates won the seats lost by the Republicans. This diversity led to discord on some divisive issues. A bill to expand federal background checks for gun purchases created conflict within the caucus when twenty-six moderate Democrats joined Republicans in amending the legislation, adding a provision requiring that Immigration and Customs Enforcement (ICE) be notified if an illegal immigrant sought to purchase a gun.[12] Similarly, in June 2019, the Trump administration asked Congress for extra funding to round up, house, and process the hundreds of thousands of migrants who had arrived at the border. Liberal Democrats in the House balked at the request, fearing it would only enable the president's harsh immigration tactics and insisted on adding restrictions and standards for the care of immigrants, especially children. However, because the bill also proposed a cut in funding for ICE, centrist Democrats refused to go along and Speaker Nancy Pelosi had to agree to pass the Senate bill that did not contain the House's restrictions.[13]

The president may find negotiating with the opposition party in Congress easier if that party's supporters in the public favor compromise. In effect, party identifiers might cut their representatives some slack in working with the president. In the abstract, people favor compromise among political leaders.[14] However, when in March 2017 the Gallup Poll asked whether Democratic leaders in Congress should compromise with the Trump administration, the responses were telling. Predictably, Republicans, by a wide margin, thought that congressional Democrats should compromise. Democrats, however, had a different view. Fifty-seven percent said it was more important for their leaders to stick to their beliefs rather than compromise, while only 15 percent favored compromise.[15] In January 2018, 63 percent of Democrats and Democratic leaners said Democratic congressional leaders should stand up to Trump on important issues, even if that meant getting less done in Washington.[16] By January 2019, that number had increased to 70 percent.[17]

These findings are consistent with experimental work that finds that partisanship trumps preferences for bipartisan legislating.[18] Indeed, the Pew Research Center found that most Republicans and Democrats in the public want compromise on their terms. Majorities of Democrats (62 percent) and Republicans (58 percent) said their party should get more of what it wants on the key issues facing the nation.[19] In November 2018, 80 percent of Democrats and Democratic leaners thought Trump should cooperate with Democratic leaders in Congress over the following two years, but only 46 percent thought Democratic congressional leaders should cooperate with Trump. Unsurprisingly, Republicans had a different view. Eight-seven percent of them thought Democratic leaders should cooperate with the president.[20]

Moreover, Trump was such a polarizing figure that he seemed to have discouraged the acceptance of compromise even further. The percentage of Democrats and Democratic leaners who answered that they liked elected officials who made compromises with people with whom they disagreed declined from 69 percent in 2017 to 46 percent in 2018. Republicans and Republican leaners, who were not enthusiastic about compromise in 2017 (46 percent said they liked officials who did it), stayed about the same (44 percent) in 2018.[21]

Given the broad influences of ideology and constituency, it is not surprising that presidential leadership itself demarcates and deepens cleavages in Congress. As Frances Lee has shown, the differences between the parties and the cohesion within them on floor votes are typically greater when the president takes a stand on issues. When the president adopts a position, members of his party have a stake in his success, while opposition party members have a stake in the president losing. Moreover, both parties take cues from the president that help define their policy views, especially when the lines of party cleavage are not clearly at stake or already well established.[22]

Because of the high level of partisan polarization in the 115th and 116th Congresses and the loathing of Democrats for Donald Trump, there was little reason to expect much bipartisan cooperation. Additionally, any Democrat who wanted to run for president in 2020 recognized that

collaborating with Trump would likely be a liability in the primaries—
and a large number of Democratic senators were interested in running.

With little hope of bipartisan support, Republicans thus chose to rely
heavily on procedures that bypassed the Democrats. The Republican
leadership wrote the health care bills away from the glare of committee
hearings and criticism. They also chose to use the filibuster-proof budget
reconciliation process that ostensibly eliminated the need to court Democratic votes—and also decreased the chances of receiving them. (Ironically,
these tactics only served to highlight internal Republican Party disagreements over health care policy.[23]) Trump made no effort to court Democrats.
He had no face-to-face meetings with Senate Minority Leader Charles
Schumer or House Democratic Leader Nancy Pelosi between late January
and the beginning of September 2017.

Partisan and ideological polarization did not mean that Democrats had
no interest in working with Trump. In the first days of his presidency,
even as anti-Trump activists demanded total resistance, liberal Democrats
were willing to cut a deal on an infrastructure plan. "If they had been
willing to do a real infrastructure package, then I would have been willing
to participate," commented Democratic Senator Brian Schatz.[24] As one
reporter put it:

> Rather than taking advantage of his honeymoon phase to pick an issue on
> which Democrats from conservative states might be amenable—fixing the na-
> tion's crumbling infrastructure, cutting taxes or stiffening immigration laws—
> Trump raced toward the most partisan corner of the room, pushing to repeal
> the health care law with no input from Democrats, in a manner that has proved
> deeply unpopular.[25]

It is not surprising that Democrats honored the demand of Schumer that
they stick together in their refusal to help the president until repeal of the
Affordable Care Act was taken off the table.

It is also the case that infrastructure was a relatively low priority for
congressional Republicans. They wanted to repeal Obamacare, both because they opposed the policy and because reducing health care expen-
ditures would ease the path for high-priority tax cuts. Moreover, many
Republicans were not eager to spend large amounts of money on public
works, especially when they were trying to reduce revenues. Trump himself had unequivocally promised to deal with health care immediately after
taking office.

The polarization of party elites has been asymmetrical, with most of it the result of the rightward movement of the Republicans.[26] According to Mann and Ornstein, the Republicans have become ideologically extreme; scornful of compromise; contemptuous of facts, evidence, and science; and dismissive of the legitimacy of the opposition; and are at war with government.[27] Democrats are interested in governing, but many Republicans are not. In 2013 when House Republican Majority Leader Eric Cantor proposed a plan to address the problem of those Americans with preexisting health conditions who either have lost their insurance or cannot obtain it, his colleagues rebuffed him. Instead of dealing with the problem, they chose to vote to repeal the Affordable Care Act for the thirty-seventh time. The next year, Cantor lost a primary to retain the Republican nomination in his district. Such an environment makes it difficult to craft legislation that will receive bipartisan support.

Republican Cohesion

Unified government is no guarantee of success if the governing party is fractured. Thus, we need to ask if Trump's party cohort was likely to agree with the his initiatives. In other words, how cohesive was the president's party in Congress?

Fostering Cohesion

There was likely to be agreement among fellow partisans on the broad orientation to government and public policy. Most congressional Republicans shared the president's views on health care, taxes, and regulation, issues that had been at the core of the party's stances for years. Moreover, shared electoral goals and emotional commitments should have facilitated agreement on both policy ends and the means to achieve them.

SUPPORT IN THE MASS PARTY. A key resource for President Trump in fostering party unity was his strong support among Republicans in the public. In 2016, he won in 218 of the 241 Republican districts, in most by comfortable margins.[28] Conservative Republicans, those most likely to vote in primaries, reliably accorded the president about a 90 percent approval rating.[29] The NBC News/*Wall Street Journal* poll asked Republicans (including leaners) "Do you consider yourself to be more of a supporter of

Donald Trump or more of a supporter of the Republican Party?" twelve times from September 2017 through December 2018. An average of 56 percent replied that they considered themselves more a supporter of Trump than of the Republican Party. In another poll, thirty-nine percent of Republicans in the public said that congressional Republicans had an obligation to support Trump's policies, even if they disagreed with him.[30]

In February 2017, 52 percent of Republicans and Republican leaners told pollsters that if there were a disagreement on an issue, they would be more likely to trust Donald Trump; 34 percent said they would be more likely to trust Republican leaders in Congress.[31] The public was even more supportive in July of that year, when 67 percent of those who voted for Trump said they would back him over their congressional representative, and just 7 percent indicated they would side with the lawmaker from their district.[32] The figure increased to 71 percent in August.[33] That same month, 53 percent of Republicans in districts with Republican representatives said their members had not been supportive enough of Trump.[34]

In October 2017, 60 percent of Republicans and Republican leaners said it was bad for the party when Republican members of Congress openly criticized President Trump when they disagreed with him. A 55 percent majority also agreed that it was a good thing for the party that some Republicans critical of Trump were not running for reelection. Voters who supported Trump in the 2016 election were even more unified, with 65 percent saying it was a bad thing for the party for Republicans to take on Trump, and an equal number saying it was good for the GOP to have Trump critics retiring.[35] Moreover, 63 percent of Republicans reported that they had more confidence in Trump dealing with the major issues facing the country, compared with 29 percent who had more confidence in Congress.[36] The following May, 64 percent of Republicans still had more confidence in Trump, compared with 26 percent with more confidence in Congress.[37]

Senate Majority Leader Mitch McConnell's approval rating nosedived after the president criticized him.[38] Similarly, Republican senator Bob Corker's poll numbers plunged amidst his feuding with Trump. Senators Ted Cruz of Texas and John McCain and Jeff Flake of Arizona also "saw their numbers decline—often precipitously"—among Republican voters after they ran afoul of Trump. Flake announced his retirement when it was clear he could not win the Republican primary to run again for his own job.[39]

After Trump made a deal on the debt ceiling with the Democrats in September 2017, 61 percent of Republicans approved of the deal. Only

28 percent disapproved, despite being told that Republican leaders opposed the deal. Forty-five percent of Republicans said they agreed more with Trump; 17 percent said they agreed with McConnell and Ryan. Fifty-two percent saw the deal as an effective act of bipartisanship; only 8 percent felt it was a betrayal of Republican Party. In general, if Trump and congressional Republicans disagreed, 60 percent of Republicans in the public were more likely to support Trump, while only 14 percent chose to side with Republicans in Congress.[40]

Given his popularity with his fellow partisans, the fear congressional Republicans had of losing in a primary if they opposed the White House's wishes was a source of strength for the president. Most Republicans chose not to take sides when McCain, Corker, and Flake criticized the president—even though they may have agreed with their colleagues. They wanted to avoid alienating Trump's base ahead of the 2018 midterm elections.[41] When Republican candidates for Congress criticized the president, they promptly suffered a substantial decline in fundraising.[42]

Even Lindsey Graham, who was once the object of Trump's scorn and who continued to have "concerns about what the president says and how he behaves," found it useful to get close to the president. "He's very popular in my state," Graham said. "When I help him, it helps me back home."[43] Graham was correct. After his strident defense of Supreme Court nominee Brett M. Kavanaugh and reliably siding with Trump, his approval rating among South Carolina Republicans rose from 51 percent in April 2018 to 74 percent less than a year later.[44]

The president's popularity with his base was reflected in the desire of Republicans, even those who once shunned him, to win his endorsement. Because the president governed more like a conventional Republican than the populist he campaigned as in 2016, there was little appetite among conservatives for electing Trump skeptics—even among those offended by the president's coarse behavior. Mitt Romney, who in 2016 excoriated Trump as an amoral con man, graciously accepted the president's endorsement. Bob Corker, who once suggested that the president required day care and that he might blunder the country into World War III, mounted a charm offensive to win the president's support—a prerequisite if the senator was to delay his retirement plans and capture a Republican nomination in Tennessee (he ultimately did not receive the endorsement and did not enter the race).

Dean Heller needed Trump's help in his primary battle in Nevada against conservative businessman Danny Tarkanian. Trump persuaded

Tarkanian to withdraw from the race, increasing the senator's chances of winning the general election. The president also convinced Mississippi state senator Chris McDaniel to drop his challenge to Senator Roger Wicker. By making clear he would support Heller and Wicker in their primaries, Trump effectively starved their challengers of the political oxygen they needed to win over conservative activists.[45] Similarly, Martha McSally could not afford to alienate the president's supporters as she sought the nomination to replace Jeff Flake in Arizona, where she faced Joe Arpaio, whom Trump pardoned, and Kelli Ward, a vigorous Trump supporter.

Candidates in Republican primaries in 2018 focused on demonstrating their loyalty to the president[46]—and for good reason. Representative Mark Sanford criticized the White House: "It's a cult of personality," he declared. "He's [Trump] fundamentally, at the core, about Donald Trump. He's not about ideas. And ideas are what parties are supposedly based on."[47] Sanford faced a 2018 primary challenge from a state legislator who charged that the congressman had been insufficiently loyal to the president. After Trump tweeted his lack of support for Sanford and his backing of the congressman's opponent a few hours before the polls closed, [48] Sanford lost. No one missed the message: it was not wise for Republicans to cross the president. Similarly, Alabama Representative Martha Roby withdrew her support of Trump's candidacy after the *Access Hollywood* tapes were released in October 2016. She was forced into a runoff after receiving only 39 percent of the primary vote in June 2018.

Trump's support among Republicans in the public made life difficult for congressional Republicans in other ways. Many of them opposed his policy of separating children from their parents at the Mexican border, and they feared an electoral backlash from the border crisis captured in images of children in metal cages. However, they did not want to draw the wrath of Trump's loyal base, who were clamoring for a crackdown on illegal immigration. Many resolved the dilemma by criticizing the policy but not the policymaker. When the president made racist comments, including telling four Democratic congresswomen of color to "go back" where they came from, criticism from congressional Republicans was directly related to Trump's victory margin in their districts.[49] The USMCA (discussed in chapter 8) disappointed many Republicans, who complained that the White House negotiated only with Democrats. Yet the president could ignore them. "The same Republicans who are complaining they are not included are also too scared to vote against [Trump]. So why would he bother negotiating with them?" explained an aide to a Republican senator.[50]

The tide seemed to ebb in June 2020 as Trump suffered from poor ratings of his handling of the coronavirus pandemic and the issue raised by police violence and the resulting protests. Republicans rejected the president's recommendations in primaries in North Carolina, Kentucky, Colorado, and Virginia. In the first case, the president endorsed Lynd Bennet for the seat vacated by Mark Meadows, who resigned to become Trump's chief of staff. She lost to a twenty-four-year old political neophyte. In Kentucky, the president called for the sitting representative, Thomas Massie, to be thrown out of the Republican party when he attempted to hold up a giant coronavirus relief package. Massie won renomination overwhelmingly. In Colorado, Lauren Boebert, a gun-rights activist who refused to close her restaurant to dine-in patrons during the coronavirus pandemic, defeated five-term representative Scott Tipton, whom Trump endorsed. Another of the president's endorsees, Representative Denver Riggleman of Virginia, lost his seat after officiating at a same-sex wedding.

GENERAL ELECTION INCENTIVES.   In late 2018, the incentives to make the president look good by providing him victories were stronger than ever. The high correlation between presidential and congressional voting and the decline in split-ticket voting, which I discuss below, tethered Republicans to Trump. It is increasingly the case that "all politics is national."[51] Vote choices in midterm elections have increasingly become referenda on the president.[52]

Although Trump was not on the ballot in 2018, evaluations of him were at the core of the midterm elections and uppermost in voters' minds. Indeed, Trump urged supporters to view the election as a referendum on him, entreating them to "pretend I'm on the ballot." In West Virginia, where he was promoting Senate candidate Patrick Morrisey, he declared that "a vote for Morrisey is a vote for me."[53]

The president succeeded in tying votes for congressional candidates to evaluations of himself—although this was of little strategic value to winning the House and little help in holding the Senate.[54] Sixty-four percent of the public reported that Trump was a consideration in their votes, with 39 percent saying their ballot was a vote against Trump and 25 percent saying it was a vote for him.[55] As Gary Jacobson shows, reactions to Trump played a greater role in congressional voting that for any previous president. Thus, the 2018 midterm elections were the "most partisan, nationalized, and president-centered midterm elections yet observed."[56]

Thus, it was much better for Republicans if Trump was high in the polls, and giving him successes had the potential to boost his approval ratings. According to Raúl Labrador, a cofounder of the House Freedom Caucus, "We want to make sure that we help the country see that we're getting things done."[57] Thus, Republicans enacted a major tax bill in late 2017 despite voter opposition, resistance from organized interests, and considerable uncertainty about its policy consequences because of concern with their party's reputation for productivity.[58] Moreover, congressional Republicans were reluctant to discuss the president's personal conduct or management of the White House and routinely defended him against charges of collusion with Russia during the 2016 campaign. They were also steadfast in opposing his impeachment in the House and conviction in the Senate.

This loyalty continued in the 2020 election. Despite the president's low approval ratings, most vulnerable Republican senators stuck with Trump. They felt they could not afford to anger voters in their party's base, who retained their enthusiasm for the president. An exception was Senator Susan Collins, who declined to support Trump for reelection. Similarly, Senator Lisa Murkowski praised former defense secretary Jim Mattis's criticisms of the president, saying they were "honest and necessary and overdue," and added that she was "struggling" with supporting Trump for reelection.[59]

COATTAILS.   Not all potential sources of party cohesion worked for Trump, however. The president hoped that loyalty to him as party leader would be a useful adhesive for congressional Republicans, but he was disappointed. He lamented in a tweet on July 23, 2017: "It's very sad that Republicans, even some that were carried over the line on my back, do very little to protect their President."[60] He felt he had coattails and that Republicans owed him loyalty as a result.

However, about 90 percent of Republican members of the House ran ahead of Trump in their districts; they did not win on his coattails. He ran ahead of only five of the twenty-two winning Republican senators—Roy Blunt (MO), Lisa Murkowski (AK), Rand Paul (KY), Todd Young (IN), and John Boozman (AR). Only one of the five, Blunt, had a close race and may have owed his election to Trump. The lack of competition in nearly all House seats and most Senate seats (see below) provides little potential for coattails to determine the winner.[61]

Running behind does not in itself prove Trump had weak coattails, but it hardly provides the basis for inferring them. One study found that those Republicans who endorsed Trump's nomination did about 1.7 percentage points worse than those who did not endorse him, while Trump did 1.4 percentage points better in districts where the incumbent Republican endorsed him. In other words, there is evidence of negative and reverse coattails.[62] It is not surprising, then, that scholars have found little relationship between Republican legislators' relative electoral performances and their legislative support for the president.[63]

Splintering the Party

Despite the forces pushing toward party cohesion, there was substantial ideological dispersion among Republicans, as figures 6.1 and 6.2 show. Indeed, under Trump, Republicans were more ideologically fractured than were Democrats. Ideological conflict within the Republican Conference caused Speaker John Boehner to resign in 2015 and bedeviled the leadership efforts of his successor, Paul Ryan, who chose to leave Congress after 2018. Since Republicans took control of the House in 1994, they have elected five speakers, with an average tenure of just five years. Republicans on the ends of the Republican ideological spectrum were less supportive of the president than those in the middle of the scale.[64]

HEALTH CARE. Health care is a prime example of the difficulty Republicans had in reaching consensus on policy. With Barack Obama in the White House, congressional Republicans could please conservative activists with votes to demonstrate their opposition to the Affordable Care Act without worrying about the policy consequences of their actions. As long as repealing Obamacare was merely a slogan used to rally disaffected voters, it was easy to ignore this tension. Once congressional leaders had to take responsibility for policy, however, legislating became more difficult. "In the 25 years that I served in the United States Congress, Republicans never, ever, one time agreed on what a health care proposal should look like," former Speaker of the House John Boehner recalled. "Not once."[65]

In March 2017, House Republicans were poised to make the first move toward fulfilling the president's promise to repeal and replace the Affordable Care Act. However, Speaker Paul Ryan ran into opposition from the Freedom Caucus and some moderates. When it became clear that the Freedom Caucus was not going to support Ryan's bill, Ryan and Trump tried to appeal to the group by removing requirements that insurers cover mental health and maternity care. Tuesday Group members balked, however, and Ryan pulled the bill. The second version, the one that ultimately passed the House, made many concessions to Freedom Caucus Republicans at the expense of moderate Republicans' concerns.

It is not surprising, then, that no health care proposal could win Senate approval, especially when the Republicans' margins were small. The most conservative members argued that their leaders' plans left too much of Obamacare in place, while the more moderate senators and representatives worried that the plans would deny health care to too many of their constituents. Senator Lisa Murkowski reportedly told Trump at a White House lunch, "With all due respect, Mr. President, I didn't come here to represent the Republican Party. I am representing my constituents and the state of Alaska."[66] When asked why he had failed to achieve as much as he wished, Trump assigned some of the blame to congressional Republicans. "You have certain factions," he said. "You have the conservative Republicans. You have the moderate Republicans. So you have to get them together, and we need close to a hundred percent. That's a pretty hard thing to get."[67]

DEBT CEILING. The president also faced a fractured party in September 2017 when he was forced to accept the Democrats' deal to accept a short-term waiver of the debt ceiling. When it came time to vote on the bill, only 60 percent of Republicans in the House and two-thirds in the Senate voted to suspend the debt limit. Democrats, however, unanimously supported it. As Frances Lee points out, "That's precisely the opposite of what we see historically." The president's party typically supports raising the debt ceiling and the opposition party makes points criticizing his stewardship. But many Republicans, especially those elected after 2010 who had never served under a Republican president and thus never had responsibility for governing, insisted on spending cuts in exchange for supporting debt-limit increases.[68] Lacking the votes from his own party, Trump had no choice but to turn to the Democrats.

TAX CUTS. The most important legislative victory for Republicans was tax cuts, probably the area of policy on which they had the most agreement. Thus, cutting taxes was easier than virtually any other legislative task for Republicans. Moreover, conservative groups went all out in support of tax cuts,[69] and Republicans felt impelled to act. Having failed to repeal the Affordable Care Act, Republicans felt intense pressure to pass a tax measure, lest they go home to their constituents—and especially their donors[70]—empty handed. "If we fail on taxes, we're toast," declared Lindsey Graham. "Cutting taxes is in the Republican DNA."[71]

The Republican default position of cutting taxes greased the legislative path. As Mitch McConnell reflected, "All of my members, from Collins to Cruz, were just more comfortable with this issue," referring to the centrist Susan Collins of Maine and the conservative Ted Cruz of Texas. "Everybody really wanted to get to yes. There was a widespread belief that this was just a good thing to do for the country and for us politically." This basic agreement facilitated discussion and compromise within the Republican caucus. "We had endless meetings getting everybody comfortable with the substance," McConnell said. "That was a stark contrast with a lot of the meetings we had on health care."[72]

Nevertheless, Republicans found it difficult to agree about which existing tax breaks they should eliminate to pay for the new tax cuts and how important shrinking the deficit was.[73] As a result, negotiators had to scale back their plan. As commentator Ryan Lizza put it, "Tax reform is hard; tax cuts are easy."[74]

TRADE POLICY. It was even more difficult for Republicans to reach consensus on trade policy, another Trump marquee issue. The president withdrew from the Trans-Pacific Partnership during his first week in office after calling the trade deal a "disaster" and a "rape of our country" during his presidential campaign. In February 2018, twenty-five Republican senators, including Senate Majority Whip John Cornyn, sent President Trump a letter asking him to "reengage with the Trans-Pacific Partnership."[75] This request was another attempt by Republican lawmakers to move Trump to a softer stance on trade.

The senators had their work cut out for them. The same day they sent the letter, commerce secretary Wilbur Ross released a report recommending that the president heavily restrict steel and aluminum imports by applying a large tariff or quota to them.[76] When the White House announced the possibility of such tariffs, 107 House Republicans sent the president a letter expressing concern about broad tariffs and calling for him to focus any action on unfair trading partners, especially China.[77] A number of prominent Republicans, including Senate Finance Committee chair Orrin Hatch and House Speaker Paul Ryan, opposed the president's efforts to raise tariffs. Republicans feared that a trade war could offset whatever economic benefit midterm voters saw from their tax bill. Although some congressional Republicans did end up supporting the president's aggressive trade practices,[78] many defended their constituents' and contributors' interests by speaking out to confront the Trump administration's protectionism.[79]

In June 2018, eight Republicans signed on to legislation authored by Bob Corker, the chair of the Senate Foreign Relations Committee, which would give Congress authority to approve presidential tariffs.[80] Trump personally asked Corker to back off, but the senator refused. However, Senate leaders, who were extremely cautious about confronting the president so directly, blocked the amendment from coming to a vote. Corker called his party's deference to Trump "cultish."[81] In response to the leadership's obstruction, Republican Jeff Flake informed the chair of the Senate Judiciary Committee that he would oppose any Trump circuit court nominee, all but guaranteeing the death of a nomination, until the Senate voted on Corker's amendment.[82]

At the same time, conservative groups funded by the Koch brothers announced they would begin a multimillion-dollar advertising campaign to promote free trade, including calling on Trump to scrap tariffs that he had threatened as well as those already in place.[83]

Republican leaders displayed little appetite for sweeping legislation. Instead, they seemed content to advance more targeted measures. After a call with Chinese president Xi Jinping, President Trump tweeted on May 13, 2018, that in order to save Chinese jobs, he wanted to ease penalties baring Chinese telecom giant ZTE from buying American products for seven years. ZTE had violated US sanctions on Iran and North Korea and had illegally copied US technology. Trump's decision was met with vociferous objections from members of Congress, who accused the president of putting national security at risk. A bipartisan group of senators, led by Republican Marco Rubio, introduced an amendment to reinstate sanctions against ZTE. On June 7, 2018, he tweeted, "I assure you with 100% confidence that #ZTE is a much greater national security threat than steel from Argentina or Europe."[84] On June 18, the Senate voted 85–10 to reinstate tough penalties on ZTE and prohibit the federal government from purchasing or leasing equipment from ZTE or another Chinese company, Huawei, that they believed to have been a national security threat, or from subsidizing the companies in any way.

IMMIGRATION. Republicans were also divided on immigration. Business-friendly Republicans tended to favor comprehensive reform, arguing for the economic benefits of allowing the entry of needed workers.

Social conservatives tended to oppose any proposals that they deemed "amnesty"—forgiving individuals who were in the United States without papers and providing them a way to remain. These clashing views explain why Republican leaders resisted pressure to consider immigration bills on the House floor since their party took control of the House in the 2010 elections. In 2013, several prominent Republican senators worked on a bipartisan immigration bill but could garner only eleven Republican votes on the Senate floor, and it never came to the House floor. When the Senate voted on several options for immigration reform in February 2018, the White House's proposal received the fewest votes. (I detail the negotiations over immigration reform in chapter 8.)

Paul Ryan suffered a humiliating defeat in May 2018 when the twice-a-decade farm bill failed on a 213–198 vote. Thirty Republicans voted to protest his refusal to schedule an immediate vote on a restrictive immigration bill sponsored by the chair of the House Judiciary Committee. Republican moderates, for their part, were moving in the opposite direction, shrugging off the pleas of their leaders as they worked toward forcing votes on legislation to protect from deportation young immigrants brought to the country illegally as children.[85]

In June 2018, moderate House Republicans filed a discharge petition to force a vote on a series of immigration proposals. The petition was just two votes short of success when Republican leaders, who feared a conservative political backlash if a Republican House advanced such legislation, undertook a furious push to stymie the moderates. It partially succeeded: the moderates only secured the promise of a vote on a moderate piece of legislation alongside a more conservative bill.

Conservatives opposed the more moderate measure—which failed—concluding that it amounted to "amnesty" for those brought to the United States illegally when they were children without doing enough to seal the southwestern border and otherwise deter future illegal immigration. Several hard-liners declared there was nothing leaders could do to convince them to vote for the compromise bill. "I'm a big fat 'no,' capital letters," said Representative Lou Barletta. "It's amnesty, chain migration, and there's no guarantee that the wall will be built." Meanwhile, Texas congressman Will Hurd, a key moderate voice on immigration, announced that he would oppose the legislation, in part because of the inclusion of funding for Trump's proposed border wall, which Hurd called "an expensive and ineffective 4th-century border security tool that takes private property away from hundreds of Texans."[86]

DIVERSITY AMONG REPUBLICANS IN THE PUBLIC. The diversity of ideologies among congressional Republicans reflected a diversity of views
among their fellow partisans in the public. The Pew Research Center
created a political typology of the public, dividing Republicans into four
groups (table 6.2). In 2017, it found that a group it termed "core conservatives" represented 31 percent of all Republicans and Republican-leaning
Independents and 43 percent of politically engaged Republicans. A large
majority of them supported US involvement in the global economy and
were not anti-immigrant. Another group, the "new era enterprisers," was
almost as large (although less politically active). Members of this group
were even more strongly supportive of immigrants and globalization than
were core conservatives. "Market skeptic conservatives" were spilt on the
two issues, and only the "country first conservatives," the smallest of the
four groups, were critical of immigration and globalization. There were
also notable splits on the cost of environmental protection laws and on
homosexuality.

TABLE 6.2. **Opinion among Republicans on issues, 2017**

Republicans (%)	Core conservatives	Country first conservatives	Market skeptic conservatives	New era enterprisers
Public	13	6	12	11
Registered voters	15	7	12	11
Politically engaged	20	6	10	9
Issue	Agree (%)			
Approve of Donald Trump	93	84	66	63
US involvement in the global economy is good for creating new markets and growth	68	39	50	76
Immigrants are a burden US by taking jobs housing	43	76	55	23
Stricter environmental laws cost jobs and hurt the economy	92	70	39	34
Homosexuality should be discouraged by society	37	70	31	28

Source: Pew Research Center polls, June 8–18, 2017, and June 27–July 9, 2017.

Resistance to Compromise

A number of factors discouraged Republicans from compromising and thus fashioning viable legislation that both the president and the Congress could support. One was a lack of experience. For example, in the 115th Congress, only fifty-one House Republicans had served under a Republican president and passed major policy reforms. They had little experience in devising complex legislation and building majority coalitions.

Equally important constraints on compromise, however, were ideological and constituency pressures not to do so, as we saw earlier in this chapter. It is difficult to legislate when relatively few members of your own party have the inclination to focus on policy details, embrace compromise, and accept the inherent trade-offs that come with change.

IDEOLOGICAL RIGIDITY. The Republican contingent in the House was further to the right in 2017–2018 than at any point in history.[87] With more than 150 members in 2017, the Republican Study Committee (RSC) was the largest caucus in Congress. Its philosophy of governance would vex any leader: members considered themselves conservatives first and Republicans second. They did not come to Washington to play for the Republican team; they came to fight for conservative principles. (Their website declared, "We believe that more government is the problem, not the solution, for the toughest issues facing our nation."[88]) If fighting for their ideological principles meant voting against party interests—and a Republican president—so be it. For core RSC believers, ideological purity trumped legislative accomplishment.[89] Nevertheless, the RSC maintained a relatively low profile in the Trump era, reflecting the size and diversity of its membership and a focus on circulating legislative bulletins and policy memos on Capitol Hill.

More conservative, more combative, and more cohesive was the House Freedom Caucus, formed as a splinter group to the RSC in 2015. It had thirty-one members in mid-2017 (after two members from Texas resigned). Holding views that were the antithesis of Donald Trump's emphasis on legislative victories rather than ideological principles, Freedom Caucus members were rigidly ideological and agreed to vote as a bloc if they had 80 percent of the group in agreement. They were likely to prove an obstacle to legislative success and were an early object of the president's wrath.[90]

On the issue of immigration, the conservatives did not hesitate to threaten Paul Ryan. Representative Mark Meadows, the chair of the Freedom

Caucus who was instrumental in the ouster of Speaker John Boehner, suggested that a misstep could cost Ryan his job. "I can say that it is a defining moment for this speaker," Meadows proclaimed. "If he gets it wrong, it will have consequences for him." According to Representative Charlie Dent, "It's hard for anyone to be a strong speaker in the traditional sense around here because the speaker is only as strong as his conference allows him to be." "And because on many issues the speaker cannot get 218 Republican votes, that weakens his position."[91]

It was especially challenging to build a winning coalition with those affiliated with the Tea Party. These members tended to view politics as a struggle for survival rather than a negotiation among opposing views.[92] Representatives and senators associated with the Tea Party did not necessarily consider their primary function to be making government work, contrary to long-held views of many Americans.

To further muddy the Republican mix, there were more than seventy members of the House (and a few senators) in the Republican Main Street Partnership.[93] Their mission was to serve as "the governing wing of the Republican Party," and they emphasized pragmatic government and offered institutional support to centrist members. These members included the approximately fifty members of the House Tuesday Group, which was founded to counterbalance the conservative trend in the Republican Conference. Centrist members were less vocal and less cohesive than the Freedom Caucus and thus were less problematic for the party leadership.[94]

ACTIVIST OPPOSITION. Equally important as a curb on compromise was the fact that when elected officials interacted with the more politically engaged voters within their reelection constituencies—the voters who were the most attentive to what they were doing, the most likely to influence their friends and neighbors, the most likely to donate money to their campaigns, and the most likely to vote in primary elections—the divide between their supporters and their opponents was even greater than it was among rank-and-file voters. Active supporters of Republican elected officials and those who voted in the party's primaries were generally very conservative[95]—a majority of Republican voters in the Obama years wanted their party's leaders to move further to the right[96]—and they were the least likely of all ideological groups to favor compromise.[97]

In both parties, donors are more ideologically extreme than other partisans, including primary voters.[98] In September 2017, Senator Cory

Gardner, who was in charge of the Republican's midterm reelection effort, warned his colleagues that campaign fundraising was drying up because of widespread disappointment among donors over the inability of the Republican Senate to repeal the Affordable Care Act or do much of anything else. Senator Charles Grassley told reporters that he could count ten reasons the new health proposal should not reach the floor but that Republicans needed to press ahead regardless in order to fulfill their long-standing promise to repeal and replace the Affordable Care Act. "Republicans campaigned on this so often that we have a responsibility to carry out what you said in the campaign. That's pretty much as much of a reason as the substance of the bill."[99]

Activists have little tolerance for what they see as nonperformance.[100] On October 11, 2017, Senate Conservatives Fund president Ken Cuccinelli II, Tea Party Patriots cofounder Jenny Beth Martin, FreedomWorks president Adam Brandon, For America president David Bozell, and chair of ConservativeHQ.com Richard Viguerie, issued a joint call for Mitch McConnell and his top deputies to step down. If he did not, they threatened, they would wage an effort against him in the 2018 midterm elections that would take the form of television ads and other advocacy in individual campaigns where his allies were on the ballot.[101] At the same time, Steve Bannon was seeking challengers to sitting Republican senators in 2018. To win his endorsement and the funding that came with it, he asked potential candidates to pledge not to vote for McConnell as Republican leader.[102]

Although the general public has supported protecting the beneficiaries of DACA, as we saw in chapter 4, few House Republican constituencies contained a significant percentage of Latinos, so few faced constituency pressures to enact immigration reform.[103] When it looked like Trump had cut a deal regarding DACA in September 2017, many of his diehard supporters exploded in anger. Representative Steve King of Iowa, one of the strongest Republican immigration hawks, issued a dramatic warning to the president, tweeting "Trump base is blown up, destroyed, irreparable, and disillusioned beyond repair. No promise is credible." Conservative radio talk show host Laura Ingraham mocked the president for seeming to shelve the pledge that had animated his supporters since his campaign's launch: "Exactly what @realDonaldTrump campaigned on. Not," she tweeted. Conservative polemicist Ann Coulter, author of *In Trump We Trust*, tweeted, "At this point, who DOESN'T want Trump impeached?" "Deep State Wins, Huge Loss for #MAGA," added Fox Business anchor

Lou Dobbs. In the unkindest cut of all, Breitbart ran an article with a bright red headline: "Amnesty Don."[104]

Similarly, in late 2018, when it appeared as though he would forgo funding for a wall on the Mexican border in order to keep the government funded, Rush Limbaugh criticized the deal as "Trump gets nothing and the Democrats get everything." Another conservative firebrand, Ann Coulter, published a column on Breitbart titled "Gutless President in Wall-less Country."[105] In a national address on January 19, 2019, the president offered to protect Dreamers for three years in exchange for wall funding. Coulter immediately tweeted, "Trump proposes amnesty. We voted for Trump and got Jeb!" Breitbart characterized the deal with the headline: "Three Year Amnesty."[106] James Carafano of the conservative Heritage Foundation said the so-called amnesty "undermines our citizen's confidence in the rule of law." Even when Trump changed tack and said he would not sign a budget deal that would avert a government shutdown, Coulter would not let up, tweeting, "BREAKING: Doctors announce world's first successful spine transplant."[107]

Electoral incentives reinforced the demands of party activists. Of the 241 Republicans elected to the House in 2016, just 18—7 percent—represented competitive congressional districts.[108] Only 15 Republicans were elected with margins under 10 percentage points. In 2018, only two House Republicans won with less than 50 percent of the vote.[109]

Thus, most congressional Republicans were far more afraid of losing a primary to a more conservative challenger than a general election to a Democrat. For many Republicans, a deal was more dangerous than no deal. The Right's demonstrated capacity to challenge[110] and punish incumbent Republicans in primaries discouraged compromise.[111] As a result, many of these representatives were content to lose on principle, because compromise and conciliation—the actual work of politics—were the only things that could cost them their jobs. Consequently, in early 2019 when the president declared a national emergency—contrary to years of Republican orthodoxy—to fund a border wall, twelve Republicans voted to overturn his decision. Only one of them (Susan Collins) was up for reelection in 2020, and she represented a state Trump lost in 2016. The other, Lamar Alexander, was retiring.

Moderating Pressures?

Most constituency pressures pushed Republicans to the right, as we saw earlier in this chapter, but in a few states and districts, constituency influences could have been moderating. These pressures, however, did not necessarily help the president. In 2016, ten Republican House members won in Democratic-leaning districts.[112] Twenty-five House Republicans (10 percent) represented districts won by Hillary Clinton. On average, these members won with only 56 percent of the 2016 vote—10 points lower than their fellow partisans[113] (although only three won by less than 5 percent of the vote[114]). Two-thirds of them were more liberal than the average Republican.[115] Nine of them voted against the Republican House health care bill. Similarly, House Republicans representing competitive and ideologically moderate districts were the most likely to break ranks with the party and oppose the president's firing of FBI director James Comey.[116] They were also much more likely to sign the June 2018 discharge petition that would have forced consideration of competing immigration bills.[117]

Three members of the Senate in the 115th Congress represented states won by Clinton: Cory Gardner (Colorado), Susan Collins (Maine), and Dean Heller (Nevada). Collins and Heller were holdouts on health care. The two Republican senators who faced the toughest reelection fights in 2018—Heller and Jeff Flake of Arizona—were frequent critics of Trump and his administration, which they saw as a drag on their political prospects.[118] Flake even wrote a book, *Conscience of a Conservative*, in which he lambasted Trump. On October 24, 2017, he gave a dramatic speech on the Senate floor in which he announced that he would not seek reelection in 2018 and declared he would "no longer be complicit or silent" in the face of the president's "reckless, outrageous and undignified" behavior that was "dangerous to democracy." He deplored the "casual undermining of our democratic ideals" and "the personal attacks, the threats against principles, freedoms and institutions, the flagrant disregard for truth and decency" that he said had become prevalent in American politics in the era of Trump.[119]

Moving to the center often makes good sense for the general election, but as we have seen, may be costly in the primaries. Ultimately, Flake dropped out of the race and Heller moved closer to the president. Similarly, overall the representatives from districts Clinton won were as loyal to Trump as those from districts Trump won. Ideology dominated roll-call voting. Republicans' support for Trump's policies was unaffected by Trump's vote in their district or state.[120]

As we have seen, the Republican losses in the 2018 midterms had the perverse effect of increasing Republican unity in the House because of the loss of moderate Republicans, but it did nothing ease the path of deal making. Moreover, in 2018, only three House Republicans won in Clinton districts (Will Hurd of Texas, John Katko from New York, and Brian Fitzpatrick of Pennsylvania). All of them had made moves to *separate* themselves from the president, such as opposing the 2017 effort to repeal the Affordable Care Act.

Democrats' Constituencies

Even if Democrats were ideologically predisposed against the proposals from a Republican president, were there cross-pressures in their constituencies that would counter their ideological predilections? Was there potential for the president to win support among Democrats for his initiatives?

One of the most important political trends in the past half century has been the polarization of the congressional parties' respective electoral bases.[121] The partisan realignment of the South[122] and the sorting of conservatives and liberals outside the South into the Republican and Democratic parties, respectively, has increased the level of consistency between party identification and ideology.[123] As a consequence, Democratic and Republican elected officials today represent electoral coalitions with strongly diverging policy preferences across a wide range of issues. Thus, the electoral constituencies of the House Democrats contain relatively few Trump supporters, and there is not much ideological division among Democrats.[124]

The decline in shared constituencies between President Trump and Democratic members of Congress reflects an increase in party loyalty and thus a falloff in ticket splitting among voters. Party-line voting reached its highest level ever for House and Senate elections in 2016, with defection rates of 11 percent in House elections and 10 percent in Senate elections.[125] The 2018 midterm elections reflected even greater partisan loyalty, 95 percent, the highest of any exit poll going back to the first in 1982.[126] Much of this coherence in voting was the result of views about the president.[127]

As a result of this individual-level behavior, in 2016 only thirty-five House districts (8 percent) split their verdicts—preferring the president of one party and the House candidate of the other. Only twelve House Democrats (6 percent) were elected to seats in districts Trump won in 2016 (although every one of them was more conservative than the average House Democrat).[128] (An additional Democrat won in a special election in a Trump district in 2018.) Only seven represented districts tilting Republican, while thirteen others represented competitive districts.[129]

Just as losses in the 2018 midterm elections resulted in a more conservative House Republican caucus, election gains added moderates to the House Democratic caucus. There was a large cohort of new members from battleground districts,[130] and thirty-one Democrats represented districts Trump carried in 2016. As we have seen, constituency cross-pressures did emerge in 2019, but Trump's unusually small legislative agenda in the 116th Congress and Nancy Pelosi's deft management of the House calendar limited the potential for the White House to draw Democratic support.

Split outcomes are typically more common in Senate elections, because states tend to be more politically heterogeneous and more evenly partisan balanced than congressional districts. Nevertheless, in 2016, for the first time in history, no state elected a senator from a different party than that of the candidate its voters supported for president. As a result, no Democratic senator was elected in a state Trump won. Five of the six Senate seats that switched parties in 2018 went to the party that had won the state's 2016 presidential vote. As a result, the number of senators representing states won by their party in the most recent presidential election reached an all-time high of eighty-nine for the 116th Congress.[131]

However, twelve Democratic senators represented states won by Trump: Joe Manchin (West Virginia), Joe Donnelly (Indiana), Jon Tester (Montana), Heidi Heitkamp (North Dakota), Clare McCaskill (Missouri), Tammy Baldwin (Wisconsin), Gary Peters and Debbie Stabenow (Michigan), Bill Nelson (Florida), Robert Casey (Pennsylvania), Sherrod Brown (Ohio), and (since 2018) Doug Jones (Alabama). Interestingly, all but Peters and Jones were up for reelection in 2018. Six of them—Jones, Donnelly, McCaskill, Tester, Heitkamp, and Manchin—represented clearly Republican states.

Some Republicans thought that a Trump win in these states would scare the Democratic senators into acceptance of the Republican agenda— perhaps even into voting to repeal President Obama's signature health care law, especially if they were up for reelection.[132] Yet none of these senators voted for any Republican proposal on health care or taxes.

The closest Trump came to receiving support on a major policy issue is when Donnelly, Heitkamp, Jones, Manchin, and McCaskill voted for a spending bill to avoid a government shutdown in January 2018. The public favored approving the budget agreement more than continuing the

DACA program,[133] knowing there was time to fix DACA later in the year. Polling done in early December 2017 by the Senate Majority PAC found that in more conservative states, voters would fault Democrats if DACA was what prompted a government shutdown.[134] The same five senators plus Angus King of Maine and Bill Nelson of Florida voted to confirm Mike Pompeo as secretary of state.

Jon Tester voted against the appointments of health and human services secretary Alex Azar and secretary of state Mike Pompeo. He also opposed Gina Haspel, Trump's controversial choice to lead the CIA. The senator earned Trump's wrath in earnest after raising alarms about misconduct allegations surrounding Ronny Jackson, the White House physician whose nomination by the president to lead the Department of Veterans Affairs was derailed.

Constituency pressures did not turn Democrats into conservatives, but the six senators from reliably Republican states gave the president the highest levels of support among Democrats (table 6.3) in 2017 and 2018.[135] Things were different in the more competitive Trump states, however. Only Bill Nelson of Florida gave him more than 17 percent support. Here the relationship between Trump's vote and support for his initiatives broke down, and Democratic senators supported the president at the very low rate typical of most of their colleagues.

If the president had maintained the public's approval in the states he won in 2016, there would have been considerable pressure on Democrats from those states to support him. However, the Gallup Poll found that among the states Trump won and that were represented by a Democratic senator, only in West Virginia, North Dakota, and Montana did he average at least 50 percent approval in 2017, and only in those states did his approval exceed his disapproval (table 6.4). He also had a high level of disapproval in Montana.[136] In 2018, he added only Missouri to these states.[137]

Polls taken in August 2017 found that about two-thirds of adults in these Trump states, including one-fifth of those who had voted for him, said they were embarrassed by Trump.[138] As one senator said, approval ratings as low as Trump's make it "tough to get Democrats to come over. You can have the [Republican] base, but that doesn't move red-state Democrats."[139]

Members of Congress are particularly responsive to their primary constituencies. The Pew Research Center found that Democrats and Democratic leaners were much more concerned that their representatives in Congress would not do enough to oppose Donald Trump and his policies

TABLE 6.3. **Presidential support of Democratic senators from states Trump won**

State	Trump support, 2016 (%)	Senator	Presidential support (%)*	
			2017	2018
West Virginia	69	Joe Manchin	55	46
North Dakota	63	Heidi Heitkamp	49	48
Alabama	62	Doug Jones	—	47
Indiana	57	Joe Donnelly	43	55
Missouri	57	Claire McCaskill	37	43
Montana	56	Jon Tester	25	36
Ohio	52	Sherrod Brown	8	5
Florida	49	Bill Nelson	24	32
Pennsylvania	48	Bob Casey	9	17
Michigan	48	Gary Peters	13	16
Michigan	48	Debbie Stabenow	9	9
Wisconsin	47	Tammy Baldwin	5	15

*Support on roll-call votes on which president took a stand and on which the winning side was supported by fewer than 80 percent of those voting.

TABLE 6.4. **Trump approval in states he won that were represented by Democratic senators, 2017**

State	Approval (%)	Disapproval (%)	Democratic senator(s)
West Virginia	61	35	Joe Manchin
North Dakota	57	39	Heidi Heitkamp
Montana	52	45	Jon Tester
Missouri	47	48	Claire McCaskill
Ohio	45	50	Sherrod Brown
Indiana	44	51	Joe Donnelly
Pennsylvania	42	53	Bob Casey
Wisconsin	41	55	Tammy Baldwin
Florida	41	53	Bill Nelson
Michigan	40	55	Debbie Stabenow; Gary Peters

Source: Gallup polls.

than they were that congressional Democrats would go too far in their opposition (72 percent vs. 20 percent).[140] In the Gallup polls for 2017 and 2018, Democratic approval of Trump's handling of the presidency averaged less than 10 percent.[141] It is not surprising that California Democrats refused to endorse the reelection of Senator Diane Feinstein at their 2018 party convention. Her fellow Democrats rebuked her for being too willing to work with the president.

Party differences in electoral bases are strongly related to party differences in presidential support and roll-call voting.[142] Given the clear preferences of their supporting coalition, congressional Democrats had every reason to resist most of Trump's initiatives vigorously. Congressional Democrats were responding rationally to their incentives for reelection when they opposed the president. The number of Democrats in the 115th Congress who saw as politically advantageous cutting a deal with the president on a core issue was close to zero. Given their constituents' views, it is not surprising that no Democrat in either chamber voted for any of the various health care bills proposed by the Republican congressional leadership or the tax bill that the president signed in December 2017.

The electoral coalitions of the two parties are increasingly divided by race as well as by party and ideology. Although the most salient demographic fact about America is that it is becoming more diverse, Republican districts are overwhelmingly white. Differences in cultural values and attitudes toward government accompany these differences in the racial composition of constituencies,[143] making it more difficult to achieve bipartisan compromises. Trump's anti-immigrant stances and his toleration of white nationalists in his coalition have intensified the saliency of these differences.

The competition for political advantage also inhibits bipartisanship. Since 1980, there has been heavy competition to control each house of Congress. Parties with a president or majority must focus on legislating while minority parties can focus on political messaging. Representatives and senators believe it is necessary to define and dramatize party differences to energize supporters and persuade undecided voters to support them. To do this, the minority forces roll calls that yield party-line divisions, publicize partisan controversies, raise more campaign money, and make the case for their party to take control. Even when they lose the vote, they may feel they have won politically because they are better positioned in the next election. Unsurprisingly, such adversarial behavior impedes bipartisan cooperation.[144]

Similarly, Adam Bonica and Gary Cox argue that the close partisan competition for control of the House since 1994 has caused activists, donors, and, indirectly, voters to focus on the national battle for majority status and thus reduced individual members' ability to escape blame for their parties' actions. Representatives could deviate from their district preferences and pay a lower electoral penalty because they would be blamed in any event. This dynamic has encouraged House members to become ideologically more extreme.[145]

Structure of Choice

The structure of the choices facing Congress can help or hinder the president's legislative agenda. Congress can take no vote, vote down, or pass a presidential initiative. Because Congress cannot act on every proposal and because there are many ways to prevent action in the US system of separation of powers, most proposals founder. The default position is for Congress to take no action. Although White House initiatives are likely to receive some congressional attention, many never come to a vote.[146]

From the standpoint of the White House seeking support for a presidential initiative, there are two critical components of these choices. The first is the presence or absence of broad political incentives to act on an issue. More specifically, are there political incentives for the opposition to act positively to support the president? Typically, there are not. Indeed, the opposition party usually opposes presidential initiatives. Democrats were in no hurry to enact Trump's proposals regarding taxes, immigration, or environmental protection, for example. Nor were they eager to repeal the Affordable Care Act or replace it with much less health care coverage.

The second component of the structure of congressional choice is the beneficiary of a failure to act. If the president opposes congressional initiatives, he benefits from the default position. However, if he wishes Congress to pass legislation—and all contemporary presidents do—the advantage usually shifts to the opposition. Most policies, from tax cuts to defense spending, do not take effect without positive action from Congress.

However, whether by design or accident, the president changed the structure of several decisions facing the legislature. By passing off responsibility for policy initiatives to Congress, he altered the incentives for action. In scrapping DACA, he ordered a six-month phase out and challenged Congress to use that time to pass legislation authorizing the program. Democrats certainly had an incentive to do so. The president also hoped the Democrats' desire to protect the Dreamers would put the Democrats in a political bind and give him leverage to pass his own initiatives regarding immigration.[147] The strategy seemed to be working until February 2018, when the administration opposed a bill that would have given the president $25 billion for a wall on the Mexican border and protected hundreds of thousands of young immigrants from deportation. The bill failed, and with it any hope for reform that year. As a Senate aide presciently put it, "To his credit, he leveraged his DACA position to get

Democrats to vote for his wall—and yet he still turned it down. He's not going to get another shot this clean to get a wall. He tossed that away for good."[148]

The president also attempted to gain legislative leverage on immigration from his policy of separating immigrant parents from their young children at the southern border. According to senior Trump aides, the president believed he could use the children as bargaining chips to force Democrats to negotiate a broader deal on immigration, which might include money for a border wall and reductions in the number of *legal* immigrants who are allowed into the United States. The president suggested he would not change the policy unless Democrats agreed to his other demands on immigration, including funding a border wall, tightening the rules for border enforcement, and curbing legal entry.[149] This maneuver was also unproductive.

Similarly, the president's decision to cut off critical payments to health insurance companies ratcheted up the pressure on Congress to take action to protect consumers from soaring premiums. The president suggested that he was trying to compel the Democrats to negotiate a compromise. "If the Democrats were smart, what they'd do is come and negotiate something where people could really get the kind of health care that they deserve," he told reporters.[150] Trump was not interested in reinstating payments to insurance companies, but he was interested in Democratic support for a replacement for the Affordable Care Act. However, Democrats were convinced that any blame for rising premiums and shrinking choices would fall on Republicans, who controlled the White House and Congress. After spending the year trying to preserve the Affordable Care Act, Democrats were in no mood to make major concessions.[151]

In decertifying the Iran nuclear deal, Trump pressed Congress to come up with ways to curb Tehran's destabilizing activities before he pulled out of the agreement altogether. Again, those who were concerned about terminating the agreement had an incentive to work on the issue. It is clear that Trump was not interested in preserving the agreement, however, and nothing was done on it.

Conclusion

Donald Trump entered office with aspirations for transformational policy change, much of which would have to be approved by Congress. Despite the president's many unique characteristics, we can employ the framework of the president's strategic position to understand that the president's opportunity structure was mixed. He lacked an electoral mandate but was fortunate enough to preside over a unified government in his first two years in office. Nevertheless, Republican cohesion was imperfect, partisan polarization was high, and there was little public pressure for Democrats to abate their strong opposition. The structure of most of the choices before Congress did not favor the president. Thus, we should not expect the president to have enjoyed notable success in obtaining congressional support for most of his major initiatives.

Making strategic assessments by asking a few key questions about the president's political environment provides us crucial leverage for evaluating a president's likely success in obtaining the support of Congress for his initiatives. In addition, understanding the president's strategic position provides a firm foundation for the next step in analysis of presidential leadership of Congress: the president exploiting the opportunities in his environment.

CHAPTER SEVEN

No Deal: Negotiating with Congress

Donald Trump and his Republican copartisans in Congress faced 2017 with great ambitions. They would quickly repeal and replace the Affordable Care Act, slash taxes and rewrite the tax code, pass a budget dramatically reducing the size of government, overturn Obama-era regulations, and raise the debt limit. Then they would move on to transform immigration policy and launch a massive investment in the nation's infrastructure.

As we have seen, the president began his tenure with one important advantage in his strategic position—Republican majorities in both houses of Congress. However, he did not receive a mandate from the people, the Republican Party had some important fractures, the parties were highly polarized, and his low support among the public from his first day in office provided Democrats with few incentives to support him. Moreover, the structure of the choices before Congress offered little help to the White House.

Recognizing and exploiting opportunities for change—rather than creating opportunities through persuasion—are the essential presidential leadership skills. To succeed, presidents have to evaluate the opportunities for change in their environments carefully, fashion strategies and tactics to exploit them, and execute these approaches skillfully. Successful leadership also requires that the president have the commitment, resolution, and adaptability to take full advantage of opportunities that arise.

Given the president's mixed opportunity structure, he was going to have to negotiate with both Democrats and Republicans to achieve his policy goals. From his perspective, that necessity did not pose much of a challenge. Donald Trump was a self-proclaimed deal maker who believed negotiating skills are the key to great leadership—and that he possessed these talents. The author of the *Art of the Deal*, he had decades of experience in negotiating contracts in the world of business. As a result, the White House devoted little attention to constraints on presidential persuasion or the most effective way to negotiate.

Despite his extravagant claims regarding his deal-making skills, Trump struggled to close deals as president. At the core of the president's problem was his approach to policymaking. His issue stances were typically unclear, uninformed, and inconsistent. Moreover, he often adopted a reactive posture and easily lost focus. In sum, the president was an unskilled, unreliable, and untrustworthy negotiator.

Passivity

In his inaugural address, Donald Trump announced, "Now arrives the hour of action." Once in the Oval Office, however, the president was unusually passive. His lack of detailed policy proposals certainly contributed to this stance, but it is nevertheless surprising that he seemed to have abdicated his role as a master dealmaker and positioned himself as dependent on congressional initiatives and sometimes as powerless in the face of entrenched Washington interests. As Mitch McConnell described the president's approach, "He sends up the nominees and signs the bills."[1]

"Ever since we've been here, we've really been following *our* lead," said Republican senator Bob Corker. "Almost every bit of this has been 100 percent internal to Congress."[2] According to Tim Alberta, when Trump entered office, he effectively contracted out policymaking decisions to Paul Ryan and McConnell, and he signed on to Republican orthodoxy on repealing Obamacare, cutting taxes, rebuilding the military, slashing regulations, reforming the Department of Veterans Affairs, and confirming conservative judges. According to Corker, "That was our agenda—it wasn't his agenda."[3]

The president seemed to agree. Commenting on the lack of progress on legislation, the president initially acknowledged that "we're not getting the job done." Reflecting his passive approach to legislating, however, he quickly shifted course and proclaimed, "And I'm not going to blame myself. I'll be honest: *They* are not getting the job done," he said, referring to Congress.[4]

In an interview on the weekend before his inauguration, the president-elect employed unequivocal terms to declare that he had nearly completed a plan to replace President Obama's signature health care law and was ready to unveil it alongside Speaker Paul Ryan and Senate Majority Leader Mitch McConnell. "It's very much formulated down to the final strokes. We haven't put it in quite yet but we're going to be doing it soon," Trump said. There was going to be "insurance for everybody" and "much lower deductibles," Trump promised. "There was a philosophy in some circles that if you can't pay for it, you don't get it. That's not going to happen with us." People covered under the law could "expect to have great health care. It will be in a much simplified form. Much less expensive and much better."[5] The White House never produced such a plan. Indeed, in one of the most telling remarks of his presidency, Trump exclaimed to a meeting of governors on February 27, 2017, "Nobody knew health care could be so complicated."[6] Trump devoted only a modest amount of time to mastering health care policy, so the White House largely delegated the development of a health care bill to Capitol Hill.

Health care was not an exception. The administration simply never invested in developing policies. As a candidate Trump pledged a $1 trillion program to reconstruct the nation's roadways, waterworks, bridges, and electrical grid—and create "millions" of new jobs in the process. A year into his presidency, he had yet to produce the detailed plan he promised to deliver "very soon" or even to name any members to a new board he claimed would green-light big projects. When Trump finally delivered a fifty-three-page plan to Congress in February 2018, the document was widely panned by Democrats and largely met with silence from Republicans. The president then dropped the initiative, saying little about it and holding no public events to build support for it.

When the president announced in August 2017 his support for a bill to cut legal immigration by half, he was backing a modified version of a bill introduced by Republican senators Tom Cotton and David Perdue from the previous April.

On September 5, 2017, Trump announced he was phasing out DACA on the grounds that he lacked the power to establish such a program on his own. He gave Congress six months to fix the program before it expired. The president offered no guidelines for action. He simply pitched the issue to the legislature. In the first White House briefing following the president's announcement, press secretary Sarah Huckabee Sanders reiterated where responsibility lay, declaring, "If Congress doesn't want to do the job that they were elected to do, then maybe they should get out of the way and let someone else do it."[7] There seemed to be little role for the

White House beyond general exhortation. "The president's position has been that he's called on Congress to come up with a permanent solution and a fix to this process," declared Sanders.[8] This passivity lost the president the opportunity to trade renewing DACA for Democratic support for building a wall along the Mexican border.[9]

When in October 2017 Trump declined to certify Iran's compliance with the 2015 nuclear agreement, he essentially left it up to Congress to decide whether to reimpose punitive economic sanctions. He made no proposals. His approach allowed him to demonstrate to his supporters that he had disavowed the accord while bowing to the reality that the United States would isolate itself from its allies if it sabotaged a deal with which most nations viewed Iran as complying. Nevertheless, the lack of guidance meant that Congress was unlikely to act and provided the president little leverage to force Iran and the other parties to the deal back to the negotiating table to make changes in the agreement.[10]

After the February 2018 shooting at a high school in Parkland, Florida, that left seventeen dead, Trump appeared on television and called for raising the age limit to purchase rifles and backed legislation for near-universal background checks. He later told lawmakers that while the NRA has "great power over you people, they have less power over me." Within a month, however, he bowed to the NRA and embraced its agenda of arming teachers and adopting incremental improvements to the background check system. As the president tweeted regarding the higher age limit, "Not much political support (to put it mildly)." Thus, the White House conceded defeat without making any serious effort to change the gun laws.[11]

Following two mass shootings in the summer of 2019, the president again called for stronger gun control. Yet he did not deliver a policy proposal. Once again, he drew back after hearing from the NRA. Rather than the White House setting an agenda, it was Congress who was courting the president, seeking for him to take a stand. Nancy Pelosi and Charles Schumer, the top two Democrats in Congress, tried to tap into Trump's penchant for drama, promising to join the president for a "historic signing ceremony at the Rose Garden" if he got behind a more expansive, House-passed background checks bill.[12] In the end, little happened. When Attorney General William Barr proposed ideas for gun control to Senate Republicans, the White House quickly disavowed the proposal. As Republican senator Josh Hawley inquired, "My question was: 'Where is the president on this?' And I asked this question directly: 'Is this something the president supports?' And they didn't have an answer for that."[13] Mitch McConnell explained, "Until the White House gives us some indication of what the president is willing to sign, we are waiting to see what it looks like."[14]

It is not uncommon for recent presidents to set broad goals and let Congress work out the details of legislation, but other presidents have been more proactive than Trump. On some issues, such as tax cuts, congressional Republican leaders were more than content to take the lead. On other matters such as immigration and gun control, however, they sought White House direction and political cover.[15] It often did not arrive.

Although very early on Republican congressional leaders said that they were comfortable with Trump's approach,[16] it did not work well. It is difficult to pass complex and controversial legislation without clear leadership from the White House on *both* an overall framework and on key components. As we have seen, congressional Republicans were not always able to overcome their divisions on their own. The failure of the White House to advance coherent policy prescriptions left them without the adhesive of presidential leadership.[17]

In addition to the failure to win passage of significant presidential initiatives, the passive approach to legislating had several other negative consequences for the president. First, Trump often lost the opportunity to shape the details of legislation that did pass. When Congress crafted a two-year budget agreement without him in March 2018, it included almost nothing for his high-priority border wall but did contain a large increase in other domestic spending that he opposed—with a subsequent ballooning deficit that was contrary to his campaign promise to put the government's fiscal house in order. The bill also averted a government shutdown, the prospect of which the president wanted to use as leverage for obtaining immigration reform, a topic I discuss in detail below.

The president was so disengaged from the budget battle that he did not issue a veto threat until *after* the bill passed, when it could have no impact on congressional voting. (He signed the bill shortly after.) After reaching the budget deal with his Republican counterpart, Senate Minority Leader Charles Schumer said he had learned to proceed without bothering with the president. "Often times we can get a lot more done working with one another and let the White House just sit on the sidelines, because you don't know what their positions are," he said.[18]

Another consequence of a passive mode is that, lacking specific proposals, the president was in no position to sequence their consideration to his advantage. Trump followed the lead of Paul Ryan, who put together a sequencing chart for legislation during the transition period, which the president-elect accepted.[19] Thus, for example, he consented to the congressional leadership's plan to focus first on Republican-only health care proposals that were sure to exacerbate partisan tensions and ultimately proved to be a time-consuming embarrassment for the White House.

A second key element of the Republican plan was to employ not one but two reconciliation bills, one for health care and the other for tax reform, to avoid a filibuster in the Senate. Because there can only be one reconciliation bill at a time, their idea was to pass health care, which would provide some budgetary space for tax cuts, and then move on to tax reform, but that strategy was based on the premise of passing health care quickly. In addition, the rules, especially in the Senate, strictly limit the types of provisions that can be included in a reconciliation bill, making it more difficult to please the Republican caucus and subjecting moderate Republicans in the House to controversial votes that would never pass in the Senate. Moreover, seeking to pass legislation on a party-line vote focused media attention on Republican divisions and freed the Democrats from blame when the health care effort failed.[20]

The choice to make repealing the Affordable Care Act conservatives' first legislative effort was generally considered a misstep, according to Senator Lindsey Graham. Moreover, the half-measure that Republicans ultimately achieved contributed to destabilizing insurance markets. "The good news is we repealed the individual mandate," Graham said. "The bad news is we now own care, for sure."[21] Aside from Trump himself, the issue of health care was biggest burden the Republicans carried into the midterm elections.

In 2017, governors from both political parties told Congress that they supported immediate action on modest, bipartisan steps to repair the Affordable Care Act without repealing it. Once again, the White House seemed to be in a reactive mode, playing no role in fashioning a solution to the problems experienced by health insurance markets. Kellyanne Conway, a top advisor to Trump, reflected the president's passivity when she told Fox News, "The president is ready. He's ready with pen in hand to sign health care reform."[22]

When no option attracted a majority of senators, the president announced an end to subsidies, known as cost-sharing reductions, to health insurers that help low-income Americans pay out-of-pocket medical expenses, calling them unconstitutional. He then left it to Congress to decide whether to appropriate funding for the subsidies. When senators Lamar Alexander and Patty Murray reached agreement on a short-term plan to fund the subsidies, the White House offered contradictory responses (discussed below) and made no effort to forge a coalition behind it.

Everyone was confused, leaving the policy in limbo. When a majority of senators seemed to support the Alexander-Murray bill, Mitch McConnell said he would be willing to bring it up for debate if the president signaled his support. "If there's a need for some kind of interim step here to stabilize the market, we need a bill the president will actually sign," McConnell said. "And I'm not certain yet what the president is looking for here, but I'll be happy to bring a bill to the floor if I know President Trump would sign it."[23]

A passive approach to legislating also forced the president to sell others' versions of policies, not his own. Whatever House or Senate Republicans produced on health care became his policy. If they made critical changes in the alternative of the moment, these alterations then became his new policy. He would have been more effective—and had more credibility—building coalitions in support of his own initiatives.

In March 2019, the president surprised congressional Republicans by abruptly ordering his administration to ask a federal court to invalidate the entire Affordable Care Act and then promised a Republican replacement. That is all he did, however. The White House had no plan to offer Congress. Trump tried to pressure Republicans to produce a replacement for the ACA,[24] but they had little appetite to take on an issue that benefited Democrats during the midterm elections and might put them in peril in 2020. Moreover, there was no realistic prospect for success in a divided Congress. Mitch McConnell asked the president to back off. "I made it clear to him that we were not going to be doing that in the Senate," he told reporters.[25]

In 2019, the president faced a Democratic House, which controlled the legislative agenda. Trump took a stand on only sixty-two votes in the House. He opposed passage on 95 percent of these votes. The only times he backed an action was on a Democratic-supported budget cap adjustment, a consensual defense authorization, and the USMCA.

Congressional Quarterly identified 190 Senate votes on which the president took a stand in 2019. However, 161 (85 percent) of these were votes confirming nominations. The president took stands on only 29 substantive legislative matters during the entire year. Moreover, only 11 of these were stands supporting an action. Four of the 11 votes were on cloture, and these were the only contentious issues on which the president took a positive stand in 2019. The other 7 bills were consensual: appropriations or authorization bills, a spending cap adjustment, and acceptance of North Macedonia into NATO membership. The rest of the time, the White House opposed initiatives, principally in foreign policy. The number of opposing stances would have even been greater if Mitch McConnell had not refused to take up nearly 300 bills passed by the Democratic House, including those dealing with gun control, voting rights, immigration, and drug pricing. As Congressional Quarterly put it, although Trump repeatedly railed against the "do nothing Democrats, "he has largely ceded the agenda to Republicans in Congress by neglecting to offer even an outline of goals."[26] But the Senate majority did not take up the slack, voting only 108 times on legislation (including matters on which the president did not take a stand), the fewest in at least two generations.[27]

The president often spoke and tweeted about the need to lower drug prices. He called on Congress to pass bipartisan legislation in his February 2020 State of the Union message and personally recognized Senator Charles Grassley for his leadership on the issue. Yet, Trump did not lobby individual senators to support the measure or personally pressure Republicans, including Mitch McConnell, for action.[28]

There are two policy areas in which the president adopted an active posture. The first was tax cuts, where he was not only active but also somewhat specific and consistent in his policy stances. He repeatedly pushed Republican leaders to deliver a bill quickly, kept in touch with the negotiations in Congress, and eagerly worked to build public pressure on Congress.[29] Although he typically left the details to Congress, he did intervene to push down corporate and individual tax rates, oppose meddling with tax-advantaged 401(k) plans, and repeal the individual mandate in Obamacare. For example, on October 23, 2017, Trump tweeted, "There will be NO change to your 401(k). This has always been a great and popular middle class tax break that works, and it stays!" On November 13, after a day of meetings in the Philippines, Trump took to Twitter again to post, "I am proud of the Rep. House & Senate for working so hard on cutting taxes {& reform.} We're getting close! Now, how about ending the unfair & highly unpopular Indiv Mandate in OCare & reducing taxes even further? Cut top rate to 35% w/all of the rest going to middle income cuts?" "The president feels very strongly about including this at some step before the final process," House Ways and Means Committee chair Kevin Brady said. "He's told me that twice by phone and once in person."[30]

In the case of tax policy, on which Republicans had broad agreement, the president's interventions were not always appreciated. Congressional leaders pushed back on the administration's efforts—including those of secretary of the treasury Steven Mnuchin—to promote policy details, giving tax writers more freedom to maneuver and craft a bill that could pass.[31] Reflecting this lack of enthusiasm for White House intervention, Republican senator Bob Corker declared, "I would just like him to leave it to the professionals for a while and see if we can do something that's constructive."[32] Thus, the president was not involved in cobbling the complex bill together. As I discuss later, he made a few calls and made a superfluous visit to Capitol Hill near the conclusion of the process.[33]

In the end, the president got much, but by no means all, of what he wanted. He asked for a 15 percent corporate income tax rate and ended up with a 21 percent rate. He supported a top rate for individual income taxes of 35 percent; Congress passed a 37 percent rate. Lawmakers did not eliminate the estate tax as the president requested, but they did limit it. Congress also did little to implement a Trump proposal to change the special treatment of "carried interest" that gives hedge fund managers and private equity partners lower tax rates on their income.

The second policy on which Trump was active was immigration, which dominated his legislative focus in his second year in office. As I show below, however, the president's activity often impeded negotiations and was unsuccessful in achieving the White House's policy goals.

The coronavirus pandemic forced a third issue on the White House in 2020. Nevertheless, the president was initially passive. Sarah Binder explained that House and Senate Democratic leaders acted together in the second week of March to forge a response plan, preempting the White House. They set the agenda with a list of concrete policy steps to help mitigate the impending emergency. In contrast, House and Senate Republicans were relatively mute, deferring to President Trump and his economic team to float potential options. Even after the president's nationally televised speech, the administration's policy agenda remained in flux.[34] Some of its ideas appeared slapdash and not carefully vetted.[35]

Confusion

To lead others to adopt a policy, one must first have one. Grand aspirations to "Make America Great Again" or provide inexpensive and better quality health insurance for all are not substitutes for operational plans to achieve them. The administration's vagueness on its policy stances contributed to the Trump presidency's lack of success in passing significant legislation. Because the president did not hold firm positions on many important subjects, he was poorly positioned to send signals to his supporters as to what he wanted and to interlocutors as to what he would accept.

The president himself seemed unfamiliar with the details of policies, leaving him vulnerable to misstatements and contradictions and increasing the difficulty of persuading the public or members of Congress to support initiatives. Indeed, Trump often seemed more interested in simply passing something and declaring success than with the content of legislation. He was willing to let others take charge of both the process and the substance.

Unsurprisingly, Trump disputed reports of his lacking a detailed understanding of legislation. "I know the details of taxes better than anybody. Better than the greatest C.P.A. I know the details of health care better than most, better than most." He added that he knew more about "the big bills" debated in the Congress "than any president that's ever been in office."[36] It is no exaggeration to characterize his protestations as blatant hyperbole.

Although Congress is certainly capable of taking the initiative, to avoid embarrassing conflicts lawmakers—especially members of the president's party—want to know where the president stands before it takes action. As Senator John Thune, the Republican leading infrastructure efforts in the Senate, put it, "We're sort of waiting on the administration to tell us what it is exactly they want to do."[37] In the middle of the failed effort to achieve immigration reform in January 2018, Mitch McConnell pleaded for guidance from the White House: "I'm looking for something that President Trump supports, and he's not yet indicated what measure he's willing to sign," McConnell declared. As soon as we figure out what he is for, then I would be convinced that we were not just spinning our wheels going to this issue on the floor, but actually dealing with a bill that has a chance to become law and therefore solve the problem."[38]

The president did have specific views on a few issues, of course. As we have seen, he intervened in Congress's writing of tax cut legislation to limit changes to 401(k) accounts and to maintain the pressure for pushing down the marginal rates for individuals and corporations.

One of the hallmarks of the Trump presidency was immigration reform. The president made it a centerpiece of his campaign, issued controversial executive orders restricting immigration immediately after taking office, and repeatedly sought legislation to limit legal immigration and increase barriers to illegal immigration, most notably by building a wall along a significant portion of the US border with Mexico. Nevertheless, lawmakers often found it difficult to discern just where he stood.

Immigration was the key legislative issue for the White House in 2018, and the president and Congress engaged in substantial efforts to pass an immigration bill. Republicans, however, could not figure out what Trump would sign.[39] In June, House Republican leaders planned to hold votes on two competing immigration bills: one hardline and one more moderate. During a wide-ranging interview on *Fox & Friends* on June 15, the president said he would oppose a compromise immigration bill cobbled together by House Republicans. "I certainly wouldn't sign the more moderate one," Trump declared. As late as the previous evening, White House officials were closely coordinating with House Republican leaders over the bill, with the understanding that Trump would endorse it and ultimately sign it if it passed. The administration even drafted and circulated a Statement of Administration Policy indicating that Trump's advisors would recommend that he sign it into law.[40] Moreover, in a tweet on the afternoon of June 15, Trump listed his priorities on immigration that hewed closely to the framework of the compromise bill, while never explicitly reversing his opposition.

The president's words created widespread confusion among Republicans on Capitol Hill and dealt a significant blow to Republican leaders who had been scrambling to rally support for the bill. House Republican leaders had planned to whip support for the compromise measure on the 15th but decided to delay until they received more clarity from the White House on what Trump meant.[41] Shortly after Trump's comments on Fox, Representative Jim Jordan, an influential leader of the conference's conservative wing, said he would not support a more moderate immigration bill that the president would not sign.[42]

Senior aides in the White House quietly insisted that the president had misspoken, but it took hours for the White House to say that aloud. Finally, early Friday evening, Raj Shah, a White House spokesperson, issued a statement pledging Trump's support for the compromise bill as well as for the hardline measure sponsored by Representative Robert W. Goodlatte. Shah said the president's opposition referred to an effort by moderate Republicans to use a so-called discharge petition to force the House to vote on narrower legislation to protect the Dreamers.[43] This explanation was highly suspect.

On June 19, the president met with House Republicans on Capitol Hill, but he offered little guidance and declined to state a preference between the two bills. He did say he would sign either before veering off subject. He took no questions and vowed to rewrite Republican immigration legislation to his liking, although he did not specify what he wanted to change.[44] The president also delivered a pointed dig at Representative Mark Sanford, a Trump critic who lost his primary election the previous week.[45] "I think the president needs to understand that that may have actually lost him votes in that meeting," Representative Raúl R. Labrador said. "The reason he was there was to emphasize that he had our backs, and I think a different message was sent."[46]

Confusion was widespread. "He didn't really tell us what bill to vote for," said Representative Markwayne Mullin.[47] "That weighs a lot in my decision-making, what the president says," Representative James Comer said. "The president needed to come out and strongly endorse this compromise plan. It doesn't appear that he has."[48] Adding to the confusion on Capitol Hill, some House Republicans left the evening meeting with the impression that Trump was endorsing the compromise bill. "The president gave unwavering support of the compromise bill," said Representative Jeff Denham. Yet when Representative Ted Yoho asked his colleague F. James Sensenbrenner in front of reporters whether he knew which bill Trump was promoting at the meeting—the compromise or the hardline measure—Sensenbrenner said he did not.[49]

Many lawmakers felt that Trump did not explicitly call on them to pass the compromise measure, leaving them free to vote only for the more conservative alternative. "I'm going to need the president's call," declared Representative Dave Brat.[50] Representative Bradley Byrne, a deputy whip who was involved in vote-counting discussions, added, "If the president said to a given bill, 'That's my bill; that's the one I want'—I think that would have a pretty significant impact on our discussions. But he hasn't done that, and so we're continuing to work without that."[51]

It is not surprising that the bill failed on June 27 on a vote of 301–121, despite a last-minute tweet of support from Trump, the backing of the Republican leadership, and weeks of negotiations between conservatives and moderate Republicans who sought an intraparty compromise. Nearly as many Republicans voted against the bill (112) as for it (121). All 189 Democrats who voted opposed the bill.

Following the historic government shutdown in December 2018–January 2019, Congress was hard at work trying to negotiate a budget and prevent a recurrence. However, Republicans were hampered in their bargaining because they did not know what the president would support in the end.[52] I discuss this incident in detail in the next section. In June 2019, the White House created yet further uncertainty about the budget and raising the debt limit. Some Senate Republicans complained that they still did not know exactly what the White House would support when it came to any of the financial issues they were confronting. "I think that's what we're trying to find out," explained Republican Senate Whip John Thune. "Our members are ready to move, but they don't want to move unless the White House is on board."[53]

Inconsistency

Being a trustworthy negotiator requires consistency in policy stances. However, the president often changed his mind and equivocated. According to Representative Charlie Dent, President Trump "can shift on a dime, and he has many unformed policy positions. We have to worry about him shifting positions."[54] Indeed, worry they did. The underinformed and impulsive chief executive frequently took contradictory stances, undermining his supporters and leaving everyone in doubt as to where he stood and what he was willing to sign. He often promised to support a proposal only to renege days, or even hours, later.

The confusion about Trump's views was not the result of a careful plan to mask what was acceptable to him and thus increase his bargaining power and strengthen him in negotiations with Congress. Instead, the president's contradictory statements seemed to be responses to his environment, including the desires of those with whom he was negotiating, the urgings of advisors and visitors in the White House, and the arguments of advocates appearing on television. He also appeared to be torn between a desire to declare a "win" and a wish to please his base.

Along with the president's lack of substantive plans for public policies and strategies for achieving them, his contradictory stances made it difficult for everyone, including his potential allies, to discern his views. His inconsistency discouraged potential supporters from taking risks to support his stances, knowing that the president might suddenly change his mind.

At the same time, adversaries concluded that they could not trust his word. "Negotiating with President Trump is like negotiating with Jell-O," complained Charles Schumer. "It's next to impossible."[55] Senate Minority

Whip Richard Durbin lamented, "I'm sorry to say, I found the president to be totally unreliable when it came to the DACA issue." "His effectiveness is compromised as long as his word is unreliable."[56]

The president may have drawn from his experience in the world of real estate, but it did not prepare him well for negotiating with Congress. In New York, Trump was known to back away from nearly completed agreements as a tactic to obtain even better deals. In Washington, he could not walk away from many of the problems on his desk, such as funding the government. And his interlocutors did not respond well to being played.

On November 28, 2017, leaders were in the midst of negotiating a bill to fund the government and prevent a shutdown. Conservatives had criticized Trump for dealing with Democratic leaders Charles Schumer and Nancy Pelosi, whom he met at the White House that afternoon, along with Mitch McConnell and Paul Ryan. The president began the day by denouncing the Democrats on Twitter: "Problem is they want illegal immigrants flooding into our Country unchecked, are weak on Crime and want to substantially RAISE Taxes. I don't see a deal!"[57]

Schumer and Pelosi then canceled their meeting with Trump. Pelosi took to Twitter, mimicking the president's social media tone: "he's more interested in stunts than in addressing the needs of the American people," Pelosi tweeted. "Poor Ryan and McConnell relegated to props. Sad!" She and Schumer then issued a statement summarizing the negotiating situation. "Given that the President doesn't see a deal between Democrats and the White House, we believe the best path forward is to continue negotiating with our Republican counterparts in Congress instead."[58] "The staffs were making great progress until the president stepped in," Schumer explained. "We were very close on a number of issues." Trump had simply got in the way of what were "serious, mature negotiations" on a major piece of legislation.[59]

Health Care

President Trump campaigned against cuts in the big entitlement programs, including Medicaid, and promised health care for all. Yet he supported the House and Senate bills that slashed future spending on Medicaid, which the Congressional Budget Office estimated would cause millions to lose their access to health care.

In May 2017, the president lauded the House health care bill as a "great plan" that was "very, very incredibly well-crafted."[60] On June 13, however he derided the same bill as "mean."[61] On May 28, Trump tweeted that "we [should] add more dollars to Healthcare and make it the best anywhere."[62] Several days earlier, however, he proposed cutting between $800 billion and $1.4 trillion in future spending on Medicaid. On May 30, press secretary Sean Spicer would not say where Trump wanted to add more money to health care. One might speculate Spicer's nonresponse reflected the fact that the president had no idea.[63] Days later, deputy press secretary Sarah Huckabee Sanders said that Trump did not necessarily support cuts to Medicaid—even though his budget and the Senate bill would make such cuts.[64]

On June 27, Trump announced that it would be "okay" if a health care bill did not reach his desk. The next month he declared that he would be "very angry" if the Senate failed to pass a bill. Trump further muddied the waters on June 30, floating the possibility on Twitter that lawmakers could repeal the ACA now and replace it later—a view that administration officials had stressed was not their preference and contrary to the view the president took earlier in the year, when he demanded that replacement accompany repeal.[65] He reiterated this view on July 17. On July 18, however, the president declared it was time to give up on trying to repeal the ACA and just let it fail. Later that morning he changed his mind yet again, calling for repealing the ACA. The next day Trump had another opinion, telling Republican senators, "People should not leave town unless we have a health insurance plan, unless we give our people great health care."[66]

On October 17, 2017, Republican senator Lamar Alexander and Democratic senator Patty Murray reached a deal to provide funding for subsidies to health insurers to reimburse them for discounts they were required to provide to millions of low-income people who had coverage under the ACA and that President Trump said that he would cut off. The president appeared to give his blessing to the agreement, saying he was aware of the deal and describing the effort as very close to a "short-term" solution. "The solution will be about a year or two years. And it will get us over this intermediate hump," Trump explained during a news conference.[67]

That evening he expressed a different view, however, declaring that "I continue to believe Congress must find a solution to the Obamacare mess instead of providing bailouts to insurance companies."[68] The next day, the president tweeted, "I am supportive of Lamar as a person & also of the process, but I can never support bailing out ins co's who have made a fortune w/ O'Care."[69] Nevertheless, the president later told reporters and Alexander that he was not closing the door on a deal. Speaking to journalists, Trump praised the bipartisan effort, saying, "If something can happen, that's fine, but I won't do anything to enrich the insurance companies." As two reporters put it, "For both sides, the president's conflicting signals have created a chaotic situation where even some of Trump's aides have found themselves scrambling to keep up with the latest developments."[70] Republican leaders said the only thing holding them back from a vote was the mixed messages from the president.[71] "There was a lot of momentum building for Lamar's effort, until the president changed his mind after encouraging him twice to move ahead," commented Republican senator Bob Corker. "You know, who knows where he'll be? Maybe where he is this very second?"[72]

DACA and Immigration

On September 5, 2017, Trump announced he was phasing out the DACA on the grounds that he lacked the power to establish such a program on his own. He gave Congress six months to fix the program before it expired. Later that day he used soft language to discuss his decision. "I have a great heart for the folks we're talking about, a great love for them," the president said of the Dreamers. "I have a love for these people. And hopefully now Congress will be able to help them and do it properly. . . . We have to be able to do something." Minutes later, the president returned to tough talk as he tweeted: "I look forward to working w/ D's + R's in Congress to address immigration reform in a way that puts hardworking citizens of our country 1st." Hours later, Trump tweeted again and seemed to offer yet another position: "Congress now has 6 months to legalize DACA. . . . If they can't, I will revisit this issue!"[73] By vowing to "revisit this issue," Trump inadvertently took Congress off the hook by appearing to suggest that if lawmakers could not agree, they need not worry because he might take action himself to protect the younger immigrants. Yet he had already argued earlier in the day that he did not have the power to do that.

The White House said it would insist that any immigration legislation protecting the Dreamers also include elements to strengthen enforcement, including, presumably, money for the wall along the Mexican border that Trump made a centerpiece of his presidency. However, on September 13, Trump's immigration policy advisor, Stephen Miller, told people that the administration would never allow a version of the replacement legislation, known as the Dream Act, to pass. Reversing yet again, that evening the president appeared to cut a deal with Charles Schumer and Nancy Pelosi to protect Dreamers from deportation and to enact border security measures that did not include building a physical wall. When word about deemphasizing the wall set off alarm bells among Trump's hardline immigration base, the White House responded the next day that there was, in fact, no deal. The president contradicted his spokesperson in a matter of hours, however. "The wall will come later," he said, adding that he was "fairly close" to a deal along the lines of what Pelosi and Schumer has announced.[74] There was, of course, no such deal.

Because of Republican pushback, whatever deal the president made with the Democratic leaders began to unravel. By September 14, the president clarified that he was not considering allowing Dreamers to become citizens, putting him at odds with Schumer and Pelosi, who believed he supported the idea. Equally important, Republican leaders, who were not part of the discussions, reminded everyone that any deal Trump reached with Democrats would still have to go through the Republican-controlled Congress. Senate Judiciary Committee chair Charles Grassley was irritated at being kept out of the loop and tweeted for Trump to have someone brief him. He also complained that Trump's moves "undercut" his own efforts to work with Democrats on immigration policy.[75] Republican senator Tom Cotton dismissed as "spin" the idea that Schumer and Pelosi had a deal with Trump. "There has to be a negotiation that occurs between the House and the Senate," he said.[76]

On December 29, 2017, Trump tweeted, "The Democrats have been told, and fully understand, that there can be no DACA without the desperately needed WALL at the Southern Border and an END to the horrible Chain Migration & ridiculous Lottery System of Immigration etc. We must protect our Country at all cost!" He repeated these demands in a tweet on January 4: "We must BUILD THE WALL, stop illegal immigration, end chain migration & cancel the visa lottery. The current system is unsafe & unfair to the great people of our country—time for change!" He reiterated his demands at various points over the following months.[77]

On the other hand, in a meeting with a bipartisan group of lawmakers on January 9, 2018, Trump signaled a willingness to sign any deal worked out between Democrats and Republicans. "I mean, I will be signing it. I'm not going to say, 'Oh, gee, I want this or I want that,'" he said. "I think my positions are going to be what the people in this room come up with," Trump said. "I am very much reliant on the people in this room." He even agreed to a bill on DACA with no conditions until House Majority

Leader Kevin McCarthy and Republican senator David Purdue explained what "a clean bill" meant. (When the White House released its official transcript of the meeting, the president's agreement was missing.) That afternoon, Trump clarified on Twitter that "Our country needs the security of the Wall on the Southern Border, which must be part of any DACA approval." During the meeting the president also offered a plan in which "We do a Phase 1, which is DACA and security, and we do Phase 2, which is comprehensive immigration." This position, of course, contradicted his previous demand for restrictions on legal immigration as part of any DACA deal.[78]

Also notable about the January 9 meeting was a four-page document summarizing the administration's "must haves" in an immigration bill provided by secretary of homeland security Kirstjen Nielsen. Trump told the bipartisan gathering that the document did not represent all of his positions, that he was not familiar with its contents, and that he did not appreciate being caught off-guard. He asked the group to disregard the summary.[79]

The next day, the president gave seemingly contradictory stances in a matter of seconds. He affirmed that he would be open to signing "just about any immigration deal," as a reporter put it, that lawmakers sent him. But asked if he would be willing to sign a deal that did not include funding for a border wall, he responded, "No, no, no, it's got to include the wall."[80]

Two days later, the president rejected a proposal to provide a pathway to citizenship for Dreamers and grew frustrated with lawmakers in the Oval Office when they discussed protecting immigrants from Haiti, El Salvador, and African countries as part of a bipartisan immigration deal. "Why are we having all these people from shithole countries come here?" Trump exclaimed. In addition, the president singled out Haiti, telling lawmakers that immigrants from that country must be left out of any deal. Trump had seemed amenable to a deal earlier in the day during phone calls with lawmakers, but shifted his position in the meeting and did not seem interested in the bipartisan compromise.[81]

It is not surprising that Trump's insulting language regarding black immigrants caused a firestorm of criticism and set back efforts to reach an agreement on immigration. As Senator Lindsey Graham exclaimed, "So Tuesday, we had a president that I was proud to golf with, call my friend, who understood immigration had to be bipartisan, you had to have border security. But he also understood the idea that we had to do it with compassion." Graham flung his arms apart and concluded: "Now I don't know where that guy went. I want him back."[82]

Adding to the confusion were comments by White House Chief of Staff John Kelly to congressional Democrats and then in a televised interview on January 17. Kelly said that some of President Trump's campaign promises on immigration were "uninformed" and that his position on a border wall had "evolved." "Certain things are said during the campaign that are not fully informed," Kelly explained.[83] In a series of Twitter posts the next day, Trump tweeted that his position had not changed, directly contradicting his own chief of staff. "The Wall is the Wall," he wrote. "It has never changed or evolved from the first day I conceived of it."[84]

On January 19, worried about being blamed for a government shutdown, Trump invited Charles Schumer to the White House. Over cheeseburgers in the president's private dining room just off the Oval Office, they discussed a comprehensive deal that would include an immigration component, keep the government open, provide disaster relief, and set budget caps. Schumer signaled he would be open to considering funding for Trump's border wall and providing more defense spending, but he wanted the president to agree to a five-day measure to keep the government open to give both sides time to negotiate something longer term. Republicans pressured Trump not to cut a deal, and John Kelly called Schumer to tell him that his immigration proposal was too liberal for the administration. Schumer wondered aloud to his members about what, exactly, had changed. "What happened to the President Trump who asked us to come up with a deal and promised that he would take heat for it?" Schumer asked on the Senate floor shortly after the government shutdown had begun at midnight on January 20, "What happened to that president? He backed off at the first sign of pressure."[85]

As part of the agreement to end the federal government shutdown of January 20–22, McConnell promised a "fair and open" immigration debate on the Senate floor. Matters took a downturn on January 23, however, when Schumer rescinded his offer to fully fund the president's border wall because of the president's rejection of the rest of the immigration package. The White House refused to even acknowledge that Schumer's offer was ever made, although Senate leaders on both sides of the aisle confirmed that it was. Trump responded by posting on Twitter that "Cryin' Chuck Schumer fully understands, especially after his humiliating defeat, that if there is no Wall, there is no DACA." In response to this confusion, Republican senator Lindsey Graham said he had a message for the administration. "To my friends at the White House: You've been all over the board. You haven't been a reliable partner, and the Senate is going to move. Please be constructive as we go forward. If you've got any ideas, let us know."[86]

The next day, the president made an unscheduled appearance at a briefing from a senior official detailing the administration's plans to stick to a restrictive immigration agenda. The president said he was open to a path to citizenship for the Dreamers—just days after rejecting a bipartisan plan with that as its centerpiece. Trump once again seemed to undercut his administration's message, telling reporters at the White House that he would allow the young immigrants to "morph into" citizens over a period of time.[87] The following day, however, he reiterated that the price for such relief for immigrants was Democratic support for the other aspects of his immigration proposal.[88] Trump later told congressional Republicans that his offer was meant to force Democrats into a political bind while showing Republicans were serious about a solution after years of inaction.[89]

On February 6, as the federal government faced another shutdown, the president revived his threat to shut down the federal government if Congress could not agree on a spending deal that tightened the nation's immigration laws—and to blame the Democrats. "If we have to shut it down because the Democrats don't want safety, let's shut it down," Trump proclaimed. Later, however, his press secretary explained that the president did not view the spending bill and immigration as "mutually exclusive," meaning that he would not necessarily precipitate a shutdown if Congress agreed on spending without meeting his demands on immigration.[90]

The government shut down for five and a half hours before the president signed a spending bill on February 9 that did not include immigration reform. On February 15, the Senate voted on four immigration bills to address the plight of those covered by DACA. Every single one failed to receive the sixty votes required to advance. The White House threatened to veto[91] the option that was the product of the broadest bipartisan compromise, with a fix for DACA and substantial border security funding but with minimal changes to legal immigration rules. It received fifty-four votes. Trump's preferred immigration plan—including a pathway to citizenship for Dreamers, $25 billion for a southern border wall, and substantial curtailment of family immigration and elimination of the diversity visa lottery program—received only thirty-nine votes, while sixty senators opposed it.

In March, the White House tried to revive discussions of immigration policy, offering three years of protections for current DACA permit holders in return for $25 billion in border wall funding. Democrats rebuffed the offer, asking for a pathway for citizenship to a broader population of about 1.8 million Dreamers. Trump would only support such a policy if he secured significant changes in legal immigration. Then the president asked for three years of wall funding and some increase in enforcement spending in return for three years of DACA protections. Again, he could not cut a deal.[92]

In the end, the president received only $1.6 billion for more than ninety miles of physical barriers along the border with Mexico, as well as related technology, a sum far short of the $25 billion he sought in order to construct the expansive border wall that he promised in his campaign for president. In fact, the appropriations bill passed on March 23 specifically stated that border funding was only permitted for "operationally effective designs deployed" as of May 5, 2017, "such as currently deployed steel board designs, that prioritize agent safety." It appeared to preclude building the wall prototypes Trump had been touting. "President Trump had an opportunity to deliver on two promises. One, build the wall. Two, to sign a 'bill of love' for dreamers. His desire to slash legal immigration and increase immigration enforcement makes delivering on these promises impossible," said Ali Noorani, the executive director of the National Immigration Forum. "To put it another way: Trump had two birds in hand; now he's got nothing."[93]

On May 9, 2018, a group of moderate House Republicans filed a discharge petition to force votes on legislation that included protections for Dreamers. This action plus the national controversy over the administration's highly unpopular policy of separating immigrant families at the border (see chapter 3) prompted Republican leaders to convene negotiations aimed at writing a consensus Republican bill that could pass the House to forestall passage of more liberal bipartisan bills that would pass with mostly Democratic votes.

On June 21, the House rejected by a 231–193 vote a hardline measure that would have significantly limited legal immigration, would not guarantee Dreamers a path to permanent legal residency, and included controversial enforcement measures such as the mandatory use of a worker verification program.

The alternative bill represented a more moderate approach, providing $25 billion for Trump's border wall, reducing legal immigration, offering a pathway to citizenship to Dreamers, and keeping migrant families together in detention centers. As of 4 p.m. on June 21, Trump was making calls to Capitol Hill and demanding that the House act.[94] In a last-ditch effort, he called Judiciary Committee chair Bob Goodlatte and told him he backed the second bill. Goodlatte delivered the president's message, but it did little to persuade opponents. Lacking the votes to pass the bill, House leaders delayed the vote.[95]

Despite his efforts to persuade House members to support immigration bills, the president undermined prospects for success in the House when he cast doubt on whether any Republican immigration legislation could pass the Senate. On the morning of June 21, he tweeted "What is the purpose of the House doing good immigration bills when you need 9 votes by Democrats in the Senate, and the Dems are only looking to Obstruct (which they feel is good for them in the Mid-Terms). Republicans must get rid of the stupid Filibuster Rule-it is killing you!"[96]

The tweet signaled to wavering House Republicans that the bills up for a vote were not going to make it into law—and therefore undermined any incentive for lawmakers to risk a conservative backlash by voting for the more moderate alternative. "Wow, this undermines getting undecided GOP members to support the compromise," tweeted Representative Ryan Costello.[97]

The mercurial chief executive added further to the leaders' burdens the next day when he tweeted, "Republicans should stop wasting their time on Immigration until after we elect more Senators and Congressmen/women in November." This communication hardly encouraged representatives to take risks to pass a bill. "We reached, I think, a good consensus, and suddenly we wake up to another tweet," lamented Representative Dennis Ross.[98]

Nevertheless, the House pressed forward with a vote on the more moderate bill. Hours before the vote on June 27, Trump fired off a tweet in all caps urging the chamber to pass the faltering legislation. "HOUSE REPUBLICANS SHOULD PASS THE STRONG BUT FAIR IMMIGRATION BILL . . . TODAY, EVEN THOUGH THE DEMS WON'T LET IT PASS IN THE SENATE. PASSAGE WILL SHOW THAT WE WANT STRONG BORDERS & SECURITY WHILE THE DEMS WANT OPEN BORDERS = CRIME. WIN!"[99] Later that afternoon, the legislation was soundly defeated, 301 to 121.

Three days later, Trump falsely claimed on Twitter that he had "never pushed the Republicans in the House to vote for" either bill.[100] On July 5, in the latest in an oscillating series of directives about how quickly law-makers should move on immigration, he was urging Congress to "FIX OUR INSANE IMMIGRATION LAWS NOW."[101]

The president also made inconsistent statements about executive ac-tions regarding immigration. He had argued for days that only Congress could solve the border crisis. When he instead bowed to pressure and is-sued an executive order reversing the family separation policy on June 20, Trump undermined the Republican effort to pass a bill.[102]

The battle over immigration reform reflects the president's inability to negotiate a deal—even when doing so would have yielded a signature domestic policy achievement and delivered the US-Mexico border wall he repeatedly promised during his campaign. Along the way, Trump demon-strated the vagueness, shifting positions, contradictory stances, and gen-eral unreliability as a negotiator that characterized his tenure. Moreover, the president hamstrung himself by insisting on provisions that could not attract enough support on Capitol Hill.

Government Shutdown, 2018–2019

On December 22, 2018, significant portions of the federal government shut down and remained that way for five weeks, the longest shutdown in American history. The shutdown was provoked by the White House and illustrates the legislative miscalculation and mismanagement of the administration and the ineptitude of Trump as a negotiator.

Following a familiar pattern, the president eschewed strategic planning and preparation in favor of day-to-day tactical maneuvering and trust-ing his gut.[103] Even before the shutdown, he lost significant negotiating leverage by declaring, "I am proud to shut down the government for bor-der security. I will take the mantle. I will be the one to shut it down."[104] This statement befuddled Republicans. "I don't understand the strategy, but maybe he's figured it out and he'll tell us in due course," said John Cornyn. "But I don't understand it."[105]

Then, the president dove into the fight with no clear endgame.[106] On December 16, the *Washington Post* reported that the White House had no plan to resolve the impasse. "That's me with my hands up in the air," said Cornyn. "There is no discernible plan—none that's been disclosed."[107]

There was little coordination with his party. Senate Majority Leader Mitch McConnell and House Speaker Paul Ryan left the Capitol at the beginning of the shutdown, neither making an effort to back up Trump with news conferences or votes that would demonstrate commitment to the cause, the normal course of action for the president's Capitol Hill allies in the periodic shutdowns since the Clinton administration. Republican leaders did not even convene conference calls of the rank and file to map out a strategy to defend Trump.[108]

The president found that his arsenal of bluster, falsehoods, threats, and theatrics were inadequate in negotiating with seasoned legislators. He met with Nancy Pelosi and Charles Schumer at the White House on December 11, 2018. What was supposed to be a private meeting ended up being partially televised, which Trump thought would be to his advantage. He called the leaders by their first names and did his best to bully and belittle them. He taunted Schumer, telling him, "You don't want to shut down the government, Chuck," referring to a brief shutdown in January 2018. "The last time you shut it down, you got killed."[109] Schumer was not moved.

Trump tried to undercut the Speaker's position by raising questions about her job security. "Nancy's in a situation where it's not easy for her to talk right now," he said, appearing to allude to Pelosi's struggle to garner the votes to be elected speaker. It did not work. "Please don't characterize the strength that I bring to this meeting as the leader of the House Democrats who just won a big victory," Pelosi shot back.

It is no secret that negotiations are best done in private. James Madison remembered that in writing the Constitution:

It was . . . best for the convention for forming the Constitution to sit with closed doors, because opinions were so various and at first so crude that it was necessary they should be long debated before any uniform system of opinion could be formed. Meantime the minds of the members were changing. . . . Had the members committed themselves publicly at first, they would have afterwards supposed consistency required them to maintain their ground, whereas by secret discussion no man felt himself obliged to retain his opinions any longer than he was satisfied of their propriety and truth, and was open to the force of argument. Mr. Madison thinks no Constitution would ever have been adopted by the convention if the debates had been public.[110]

Trump appears never to have learned this lesson. Indeed, he thought the meeting with Pelosi and Schumer went very well.[111]

The day after he delivered a prime-time Oval Office address on behalf of his position on building a border wall, Trump abruptly walked out of a private meeting with Democratic leaders at the White House. A "total waste of time," Trump fumed on Twitter, lending credence to Schumer's accusations that the president is prone to "temper tantrums" when he does not get his way.[112]

Two years of contradictory statements and actions had built up a profound distrust of the president as a negotiator, a feeling strengthened by the president's fluctuating positions on the shutdown. On December 18, White House press secretary Sarah Huckabee Sanders told Fox News that because the administration had a "number of different funding sources we could use" to pay for the wall, the administration would be willing to compromise over border security in the spending bills pending in Congress. "At the end of the day we don't want to shut down the government, we want to shut down the border," she said.[113]

Two days later, Trump said in a series of Twitter posts that he would continue to press Democrats for wall funding in the coming year, implying that he would sign an appropriations bill that did not include funds for a border wall. Later that day, in the face of criticism from his base, the president declared, "Any measure that funds the government must include border security." In an emergency meeting with House Republican leaders, he threatened to veto the Senate stopgap funding measure, overturning the plan they were patching together to avoid a shutdown.[114] Paul Ryan hastily canceled a planned news conference after he spoke by phone with Trump. At the same time, he was unsuccessfully working the phones trying to sell Republican senators on a plan to force red-state Democrats to vote for wall funding and avoid a shutdown.[115]

On December 21, the president tweeted a warning that a partial government shutdown "will last for a very long time" if Democrats did not vote funds for a border wall.[116] After the government shutdown began at midnight, he tweeted, "The Democrats now own the shutdown!"[117] contradicting his statement of ten days earlier.

Earlier in 2018, the Democrats offered Trump a deal to trade $25 billion in wall funding in exchange for protecting the Dreamers. Even Bernie Sanders said he would vote for wall funding. However, Trump, egged on by hardline foes of immigration, demanded Democrats also agree to deep cuts in legal immigration, at which they balked.[118] On January 2, 2019 the president rejected suggestions from Republican senators that negotiators revive the compromise that would twin border wall money with legislation to shield Dreamers.[119] Yet on January 19, the president gave an address offering temporary protection for Dreamers and temporary protected status for immigrants from some Latin American and African nations in exchange for funding for the wall.

On January 2, in a meeting with Democratic leaders, Trump rejected their offer to temporarily fund agencies while negotiating over a border wall, saying "I would look foolish if I did that."[120] On January 25, that is exactly the deal he accepted.

The president also vacillated between threatening to declare a national emergency on December 18, January 10, and January 24, and professing to prefer a negotiated deal with Democrats on January 4 and 11.[121] When he announced a deal to reopen the government on January 25, he added, "If we don't get a fair deal from Congress, the government will either shut down on February 15, or I will use the powers afforded to me under the laws and Constitution of the United States to address this emergency."[122] Acting White House chief of staff Mick Mulvaney reiterated the point two days later on *Fox News Sunday*.

Democrats expressed doubt that the president could be trusted to stick with any deal he made. Senate Democratic Whip Richard Durbin pointed to a round of immigration negotiations with the White House a year earlier. At more than one point, Democrats thought they had a deal with Trump to provide some wall funding in exchange for giving legal status to some undocumented immigrants—only to have him reject it in public.

Even Republicans were sympathetic. Mitch McConnell complained to allies about how unreliable the president was as a negotiator, as well as how he listened to unproductive forces.[123] With a lack of clarity from the White House, even the president's copartisans were unsure what he would accept to end the standoff. Lindsey Graham told reporters, "Democrats keep saying, 'We don't trust it until Trump will sign it. That's not an unreasonable request." "It's always difficult when the person you're negotiating with is someone who changes their mind," added Republican senator John Cornyn.[124] In what the president must have found a galling statement, Senator Lamar Alexander published an op-ed urging Trump to emulate Barack Obama in negotiating with Democrats to end the shutdown and secure funding for a border wall.[125]

"It's very difficult to be successful if there's not predictability, reliability, and trust," said Phil Schiliro, who served as President Obama's legislative affairs chief in his first term. "For there to be a successful negotiation and for people to move off the position they came in with, members want to know that there's going to be closure and agreement and cover at the end of the day."[126]

Equally damaging to his credibility, Trump dispatched aides to negotiate with lawmakers, only to undercut their offers. The president repeatedly undermined Vice President Pence, to whom he delegated the task of negotiating an end to the stalemate. On December 19, the Senate unanimously passed a short-term spending bill without border wall funding to avert a government shutdown. John Cornyn said he and every other senator believed the president would sign the bill, acting on private assurances from Pence. The vice president said he told senators the president was undecided, but that is not how they remembered it.[127]

In December, Pence floated the idea to Democrats of splitting the difference and appropriating $2.5 billion for wall funding. Trump publicly rejected the idea on January 2.[128] Indeed, even as Pence and Mick Mulvaney were relaying the proposal to Democrats shortly after the shutdown began, a senior administration official was holding a briefing call with reporters stating that the president would accept no less than $5 billion.[129] On January 10, the vice president stated that the president would not accept a deal trading wall funding for the protection of Dreamers. Later in the day, Trump said he would indeed consider such a compromise.[130]

This seemingly capricious behavior confirmed the concerns of Democratic leaders that they could not trust senior White House officials to broker any compromise that would not then be rejected by a mercurial president who had often shifted his position at the last moment.[131] When the shutdown ended, Nita Lowey, chair of the House Appropriations Committee and a leader in the subsequent talks over border security, wondered, "Is this going to be a Trump negotiation, negotiated in good faith, or is he going to say one thing through his advisors and another when he hears from Rush Limbaugh and Ann Coulter?" "I'm an appropriator; I'm used to making deals," Lowey said, but also added, "I don't know how this negotiation is going to go."[132]

On January 24, the Senate voted on two bills to reopen the government. One included funds for Trump's border wall. Neither mustered the sixty votes required for passage, but the Trump-backed bill received only fifty votes, while six Republican senators supported the Democratic option, which won fifty-two votes. Other Republicans privately voiced frustration with Vice President Pence and Senate Majority Leader McConnell during a contentious closed-door luncheon.[133]

The news was filled with reports of slowdowns at airports, degradation of national parks, delays in tax refunds, and an FBI director angrily decrying agents working without pay and others not being allowed to work at all. There were also hardship stories of government employees lining up at food banks and working without pay—and the administration's lack of empathy for them. Consumer confidence in the economy was falling, as were the president's approval ratings. As we saw in chapter 4, the public blamed Trump for the shutdown and supported neither his border wall nor his rationale for it. Meanwhile, Nancy Pelosi refused to issue an invitation for him to deliver his State of the Union address.

Frustrated and eager to deliver his address,[134] on January 25, the president bit the bullet and agreed to reopen the government for three weeks while negotiations continued over border security. After the longest government shutdown in history, Trump surrendered with nothing to show for the battle, taking essentially the same deal that he rejected in December.

The president did his best to cover himself. Cabinet officers and White House aides lined up and applauded when the president emerged from the Oval Office as if he were claiming victory in his confrontation with the Democrats in Congress. Speaking in the Rose Garden, he declared he was "very proud to announce today that we have reached a deal to end the shutdown."[135]

Supporters of a border wall were not fooled, excoriating Trump for caving to the Democrats. "Good news for George Herbert Walker Bush: As of today, he is no longer the biggest wimp ever to serve as President of the United States," Ann Coulter tweeted.[136] Breitbart ran the banner headline: "Government Open . . . And Border. No Wall." The *Daily Caller* was more succinct in its headline: "TRUMP CAVES." According to The *Washington Examiner*, "Trump blinks."[137] Nevertheless, right after the shutdown ended, only 37 percent of the public wanted Trump and Republicans to keep working to fund the border wall.

Peter Wehner, a senior fellow at the conservative Ethics and Public Policy Center who worked for presidents Ronald Reagan, George H. W. Bush, and George W. Bush, tweeted that "In the showdown with Nancy Pelosi, Trump's been exposed as pitifully weak, all bluster, a pathetic negotiator. Pelosi rolled him in every way. Egged on by right wingers, the whole thing was buffoonish from start to finish. *This* is how Trump's Art of the Deal works in real life."[138]

Trump had put himself in an untenable position. We saw in chapter 4 how unpopular the president, the shutdown, and the border wall were. If he had maintained the shutdown, he would have likely fallen further in the polls. If he had struck a deal with the Democrats, it would not have been a good one, as they had a stronger bargaining position. The public opposed the president declaring a national emergency to build the wall. Any competent public official should have foreseen the weakness of his bargaining position. As Nate Silver summarized the politics of the shutdown:

It's been obvious the whole time that it was liable to end in political (if not also literal) disaster. Trump was an unpopular president using an unpopular technique to push for an unpopular policy, and he was doing it just after Republicans had lost 40 seats to Democrats in the midterm elections while Trump tried to scaremonger voters on immigration. I can certainly think of lapses in presidential judgment that were more consequential in hindsight than the shutdown, but not all that many that were so obvious in advance.[139]

As Congress negotiated a budget in the three-week period after the deal to end the shutdown, Nancy Pelosi said she would be willing to endorse any bipartisan border security agreement that emerged from House-Senate negotiations. She also told Pence that she hoped the White House would adhere to "the same hands-off policy" and let the bipartisan group of House and Senate lawmakers reach agreement without Trump's interference.[140] Asked whether it would help if Trump stayed out of it and let lawmakers negotiate among themselves, Republican senator Shelley Moore Capito laughed and replied, "That would be nice."[141]

Surveillance

In 2008, Congress modified the Foreign Intelligence Surveillance Act (FISA) to legalize warrantless surveillance of foreigners abroad, even if they were talking to Americans. A bipartisan group of lawmakers, which included some of the most conservative and most liberal members of the House, proposed requiring officials to obtain court warrants before hunting for and reading private e-mails and other messages of Americans that were swept up by the program that targeted foreigners' communications in counterterror and espionage cases. Their goal was to uphold Fourth Amendment privacy rights in light of twenty-first-century communications technology and surveillance powers. The House was to vote on the proposal on January 11, 2018.

The Trump administration and Republican House leaders opposed the change, arguing that it would impede efforts to protect the country. On January 10, the White House press secretary issued a statement asking that lawmakers to vote against the amendment. However, on the morning of January 11, Trump's Twitter post seemed to encourage representatives to support limiting the law. It appears that the president sent his tweet shortly after Fox News analyst Andrew Napolitano gave his support to the bill on *Fox & Friends*. Napolitano appealed directly to the president to support the bill, reminding Trump that his "woes" began with surveillance. In his tweet, the president quoted verbatim the Fox headline from Napolitano's appearance and suggested that the FISA law had been used by the Obama administration to "so badly surveil and abuse the Trump Campaign."[142]

The tweet enraged Republican leaders on Capitol Hill and left leaders in both parties and the president's staff scrambling to secure votes. Paul Ryan spent thirty minutes on the phone with the president, explaining the differences between domestic and foreign surveillance, as many fellow Republicans reacted in disbelief and befuddlement. White House Chief of Staff John Kelly also directly intervened with Trump, reiterating the program's importance. The president issued a correction 101 minutes after the initial tweet, stating that "today's vote is about foreign surveillance of foreign bad guys on foreign land. We need it! Get smart!"[143]

CHIP

With a possible government shutdown looming on January 19, 2018, House Republican leaders were pressuring Democrats to vote for a stopgap spending bill, arguing that opposing it would effectively block a six-year extension of the Children's Health Insurance Program (CHIP) that was attached to the bill as a sweetener for lawmakers in both parties. On January 17, the Trump administration released an official statement endorsing the measure, including the extension of funding for CHIP. The next day, however, the president took to Twitter to say that CHIP should not be included in any short-term spending bill.

Trump did not seem to fully grasp just how problematic his CHIP tweet was for his own party. He may not have understood that CHIP itself was receiving a long term extension, even as the spending bill appropriated funds in the short term. Minutes after tweeting his criticism, Trump spoke by phone with Mitch McConnell. Trump praised the Republican bill, did not resist when McConnell explained his plan to forge ahead with it, and made no mention of his tweet. Trump also reassured Paul Ryan that he liked the bill as it was. The whole episode left congressional leaders puzzled: Why, they wondered, would the president tweet something negative about their legislation and rattle Republican lawmakers without ever raising concerns with them—and then act as if nothing had happened?[144] "We don't have a reliable partner at the White House to negotiate with," complained Senator Lindsey Graham.[145]

Gun Control

Following a mass shooting in Parkland High School in Florida, in a televised meeting in the Cabinet Room, the president embraced a set of gun
control measures, including expanding background checks, keeping guns
from the mentally ill, securing schools, and restricting gun sales from
some young adults.[146] It was soon clear, however, that the White House
would not really be pushing these proposals.

In the summer of 2019, two mass shootings once again raised the salience
of gun control. Immediately after the shootings, the president opened the
door to expanded background checks and other proposals to keep guns
away from unstable people and elicited a promise from Mitch McConnell
to engage in talks about potential legislation. He expressed confidence that
he could rally recalcitrant Republicans around legislation strengthening
background checks and persuade the nation's powerful gun lobby to drop
its long-standing opposition to such measures, tasks that had proved elusive
following other mass shootings on his watch. Trump acknowledged that
previous efforts to strengthen background checks "went nowhere." "But
there's never been a president like President Trump," he boasted. "I have a
great relationship with the Republican senators, and I really think they're—
they're looking for me to make—give them a signal," Trump declared.[147]

Indeed they were, but the president's signals were confusing and contradictory. After talking to NRA chief executive Wayne LaPierre, the
president backed away from his position, arguing that there were sufficient background checks in place and the focus should instead be on mental health. Then the president muddled the issue yet again on August 21.
"I have an appetite for background checks," he told reporters. "We'll be
doing background checks. We're working with Democrats. We're working
with Republicans."[148] In the end, nothing happened at all on gun control.

Budget

The budget is a key presidential document, typically setting forth both the
president's priorities and his approach to fiscal policy. Trump's budgets
did neither. What the Office of Management and Budget sent to Congress
did not really reflect the president's policies, because he delegated an unprecedented level of discretion to his budget directors. It is not surprising that Congress felt free to ignore proposals for steep cuts in the State
Department, the EPA, medical research, public broadcasting, and a wide

array of other domestic programs. No more unexpected was the disconnect between the proposed slashes in domestic spending and the spending bill the president signed in March 2018. When it came to obvious differences between budget projections and anticipated tax cuts, OMB director Mick Mulvaney was clear. "I wouldn't take what's in the budget as indicative of what our proposals are," he admitted.[149]

Trade

Farm-state Republicans, concerned about the damage the administration's trade policies would do to their states, were pleased following a White House meeting in which the president told them he would reconsider his decision to abandon a Pacific Rim trade deal that would benefit their farmers. However, Trump soon made clear through Twitter and his top aides that he had little interest in reengaging in the Trans-Pacific Partnership trade pact—despite what he told the lawmakers. "No. Did he do that?" sarcastically asked Pat Roberts, chair of the Senate Committee on Agriculture, Nutrition, and Forestry, in response to a question about Trump's recent reversal on TPP. "I thought we had him lassoed pretty tight on that." Other senators who attended the meeting expressed frustration at the conflicting signals from the president. "The question you always have coming out of a meeting over there is, is the same position going to be true tomorrow?" lamented Republican senator John Thune.[150]

War Powers

In January 2020, the House was set to vote to repeal the authorization for use of military force that Congress passed before the invasion of Iraq in 2003. Trump at first appeared to give Republicans permission to support the measure. On January 29, he tweeted, "I want everyone, Republican and Democrat, to vote their HEART!" By the evening, however, he reversed his stance, tweeting that the repeal was an attempt by Nancy Pelosi to "take away authority Presidents use to stand up to other countries and defend AMERICANS." "Stand with your Commander in Chiefs!" the president ordered.[151]

Professional Reputation

Richard Neustadt famously wrote that one of the president's most important sources of influence was his professional reputation. By that, he meant that other power holders believe the president has the skill and will to use his advantages. As he put it:

> The men who share in governing do what they think they must. A president's effect on them is heightened or diminished by their thoughts about his probable reaction to their doing. And they base their expectations on what they see of him. And they are watching all the time.[152]

Although he routinely touted his skill as a dealmaker, Donald Trump had a weak professional reputation. His vague, inconsistent, uninformed, and impulsive stances undermined the ability of members of Congress to anticipate his reactions. He repeatedly backed down from his positions once he came under pressure. Some of the policy proposals he floated, such as his family separation policy at the border and his threats to close the border entirely, involved administrative discretion. Often he was unclear or changed his mind about legislative matters. It is normal bargaining strategy to maintain uncertainty about the specifics of the deal one will ultimately accept. However, confusion caused by ambiguity, and especially inconsistency, did not serve President Trump well in his relations with Congress.

In his business dealings, Trump's negotiating protocol typically prioritized "take it or leave it offers." That strategy assumes that negotiators can always turn to other bargaining partners to make a different deal. In real estate, for example, Trump liked to keep several balls in the air "because most deals fall out."[153] Unlike business transactions, in which there are many possible deals with many possible partners, the president has no alternative but to deal with Congress. Republican Darrell Issa of California said few members of Congress feared permanent retaliation from the president. "He comes from the private sector, where your business partner today isn't always your business partner tomorrow," Issa said. In Washington, "Just because you're one way today doesn't mean you're written off."[154] Members of Congress understood this fact of legislative life, even if the president did not.

Selling

On the stump, Trump boasted that he could make deals better than anyone else, sometimes pointing to his book, *The Art of the Deal*, as evidence of his expertise. He and his aides assured the public that he was "the closer." But when it came to repealing and replacing Obamacare, he faltered. He never tried to deal with the Democrats, and he never failed to lambast them for their lack of support. Equally important, he found it difficult to convince fellow Republicans to support the option of the moment.

It is not that he did not try. By the time House Republican leaders pulled their rewrite of Obamacare from consideration in late March 2017, Trump had personally lobbied 120 lawmakers, either in person or on the phone. According to White House press secretary Sean Spicer, the president "left everything on the field."[155] He even kept an open phone line just off the House floor in case someone needed last-minute arm twisting. As he told the entire Republican House contingent, "I am in with White House waiting if anybody needs anybody, if anybody wants to see me, you guys just let me know."[156]

Trump endeavored to cajole and charm members of Congress into support. He invited senators and representatives to the White House for bowling, gave others rides on Air Force One, and grinned for pictures with dozens of members in the Oval Office. There were East Room meetings, evening dinners, and lunches. In all of these settings, the president was happy to remind lawmakers of his margins of victory in their districts and his popularity among the Republican base. Trump was also candid in stating his view that not supporting the bill would be an act of betrayal,[157] and he gave reassurances that he would be responsive to members' concerns.[158]

As political scientists now know, schmoozing does not take the president far.[159] Among the lawmakers Trump courted most intensely on health care was Mark Meadows, the chair of the House Freedom Caucus. Trump brought him to the Oval Office, called him regularly, and directed White House chief strategist Stephen K. Bannon to call or text him daily. He even brought him to Mar-a-Lago, his private club in Florida, to discuss the bill. According to Meadows, "If this was about personalities, we'd already be at 'yes.' He's charming, and anyone who spends time with him knows that. But this is about policy, and we're not going to make it about anything else." Similarly, Representative Leonard Lance recollected, "He's got this wit about him that I enjoy, but I'm a 'no' vote." Trump called Dave Brat of Virginia. "C'mon, Brat, what's going on with this thing?" Trump asked. Recollected Brat, "He puts on the hard sell. . . . Humor, heart, personality." Trump ended the call with a plea: "Dave, c'mon, we're going to get it right." But Brat was unmoved.[160]

Trump was more successful with Joe Barton of Texas and Gary Palmer of Alabama, however.[161] Yet when he delivered an ultimatum to lawmakers to approve the measure, or reject it and he would move on to his other legislative priorities,[162] the leadership had to pull the bill for lack of support.[163] It was not until the House Republican leadership modified its bill that it was able to win on a 217–213 vote.

When the Senate took up health care, Republican leader Mitch McConnell made it known that he preferred to limit Trump's involvement to being an encourager, not a dealmaker. He and other senators preferred to negotiate with Vice President Pence than with Trump or his top lieutenants.[164] Trump and his aides left it to McConnell to take the lead in crafting the legislation and in figuring out how to persuade hesitant senators.[165]

Eventually, the president reached out to a few reluctant conservatives like Senators Mike Lee, Ted Cruz, and Rand Paul. Yet he became an active participant only when it became clear that Republican leaders were postponing a vote until after the summer recess. At McConnell's request, Trump summoned all fifty-two Republican senators to the White House for some last-ditch diplomacy and to show senators that the White House was fully engaged.[166] At this meeting the president issued some new threats (discussed in the next chapter), but they seemed to have little effect. A last-minute call to John McCain before the final vote was no more successful.[167]

When the Senate tried to pass a health care bill again in September, Trump fared no better. Senator Susan Collins delivered a scathing assessment of the bill in a statement, saying the fourth version that the senators had produced in an effort to win new votes "is as deeply flawed as the previous iterations." The senator said the administration had lobbied her hard to endorse the bill—and she received a call from the president himself.[168] Nevertheless, she refused to support the bill.

Occasionally the president also offered specific benefits. He called Senator Charles Grassley, chair of the Senate Judiciary Committee, to assure him that he supported ethanol-related matters such as subsidies and renewable fuel standards. These issues were not on the agenda of the Senate, but Grassley was about to interview the president's son as part of his committee's Russia probe. The senator seemed pleased to receive the president's pledges.[169]

Apparently, many members of Congress used Trump's overtures to seek particularistic favors, such as visiting with their families or dining with their wives. The president said that Luther Strange was the only Republican senator who did not solicit a personal favor when the president lobbied them for their votes to repeal the Affordable Care Act.[170]

Throughout Congress's consideration of health care, the president displayed one important disadvantage. He could not speak fluently about the details of the various bills before the House and Senate. He focused his case in purely transactional terms, on the political risks (losing electoral support) and rewards (winning support) of passage, and treaded gingerly on the actual provisions of the legislation.[171] For members of Congress interested in substance, and we have seen that there were many, Trump's arguments were unconvincing. Senators' and representatives' positions on major issues of public policy are generally cemented by core principles, and principles are less susceptible to transactions such as increasing the appropriation for a policy to compensate for restricting immigration.

Perhaps recognizing this dynamic and frustrated at his inability to deal, Trump raised the possibility of reinstating earmarks to grease the wheels of coalition building. "You know, our system lends itself to not getting things done," he told a bipartisan group of lawmakers in January 2018. "I hear so much about earmarks, the old earmark system, how there was a great friendliness when you had earmarks." "They went out to dinner at night, and they all got along, and they passed bills. That was an earmark system. And maybe we should think about it." Republicans, however, opposed the idea, which went nowhere.[172]

Trump's lack of success in selling policy was not limited to health care. As we have seen, the president made a series of pleas and demands for support for immigration bills, all of which failed to win majority support. Individual calls for support did no better.[173] On May 17, 2018, the president tweeted his support for the House farm bill, writing, "Tomorrow, the House will vote on a strong Farm Bill, which includes work requirements. We must support our Nation's great farmers!"[174] The bill failed on a vote of 198–213 as a result of conservative Republican opposition.

Even on taxes, where Republicans displayed more unity than on immigration, the president's efforts were not always appreciated. As Republican Bob Corker put it, "I would just like him to leave it to the professionals for a while and see if we can do something that's constructive."[175] Similarly, Democratic leader Charles Schumer said the key to getting things done on Capitol Hill was for the president to take a back seat.[176] Thus, Republicans kept Trump away from the tax negotiations as long as they could, with positive results.[177] Mitch McConnell consulted regularly with the president about the influence he could apply on wavering members—or those of whom he should steer clear.[178] Trump made some phone calls but was not involved in cobbling the bill together. When he visited the Capitol near the end of the process, his talk was mostly off point.[179]

Nevertheless, the president was a relentless salesman, cajoling Republican senators on the golf course and on Capitol Hill, giving Democratic senators rides on Air Force One, calling fierce critics such as John McCain to find common cause, deploying his daughter Ivanka, and tweeting continuously to generate enthusiasm. He paid a lot of attention to Ron Johnson and Susan Collins, who had qualms about parts of the bill.[180]

Yet, there were problems with his efforts to persuade Democrats. In a bipartisan meeting with members of the Senate Finance Committee at the White House, the president joked with Ron Wyden, the committee's ranking Democrat: "I'm sure we'll have unanimous support. I have no doubt, right? Right, Ron? I think. Right?" Senators chuckled. Once the press corps left the room, however, there was an immediate disconnect between Trump and some of the Democrats. Robert Casey told the president, "It's good to have this meeting, but I have to tell you, this plan, in my judgment, is a giveaway to the rich." Casey said he and other Democrats there wanted to make clear to Trump that bipartisan support could not be willed by the president's liveliness. It had to be carefully negotiated. As the meeting wrapped up, Trump vaguely warned that he might hound senators who voted against the bill by visiting their states and rallying against them ahead of the midterm elections. "He said if those people didn't support a tax cut, it could be pretty tough," recalled Casey.[181]

Democrats were confused about what the tax cuts would be. In early October 2017, Senator Heidi Heitkamp told constituents that the emerging White House plan seemed to be the kind of bill she would support. "I've met with the president's people four or five times now, and they've told me, no, this really is going to be a middle-class tax cut," Heitkamp said. Ten days later, however, Heitkamp told reporters that the administration's plan remained a mystery, lamenting that "I still don't know what it is."[182] The fundamental problem was that Trump did not know the details of the plan himself. In the end, no Democrat voted for the tax plan.

A crucial part of selling a policy is obtaining the public's backing. We saw in chapter 4 that the president was not successful in expanding public support for his initiatives. Although he did make some inroads among Republicans on immigration, even these modest gains did little to encourage congressional support within his party.

The White House made an effort to ensure that candidates Trump backed in 2018 were loyal to his policies.[183] Trump's support was valuable in the primaries, and he campaigned aggressively for Republicans in the general election. Nevertheless, he could not maintain a Republican majority in the House. Although the president was active in support of Republican Senate candidates in the midterm general elections, making dozens of appearances on their behalf, almost all in states with competitive contests, research has found that this activity had little or no impact on either voter turnout or on the performance of Republican candidates in these races.[184] In October and November 2018, he campaigned in only two states he did not win in 2016: Nevada and Illinois. Democrats picked up a Senate seat and a governor's mansion in those states, respectively.[185] The losses in the 2018 midterm elections did little to encourage congressional Republicans to defer to the White House's wishes.

Impeachment was different, however. Republicans remained solidly in support of the president. The firm support of the Republican base for Trump no doubt encouraged such loyalty. Taking no chances, however, White House outreach went into overdrive. Acting White House chief of staff Mick Mulvaney and other top officials hosted weekend getaways for Republicans at Camp David. The White House also included Republican lawmakers when the president attended sporting events, including the Ultimate Fighting Championship in New York, the World Series in Washington, and a football game in Tuscaloosa, Alabama. During the impeachment inquiry, the White House also invited a group of Republican senators to have lunch with Trump every Thursday, had other members of Congress to dinner, and invited some of them to movie nights in the East Wing. In all these settings, the conversations were low-key. The goal was to create goodwill and make it more difficult for members to vote to impeach or convict the president. By November 22, 2019, Trump had met with or reached out personally to one hundred House Republicans since the impeachment inquiry was launched, and fifty of the fifty-three Senate Republicans had attended a White House lunch[186]

A short while later, the coronavirus pandemic hit the United States. In March 2020, Congress passed a coronavirus relief bill that included free coronavirus testing, an increase in family medical leave, paid sick leave, and unemployment insurance, and increased spending on health insurance for the poor and food programs for children and the elderly. Trump pushed for a suspension of payroll taxes through the end of the year. In a tweet on March 13, he said such a cut was essential to any recovery package. "Only that will make a big difference!" he wrote.[187] Both Republicans and Democrats were cool to the idea, however, and it went nowhere. Negotiations did not involve the president. Instead, Nancy Pelosi dealt with treasury secretary Steven Mnuchin.[188] Ultimately, Trump endorsed the legislation, which passed without the president's tax cut but with bi-partisan backing.

Conclusion

Despite his claims, Donald Trump was not an effective negotiator, nor could he make a sale and close a deal. His passivity, vagueness, inconsistency, and lack of command of policy made him an unskilled, unreliable, and untrustworthy negotiator. He was no more successful in closing deals and convincing wavering members to support him. Ann Coulter termed him "the worst negotiator God ever created," and suggest he add a chapter to *The Art of the Deal* entitled "How to Give Up Everything in Return for Nothing."[189] In the next chapter I focus on the president's approach to bipartisanship and party leadership, including his unusual use of threats and criticism. I also examine Trump's success in winning congressional support.

CHAPTER EIGHT

At the Margins

D onald Trump came to office with an ambitious agenda for policy change, most of which required legislative approval. To obtain congressional support, he employed a variety of strategies for governing. One approach centered on creating opportunities for change in Congress by appealing to the public. We saw in chapter 2 that there was little prospect for such a strategy to succeed, in chapter 3 that he was not a skilled communicator, and in chapter 4 that, indeed, his efforts failed. The president found it difficult to move the public. Nevertheless, he enjoyed the advantage of support among rank-and-file Republicans.

Aside from moving the public, there are two other presidential strategies for governing in Congress: obtaining bipartisan support and leading one's own party. These strategies are not necessarily mutually exclusive, and most presidents try both. Although senators and representatives of the president's party usually form the core of his governing coalition, the White House often has no choice but to seek additional votes from the opposition.

This chapter focuses on the president's approach to bipartisan and party leadership. On the one hand, Trump followed traditional patterns of working closely with Republican leaders and soliciting the votes of Democrats. Yet, he could not resist his combative urges. Machiavelli said it is better for a leader to be feared than loved, and the president took this advice to heart. He told the *Washington Post*, "Real power is—I don't even want to use the word: 'fear.'"[1] It is not surprising, then, that he frequently—and publicly—disparaged and threatened members of Congress, including Republicans.[2]

Bipartisanship?

The Framers created a deliberative democracy that requires and encourages reflection and refinement of the public's views through an elaborate decision-making process. Those opposed to change need only win at one point in the policymaking process—say in obtaining a presidential veto—whereas those who favor change must win every battle along the way. To win all these conflicts usually requires the support of a sizable majority of the country, not just a simple majority of 51 percent. As a result, the Madisonian system calls for moderation and compromise.

The principal mechanism for overcoming the purposefully inefficient form of government established by the Constitution is the extraconstitutional institution of political parties. Representatives and senators of the president's party are almost always the nucleus of coalitions supporting the president's programs. Thus, parties help overcome the fractures of shared powers. Yet, unless one party controls both the presidency and Congress and has very large majorities in both houses of Congress, little is likely to be accomplished without compromise.

When parties are broad, there is potential for compromise, because there will be some ideological overlap among members. When the parties are unified and polarized, however, they exacerbate conflict and immobilize the system. Critical issues such as immigration, environmental protection, taxation, and budgeting go unresolved. We expect political parties in a parliamentary system to take clear stands and vigorously oppose each other. Such a system usually works because the executive comes from the legislature and can generally rely on a supportive majority to govern. Partisan polarization has given the United States parliamentary-style political parties operating in a system of shared powers, virtually guaranteeing gridlock. Moreover, minority interests that want to stop change are likely to win, raising troubling questions about the nature of our democracy.

For the US system to work, then, there must be a favorable orientation toward compromise. Such a temperament is found in the very roots of the nation. Recalling the events of the Philadelphia Constitutional Convention, James Madison observed that "the minds of the members were changing" throughout the convention, in part due to a "yielding and accommodating spirit" that prevailed among the delegates.[3]

Because presidents typically require substantial support from the opposition party to pass significant legislation, bipartisanship is a central concern for the White House.[4] Of course, divided government magnifies the president's need for bipartisan support. However, polarization diminishes the likelihood of receiving it.[5] After analyzing Trump's prospects for success in winning bipartisan support in chapter 6, I predicted there was little chance of obtaining it for his core initiatives.

A bipartisan strategy put strains on both sides. The White House knew it was unlikely to receive much support from the Democrats, and the president complained frequently about his frustrations with them. Nevertheless, the president had no option but to try to win over some Democrats. A key question is how well he handled the challenge.

High Points

We saw in chapter 7 that the president made little attempt to engage Democrats on his failed effort to pass health care legislation. By September 2017, he had no choice but to turn to the opposition party.

The government once again approached the debt limit. In July, Steve Mnuchin told Congress that the limit would be hit in late September, and that he was implementing extraordinary measures to keep the government afloat. Negotiations between the White House and Congress broke down in August, with Trump criticizing Republican leaders Paul Ryan and Mitch McConnell for creating "a mess" with the debt ceiling.[6] Debt limit negotiations were further complicated when the president threatened to veto spending bills and cause a government shutdown if Congress did not appropriate funds for a border wall with Mexico.[7]

Administration officials sent mixed signals, with Mnuchin supporting a "clean" debt limit increase that had no other language, but OMB director Mick Mulvaney insisted that the increase should be tied to spending cuts. Although he quickly backed off that position, congressional conservatives saw it as an opening to push for policy concessions (as they did in 2011 and 2013).[8] Other congressional Republicans wanted to tie a debt ceiling vote to other pressing matters, such as disaster relief in response to damage caused by Hurricane Harvey.

Republican leaders had been planning to tie Harvey aid to a bill to raise the debt ceiling for at least eighteen months (since after the November 2018 midterm elections). Democrats offered to extend the debt ceiling and budget fight for three months and revisit it in December. Paul Ryan called that proposal "ridiculous and disgraceful." He also noted, "What the President doesn't want to do is to give more leverage where it shouldn't occur on the debt ceiling." Nevertheless, Trump made a snap decision to accept the Democrats' deal—much to the surprise and irritation of members of his own party—and the humiliation of Ryan.[9] Knowing that the president was more popular with Republican voters than they were, Republican leaders had no choice but to get on board.

Democrats believed that extending the debt limit and budget decisions into December would increase their leverage to win concessions from Republicans on spending, immigration, and health care issues. Conservatives agreed, which is why they opposed the deal. The short-term extensions for the debt ceiling and government funding also meant that the issues would continue for months, just as Republicans were hoping to coalesce around a plan to cut taxes. Apparently, the president was thinking of tax policy himself but had a different view. "We believe that helping to clear the decks in September enables us to focus on tax reform," White House director of legislative affairs Marc Short told reporters. "I think it puts pressure on all of us to get tax reform done before December."[10] Setting aside his opposition to the deal, Mnuchin agreed.[11]

The debt ceiling deal was the first time Trump reached across the aisle to resolve a major dispute. After weeks of criticizing Republican leaders for failing to pass legislation, the president signaled that he was willing to cross party lines to score some much-desired legislative victories. His meeting with the House and Senate Democratic leaders was the first time he had seen Senator Charles Schumer in person since shortly after his inauguration in January. Since then, they had spoken by phone only once or twice.[12]

Nevertheless, the bipartisan deal was not the result of a sudden change of heart. If the president wanted to manage the debt ceiling, keep the government open, and pass aid for the victims of Hurricane Harvey, he had no choice but to deal with the Democrats. Republicans would not give Trump what he wanted, so they were in no position to drive a hard bargain and had to cede power to the minority. As Representative Mark Walker, chair of the Republican Study Committee, remarked, "If Republicans won't work with the president . . . then maybe he goes and finds somebody who's willing to."[13]

The Democrats understood the situation well. House Minority Leader Nancy Pelosi summed it up clearly: "Here the currency of the realm is the vote. You have the votes, no discussion necessary. You don't have the votes, three months."[14] "If they had the votes, we wouldn't have been having the meeting. The clarity of that situation I think the president was fully aware of." The Democrats went into the meeting with the president prepared to deliver the votes he needed, but on their terms.[15] He had no option but to accept.

Congressional Republicans were less obliging. Stung by the president's deal, Mitch McConnell argued that the short-term waiver of the debt ceiling preserved the treasury's ability to apply "extraordinary measures" and shift money within government accounts to pay off debt and extend federal borrowing power, delaying the need for another increase in the debt limit well beyond December. Thus, he claimed, the Democrats would lose their leverage at the time Congress needed to pass the spending bill, including further hurricane relief, and Republicans could vote for spending without also voting to raise the debt limit. Democrats responded that the Republicans would still need their votes for the spending bill, giving them leverage over it and other issues such as immigration and health care. Moreover, separating the spending and debt bills would give the Democrats a second round of opportunity to exercise leverage when the debt ceiling came due, and their votes would be necessary, as some Republicans would be reluctant to raise the ceiling so close to the midterm elections.[16]

On September 8, 2017, the president called Pelosi and Schumer to reinforce his willingness to keep working across party lines. He was effusive about their consensus, telling reporters that the debt ceiling deal may signal a new era of bipartisanship. "I think we will have a different relationship than we've been watching over the last number of years. I hope so," he declared.[17]

In another gesture toward bipartisanship, on September 7, Trump responded to a request from Pelosi and tweeted that young, undocumented immigrants who received temporary work visas under the DACA program did not need to worry about his administration acting against them over the next six months. "For all of those (DACA) that are concerned about your status during the 6-month period, you have nothing to worry about—No action!" the president tweeted. Trump also signaled support for a Democratic effort to pass legislation that would shield those covered by the DACA program from deportation. Referring to the Senate and House minority leaders Charles Schumer and Nancy Pelosi, the president declared, "Chuck and Nancy want to see something happen—and so do I."[18]

The president argued that he had no choice but to collaborate with the Democratic minority to get business done, especially because the opposition had the power to block bills in the Senate, where Republicans did not have the sixty votes required to overcome a filibuster. "Republicans, sorry, but I've been hearing about Repeal & Replace for 7 years, didn't happen!" he wrote in a series of morning tweets, referring to the failure of party leaders to pass legislation overturning the Affordable Care Act. "Even worse, the Senate Filibuster Rule will never allow the Republicans to pass even great legislation. 8 Dems control—will rarely get 60 (vs. 51) votes. It is a Repub Death Wish!"[19] A few days later the president goaded Congress to "move fast" on what he called the "biggest Tax Cut & Tax Reform package in the history of our country," a swipe at Republicans' inability to resolve their differences over tax legislation.[20]

Trump had lost confidence in his own party's leadership. "Republicans have shown they can't keep 50 out of 52 members in line, even after six years of promise to repeal and replace Obamacare when given the opportunity," said Marc Short. Another senior White House official explained that Trump saw Schumer as an exciting and energetic contrast to McConnell.[21] The president came to believe that he could not trust Republicans to pass bills by themselves and saw it as his responsibility to create a better environment for garnering support for his legislative agenda. He was more interested in winning than in the specifics of a bill, according to one congressional Republican. Moreover, he wanted to teach the intractable conservatives in his party that he liked them but did not need them.[22]

On September 13, 2017, the president hosted a dinner with Schumer and Pelosi during which they discussed immigration, tax reform, infrastructure, and China trade issues.[23] Mitch McConnell and Paul Ryan were not included among the guests, sending the message that Trump was willing to exclude the leadership of his own party in the interest of scoring fast legislative victories.[24]

The president also displayed rhetorical flexibility toward a few Democrats. For example, at a signing ceremony in 2018, he thanked Senator Heidi Heitkamp for her support of legislation that rolled back banking regulations passed in response to the 2008 financial crisis[25]—much to the irritation of Kevin Cramer, her opponent in the November election.[26] Heitkamp was also one of just seven Democrats who voted to confirm Trump's pick of Mike Pompeo for secretary of state and one of the six who voted for Gina Haspel to be CIA director.

Reversion to the Mean

How long would any respite from partisan warfare last? "Seeing is believing," declared Charles Schumer.[27] There was good reason to be skeptical.

"Looking to the long term, trust and reliability have been essential ingredients in productive relationships between the president and Congress," reflected Phil Schiliro, who served as director of legislative affairs under Barack Obama. "Without them, trying to move a legislative agenda is like juggling on quicksand. It usually doesn't end well."[28] Trump was not a reliable partner and kept pushing the envelope, undermining his ability to win bipartisan support.

The critical stumbling block to passing a Dream Act to replace DACA was the level of additional border security and enforcement Trump would require. On October 8, the White House delivered to Congress a long list of hardline immigration measures the president demanded in exchange for any deal to protect the Dreamers, including the construction of a wall across the southern border; the hiring of 10,000 immigration agents, 370 additional immigration judges, and 1,000 government lawyers; tougher laws for those seeking asylum; and denial of federal grants to "sanctuary cities." The White House also demanded the use of the E-Verify program by companies to keep illegal immigrants from getting jobs; an end to people bringing their extended family into the United States; a hardening of the border against thousands of children fleeing violence in Central America; and limits on legal immigration. A White House official added that Trump was not open to a deal that would eventually allow the Dreamers to become United States citizens.[29]

Democratic leaders in Congress reacted negatively, declaring the demands threatened to undermine the president's pledge to work across the aisle to protect the Dreamers through legislation. Schumer and Pelosi denounced the president's demands as failing to "represent any attempt at compromise." They called them little more than a thinly veiled effort to scuttle negotiations before they began in earnest.[30] Pelosi threatened to withhold support for must-pass spending bills later in the year if Congress could not reach agreement on how to protect Dreamers from deportation. The Congressional Hispanic Caucus went further and insisted on a path to citizenship for the Dreamers.

Advocates on both sides of the debate said they did not interpret the administration's principles as nonnegotiable but as an opening bid,[31] but no one really knew whether the president was trying to please his base with symbolic gestures, had given up on compromising with the Democrats, or was seeking to extract as many concessions as possible from them.

Making matters worse, Trump reached out to Schumer to propose yet another effort to repeal and replace the Affordable Care Act. The president announced his phone call in a tweet on October 7: "I called Chuck Schumer yesterday to see if the Dems want to do a great Health-Care Bill. ObamaCare is badly broken, big premiums. Who knows!"[32] Schumer rebuffed the president, however, telling him that Democrats would work with the White House only on fixing the weaknesses in the Affordable Care Act, not on replacing it. An aide to Schumer said the timing of Trump's call was particularly awkward, given that the administration had just announced rules to expand the right of employers to deny women coverage for contraception on religious grounds—a move widely condemned by Democrats. The Trump administration, the aide stated, needed to stop sabotaging the law before bipartisan negotiations could begin.[33]

Further decreasing the potential for bipartisan cooperation, on October 12, the president decided to cut off critical payments to health insurance companies. Experts predicted the move could cause chaos in insurance markets, sending insurers fleeing from the Affordable Care Act's marketplaces, raising the federal government's costs, and pricing some consumers out of the market. About seven million people benefitted from the cost-sharing subsidies. The decision came just hours after the president signed an executive order that also undermined the health law by encouraging the development of lower-cost insurance policies not subject to the Affordable Care Act's rigorous coverage standards. The president's decision, by destabilizing insurance markets and driving up premiums, could also adversely affect millions of others who bought insurance on their own and did not receive federal subsidies.

The president suggested that he was trying to move Democrats to the negotiating table by ratcheting up the pressure on Congress to act to protect consumers from soaring premiums. Republicans were divided, however. Some worried that ending the subsidies would hurt their constituents. Others were loath to do anything that could be seen as propping up the health law that they had promised to repeal.[34] In general, most Republicans were not devoting time and energy to cutting a bipartisan deal to save the insurance subsidies and were not broadly supportive of the deal worked out by Republican senator Lamar Alexander and Democratic senator Patty Murray.[35]

In a year-end interview in 2017, Trump expressed frustration and anger at Democrats, who he said refused to negotiate on legislation. He highlighted Senator Joe Manchin, who he said was representative of Democrats who claimed to be centrists but refused to negotiate on health care or taxes. "He talks. But he doesn't do anything. He doesn't do," the president asserted. " 'Hey, let's get together, let's do bipartisan.' I say, 'Good, let's go.' Then you don't hear from him again." Nonetheless, Trump said he still hoped Democrats would work with him on bipartisan legislation in the coming year to overhaul health care, improve the country's crumbling infrastructure, and help young immigrants brought to the country as children.[36]

TAX CUTS.   Yet it seems that the president did not exploit his opportunities. Tax cuts were the primary agenda item for the White House and Republicans in the fall of 2017, and Trump at one point concluded he would need the Democrats to pass them. Nevertheless, the White House and the Republican congressional leadership omitted Democrats from discussions as they drafted the legislation. The president also relied more on threats than negotiations.

When he staged his first event to promote his tax reform proposal, in Missouri in late August, the president singled out the state's Democratic senator, Claire McCaskill, who faced reelection in 2018, for a pointed threat. "She must do this for you," the president said. "And if she doesn't do it for you, you have to vote her out office."[37]

A week later, Trump visited North Dakota to advocate tax cuts. This time, he included the state's Democratic senator, Heidi Heitkamp, in his traveling delegation aboard Air Force One. Trump won North Dakota by 36 percentage points in 2016, so Heitkamp was fighting an uphill battle for reelection in 2018. She probably concluded that being seen as friendly with the president was a political advantage. Trump did not disappoint. He called her onto the stage with her Republican colleagues in Congress. "Everyone's saying, 'What's she doing up here?' " Trump asked. "But I'll tell you what—good woman. And I think we'll have your support. I hope we'll have your support. And thank you very much, senator." The president also included a threat, however. "If Democrats don't want to bring back your jobs, cut your taxes, raise your pay, and help America win, voters should deliver a clear message: Do your job to deliver for America, or find a new job. Do something else. Just do something else."[38]

The White House did little to follow up with Heitkamp. She was eager to reengage, and in October approached a senior administration official to say she hoped to continue working with them on taxes. Nevertheless, she heard little after that. Other Democrats had similar experiences. When reports surfaced that Trump might want to visit Montana to put pressure on Democratic senator Jon Tester to support a tax deal, the senator sent a letter to the White House saying he wanted to collaborate "in an open and transparent manner" and that he would be happy to meet with Trump if he opted to visit his home state. In the weeks that followed, Tester's aides heard from lower-level White House staffers, but Trump did not contact the senator, nor did any other senior Republican. Similarly, Claire Mc-Caskill, who sat on the Senate Finance Committee, spent weeks pushing the White House to work more closely with Democrats on the tax plan. Even though she was up for reelection in 2018 and represented a state Trump won handily, she resisted the White House's tax plan. Joe Manchin told Mike Pence he wanted "to be involved and help in any way I can." After that, Manchin met twice with Marc Short but was not involved in substantive negotiations on the tax bill.[39]

The president did hold a bipartisan gathering of House members on September 12, and then hosted several moderate Senate Democrats, including Joe Donnelly, Heidi Heitkamp, and Joe Manchin, for a bipartisan working dinner that evening to discuss tax reform and infrastructure projects. Being seen as working with Trump could be a boost for their 2018 reelections.[40] Moreover, the next day the president told reporters, "The rich will not be gaining at all with this plan. I think the wealthy will be pretty much where they are." He added about their tax rates, "If they have to go higher, they'll go higher."[41] Thus, the president seemed to give Democrats what they most wanted from tax reform.

Trump soon reverted to his more aggressive approach, however, apparently concluding that he did not have to negotiate with the Democrats on taxes. In late September, he invited Donnelly, who was up for reelection 2018, to join him on Air Force One to travel to Indiana, where he was speaking on taxes. During their conversations on Air Force One, the president pledged that they could work together on taxes and build a bond. He also asked the senator to ride with him in the presidential motorcade. In front of the large crowd at the state fairgrounds, however, Trump abruptly changed his tone. "If Senator Donnelly doesn't approve it—because, you know, he's on the other side—we will come here, we will campaign against him like you wouldn't believe," he threatened.[42]

Donnelly was not amused. "This is something I have not experienced before," he said. "I actually told his folks, 'You have one of the most unusual sales tactics I have ever seen. In my experience when you are trying to have someone like your product or buy your product, you're usually nice to your customer.'" More important, the ultimatum did little to get the president closer to winning Donnelly's support. "I happen to be an Irish-American," he said, adding, "Threatening me is like waving the red flag in front of the bull."[43]

Trump's actions in mid-October illustrated his schizophrenic approach to bipartisanship. On October 16, he predicted, "We may get no Democrat support and that's because they are obstructionist and they basically want us to do badly."[44] The next evening, however, the president's daughter and son-in-law hosted a bipartisan dinner at their home that included Senators Joe Manchin, Heidi Heitkamp, and Claire McCaskill to discuss tax policy. Nevertheless, on October 18, Trump tweeted, "The Democrats will only vote for tax increases. Hopefully, all Senate Republicans will vote for the largest tax cuts in U.S. history."[45] Later in the day, he told a bipartisan group of senators on the Finance Committee that he wanted Democrats' help in cutting taxes. He also advised Democrats that they had political incentives to support the plan, declaring he would not want to be a Democrat in 2018 or 2020 who voted against a tax cut plan. After the meeting, the White House released a statement stating, "The administration looks forward to continued opportunities to reach across the aisle in an effort to provide tangible quality of life improvements for the American people." However, Trump did not commit to make any changes that would scale back tax benefits for the wealthy, which had long been a demand of Democrats.[46]

There was another meeting between a number of Democratic senators, Marc Short, and Gary Cohn, director of the National Economic Council, in November 2107. Despite being shut out of the tax debate, the Democrats insisted they were eager to reach accord with Republicans.[47] Once again, the administration made no concessions and no effort to include Democrats in writing the bill. This pattern of symbolic gestures and ultimate exclusion characterized the crafting of the tax bill.[48]

ERRATIC BEHAVIOR.   In chapter 7, we saw that 2018 was not a year distinguished by bipartisanship on presidential initiatives. The president started campaigning early in the midterm elections and actively sought to maintain Republican majorities in Congress. He attacked Nancy Pelosi and demonized the Democrats in apocalyptic terms, claiming they were too dangerous to govern.

Nevertheless, in a White House press conference the day after the Democrats won the House, the president declared, "The election's over. Now everybody is in love." Trump said he looked forward to working with the Democrats on "a beautiful bipartisan-type situation" and thought the two sides could find common ground on rebuilding the nation's infrastructure, lowering the cost of prescription drugs, and refashioning trade policy. "Now we have a much easier path because the Democrats will come to us with a plan for infrastructure, a plan for health care, a plan for whatever they're looking at, and we'll negotiate," Trump declared. He added, "From a deal-making standpoint, we are all much better off the way it turned out" than if Republicans had kept control of the House.[49]

As was his wont, Trump coupled this invitation to compromise with a threat, promising to react aggressively to any attempt to investigate possible corruption in his administration, his personal finances, or his conduct in office. He vowed to respond with "warlike posture" that would extinguish any hopes for bipartisan progress. "They can play that game, but we can play it better, because we have a thing called the United States Senate," Trump said, referring to the enlarged GOP Senate majority following the election. "I could see it being extremely good for me politically because I think I'm better at that game than they are, actually, but we'll find out."[50] The partial government shutdown that occurred in December 2018–January 2019 undercut whatever potential there was for bipartisanship. We saw in chapter 7 that Trump mishandled the episode and, naturally, blamed the Democrats. The White House sought support from centrist Democrats and failed completely. Many would not even accept a meeting with the president.[51]

After the Democrats took charge of the House in January 2019, they channeled some of their energy into vigorously investigating Trump and his administration. The president's response was one of broad defiance in which he claimed the Democrats were only playing politics, vowed to fight *all* subpoenas, filed lawsuits against corporations to bar them from responding to subpoenas, and ordered aides and former aides not to testify. The president abandoned even the pretense of negotiating accommodations and compromise with his political opponents. This strategy set the stage for open warfare with House Democrats heading into the 2020 election.

The president found he needed the Democrats, yet he could not refrain from annoying them. For example, in May 2019, the president announced he was directing a bipartisan group of lawmakers to create legislation that would provide relief for people who were surprised by bills they received from out-of-network health care providers after both emergency and scheduled medical visits. Yet he also took the occasion to attack some

Democrats, including Representative Jerrold Nadler, the chair of the House Judiciary Committee, bragging, "I beat him all the time."[52]

Similarly, surprised by bipartisan blowback that threatened to scuttle his rewrite of NAFTA, he solicited Democrats' feedback on what he needed to do to win their support. Democrats had treaded cautiously rather than flatly reject the deal, at least partially because US trade representative Robert Lighthizer had kept them and union leaders updated on developments and sought their input.[53] Within a month of his meeting with Democrats, however, Trump threatened Mexico with tariffs on all its exports, infuriating members of both parties.

Ironically, the impeachment of the president provided some opportunities for bipartisanship in trade policy. In December 2019, the House voted 385–41 to pass the USMCA. Earlier the president had called it "the most important trade deal we've ever made by far."[54] Hyperbole aside, and there was plenty, the president trumpeted the agreement as a signal success and a 2016 campaign promise kept.

Marc Short, now chief of staff to Vice President Pence, argued that the Democrats only agreed to support the trade pact because they were feeling constituency pressure, at least partially the result of Pence's visits to swing districts represented by vulnerable Democrats. By contrast, Democrats claimed the deal materialized because they extracted nearly every concession they wanted from the administration, including strong enforcement mechanisms. The president needed to show success during the impeachment process, and this need provided leverage to the Democrats. According to Nancy Pelosi, "We ate their lunch."[55]

Some Republicans, especially those committed to conservative trade policies, agreed. "The only reason Pelosi moved on USMCA is because she took Lighthizer, flipped him upside down, and shook all the money out of him and destroyed him," said one Republican leadership aide. This person added: "Democrats won on substance; Trump won on the politics of USMCA. And that's because Trump doesn't care about substance."[56] "Taken as a whole, it looks more like an agreement that would've been negotiated under the Obama administration," declared Senator Rob Portman, a former trade representative during the George W. Bush administration. "There are some aspects to it that Democrats have been calling for, for decades." Senator Patrick J. Toomey, one of the most ardent critics of the deal, called the pact "a complete departure from the free trade agreements we've pursued through our history" and urged fellow Republicans to vote it down.[57] Mitch McConnell was candid about his view of the agreement on its merits. "From my perspective, it's not as good as I had hoped." Senator John Cornyn added, "My concern is that what the administration presented has now been moved demonstrably to Democrats, the direction they wanted. And anything that gets the AFL-CIO's endorsement . . . could be problematic."[58]

In fact, the outcome was the result of months of negotiations that took place without Nancy Pelosi or Donald Trump ever speaking directly and with little involvement of the president. Instead, Democrats worked directly with Lighthizer, who agreed to make numerous adjustments to garner their support. Trump's desire to pass the bill accorded Pelosi leverage, an opportunity she exploited aggressively. House Democrats and their Senate counterparts achieved substantial changes. They jettisoned pharmaceutical protections sought by drug companies and added provisions ensuring higher labor standards in Mexico, quicker dispute resolutions, a rollback of a special system of arbitration for corporations that had drawn bipartisan condemnation, higher environmental standards, higher thresholds for how much of a car must be made in North America in order to avoid tariffs, the inclusion of additional provisions designed to help identify and prevent labor violations, particularly in Mexico, and stronger enforcement of all elements of the deal.[59] The Senate passed the agreement by a lopsided bipartisan vote of 89–10. Reflecting the Democrats' role in achieving this unity, Democratic senator Sherrod Brown exclaimed, "I never thought I'd be voting for a trade agreement during my Senate tenure that I wrote a big part of."[60]

Also in December 2019, Congress unveiled a defense bill that included twelve weeks of paid parental leave for federal workers, despite the additional government spending that the new benefits would entail and the opposition of Republicans. The parental leave provision was part of a deal that included a Space Force branch of the military supported by the president. When Trump gave Democrats what they wanted, they were willing to support him.

Immigration was a continuous source of partisan strain. At various points in 2019, the administration announced that it would be carrying out nationwide raids to deport undocumented families. If the plans had gone forward, some immigrant children—many of whom are American citizens because they were born in the United States—would have faced the possibility of being forcibly separated from their undocumented parents. The president tried to leverage the threat of the raids to win Democratic support for changes in asylum law and other aspects of immigration policy they had long opposed. In the end, the Democrats did not budge, and the raids that did occur arrested only a modest number of people.

A bipartisan effort in May 2020 produced legislation that would revive expired FBI tools to investigate terrorism and espionage and add privacy protections for Americans subjected to wiretapping for national security purposes. The bill appeared poised to become law after approval of both the House and Senate. However, just as the House was to vote on a final compromise version, the president abruptly announced that the reforms did not go far enough and threatened to veto the bill if it passed. Trump did not put forward any alternative, and it appeared that he was largely interested in keeping alive his grievances about the FBI investigation into whether his campaign was involved with Russia's efforts to interfere in the 2016 election. House Democrats had to withdraw the bill and send a previously passed version to the conference committee to be reconciled with the Senate version. Months followed with no action by either the White House or the Republican Senate.

CORONAVIRUS PANDEMIC RELIEF. In the wake of the coronavirus pandemic of 2020, Congress passed several bills in the spring, the total cost of which was about $3 trillion. One provided $8 billion of emergency funding for the health care system. A second offered paid sick and child care leave, expanded food assistance for the poor and elderly, extended unemployment insurance, increased spending on health insurance for the poor, and provided free coronavirus testing at a cost of $100 billion. The third bill was of historic proportions, spending $2.3 trillion on aid to state and local governments; grants for states to adjust elections; loans and grants to airlines; grants to hospitals and health care providers; funds for FEMA, the Department of Defense, and Congress; checks to individual Americans; loans and tax cuts for businesses; and expanded unemployment assistance.

The president had little direct role in the negotiations with Congress. Instead, Democratic leaders dealt largely with treasury secretary Steven Mnuchin. Trump insisted on instituting a broad payroll tax cut to stimulate the economy. On March 13, for example, he tweeted that such a cut was essential to any recovery package. "Only that will make a big difference!" he wrote.[61] Nevertheless, lawmakers in both parties reacted coolly to the proposal, expressing qualms about its cost and the fact that it was not targeted to those directly affected by the pandemic. None of the bills included a payroll tax cut. Although sending checks to citizens was a congressional initiative, Trump insisted on his name being printed on each check.

In the giant $2.3 trillion bill, Republicans balked at some of the Democrats' demands. Mitch McConnell twice called up a bill that included only Republicans' priorities, daring Democrats to vote against it. The Senate majority leader's gambit failed: Democrats stuck together, and some of their demands even attracted GOP support—including oversight and transparency rules for new corporate lending programs. The Democrats also extracted changes focused on greater protections for workers.

The negotiations over a fourth bill followed a similar pattern. The president and Republicans wanted a clean bill providing $250 billion of additional funding for small businesses. The Democrats wanted to include a similar amount for hospitals, state and local governments, and food stamp recipients. They also wanted to ensure that much of the business funding went through community-based financial institutions serving farmers and businesses and nonprofits owned by families, women, minorities, and veterans, and they proposed new disclosure requirements on the administration and new guidelines to streamline the lending process.

"We do not have time for the partisan games, and we don't want that, the obstruction or the totally unrelated agendas," Trump declared.[62] He also continued his pattern of insulting his opponents in highly personal terms. On April 16, he tweeted, "'Crazy' Nancy Pelosi, you are a weak person. You are a poor leader. You are the reason America hates career politicians, like yourself," adding that "She is totally incompetent & controlled by the Radical Left, a weak and pathetic puppet. Come back to Washington and do your job!" On April 19, he opined that "Nervous Nancy is an inherently 'dumb' person."[63]

Republican leaders refused to negotiate with the Democrats. Democratic leaders dealt with Mnuchin, however, and used the president's desire for money for small businesses as leverage. As was the case in the previous bills, the Democrats won substantial concessions from the White House. In addition to grants and loans to small businesses, the law added $75 billion for hospitals and $25 billion for a new coronavirus testing program with a mandate that the Trump administration establish a strategy to help states vastly step up the deployment of tests throughout the country—a move Republicans had opposed. An additional $60 billion was added to the bill reserved for lending by small- and medium-size financial institutions, and there were requirements for participation by lending institutions serving minority or underserved areas, language sought by the Congressional Hispanic Caucus and others.

The pandemic lasted longer than many officials anticipated, requiring yet another relief measure. In May, House Democrats passed a bill providing an additional $3.4 trillion in relief. This package continued the $600 unemployment payments that were cushioning millions of Americans from the worst of the recession through January 2021 and also included billions of dollars for state and local governments and schools, food and rental assistance, and additional aid for election security and the Postal Service.

Senate Republicans waited until late July to unveil their own $1 trillion plan, arguing that they needed time to assess how the previous aid bills were working, all the while hoping the coronavirus would abate. They presented their plan just before protections against eviction and expanded unemployment benefits were to expire. The small business program, considered crucial to preventing a total economic collapse, was also soon set to end. Republicans could not pass any bill, however, because they were divided. One group, including endangered incumbents, wanted to act, while a second group of fifteen to twenty senators wanted to do nothing at all.[64] McConnell told reporters, "There are some members who think we've already done enough, other members who think we need to do more. This is a complicated problem."[65] The Republican plan would slash jobless benefits—in an unworkable way, according to many experts—and failed to provide aid for struggling state and local governments. It also rejected the administration's plan to omit money for coronavirus testing and to defund schools that failed to resume in-person classes in the fall.

Once again, the president played little direct role in the negotiations. Instead of providing a strategy or a set of proposals behind which Republicans could rally, he undercut his own party. A day after the McConnell announced the Republican plan, Trump dismissed it as "sort of semi-irrelevant."[66] He sent mixed signals on the only provision that McConnell called a "red line" in the measure—a broad legal liability shield for businesses.[67]

Trump did continue to insist on a payroll tax cut, however. For example, he told an interviewer, "I would consider not signing it if we don't have a payroll tax cut."[68] Ultimately, the White House backed down. The idea was unpopular among Republicans in Congress and had no chance of passage. Trump blamed the Democrats, however. On July 23, he tweeted, "The Democrats have stated strongly that they won't approve a Payroll

Tax Cut (too bad!). It would be great for workers. The Republicans, therefore, didn't want to ask for it. Dems, as usual, are hurting the working men and women of our Country!"[69]

The president also wanted to include funding for a new FBI building—on the site of the current building—in the bill. It was probably not a coincidence that the FBI was located across the street from his hotel and posed potential competition if it moved, opening the location to commercial development and competition for Trump's enterprise. Republicans balked at Trump's request. Senator Graham declared, "I don't know— that makes no sense to me. I'd be fine, OK, with stripping it out."[70] Rick Scott added, "I just don't get it, I mean, how's it tied to the coronavirus? During the pandemic, let's focus on solving the problem."[71] The president responded to Republican resistance by telling them "should go back to school and learn."[72]

Previous efforts to convene a bipartisan meeting of the minds at the White House had proved disastrous, and the president had a toxic relationship with Nancy Pelosi. With Senate Republicans split, treasury secretary Steven Mnuchin and Mark Meadows, the White House chief of staff, took the lead on negotiating with the House Democrats. They refused to go above $400 a week for unemployment benefits and were unwilling to agree to more than $150 billion in additional aid to state and local governments, although they did stop pushing for cuts to coronavirus testing and the Centers for Disease Control and Prevention. They also insisted on a five-year liability shield aimed at protecting health-care providers, schools, employers, and others from lawsuits from people who become ill from the virus.

On August 3, the *New York Times* reported:

> On the first day of the first full week when tens of millions of Americans went without the federal jobless aid that has cushioned them during the pandemic, President Trump was not cajoling undecided lawmakers to embrace a critical stimulus bill to stabilize the foundering economy. He was at the White House, hurling insults at the Democratic leaders whose support he needs to strike a deal."[73]

Although the president received regular updates on the negotiations, he did little to persuade reluctant legislators. When asked why Trump did not simply bring congressional leaders to the Oval Office and keep everyone there until there was a deal, White House chief of staff Mark Meadows prompted laughter when he replied, "You've seen that movie before."[74]

Reflecting the failure of the negotiations with the Democrats, on August 8, Trump signed one executive order and three memoranda actions aimed at restoring some enhanced unemployment benefits, deferring payroll taxes and student loan payments, and protecting renters and homeowners against eviction. However, state officials, businesses, economists, and Democrats criticized the president's actions as confusing, unworkable, inadequate, and possibly unconstitutional. Even the president conceded at his news conference announcing his actions that they left unaddressed multiple critical needs,[75] including billions of dollars to help schools safely reopen; a second round of $1,200 stimulus payments; and a replenishing of funds for the Paycheck Protection Program for small businesses. A few days later, the White House acknowledged that the president's actions would only guarantee $300 per week in unemployment benefits, not the $400 he had initially claimed. The assistance to renters and homeowners was largely symbolic.

Taking unilateral action was a familiar tactic of a president who portrayed himself as the ultimate dealmaker, but who in practice showed little skill for negotiating with Congress. His executive actions also amounted to an about-face from his promise as a presidential candidate to cut deals and not rely on executive orders. "We have a president that can't get anything done so he just keeps signing executive orders all over the place," Trump said on MSNBC's "Morning Joe" in January 2016, adding that he preferred "the old fashioned way, get everybody into a room and get something people agree on."[76] Similarly, he told the audience at a Republican primary debate in March 2016, "We don't want to continue to watch people signing executive orders because that was not what the Constitution and the brilliant designers of this incredible document had in mind. We need people that can make deals."[77]

Trump's analysis was correct, but it did not foreshadow his own behavior. Instead, as we have seen on funding the border wall, gun control, and immigration, he regularly pivoted to signing executive orders—with great fanfare—after failing to negotiate legislative deals that would have broader and more long-lasting impact.

Disparaging Democrats

Undermining the potential for bipartisanship was the president's personal style of criticizing those who disagreed with him. Unsurprisingly, the president did not hesitate to disparage Democrats, both as a group and as individuals. He seemed more interested in destroying enemies than producing legislative products. Frightening people about the evils of the opposition is often the most effective means of obtaining attention and rousing one's supporters, but such rhetoric discourages the comity necessary for building coalitions. It is difficult to compromise with someone who relentlessly vilifies you.

A few examples illustrate Trump's approach. At various points, the president blamed Democrats for his problems with health care reform and proclaimed in anger that the lack of support from Democrats in both chambers meant that they would "own" Obamacare when it exploded.[78] He typically criticized Democrats as obstructionists, as when he told reporters, "The Democrats have terrible policy. They are very good at, really, obstruction."[79]

On July 24, 2017, ahead of a crucial Senate vote on health care, Trump delivered an afternoon address from the White House Blue Room. Calling the Democrats' signature achievement during the Obama presidency a "big fat ugly lie," he chided Senate Democrats for their refusal to support the Republican health care bill, which was designed to undo as much of Obamacare as possible and the development of which they were given no role. "The problem is we have zero help from the Democrats. They're obstructionists—that's all they are," Trump declared. "The Democrats aren't giving us one vote, so we need virtually every single vote from the Republicans. Not easy to do." Heating up his rhetoric further, he continued to deride Democrats: "They run out. They say, 'Death, death, death.' Well, Obamacare is death. That's the one that's death."[80] Such words were unlikely to win the hearts, much less the votes, of Democrats.

On January 30, 2018, President Trump delivered his first State of the Union address, asking for unity. "Tonight, I call upon all of us to set aside our differences, to seek out common ground, and to summon the unity we need to deliver for the people we were elected to serve." He also called for a compromise on immigration policy "where nobody gets everything they want, but where our country gets the critical reforms it needs." There was a dichotomy between the teleprompter Trump and the Twitter Trump, however. Within days, he accused Democrats of doing nothing to help Dreamers and not caring about violent MS-13 gang members "pouring" into the United States.

Most dramatically, in a rambling speech at a factory near Cincinnati, he complained about the Democrats' failure to applaud during his speech. Trump told the crowd "they were like death and un-American. Un-American. Somebody said, 'treasonous.' I mean, yeah, I guess, why not? Can we call that treason? Why not? I mean, they certainly didn't seem to love our country very much."[81]

The president's insults came as he was seeking bipartisan support for immigration reform and rebuilding the nation's infrastructure, two of his marquee initiatives. "Treason is not a punchline, Mr. President," declared Jeff Flake on the Senate floor, wondering aloud why Trump would follow up a State of the Union address that seemed designed to foster unity with such a divisive comment.[82]

Although White House press secretary Sarah Huckabee Sanders said Trump "was clearly joking," Democrats were outraged by the president's comments. Sanders made it worse when she added, "it's un-American not to be excited" about progress being made on unemployment and other measures of economic strength. "Democrats are going to have to make a decision at some point really soon: Do they hate this president more than they love this country? And I hope the answer is no," she declared.[83]

The president told lawmakers in early January 2018, "I'll take all the heat you want to give me, and I'll take the heat off both the Democrats and the Republicans" on the immigration issue.[84] Actually, he emphasized turning up the temperature on the opposition. For example, in early December 2017 he declared, "The Democrats are really looking at something that is very dangerous for our country." "They want to have illegal immigrants pouring into our country, bringing with them crime, tremendous amounts of crime."[85]

Trump attacked individual Democrats as well as their party. After only a few days in office, the president mocked Senate Democratic leader Charles Schumer: "I noticed Charles E. Schumer yesterday with fake tears. I'm gonna ask him who is his acting coach because I know him very well, I don't see him as a crier. If he is, he's a different man. There's about a five percent chance that it was real, but I think they were fake tears."[86] In a March 28, 2017 tweet, Trump called Schumer a "head clown." It is not clear what possible legislative benefit could result from such rhetoric. It certainly was unlikely to advance the cause of bipartisanship.

Nevertheless, the president continued his insults. At the beginning of 2018, Schumer voiced opposition to the White House's immigration proposal aimed at breaking a congressional impasse over a long-term budget deal. In a tweet, Trump taunted the Senate minority leader for taking a political "beating" in the recent government shutdown fight and accusing him of making an immigration deal "increasingly difficult." Using the derogatory nickname "Cryin' Chuck" again, the president mocked Schumer for being "unable to act on immigration."[87] At a luncheon before his 2019 State of the Union message, he told television news anchors that the Democratic leader "can be a nasty son of a bitch."[88]

On April 2, 2020, during the coronavirus pandemic, Trump complained about partisanship during his daily briefing with reporters. At the same time, he released a letter to Schumer, mocking the senator for being "missing in action" and too busy with the "impeachment hoax" to prepare for the COVID-19 outbreak that was ravaging his home state of New York—as if that was Schumer's responsibility. "I've known you for many years," the president added, "but I never knew how bad a senator you are for the state of New York, until I became president."[89]

While in France to commemorate the seventy-fifth anniversary of the D-Day landings, Trump took the opportunity to pronounce Nancy Pelosi "a nasty, vindictive, horrible person" for her commenting that she would like to see him in prison. "She is a disaster," he added. The president also described Schumer as a "jerk."[90] The next day, he called Pelosi "a disgrace to herself and her family."[91] A week later, Trump called her criticism of him a "fascist statement." "When Nancy Pelosi makes a statement like that, she ought to be ashamed of herself," he declared. "It's a disgrace."[92]

The president accused Adam Schiff, then the ranking minority member of the House Intelligence Committee, of being "one of the biggest liars and leakers in Washington," and mocking him as "Little Adam Schiff." "Adam leaves closed committee hearings to illegally leak confidential information. Must be stopped!" the president demanded.[93] Similarly, he often attacked Senator Richard Blumenthal for exaggerating his military service. On January 29, 2019, for example, he tweeted, "How does Da Nang Dick (Blumenthal) serve on the Senate Judiciary Committee when he defrauded the American people about his so called War Hero status in Vietnam, only to later admit, with tears pouring down his face, that he was never in Vietnam. An embarrassment to our Country!"[94]

We discussed earlier how Trump publicly threatened Democratic senators Joe Donnelly, Claire McCaskill, and Joe Manchin with defeat if they failed to support tax cuts. Manchin argued that Trump had not really made the transition from negotiating tactics that work in the private sector—like bluster and intimidation—to those that work in the public sector. "It takes a little more diplomacy in the public sector," Manchin said.[95]

Donnelly was in the front row at a White House signing ceremony for "right-to-try" legislation—allowing people with life-threatening illnesses to bypass the Food and Drug Administration to obtain experimental medications—that the senator had helped to write. "Senator Donnelly, thank you very much," Trump said. "That's really great. Appreciate it. Thank you." Shortly after the event, Donnelly issued a statement that highlighted Trump's praise. "I was proud to join President Trump at the White House, as he signed my right to try bill into law," the senator said. Earlier in the month, however, Trump traveled to Elkhart, Indiana, to tout the candidacy of Mike Braun, Donnelly's challenger. At a rally in the state, Trump disparagingly labeled Donnelly "Sleepin' Joe" and ticked off other White House priorities the first-term senator had opposed. "Joe Donnelly voted no on tax cuts, no on better health care, and he voted no on canceling job-killing regulations, which may be even more important than those incredible tax cuts," Trump told the crowd.[96]

In yet another departure from the norms of party competition, Trump publicly and privately campaigned for the Israeli government to block Democratic representatives Ilhan Omar of Minnesota and Rashida Tlaib of Michigan from visiting Israel. "It would show great weakness if Israel allowed Rep. Omar and Rep. Tlaib to visit," Trump tweeted. "They hate Israel & all Jewish people, & there is nothing that can be said or done to change their minds. Minnesota and Michigan will have a hard time putting them back in office. They are a disgrace!"[97]

It is rare for a government entity to directly criticize a sitting member of Congress. However, the president broke from the practice of past administrations of refraining from posting overtly partisan content, singling out public figures on official accounts. The White House used its official Twitter account to attack two Democratic senators who opposed the president's immigration agenda, falsely equating their criticisms of the Immigration and Customs Enforcement agency with support for criminals and murderous gangs. "@SenWarren, why are you supporting criminals moving weapons, drugs, and victims across our nation's borders?" asked a tweet addressed to Senator Elizabeth Warren from the @WhiteHouse account. "@SenKamalaHarris, why are you supporting the animals of MS-13?" queried a tweet posted by the same account about an hour later to Senator Kamala Harris, which referred to the transnational gang with roots in El Salvador.[98]

Criticism of Trump's Iranian policy heated up after US drones killed Iranian general Qasem Soleimani. On January 13, 2020, the president retweeted a volley of incendiary posts accusing Nancy Pelosi of supporting the Iranian regime. One of them included a fake photo of the Speaker and Senate Minority Leader Schumer wearing photoshopped Islamic head coverings and standing in front of the Iranian flag. Another retweet showed a graphic picture of what appeared to be a man's body, along with the claim that Pelosi "supports this mullahs' crime." The tweet was later removed from Twitter and replaced with a note saying it "violated the Twitter Rules."[99]

The Case of Infrastructure

Observers have always viewed infrastructure development as a prime opportunity for the two parties to come together to create jobs and bolster economic growth. There was widespread agreement that the country's bridges, railroads, broadband, and other structures were badly fraying and in need of repair and rebuilding. If approved, the policy would have been the most significant bipartisan achievement of Trump's presidency. The issue illustrates the president's problematic approach to bipartisanship.

On one level, the president was upbeat about the prospects of working with the Democrats. On December 22, 2017, he tweeted, "At some point, and for the good of the country, I predict we will start working with the Democrats in a Bipartisan fashion. Infrastructure would be a perfect place to start. After having foolishly spent $7 trillion in the Middle East, it is time to start rebuilding our country!"[100] As we have seen, however, the White House never developed an infrastructure plan, and it never involved the Democrats in any effort to do so.

After the 2018 midterm elections, the president again named infrastructure as a policy on which he hoped to work with the new Democratic House majority. Democrats were conflicted. How would they balance investigating the president with cooperating with him in areas of mutual interest?[101] They did move forward, however, and Trump and the Democrats reached a tentative accord on a $2 trillion price tag—proposed by the president himself—in early May 2019. However, this agreement ran into immediate opposition from Republicans, including acting White House chief of staff Mick Mulvaney and Senate Majority Leader Mitch McConnell, who balked at the hefty price tag, and from conservative allies who were pushing lawmakers to block it.[102]

On May 21, the president complicated the effort further when he sent Democratic leaders a letter saying that infrastructure should wait until after Congress passed the USMCA, his revised version of NAFTA.[103]

The next day, the president walked into the White House Cabinet Room, ostensibly for a meeting with Democratic congressional leaders on an infrastructure bill. He never took his seat, however, and shook no hands. Instead, he lashed out at Nancy Pelosi for accusing him of a cover-up and declared that he could not work with the Democrats until they stopped investigating him. After just three minutes, and before anyone else could speak, he marched out into the Rose Garden and delivered a statement bristling with anger, demanding Democrats "get these phony investigations over with." Trump followed up his comments with a series of tweets, charging in one that the "Democrat leadership is tearing the United States apart."[104]

May 23 saw a further escalation of the spat in which each questioned the other's mental fitness. At a news conference, the president called Pelosi "crazy Nancy" and proclaimed, "she's a mess" and She's lost it." after the Speaker told reporters that Trump's family and White House aides "should stage an intervention for the good of the country." He also questioned Pelosi's intellectual capacities, saying that she was incapable of understanding the details of a proposed new trade agreement with Canada and Mexico. In contrast, the president reprised his self-assessment as an "extremely stable genius."[105] Later in the day, Trump shared a video on Twitter that spliced together several verbal stumbles of Pelosi at a press conference earlier in the day. Meanwhile, some Trump allies distributed a video, which rapidly spread across social media, which slowed the sound to make it look like Pelosi was drunkenly slurring her words.

There was reason to think that Trump's eruption was staged to end negotiations over infrastructure spending, because he had not come up with a way to pay for such an enormous package.[106] Despite his insults of the Democratic leaders, and with seemingly little sensitivity to their impact, the day after the aborted White House meeting he nevertheless demanded that the House pass his revised trade agreement with Canada and Mexico.

Whatever the president's motivation, his blowup was reminiscent of a meeting in January 2019 when he erupted at Pelosi during the partial government shutdown as he sought money for his promised border wall. After she refused to go along, he snapped, "bye-bye" and stormed out, later blasting the negotiations as a "waste of time."[107] Trump was still relying on a negotiating style that had proven to be a failure, but it was his *modus operandi* and he seemed unable to adapt. He was neither a reliable nor a skilled negotiator. Moreover, his own party constrained his ability to win Democratic support.

Impeachment

The final break in the president's relations with Democrats occurred when the House opened an impeachment inquiry in September 2019. Calls for the president's impeachment had grown among Democrats throughout his tenure, but the immediate catalyst for the inquiry was Trump's efforts to pressure the Ukraine to investigate Joe Biden and his son, Hunter. For most reluctant Democrats, this behavior was the final straw, and Nancy Pelosi agreed to begin the inquiry. As we discussed in chapter 5, Trump frenetically sought to delegitimize the proceedings and refused to cooperate. He also grew increasingly abusive in his criticism of the opposition.

On October 16, 2019, congressional leaders met with the president to be briefed on fighting in Syria. Trump began the proceedings in the Cabinet Room by making it clear that he did not want to be there. "They said you wanted this meeting," he told his guests. "I didn't want this meeting, but I'm doing it." The atmosphere deteriorated further, with the president ultimately calling Nancy Pelosi a "third-grade" or a "third-rate" politician.[108] At that point, the Democratic leaders walked out of the meeting.

Later in the day, Trump tweeted a picture of Pelosi standing in the Cabinet Room pointing her finger at the president. He thought it showed her in an "unhinged meltdown."[109] To Democrats—and some Republicans—however, the picture conveyed the Speaker standing up to the president after the House overwhelmingly voted to condemn his decision to pull out of northern Syria. Indeed, Pelosi made the photo her Twitter profile picture.[110]

As the impeachment inquiry accelerated, the president's criticism of Democratic leaders went into overdrive. For example, on November 1, 2019, he called Pelosi and House Intelligence Committee chair Adam Schiff "corrupt politicians."[111] The day after his acquittal during a televised speech at the White House, he assailed Pelosi and Schiff. "They're vicious and mean," Trump said. "Adam Schiff is a vicious, horrible person. Nancy Pelosi is a horrible person."[112]

Unsurprisingly, the president had additional grievances. Joe Manchin voted with Trump more than any other Democrat in the Senate and was the only Democratic vote in favor of confirming Brett Kavanaugh to the Supreme Court. When he voted to convict the president of impeachable offenses, however, Trump was enraged. On February 8, he called Manchin a "puppet Democrat Senator" who was "weak & pathetic." He gave the senator a new nickname: "Joe Munchkin" and suggested that Manchin was too stupid to understand a transcript of his telephone call with President Volodymyr Zelensky of the Ukraine. Adding insult to injury, the president took credit for the senator's signature legislative achievement: a bipartisan bill to secure miners' pensions. Manchin was not cowed, however.

"The people of America and the people of West Virginia want some adults in the room," he said, and Trump was not behaving like one.[113]

Democratic Support

The best test of the success of a bipartisan effort is the support the president wins from the opposition. One would not expect a high level of support, but Donald Trump's record is especially dismal. Table 8.1 shows that House Democrats voted with the president only 9 percent of the time on contested votes during 2017–2019, the lowest level they had ever accorded a Republican president. Trump did not do much better in the Senate, where Democrats supported the president's stand only 13 percent of the time. Once again, this level of opposition support was the lowest ever for a Republican president.

Examining votes on specific issues clarifies the division further. Not a single Democrat in either House supported any version of the Republican, Trump-backed efforts to repeal and replace the Affordable Care Act. Similarly, no Democrat voted for the 2017 tax cuts, despite the president's campaigning and threats. The president did no better on his signature efforts to alter immigration policy. For example, when the Senate voted on February 15, 2018, on a bill the president favored, only three Democrats (Heitkamp Donnelly, and Manchin) supported him. He won no House Democratic votes for either version of the immigration bill voted on in June 2018. Only Manchin voted to fund his $5.7 billion request for a border wall during the 2018–2019 government shutdown. Thus, when the

TABLE 8.1. **Democratic support for Republican presidents**

President	Support (%)*	
	House	Senate
Eisenhower	42	36
Nixon/Ford	39	33
Reagan	29	31
G. H. W. Bush	27	29
G. W. Bush	19	18
Trump**	9	13

*On roll-call votes on which the winning side was supported by fewer than 80 percent of those voting.
**2017–2019.

chips were down, the president could not rely on the Democrats to give him a winning coalition.

Part of the president's problem was the increasing polarization in Congress, discussed in chapter 6. Democratic support has decreased for every succeeding Republican president since Eisenhower's tenure in the 1950s. It is difficult to say how much Trump contributed to intensifying this polarization, but it is reasonable to argue that his approach to bipartisanship left much to be desired, and his disparaging of Democrats, collectively and individually, only reinforced the opposition's disinclination to grant him the benefit of the doubt. The president's alienation of the Democrats' constituents made it even more difficult for them to compromise with the White House.

Congressional Initiatives

A number of important bills that were not presidential initiatives passed with bipartisan support in the 115th Congress. Congress approved a law intended to address the opioid crisis by, among other things, expanding the availability of addiction treatment. It took a bipartisan approach to the legislation, while the White House adopted a mostly hands-off but supportive approach. Other bipartisan, Congress-led efforts resulted in a major overhaul and extension of veterans' educational benefits; a bill designed to help veterans obtain health care;[114] the Music Modernization Act, which rewrote music copyright and royalty rules for the digital age; and the first comprehensive NASA authorization bill in more than six years.

Two important bills passed late in the 115th Congress. Lawmakers approved a twice-a-decade farm bill. The legislation was largely the work of bipartisan bargaining among members of Congress. The primary contribution of the Trump administration was a proposal to add new work requirements for many food stamp recipients. The bill passed by wide margins in both the House (369–47) and the Senate (87–13), but it did so after scrapping the president's proposal.

The other significant legislation dealt with reforming the criminal justice system. An unusual alliance of liberal groups such as the ACLU and the Center for American Progress and conservative groups such as those funded by the Koch brothers and law enforcement organizations supported the bill. Conservatives saw an opportunity to reduce the high costs of the nation's growing prison population, while liberals were enthusiastic about shortening mandatory minimum sentences for some nonviolent drug offenses and reducing the sentencing disparity between crack and powder cocaine offenders. Both sides liked incentives and new programs aimed at improving prison conditions and preparing prisoners for reentry into their communities. This First Step Act had a lengthy gestation period and was the product of years of bipartisan cooperation in Congress. Trump did not endorse the bill until November 14, 2018. The president's essential contribution was encouraging Mitch McConnell to bring it to the floor.[115] When he did, eighty-seven senators voted for it on December 18.

In 2020, Congress passed the Great American Outdoors Act, a measure that for the first time guaranteed maximum annual funding for the Land and Water Conservation Fund, the premiere federal program to acquire and preserve land for public use. The president signed the bill, although his budget earlier in the year proposed eliminating spending on the program altogether. The bill received widespread bipartisan support, and two Senate Republicans from the West facing tough reelection fights—Cory Gardner of Colorado and Steve Daines of Montana—seized on the measure as beneficial both for their states and for their election prospects. They talked Trump into signing the bill.[116]

When the White House stayed out of the negotiations and when the issues had the potential for consensus, Congress was able to legislate.

Even when the president tried to intervene in a congressional initiative, legislators could ignore him. A bill providing billions in financial aid to places across the country besieged by natural disasters since 2017 was a high priority in 2019. Trump called for Republicans to "stick together" and reject the "BAD DEMOCRAT" bill,[117] apparently because it provided help to Puerto Rico. He also wanted the bill to include additional funding for border security.[118] Congress, by votes of 85–8 in the Senate and 354–58 in the House, easily passed the bill, which did not include the border funding the president requested.

Leading the Party

Managing and maintaining a supportive majority coalition of those predisposed to support the president, members of his party, has always been the key strategy for winning votes in Congress. The difficulty of winning support from the opposition party has only increased the White House's reliance on party leadership. President Trump enjoyed a comfortable majority in the House and a narrow one in the Senate during 2017–2018. By 2019, Democrats had taken the House, greatly reducing the prospects of passing significant White House proposals.

It is common for presidents to rely on party leaders and to receive support from them, and Trump was no exception. His relationships with them were sometimes stormy, however. We have seen how he publicly criticized Mitch McConnell, especially over the failure of the Senate to pass a health care bill in 2017, a departure from the modern tradition. McConnell sometimes voiced differences with the president in public. Recognizing he had a problem, Trump held an impromptu news conference with McConnell, claiming their relationship was "outstanding." He also promised to try to talk former aide Steve Bannon out of at least some of his plans to field hard-right primary candidates to challenge sitting Republicans.[119] (Taking nothing for granted, McConnell's allies launched a concerted effort to personally attack Bannon in hopes of blunting his impact in Republican primaries.[120])

Trump also followed the well-developed White House routines of providing favors and amenities for congressional party members. He even created opportunities for favors. On September 4, 2019, he tweeted, "At the request of Senator Thom Tillis, I am getting the North Carolina Emergency Declaration completed and signed tonight." Tillis was a Republican facing a tough reelection fight in 2020. Under federal law, however, requests for disaster declarations are made by governors. Roy Cooper, the Democratic governor of North Carolina had made such a request two days before.[121]

In addition, the president was accessible, routinely calling some members of Congress. His calls tended to be unfocused, however, and often did not concentrate on policy development. Instead, he may have chatted about golf, some news in a member's state, or something he saw on television. Sometimes, he batted around ideas with senators, asking for their thoughts about a policy move or a nomination. Congressional Republicans reciprocated, dialing up the president directly to gauge his thinking or to express a complaint. They knew that ultimately no one spoke for Trump but Trump himself. Lawmakers rarely had to wait for Trump to return their calls, as he was prone to taking them immediately. Republican senators said they also called Trump just to offer positive reinforcement and praise.[122] Mitch McConnell was among the most frequent of the president's phone partners, as were Paul Ryan and Kevin McCarthy.[123]

Working with Republican leaders had advantages for the president, in addition to rounding up votes. Ryan and McConnell were able to use

their control over the congressional agenda to aid the president by rush-
ing votes before Congressional Budget Office estimates were available
to avoid evidence that repealing the Affordable Care Act would increase
the number of uninsured and the cost of health insurance—which would
make it more difficult to secure votes. Similarly, the leaders brought tax
measures to a vote before Joint Tax Committee estimates of their consequences were available.[124] When it came time for the Senate trial on
impeachment, McConnell made it clear he was "taking my cues" from the
White House and that he would follow White House counsel Pat Cipollone's lead. "Everything I do during this, I'm coordinating with the White
House counsel," he announced.[125]

Despite the veneer of normality, Trump was a disruptive influence on
the Republican caucuses on Capitol Hill. His negotiating style made it
more difficult to form winning coalitions. More important, his rhetoric
and policy stances on spending, immigration, trade, and foreign policy
strained the party, while the president's ill-considered broadsides against
opponents, international leaders, and domestic activists increased the
burdens of defending him. As conservative commentator Max Boot put it:

> Republicans now found themselves making excuses for a boorish, ignorant
> demagogue who had no respect for the fundamental norms of democracy and
> no adherence to conservative principles. The party of fiscal conservatism ex-
> cused a profligate president who added $2 trillion in debt and counting. The
> party of family values became cheerleaders for what Democratic presidential
> candidate Pete Buttigieg has witheringly and accurately called the "porn star
> presidency." The party of law and order became accomplices to the president's
> obstruction of justice. The party of free trade did nothing to stop the presi-
> dent from launching trade wars. The party of moral clarity barely uttered a
> peep at the president's sickening sycophancy toward the worst dictators on the
> planet—or his equally nauseating attacks on America's closest allies. The party
> that once championed immigration eagerly joined in the president's xenopho-
> bic attacks on refugee caravans. And the party that long castigated Democrats
> for dividing Americans by race pretended not to notice—or even cheered—
> when the president made openly racist appeals to white voters.[126]

In addition, the president lacked a strategic sense. The issue of infrastructure is a good example. We have seen that the White House had
several rollouts of an infrastructure initiative, but it often stepped on its
own story. Equally important, the administration never developed a plan

to present to Congress, nor did it prepare the groundwork of building a supportive coalition. Instead of enumerating problems with the nation's infrastructure and specifying what the president's plan was to remedy, it simply announced an aspiration. Similarly, the White House offered no plan for funding the spending.

The most distinctive aspect of Trump's party leadership, however, was his criticism of and threats against members of his own party.

Intimidation

We saw in chapter 7 that Donald Trump was not an effective negotiator or dealmaker. He had difficulty making a sale or closing a deal. His passivity, vagueness, inconsistency, and lack of command of policy made him an unskilled, unreliable, and untrustworthy negotiator. His lack of success at legislative leadership and his customary way of dealing with others led him to try intimidation to sway members of his party.

On March 21, 2017, Trump went to Capitol Hill to speak to the House Republican Conference about the leadership's health care bill. The president told Mark Meadows, the chair of the House Freedom Caucus, whose members Trump had lobbied intensively, to stand up and take some advice. "I'm gonna come after you, but I know I won't have to, because I know you'll vote 'yes,'" asserted the president. Nevertheless, after the meeting, Meadows told reporters that the president had not convinced him or other caucus members. "I didn't take anything he said as threatening anybody's political future," said Meadows. "Oh, he was kidding around," said Hal Rodgers of Kentucky, a supporter of the bill. "I think."[127]

The bill failed to come to a vote, and Trump was angry. On March 26, he blamed conservative interest groups and far-right Republican lawmakers, tweeting, "Democrats are smiling in D.C. that the Freedom Caucus, with the help of Club for Growth and Heritage, have saved Planned Parenthood & Ocare!"[128] Less than an hour later, White House Chief of Staff Reince Priebus appeared on television to echo his boss's sentiments, saying his missive hit "the bull's eye." As if to rub salt in the Republicans' wound, Priebus hinted that Trump might try forging more consensus with moderate Democrats in future legislative battles. Priebus pointed to the Freedom Caucus and the Tuesday Group for heavily resisting the health care bill. Although one member of the Freedom Caucus, Ted Poe of Texas, resigned from the group and criticized its opposition to the health care bill, there was little sign of successful intimidation.[129]

Trump was not finished, however. In the early hours of March 30, the president tweeted, "The Freedom Caucus will hurt the entire Republican agenda if they don't get on the team, & fast. We must fight them, & Dems, in 2018!" That afternoon, Trump stepped up his Twitter attacks on the caucus, singling out three of its members by name. "Where are @Rep-MarkMeadows, @Jim_Jordan and @Raul_Labrador? #RepealANDReplace #Obamacare," he asked, claiming that with their support "we would have both great healthcare and massive tax cuts & reform." Trump's aides reported the president intended his tweets to make members of the Freedom Caucus think twice about crossing him again after they blocked his Affordable Care Act repeal the previous week.[130]

Many in the bloc met Trump's threat with defiance. Republican Justin Amash of Michigan responded to Trump's tweet with a taunting reference to the president's promise to "drain the swamp" of Washington: "It didn't take long for the swamp to drain @realDonaldTrump. No shame, Mr. President. Almost everyone succumbs to the D.C. Establishment." Amash also told reporters that Trump's tactic would have been "constructive in fifth grade. It may allow a child to get his way, but that's not how our government works." "Intimidation may work with some in the short term, but it never really works in the long run," said Republican Mark Sanford of South Carolina. Tom Garrett of Virginia, another Freedom Caucus member, was even more blunt. "Stockholm Syndrome?" he asked on Twitter above a copy of Trump's taunting post, suggesting the president had become captive to the Republican establishment he gleefully flayed during the campaign.[131] When White House chief strategist Stephen Bannon told Freedom Caucus members that they must stop waffling and vote for the legislation, Republican Joe Barton of Texas icily told Bannon that the only person who ordered him around was "my daddy"—and that his father was unsuccessful in doing so.[132]

House Freedom Caucus members were electorally secure, representing solidly conservative districts. They typically won with greater margins of the vote than Trump received in their districts. They were also very conservative, unlikely to generate primary opposition from the right. Moreover, the Freedom Caucus acted as a bloc, making it more difficult for opponents to focus on individual members, and it received substantial outside support, such as from the Koch Industries Inc. PAC, which lessened its reliance on Republican Party coffers.[133] Two Koch-aligned groups pledged to spend upward of $1 million on ads defending any Republican who voted against the replacement legislation. (Some of the same groups began an online advertising campaign attacking the border tax proposal.[134]) It is no surprise that leaders of conservative groups, including Heritage Action for America, FreedomWorks, and the Family Research Council, expressed sharp indignation at Trump when he criticized the Freedom Caucus.[135]

Nevertheless, Trump kept up his threats. In April, during the push for the revised health care bill in the House, the president sent an emissary to Sanford to tell him, "The president hopes you vote against this because he wants to run somebody against you if you do." Sanford said Trump "has made those kinds of threats to any number of members. . . . But I don't think it's productive to his own legislative agenda. It doesn't make anybody's day when the president of the United States says, 'I want to take you out.' "[136]

After a revised health care bill passed the House, the focus turned to the Senate. Once again, the president won few, if any votes, and some of his efforts seemed to be counterproductive.

Senator Dean Heller of Nevada, the only Republican running in 2018 from a state won by Hillary Clinton, was a consistent holdout from supporting the versions of the Senate health care bill cobbled together by Mitch McConnell. Heller followed the lead of Nevada's Republican governor, Brian Sandoval, who was far more popular in his state than Trump and never backed off his opposition to the health measures, even after a phone call from the president and a series of one-on-one meetings with senior administration officials at the National Governors Association annual meeting.[137]

Trying to exert pressure on Heller, Trump sat next to him during a July 19 White House meeting with Republican senators, convened to rekindle interest in voting on a clean repeal of the health care law before the August recess. At the lunch, the president also threatened electoral consequences for senators who opposed him, suggesting that Heller could lose his reelection bid in 2018 if he did not back the effort. The president began with a lightly veiled threat, urging the senator to back his third push for a Senate repeal. "This was the one we were worried about," Trump said, turning to Heller. "Look, he wants to remain a senator, doesn't he?" Trump asked. "You weren't there. But you're gonna be," the president said. "And I think the people of your state, which I know very well, I think they're gonna appreciate what you hopefully will do." The president also invited conservative opposition against anyone else who stood in the way. "Any senator who votes against starting debate is really telling America that you're fine with Obamacare," he declared.[138]

There was no sign that the president changed any minds, however. Other stories emerged of the president trying to employ some Oval Office muscle on Republican senator Ron Johnson of Wisconsin. Johnson, however, noted that he received more votes than did Trump in 2016. In addition, few Republicans were up for reelection in 2018, making a threat of retaliation somewhat toothless. One Republican senator put it bluntly: the president, he said, scared no one in the Senate, not even the pages.[139] After he returned from lunch at the White House, Dean Heller reflected, "That's just President Trump being President Trump."[140]

In the meantime, conservative activists were aggressively targeting centrist Republicans who opposed the Senate bill. A pair of conservative groups launched an "Obamacare Repeal Traitors" website attacking Republican senators Lisa Murkowski of Alaska, Rob Portman from Ohio, and Shelley Moore Capito of West Virginia. The Trump-aligned super PAC, America First Action, started an ad campaign against Heller with the White House's blessing. Mitch McConnell called the president's chief of staff, Reince Priebus, to complain that the attacks were "beyond stupid."[141] Trump allies also encouraged major GOP donors to reach out to senators who opposed the bill. For example, Las Vegas casino moguls Sheldon Adelson and Steve Wynn both spoke with Heller to prod him along.[142]

Lisa Murkowski was one of only two Republicans to vote against starting debate on health care. On July 26, the president tweeted "Senator @lisamurkowski of the Great State of Alaska really let the Republicans, and our country, down yesterday. Too bad!"[143] If publicly criticizing a crucial vote was not enough, Ryan Zinke, the interior secretary, called both Murkowski and Alaska's other senator, Dan Sullivan, blatantly warning them that the administration might change its position on several issues, given Murkowski's vote. Since Trump took office, the Department of the Interior had indicated it was open to constructing a road through the Izembek National Wildlife Refuge and drilling in the Arctic National Wildlife Refuge while expanding energy exploration elsewhere in the state. However, Zinke suggested, these policy shifts might now be in jeopardy. The senator also received what she described as "not a very pleasant call" from President Trump about her decision to cast her vote against moving the health care effort forward. Apparently, Trump and Zinke did not appreciate the fact that Murkowski was the chair of the Senate Energy and Natural Resources Committee, which has oversight of the Department of the Interior. She was also the chair of the Senate Appropriations subcommittee with jurisdiction over the department. Thus, she was positioned to do more to Zinke than he could do to her.[144]

More broadly, the president was furious at Senator Jeff Flake when he called on him to withdraw from the presidential race after the emergence of the *Access Hollywood* tape. As a candidate, Trump told a small group of Arizona Republicans that he would spend $10 million to defeat Flake in the 2018 Senate primary. Once in the White House, Trump and his aides openly tried to recruit a primary challenger to Flake.[145] Not only did these efforts fail to turn Flake into a Trump enthusiast, but they also irritated Republican leaders. Commenting on White House meddling in the Arizona primary, John Cornyn said, "I don't think that's productive."[146]

Trump wasted no time in attacking other Republican senators. In his first major act as president, he issued an executive order banning immigration from some Middle Eastern countries. In response, Senators John McCain and Lindsey Graham issued a joint statement in which they characterized the order as "hasty" and "not properly vetted." They argued that the president's policy would "become a self-inflicted wound in the fight against terrorism" by serving to aid terrorist recruitment more than it would improve national security. In a series of tweets, the president attacked McCain and Graham, accusing them of "looking to start World War III" and claimed that the senators were "sadly weak on immigration."[147]

On July 14, during the heat of the Senate debate on health care, Vice President Mike Pence addressed the National Governors Association in Providence, Rhode Island.

> Gov. [John] Kasich isn't with us, but I suspect that he's very troubled to know that in Ohio alone, nearly 60,000 disabled citizens are stuck on waiting lists, leaving them without the care they need for months or even years.[148]

However, the waiting lists were unrelated to Medicaid expansion, sparking negative commentary and reportedly making Kasich newly furious about the hardball tactics.[149]

Trump addressed a Boy Scouts jamboree in West Virginia in July. White House aides told Republican senator Shelley Moore Capito from that state that she could only accompany the president on Air Force One if she committed to voting for the health care bill. She declined the invitation, noting that she could not commit to voting for a measure she had not seen.[150]

Even on his August vacation, the president fought with senators of his party. In a retort to their criticism of his response to the violence in Charlottesville, Virginia, the president lashed out at Lindsey Graham as "publicity seeking." He added that Graham "just can't forget his election trouncing. The people of South Carolina will remember!" he threatened. Trump also described Jeff Flake as "WEAK on borders, crime and a non-factor in the Senate. He's toxic!" and praised Flake's Republican primary opponent.[151]

In addition, the president engaged in a public spat with Mitch McConnell over the latter's comment that he had "excessive expectations" for Congress.[152] He then retweeted *Fox & Friends* headlines: "Senators learn the hard way about the fallout from turning on Trump" and "Trump fires new warning shot at McConnell, leaves door open on whether he should step down." Trump also berated McConnell in a phone call that quickly devolved into a profane shouting match.[153]

On August 24, the president was at it again, tweeting, "The only problem I have with Mitch McConnell is that, after hearing Repeal & Replace for 7 years, he failed! That should NEVER have happened!" He added in another tweet: "I requested that Mitch M & Paul R tie the Debt Ceiling legislation into the popular V.A. Bill (which just passed) for easy approval. They . . . didn't do it so now we have a big deal with Dems holding them up (as usual) on Debt Ceiling approval. Could have been so easy—now a mess!"[154]

Before the crucial Senate vote on the Republican health care bill in September, Trump tweeted that any Republican who opposed the measure "will forever (future political campaigns) be known as 'the Republican who saved ObamaCare.' "[155] Hours later, John McCain cast the deciding vote killing the bill and became the focus of the president's ire. Trump distributed a video that showed the Arizona Republican opposing the Affordable Care Act in the past. "A few of the many clips of John McCain talking about Repealing & Replacing O'Care," Trump said in a tweet that accompanied the video. "My oh my has he changed—complete turn from years of talk!"[156] During a radio interview, Trump called McCain's opposition "a tremendous slap in the face to the Republican Party."[157] In other tweets, the president claimed McCain had let his state and his best friend, Lindsey Graham, down and been deceived by Democrats.[158]

After the last vote on health care failed to garner a majority in the Senate, Trump adopted an antagonistic posture. He lashed out at "some Republicans" in the Senate whom he accused of refusing to go along with their party, apparently talking about failed votes to repeal the Affordable Care Act. "There are some Republicans, frankly, that should be ashamed of themselves."[159] In addition, the president declared that the senators

looked like "fools," and tweeted, "Unless the Republican Senators are total quitters, Repeal & Replace is not dead! Demand another vote before
voting on any other bill!"[160]

In a petty move, Trump threatened to remove the subsidies members
of Congress received to help offset the costs of their health insurance
purchased through the District of Columbia's insurance exchanges, as required under the Affordable Care Act. Budget director Mick Mulvaney
echoed the president's sentiments. In addition, the president insisted that
the Senate eliminate the filibuster. White House press secretary Sarah
Huckabee Sanders blamed the Republican-controlled Congress for the
lack of major accomplishments this year.[161]

Senators were not impressed. "We've got other things to do," responded Republican senator John Thune. "It's time to move on," agreed
his Republican colleague Roy Blunt. John Cornyn advised Mulvaney to
do his job and let the senators do theirs. Mitch McConnell made it clear
that the Senate would not be dealing with health care for a while and
that he had no plans to scuttle the filibuster.[162] "We work for the American people. We don't work for the president," added Republican senator Tim Scott.[163] Asked if Trump's repeated insistence on jettisoning the
filibuster was hindering progress, Senate Finance Committee chair Orrin
Hatch replied, "It doesn't help." "He'd like to get more cooperation up
here. And he's not getting very much, to be honest with you."[164] Similarly,
asked if a large portion of the Republican caucus had lost patience with
the president's unpredictable ways, one GOP senator replied. "Yeah—it's
just endless chaos."[165]

No doubt the president hoped his messages would encourage senators to toe the White House line. He was wrong. In private, McConnell
described Trump as entirely unwilling to learn the basics of governing
and expressed uncertainty that the president would be able to salvage
his administration after a series of summer crises. Senator Bob Corker
rebuked Trump for failing to "demonstrate the stability, nor some of the
competence" required of presidents.[166] (Trump responded by tweeting on
August 25, "Strange statement by Bob Corker considering that he is constantly asking me whether or not he should run again in '18. Tennessee
not happy!"[167])

In early October, the president's feud with Corker escalated. The senator told reporters that secretary of state Rex Tillerson, defense secretary
Jim Mattis, and White House chief of staff John Kelly "are those people
that help separate our country from chaos." Corker charged that Trump

was treating his office like "a reality show," with reckless threats toward other countries that could set the nation "on the path to World War III." The president posed such an acute risk, the senator said, that a coterie of senior administration officials must protect him from his own instincts. "I know for a fact that every single day at the White House, it's a situation of trying to contain him," the senator said. He also charged that Trump had repeatedly undermined diplomacy with his tweets. "I know he has hurt, in several instances, he's hurt us as it relates to negotiations that were under-way by tweeting things out."[168]

Trump, of course, could not resist insulting the senator, even though he chaired the Foreign Relations Committee and was a critical vote on the tax cut bill. The president tweeted that Corker decided not to seek reelec-tion because he "didn't have the guts." The senator, the president said, had "begged" for his endorsement. "I said 'NO' and he dropped out (said he could not win without my endorsement)."[169] Corker flatly disputed that account, saying Trump had urged him to run again, and promised to en-dorse him if he did.[170] The president also claimed Corker had asked to be secretary of state. "I said 'NO THANKS.'" Later, the president charged "Bob Corker gave us the Iran Deal, & that's about it. We need Health-Care, we need Tax Cuts/Reform, we need people that can get the job done!"[171] Corker responded in his own tweet: "It's a shame the White House has become an adult day care center. Someone obviously missed their shift this morning."[172]

The president also ridiculed Corker's height, assigning him a deroga-tory new nickname—"Liddle Bob"—and suggested the *New York Times* had tricked him when he told a reporter that the president was reckless and could stumble into a nuclear war.[173] Two weeks later, when Corker commented on the *Today* show that Trump should step aside and leave tax legislation to Congress,[174] Trump countered that Corker "couldn't get elected dog catcher in Tennessee" and was incompetent to head his committee.[175] Corker characterized Trump's statements about him as the "same untruths from an utterly untruthful president."[176]

Corker also claimed nearly every Senate Republican shared his con-cerns about Trump. "Look, except for a few people, the vast majority of our caucus understands what we're dealing with here," he said, adding that "of course they understand the volatility that we're dealing with and the tremendous amount of work that it takes by people around him to keep him in the middle of the road." The senator added, "I don't know why the president tweets out things that are not true." "You know he does it, everyone knows he does it, but he does."[177] In another interview, Corker reflected, "I don't know why he lowers himself to such a low, low standard and is debasing our country."[178]

McConnell and his allies were incredulous that the president would anger a senator just a week before a budget vote that was critical to tax cuts, when just three defections could thwart the party's fifty-two-vote majority. "He's an important part of our team, and he's a particularly important part of the budget debate, which will be on the floor next week," McConnell said pointedly.[179]

Other Republicans were critical of the president's condemnation of their colleagues. "It's entirely counterproductive for the president to be picking fights with Republican senators who he will need for important agenda items that they both agree on," reflected Representative Charlie Dent. "Does he think that Democratic senators will be more cooperative than John McCain and Jeff Flake and Susan Collins? It doesn't seem to make any sense."[180] Representative Tom Cole added, "It doesn't help at this point . . . to be throwing rocks at one another. You don't, I think, do a lot of good by torching your teammates, particularly by name, individually."[181]

In 2018, Senator Jeff Flake declared that Trump had "debased" the presidency and that the nation's leadership "may have hit bottom." Asked in the interview for examples of how Trump has degraded the presidency, Flake singled out his name-calling. "When you refer to your opponents in the legislature, for example, in the Congress, and call them losers and clowns and nicknames for people—that's debasing the presidency. That's not presidential," he said.[182] Unwilling to roll with the punches, Trump tweeted a response on June 7. "How could Jeff Flake, who is setting record low polling numbers in Arizona and was therefore humiliatingly forced out of his own Senate seat without even a fight (and who doesn't have a clue), think about running for office, even a lower one, again?" Trump wrote. "Let's face it, he's a Flake!"[183]

Former Republican presidential nominee Mitt Romney took office as a senator in 2019. He was an early critic of the president's behavior in seeking foreign assistance against his political opponents. On October 4, he tweeted, "By all appearances, the President's brazen and unprecedented appeal to China and to Ukraine to investigate Joe Biden is wrong and appalling." Trump responded harshly to Romney's criticism, calling him a pompous "ass" and "a fool" who should be impeached.[184] (Senators cannot be impeached.) On October 23, the president reached a new low, calling "The Never Trumper Republicans" "human scum."[185]

Even staunch supporters were the subjects of the president's ire. He dismissed as "crazy" a proposal by some Senate Republicans, including Ted Cruz, to expedite processing of immigrant families by hiring hundreds of new immigration judges. Trump suggested that many of the judges would be corrupt and that some of the lawyers involved were "bad people."[186] In a conference call with reporters before voting began on immigration reform bills in February 2018, a senior White House official lashed out at Lindsey Graham. The official accused Graham of attacking Homeland Security officials and standing in the way of needed immigration changes. "Senator Graham has been an obstacle for those reforms," the official said, and he accused Graham of misleading other senators about the damage the proposal would do."[187]

Shortly before the 2018 midterm elections, Trump threatened to end birthright citizenship with an executive order (which he lacked the power to do). A number of Republicans, including Speaker Paul Ryan, tried to separate themselves from the president on the issue. Angered, the president tweeted that this was an issue that Ryan "knows nothing about."[188]

In an interview after he retired from Congress, Ryan disclosed that Trump "didn't know *anything* about government" and operated on ill-informed "knee-jerk reactions." Thus, Republican congressional leaders had to work quietly to stop him from making bad decisions.[189] Trump struck back, calling Ryan a "long running lame duck failure" who had an "atrocious" record of achievement. "Couldn't get him out of Congress fast enough!" Trump tweeted.[190]

Trump insulted prominent Republicans in more subtle ways as well. John McCain was a frequent Trump critic. In addition to opposing the president on health care and immigration, he denounced the "half-baked, spurious nationalism" that he saw overtaking American politics.[191] Trump was never a gracious recipient of criticism. When he gave a speech at Fort Drum, New York, commemorating the signing of a defense spending bill named for John McCain, Trump failed to mention the ailing senator. When McCain died, the president refused to release a statement prepared by his aides that praised the Republican's life and heroism. Instead, he issued a tweet that did not include any kind words for McCain. White House aides had to post statements from other officials praising the war hero.[192]

Not only did the president's criticism do little to win support on particular bills, but in the long run it was also self-defeating. For example, although Trump succeeded in denying both Jeff Flake and Mark Sanford renominations, the Democrats won both seats in the subsequent election.

Trump's Success

A week before the 2016 presidential election, Donald Trump traveled to the Philadelphia suburbs to deliver a health care policy speech that was light on details and heavy on ambitious promises. In a hotel ballroom, Trump promised to convene a special session of Congress as soon as he was sworn in—a perplexing idea, as Congress would already be in session—so that lawmakers could "immediately repeal and replace Obamacare." All of this would happen "very, very quickly," he vowed.[193]

The new president came to Washington boasting of his prowess as a leader, able to cut deals, "drain the swamp" in Washington, and transform public policy. Once in office, he repeatedly claimed that his stewardship had led to uncommon success with Congress, declaring that he had signed more legislation than any president since Franklin D. Roosevelt. On July 17, he declared at a White House event, "We've signed more bills—and I'm talking about through the legislature—than any president, ever."[194] He was wrong.

At first glance, it may seem as though Trump was extraordinarily successful as a legislative leader. He won nearly every roll-call vote on which he took a stand in 2017 (99 percent) and 2018 (93 percent). The president achieved these results because he received high levels of support from Republicans (table 8.2). In fact, Trump obtained a higher level of support from Republicans in both the House and the Senate than any other Republican president in the modern age. There is little variance among the members. For example, in 2017, forty-seven of the fifty-one Republican senators supported Trump at least 95 percent of the time. In 2018, the same number supported the president on 91 percent of the votes.

This impressive backing is the mirror image of his record low levels of support among Democrats. Polarization cuts two ways, aiding as well as thwarting the president's ability to win votes in Congress. Republican support has increased for every succeeding Republican president since Eisenhower (with the minor exception of the Senate in the Nixon/Ford era). It is unlikely that Trump's stewardship as party leader was responsible for the uniformity of Republican support, however. There was nothing in his behavior that would encourage us to credit his leadership skills for his success. The increasingly conservative views of Republican senators and the president's support among their constituents are the most likely

TABLE 8.2. **Republican support for Republican Presidents**

President	Support (%)[*]	
	House	Senate
Eisenhower	63	69
Nixon/Ford	64	63
Reagan	70	74
G. H. W. Bush	73	75
G. W. Bush	83	86
Trump[**]	92	95

[*]On roll-call votes on which the winning side was supported by fewer than 80 percent of those voting.
[**]2017–2019.

explanations. Jon Bond found that Trump did about what one would expect in the political environment in which he operated.[195]

Another explanation for the president's high level of Republican support is the small size of the agenda that reached the floor of Congress.
According to Congressional Quarterly, in 2017 Trump took stands on
only thirty-six votes in the House, representing 5.1 percent of the votes
taken and the lowest percentage in the history of calculating presidential
support, which stretches back nearly seven decades. He took even fewer
stands on legislative votes (those not on nominations) in the Senate—
twenty-three.[196] In 2018, the president was even less active, taking stands
on only thirty votes in the House and sixteen legislative votes in the Senate.[197] He lost seven of these sixteen votes, despite Republicans holding a
Senate majority.

In 2017–2018, Republican congressional leaders had substantial control over the legislative agenda and kept issues that would divide the majority and alienate a bloc of members from coming to the floor.[198] Equally
important, the leaders hesitated to bring legislation to the floor that the
president would not support—and which might attract opposition.[199] For
example, during the government shutdown in December 2018 and January 2019, Mitch McConnell refused to bring to the floor any bill to resolve
the issue that the president said he would not sign.

In addition, nearly one-third of the laws passed by the 115th Congress
were ceremonial in nature. One hundred and nine pieces of legislation
renamed post offices, courthouses and the like—one-fourth of the Congress' total legislative output.[200]

In 2019, the tables were turned when the Democrats took over the

House. The president won only five of sixty-two votes (8 percent) on which he took a stand, the lowest percentage on record. Two of the president's five victories (the Fiscal 2020 Defense Authorization Conference Report and the USMCA) were on near-unanimous votes on which the Democrats had negotiated effectively to win important concessions from the administration. Although the White House supported the Budget Cap Adjustment bill, two-thirds of House Republicans did not, indicating how well the Democrats had bargained. The president was not able to obtain majority support for his other two "victories" (a veto override attempt of the National Emergency Disapproval Resolution and the Further Continuing Fiscal 2019 Appropriations bill), but he was able to win the support of enough representatives to prevent the opposition from acquiring the two-thirds majorities the bills required to pass.

The Republicans strengthened their control of the Senate with the 2018 elections and continued to provide the president with victories, especially on nominations. Nevertheless, Trump lost eleven of the twenty-nine votes that were not on nominations. Five of his eighteen victories were on veto override attempts on which he failed to win a majority of the vote. So even with a Republican majority, the president failed to win a majority of the vote on sixteen of twenty-nine (55 percent) of legislative votes.

Passing Legislation

Trump did enjoy some successes, of course. Tax cuts, a high-priority item for both him and his party, passed. The White House was also able to use the tax bill to open oil and gas exploration in the Arctic National Wildlife Refuge and end the individual mandate established by the Affordable Care Act. In addition, Republicans exploited the Congressional Review Act to overturn sixteen agency rules adopted in the last sixty days of the Obama administration. Congress had made use of the 1995 law only once before—in 2001 to rescind a Clinton administration Labor Department ergonomics rule. In each case, Republicans had to employ a procedure that avoided filibusters to accomplish their goals.

The White House also enjoyed a notable success in winning approval of the USMCA. As we have seen, this victory occurred only after the Democrats won a series of major concessions. The bills designed to provide relief in response to the coronavirus pandemic were even more the product of Democratic as well as Republican initiatives.

The most notable fact about Trump's legislative record, however, is the relative absence of passage of significant presidential initiatives.

Prominent among the legislation that did *not* pass were bills dealing with health care reform, infrastructure spending, and immigration—policies central to Trump's presidential campaign. The president's budgets proposed deep cuts in nondefense discretionary spending. Congress, including many Republicans, simply ignored the president's requests and passed bills that reversed his proposed cuts.[201] In May 2018, the White House submitted a $15 billion rescission package to Congress. The Republican Senate rejected the bill.

To cap off the president's first two years, the 115th Congress ended without funding large portions of the federal government, precipitating the longest government shutdown in US history. It is clear that the episode was not an example of successful presidential leadership. Ultimately, Trump won only $1.375 billion for building a wall, less than he could have obtained months earlier. Sean Hannity, perhaps Trump's most reliable media supporter, declared to his Fox News audience on February 11, 2019, "Any Republican that supports this garbage compromise, you will have to explain."[202] Mark Meadows, the head of the House Freedom Caucus and the most vocal supporter of a border wall in Congress, complained to the same network, "Only in Washington, D.C., can we start out with needing $25 billion dollars for border-security measures and expect applause at $1.37 [billion]."[203]

After the president failed to win funding to build a border wall in 2019, he declared a national emergency in order to reprogram defense funds to wall building. Never before had a president asked for funding, Congress refused to provide it, and the president then used the National Emergencies Act of 1976 to spend the money anyway.

The House voted 245–182 to overturn the president. Attention then focused on the Senate. There was little chance that Congress could override a presidential veto, but the White House nevertheless made a frenzied effort to avoid a rebuke in the upper chamber. Trump sought to frame the vote as not only a declaration of support for his border security policy, but also as a sign of personal loyalty in a time of divided government. On Twitter, he referred to it as a vote on "Border Security and Crime!!!" and urged Republican senators, "Don't vote with Pelosi!"[204] He also warned Republicans of the electoral consequences of defying his will and dismissed concerns about the constitutional precedent of his order.[205]

In the end, twelve of fifty-three Republican senators voted against the president as the Senate passed the resolution of disapproval, 59–41. The vote marked the first time Congress had ever sought to terminate a national emergency order with a resolution of disapproval. It was also a rejection of the president on his signature campaign issue. On September 25, the Senate again voted to terminate the national emergency. The vote was 54–41, as five of the votes for termination were absent. The House followed suit, forcing the president to once again veto the resolution of disapproval.

In general, despite its high priority on the White House's agenda, there was little legislative change in immigration law. Congress enacted none of the big changes to immigration policy for which Trump called. Not only could he not win funding for a border wall, but he also failed to win legislative policy changes in the number of legal immigrants the United States would commit to accepting or the skills or family connections of those it would accept. Dreamers did not win permanent legal status, and there has been no law regarding those seeking asylum.

In 2019, Congress passed a two-year budget deal that raised spending by hundreds of billions of dollars over existing caps and allowed the government to keep borrowing to cover its debts. Before the House vote, the president tweeted on July 25, "House Republicans should support the TWO YEAR BUDGET AGREEMENT which greatly helps our Military and our Vets. I am totally with you!"[206] Nevertheless, only 65 Republicans voted for the bill while 132 voted against it.

PUSHBACK.   Congress displayed its independence in other ways. In response to Trump's public disparaging of Attorney General Jeff Sessions, several of Sessions's former Senate colleagues rallied behind him and strongly cautioned the president that "there will be holy hell to pay," in the words of Lindsey Graham, if Sessions were fired.[207] Republican Senate Judiciary Committee chair Charles Grassley said that he would not make time in the Senate schedule to consider a new attorney general nominee. Before leaving for its 2017 summer recess, the Senate set up a system to prevent the president from appointing senior administration officials to posts that required confirmation in the senators' absence. The goal was to prevent Trump from dismissing Sessions and then appointing someone without Senate confirmation who would be willing to fire Special Counsel Robert Mueller. In addition, two bipartisan pairs of senators unveiled legislation to prevent the president from firing Mueller without cause.[208]

In chapter 4, we discussed the president's policy of separating the children of illegal immigrants and asylum seekers from their parents at the border. Republican Orrin Hatch and twelve other senators sent a letter

to the Department of Justice, asking the administration to stop the separation of families until Congress could pass legislation. Mitch McConnell said that "all of the members of the Republican conference support
a plan that keeps families together," endorsing quick passage of a narrow bill to provide legal authority to detain parents and children together
while the courts considered their status.[209] The policy was so unpopular
that even stalwart Republican supporters—from the Chamber of Commerce to evangelist Franklin Graham—urged the president to reverse his
stance. As the public outcry against the policy grew, the president ended
the practice.

Trump also endured symbolic defeats in the domestic arena. On August 16, 2018, senators unanimously voted to separate themselves from
the president's attacks on the media. They adopted a resolution affirming
support for a free press and declaring, "The press is not the enemy of the
people." The resolution reaffirmed "the vital and indispensable role that
the free press serves to inform the electorate, uncover the truth, act as
a check on the inherent power of the government, further national discourse and debate, and otherwise advance the most basic and cherished
democratic norms and freedoms of the United States."[210]

Republican senator Ben Sasse was outraged when the president raised
questions about the television networks' licenses and declared that it's
"frankly disgusting the way the press is able to write whatever they want
to write." The senator issued a press release in which he asked the president if he was recanting his oath to "preserve, protect and defend the First
Amendment."[211]

In September 2017, the House and Senate unanimously passed a joint
resolution urging Trump to denounce racist and anti-Semitic hate groups,
sending a blunt message of dissatisfaction with the president's initial, equiv-
ocal response to the white nationalist violence in Charlottesville, Virginia,
in August. Trump ultimately signed the resolution. The president was by
no means done with race baiting, however. In July 2019, he advised four
Democratic congresswomen of color to go back where they came from.[212]
In response, the House passed a resolution condemning the president for
his "racist comments."

FOREIGN POLICY. Trump's foreign policy stances often went against the
grain of established Republican policy. Although Congress often finds
it difficult to thwart a president in the area of international relations, it
can send important symbolic messages that may be embarrassing and

politically costly to the White House. The 115th Congress was unusually active in doing so, despite its Republican majorities, and this opposition to the president continued in the 116th Congress. Symbolic votes can matter, because the public is more likely to notice conflict in Washington when the elite consensus breaks down. Dissent further undermines a struggling White House. Moreover, negative congressional votes—even when they fail—can shape future foreign policy by increasing the political costs to the president of persisting in a course of action.[213]

In July 2017, Congress passed by veto-proof margins a bill containing toughened sanctions on Russia, Iran, and North Korea—but aimed primarily at punishing Russia for its interference in the 2016 elections. The White House opposed the law, and Republican Senate Foreign Relations chair Bob Corker described the president and White House officials as "non-existent" as lawmakers worked out a final bill.[214] The law represented an emboldened Congress, including Republicans, pushing back against the White House. Trump reluctantly signed the measure on August 2 to avoid the humiliation of a veto override. At the same time, the president issued two signing statements in which he made bold declarations of executive power. The second one ended with a gratuitous assertion:

> I built a truly great company worth many billions of dollars. That is a big part of the reason I was elected. As President, I can make far better deals with foreign countries than Congress.[215]

Ironically, Trump's assertion of power and his criticism of the legislature was likely to make Congress even less likely to defer to him or to grant him discretion.

Free trade has been a central tenet of Republican policy for decades and runs counter to Trump's protectionist approach. On July 10, 2018, the Senate passed a nonbinding measure calling for Congress to have a role in tariffs imposed on the basis of national security, an implicit rebuke of the president's move to tax imported steel and aluminum from Canada, Mexico, the European Union, and other trading partners.

In 2019, Trump more than doubled tariffs on $200 billion in Chinese goods, provoking China to retaliate with tariffs on US agricultural and other products. Then he expanded the trade war further, taking steps to levy tariffs on an additional $300 billion in Chinese goods. Senate Republicans expressed concern that the president's escalating trade war was hurting their constituents. Some, including Senate Finance Committee chair Charles Grassley, took the unusual step of openly criticizing a president from their own party.[216]

On May 30, 2019, the president announced that he would impose a 5 percent tariff on all goods imported from Mexico on June 10, and then increase the levies each month if that country did not agree to do more to stop immigrants from reaching the US border. Republican lawmakers warned White House officials that the tariffs could imperil the chances of passing an overhaul of NAFTA, but Trump remained undeterred. Republican senators then warned that they were prepared to block the president's efforts to impose tariffs on Mexican imports and that they had enough votes to override a veto. "There is not much support in my conference for tariffs, that's for sure," said Mitch McConnell.[217] In the end, Trump backed down and levied no tariffs. Although he announced a deal with Mexico, it had agreed to the main provisions months earlier.[218]

Donald Trump and Vladimir Putin held a press conference in Helsinki on July 17, 2018, in which the president expressed doubts about US intelligence conclusions that the Russian government tried to influence the outcome of the 2016 US presidential election. Instead, he indicated he believed Putin's denials. At least thirteen Republican senators denounced his comments, as did Paul Ryan and other Republican members of the House.[219] On July 19, 2018, Republican representative Will Hurd penned an op-ed in the *New York Times* titled "Trump Is Being Manipulated by Putin."[220] John McCain excoriated the president: "Today's press conference in Helsinki was one of the most disgraceful performances by an American president in memory. The damage inflicted by President Trump's naiveté, egotism, false equivalence, and sympathy for autocrats is difficult to calculate. But it is clear that the summit in Helsinki was a tragic mistake."[221]

On November 28, 2018, the Senate voted 63–37 to advance a resolution that would end US military support for the Saudi-led war effort in Yemen, except for operations against al-Qaeda. Fourteen Republicans joined all forty-nine Democrats in supporting it. Two weeks later, on December 13, 2018, the Senate voted to end US military support for Saudi Arabia's war in Yemen. The 56–41 vote marked the first time the Senate utilized powers granted under the 1973 War Powers Resolution, which gives Congress the power to demand an end to military actions. Seven Republicans joined with all forty-nine Democrats to support the measure. Immediately after the vote on the Yemen war, the Senate voted unanimously for a nonbinding resolution officially blaming Saudi crown prince Mohammed bin Salman for the killing of journalist Jamal Khashoggi. With both votes, senators diverged sharply from Trump, who maintained steadfast support for Saudi Arabia and Prince Mohammed, even though the CIA concluded that the prince ordered the assassination of Khashoggi inside the Saudi consulate in Istanbul.

The House may very well have passed the Senate resolution on Yemen. Republican leaders were so concerned that it would do so that on the first day of their lame-duck session following the midterm elections, they proposed a rule change to block a vote on matter. The change nullified parts of the War Powers Resolution, specifically for the Yemen bill, that would have allowed lawmakers to force a vote on the measure. Thus, the leaders spared the president from having to veto the resolution.[222]

A Democratic majority took over in January 2019, however, and on February 13, it voted to end American military assistance for Saudi Arabia's war in Yemen. The Senate followed suit on March 13, with seven Republican senators again opposing the president. The resolution was a rebuke to the president, who was forced to veto it.

In June, the Senate passed three measures to block President Trump from using his emergency authority to complete several arms sales benefiting Saudi Arabia and the United Arab Emirates and also registering growing anger with the administration's use of emergency power to cut lawmakers out of national security decisions. Seven Republican senators broke with the president—short of the support needed to overcome a veto but another slap at the White House. In July, the House followed suit, forcing the president to exercise his veto.

In December 2018, the president abruptly tweeted plans for a US pullout from Syria, overruling his generals and civilian advisors and claiming that the Islamic State had been defeated. Trump also ordered the military to develop plans to remove up to half of the fourteen thousand US forces in Afghanistan. The next month, Mitch McConnell introduced an amendment warning that "the precipitous withdrawal of United States forces from either country could put at risk hard-won gains and United States national security" and arguing that "it is incumbent upon the United States to lead, to continue to maintain a global coalition against terror and to stand by our local partners."[223] On February 4, 2019, the Senate approved the amendment by a vote of 70 to 26. Only four Republican senators voted to support the president.

In 2018, the United States sanctioned companies controlled by Russian oligarch Oleg Deripaska, an ally of Vladimir Putin, for furthering "the Kremlin's global malign activities, including its attempts to subvert Western democracy." On January 17, 2019, the House voted 362 to 53, including 136 Republicans, formally to disapprove of plans to relax sanctions against Deripaska's companies. A similar resolution narrowly failed in the Senate, falling three votes shy of clearing the 60-vote threshold to advance it to a final vote, despite winning the support of eleven Republican senators.

Several times over the course of 2018, Trump privately told aides he wanted to withdraw the United States from NATO.[224] On January 22, 2019, the House voted 357–22 to reaffirm the lawmakers' support for the alliance and to specify that the administration could spend no US funds to withdraw the United States from it.

In June 2019, the House voted to repeal the 2001 Authorization for the Use of Military Force, which passed in the days following the 9/11 terrorist attacks and accorded President George W. Bush the authority to go to war with al-Qaeda and any related organizations. The primary goal of the House action was to constrain President Trump from attacking Iran. Mitch McConnell refused to bring the bill to the Senate floor, but the Senate voted 50–40 for a bipartisan measure that would have required the president to obtain Congress's permission before striking Iran. The bill lacked the necessary 60 votes to pass. Nevertheless, four Republicans voted for it. On July 12, the House voted 251–170 to curb Trump's ability to strike Iran militarily, adopting a bipartisan provision that would require the president to obtain Congress's approval before authorizing military force against Tehran.

On January 9, 2020, the House passed on a vote of 224–195 a nonbinding resolution directing the president to terminate the use of US armed forces to engage in hostilities against Iran unless Congress had declared war or enacted a specific authorization or unless military action was necessary to defend against an imminent attack. On January 30, it passed a measure that would block funding for any use of offensive military force in or against Iran without congressional approval. It passed 228–175, with four Republicans supporting it. A second measure would repeal the authorization for use of military force that Congress passed to facilitate the Iraq invasion in 2003. It passed by a vote of 236 to 166, with eleven Republicans supporting it.

On March 11, the House gave final approval to a resolution aimed at forcing President Trump to receive explicit approval from Congress before taking further military action against Iran. The Senate had already passed a resolution on February 13, limiting the president from ordering future strikes against Iran without first seeking Congress' explicit permission. Eight Republicans joined all Democrats in voting 55–45 for the measure, forcing the president to veto it.

This resolution was only the third time the Senate had used its authority under the 1973 War Powers Resolution to block a president from using military force abroad. All three efforts were attempts to rein in Trump—and all occurred with Republican majorities in the Senate.

In August 2019, the OMB sent a letter to the State Department and the US Agency for International Development, notifying them of a temporary freeze on funds that Congress had already approved and the potential cancellation of up to $4 billion of dollars in foreign aid. Senior Republicans and Democrats complained that the move would undermine Congress's authority to appropriate funds. Within weeks, the White House scrapped the plans.[225]

On December 6, 2019, the House passed a symbolic measure backing a two-state solution to the Israeli-Palestinian conflict—an implicit rebuke to President Trump that passed mostly along party lines. The legislation declared that "only the outcome of a two-state solution . . . can both ensure the state of Israel's survival as a Jewish and democratic state and fulfill the legitimate aspirations of the Palestinian people for a state of their own."[226] It also noted longtime US opposition to "settlement expansion, moves toward unilateral annexation of territory, and efforts to achieve Palestinian statehood status outside the framework of negotiations with Israel"—an implicit critique of Trump's moves to legitimize Israel's increasingly assertive behavior in the West Bank and Golan Heights. Six days later, the Senate voted unanimously—and over the objections of the Trump administration—to recognize the 1915 mass killings of an estimated 1.5 million Armenians at the hands of the Ottoman Empire as a genocide.

Perhaps the most damning action of Congress regarding Trump and national security was its opening of an impeachment inquiry against the president in response to a whistleblower complaint that Trump had attempted to trade US aid for an investigation into possible Democratic nominee Joe Biden and his son Hunter. When the administration showed reluctance to turn over the complaint to Congress, the Senate voted unanimously to urge the release of the document on September 24, 2019.

On October 6, in a phone call with Turkish president Recep Tayyip Erdogan, Trump agreed to a withdrawal of American forces from northern Syria. On October 9, Turkey launched an attack against America's Kurdish allies. Trump's decision was widely condemned by Republicans and Democrats alike, and on October 16, the House adopted a resolution on a 354–60 vote that rebuked Trump's policy. All of the elected Republican leaders supported the measure, which upbraided the withdrawal as "beneficial to adversaries of the United States government" and called on Erdogan to immediately end unilateral military action in northern Syria.[227] Two days later, Mitch McConnell wrote an op-ed in the *Washington Post* criticizing president' policy. When Turkey did not end its assault on the Kurds, on October 29, the House voted 403–16 to impose a series of sweeping sanctions on Turkey. The measure drew broad support from Republicans, including the party's leaders.

NOMINATIONS. The president won the Senate floor votes on his nominations, but a number of them did not make it that far. In December 2017, for example, the Senate Banking Committee voted down Trump's nomination of Scott Garrett to head the Export-Import Bank. The vote on Garrett was the first time in more than three decades that a president's party controlled the Senate and defeated one of his nominees in a committee vote. (The last time that happened was on June 5, 1986, when the Judiciary Committee voted against the nomination of Jeff Sessions to be a district court judge.[228])

The president's nominee for secretary of labor, Andrew Puzder, had to withdraw in 2017 in the face of Senate opposition. Trump selected Ronny L. Jackson to head the Department of Veterans Affairs, but Jackson withdrew in the face of bipartisan criticism of his suitability for the job. In 2019, two proposed nominees for the Federal Reserve's board of governors, Herman Cain and Stephen Moore, ran into opposition from some Republicans as well as Democrats and withdrew from consideration. Patrick Sheehan withdrew as nominee for secretary of defense, and Heather Nauert withdrew from consideration as ambassador to the United Nations that same year. Trump withdrew the nomination of John Ratcliffe as director of national intelligence in response to criticism of his lack of credentials and embellishment of his resumé. The White House also withdrew six other ambassadorial nominations. In addition, the nominees for undersecretary of the departments of Agriculture and State, secretaries of the Army and Navy, deputy secretary of the departments of Commerce and Treasury, the director of US Immigration and Customs Enforcement (two), the administrator of FEMA, and many others ran into trouble. Either they withdrew from congressional consideration on their own accord or the White House decided to pull the plug on their nominations to avoid embarrassment.

Trump could claim impressive success in populating the federal judiciary. We would expect such a level of accomplishment with a Republican Senate, party agreement on judicial philosophy, and a lack of opportunity for Democrats to filibuster judicial nominations. Nevertheless, the votes on the president's nominations to judgeships were by far the most contentious since the Senate expanded to one hundred members in 1959.[229] Moreover, a surprising number of nominations, including those of Matthew Petersen, Ryan Bounds, Brett Talley, Jeff Mateer, Thomas A. Farr, and Michael Bogren, lacked the votes for confirmation. Either the White House withdrew their nominations or the candidate withdrew from consideration.

Most important, however, confirming judges was no substitute for legislation. Commenting on the Senate keeping up a steady pace of judicial confirmations, even as the chamber failed to pass major legislation such as a coronavirus relief bill, Republican Marco Rubio noted, "We're going to have to move toward each other to get something done. At some point," he added, chuckling, "we'll run out of judges."[230]

Conclusion

Donald Trump came to office with a problematic strategic position in dealing with Democrats. Successful bipartisanship would take a skilled legislator, one sensitive to the nuances of coalition building. The president did not rise to the challenge. His shifting positions, inconsistent behavior, willingness to exclude the opposition in developing policies, and use of threats and ridicule squandered whatever potential for compromise might have existed. As a result, he received historically low levels of support from Democratic senators and representatives.

The president's relations with his own party presented another challenge, one that the president could not negotiate successfully. Although he received high levels of support from Republicans in both chambers of Congress and although their leaders kept votes that he might lose off the agenda, little significant legislation passed at his behest. Some of his signature issues split the party, and when he could not convince members to support him, he turned to his customary tools of threats and disparagement. They gained him little. Moreover, some Republicans joined with Democrats to pass resolutions that forced Trump to endure symbolic defeats. It is not possible to characterize Trump as a successful party leader.

PART 3

Trump as a Leader

CHAPTER NINE

Plus ça Change

This is a book about Donald Trump as president. It is also a broader analysis of presidential leadership. Donald Trump entered the White House determined to transform public policy. To accomplish many of his goals would have required the backing of the American people and, ultimately, the approval of Congress. To obtain public and congressional support would have necessitated effective leadership.

The president was not very successful in winning support for his initiatives from either the public or Congress. Why did he fail? Did his strategic position, his opportunity structure, allow him to create opportunities for change? Alternatively, did it constrain him, offering little chance to persuade others to support his policies? Even if Trump had the potential for persuasion, was he able to exploit his public relations and negotiating skills to make the most of existing opportunities? Alternatively, was his performance wanting, squandering whatever potential for success he had?

Leading the Public

In 1976, pollster Patrick Caddell wrote a memo to president-elect Jimmy Carter entitled, "Initial Working Paper on Political Strategy." In it, Caddell argued, "governing with public approval requires a *continuing* political campaign." He also suggested implementing a working group to begin planning the *1980* presidential campaign.[1] Donald Trump adopted Caddell's advice. He filed for reelection the day of his inauguration, spent millions on advertising by mid-2019, and held dozens of election-style rallies throughout his tenure, the first in February 2017.

The president certainly could not take the public's backing for granted. His strategic position with public opinion was not strong and provided him little in the way of opportunity for winning broad public support for his initiatives. He began his tenure without the advantage of a public mandate for governing. Moreover, the public did not embrace the conservative direction of the president's policies.

It is hypothetically possible that the president could persuade the public to change their minds. There were many obstacles to success in this endeavor, however. Perhaps most important was the highly polarized nature of public opinion; affective polarization and motivated reasoning left little room for presidential persuasion. In addition, long-term factors, ranging from attention to and understanding of the president's messages to predispositions, misinformation, and loss aversion, constrained the movement of opinion.

Under these circumstances, it was not difficult to predict that public opinion would not respond positively to Trump's persuasive efforts. Instead, those not already inclined to agree with the president would resist his views. Many in the public always were inclined to support the president's policies, of course, but the prospects of expanding his coalition and sending a strong signal to Congress were dim.

Nevertheless, Trump was a seasoned and skilled communicator, especially adept at attracting attention to himself and his views. As president, he easily dominated the news. Ironically, the media served as his megaphone. Nevertheless, he faced the perennial challenges of reaching the public, focusing its attention, and framing the terms of debate. Often, Trump was his own worst enemy, creating distractions from his core message and alienating the public with his divisive approach to governing. His impulsive, undisciplined communications and provocative tweets were not effective tools of persuasion.

There was more to the president's bungling, however. In addition to his lack of message discipline and a communications strategy, Trump had a distinctive style of public discourse. Its principal characteristics were *ad hominem* attacks aimed at branding and delegitimizing critics and opponents, exaggerated threats and inappropriate offers of reassurance, blurred distinctions between fact and fiction, encouragement of cultural divisions and racial and ethnic tensions, and challenges to the rule of law. This inflammatory rhetoric did not aid him in expanding his coalition. Instead, the public found him untrustworthy and chose not to follow his lead, making it more difficult for him to govern effectively.

Not all of the White House's public relations efforts are designed to alter opinions. Instead, the audience for much of presidential rhetoric is those who already agree with the president. Perhaps the most important function of a coalition builder is consolidating one's core supporters. Doing so may require reassuring them as to one's fundamental principles, strengthening their resolve to persist in a political battle, or encouraging them to become more active on behalf of a candidacy or policy proposal.

Maintaining preexisting support or activating those predisposed to back him can be crucial to a president's success. Important policies usually face substantial opposition. Often opponents are virulent in their criticism. Presidents will not unilaterally disarm and remain quiet in the face of such antagonism. Instead, they engage in a permanent campaign just to maintain the status quo. When offered competing views, people are likely to respond according to their predispositions. Thus, the White House must act to encourage motivated reasoning and reinforce the predispositions of its supporters.

President Trump was more successful in solidifying his core supporters—those who already agreed with him—than in persuading others to adopt new views. Although we cannot know for certain, it appears that his rallies, tweets, and other communications—along with affective polarization and motivated reasoning—kept Republicans in his camp, making it more difficult for congressional Republicans to challenge him. Nevertheless, his inability to expand public support for either himself or his policies cost him the Republican majority in the House and thus the potential for legislative success in the 116th Congress.

Presidents also go public to demonstrate preexisting public support when that support lies in the constituencies of members of Congress who are potential swing votes. The president focused on moderate Democratic senators from states he won in 2016 and in which he maintained his strongest approval as president. He held rallies in states like North Dakota, West Virginia, Montana, Indiana, and Missouri. He may well have reinforced his supporters' views, but this solidification seemed to have only limited effect on the senators whose votes he sought to pass major initiatives on health care, taxes, and immigration. Typically, they opposed him.

In the end, public opinion about the president and his policies was much as we expected after evaluating the president's strategic position. Opinion was remarkably stable, providing Trump with a solid base of support. Nevertheless, this coalition was not large enough to produce pluralities, much less majorities, in favor of either his policies or his handling of them. Indeed, he often seemed to turn the public in the opposite direction.

In addition, it appears that Trump's efforts to influence the public were detrimental to the polity. His rhetoric encouraged incivility in public discourse, accelerated the use of disinformation, legitimized the expression of prejudice, increased the salience of cultural divisions and racial and ethnic tensions, and undermined democratic accountability. Although most people rejected both the tone and substance of the president's messages, many Republicans did not. Especially for his copartisans, he distorted their knowledge about politics and policy, warped their understanding of policy challenges, and chipped away at their respect for the rule of law.

Donald Trump was a unique chief executive who came to office with more experience as a self-promoter and public personality than did any previous chief executive. If these personal characteristics were key to leading the public, we should have found him successfully doing so, especially on policies such as tax cuts that on their face should not have been difficult sells to the American people. Yet, his skills and experience were not enough to persuade the public to support his initiatives. Part of the explanation for the president's record is no doubt his own lack of proficiency in governing. Yet no matter how skilled the president and no matter which policies he touted, the odds were against him, because his opportunity structure was weak. The Trump presidency is another example of a president failing to move the American people to support his priority policies, providing further evidence that presidential power is not the power to persuade.

Presidents seek public approval for themselves and their policies for several reasons. First-term chief executives want to win reelection, and those in their second terms want history to remember them well. In the short term, presidents want to pass legislation.

Leading Congress

Congress continually frustrated President Trump, passing little significant legislation at his behest. He was even less successful after Democrats gained control of the House in the 2018 midterm elections. He could not win support for new health care policy, immigration reform, or infrastructure spending. Government shutdowns and symbolic slaps at his foreign policies characterized his tenure, even when Republicans were in control of the legislature. Trump was successful in preventing bills he opposed from passing,[2] as are most presidents with party majorities in Congress, but he struggled to win enactment of legislation.

Once again, it is useful to begin with an analysis of the president's strategic position to explain his lack of success. Trump's opportunity structure was mixed. His primary advantage—and it was a considerable one—was presiding over a unified government in his first two years in office. Both chambers of Congress had a stake in his success. Moreover, Republicans in Congress agreed with many of his proposals, most notably, tax cuts.

Nevertheless, Republican cohesion was imperfect, partisan polarization was high, and there was little public pressure for Democrats to abate their strong opposition. The structure of most of the choices before Congress did not favor the president. Moreover, with his failing to win the popular vote and his low standing with the public, he lacked the impression of an electoral mandate. Thus, it is not surprising that Trump failed to obtain sufficient congressional support for most of his major initiatives.

Of course, the president came to the Oval Office claiming a unique proficiency in negotiating deals. Was he able to exploit his experience to create opportunities for change beyond those provided by his strategic position? He was not. Once in office, he floundered. His passivity, vagueness, inconsistency, and lack of command of policy made him an unskilled, unreliable, and untrustworthy negotiator. He was not successful in closing deals and convincing wavering members, principally Republicans, to support him. His shifting positions, inconsistent behavior, exclusion of Democrats in developing policies, and use of threats and ridicule squandered whatever potential for compromise might have existed. As a result, he received historically low levels of support from Democratic senators and representatives. His high levels of support from Republicans in both chambers of Congress were largely the product of agreement on policy and party leaders keeping votes he might lose off the agenda. When they were resistant, the president could not convince Republicans to defer to him, and his customary tools of threats and disparagement gained him little.

Presidential Leadership

The challenges of governing have rarely been greater. The distance between the parties in Congress, as well as between identifiers with the parties among the public, is the greatest in a century. The public accords Congress extraordinarily low approval ratings, but activists allow its members little leeway to compromise. The inability of Congress and the president to resolve critical problems results in constant crises in financing the government; endless debate over immigration, health care, environmental protection, and other crucial issues; and a failure to plan effectively for the future. The president is the official with the greatest potential to overcome these obstacles, but presidents frequently fail to do so. Donald Trump was no exception.

The president failed at persuasion, but his tenure provides further evidence about the nature of presidential leadership. Although it may be appealing to explain major policy changes in terms of persuasive personalities, public opinion is too biased, the political system is too complicated, power is too decentralized, and interests are too diverse for one person, no matter how extraordinary, to dominate. Neither the public nor Congress is likely to respond to the White House's efforts at persuasion. Presidents cannot create opportunities for change. There is overwhelming evidence that presidents, even "great communicators," rarely move the public in their direction. Indeed, the public often moves *against* the position the president favors. Similarly, there is no systematic evidence that presidents can reliably employ persuasion to move members of Congress to support them.

The context in which presidents operate is the key element in their leadership. Making strategic assessments by asking a few key questions about their political environment provides us crucial leverage for evaluating presidents' likely success in obtaining the support of the public and Congress for their initiatives. Understanding the nature and possibilities of leadership puts us in a better position to evaluate both the performance of presidents and the opportunities for change.

Successful leadership, then, is not the result of the dominant chief executive of political folklore who reshapes the contours of the political landscape, altering his strategic position to pave the way for change. Rather than creating the conditions for important shifts in public policy, such as attracting bipartisan congressional support or moving public opinion in their direction, effective leaders are facilitators who work at the margins of coalition building to recognize and exploit opportunities in their environments. When the various streams of political resources converge to create opportunities for major change, presidents can be critical facilitators in engendering significant alterations in public policy.

Recognizing and exploiting opportunities for change—rather than creating opportunities through persuasion—are the essential presidential leadership skills. Exploiting opportunities requires that the president possess the analytical insight necessary to identify opportunities for change and the skills necessary to take advantage of them. As Edgar advised in *King*

Lear, "Ripeness is all."[3] To succeed, presidents have to evaluate the opportunities for change in their environments carefully and orchestrate existing and potential support skillfully.

How did Donald Trump measure up to these tests of leadership? He failed. With negligible knowledge about either government or public policy and even less respect for democratic norms and civil discourse, he lacked the ability to envision a strategy for governing and the self-discipline to execute one. Moreover, his impulsiveness and compulsion to satisfy his personal needs and govern by grievances created distractions from even inchoate strategies.

The president seemed to have no idea how to expand his minority coalition and had slight interest in doing so. Having won the presidency while losing the popular vote, he wrote off the majority of the public and confined his attention to the minority who already agreed with him. His genius for politics focused on playing to his base, with all its attendant detriments for the success of his presidency and the health of the polity. The promotion of policies and reaction to criticism can take a wide range of forms. It is possible to assert values and policies without incendiary rhetoric, but that was not Trump's way. Instead, he preferred to excoriate opponents, fuel fear, and mislead and divide the country.

Although he possessed the perseverance and resiliency necessary for leadership, the president could not exploit the opportunities provided by the Republican majorities in both houses of Congress in his first two years in the White House and a Republican Senate in the next two years. Although his copartisans had strong incentives to make him—and themselves—look good by passing significant legislation, Trump squandered the potential. He could not fashion winning coalitions for priority initiatives such as health care and immigration. There was little prospect for winning support from Democrats on many issues, but he wasted whatever chance there was to compromise on policies such as immigration and infrastructure development. The president was not a competent negotiator. Contrary to his frequent claims, he had not mastered the art of the deal. Threats, intimidation, and criticism, common modes of interaction for him, are not the keys to success in presidential politics, even for a president with a loyal base.

Donald Trump's response to his failure to persuade was to push the boundaries of presidential power and violate the norms of the presidency. The president turned increasingly to unilateral action. His remark that "I have an Article II, where I have to the right to do whatever I want as president"[4] reflected his orientation. Even more startling, in a televised press briefing on April 13, 2020, he claimed that it was he, not the nation's governors, who would decide when to end stay-at-home and shelter-in-place orders in response to the coronavirus pandemic. Without citing any constitutional basis, Trump declared, "The President of the United States calls the shots," and "when somebody is the President of the United States, the authority is total."[5] Having failed to lead both the public and Congress, the president had forsaken leadership.

*　*　*

The presidential election dominated the summer and fall of 2020, but it did not alter the patterns of Trump's presidency. The pandemic surged, unemployment increased, and business failures mounted. Nevertheless, the president was passive, nursing his grievances and generally remaining disengaged from negotiations with Congress. He was also wildly inconsistent and confusing, ordering a stop to negotiations on a pandemic relief bill, calling for immediate action on a modest measure a few hours later, and then, three days after that, advising his followers to "Go Big." Even worse, Trump persisted in prevaricating, demeaning opponents, fueling fear, stoking division, and challenging the rule of law.

He could not persuade the public to reelect him, losing by 7 million votes. His refusal to concede defeat to Joe Biden needlessly delayed the presidential transition, and his propagation of misinformation about the election process threatened to undermine a central pillar of democracy. Ultimately, the House impeached him for inciting insurrection, and leading social media platforms cut off his access. Republicans lost both the House and the Senate, and the president left his party in disarray. On average, he had the lowest approval of any modern chief executive.

Graceless to the end, Trump refused to attend Biden's inauguration. The president who lost the popular vote in 2016 and found it necessary to exaggerate the size of the crowds at his inauguration left office as he entered it, a whiner not a winner.

Notes

Preface

1. George C. Edwards III, "Can Donald Trump Persuade American to Support His Agenda? It's Not Likely," *Washington Post*, December 27, 2016.
2. See, e.g., George C. Edwards III, *Predicting the Presidency: The Potential of Persuasive Leadership* (Princeton, NJ: Princeton University Press, 2016); Edwards, *Overreach: Leadership in the Obama Presidency* (Princeton, NJ: Princeton University Press, 2012); Edwards, *The Strategic President: Persuasion and Opportunity in Presidential Leadership* (Princeton, NJ: Princeton University Press, 2009); Edwards, *On Deaf Ears: The Limits of the Bully Pulpit* (New Haven, CT: Yale University Press, 2003); Edwards, *At the Margins: Presidential Leadership of Congress* (New Haven, CT: Yale University Press, 1989); and Edwards, *Governing by Campaigning: The Politics of the Bush Presidency*, 2nd ed. (New York: Longman, 2007).

Chapter One

1. "Full Text: Donald Trump Announces a Presidential Bid," *Washington Post*, June 16, 2015, https://www.washingtonpost.com/news/post-politics/wp/2015/06/16/full-text-donald-trump-announces-a-presidential-bid/?arc404=true
2. James MacGregor Burns, *Leadership* (New York: Harper & Row, 1978), 2.
3. Richard E. Neustadt, *Presidential Power and the Modern Presidents* (New York: Free Press, 1990), 11.
4. Neustadt, *Presidential Power*, 10.
5. Neustadt, *Presidential Power*, 37 (original emphasis).
6. Neustadt, *Presidential Power*, 40.
7. Neustadt, *Presidential Power*, 32.
8. George C. Edwards III, *On Deaf Ears: The Limits of the Bully Pulpit* (New Haven, CT: Yale University Press, 2003).

9. Edwards, *On Deaf Ears*; George C. Edwards III, *Predicting the Presidency: The Potential of Persuasive Leadership* (Princeton, NJ: Princeton University Press, 2016); Edwards, *Overreach: Leadership in the Obama Presidency* (Princeton, NJ: Princeton University Press, 2012), chap. 3; Edwards, *The Strategic President: Persuasion and Opportunity in Presidential Leadership* (Princeton, NJ: Princeton University Press, 2009), chaps. 2–3; and Edwards, *Governing by Campaigning: The Politics of the Bush Presidency*, 2nd ed. (New York: Longman, 2007).

10. See Edwards, *The Strategic President*, chaps. 2–3, 6.

11. Lawrence R. Jacobs and Robert Y. Shapiro, *Politicians Don't Pander* (Chicago: University of Chicago Press, 2000), 45, 106, 136.

12. Barack Obama, speech at the Democratic Party of Wisconsin Founders Day Gala, Milwaukee, Wisconsin, February 16, 2008.

13. David Axelrod, *Believer: My Forty Years in Politics* (New York: Penguin Press, 2015), 371–77.

14. Quoted in Ronald Suskind, *Confidence Men: Wall Street, Washington, and the Education of a President* (New York: Harper, 2011), 370.

15. See, e.g., Edwards, *Predicting the Presidency*, 190–94.

16. See, e.g., William G. Howell, *Politics without Persuasion* (Princeton, NJ: Princeton University Press, 2003); Kenneth R. Mayer, *With the Stroke of a Pen: Executive Orders and Presidential Power* (Princeton, NJ: Princeton University Press, 2001).

17. Edwards, *Predicting the Presidency*; James N. Druckman and Lawrence R. Jacobs, *Who Governs? Presidents, Public Opinion, and Manipulation* (Chicago: University of Chicago Press, 2015), chap. 6; Edwards, *Overreach*; Edwards, *The Strategic President*; B. Dan Wood, *The Myth of Presidential Representation* (New York: Cambridge University Press, 2009); Wood, *The Politics of Economic Leadership* (Princeton, NJ: Princeton University Press, 2007); Richard Fleisher, Jon R. Bond, and B. Dan Wood, "Which Presidents Are Uncommonly Successful in Congress?" in *Presidential Leadership: The Vortex of Presidential Power*, ed. Bert Rockman and Richard W. Waterman (New York: Oxford University Press, 2007); Edwards, *Governing by Campaigning*; Edwards, *On Deaf Ears*; Jon R. Bond and Richard Fleisher, *The President in the Legislative Arena* (Chicago: University of Chicago Press, 1990); and George C. Edwards III, *At the Margins: Presidential Leadership of Congress* (New Haven, CT: Yale University Press, 1989).

18. Edwards, *Predicting the Presidency*, 190–94.

19. Edwards, *On Deaf Ears*, chap. 3.

20. Edwards, *The Strategic President*, 192–99; Edwards, *Overreach*.

21. Stephen Skowronek, *The Politics Presidents Make: Leadership from John Adams to Bill Clinton*, rev. ed. (Cambridge, MA: Harvard University Press, 1997). See also his remarks at the Annual Meeting of the American Political Science Association, Philadelphia, August 31–September 3, 2006.

22. Bruce Miroff, *Presidents on Political Ground: Leaders in Action and What They Face* (Lawrence: University Press of Kansas, 2016).

23. Edwards, *Predicting the Presidency*; Edwards, *Overreach*; Edwards, *The Strategic President*.

24. Neustadt, *Presidential Power*, 4.

25. For a broad attempt to do so, see Byron E. Shafer and Regina L. Wagner, "The Trump Presidency and the Structure of Modern American Politics," *Perspectives on Politics* 17 (June 2019): 340–57.

26. Edwards, *Predicting the Presidency*; Edwards, *Overreach*; Edwards, *The Strategic President*.

Chapter Two

1. ABC News poll, October 20–22, 2016.

2. 2016 American National Election Study.

3. *HuffPost*/YouGov poll, November 10–14, 2016.

4. *Washington Post*–Schar School poll, November 11–14, 2016.

5. Gallup poll, January 20–22, 2017.

6. Lydia Saad, "Conservative-Leaning States Drop From 44 to 39," Gallup Poll, February 6, 2018; Jeffrey M. Jones, "Conservatives Greatly Outnumber Liberals in 19 U.S. States," Gallup Poll, February 22, 2019.

7. Gallup polls, May 1–10, 2018, and May 3–7, 2017.

8. Lydia Saad, "Democrats Growing More Economically Liberal," Gallup Poll, August 11, 2017. See also Samantha Smith, "Democratic Voters Are Increasingly Likely to Call Their Views Liberal," Pew Research Center, September 7, 2017.

9. Christopher Ellis and James A. Stimson, *Ideology in America* (New York: Cambridge University Press, 2012); Shawn Treier and D. Sunshine Hillygus, "The Nature of Political Ideology in the Contemporary Electorate," *Public Opinion Quarterly* 73 (Winter 2009): 679–703; Christopher Ellis and James A. Stimson, "Symbolic Ideology in the American Electorate," *Electoral Studies* 28 (September 2009): 388–402; William G. Jacoby, "Policy Attitudes, Ideology, and Voting Behavior in the 2008 Election" (paper presented at the Annual Meeting of the American Political Science Association, Toronto, Canada, September 3–6, 2009); James A. Stimson, *Tides of Consent: How Public Opinion Shapes American Politics* (New York: Cambridge University Press, 2004); Pamela J. Conover and Stanley Feldman, "The Origins and Meaning of Liberal/Conservative Identifications," *American Journal of Political Science* 25 (October 1981): 617–45; David O. Sears, Richard L. Lau, Tom R. Tyler, and Harris M. Allen, "Self-Interest vs. Symbolic Politics in Policy Attitudes and Presidential Voting," *American Political Science Review* 74 (September 1980): 670–84.

10. Donald R. Kinder and Nathan P. Kalmoe, *Neither Liberal Nor Conservative: Ideological Innocence in the American People* (Chicago: University of Chicago Press, 2017); Philip E. Converse, "The Nature of Belief Systems in Mass Publics," in *Ideology and Discontent*, ed. David E. Apter (New York: Free Press, 1964).

11. "Political Polarization in the American Public," Pew Research Center, June 12, 2014; Teresa E. Levitin and Warren E. Miller, "Ideological Interpretations of Presidential Elections," *American Political Science Review* 73 (September 1979): 751–71.

12. Robert Huckfeldt, Jeffrey Levine, William Morgan, and John Sprague, "Accessibility and the Political Utility of Partisan and Ideological Orientations," *American Journal of Political Science* 43 (July 1999): 888–911; Kathleen Knight, "Ideology in the 1980 Election: Ideological Sophistication Does Matter," *Journal of Politics* 47 (July 1985): 828–53; Levitin and Miller, "Ideological Interpretations of Presidential Elections"; James A. Stimson, "Belief Systems: Constraint, Complexity, and the 1972 Election," *American Journal of Political Science* 19 (July 1975): 393–417.

13. Paul Goren, Christopher M. Federico, and Miki Caul Kittilson, "Source Cues, Partisan Identities, and Political Value Expression," *American Journal of Political Science* 53 (October 2009): 805–20; Christopher M. Federico and Monica C. Schneider, "Political Expertise and the Use of Ideology: Moderating the Effects of Evaluative Motivation," *Public Opinion Quarterly* 71 (Summer 2007): 221–52; William G. Jacoby, "Value Choices and American Public Opinion," *American Journal of Political Science* 50 (July 2006): 706–23; Paul Goren, "Political Sophistication and Policy Reasoning: A Reconsideration," *American Journal of Political Science* 48 (July 2004): 462–78; Paul Goren, "Core Principles and Policy Reasoning in Mass Publics: A Test of Two Theories," *British Journal of Political Science* 31 (January 2001): 159–77; Huckfeldt et al., "Accessibility and the Political Utility"; William G. Jacoby, "The Structure of Ideological Thinking in the American Electorate," *American Journal of Political Science* 39 (April 1995): 314–35; Jacoby, "Ideological Identification and Issue Attitudes," *American Journal of Political Science* 35 (January 1991): 178–205; Stanley Feldman, "Structure and Consistency in Public Opinion: The Role of Core Beliefs and Attitudes," *American Journal of Political Science* 32 (May 1988): 416–40; Sears et al., "Self-Interest vs. Symbolic Politics."

14. Thomas J. Rudolph and Jillian Evans, "Political Trust, Ideology, and Public Support for Government Spending," *American Journal of Political Science* 49 (July 2005): 660–71; William G. Jacoby, "Issue Framing and Government Spending," *American Journal of Political Science* 44 (October 2000): 750–67; William G. Jacoby, "Public Attitudes toward Government Spending," *American Journal of Political Science* 38 (April 1994): 336–61.

15. NBC/*Wall Street Journal* poll, April 17–20, 2017.

16. NBC News/*Wall Street Journal* poll, April 17–20, 2017; NBC News/*Wall Street Journal* poll, January 13–17, 2018; Pew Research Center polls, December 4–18, 2017, February 26–March 11, 2018, September 24–October 7, 2018, March 18–April 1, 2019, and September 3–15, 2019. See also Gallup poll, September 6–10, 2017.

17. Pew Research Center polls, April 5–11, 2017, and March 20–25, 2019. See also Fox News poll, February 10–13, 2018 (registered voters).

18. Pew Research Center polls, June 8–18, 2017, September 18–24, 2018, July 22–August 4, 2019, September 3–15, 2019, and September 16–29, 2019; Gallup polls, November 2–8, 2017, and November 1–11, 2018.

19. Gallup polls, March 1–8, 2018, and March 1–10, 2019.

20. Pew Research Center poll, March 27–April 9, 2018.

21. See also Paul C. Light, *Introducing the Next Government Reform Majority: What Americans Want from Reform in 2018* (Washington DC: Brookings Institution, 2018).

22. Robert S. Erikson, Michael B. MacKuen, and James A. Stimson, *The Macro Polity* (New York: Cambridge University Press, 2002), chap. 9.

23. Erikson et al., *The Macro Polity*, 344, 374.

24. Stuart N. Soroka and Christopher Wlezien, *Degrees of Democracy* (New York: Cambridge University Press, 2010).

25. "Political Polarization in the American Public"; Alan I. Abramowitz, *The Disappearing Center* (New Haven, CT: Yale University Press, 2010); Logan Dancey and Paul Goren, "Party Identification, Issue Attitudes, and the Dynamics of Political Debate," *American Journal of Political Science* 54 (July 2010): 686–99; Michael Bang Petersen, Rune Slothuus, and Lise Togeby, "Political Parties and Value Consistency in Public Opinion Formation," *Public Opinion Quarterly* 74 (Fall 2010): 530–50; Matthew Levendusky, *The Partisan Sort* (Chicago: University of Chicago Press, 2009); Adam J. Berinsky, *In Time of War: Understanding American Public Opinion from World War II to Iraq* (Chicago: University of Chicago Press, 2009). See also Morris P. Fiorina, with Samuel J. Abrams and Jeremy C. Pope, *Culture Wars? The Myth of Polarized America*, 3rd ed. (New York: Pearson Longman, 2011); Joseph Bafumi and Robert Y. Shapiro, "A New Partisan Voter," *Journal of Politics* 71 (January 2009): 1–24; Geoffrey C. Layman, Thomas M. Carsey, and Juliana Menasce Horowitz, "Party Polarization in American Politics: Characteristics, Causes, and Consequences," *Annual Review of Political Science* 9 (2006): 83–110; Gary C. Jacobson, *A Divider, Not a Uniter: George W. Bush and the American Public*, 3rd ed. (New York: Longman, 2011).

26. Melanie Freeze and Jacob M. Montgomery, "Static Stability and Evolving Constraint: Preference Stability and Ideological Structure in the Mass Public," *American Politics Research* 44 (May 2016): 415–47; Steven W. Webster and Alan I. Abramowitz, "The Ideological Foundations of Affective Polarization in the U.S. Electorate," *American Politics Research* 45 (July 2017): 621–47; "The Partisan Divide on Political Values Grows Even Wider," Pew Research Center, October 5, 2017; "A Wider Ideological Gap Between More and Less Educated Adults," Pew Research Center, April 26, 2016; Caitlin E. Jewitt and Paul Goren, "Ideological Structure and Consistency in the Age of Polarization," *American Politics Research* 44 (January 2016): 81–105.

27. "The Partisan Divide on Political Values Grows Even Wider"; "Political Polarization in the American Public"; Andrew Garner and Harvey Palmer, "Polarization and Issue Consistency Over Time," *Political Behavior* 33 (June 2011): 225–46; Paul Goren, "Party Identification and Core Political Values," *American Journal of Political Science* 49 (October 2005): 881–96.

28. Nolan McCarty, Keith T. Poole, and Howard Rosenthal, *Polarized America: The Dance of Ideology and Unequal Riches* (Cambridge, MA: MIT Press, 2006).

29. "Political Polarization in the American Public."

30. Frank Newport and Andrew Dugan, "Partisan Differences Growing on a Number of Issues," Gallup.com, August 3, 2017.

31. "The Partisan Divide on Political Values Grows Even Wider."

32. "The Partisan Divide on Political Values Grows Even Wider."

33. "In a Politically Polarized Era, Sharp Divided in Both Partisan Coalitions," Pew Research Center, December 17, 2019. See also Larry M. Bartels, "Under Trump, Democrats and Republicans Have Never Been More Divided—on Nearly Everything," *Washington Post*, May 21, 2020.

34. Larry M. Bartels, "Partisanship in the Trump Era," *Journal of Politics* 80 (October 2018): 1483–94.

35. Jonathan M. Ladd, Joshua A. Tucker, and Sean Kates, *2018 American Institutional Confidence Poll: The Health of American Democracy in an Era of Hyper Polarization* (Baker Center for Leadership & Governance, Georgetown University, and the John S. and James L. Knight Foundation, 2018), 14–15. Poll was conducted June 12–July 19, 2018.

36. Amina Dunn, John Laloggia, and Carroll Doherty, "In Midterm Voting Decisions, Policies Took a Back Seat to Partisanship," Pew Research Center, November 29, 2018.

37. Bartels, "Under Trump, Democrats and Republicans Have Never Been More Divided"; Lilliana Mason, *Uncivil Agreement: How Politics Became Our Identity* (Chicago: University of Chicago Press, 2018); Shanto Iyengar and Masha Krupenkin, "Partisanship as Social Identity; Implications for the Study of Party Polarization," *The Forum* 16, no. 1 (2018): 23–45; Matthew S. Levendusky, "Americans, Not Partisans: Can Priming American National Identity Reduce Affective Polarization?" *Journal of Politics* 80 (January 2018): 59–70; Alan I. Abramowitz and Steven Webster, "The Rise of Negative Partisanship and the Nationalization of U.S. Elections in the 21st Century," *Electoral Studies* 41 (March 2016): 12–22; Lilliana Mason, "A Cross-Cutting Calm: How Social Sorting Drives Affective Polarization," *Public Opinion Quarterly* 80 (January 2016): 351–77; Shanto Iyengar and Sean J. Westwood, "Fear and Loathing across Party Lines: New Evidence on Group Polarization," *American Journal of Political Science* 59 (July 2015): 690–707; Shanto Iyengar, Gaurav Sood, and Yphtach Lelkes, "Affect, Not Ideology: A Social Identity Perspective on Polarization," *Public Opinion Quarterly* 76 (January 2012): 405–31.

38. Pew Research Center polls, July 30–August 12, 2018, and September 3–5, 2019; Daniel Yudkin, Stephen Hawkins, and Tim Dixon, *The Perception Gap: How False Impressions Are Pulling Americans Apart* (More in Common, June 2019).

39. Douglas J. Ahler and Gaurav Sood, "The Parties in Our Heads: Misperceptions about Party Composition and Their Consequences," *Journal of Politics* 80 (July 2018): 964–81.

40. Pew Research Center polls, March 2–28, 2016, and April 5–May 2, 2016. See also 2018 American Institutional Confidence poll, June 12–July 19, 2018.

41. Pew Research Center poll, June 8–18, 2017.

42. Pew Research Center poll, March 7–14, 2018. See also Pew Research Center poll, September 3–5, 2019.

43. Marc J. Hetherington and Jonathan D. Weiler, *Prius or Pickup? How the Answers to Four Simple Questions Explain America's Great Divide* (Boston, MA: Houghton Mifflin Harcourt, 2018); Marc J. Hetherington and Jonathan D. Weiler, *Authoritarianism and Polarization in American Politics* (New York: Cambridge University Press, 2009).

44. Kevin K. Banda, Thomas M. Carsey, and Serge Severenchuk, "Evidence of Conflict Extension in Partisans' Evaluations of People and Inanimate Objects," *American Politics Research* 48 (March 2020): 275–85; Christopher McConnell, Neil Malhotra, Yotam Margalit, and Matthew Levendusky, "The Economic Consequences of Partisanship in a Polarized Era," *American Journal of Political Science* 62 (January 2018): 5–18; Jonathan Mummolo and Clayton Nall, "Why Partisans Don't Sort: How Quality and Resource Constraints Prevent Political Segregation," *Journal of Politics* 79 (January 2017): 45–59; Gregory A. Huber and Neil Malhotra, "Political Homophily in Social Relationships: Evidence from Online Dating Behavior," *Journal of Politics* 79 (January 2017): 269–83; Stephen P. Nicholson, Chelsea M. Coe, Jason Emory, and Anna V. Song, "The Politics of Beauty: The Effects of Partisan Bias on Physical Attractiveness," *Political Behavior* 38 (December 2016): 883–98.

45. Daniel Diermeier and Christopher Li, "Partisan Affect and Elite Polarization," *American Political Science Review* 113 (February 2019): 277–81.

46. Steven Levitsky and Daniel Ziblatt, *How Democracies Die* (New York: Crown, 2018).

47. Marc J. Hetherington, and Thomas J. Rudolph, *Why Washington Won't Work: Polarization, Political Trust, and the Governing Crisis* (Chicago: University of Chicago Press, 2015).

48. Alan I. Abramowitz, *The Great Alignment* (New Haven, CT: Yale University Press, 2018), 109–13; Lori Bougher, "The Correlates of Discord: Identity, Issue Alignment, and Political Hostility in Polarized America," *Political Behavior* 39 (September 2017): 731–62; Webster and Abramowitz, "The Ideological Foundations of Affective Polarization"; Jon C. Rogowski and Joseph L. Sutherland, "How Ideology Fuels Affective Polarization," *Political Behavior* 38 (June 2016): 485–508.

49. Morris P. Fiorina, *Unstable Majorities: Polarization, Party Sorting, and Political Stalemate*. Stanford, CA: Hoover Press, 2017); Lilliana Mason, "'I Disrespectfully Agree': The Differential Effects of Partisan Sorting on Social and Issue Polarization," *American Journal of Political Science* 59 (January 2015): 128–45; Matthew S. Levendusky, "Clearer Cues, More Consistent Voters: A Benefit of Elite Polarization," *Political Behavior* 32 (March 2010): 111–31.

50. Kinder and Kalmoe, *Neither Liberal Nor Conservative*; Alexander G. Theodoridis, "Me, Myself, and (I), (D), or (R)? Partisanship and Political Cognition Through the Lens of Implicit Identity," *Journal of Politics* 79 (October 2017): 1253–67; Alexa Bankert, Leonie Huddy, and Martin Rosema, "Measuring Partisanship as a Social Identity in Multi-Party Systems," *Political Behavior* 39 (March 2017): 103–32; Leonie Huddy, Lilliana Mason, and Lene Aaroe, "Expressive Partisanship: Campaign Involvement, Political Emotion, and Partisan Identity," *American Political Science Review* 109 (February 2015): 1–17; Alexander G. Theodoridis, "Implicit Political Identity," *PS: Political Science and Politics* 46 (July 2013): 545–49; Steven Greene, "Social Identity Theory and Party Identification," *Social Science Quarterly* 85 (March 2004): 136–53; Donald P. Green, Bradley Palmquist, and Eric Schickler, *Partisan Hearts and Minds: Political Parties and the Social Identities of Voters* (New Haven, CT: Yale University Press, 2002); Steven Greene, "The Psychological Sources of Partisan-leaning Independence," *American Politics Quarterly* 28 (October 2000): 511–37; Steven Greene, "Understanding Party Identification: A Social Identity Approach," *Political Psychology* 20 (June 1999): 393–403.

51. Abramowitz, *The Great Alignment*; Mason, *Uncivil Agreement*; Lilliana Mason and Julie Wronski, "One Tribe to Bind Them All: How Our Social Group Attachments Strengthen Partisanship," *Political Psychology* 39 (February 2018): 257–77; Theodoridis, "Me, Myself, and (I), (D), or (R)?"; Alan I. Abramowitz and Steven W. Webster, "Negative Partisanship: Why Americans Dislike Parties But Behave Like Rabid Partisans," *Political Psychology* 39 (February 2018): 119–35; Yphtach Lelkes, "Affective Polarization and Ideological Sorting: A Reciprocal, Albeit Weak, Relationship," *The Forum* 16, no. 1 (2018): 67–79; Mason, "A Cross-Cutting Calm"; Daniel M. Shea, "Our Tribal Nature and the Rise of Nasty Politics," in *Can We Talk? The Rise of Rude, Nasty, Stubborn Politics*, ed. Daniel Shea and Morris Fiorina (New York: Pearson, 2013), 82–98; Bill Bishop, *The Big Sort: Why the Clustering of Like-Minded America Is Tearing Us Apart* (New York: Houghton Mifflin, 2008); and Jeffrey M. Stonecash, Mark D. Brewer, and Mack D. Mariani, *Diverging Parties: Social Change, Realignment, and Party Polarization* (Boulder, CO: Westview Press, 2003).

52. Joshua Robison and Rachel L. Moskowitz, "The Group Basis of Partisan Affective Polarization," *Journal of Politics* 81 (July 2019): 1075–79.

53. Douglas J. Ahler and Gaurav Sood, "The Parties in Our Heads: Misperceptions about Party Composition and Their Consequences," *Journal of Politics* 80 (July 2018): 964–81.

54. "Political Polarization in the American Public."

55. Pew Research Center poll, August 8–21, 2017. See also Ross Butters and Christopher Hare, "Three-Fourths of Americans Regularly Talk Politics Only with Members of Their Own Political Tribe," *Washington Post*, May 1, 2017.

56. David A. Hopkins, *Red Fighting Blue: How Geography and Electoral Rules Polarize American Politics* (New York: Cambridge University Press, 2017).

57. Shanto Iyengar, Tobias Konitzer, and Kent Tedin, "The Home as a Political Fortress: Family Agreement in an Era of Polarization," *Journal of Politics* 80 (October 2018): 1326–38.

58. John Sides, Michael Tesler, and Lynn Vavreck, *Identity Crisis: The 2016 Presidential Campaign and the Battle for the Meaning of America* (Princeton, NJ: Princeton University Press, 2018), 25–31; Spencer Piston, "How Explicit Racial Prejudice Hurt Obama in the 2008 Election," *Political Behavior* 32 (December 2010): 431–51; Michael Lewis-Beck, Charles Tien, and Richard Nadeau, "Obama's Missed Landslide: A Racial Cost?" *PS: Political Science and Politics* 43 (January 2010): 69–76; Benjamin Highton, "Prejudice Rivals Partisanship and Ideology When Explaining the 2008 Presidential Vote across the States" *PS: Political Science and Politics* 44 (July 2011): 530–35.

59. Spee Kosloff, Jeff Greenberg, Toni Schmader, Mark Dechesne, and David Weise, "Smearing the Opposition: Implicit and Explicit Stigmatization of the 2008 U.S. Presidential Candidates and the Current U.S. President," *Journal of Experimental Psychology* 139 (August 2010): 383–98.

60. Piston, "How Explicit Racial Prejudice Hurt Obama."

61. Alan I. Abramowitz, "The Race Factor: White Racial Attitudes and Opinions of Obama," *Sabato's Crystal Ball*, May 12, 2011, http://centerforpolitics.org/crystalball/articles/aia2011051201/; Abramowitz and Webster, "Negative Partisanship."

62. Michael Tesler, "The Return of Old-Fashioned Racism to White Americans' Partisan Preferences in the Early Obama Era," *Journal of Politics* 75 (January 2013): 110–23.

63. Michael Tesler, "The Spillover of Racialization into Health Care: How President Obama Polarized Public Opinion by Racial Attitudes and Race," *American Journal of Political Science* 56 (July 2012): 690–704.

64. Jeremiah Castle, "New Fronts in the Culture Wars? Religion, Partisanship, and Polarization on Religious Liberty and Transgender Rights in the United States," *American Politics Research* 47 (May 2019): 650–79.

65. Abramowitz, *The Great Alignment*; Sides et al., *Identity Crisis*, 30–31. See also Jon Green and Sean McElwee, "The Differential Effects of Economic Conditions and Racial Attitudes in the Election of Donald Trump," *Perspectives on Politics* 17 (June 2019): 358–79.

66. Janelle Wong, *Immigrants, Evangelicals and Politics in an Era of Demographic Change* (New York: Russell Sage Foundation, 2018).

67. Diana C. Mutz, "Status Threat, Not Economic Hardship, Explains the 2016 Presidential Vote," *Proceedings of the National Academy of Sciences USA* 115

(April 2018): E4330–39. See also Ashley Jardina, *White Identity Politics* (New York; Cambridge University Press, 2019).

68. Hetherington and Weiler, *Prius or Pickup?*

69. Kevin Arceneaux and Martin Johnson, *Changing Minds or Changing Channels: Partisan News in an Age of Choice* (Chicago: University of Chicago Press, 2013); Kevin Arceneaux, Martin Johnson, and Chad Murphy, "Polarized Political Communication, Oppositional Media Hostility, and Selective Exposure," *Journal of Politics* 74 (January 2012): 174–86; Natalie J. Stroud, *Niche News: The Politics of News Choice* (New York: Oxford University Press, 2011); Natalie J. Stroud, "Media Use and Political Predispositions: Revisiting the Concept of Selective Exposure," *Political Behavior* 30 (September 2008): 341–66.

70. Pew Research Center poll, November 29–December 12, 2016.

71. Pew Research Center poll, March 19–April 29, 2014.

72. Costas Panagopoulos, Donald P. Green, Jonathan Krasno, Michael Schwam-Baird, and Kyle Endres, "Partisan Consumerism: Experimental Tests of Consumer Reactions to Corporate Political Activity," *Journal of Politics* 82 (July 2020): 996–1007; Gregory J. Martin and Ali Yurukoglu, "Bias in Cable News: Persuasion and Polarization," *American Economic Review* 107 (September 2017): 2565–99; Matthew Levendusky, *How Partisan Media Polarize America* (Chicago: University of Chicago Press, 2013); Stefano DellaVigna and Ethan Kaplan, "The Fox News Effect: Media Bias and Voting," *Quarterly Journal of Economics* 122 (August 2007): 1187–234. See, however, Arceneaux and Johnson, *Changing Minds or Changing Channels*.

73. Eric Lawrence, John Sides, and Henry Farrell, "Self-Segregation or Deliberation? Blog Readership, Participation, and Polarization in American Politics," *Perspectives on Politics* 8 (March 2010): 141–57.

74. Cass R. Sunstein, *#Republic: Divided Democracy in the Age of Social Media* (Princeton, NJ: Princeton University Press, 2017).

75. John A. Henderson and Alexander G. Theodoridis, "Seeing Spots: Partisanship, Negativity and the Conditional Receipt of Campaign Advertisements," *Political Behavior* 40 (December 2018): 965–87.

76. Yphtach Lelkes, Gaurav Sood, and Shanto Iyengar, "The Hostile Audience: The Effect of Access to Broadband Internet on Partisan Affect," *American Journal of Political Science* 61 (January 2017): 5–20. But see Levi Boxell, Matthew Gentzkow, and Jesse M. Shapiro, "Greater Internet Use Is Not Associated with Faster Growth in Political Polarization Among US Demographic Groups," *Proceedings of the National Academy of Sciences U S A* 114 (October 2017): 10612–17.

77. Jeffrey M. Berry and Sarah Sobieraj, *The Outrage Industry: Political Opinion Media and the New Incivility* (New York: Oxford University Press, 2014).

78. Kathleen Hall Jamieson and Joseph N. Cappella, *Echo Chamber: Rush Limbaugh and the Conservative Media Establishment* (New York: Oxford University Press, 2008).

79. Gary C. Jacobson, "Donald Trump and the Future of American Politics" (paper prepared for delivery at the Midwest Political Science Association, April 16–19, 2020); Jacobson, *Presidents and Parties in the Public Mind* (Chicago: University of Chicago Press, 2019); Jacobson, "The Effects of the Early Trump Presidency on Public Attitudes toward the Republican Party," *Presidential Studies Quarterly* 48 (September 2018): 404–435; Jacobson, "Donald Trump, the Public, and Congress: The First 7 Months," *The Forum* 15 (November 2017): 525–45; Jacobson, "The Coevolution of Affect Toward Presidents and Their Parties," *Presidential Studies Quarterly* 46 (June 2016):1–29; Jacobson, "Partisan Polarization in American Politics: A Background Paper," *Presidential Studies Quarterly* 43 (December 2013): 688–70; Jacobson, "The President's Effect on Partisan Attitudes," *Presidential Studies Quarterly* 42 (December 2012): 683–718.

80. Jeffrey M. Jones, "Trump Job Approval Sets New Record for Polarization," Gallup Poll, January 16, 2019.

81. Gary C. Jacobson, "Extreme Referendum: Donald Trump and the 2018 Midterm Elections," *Political Science Quarterly* 134 (Spring 2019): 9–38.

82. Gallup poll, November 5–11, 2018.

83. Jeffrey M. Jones, "Trump Third Year Sets New Standard for Party Polarization," Gallup Poll, January 21, 2020.

84. Gallup poll, June 8–30, 2020.

85. CNN poll, June 14–17, 2018.

86. Matthew L. Stanley, Paul Henne, Brenda W. Yang, and Felipe De Brigard, "Resistance to Position Change, Motivated Reasoning, and Polarization," *Political Behavior* (2019), https://doi.org/10.1007/s11109-019-09526-z; Milton Lodge and Charles S. Taber, *The Rationalizing Voter* (New York: Cambridge University Press, 2013); James N. Druckman, Jordan Fein, and Thomas J. Leeper, "A Source of Bias in Public Opinion Stability," *American Political Science Review* 106 (May 2012): 430–54; Rune Slothuus and Claes H. de Vreese, "Political Parties, Motivated Reasoning, and Issue Framing Effects," *Journal of Politics* (July 2010): 630–45; Charles S. Taber, Damon Cann, and Simona Kucsova, "The Motivated Processing of Political Arguments," *Political Behavior* 31 (June 2009): 137–55; Charles S. Taber and Milton Lodge, "Motivated Skepticism in the Evaluation of Political Beliefs," *American Journal of Political Science* 50 (July 2006): 755–69; John T. Jost, "The End of the End of Ideology," *American Psychologist* 61, no. 7 (2006): 651–70; Richard R. Lau and David P. Redlawsk, *How Voters Decide: Information Processing in Election Campaigns* (New York: Cambridge University Press, 2006); Milton Lodge and Charles S. Taber, "The Automaticity of Affect for Political Leaders, Groups, and Issues: An Experimental Test of the Hot Cognition Hypothesis," *Political Psychology* 26 (June 2005): 455–82; David P. Redlawsk, "Hot Cognition or Cool Consideration: Testing the Effects of Motivated Reasoning on Political Decision Making," *Journal of Politics* 64 (November 2002): 1021–44; Ziva Kunda, "The Case for Motivated Reasoning," *Psychological Bulletin* 108 (November 1990):

480–98; Ziva Kunda, "Motivated Inference: Self-Serving Generation and Evaluation of Causal Theories," *Journal of Personality and Social Psychology* 53, no. 4 (1987): 636–47; Milton Lodge and Ruth Hamill, "A Partisan Schema for Political Information Processing," *American Political Science Review* 80 (June 1986): 505–19; Charles Lord, Lee Ross, and Mark R. Lepper, "Biased Assimilation and Attitude Polarization: The Effects of Prior Theories on Subsequently Considered Evidence," *Journal of Personality and Social Psychology* 37 (November 1979): 2098–09; Robert P. Abelson, Elliot Ed Aronson, William J. McGuire, Theodore M. Newcomb, Milton J. Rosenberg, and Percy H. Tannenbaum, *Theories of Cognitive Consistency: A Sourcebook* (Chicago: Rand-McNally, 1968); Leon Festinger, *A Theory of Cognitive Dissonance* (Palo Alto, CA: Stanford University Press, 1957).

87. Green, Palmquist, and Schickler, *Partisan Hearts and Minds*, Alan S. Gerber, Gregory A. Huber, and Ebonya Washington, "Party Affiliation, Partisanship, and Political Beliefs: A Field Experiment," *American Political Science Review* 104 (November 20120): 720–44.

88. Jennifer Jerit and Jason Barabas, "Partisan Perceptual Bias and the Information Environment," *Journal of Politics* 74 (July 2012): 672–84.

89. See David K. Sherman and Geoffrey L. Cohen, "The Psychology of Self-Defense: Self-Affirmation Theory," *Advances in Experimental Social Psychology* 38 (2006): 183–242; Abraham Tesser, "On the Confluence of Self-Esteem Maintenance Mechanisms," *Personality and Social Psychology Review* 4, no. 4 (2000): 290–99; Ruth Thibodeau and Elliot Aronson, "Taking a Closer Look: Reasserting the Role of the Self-Concept in Dissonance Theory," *Personality and Social Psychology Bulletin* 18 (October 1992): 591–602.

90. Samara Klar, Yanna Krupnikov, and John Barry Ryan, "Affective Polarization or Partisan Disdain? Untangling a Dislike for the Opposing Party from a Dislike of Partisanship," *Public Opinion Quarterly* 82 (Summer 2018): 379–90; Kevin Arceneaux and Ryan J. Vander Wielen, *Taming Intuition: How Reflection Minimizes Partisan Reasoning and Promotes Democratic Accountability* (New York: Cambridge University Press, 2017); Erik Peterson, "The Role of the Information Environment in Partisan Voting," *Journal of Politics* 79 (October 2017): 1191–204; Seth J. Hill, "Learning Together Slowly: Bayesian Learning about Political Facts," *Journal of Politics* 79 (October 2017): 1403–18; Green, Palmquist, and Schickler, *Partisan Hearts and Minds*; Alan Gerber and Donald P. Green, "Misperceptions About Perceptual Bias," *Annual Review of Political Science* 2, no. 1 (1999): 189–210; Alan Gerber Donald P. Green, "Rational Learning and Partisan Attitudes," *American Journal of Political Science* 42 (July 1998): 794–818.

91. Stephen N. Goggin and Alexander G. Theodoridis, "Seeing Red (or Blue): How Party Identity Colors Political Cognition," *The Forum* 16, no. 1 (2018): 81–95; Theodoridis, "Me, Myself, and (I), (D), or (R)?; Stephen N. Goggin and Alexander G. Theodoridis, "Disputed Ownership: Parties, Issues, and Traits in the Minds of Voters," *Political Behavior* 39 (September 2017): 675–702; Jerit and Barabas.,

"Partisan Perceptual Bias and the Information Environment"; Taber and Lodge, "Motivated Skepticism in the Evaluation of Political Beliefs"; Larry M. Bartels, "Beyond the Running Tally: Partisan Bias in Political Perceptions," *Political Behavior* 24 (June 2002): 117–50; Ziva Kundra and Lisa Sinclair, "Motivated Reasoning with Stereotypes: Activation, Application, and Inhibition," *Psychological Inquiry* 10, no. 1 (1999): 12–22; Redlawsk, "Hot Cognition or Cool Consideration?"

92. Brian J. Gaines, James H. Kuklinski, Paul J. Quirk, Buddy Peyton, and Jay Verkuilen, "Same Facts, Different Interpretations: Partisan Motivation and Opinion on Iraq," *Journal of Politics* 69 (November 2007): 957–74; Steven Kull, Clay Ramsay, and Evan Lewis, "Misperceptions, the Media, and the Iraq War," *Political Science Quarterly* 118 (Winter 2003–2004): 569–98.

93. Alan S. Gerber and Gregory A. Huber, "Partisanship, Political Control, and Economic Assessments," *American Journal of Political Science* 54 (January 2010): 153–73; Suzanna DeBoef and Paul M. Kellstedt, "The Political (and Economic) Origins of Consumer Confidence," *American Journal of Political Science* 48 (October 2004): 633–49.

94. Toby Bolsen, James N. Druckman, and Fay Lomax Cook, "The Influence of Partisan Motivated Reasoning on Public Opinion," *Political Behavior* 36 (June 2014): 235–62.

95. Matthew J. Lebo and Daniel Cassino, "The Aggregated Consequences of Motivated Reasoning and the Dynamics of Partisan Presidential Approval," *Political Psychology* 28 (December 2007): 719–46.

96. Kate Kenski and Natalie J. Stroud, "Who Watches Presidential Debates? A Comparative Analysis of Presidential Debate Viewing in 2000 and 2004," *American Behavioral Scientist* 49 (October 2005): 213–28; Lee Sigelman and Carol K. Sigelman, "Judgments of the Carter-Reagan Debate: The Eyes of the Beholders," *Public Opinion Quarterly* 48 (January 1984): 624–28; Sidney Kraus, *The Great Debates: Background-Perspective-Effects* (Bloomington: Indiana University Press, 1962).

97. Nicholas D. Duran, Stephen P. Nicholson, and Rick Dale, "The Hidden Appeal and Aversion to Political Conspiracies as Revealed in the Response Dynamics of Partisans," *Journal of Experimental Social Psychology* 73 (November 2017): 268–78.

98. Paul D. Sweeney and Kathy L. Gruber, "Selective Exposure: Voter Information Preferences and the Watergate Affair," *Journal of Personality and Social Psychology* 46, no. 6 (1984): 1208–21; Mark Fischle, "Mass Response to the Lewinsky Scandal: Motivated Reasoning or Bayesian Updating?" *Political Psychology* 21 (March 2000): 135–59.

99. See Howard Lavine, Christopher Johnston, and Marco Steenbergen, *The Ambivalent Partisan* (Oxford: Oxford University Press 2012); Brendan Nyhan and Jason Reifler, *Misinformation and Fact-Checking: Research Findings from Social Science* (Washington DC: New America Foundation, 2012); Goren et al., "Source

Cues"; Bartels, "Beyond the Running Tally"; Christopher H. Achen and Larry M. Bartels, "It Feels Like We're Thinking: The Rationalizing Voter and Electoral Democracy" (paper presented at the Annual Meeting of the American Political Science Association, Philadelphia, August 31–September 3, 2006); Larry M. Bartels, *Unequal Democracy* (Princeton, NJ: Princeton University Press, 2008), chap. 5.

100. Alison Kodjak, "We Asked People What They Know About Obamacare. See If You Know the Answers," NPR, April 3, 2017; YouGov.com poll, April 18–20, 2015.

101. CBS News poll, June 15–18, 2017.

102. Pew Research Center poll, July 13–19, 2020.

103. Steven P. Nawara, "Who Is Responsible, the Incumbent or the Former President? Motivated Reasoning in Responsibility Attributions," *Presidential Studies Quarterly* 45 (March 2015): 110–31. See also Martin Bisgaard, "Bias Will Find a Way: Economic Perceptions, Attributions of Blame, and Partisan-Motivated Reasoning during Crisis," *Journal of Politics* 77 (July 2015): 849–60.

104. Adam J. Berinsky, *In Time of War: Understanding American Public Opinion from World War II to Iraq* (Chicago: University of Chicago Press, 2009), 124.

105. See Logan Dancey and Geoffrey Sheagley, "Heuristics Behaving Badly: Party Cues and Voter Knowledge," *American Journal of Political Science* 57 (April 2013): 312–25; Bisgaard, "Bias Will Find a Way."

106. Gabriel S. Lenz, *Follow the Leader? How Voters Respond to Politicians' Policies and Performance* (Chicago: University of Chicago Press, 2012); Michael Tesler, "Priming Predispositions and Changing Policy Positions: An Account of When Mass Opinion Is Primed or Changed," *American Journal of Political Science* 59 (October 2015): 806–24.

107. James N. Druckman, Erik Peterson, and Rune Slothuus, "How Elite Partisan Polarization Affects Public Opinion Formation," *American Political Science Review* 107 (February 2013): 57–79; Geoffrey C. Layman, Thomas M. Carsey, John C. Green, Richard Herrera, and Rosalyn Cooperman, "Activists and Conflict Extension in American Party Politics," *American Political Science Review* 107 (June 2013): 324–46; Lenz, *Follow the Leader?*; Matthew Levendusky, *The Partisan Sort* (Chicago: University of Chicago Press, 2009). See also Joshua Dyck and Shanna Pearson-Merkowitz, "To Know You Is Not Necessarily to Love You: The Partisan Mediators of Intergroup Contact," *Political Behavior* 36 (September 2014): 553–80.

108. Logan Dancey and Paul Goren, "Party Identification, Issue Attitudes, and the Dynamics of Political Debate," *American Journal of Political Science* 54 (July 2010): 686.

109. Stephen P. Nicholson, "Polarizing Cues," *American Journal of Political Science* 56 (January 2012): 52–66; Joanne R. Smith, Deborah J. Terry, Timothy R. Crosier, and Julie M. Duck, "The Importance of the Relevance of the Issue to the Group in Voting Intentions," *Basic and Applied Social Psychology* 27 no. 2 (2005): 163–70.

110. John G. Bullock, "Elite Influence on Public Opinion in an Informed Electorate," *American Political Science Review* 105 (August 2011): 496–515.

111. Druckman et al., "How Elite Partisan Polarization Affects Public Opinion Formation." Party endorsements, particularly under conditions of polarization, do not appear to serve simply as cues people follow. Instead, cues seem to shape how the public views arguments put forth by different sides. See also Toby Bolsen, James N. Druckman, and Fay Lomax Cook, "The Influence of Partisan Motivated Reasoning on Public Opinion," *Political Behavior* 36 (June 2014): 235–62. But see Cheryl Boudreau and Scott A. MacKenzie, "Informing the Electorate? How Party Cues and Policy Information Affect Public Opinion about Initiatives," *American Journal of Political Science* 58 (January 2014): 48–62.

112. Penny S. Visser, George Y. Bizer, and Jon A. Krosnick, "Exploring the Latent Structure of Strength-Related Attitude Attributes," in *Advances in Experimental Social Psychology*, vol. 38, ed. Mark P. Zanna (San Diego: Academic Press, 2006).

113. Christopher H. Achen and Larry M. Bartels, *Democracy for Realists: Why Elections Do Not Produce Responsive Government* (Princeton, NJ: Princeton University Press, 2016), 286.

114. Douglas Ahler and David Broockman, "The Delegate Paradox: Why Polarized Politicians Can Represent Citizens Best," *Journal of Politics* 80 (October 2018): 1117–33.

115. Joshua Kalla and David E. Broockman, "The Minimal Persuasive Effects of Campaign Contact in General Elections: Evidence from 49 Field Experiments," *American Political Science Review* 112 (February 2018): 148–66. See also Antoine J. Banks and Heather M. Hicks, "The Effectiveness of a Racialized Counterstrategy," *American Journal of Political Science* 63 (April 2019): 305–22.

116. See Druckman et al., "How Elite Partisan Polarization Affects Public Opinion Formation."

117. Bolsen et al., "The Influence of Partisan Motivated Reasoning on Public Opinion"; Michael Bang Petersen, Martin Skov, Søren Serritzlew, and Thomas Ramsøy, "Motivated Reasoning and Political Parties: Evidence for Increased Processing in the Face of Party Cues," *Political Behavior* 35 (December 2013): 831–54.

118. James N. Druckman and Toby Bolsen, "Framing, Motivated Reasoning, and Opinions about Emergent Technologies," *Journal of Communication* 61 (August 2011): 659–88.

119. Lenz, *Follow the Leader?*

120. Michael J. Nelson and James L. Gibson, "How Does Hyperpoliticized Rhetoric Affect the US Supreme Court's Legitimacy?" *Journal of Politics* 81 (October 2019): 1512–16; Jeffery J. Mondak, "Source Cues and Policy Approval: The Cognitive Dynamics of Public Support for the Reagan Administration," *American Journal of Political Science* 37 (February 1993): 186–212.

121. Nicholson, "Polarizing Cues." On the importance of source credibility, see Adam J. Berinsky, "Rumors and Health Care Reform: Experiments in Political

Misinformation," *British Journal of Political Science* 47 (April 2017): 241–262; James N. Druckman, "Using Credible Advice to Overcome Framing Effects," *Journal of Law, Economics, and Organization* 17, no. 1 (2001): 62–82; James N. Druckman, "On the Limits of Framing Effects: Who Can Frame?" *Journal of Politics* 63 (November 2001): 1041–66; Joanne M. Miller and Jon A. Krosnick, "News Media Impact on the Ingredients of Presidential Evaluations: Politically Knowledgeable Citizens Are Guided by a Trusted Source," *American Journal of Political Science* 44 (April 2000): 301–15; James H. Kuklinski and Norman Hurley, "On Hearing and Interpreting Messages: A Cautionary Tale of Citizen Cue-Taking," *Journal of Politics* 56 (August 1994): 729–51; and John R. Zaller, *The Nature and Origins of Mass Opinion* (New York: Cambridge University Press, 1992), 42–48.

122. Lavine et al., *The Ambivalent Partisan.*

123. Kinder and Kalmoe, *Neither Liberal Nor Conservative.*

124. Jeremy Diamond, "Trump: I Could 'Shoot Somebody and I Wouldn't Lose Voters,'" CNN.com, January 24, 2016, https://www.cnn.com/2016/01/23/politics/donald-trump-shoot-somebody-support/index.html.

125. Quoted in Greg Sargent, "A GOP Senator's Remarkable Admission about Trump and Mueller," *Washington Post*, March 21, 2018.

126. Quoted in Tim Alberta, *American Carnage: On the Front Lines of the Republican Civil War and the Rise of President Trump* (New York: HarperCollins, 2019), 490–91.

127. *The Economist* poll, December 1–3, 2019.

128. Pew Research Center poll, April 7–12, 2020.

129. Robert Costa and Philip Rucker, "'Siege Warfare': Republican Anxiety Spikes as Trump Faces Growing Legal and Political Perils," *Washington Post*, December 8, 2018.

130. *HuffPost*/YouGov poll, May 29–30, 2019.

131. Michael Barber and Jeremy C. Pope, "Does Party Trump Ideology? Disentangling Party and Ideology in America," *American Political Science Review* 113 (February 2019): 38–54.

132. Jared McDonald, Sarah E. Croco, and Candace Turitto, "Teflon Don or Politics as Usual? An Examination of Foreign Policy Flip-Flops in the Age of Trump," *Journal of Politics* 81 (April 2019): 757–66.

133. Joshua Robison, "The Role of Elite Accounts in Mitigating the Negative Effects of Repositioning," *Political Behavior* 39 (September 2017): 609–28.

134. Larry Bartels, "Here's How Little Americans Have Learned about Donald Trump," *Washington Post*, February 21, 2018.

135. Croco et al., "Teflon Don or Politics as Usual?"

136. Robert Griffin, *Two Years In: How Americans' Have—and Have Not—Changed During Trump's Presidency*, Democracy Fund Voter Study Group 2019 VOTER Survey, May 2019. Survey was conducted November 17, 2018–January 7, 2019.

137. This discussion is based on Edwards, George C. Edwards III, *On Deaf Ears: The Limits of the Bully Pulpit* (New Haven, CT: Yale University Press, 2003), chaps. 4–9 and Edwards, *Predicting the Presidency: The Potential of Persuasive Leadership* (Princeton, NJ: Princeton University Press, 2016), chaps. 5–8.

138. On the importance of repetition in strengthening and increasing confidence in attitudes, see Druckman and Bolsen, "Framing, Motivated Reasoning, and Opinions"; Wesley G. Moons, Diane Mackie, and Teresa Garcia-Marques, "The Impact of Repetition-induced Familiarity on Agreement with Weak and Strong Arguments," *Journal of Personality and Social Psychology* 96 (January 2009): 32–44; Michele P. Claibourn, "Making a Connection: Repetition and Priming in Presidential Campaigns," *Journal of Politics* 70 (October 2008): 1142–59; Richard Johnston, Michael G. Hagen, and Kathleen Hall Jamieson, *The 2000 Presidential Election and the Foundations of Party Politics* (New York: Cambridge University Press, 2004); Daron R. Shaw, "The Effect of TV Ads and Candidate Appearances on Statewide Presidential Votes, 1988–96," *American Political Science Review* 93 (June 1999): 345–61; Prashant Malaviya and Brian Sternthal, "The Persuasive Impact of Message Spacing," *Journal of Consumer Psychology* 6, no. 3 (1997): 233–55; Ida E. Berger, "The Nature of Attitude Accessibility and Attitude Confidence," *Journal of Consumer Psychology* 1, no. 2 (1992): 103–23; John T. Cacioppo and Richard E. Petty, "Effects of Message Repetition on Argument Processing, Recall, and Persuasion," *Basic and Applied Social Psychology* 10, no. 1 (1989): 3–12.

139. Dennis Chong and James N. Druckman, "Dynamic Public Opinion: Communication Effects over Time," *American Political Science Review* 104 (November 2010): 663–80; Douglas A. Hibbs Jr., "Implications of the 'Bread and Peace' Model for the 2008 Presidential Election," *Public Choice* 137 (October 2008): 1–10; Seth J. Hill, James Lo, Lynn Vavreck, and John Zaller, "The Duration of Advertising Effects in the 2000 Presidential Campaign" (paper presented at the Annual Meeting of the American Political Science Association, Boston, August 28–31, 2008); Dennis Chong and James N. Druckman, "A Theory of Framing and Opinion Formation in Competitive Elite Environments," *Journal of Communication* 57 (February 2007): 99–118; Alan Gerber, James G. Gimpel, Donald P. Green, and Daron R. Shaw, "The Influence of Television and Radio Advertising on Candidate Evaluations: Results from a Large Scale Randomized Experiment" (paper presented at the Annual Meeting of the Midwest Political Science Association, Chicago, April 12–15, 2007); Diana C. Mutz and Byron Reeves, "The New Videomalaise: Effects of Televised Incivility on Political Trust," *American Political Science Review* 99 (February 2005): 1–15; Claes H. de Vreese, "Primed by the Euro," *Scandinavian Political Studies* 27 (March 2004): 45–65; James N. Druckman and Kjersten R. Nelson, "Framing and Deliberation: How Citizens' Conversations Limit Elite Influence," *American Journal of Political Science* 47 (October 2003): 729–45; David Tewksbury, Jennifer Jones, Matthew W. Peske, Ashlea Raymond,

and William Vig, "The Interaction of News and Advocate Frames: Manipulating Audience Perceptions of a Local Public Policy Issue," *Journalism and Mass Communication Quarterly* 77 (December 2000): 804–29.

140. Zaller, *The Nature and Origins of Mass Opinion*, 102–13; Danielle Shani, "Knowing Your Colors: Can Knowledge Correct for Partisan Bias in Political Perceptions?" (paper presented at the Annual Meeting of the Midwest Political Science Association, Chicago, April 20–23, 2006).

141. Ryan L. Claassen and Benjamin Highton, "Does Policy Debate Reduce Information Effects in Public Opinion? Analyzing the Evolution of Public Opinion on Health Care," *Journal of Politics* 68 (May 2006): 410–20.

142. Zaller, *The Nature and Origins of Mass Opinion*, 48; William G. Jacoby, "The Sources of Liberal–Conservative Thinking: Education and Conceptualization," *Political Behavior* 10 (December 1988): 316–32; Robert C. Luskin, "Measuring Political Sophistication," *American Journal of Political Science* 31 (November 1987): 856–99; W. Russell Neuman, *The Paradox of Mass Politics; Knowledge and Opinion in the American Electorate* (Cambridge, MA: Harvard University Press, 1986); Edward G. Carmines and James A. Stimson, "The Two Faces of Issue Voting," *American Political Science Review* 74 (March 1980): 78–91; Philip E. Converse, "The Nature of Belief Systems in Mass Publics," in *Ideology and Discontent*, ed. David E. Apter (New York: Free Press, 1964).

143. Conor M. Dowling, Michael Henderson, and Michael G. Miller, "Knowledge Persists, Opinions Drift: Learning and Opinion Change in a Three-Wave Panel Experiment," *American Politics Research* 48 (March 2020): 263–74; James H. Kuklinski, Paul J. Quirk, Jennifer Jerit, David Schwieder, and Robert F. Rich, "Misinformation and the Currency of Democratic Citizenship," *Journal of Politics* 62 (August 2000): 790–816. See also Brendan Nyhan, "Why the 'Death Panel' Myth Wouldn't Die: Misinformation in the Health Care Reform Debate," *The Forum* 8, no. 1 (2010): https://doi.org/10.2202/1540-8884.1354; Brendan Nyhan, Ethan Porter, Jason Reifler, and Thomas Wood, "Taking Fact-Checks Literally but Not Seriously? The Effects of Journalistic Fact-Checking on Factual Beliefs and Candidate Favorability," *Political Behavior* (2019): https://doi.org/10.1007/s11109 -019-09528-x. But see Thomas Wood and Ethan Porter, "The Elusive Backfire Effect: Mass Attitudes' Steadfast Factual Adherence," *Political Behavior* 41 (March 2019): 135–63; Ethan Porter, Thomas J. Wood, and Babak Bahador, "Can Presidential Misinformation on Climate Change Be Corrected? Evidence from Internet and Phone Experiments, *Research and Politics* 6 (July–September 2019): 1–10.

144. R. Kelly Garrett and Brian Weeks, "The Promise and Peril of Real-Time Corrections to Political Misperceptions," *Proceedings of the 2013 Conference on Computer Supported Cooperative Work*, (San Antonio, TX, February 23–27, 2013): 1047–58; Brendan Nyhan and Jason Reifler, "When Corrections Fail: The Persistence of Political Misperceptions," *Political Behavior* 32 (June 2010): 303–30; David P. Redlawsk, Andrew J. W. Civettini, and Karen M. Emmerson, "The

Affective Tipping Point: Do Motivated Reasoners Ever 'Get It'?" *Political Psychology* 31 (August 2010): 563–93. But see Wood and Porter, "The Elusive Backfire Effect."

145. Dancey and Sheagley, "Heuristics Behaving Badly"; Bisgaard, "Bias Will Find a Way"; Yudkin et al., "The Perception Gap."

146. Ruth Mayo, Yaacov Schul, and Eugene Burnstein, "'I Am Not Guilty' vs 'I Am Innocent': Successful Negation May Depend on the Schema Used for Its Encoding," *Journal of Experimental Social Psychology* 40 (July 2004): 433–49.

147. Stephan Lewandowsky, Ulrich K. H. Ecker, Colleen M Seifert, Norbert Schwarz, and John Cook, "Misinformation and Its Correction: Continued Influence and Successful Debiasing," *Psychological Science in the Public Interest* 13 (December 2012): 106–31; Norbert Schwarz, Lawrence J. Sanna, Ian Skurnik, and Carolyn Yoon, "Metacognitive Experiences and the Intricacies of Setting People Straight: Implications for Debiasing and Public Information Campaigns," *Advances in Experimental Social Psychology* 39 (2007): 127–61; Ian Skurnik, Carolyn Yoon, Denise C. Park, and Norbert Schwarz, "How Warnings about False Claims Become Recommendations," *Journal of Consumer Research* 31 (March 2005): 713–24.

148. Colleen Seifert, "The Continued Influence of Misinformation in Memory," *Psychology of Learning and Motivation* 41 (New York: Elsevier, 2002): 265–92; Berinsky, "Rumors and Health Care Reform."

149. Ulrich K. H. Ecker, Stephan Lewandowsky, Briony Swire, and Darren Chang, "Correcting False Information in Memory: Manipulating the Strength of Misinformation Encoding and Its Retraction," *Psychonomic Bulletin and Review*, 18 (June 2011): 570–78; John Bullock, "Experiments on Partisanship and Public Opinion: Party Cues, False Beliefs, and Bayesian Updating," PhD diss., Stanford University, 2007; Norbert Schwarz and Gerald L. Clore, "Feelings and Phenomenal Experiences," in *Social Psychology: Handbook of Basic Principles*, 2nd ed., ed. Arie W. Kruglanski and E. Tory Higgins (New York: Guilford, 1996).

150. See Rebekah H. Nagler, "Adverse Outcomes Associated with Media Exposure to Contradictory Nutrition Messages," *Journal of Health Communication* 19, no. 1 (2014): 24–40.

151. David Kahneman and Amos Tversky, "Choices, Values, and Frames," *American Psychologist* 39 (April 1984): 341–50; David Kahneman and Amos Tversky, "Prospect Theory: An Analysis of Decision under Risk," *Econometrica* 47 (March 1979): 263–92.

152. Stuart N. Soroka, *Negativity in Democratic Politics* (New York: Cambridge University Press, 2014); Susan T. Fiske, "Attention and Weight in Person Perception: The Impact of Negative and Extreme Behavior," *Journal of Personality and Social Psychology* 38, no. 6 (1980): 889–906; David L. Hamilton and Mark P. Zanna, "Differential Weighting of Favorable and Unfavorable Attributes in Impressions of Personality," *Journal of Experimental Research in Personality* 6, nos. 2–3 (1972): 204–12.

153. Richard Lau, "Two Explanations for Negativity Effects in Political Behavior," *American Journal of Political Science* 29 (February 1985): 119–38.

154. See, e.g., David W. Brady and Daniel P. Kessler, "Who Supports Health Reform?" *PS: Political Science and Politics* 43 (January 2010): 1–5.

155. Michael D. Cobb and James H. Kuklinski, "Changing Minds: Political Arguments and Political Persuasion," *American Journal of Political Science* 41 (January 1997): 88–121. On the role of emotion in political decision-making, see Joanne M. Miller, "Examining the Mediators of Agenda Setting: A New Experimental Paradigm Reveals the Role of Emotions," *Political Psychology* 28 (December 2007): 689–717; George E. Marcus, W. Russell Neuman, and Michael MacKuen, *Affective Intelligence and Political Judgment* (Chicago: University of Chicago Press, 2000); George E. Marcus, *The Sentimental Citizen* (University Park: Pennsylvania State University Press, 2002); Michael MacKuen, Jennifer Wolak, Luke Keele, and George E. Marcus, "Civic Engagements: Resolute Partisanship or Reflective Deliberation," *American Journal of Political Science* 54 (April 2010): 440–58.

156. Kevin Arceneaux, "Cognitive Biases and the Strength of Political Arguments," *American Journal of Political Science* 56 (April 2012): 271–85.

Chapter Three

1. See George C. Edwards III, *On Deaf Ears: The Limits of the Bully Pulpit* (New Haven, CT: Yale University Press, 2003); Samuel Kernell, *Going Public*, 4th ed. (Washington DC: CQ Press, 2007).

2. See Edwards, *On Deaf Ears*; Edwards, *The Strategic President: Persuasion and Opportunity in Presidential Leadership* (Princeton, NJ: Princeton University Press, 2009); Edwards, *Overreach: Leadership in the Obama Presidency* (Princeton, NJ: Princeton University Press, 2012); Edwards, *Predicting the Presidency: The Potential of Persuasive Leadership* (Princeton, NJ: Princeton University Press, 2016); Edwards, *Governing by Campaigning: The Politics of the Bush Presidency*, 2nd ed. (New York: Longman, 2007).

3. "Remarks by President Bush in a Conversation on Strengthening Social Security," Greece, New York, March 24, 2005, https://georgewbush-whitehouse.archives .gov/infocus/social-security/.

4. David Gergen, *Eyewitness to Power: The Essence of Leadership* (New York: Simon and Schuster, 2000), 54, 186. Also see Martha Joynt Kumar, *Managing the President's Message: The White House Communications Operation* (Baltimore, MD: Johns Hopkins University Press, 2007), chaps. 2–3.

5. Philip E. Converse, "The Nature of Belief Systems in Mass Publics," in *Ideology and Discontent*, ed. David E. Apter (New York: Free Press, 1964), 206–61.

6. Joe S. Foote, "Ratings Decline of Presidential Television," *Journal of Broadcasting and Electronic Media* 32 (Spring 1988): 225–30; A. C. Nielsen, *Nielsen*

Newscast (Northbrook, IL: Nielson, 1975); Edwards, *On Deaf Ears*, chap. 8; Edwards, *Governing by Campaigning*, 86–94.

7. Matthew A. Baum and Samuel Kernell, "Has Cable Ended the Golden Age of Presidential Television?" *American Political Science Review* 93 (March 1999): 99–114; Garry Young and William B. Perkins, "Presidential Rhetoric, the Public Agenda, and the End of Presidential Television's 'Golden Age,'" *Journal of Politics* 67 (November 2005): 1190–2015.

8. "Changing Channels: Americans View Just 17 Channels Despite Record Number to Choose From," Nielsen, May 6, 2014.

9. Gergen, *Eyewitness to Power*, 54. See also Kumar, *Managing the President's Message*, chap. 1.

10. Gergen, *Eyewitness to Power*, 54.

11. Scott Rasmussen, "60 Percent of U.S. Adults Underestimate Size of Personal Tax Cuts," *Ballotpedia*, September 21, 2018.

12. *HuffPost/*YouGov poll, February 5–7, 2018.

13. Pew Research Center poll, March 7–14, 2018.

14. Ariel Edwards-Levy, "The GOP Health Care Bill Is a Historically Unpopular Piece of Legislation," *HuffPost*, July 7, 2017.

15. John Wagner, "President Largely Sidesteps the Bully Pulpit in Pushing Health-Care Bill," *Washington Post*, July 2, 2017.

16. Abby Phillip and Robert Costa, "Trump Says He Wants Victories—but He Isn't Selling the GOP Agenda to Voters," *Washington Post*, July 14, 2017.

17. Sean Sullivan, "Recess Just Started for Congress, and It's Not Going to Be Much Fun for Republicans," *Washington Post*, August 3, 2017.

18. Phillip and Costa, "Trump Says He Wants Victories."

19. Philip Bump, "Trump Tweets about the Health-Care Bill a Lot. He Just Doesn't Really Make the Case for It," *Washington Post*, July 17, 2017.

20. Rachael Bade, Seung Min Kim, and Kyle Cheney, "Trump's Confederacy Fight Threatens GOP Agenda in Congress," *Politico*, August 7, 2017.

21. Kelsey Snell, "Republicans Worry Tax Reform Could Be Victim of Their Worsening Relationship with Trump," *Washington Post*, August 17, 2017.

22. Julie Hirschfeld Davis and Alan Rappeport, "Trump Proposes the Most Sweeping Tax Overhaul in Decades," *New York Times*, September 27, 2017.

23. Kathryn Dunn Tenpas, James A. McCann, and Emily J. Charnock, "Trump Makes Fewer Public Trips than Recent Presidents. Will that Hurt the Republicans in November?" *Washington Post*, January 17, 2018; Kathryn Dunn Tenpas and James A. McCann, "Compared with Recent Presidents, Trump Does Not Like to Travel—Except When He's Campaigning," *Washington Post*, January 25, 2019. See also John Wagner, "Trump and Republicans Bolster Red States, Punish Blue," *Washington Post*, September 25, 2017; Jenna Johnson, "Trump's Comfort Zone This Year: Smaller Venues and Rapturous Fans in Places Where He Remains Popular," *Washington Post*, October 22, 2018.

24. Andy McDonald, "Former White House Adviser Reveals 'Meticulous' Way Trump Dictates His Tweets," *HuffPost*, November 26, 2018.

25. Julie Hirschfeld Davis, "The Ripple Effect of a Trump Tweetstorm," *New York Times*, October 23, 2018.

26. Michael D. Shear, Maggie Haberman, Nicholas Confessore, Karen Youris, Larry Buchanan, and Keith Collins, "How Trump Reshaped the Presidency in Over 11,000 Tweets," *New York Times*, November 2, 2019.

27. Donald J. Trump (@realDonaldTrump), "Sorry folks, but if I would have relied on the Fake News of CNN, NBC, ABC, CBS, washpost or nytimes, I would have had ZERO chance winning WH," Twitter, June 6, 2017, 7:15 a.m., https://twitter.com/realDonaldTrump/status/872064426568036353; Donald Trump, interview with Tucker Carlson, *Tucker Carlson Tonight*, Fox News, March 15, 2017. See also Bob Woodward, *Fear: Trump in the White House* (New York: Simon and Schuster, 2018), 205–6.

28. Gallup poll, May 1–13, 2018.

29. Pew Research Center poll, November 21–December 17, 2018 (data collected December 2018– July 2019).

30. Shear et al., "How Trump Reshaped the Presidency."

31. *HuffPost*/ YouGov poll, October 16–17, 2018.

32. Gallup poll, May 1–13, 2018.

33. *HuffPost*/ YouGov poll, October 16–17, 2018.

34. Fox News poll, March 12–14, 2017.

35. ABC News/*Washington Post* poll, July 10–13, NBC News/*Wall Street Journal* poll, September 14–18, 2017; ABC News/*Washington Post* poll, January 15–18, 2018.

36. CNN poll, August 3–6, 2017.

37. McClatchy polls, February 15–19, 2017, and March 22–27, 2017; NPR/PBS *NewsHour* poll, June 21–25, 2017; Marist College poll, August 8–12, 2017. See also CNN poll, August 3–6, 2017.

38. CNN poll, August 3–6, 2017; Marist College poll, October 15–17, 2017; NPR/PBS *NewsHour* poll, December 4–7, 2017.

39. Donald J. Trump (@realDonaldTrump), "There is NO WAY (ZERO!) that Mail-In Ballots will be anything less than substantially fraudulent. Mail boxes will be robbed, ballots will be forged & even illegally printed out & fraudulently signed. The Governor of California is sending Ballots to millions of people, anyone . . . living in the state, no matter who they are or how they got there, will get one. That will be followed up with professionals telling all of these people, many of whom have never even thought of voting before, how, and for whom, to vote. This will be a Rigged Election. No way!" Twitter, May 26, 2020, 7:17 a.m., https://twitter.com/realDonaldTrump/status/1265255835124539392.

40. *The Economist*/ YouGov poll, July 3–4, 2017.

41. Donald J. Trump (@realDonaldTrump), "I heard poorly rated @Morning_ Joe speaks badly of me (don't watch anymore). Then how come low I.Q. Crazy Mika, along with Psycho Joe, came . . ."; ". . . to Mar-a-Lago 3 nights in a row around

New Year's Eve, and insisted on joining me. She was bleeding badly from a face-lift. I said no!" Twitter, June 29, 2017, 7:52 a.m., 7:58 a.m., https://twitter.com/real DonaldTrump/status/880408582310776832; https://twitter.com/realDonaldTrump /status/880410114456465411.

42. Donald J. Trump (@realDonaldTrump), " 'Concast' should open up a long overdue Florida Cold Case against Psycho Joe Scarborough. I know him and Crazy Mika well, used them beautifully in the last Election, dumped them nicely, and will state on the record that he is "nuts". Besides, bad ratings! #OPENJOE-COLDCASE," Twitter, May 4, 2020, 5:38 a.m., https://twitter.com/realdonald trump/status/1257258214615367680; "When will they open a Cold Case on the Psycho Joe Scarborough matter in Florida. Did he get away with murder? Some people think so. Why did he leave Congress so quietly and quickly? Isn't it obvious? What's happening now? A total nut job!" Twitter, May 12, 2020, 5:54 a.m., https://twitter.com/realdonaldtrump/status/1260161295019630592; "A blow to her head? Body found under his desk? Left Congress suddenly? Big topic of discussion in Florida . . . and, he's a Nut Job (with bad ratings). Keep digging, use forensic geniuses!" Twitter, May 23, 2020, 7:05 p.m., https://twitter.com/realdonaldtrump /status/1264346866780700675.

43. Donald J. Trump (@realDonaldTrump), "Mike Pompeo is doing a great job, I am very proud of him. His predecessor, Rex Tillerson, didn't have the mental capacity needed. He was dumb as a rock and I couldn't get rid of him fast enough. He was lazy as hell. Now it is a whole new ballgame, great spirit at State!" Twitter, December 7, 2018, 2:02 p.m., https://twitter.com/realDonaldTrump/status /1071132880368132096.

44. Dino Christenson, Sarah Kreps, and Doug Kriner, "Going Public in an Era of Social Media: Tweets, Corrections, and Public Opinion," *Presidential Studies Quarterly* 50 (forthcoming).

45. Matthew R. Miles and Donald P. Haider-Markel, "Polls and Elections: Trump, Twitter, and Public Dissuasion: A Natural Experiment in Presidential Rhetoric," *Presidential Studies Quarterly* 50 (June 2020): 436–50.

46. See also YouGov poll, May 29–20, 2020.

47. ABC News/*Washington Post* poll, January 15–18, 2018.

48. Matthew R. Miles and Donald P. Haider-Markel, "Polls and Elections: Trump, Twitter, and Public Dissuasion: A Natural Experiment in Presidential Rhetoric," *Presidential Studies Quarterly* 50 (June 2020): 436–50.

49. Donald J. Trump, *The Art of the Deal* (New York: Random House, 1987), 40.

50. Ezra Klein, "Trump Is Winning," *Vox*, January 29, 2018.

51. John Sides, Michael Tesler, and Lynn Vavreck, *Identity Crisis: The 2016 Presidential Campaign and the Battle for the Meaning of America* (Princeton, NJ: Princeton University Press, 2018), chap. 4, 135–44.

52. "The Year in News 2017," *Echelon Insights* (blog), Medium.com, December 27, 2017, https://medium.com/echelon-indicators/the-year-in-news-2017-2b8 32594b4a6.

53. Michael Scherer, "Democrats Fret over the Never-Ending Trump Show," *Washington Post*, June 17, 2019.

54. Mike Allen, "Trump Show Dominates Pandemic While Biden's Voice Fades," *Axios*, April 18, 2020.

55. Klein, "Trump Is Winning."

56. "The Year in News 2017."

57. George F. Will, "The Shabbiest U.S. President Ever Is an Inexpressibly Sad Specimen," *Washington Post*, January 18, 2019.

58. Kumar, *Managing the President's Message*, 9; James N. Druckman and Lawrence R. Jacobs, *Who Governs? Presidents, Public Opinion, and Manipulation* (Chicago: University of Chicago Press, 2015), chap. 5.

59. See Edwards, *The Strategic President*, 96–104.

60. See an interview with Bill Clinton by Jack Nelson and Robert J. Donovan, "The Education of a President," *Los Angeles Times Magazine*, August 1, 1993, 39. See also Bill Clinton, *My Life* (New York: Knopf, 2004), 556.

61. Quoted in Dan Balz, "For Obama, a Tough Year to Get the Message Out," *Washington Post*, January 10, 2010.

62. George Packer, "Obama's Lost Year," *New Yorker*, March 15, 2010, 46.

63. Quoted in Balz, "For Obama, a Tough Year to Get the Message Out."

64. Daniel Pfeiffer, *Yes We (Still) Can* (New York: Twelve, 2018), 79.

65. "Remarks by President Trump in Meeting with State and Local Officials on Infrastructure Initiative," White House transcript, Washington, DC, February 12, 2018.

66. John Wagner and Ashley Parker, "Trump's Infrastructure Push, a Marquee Campaign Promise, Is Overshadowed by Controversy and Tragedy," *Washington Post*, February 17, 2018.

67. Wagner and Parker, "Trump's Infrastructure Push."

68. Urban Dictionary, s.v. "infrastructure week," last updated September 14, 2018, https://www.urbandictionary.com/define.php?term=Infrastructure+week&=true

69. John Wagner, "Trump Says Media Coverage of Explosive Devices Slowing GOP Momentum Ahead of Elections," *Washington Post*, October 26, 2018.

70. Quoted in Josh Dawsey, "Trump Derides Protections for Immigrants from 'Shithole' Countries," *Washington Post*, January 12, 2018.

71. Philip Bump, "The White House Had a Coordinated Message This Month. Trump Didn't," *Washington Post*, July 3, 2017.

72. Philip Rucker, Sean Sullivan, and Paul Kane, "The Great Dealmaker? Lawmakers Find Trump to Be an Untrustworthy Negotiator," *Washington Post*, October 23, 2017.

73. John Cassidy, "Trump's Obsession with the 'Witch Hunt' Overshadows a Good Jobs Report," *New Yorker*, September 7, 2018.

74. Monmouth University poll, April 30–May 4, 2020.

75. Ashley Parker and Philip Rucker, "How Trump's Attempts to Win the Daily News Cycle Feed a Chaotic Coronavirus Response," *Washington Post*, April 5, 2020.

76. "Trump's Wasted Briefings," *Wall Street Journal*, April 8, 2020.

77. Quoted in Jonathan Martin and Maggie Haberman, "Trump Keeps Talking. Some Republicans Don't Like What They're Hearing," *New York Times*, April 9, 2020.

78. Quoted in Philip Rucker and Robert Costa, "Commander of Confusion: Trump Sows Uncertainty and Seeks to Cast Blame in Coronavirus Crisis," *Washington Post*, April 2, 2020.

79. Donald J. Trump (@realDonaldTrump), "Sports fans should never condone players that do not stand proud for their National Anthem or their Country. NFL should change policy!" Twitter, September 24, 2017, 5:25 p.m., https://twitter.com /realDonaldTrump/status/912080538755846144.

80. Klein, "Trump Is Winning."

81. Donald J. Trump (@realDonaldTrump), ". . . . These THUGS are dishonoring the memory of George Floyd, and I won't let that happen. Just spoke to Governor Tim Walz and told him that the Military is with him all the way. Any difficulty and we will assume control but, when the looting starts, the shooting starts. Thank you!" Twitter, May 28, 2020, 11:53 p.m., https://twitter.com/realdonaldtrump/status /1266231100780744704.

82. Quoted in Robert Costa, Philip Rucker, Yasmeen Abutaleb and Josh Dawsey, "Trump's May Days: A Month of Distractions and Grievances as Nation Marks Bleak Coronavirus Milestone," *Washington Post*, May 31, 2020.

83. See, e.g., Arthur Lupia, "Shortcuts versus Encyclopedias: Information and Voting Behavior in California Insurance Reform Elections," *American Political Science Review* 88 (March 1994): 63–76; Samuel L. Popkin, *The Reasoning Voter* (Chicago: University of Chicago Press, 1991); Paul M. Sniderman, Richard Brody, and Philip E. Tetlock, *Reasoning and Choice* (New York: Cambridge University Press, 1991); Daniel Kahneman, Paul Slovic, and Amos Tversky, *Judgment Under Uncertainty: Heuristics and Biases* (New York: Cambridge University Press, 1982); Herbert A. Simon, "A Behavioral Model of Rational Choice," *Quarterly Journal of Economics* 69 (February 1955): 99–118.

84. Richard R. Lau, "Construct Accessibility and Electoral Choice," *Political Behavior* 11 (March 1989): 5–32; Thomas K. Srull and Robert S. Wyer Jr., *Memory and Cognition in Their Social Context* (Hillsdale, NJ: Erlbaum, 1989); Robert S. Wyer Jr., and Jon Hartwick, "The Recall and Use of Belief Statements as Bases for Judgments," *Journal of Experimental Social Psychology* 20 (January 1984): 65–85; E. Tory Higgins and Gary A. King, "Accessibility of Social Constructs: Information-Processing Consequences of Individual and Contextual Variation," in *Personality, Cognition, and Social Interaction*, ed. N. Cantor and J. F. Kihlstrom (Hillsdale, NJ: Erlbaum, 1981); Thomas K. Srull and Robert S. Wyer Jr., "Category Accessibility and Social Perception: Some Implications for the Study of Person Memory and Interpersonal Judgments," *Journal of Personality and Social Psychology* 38, no. 6 (1980): 841–56; Thomas K. Srull and Robert S. Wyer Jr., "The Role of Category Accessibility in the Interpretation of Information about Persons:

Some Determinants and Implications," *Journal of Personality and Social Psychology* 37, no. 10 (1979): 1660–72.

85. Converse, "The Nature of Belief Systems in Mass Publics."

86. John R. Zaller, *The Nature and Origins of Mass Opinion* (New York: Cambridge University Press, 1992), 42–48; James H. Kuklinski and Norman Hurley, "On Hearing and Interpreting Messages: A Cautionary Tale of Citizen Cue-Taking," *Journal of Politics* 56 (August 1994): 729–51; Jeffery Mondak, "Source Cues and Policy Approval: The Cognitive Dynamics of Public Support for the Reagan Agenda," *American Journal of Political Science* 37 (February 1993): 186–212; James N. Druckman, "On the Limits of Framing Effects: Who Can Frame?" *Journal of Politics* 63 (November 2001): 1041–66. See also Joanne M. Miller and Jon A. Krosnick, "News Media Impact on the Ingredients of Presidential Evaluations: Politically Knowledgeable Citizens Are Guided by a Trusted Source," *American Journal of Political Science* 44 (April 2000): 301–15; and James N. Druckman, "Using Credible Advice to Overcome Framing Effects," *Journal of Law, Economics, and Organization* 17 (April 2001): 62–82.

87. See, e.g., Donald R. Kinder and Lynn M. Sanders, *Divided by Color: Racial Politics and Democratic Ideals* (Chicago: University of Chicago Press, 1996); Zhongdang Pan and Gerald M. Kosicki, "Framing Analysis: An Approach to News Discourse," *Political Communication* 10, no. 1 (1993): 55–75; William A. Gamson, *Talking Politics* (Cambridge: Cambridge University Press, 1992); William A. Gamson and Andre Modigliani, "Media Discourse and Public Opinion on Nuclear Power: A Constructionist Approach," *American Journal of Sociology* 95 (July 1989): 1–37; William A. Gamson and Andre Modigliani, "The Changing Culture of Affirmative Action," in *Research in Political Sociology*, vol. 3, ed. Richard D. Braungart (Greenwich, CT: JAI Press, 1987), 143.

88. There is some evidence that the president's rhetoric can prime the criteria on which the public evaluates him. See James N. Druckman and Justin W. Holmes, "Does Presidential Rhetoric Matter? Priming and Presidential Approval," *Presidential Studies Quarterly* 34 (December 2004): 755–78.

89. Quoted in Gerald M. Boyd, "'General Contractor' of the White House Staff," *New York Times*, March 4, 1986, sec. A, 22.

90. For the latter view that framing does not work by altering the accessibility to different considerations, see Druckman, "On the Limits of Framing Effects." See also Thomas E. Nelson, Rosalee A. Clawson, and Zoe M. Oxley, "Media Framing of a Civil Liberties Conflict and Its Effect on Tolerance," *American Political Science Review* 91 (September 1997): 567–84; and Miller and Krosnick, "News Media Impact."

91. Over the past generation, the research on public opinion has produced a large number of studies showing the impact of priming and framing on people's opinions. For evidence of the impact of framing effects, see John Sides, "Stories or Science? Facts, Frames, and Policy Attitudes," *American Politics Research* 44

(May 2016): 387–414; Samara Klar, "The Influence of Competing Identity Primes on Political Preferences," *Journal of Politics* 75 (October 2013): 1108–24; Dan Cassino and Cengiz Erisen, "Priming Bush and Iraq in 2008: A Survey Experiment," *American Politics Research* 38 (March 2010): 372–94; Nicholas J. G. Winter, "Beyond Welfare: Framing and the Racialization of White Opinion on Social Security," *American Journal of Political Science* 50 (April 2006): 400–20; Nicholas A. Valentino, Vincent L. Hutchings, and Ismail K. White, "Cues that Matter: How Political Ads Prime Racial Attitudes During Campaigns," *American Political Science Review* 96 (March 2002): 75–90; Thomas E. Nelson, "Policy Goals, Public Rhetoric, and Political Attitudes," *Journal of Politics* 66 (May 2004): 581–605; William G. Jacoby, "Issue Framing and Public Opinion on Government Spending," *American Journal of Political Science* 44 (October 2000): 750–67; Thomas E. Nelson and Zoe M. Oxley, "Issue Framing Effects on Belief Importance and Opinion," *Journal of Politics* 61 (November 1999): 1040–67; Joseph N. Cappella and Kathleen Hall Jamieson, *Spiral of Cynicism: The Press and the Public Good* (New York: Oxford University Press, 1997); Thomas E. Nelson, Rosalee A. Clawson, and Zoe M. Oxley, "Toward a Psychology of Framing Effects," *Political Behavior* 19 (September 1997): 221–46; Nelson, Clawson, and Oxley, "Media Framing of a Civil Liberties Conflict and Its Effect on Tolerance"; Donald R. Kinder and Lynn M. Sanders, *Divided by Color: Racial Politics and Democratic Ideals* (Chicago: University of Chicago Press, 1996); Thomas E. Nelson and Donald R. Kinder, "Issue Frames and Group-Centrism in American Public Opinion," *Journal of Politics* 58 (November 1996): 1055–78; Dennis Chong, "How People Think, Reason, and Feel about Rights and Liberties," *American Journal of Political Science* 37 (August 1993): 867–99; W. Russell Neuman, Marion K. Just, and Ann N. Crigler, *Common Knowledge: News and the Construction of Political Meaning* (Chicago: University of Chicago Press, 1992); John Zaller and Stanley Feldman, "A Simple Theory of the Survey Response: Answering Questions versus Revealing Preferences," *American Journal of Political Science* 36 (August 1992): 579–616; Stanley Feldman and John Zaller, "The Political Culture of Ambivalence: Ideological Responses to the Welfare State," *American Journal of Political Science* 36 (February 1992): 268–307; Donald R. Kinder and Lynn M. Sanders, "Mimicking Political Debate with Survey Questions: The Case of White Opinion on Affirmative Action for Blacks," *Social Cognition* 8, no. 1 (1990): 73–103; Jon A. Krosnick and Donald R. Kinder, "Altering the Foundations of Support for the President through Priming," *American Political Science Review* 84 (June 1990): 497–512; John H. Aldrich, John Sullivan, and Eugene Borgida, "Foreign Affairs and Issue Voting: Do Presidential Candidates Waltz Before a Blind Audience?" *American Political Science Review* 83 (March 1989): 123–41; Daniel Kahneman and Amos Tversky, "Rational Choice and the Framing of Decisions," in *Rational Choice: The Contrast between Economics and Psychology*, ed. Hillel J. Einhorn and Robin M. Hogarth (Chicago: University of Chicago Press, 1987); Daniel Kahneman and Amos Tversky, "Choices, Values, and Frames," *American Psychologist* 39 (April 1984): 341–50; Amos Tversky and Daniel Kahneman, "The Framing of Decisions and the Psychology of Choice," *Science* 211 (January 30, 1981): 453–58.

92. See Druckman and Jacobs, *Who Governs?*

93. Druckman and Jacobs, *Who Governs?*, chap. 5.

94. For a good discussion of this point, see Lawrence R. Jacobs and Robert Y. Shapiro, *Politicians Don't Pander* (Chicago: University of Chicago Press, 2000), 49–52.

95. See, e.g., William B. Riker, *The Art of Political Manipulation* (New Haven, CT: Yale University Press, 1986); William B. Riker, *The Strategy of Rhetoric: Campaigning for the American Constitution* (New Haven, CT: Yale University Press, 1996); William B. Riker, "The Heresthetics of Constitution Making: The Presidency in 1787, with Comments on Determinism and Rational Choice," *American Political Science Review* 78 (March 1984): 1–6.

96. Byron E. Shafer and William J. M. Claggett, *The Two Majorities: The Issue Context of Modern American Politics* (Baltimore, MD: Johns Hopkins University Press, 1995). See also James N. Druckman, Lawrence R. Jacobs, and Eric Ostermeier, "Candidate Strategies to Prime Issues and Image," *Journal of Politics* 66 (November 2004): 1180–202.

97. John R. Petrocik, "Divided Government: Is It All in the Campaigns," in *The Politics of Divided Government*, ed. Gary W. Cox and Samuel Kernell (Boulder, CO: Westview Press, 1991); John R. Petrocik, "Issue Ownership in Presidential Elections, with a 1980 Case Study," *American Journal of Political Science* (August 1996): 825–50.

98. Andrew Gelman and Gary King, "Why Are American Presidential Election Campaign Polls So Variable When Votes Are So Predictable?" *British Journal of Political Science* 23 (1993): 409–51.

99. John R. Zaller, "Elite Leadership of Mass Opinion: New Evidence from the Gulf War," in *Taken by Storm: The Media, Public Opinion, and U.S. Foreign Policy in the Gulf War*, ed. W. Lance Bennett and David L. Paletz (Chicago: University of Chicago Press, 1994), 186–209.

100. James N. Druckman, Jordan Fein, and Thomas J. Leeper, "A Source of Bias in Public Opinion Stability," *American Political Science Review* 106 (May 2012): 430–54; Adam J. Berinsky, "Assuming the Costs of War: Events, Elites, and American Public Support for Military Conflict," *Journal of Politics* 69 (November 2007): 975–97; Paul M. Sniderman and Sean M. Theriault, "The Structure of Political Argument and the Logic of Issue Framing," in *Studies in Public Opinion: Attitudes, Nonattitudes, Measurement Error and Change*, ed. Willem E. Saris and Paul M. Sniderman (Princeton, NJ: Princeton University Press, 2004); James N. Druckman and Kjersten R. Nelson, "Framing and Deliberation: How Citizens' Conversations Limit Elite Influence," *American Journal of Political Science* 47 (October 2003): 729–45; James N. Druckman, "Political Preference Formation: Competition, Deliberation, and the (Ir)relevance of Framing Effects," *American Political Science Review* 98 (November 2004): 671–86; Paul M. Sniderman, "Taking

Sides: A Fixed Choice Theory of Political Reasoning," in *Elements of Reason: Understanding and Expanding the Limits of Political Rationality*, ed. Arthur Lupia, Mathew D. McCubbins, and Samuel L. Popkin (New York: Cambridge University Press, 2000); Zaller, "Elite Leadership of Mass Opinion"; Zaller, *The Nature and Origins of Mass Opinion*, 99, chap. 9. But see Dennis Chong and James N. Druckman, "Framing Public Opinion in Competitive Democracies," *American Political Science Review* 101 (November 2007): 637–55.

101. Druckman, Fein, and Leeper, "A Source of Bias in Public Opinion Stability."

102. See Jean-Christophe Boucher and Cameron G. Thies, "'I Am a Tariff Man': The Power of Populist Foreign Policy Rhetoric under President Trump," *Journal of Politics* 81 (April 2019): 712–22; Ethan C. Busby, Joshua R. Gubler, and Kirk A. Hawkins, "Framing and Blame Attribution in Populist Rhetoric," *Journal of Politics* 81 (April 2019): 616–30; Chelsea M. Coe, Kayla S. Canelo, Kau Vue, Matthew V. Hibbing, and Stephen P. Nicholson, "The Physiology of Framing Effects: Threat Sensitivity and the Persuasiveness of Political Arguments," *Journal of Politics* 79 (October 2017): 1465–68; Dennis Chong and James N. Druckman, "Counterframing Effects," *Journal of Politics* 75 (January 2013): 1–16; James N. Druckman and Kjersten R. Nelson, "Framing and Deliberation: How Citizens' Conversations Limit Elite Influence," *American Journal of Political Science* 47 (October 2003): 729–45; Druckman, "Using Credible Advice to Overcome Framing Effects"; Donald P. Haider-Markel and Mark R. Joslyn, "Gun Policy, Opinion, Tragedy, and Blame Attribution: The Conditional Influence of Issue Frames," *Journal of Politics* 63 (May 2001): 520–43; Gregory A. Huber and John S. Lapinski, "The 'Race Card' Revisited: Assessing Racial Priming in Policy Contests," *American Journal of Political Science* 50 (April 2006): 421–40.

103. Daniel J. Hopkins, "The Exaggerated Life of Death Panels: The Limits of Framing Effects in the 2009–2012 Health Care Debate" SSRN, October 19, 2012, http://ssrn .com/abstract=2163769; Frank R. Baumgartner, Jeffrey M. Berry, Marie Hojnacki, Beth L. Leech, and David C. Kimball, *Lobbying and Policy Change: Who Wins, Who Loses, and Why* (Chicago: University of Chicago Press, 2009), chap. 9. But see Busby et al., "Framing and Blame Attribution."

104. Gregory A. Huber and Celia Paris, "Assessing the Programmatic Equivalence Assumption in Question Wording Experiments: Understanding Why Americans Like Assistance to the Poor More Than Welfare," *Public Opinion Quarterly* 77 (January 2013): 385–97; Gabriel S. Lenz, "Learning and Opinion Change, Not Priming: Reconsidering the Priming Hypothesis," *American Journal of Political Science* 53 (October 2009): 821–37.

105. Erik Peterson and Gabor Simonovits, "The Electoral Consequences of Issue Frames," *Journal of Politics* 80 (October 2018): 1283–96.

106. See Hans Noel, "The Coalition Merchants: The Ideological Roots of the Civil Rights Realignment," *Journal of Politics* 74 (January 2012): 156–73; Mark A. Smith, *The Right Talk: How Conservatives Transformed the Great Society into the*

Economic Society (Princeton, NJ: Princeton University Press, 2007); Edward G. Carmines and James A. Stimson, *Issue Evolution: Race and the Transformation of American Politics* (Princeton, NJ: Princeton University Press, 1989).

107. See, e.g., Markus Prior, *Post-Broadcast Democracy: How Media Choice Increases Inequality in Political Involvement and Polarizes Elections* (New York, NY: Cambridge University Press, 2007).

108. Converse, "The Nature of Belief Systems in Mass Publics"; William G. Jacoby, "The Sources of Liberal-Conservative Thinking: Education and Conceptualization," *Political Behavior* 10 (Winter 1988): 316–32; Robert C. Luskin, "Measuring Political Sophistication," *American Journal of Political Science* 31 (November 1987): 856–99; W. Russell Neuman, *The Paradox of Mass Politics; Knowledge and Opinion in the American Electorate* (Cambridge, MA: Harvard University Press, 1986); Edward G. Carmines and James A. Stimson, "The Two Faces of Issue Voting," *American Political Science Review* 74 (March 1980): 78–91; Zaller, *The Nature and Origins of Mass Opinion*, 48.

109. See Brian J. Gaines, James H. Kuklinski, Paul J. Quirk, Buddy Peyton, and Jay Verkuilen, "Same Facts, Different Interpretations: Partisan Motivation and Opinion on Iraq," *Journal of Politics* 69 (November 2007): 957–74; Edwards, *On Deaf Ears*, chap. 9; Larry Bartels, "Beyond the Running Tally: Partisan Bias in Political Perceptions," *Political Behavior* 24 (June 2002): 117–50.

110. See, e.g., David Remnick, "A Conversation with Maggie Haberman, Trump's Favorite Foe," *New Yorker*, July 21, 2017.

111. See, e.g., Boucher and Thies, "'I Am a Tariff Man.'" See also Busby et al., "Framing and Blame Attribution."

112. Donald J. Trump (@realDonaldTrump), "Senate Republicans are not voting on constitutionality or precedent, they are voting on desperately needed Border Security & the Wall. Our Country is being invaded with Drugs, Human Traffickers, & Criminals of all shapes and sizes. That's what this vote is all about. STAY UNITED!" Twitter, March 6, 2019, 11:54 a.m., https://twitter.com/realDonaldTrump/status/1103353074469535750; "Republican Senators are overthinking tomorrow's vote on National Emergency. It is very simply Border Security/No Crime - Should not be thought of any other way. We have a MAJOR NATIONAL EMERGENCY at our Border and the People of our Country know it very well!" Twitter, March 13, 2019, 11:48 a.m., https://twitter.com/realDonaldTrump/status/1105873274804813824.

113. Michelle Boorstein and Sarah Pulliam Bailey, "Episcopal Bishop on President Trump: 'Everything He Has Said and Done Is to Inflame Violence,'" *Washington Post*, June 1, 2020.

Chapter Four

1. Quoted in Robert Costa and Amy Goldstein, "Trump Vows 'Insurance for Everybody' in Obamacare Replacement Plan," *Washington Post*, January 15, 2017.

2. See George C. Edwards III, *On Deaf Ears: The Limits of the Bully Pulpit* (New Haven, CT: Yale University Press, 2003); Samuel Kernell, *Going Public*, 4th ed. (Washington DC: CQ Press, 2007).

3. See Edwards, *On Deaf Ears*; Edwards, *The Strategic President Persuasion and Opportunity in Presidential Leadership* (Princeton, NJ: Princeton University Press, 2009); Edwards, *Overreach: Leadership in the Obama Presidency* (Princeton, NJ: Princeton University Press, 2012); Edwards, *Predicting the Presidency: The Potential of Persuasive Leadership* (Princeton, NJ: Princeton University Press, 2016); Edwards, *Governing by Campaigning: The Politics of the Bush Presidency*, 2nd ed. (New York: Longman, 2007).

4. See George C. Edwards III, "Can Donald Trump Persuade Americans to Support His Agenda? It's Not Likely," *Washington Post*, December 27, 2016.

5. See Edwards, *Predicting the Presidency*, 83–94.

6. Gallup polls, November 9–13, 2016, and April 1–2, 2017.

7. Christopher Warshaw and David Broockman, "G.O.P. Senators Might Not Realize It, But Not One State Supports the A.H.C.A.," *New York Times*, June 14, 2017.

8. See also *Washington Post*/ABC News poll, October 29–November 1, 2017.

9. "Exit Polls," CNN.com, http://www.cnn.com/election/2018/exit-polls.

10. Fox News polls, March 12–14, 2017, and March 18–21, 2018 (registered voters); Pew Research Center poll, April 5–11, 2017; NBC/*Wall Street Journal*, September 14–18, 2017.

11. See also CBS News poll, October 27–30, 2017; ABC News/*Washington Post* polls, September 18–21, 2017, and October 29–November 1, 2017; Democracy Fund Voter Study Group poll, April 5–May 14, 2018; CNN poll, January 30–February 2, 2019.

12. ABC News/*Washington Post* polls, January 12–15, 2017, and September 18–21, 2017; Quinnipiac University polls, February 16–21, 2017, March 2–6, 2017, March 30–April 3, 2017, April 12–18, 2017, May 4–9, 2017, May 17–23, 2017 (registered voters); Pew Research Center poll, August 15–21, 2017; NBC/*Wall Street Journal* poll, September 14–18, 2017; CBS News poll, October 27–30, 2017.

13. Associated Press polls, October 12–16, 2017, and March 23–27, 2017; Gallup polls, April 5–9, 2017, and April 2–11, 2018; CBS News poll, October 27–30, 2017; ABC/*Washington Post* polls, September 18–21, 2017, and October 29–November 1, 2017; NBC News/*Wall Street Journal* poll, September 14–18, 2017; Democracy Fund Voter Study Group poll, April 5–May 14, 2018.

14. Quinnipiac University polls, November 7–13, 2017, November 29–December 4, 2017, December 6–11, 2017, January 5–9, 2018, and February 2–5, 2018 (registered voters); CBS News poll, January 13–16, 2018; Democracy Fund Voter Study Group poll, April 5–May 14, 2018; Winston Group poll, October 31–November 2, 2019 (registered voters).

15. Fox News poll, January 20–22, 2019.

16. Pew Research Center poll, September 3–15, 2019.

17. Quinnipiac University polls, May 4–9, 2917, and July 17–August 1, 2017 (registered voters); Bloomberg poll, July 8–12, 2017; Pew Research Center poll, October 25–30, 2017. But see NBC News/*Wall Street Journal* poll, September 14–18, 2017; CBS News poll, October 27–30, 2017; Democracy Fund Voter Study Group poll, April 5–May 14, 2018; Winston Group poll, October 31–November 2, 2019 (registered voters).

18. CBS News polls, October 27–30, 2017, and December 3–5, 2017.

19. See, e.g., Kate Davidson, "Treasury Secretary Steven Mnuchin: GOP Tax Plan Would More Than Offset Its Cost," *Wall Street Journal*, September 28, 2017; Alan Rappeport and Jim Tankersley, "Treasury Defends Tax Plan Cost With One-Page Analysis," *New York Times*, December 11, 2017; Jeff Cox, "Treasury Secretary Mnuchin: Trump Tweet Was 'Warning Shot' to China on Currency," CNBC, April 17, 2018.

20. Quinnipiac University poll, May 4–9, 2017 (registered voters); CNN polls, October 12–15, 2017, and November 2–5, 2017; NBC News/*Wall Street Journal* poll, October 23–26, 2017; Gallup poll, December 1–2, 2017; CBS News poll, December 3–5, 2017; Associated Press poll, March 14–19, 2018.

21. Donald J. Trump, "Executive Order: Border Security and Immigration Enforcement Improvements," January 25, 2017, https://www.whitehouse.gov/presidential-actions/executive-order-border-security-immigration-enforcement-improvements/.

22. Frank Newport and Riley Brands, "Gallup Review: Americans, Immigration and the Election," Gallup Poll, October 27, 2016.

23. Quoted in Katie Rogers and Sheryl Gay Stolberg, "Trump Resisting a Growing Wrath for Separating Migrant Families," *New York Times*, June 18, 2018.

24. *Washington Post*–Schar School poll, June 27–July 2, 2018; CBS News poll, June 14–17, 2018; CNN poll, June 14–17, 2018; Quinnipiac University poll, June 14–17, 2018 (registered voters); GW Politics polls, July 23–August 9, 2018, October 17–25, 2018, December 11–19, 2018 (all polls of registered voters).

25. Loren Collingwood, Nazita Lajevardi, and Kassra A. R. Oskooii, "A Change of Heart? Why Individual-Level Public Opinion Shifted against Trump's Muslim Ban," *Political Behavior* 40 (December 2018): 1035–72.

26. Quinnipiac University poll, February 2–6, 2017 (registered voters); CNN poll, January 31–February 2, 2017. But see *Politico*/Harvard Public Health poll, March 22–26, 2017; and Fox News poll, February 11–13, 2017 (registered voters). See also GW Politics poll, July 23–August 9, 2018 (registered voters).

27. CBS News poll, February 1–2, 2017.

28. CNN poll, January 31–February 2, 2017.

29. Collingwood et al., "A Change of Heart?"

30. Gallup poll, May 7–9, 1999.

31. Roper poll, January 1939.

32. Gallup poll, January 22–27, 1939 (asked of half the sample).

33. Gallup poll, August 30–September 4, 1946. The figure in support was 40 percent two months earlier (Gallup poll, June 28–July 3, 1946).

34. Gallup poll, February 14–19, 1947 (asked of half the sample).

35. *Foreign Affairs* survey, May 1953.

36. Gallup poll, July 25–30, 1953.

37. Gallup poll, September 19–24, 1957, and July 30oAugust 4, 1958.

38. Harris poll, May 23–27, 1975.

39. CBS New/*New York Times*, poll, July 9–11, 1979; Gallup poll, August 3–6, 1979; Roper poll, August 18–25, 1979.

40. Gallup poll, May 16–19, 1980; ABC News/Louis Harris polls, May 16–18, and June 5–9, 1980; CBS News/*New York Times* poll, June 18–22, 1980.

41. Public Attitudes toward Refugees and Immigrants poll, February 2–7, 1984.

42. NBC News/*Wall Street Journal* poll, January 23–26, 1993.

43. CNN poll, July 18–20, 2014. See also Pew Research Center poll, July 8–14, 2014.

44. Pew Research Center polls, February 7–17, 2017 (asked of half the sample of 1,503), and April 25–May 1, 2018.

45. Gallup poll, June 7–11, 2017.

46. *HuffPost*/YouGov poll, August 2–3, 2017; CBS News poll, August 3–6, 2107.

47. CNN poll, September 17–20, 2017.

48. Quinnipiac University poll, February 2–5, 2018 (registered voters).

49. Quinnipiac University poll, June 14–17, 2018 (registered voters). Also see Quinnipiac University poll, June 27–July 1, 2018.

50. Gallup poll, June 1–13, 2018. See also Democracy Fund Voter Study Group survey, April 5–May 14, 2018.

51. Pew Research Center poll, June 5–12, 2018.

52. GW Politics polls, July 23–August 9, 2018; October 17–25, 2018; December 11–19, 2018 (all polls of registered voters).

53. *The Economist*/YouGov polls, December 31, 2019–January 1, 2019, and January 12–15, 2019.

54. Gallup polls, January 21–27, 2019, and June 3–16, 2019.

55. Gallup poll, May 28–June 4, 2020. These results preceded the administration's action to end worker visas for the remainder of 2020 and the Supreme Court's decision on DACA.

56. Gallup polls, December 3–12, 2018, and July 15–31, 2019.

57. Fox News poll, July 21–23, 2019 (registered voters); CNN poll, June 28–30, 2019. In a confusing result, a Pew Research Center poll (July 22–August 4, 2019) found that 60 percent of the public wanted to make it easier for asylum seekers to win legal status in the United States, but 53 percent wished to make it more difficult.

58. ABC News/*Washington Post* poll, April 22–25, 2019.

59. NPR/PBS *NewsHour* poll, November 28–December 4, 2018.

60. Also see Gallup polls, June 7–11, 2017 (asked of half the sample), and June 3–16, 2019; Monmouth University poll, September 15–17, 2018; Quinnipiac

University polls, February 2–5, 2018, and April 6–9, 2018 (registered voters); *Huff-Post*/YouGov polls, June 26–27, 2016, and December 10–12, 2018; NBC News/*Wall Street Journal* poll, September 16–19, 2018.

61. Gallup poll, June 7–11, 2017 (asked of half the sample); Monmouth University polls, September 15–19, 2017, and April 11–15, 2019; Pew Research Center poll, July 22–August 4, 2019.

62. Program for Public Consultation poll, October 1–16, 2018 (registered voters).

63. Pew Research Center poll, April 25–May 1, 2018. See also the Pew Research Center polls of September 3–15, 2019, February 7–12, 2017, August 9–16, 2016, March 17–26, 2016, and August 27–September 13, 2015; Fox News polls, February 10–13, 2018, and April 14–16, 2019.

64. Grinnell College poll, October 17–23, 2019.

65. Justin McCarthy, "Americans More Positive about Effects of Immigration," Gallup Poll, June 28, 2017.

66. ABC News/*Washington Post* poll, September 18–21, 2017; Pew Research Center poll, June 5–12, 2018; Monmouth University poll, April 11–15, 2019.

67. CBS News poll, February 17–21, 2017; Quinnipiac University polls, April 6–9, 2018, June 27–July 1, 2018, and January 9–13, 2019 (registered voters); Pew Research Center poll, July 22–August 4, 2019.

68. Pew Research Center poll, July 22–August 4, 2019.

69. *Washington Post*–Schar School poll, June 7–July2, 2018; *HuffPost*/YouGov polls, August 2–3, 2017, and August 5–9, 2017; Quinnipiac University polls, January 12–16, 2018, January 9–13, 2019, and January 25–28, 2019 (registered voters); ABC News/*Washington Post* poll, January 15–18, 2018; GW Politics poll, July 23–August 9, 2018 (registered voters); Democracy Fund Voter Study Group survey, April 5–May 14, 2018; NBC News/*Wall Street Journal* poll, September 16–19, 2018 (registered voters); Pew Research Center polls, January 9–14, 2019, and September 3–15, 2019.

70. Gallup poll, June 1–13, 2018.

71. APM Research Lab poll, December 10–15, 2019.

72. Pew Research Center poll, December 3–23, 2019.

73. CNN polls, September 1–4, 2016, and March 1–4, 2017. See also McClatchy polls, February 15–19, 2017, and March 22–27, 2018; GW Politics polls, May 14–30, 2018, July 23–August 9, 2018, October 17–25, 2018, December 11–19, 2018 (all polls of registered voters); Pew Research Center poll, July 22–August 4, 2019. See also Democracy Fund Voter Study Group survey, April 5–May 14, 2018.

74. See also Pew Research Center poll, December 3–23, 2019; and NPR/PBS *NewsHour* poll, December 9–11, 2019.

75. CNN poll, March 1–4, 2017.

76. *Investor's Business Daily* poll, February 24–March 4, 2017; Suffolk University poll, March 1–5, 2017; NBC News/SurveyMonkey poll, August 24–29, 2017;

Morning Consult/*Politico* poll, August 31–September 3, 2017; YouGov/*The Economist* poll, September 3–5, 2017; *HuffPost*/YouGov poll, September 5–6, 2017; Monmouth University polls, September 15–19, 2017, and January 28–30, 2018; CNN polls, September 17–20, 2017, January 14–15, 2018, and January 17–18, 2018; Quinnipiac University polls, September 21–26, 2017, and December 6–11, 2017 (registered voters); Marist College polls, September 11–13, 2017, and December 4–7, 2017; ABC News/*Washington Post* polls, September 18–21, 2017, and January 15–18, 2018; PBS *NewsHour* poll, September 25–27, 2017; NBC News/*Wall Street Journal* poll, December 13–15, 2017; Pew Research Center poll, January 10–15, 2018; *Politico*/Harvard School of Public Health poll, February 21–25, 2018 (half the sample of 1,007); Democracy Fund Voter Study Group survey, April 5–May 14, 2018; Pew Research Center poll, June 5–12, 2018; CBS News poll, June 14–17, 2018; CNN poll, June 14–17, 2018; Quinnipiac University poll, June 14–17, 2018; *Washington Post*–Schar School poll, June 27–July 2, 2018; GW Politics polls, May 14–30, 2018, July 23–August 9, 2018, October 17–25, 2018, December 11–19, 2018 (all polls of registered voters); Program for Public Consultation poll, October 1–16, 2018 (registered voters).

77. Pew Research Center poll, December 3–23, 2019. See also Pew Research Center poll, June 4–10, 2020.

78. Pew Research Center poll, January 9–14, 2019; *HuffPost*/YouGov poll, January 25–27, 2019.

79. Also see Associated Press poll, January 16–20, 2019.

80. *Washington Post*/ABC News poll, January 21–24, 2019; *HuffPost*/YouGov polls, January 4–7, 2019, January 12, 2019, and January 25–27, 2019; Pew Research Center poll, January 9–14, 2019.

81. Quinnipiac University poll, January 9–13, 2019 (registered voters).

82. Associated Press poll, January 16–20, 2019; Quinnipiac University polls, January 9–13, 2019, and January 25–28, 2019 (registered voters).

83. ABC News/*Washington Post* poll, January 8–11, 2019; CNN poll, January 10–11, 2019. However, see Quinnipiac University poll, January 9–13, 2019 (registered voters).

84. CBS News poll, January 18–21, 2019. See also Quinnipiac University poll, January 25–28, 2019 (registered voters).

85. Fox News polls, January 20–22, 2019, and March 17–20, 2019; Associated Press poll, January 16–20, 2019; ABC News/*Washington Post* polls, January 8–11, 2019, and April 22–25, 2019; Quinnipiac University polls, January 9–13, 2019, and January 25–28, 2019 (registered voters); Monmouth University polls, January 25–27, 2019, and March 1–4, 2019; CNN poll, January 30–February 2, 2019 *HuffPost*/YouGov poll, February 14–15, 2019; NPR/PBS *NewsHour* poll, February 15–17, 2019; Morning Consult/*Politico* poll, February 15–19, 2019 (registered voters); NBC News/*Wall Street Journal* poll, February 24–27, 2019.

86. NPR/PBS *NewsHour* poll, February 15–17, 2019; Morning Consult/*Politico* poll, February 15–19, 2019 (registered voters).

87. NPR/PBS *NewsHour* poll, February 15–17, 2019; ABC News/*Washington Post* poll, April 22–25, 2019; Quinnipiac University poll, January 9–13, 2019; CNN poll, January 10–11, 2019.

88. Quinnipiac University polls, January 9–13, 2019, and January 25–28, 2019 (registered voters).

89. Bob Woodward, *Fear: Trump in the White House* (New York: Simon and Schuster, 2018), 208.

90. Pew Research Center Global Attitudes surveys, April 22–May 11, 2014, and May 14–June 15, 2018.

91. Pew Research Center polls, October 2–25, 2016, and April 25–May 1, 2018.

92. Pew Research Center poll, July 10–15, 2019.

93. See also The Chicago Council on Global Affairs polls, June 27–July 19, 2017, and July 12–31, 2018.

94. NBC News/*Wall Street Journal* poll, June 11–13, 2016, and August 18–22, 2018 (both polls of registered voters). See also Monmouth University poll, June 12–13, 2018.

95. Pew Research Center poll, July 10–15, 2019.

96. Quinnipiac University poll, March 3–5, 2018, April 6–9, 2018, and June 27–July 1, 2018 (registered voters); Marist College poll, March 5–6, 2018; CBS News poll, March 8–11, 2018, June 14–17, 2018, and October 14–17, 2018; ABC News/*Washington Post* poll, April 8–11, 2011; Pew Research Center polls, April 25–May 1, 2018, July 11–15, 2018, September 11–16, 2018, and September 18–24, 2018; Monmouth University poll, June 12–13, 2018, and August 15–19, 2018; Suffolk University/*USA Today* poll, June 13–18, 2018 (focused on Mexico); NBC News/*Wall Street Journal* poll, July 15–18, 2018; Gallup poll, July 16–22, 2018; Associated Press polls, August 16–20, 2018, and June 13–17, 2019; ABC News/*Washington Post* poll, August 26–29, 2018; Fox News polls, June 9–12, 2019, August 11–13, 2019, and September 15–17, 2019.

97. CBS News poll, June 14–17, 2018.

98. Scott Lincicome, "The 'Protectionist Moment' That Wasn't: American Views on Trade and Globalization," *Free Trade Bulletin*, Cato Institute, November 2, 2018; Chicago Council on Global Affairs poll, July 12–31, 2018; Monmouth University poll, June 12–13, 2018; Pew Research Center poll, July 10–15, 2019.

99. David H. Autor, David Dorn, Gordon H. Hanson, "The China Shock: Learning from Labor Market Adjustment to Large Changes in Trade" (working paper no. 21906, National Bureau of Economic Research, January 2016).

100. John Seungmin Kuk, Deborah Seligsohn, and Jiakun (Jack) Zhang, *The Partisan Divide in U.S. Congressional Communications After the China Shock* (research paper no. 2018–03, 21st Century China Center, July 23, 2018).

101. Alexandra Guisinger, "Trade Policy Is Back in the News: Will Voters Care?" *The Forum* 17, no. 4 (2020):647–74.

102. Fox News poll, January 19–22, 2020 (registered voters).

103. Pew Research Center poll, January 6–19, 2020.

104. Quinnipiac University poll, May 16–20, 2019 (registered voters).

105. Monmouth University poll, May 16–20, 2019.

106. Jeffrey M. Jones, "Trump Job Approval Sets New Record for Polarization," Gallup Poll, January 16, 2019.

107. See also ABC News/*Washington Post* poll, January 8–11, 2018.

108. Pew Research Center poll, January 9–14, 2019.

109. Pew Research Center poll, July 10–15, 2019.

110. John Sides, Michael Tesler, and Lynn Vavreck, *Identity Crisis: The 2016 Presidential Campaign and the Battle for the Meaning of America* (Princeton, NJ: Princeton University Press, 2018), 7–8, chap. 5.

111. Vanessa Williamson, Theda Skocpol, and John Coggin, "The Tea Party and the Remaking of Republican Conservatism," *Perspectives on Politics* 9 (March 2011): 25–43.

112. Larry M. Bartels, "Partisanship in the Trump Era," *Journal of Politics* 80 (October 2018): 1483–94.

113. Alan I. Abramowitz, *The Great Alignment* (New Haven, CT: Yale University Press, 2018), 18, 131, 169–70.

114. John Sides, "Race, Religion, and Immigration in 2016: How the Debate over American Identity Shaped the Election and What It Means for a Trump Presidency," Democracy Fund Voter Study Group, June 2017, https://www.voter studygroup.org/publication/race-religion-immigration-2016.

115. Quoted in Ashley Parker, "How Trumpism Has Come to Define the Republican Party," *Washington Post*, March 25, 2018.

116. Pew Research Center poll, February 4–15, 2020.

117. Quoted in Alex Isenstadt, "Louisiana Delivers Trump a Black Eye," *Politico*, November 17, 2018.

Chapter Five

1. Jennifer Kavanagh and Michael Rich, *Truth Decay* (Washington DC: Rand Corporation, 2018).

2. Maggie Haberman, Glenn Thrush, and Peter Baker, "Inside Trump's Hour-by-Hour Battle for Self-Preservation," *New York Times*, December 9, 2017.

3. See, e.g., Jasmine C. Lee and Kevin Quealy, "The 551 People, Places, and Things Donald Trump Has Insulted on Twitter: A Complete List," *New York Times*, December 28, 2018.

4. George F. Will, "The Shabbiest U.S. President Ever Is an Inexpressibly Sad Specimen," *Washington Post*, January 18, 2019.

5. Kevin Coe and Dakota Park-Ozee, "Uncivil Name-Calling in the U.S. Presidency, 1933–2018," *Presidential Studies Quarterly* 50 (June 2020): 264–85.

6. Gregory M. Walton and Mahzarin R. Banaji, "Being What You Say: The Effect of Essentialist Linguistic Labels on Preferences," *Social Cognition* 22 (No. 2, 2004): 193–213.

7. Quoted in "Lesley Stahl: Trump Admitted Mission to 'Discredit' Press," *CBS News*, May 23, 2018, https://www.cbsnews.com/news/lesley-stahl-donald-trump-said-attacking-press-to-discredit-negative-stories/.

8. Michael D. Shear, Maggie Haberman, Nicholas Confessore, Karen Youris, Larry Buchanan, and Keith Collins, "How Trump Reshaped the Presidency in Over 11,000 Tweets," *New York Times*, November 2, 2019; Lee and Quealy, "The 551 People, Places, and Things"; Philip Bump, "The People Whom President Trump Has Called Stupid," *Washington Post,* November 6, 2018; Kevin Coe and Dakota Park-Ozee, "From 'Snollygoster' to 'Son of a Bitch': Name-Calling in the U.S. Presidency, 1933–2018," *Presidential Studies Quarterly* 50 (June 2020): 264–85.

9. Quoted in Ashley Parker, "Trump's Mean Streak Spares No One—Living or Dead," *Washington Post*, December 20, 2019.

10. Donald J. Trump (@realDonaldTrump), "There has been no President in the history of our Country who has been treated so badly as I have. The Democrats are frozen with hatred and fear. They get nothing done. This should never be allowed to happen to another President. Witch Hunt!" Twitter, September 25, 2019, 6:24 a.m., https://twitter.com/realDonaldTrump/status/1176819645699043328.

11. Quoted in Maggie Haberman and Katie Rogers, "Trump Attacks Whistle-Blower's Sources and Alludes to Punishment for Spies," *New York Times*, September 26, 2019.

12. See, e.g., Peter Baker, "A White House Now 'Cannibalizing Itself,'" *New York Times*, November 20, 2019; Elsie Viebeck and Isaac Stanley-Becker, "Attacking Witnesses Is Trump's Core Defense Strategy in Fighting Impeachment," *Washington Post*, November 18, 2019.

13. E. J. Dionne Jr., Norman J. Ornstein, and Thomas E. Mann, *One Nation after Trump: A Guide for the Perplexed, the Disillusioned, the Desperate, and the Not-Yet Deported* (New York: St. Martin's Press, 2017), 9–10.

14. *HuffPost/*YouGov poll, October 16–17, 2018.

15. Quinnipiac University poll, November 29–December 4, 2017 (registered voters).

16. Pew Research Center poll, March 7–14, 2018. See also Pew Research Center poll, April 29–May 3, 2019.

17. "'Sleepy Joe' Isn't Sticking," *Axios*, July 5, 2020.

18. Emily Badger and Kevin Quealy, "Trump Seems Much Better at Branding Opponents than Marketing Policies," *New York Times*, July 18, 2017.

19. See, e.g., Letter from Counsel to the President Pat A. Cipollone to House Democratic leaders, October 8, 2019, https://www.whitehouse.gov/wp-content/uploads/2019/10/PAC-Letter-10.08.2019.pdf.

20. Quoted in Annie Karni and Peter Baker, "At Minneapolis Rally, an Angry Trump Reserves Sharpest Attack for Biden," *New York Times*, October 11, 2019.

21. See Fox News polls, May 11–14, 2019 (registered voters), June 9–12, 2019 (registered voters), July 21–23, 2019 (registered voters), and October 6–8, 2019 (registered voters); *Washington Post*–Schar School poll, October 1–6, 2019; *Washington Post*/ABC News polls, April 22–25, 2019, and June 28–July 1, 2019; Quinnipiac University polls, April 26–29, 2019 (registered voters), May 29–June 4, 2019 (registered voters), July 25–26, 2019 (registered voters), September 19–23, 2019 (registered voters), September 27–29, 2019 (registered voters), and October 4–7, 2019 (registered voters); CNN polls, April 25–28, 2019, May 28–31, 2019, and September 24–29, 2019; Pew Research Center polls, September 3–15, 2019, and October 1–13, 2019; and Suffolk University poll, June 11–15, 2019. For a comprehensive set of polls on impeachment, see "Did Americans Support Removing Trump from Office?" FiveThirtyEight, February 20, 2020; and "Impeachment Polls: Public Master List," https://docs.google.com/spreadsheets/d/e/2PACX -1vS15V8lYPUc_OH4OBss6d8NPGRnCH1lAlBBY4FYWcK6cm6iVM8dXE_4K MFOUybRe-cVvDg7ap46FPig/pubhtml?gid=39569490&single=true.

22. See Mary E. Stuckey, "'The Power of the Presidency to Hurt:' The Indecorous Rhetoric of Donald J. Trump and the Rhetorical Norms of Democracy," *Presidential Studies Quarterly* 50 (June 2020): 366–91.

23. Quoted in Jeremy W. Peters, "I Was Trump before Trump Was Trump," *New York Times*, April 22, 2018.

24. Quoted in Tony Romm, Michael Scherer, and Amy B. Wang, "Trump Looks to Rally Controversial Online Allies at White House Social Media Summit," *Washington Post*, July 9, 2019.

25. Quoted in Peter Baker and Katie Rogers, "In Trump's America, the Conversation Turns Ugly and Angry, Starting at the Top," *New York Times*, June 20, 2018.

26. "As Election Nears, Voters Divided Over Democracy and 'Respect,'" Pew Research Center, October 27, 2016. Poll on Trump was Pew Research Center poll, October 20–25, 2016.

27. Quinnipiac University polls, June 27–July 1, 2018, and July 25–28, 2019 (registered voters).

28. NPR/PBS *NewsHour* poll, October 28–29, 2018. See also NPR/PBS *News Hour* polls, June 21–25, 2017, and November 13–15, 2017; and CBS News poll, October 27–30, 2017. The NPR/PBS *NewsHour* poll (November 28–December 4, 2018) found an outlier result: only 35 percent blamed Trump and 37 percent blamed the media.

29. Pew Research Center poll, April 29–May 3, 2019. See also Pew Research Center poll, June 6-16, 2020.

30. Weber Shandwick and Powell Tate with KRC Research, "Civility in American VII: The State of Civility, June 13, 2017, https://www.webershandwick.com /news/civility-in-america-vii-the-state-of-civility/.

31. Donald J. Trump (@realDonald Trump), "The FAKE NEWS media (failing @nytimes, @NBCNews, @ABC, @CBS, @CNN) is not my enemy, it is the

enemy of the American People," Twitter, February 17, 2017, 3:58 p.m., https://twitter.com/realDonaldTrump/status/832708293516632065.

32. Justin Wise, "Trump: What You're Seeing in the News 'Is Not What's Happening,'" *The Hill*, July 24, 2018.

33. Josh Dawsey and Felicia Sonmez, "Trump Takes Aim at Media after Home-made Bombs Sent to Clinton, Obama and CNN," *Washington Post*, October 24, 2018. See also Philip Rucker and Josh Dawsey, "Trump Vows 'Beautiful' Deals with Democrats but Threatens 'Warlike' Retaliation to Probes," *Washington Post*, November 7, 2018.

34. Aaron Blake, "Trump Claims His Intelligence Chiefs Said They Were 'Totally Misquoted.' They Spoke in Public," *Washington Post*, January 31, 2019; Shane Harris, "Intelligence Officials Were 'Misquoted' after Public Hearing, Trump Claims," *Washington Post*, January 31, 2019.

35. Lena H. Sun, "CDC Director Warns Second Wave of Coronavirus Is likely To Be Even More Devastating," *Washington Post*, April 21, 2020.

36. "Remarks by President Trump, Vice President Pence, and Member of the Coronavirus Task Force in Press Briefing," April 22, 2020, White House transcript, White House, Washington, DC.

37. "Remarks by President Trump, Vice President Pence, and Member of the Coronavirus Task Force in Press Briefing," April 13, 2020, White House transcript, White House, Washington, DC.

38. See also Pew Research Center poll, June 4–10, 2020.

39. See also Monmouth University poll, March 2–5, 2018.

40. "Full Transcript of Donald Trump's Acceptance Speech at the RNC," *Vox*, July 22, 2016, https://www.vox.com/2016/7/21/12253426/donald-trump-acceptance-speech-transcript-republican-nomination-transcript.

41. "Remarks of President Donald J. Trump—as Prepared for Delivery, Inaugural Address," January 20, 2017, White House transcript, White House, Washington, DC.

42. See, e.g., Max Boot, "Trump's Claim of a 'War on Thanksgiving' Is Absurd—but Also Sinister," *Washington Post*, November 28, 2019.

43. Fox News poll, July 16–18, 2017 (registered voters); Quinnipiac University polls, February 2–6, 2017 (registered voters), and March 16–21, 2017 (registered voters).

44. United States Government Accountability Office, *Issues Related to State Voter Identification Laws* (Washington DC: US Government Printing Office, February 27, 2015); Ray Christensen and Thomas J. Schultz, "Identifying Election Fraud Using Orphan and Low Propensity Voters," *American Politics Research* 42, no. 2 (2014): 311–37; John S. Ahlquist, Kenneth R. Mayer, and Simon Jackman, "Alien Abduction and Voter Impersonation in the 2012 U.S. General Election: Evidence from a Survey List Experiment" *Election Law Journal* 13 (December 2014): 460–75; Corbin Carson, "Exhaustive Database of Voter Fraud Cases Turns

Up Scant Evidence That It Happens," *News21*, August 12, 2012, https://voting rights.news21.com/article/election-fraud-explainer/; M. V. Hood III and William Gillespie, "They Just Do Not Vote Like They Used To: A Methodology to Empirically Assess Election Fraud," *Social Science Quarterly* 93 (March 2012): 76–94; Testimony of Professor Justin Levitt, Loyola Law School, Los Angeles Before the United States Senate Committee on the Judiciary Subcommittee on the Constitution, Civil Rights and Human Rights, "New State Voting Laws: Barriers to the Ballot?" September 8, 2011; Lorraine C. Minnite, *The Myth of Voter Fraud* (Ithaca, NY: Cornell University Press, 2010); U.S. Election Assistance Commission, *Election Crimes: An Initial Review and Recommendations for Future Study*, December 2006, https://www.eac.gov/sites/default/files/eac_assets/1/6/Initial_Review _and_Recommendations_for_Further_Study.pdf.

45. "Full Transcript of Donald Trump's Acceptance Speech at the RNC."

46. Pew Research Center poll, October 25–November 8, 2016 (registered voters).

47. John Gramlich, "Voter's Perceptions of Crime Continue to Conflict with Reality," Pew Research Center, November 16, 2016. See also Gramlich, "5 Facts about Crime in the U.S.," Pew Research Center, January 3, 2019.

48. President Donald Trump, Remarks to Major County Sheriffs and Major Cities Chiefs Association joint conference, February 13, 2019, White House transcript, Washington, DC.

49. Donald J. Trump (@realDonaldTrump), "Will be going to North Dakota today to discuss tax reform and tax cuts. We are the highest taxed nation in the world - that will change," Twitter, September 6, 2017, 5:47 a.m., https://twitter.com /realDonaldTrump/status/905381817695526912; Organization for Economic Cooperation and Development, *Revenue Statistics 2017* (OECD, 2018), table 2.

50. Fox News polls, March 12–14, 2017 (registered voters), and March 18–21, 2018 (registered voters).

51. Miriam Valverde, "Trump Misleads in Claim about Terrorism Convictions since 9/11," *Politifact*, March 2, 2017, https://www.politifact.com/factchecks/2017 /mar/02/donald-trump/trump-misleads-claim-about-terrorism-convictions-9/.

52. Benjamin Wittes, "The Justice Department Finds 'No Responsive Records' to Support a Trump Speech," *Lawfare* (blog), July 31, 2018 https://www.lawfare blog.com/justice-department-finds-no-responsive-records-support-trump-speech.

53. Ashley Parker, Philip Rucker, and Josh Dawsey, "Trump and Republicans Settle on Fear—and Falsehoods—as a Midterm Strategy," *Washington Post*, October 22, 2018.

54. "Remarks by President Trump at the Signing Ceremony for S. 3021, America's Water Infrastructure Act of 2018," White House transcript, White House, Washington, DC.

55. Jeffrey S. Passel and D'Vera Cohn, "U.S. Unauthorized Immigrant Total Dips to Lowest Level in a Decade," Pew Research Center, November 27, 2018.

56. "Remarks by President Trump After Meeting with Congressional Leadership on Border Security," Donald Trump, speaking at the White House, January 4, 2019, White House transcript, White House, Washington, DC.

57. "Full Transcript of Donald Trump's Acceptance Speech at the RNC."

58. "Remarks by President Trump at South Dakota's 2020 Mount Rushmore Fireworks Celebration, Keystone, South Dakota," July 3, 2020, White House transcript, White House, Washington, DC.

59. "Remarks by President Trump at the 2020 Salute to America," July 4, 2020, White House transcript, White House, Washington, DC.

60. Morgan Marietta, Tyler Farley, Tyler Cote, and Paul Murphy, "The Rhetorical Psychology of Trumpism: Threat, Absolutism, and the Absolutist Threat," *The Forum* 15 (July 2017): 313–32.

61. See Roderick P. Hart, "Donald Trump and the Return of the Paranoid Style," *Presidential Studies Quarterly* 50 (June 2020): 348–65.

62. William Davies, *Nervous States: Democracy and the Decline of Reason* (New York: Norton, 2019).

63. See Jennifer Petriglieri, "Under Threat: Responses to and the Consequences of Threats to Individuals' Identities," *Academy of Management Review* 36 (October 2011): 641–62; Thomas Pyszczynski, Sheldon Solomon, and Jeff Greenberg, *In the Wake of 9/11: The Psychology of Terror* (Washington DC: American Psychological Association, 2003).

64. Rachel Marie Blum and Christopher Sebastian Parker, "Trump-ing Foreign Affairs: Status Threat and Foreign Policy Preferences on the Right," *Perspectives on Politics* 17 (September 2019): 737–55; Bethany Albertson and Shana Kushner Gadarian, *Anxious Politics: Democratic Citizenship in a Threatening World* (New York: Cambridge University Press, 2015); Shana Kushner Gadarian, "The Politics of Threat: How Terrorism News Shapes Foreign Policy Attitudes," *Journal of Politics* 72 (April 2010): 469–83; Ted Brader, Nicholas A. Valentino, and Elizabeth Suhay, "What Triggers Public Opposition to Immigration? Anxiety, Group Cues, and Immigration Threat," *American Journal of Political Science* 52 (October 2008): 959–78; Leonie Huddy, Stanley Feldman, and Christopher Weber, "The Political Consequences of Perceived Threat and Felt Insecurity, *Annals of the American Academy of Political and Social Science* 614 (November 2007): 131–53.

65. Joanne M. Miller and Jon A. Krosnick, "Threat as a Motivator of Political Activism: A Field Experiment," *Political Psychology* 25 (August 2004): 507–23.

66. Albertson, and Gadarian, *Anxious Politics*; Jennifer Merolla and Elizabeth Zechmeister, "Evaluating Political Leaders in Times of Terror and Economic Threat: The Conditioning Influence of Political Partisanship," *Journal of Politics* 75 (May 2013): 599–612; Mark Landau, Sheldon Solomon, Jeff Greenberg, et al., "Deliver Us From Evil: The Effects of Mortality Salience and Reminders of 9/11 on Support for President George W. Bush." *Personality and Social Psychology Bulletin* 30 (September 2004): 1135–50; Stanley Feldman and Karen Stenner, "Perceived Threat and Authoritarianism," *Political Psychology* 18 (December 1997): 741–70.

67. Pascal Boyer and Nora Parren, "Threat-Related Information Suggests Competence: A Possible Factor in the Spread of Rumors," *PLoS One* 10, no. 6 (2015): https://doi.org/10.1371/journal.pone.0128421.

68. Morgan Marietta, "The Absolutist Advantage: Sacred Rhetoric in Contemporary Presidential Debate" *Political Communication* 26, no. 4 (2009): 388–411.

69. Interview with Lesley Stahl, "President Trump on Christine Blasey Ford, his relationships with Vladimir Putin and Kim Jong Un and More," CBS News.com, October 15, 2018, https://www.cbsnews.com/news/donald-trump-full-interview-60-minutes-transcript-lesley-stahl-2018-10-14/.

70. "Remarks by President Trump before Marine One Departure," November 26, 2018, White House transcript, White House, Washington, DC.

71. Aaron Blake, "President Trump's Full *Washington Post* Interview Transcript, Annotated," *Washington Post*, November 28, 2018.

72. Pew Research Center poll, January 10–15, 2018 (half sample).

73. Pew Research Center polls, September 24–October 7, 2018, February 19–March 4, 2019, and September 3–15, 2019.

74. AP–NORC poll, November 14–19, 2018.

75. Monmouth University poll, November 9–12, 2018. See also Yale Program on Climate Change Communication and the George Mason University Center for Climate Change Communication poll, November 28–December 11, 2018.

76. AP NORC poll, March 14–18, 2019.

77. Fox News poll, May 11–14, 2019. See also Fox News poll, February 10–12, 2019.

78. *Washington Post*/Kaiser Family Foundation poll, July 9–August 5, 2019. See also *Climate Change in the American Mind* poll, April 7–17, 2020.

79. Pew Research Center poll, October 1–13, 2019.

80. Pew Research Center poll, July 10–15, 2019. See also Gallup poll, March 1–10, 2019.

81. Pew Research Center poll, October 1–13, 2019.

82. Gallup poll, March 1–10, 2019.

83. Donald J. Trump (@realDonaldTrump), "Russia started their anti-US campaign in 2014, long before I announced that I would run for President. The results of the election were not impacted. The Trump campaign did nothing wrong - no collusion!" Twitter, February 16, 2018, 2:18 p.m., https://twitter.com/realdonaldtrump/status/964594780088033282.

84. Quoted in Ashley Parker and David E. Sanger, "Donald Trump Calls on Russia to Find Hillary Clinton's Missing Emails," *New York Times*, July 27, 2016.

85. Carol D. Leonnig, David Nakamura, and Josh Dawsey, "Trump's National Security Advisers Warned Him Not to Congratulate Putin. He Did It Anyway," *Washington Post*, March 20, 2018.

86. "Remarks by President Trump and President Putin of the Russian Federation in Joint Press Conference," July 16, 2018, White House transcript, White House, Washington, DC.

87. See, e.g., Pew Research Center polls, February 18–22, 2015, January 4–9, 2017, February 28–March 12, 2017, January 10–15, 2018; and the Pew Research Center Global Attitudes survey, spring 2019.

88. *Washington Post*/ABC News poll, July 18–20, 2018.

89. Quinnipiac University poll, July 12–23, 2018 (registered voters).

90. Dina Smeltz, "Republicans Used to Fear Russians. Here's What They Think Now," *Washington Post*, February 16, 2017.

91. *USA Today*/Suffolk University poll, December 11–16, 2018 (registered voters).

92. Pew Research Center poll, July 10–15, 2019.

93. Chicago Council on Global Affairs polls, June 10–27, 2016, and June 27–July 19, 2017.

94. Pew Research Center polls, October 25–November 8, 2016, and July 30–August 12, 2018.

95. "Remarks by President Trump, Vice President Pence, and Members of the Coronavirus Task Force in Press Conference," February 27, 2020, White House transcript, White House, Washington, DC.

96. Donald J. Trump (@realDonaldTrump), "retweet," Twitter, 11:45 p.m., March 9, 2020. This retweet has been deleted from the Trump Twitter archive. Fox Business ended her contract later that month.

97. Peter Baker, "For Trump, Coronavirus Proves to Be an Enemy He Can't Tweet Away," *New York Times*, March 8, 2020.

98. "Remarks by President Trump, Vice President Pence, and Members of the Coronavirus Task Force in Press Briefing," March 19, 2020, White House transcript, White House, Washington, DC.

99. "Remarks by President Trump, Vice President Pence, and Members of the Coronavirus Task Force in Press Briefing," March 20, 2020, White House transcript, White House, Washington, DC.

100. "Remarks by President Trump, Vice President Pence, and Members of the Coronavirus Task Force in Press Briefing," March 20, 2020, White House transcript, White House, Washington, DC.

101. CBS News poll, March 21–23, 2020; Quinnipiac University poll, March 5–8, 2020; *Axios* poll, March 5–9, 2020; *Economist* poll, March 8–10, 2020; NBC News/*Wall Street Journal* poll, March 11–13, 2019; NPR/PBS *NewsHour* poll, March 13–14, 2020; Kaiser Family Foundation poll, March 11–15, 2020. See also Michael Tesler, "Red States Are Finally Starting to Google 'Coronavirus,'" *Washington Post*, March 16, 2020; Pew Research Center poll, March 10–16, 2020.

102. Pew Research Center poll, March 19–24, 2020; Reuters poll, March 2–3, 2020.

103. CBS News polls, March 21–23, 2020, and April 7–9, 2020; Monmouth University poll, April 3–7, 2020; NPR/PBS *NewsHour* poll, March 13–14, 2020; NBC News/*Wall Street Journal* poll, April 13–15, 2020; CNN poll May 7–10, 2020. See

also *Axios* poll, March 9–13, 2020; Kaiser Family Foundation poll, March 25–30, 2020.

104. Pew Research Center poll, April 7–12, 2020.

105. ABC News/*Washington Post* poll, July 12–15, 2020.

106. Quoted in Isaac Chotiner, "The Coronavirus and Building a Better Strategy for Fighting Pandemics," *New Yorker*, March 21, 2020, https://www.new yorker.com/news/q-and-a/the-coronavirus-and-building-a-better-strategy-for -fighting-pandemics.

107. See, e.g., PolitiFact (https://www.politifact.com/); *Washington Post* Fact Checker (https://www.washingtonpost.com/news/fact-checker/), *New York Times* Fact Checks (https://www.nytimes.com/spotlight/fact-checks).

108. Glenn Kessler, "A Year of Unprecedented Deception: Trump Averaged 15 False Claims a Day in 2018," *Washington Post*, December 30, 2018.

109. Glenn Kessler, Salvador Rizzo, and Meg Kelly, "President Trump Made 8, 158 False or Misleading Claims in His First Two Years," *Washington Post*, January 21, 2019.

110. Glenn Kessler, Salvador Rizzo, and Meg Kelly, "President Trump Has Made More than 20,000 False or Misleading Claims, *Washington Post*, July 13, 2020. See also Glenn Kessler, Salvador Rizzo, and Meg Kelly, *Donald Trump and His Assault on Truth* (New York: Scribner, 2020).

111. Mike McIntire, Karen Yourish, and Larry Buchanan, "In Trump's Twitter Feed: Conspiracy-Mongers, Racists, and Spies," *New York Times*, November 2, 2019; Shear et al., "How Trump Reshaped the Presidency"; Aaron Blake, "23 Bizarre Conspiracy Theories Trump Has Elevated," *Washington Post*, August 12, 2019.

112. Quoted in Philip Rucker and Carol Leonnig, *A Very Stable Genius: Donald J. Trump's Testing of America* (New York: Penguin, 2020), 191–92.

113. Amanda Carpenter, *Gaslighting America: Why We Love It When Trump Lies to Us* (New York: Broadside Books, 2018).

114. John Wagner, " 'When I Can, I Tell the Truth': Trump Pushes Back Against His Peddling of Falsehoods," *Washington Post*, November 1, 2018.

115. Donald J. Trump, interview with George Stephanopoulos, *20/20,* ABC News, June 16, 2019.

116. Donald J. Trump, with Tony Schwartz, *Trump: The Art of the Deal* (New York: Random House, 1987), 40.

117. Maggie Haberman, "A President Who Believes He Is Entitled to His Own Facts," *New York Times*, October 18, 2018.

118. Blake, "President Trump's Full *Washington Post* Interview Transcript, Annotated."

119. See, e.g., Aaron Blake, "Rex Tillerson on Trump: 'Undisciplined, Doesn't Like to Read' and Tries to Do Illegal Things," *Washington Post*, December 7, 2018; Bob Woodward, *Fear: Trump in the White House* (New York: Simon and Schuster, 2018), 271, 276.

120. Sheryl Gay Stolberg, Maggie Haberman, and Peter Baker, "Trump Was Repeatedly Warned that Ukraine Conspiracy Theory Was 'Completely Debunked,'" *New York Times*, September 30, 2019.

121. Maggie Haberman and Mark Landler, "A Week after the Midterms, Trump Seems to Forget the Caravan," *New York Times*, November 13, 2018; Philip Rucker and Josh Dawsey, "From Dire Warnings to Happy Talk: Trump changes His Tune after the Midterms," *Washington Post*, November 19, 2018.

122. Interview with Chris Wallace on *Fox News Sunday*, November 18, 2018.

123. John Wagner, "Anthony Scaramucci: Trump Is Not 'a Liar,' as Previously Said. He's an 'Intentional Liar' Who Uses 'a Methodology of Mistruth,'" *Washington Post*, October 25, 2018.

124. Julie Hirschfeld Davis, "In a Fox-Inspired Tweetstorm Trump Offers a Medley of Falsehoods and Misstatements," *New York Times*, July 3, 2018; Josh Dawsey, Damian Paletta, and Erica Werner, "In Fundraising Speech, Trump Says He Made Up Trade Claim in Meeting with Justin Trudeau," *Washington Post*, March 15, 2018.

125. *Washington Post*/ABC News poll, April 17–20, 2017.

126. Pew Research Center poll, September 18–24, 2018. See also ABC News/*Washington Post* poll, January 21–24, 2019.

127. *Washington Post* Fact Checker poll, November 29–December 10, 2018. See also Pew Research Center poll, January 9–14, 2019.

128. *USA Today*/Suffolk University poll, December 11–16, 2018 (registered voters).

129. Quinnipiac University poll, March 1–4, 2019.

130. Pew Research Center poll, March 20–25, 2019. See also CNN polls, August 3–6, 2017, November 2–5, 2017, September 5–9, 2019, and November 21–24, 2019; ABC News/*Washington Post* poll, May 25–28, 2020.

131. Pew Research Center poll, January 8–13, 2020.

132. Pew Research Center poll, February 4–15, 2020.

133. *USA Today*/Suffolk University poll, April 21–25, 2020.

134. Pew Research Center poll, January 6–19, 2020.

135. McIntire et al., "In Trump's Twitter Feed."

136. Logan Dancey and Geoffrey Sheagley, "Heuristics Behaving Badly," *American Journal of Political Science* 57 (April 2013): 312–25; Martin Bisgaard, "Bias Will Find a Way: Economic Perceptions, Attributions of Blame, and Partisan-Motivated Reasoning during Crisis," *Journal of Politics* 77 (July 2015): 849–60.

137. Conor M. Dowling, Michael Henderson, and Michael G. Miller, "Knowledge Persists, Opinions Drift: Learning and Opinion Change in a Three-Wave Panel Experiment," *American Politics Research* 48 (March 2020): 263–74; James H. Kuklinski, Paul J. Quirk, Jennifer Jerit, David Schwieder, and Robert F. Rich, "Misinformation and the Currency of Democratic Citizenship," *Journal of Politics*

62 (August 2000): 790–816. See also Brendan Nyhan, "Why the 'Death Panel' Myth Wouldn't Die: Misinformation in the Health Care Reform Debate," *The Forum* 8, no. 1 (2010): https://doi.org/10.2202/1540-8884.1354; Brendan Nyhan, Ethan Porter, Jason Reifler, and Thomas Wood, "Taking Fact-Checks Literally but Not Seriously? The Effects of Journalistic Fact-Checking on Factual Beliefs and Candidate Favorability," *Political Behavior* (2019): https://doi.org/10.1007/s11109 -019-09528-x.

138. Eli Saslow, "'Nothing on This Page Is Real': How Lies Become Truth in Online America," *Washington Post*, November 17, 2018.

139. Soroush Vosoughi, Deb Roy, and Aral Sinan, "The Spread of True and False News Online," *Science* 359 (6380): 1146–51.

140. Stephan Lewandowsky, Ulrich K. H. Ecker, Colleen M Seifert, Norbert Schwarz, and John Cook, "Misinformation and Its Correction: Continued Influence and Successful Debiasing," *Psychological Science in the Public Interest* 13 (December 2012): 106–31; Norbert Schwarz, Lawrence J. Sanna, Ian Skurnik, and Carolyn Yoon, "Metacognitive Experiences and the Intricacies of Setting People Straight: Implications for Debiasing and Public Information Campaigns," *Advances in Experimental Social Psychology* 39 (2007): 127–61; Ian Skurnik, Carolyn Yoon, Denise C. Park, and Norbert Schwarz, "How Warnings about False Claims Become Recommendations," *Journal of Consumer Research* 31 (March 2005): 713–24.

141. Ruth Mayo, Yaacov Schul, and Eugene Burnstein, "'I Am Not Guilty' vs 'I Am Innocent': Successful Negation May Depend on the Schema Used for Its Encoding," *Journal of Experimental Social Psychology* 40 (July 2004): 433–49.

142. Danielle C. Polage, "Making up History: False Memories of Fake News Stories," *Europe's Journal of Psychology* 8, no. 2 (2012): 245–50.

143. Lynn Hasher and David Goldstein, "Frequency and the Conference of Referential Validity," *Journal of Verbal Learning and Verbal Behavior* 16 (February 1977): 107–12.

144. R. Kelly Garret and Brian Weeks, "The Promise and Peril of Real-Time Corrections to Political Misperceptions," *Proceedings of the 2013 Conference on Computer Supported Cooperative Work* (San Antonio, TX, February 23–27, 2013): 1047–58; Brendan Nyhan and Jason Reifler, "When Corrections Fail: The Persistence of Political Misperceptions," *Political Behavior* 32 (June 2010): 303–30; David P. Redlawsk, Andrew J. W. Civettini, and Karen M. Emmerson, "The Affective Tipping Point: Do Motivated Reasoners Ever 'Get It'?" *Political Psychology* 31 (August 2010): 563–93.

145. J. Eric Oliver and Thomas J. Wood, "Conspiracy Theories and the Paranoid Style(s) of Mass Opinion," *American Journal of Political Science* 58 (October 2014): 952–66.

146. Andrew Kohut, "Little Voter Discomfort with Romney's Mormon Religion," Pew Research Center, July 26, 2012, 2.

147. Ulrich K. H. Ecker, Stephan Lewandowsky, Briony Swire, and Darren Chang, "Correcting False Information in Memory: Manipulating the Strength of Misinformation Encoding and Its Retraction," *Psychonomic Bulletin and Review*, 18 (June 2011): 570–78. See also John Bullock, "Experiments on Partisanship and Public Opinion: Party Cues, False Beliefs, and Bayesian Updating," PhD diss., Stanford University, 2007.

148. Fairleigh Dickinson University poll, December 8–15, 2014.

149. Harris Interactive poll, October 16–20, 2008.

150. *Politico*/Morning Consult poll, July 20–24, 2017 (registered voters).

151. Quinnipiac University polls, February 2–6, 2017, and March 16021, 2017 (both of registered voters).

152. Philip Bump, "The Media Consumers Most Likely to Believe Trump's Falsehoods? Fox News Watchers," *Washington Post*, December 14, 2018.

153. *Washington Post* Fact Checker poll, November 29–December 10, 2018.

154. James Pfiffner, "Trump's Lies Corrode Democracy," Brookings Institution, April 13, 2018.

155. Pew Research Center poll, January 7–21, 2019.

156. Timothy Snyder, *On Tyranny: Twenty Lessons from the Twentieth Century* (New York: Tim Duggan Books, 2017), 65, 71.

157. Hannah Arendt, *The Origins of Totalitarianism* (Cleveland, OH: Meridian Books, 1958), 350.

158. On this point, see Matthew A. Baum and Philip B. K. Potter, "Media, Public Opinion, and Foreign Policy in the Age of Social Media," *Journal of Politics* 81 (April 2019): 747–56.

159. Donald J. Trump (@realDonaldTrump), "So interesting to see "Progressive" Democrat Congresswomen, who originally came from countries whose governments are a complete and total catastrophe, the worst, most corrupt and inept anywhere in the world (if they even have a functioning government at all), now loudly . . . . . . and viciously telling the people of the United States, the greatest and most powerful Nation on earth, how our government is to be run. Why don't they go back and help fix the totally broken and crime infested places from which they came. Then come back and show us how. . . ." Twitter, July 14, 2019, 7:57 a.m., https://twitter.com/realDonaldTrump/status/1150381395078000643.

160. See, e.g., Donald J. Trump (@realDonaldTrump), "Looks what's going on here. Where are the protesters? Was this man arrested?" Twitter, June 22, 2020, 9:35 p.m., https://twitter.com/realdonaldtrump/status/1275256115710885889.

161. Donald J. Trump (@realDonaldTrump), Twitter, June 18, 2020, 7:12 p.m., https://twitter.com/realdonaldtrump/status/1273770669214490626. The video has been removed from the Trump Twitter archive.

162. Felicia Sonmez, "Trump, without Evidence, Accuses Obama of 'Treason,'" *Washington Post*, June 22, 2020.

163. Maggie Haberman and Annie Karni, "The President's Shock at the Rows of Empty Seats in Tulsa," *New York Times*, June 21, 2020.

164. See, e.g., Donald J. Trump, interview with Brian Kilmeade on *Fox & Friends*, June 22, 2020.

165. Donald J. Trump (@realDonaldTrump), ". . . . horrible BLM chant, 'Pigs In A Blanket, Fry 'Em Like Bacon'. Maybe our GREAT Police, who have been neutralized and scorned by a mayor who hates & disrespects them, won't let this symbol of hate be affixed to New York's greatest street. Spend this money fighting crime instead!" Twitter, July 1, 2020, 8:48 a.m., https://twitter.com/realdonald trump/status/1278324681477689349.

166. See, e.g., Michael Tesler, *Post-Racial or Most Racial? Race and Politics in the Obama Era* (Chicago: University of Chicago Press, 2016); Marisa Abrajano and Zoltan L. Hajnal, *White Backlash: Immigration, Race, and American Politics* (Princeton, NJ: Princeton University Press, 2015). See also Tali Mendelberg, *The Race Card: Campaign Strategy, Implicit Messages, and the Norm of Equality* (Princeton, NJ: Princeton University Press, 2001).

167. John Sides, Michael Tesler, and Lynn Vavreck, *Identity Crisis: The 2016 Presidential Campaign and the Battle for the Meaning of America* (Princeton, NJ: Princeton University Press, 2018), chaps. 5 and 8.

168. *The Economist*/YouGov poll, October 22–26, 2016 (registered voters).

169. Associated Press polls, February15–19, 2018, and August 31–September 16, 2017. See also Quinnipiac University polls, February 2–5, 2018, and June 27–July 1, 2018, and July 25–28, 2019 (registered voters). But see YouGov/*The Economist* poll, July 21–23, 2019.

170. Quinnipiac University poll, January 12–16, 2018 (registered voters).

171. Quinnipiac University polls, June 27–July 1, 2018, November 14–19, 2018, and July 25–28, 2019 (registered voters).

172. Fox News poll, July 21–23, 2019 (registered voters); YouGov/*The Economist* poll, July 21–23, 2019.

173. Fox News poll, July 21–23, 2019 (registered voters).

174. *Washington Post* -Ipsos poll, January 2–8, 2020.

175. Pew Research Center poll, February 4–15, 2020. See also YouGov poll, May 29–30, 2020.

176. Pew Research Center poll, January 22–February 5, 2020. See also YouGov poll, May 29–30, 2020; Pew Research Center poll, June 4–10, 2020.

177. Pew Research Center poll, June 4–10, 2020.

178. Sides et al., *Identity Crisis*, 85–87; Michael Tesler, "In a Trump-Clinton Match-Up, Racial Prejudice Makes a Striking Difference," *Washington Post*, May 25, 2016; Tehama Lopez Bunyasi, "The Role of Whiteness in the 2016 Presidential Primaries," *Perspectives on Politics* 17 (September 2019): 679–98.

179. Sides et al., *Identity Crisis*; Alan I. Abramowitz, *The Great Alignment* (New Haven, CT: Yale University Press, 2018), chaps. 6–7; Michael Tesler, "Views about Race Mattered More in Electing Trump than in Electing Obama," *Washington Post*, November 22, 2016; Michael Tesler, The Education Gap among Whites This Year Wasn't about Education. It Was about Race," *Washington Post*,

November 16, 2016. See also Nazita Lajevardi and Marisa Abrajano, "How Negative Sentiment toward Muslim Americans Predicts Support for Trump in the 2016 Presidential Election," *Journal of Politics* 81 (January 2019): 296–302; Blum and Parker, "Trump-ing Foreign Affairs"; James G. Gimpel, "From Wedge Issue to Partisan Divide: The Development of Immigration Policy Opinion after 2016,"*The Forum* 17, no. 3 (2019): 467–86; Janelle S. Wong, "Race, Evangelicals and Immigration," *The Forum* 17, no. 3 (2019): 403–19; Deborah J. Schildkraut, "The Political Meaning of Whiteness for Liberals and Conservatives," *The Forum* 17, no. 3 (2019): 421–46; Ashley Jardina, "White Consciousness and White Prejudice: Two Compounding Forces in Contemporary American Politics," *The Forum* 17, no. 3 (2019): 447–66.

180. Christian S. Crandall, Jason M. Miller, Mark H. White II, "Changing Norms Following the 2016 U.S. Presidential Election: The Trump Effect on Prejudice," *Social Psychology and Personality Science* 9, no. 2 (2018): 186–92. See also Benjamin Newman, Jennifer L. Merolla, Sono Shah, et al., "The Trump Effect: An Experimental Investigation of the Emboldening Effect of Racially Inflammatory Elite Communication," *British Journal of Political Science* (2020): https://doi.org/10.1017/S0007123419000590.

181. OZY Media, WGBH poll, September 11–13, 2017; Quinnipiac University polls, June 27–July 1, 2018, and August 9–13, 2018 (registered voters).

182. Brian F. Schaffner, "Political Rhetoric and Expressions of Prejudice among the American Public," working paper, Tufts University, 2019. See also Richard Fording and Sanford F. Schram, *Hard White: Outgroup Hostility and the Mainstreaming of Racism in America* (New York: Oxford University Press, 2020).

183. Daniel J. Hopkins and Samantha Washington, "The Rise of Trump, the Fall of Prejudice? Tracking White Americans' Racial Attitudes 2008–2018 via a Panel Survey," unpublished manuscript, April 17, 2019.

184. Pew Research Center polls, January 22–February 5, 2019.

185. "Hate Crime Statistics, 2017," Federal Bureau of Investigation website, https://ucr.fbi.gov/hate-crime/2017. There was also an increase in the number of agencies reporting hate crimes.

186. Ayal Feinberg, Regina Branton, and Valerie Martinez-Ebers, "The Trump Effect? Political Rallies and Hate Crime Contagion" (paper presented at the Annual Meeting of the Western Political Science Association, San Diego, California, April 18, 2019).

187. "Hate Crime Statistics, 2018," Federal Bureau of Investigation website, https://ucr.fbi.gov/hate-crime/2018/hate-crime.

188. "White Supremacists Double Down on Propaganda in 2019," Anti-Defamation League, February 11, 2020, https://www.adl.org/blog/white-supremacists-double-down-on-propaganda-in-2019.

189. Niall McCarthy, "Most Countries Overestimate Their Muslim Population," *Statista*, December 15, 2016. Based on Ipsos MORI publication, Bobby Duffy, *The Perils of Perception* (London: Atlantic Books, 2018).

190. See, e.g., David Horowitz, "I'm a Uniter, Not a Divider," *Salon*, May 6, 1999.

191. "Barack Obama's Remarks to the Democratic National Convention," *New York Times*, July 27, 2004.

192. Jeffrey Goldberg, "James Mattis Denounces President Trump, Describes Him as a Threat to the Constitution," *The Atlantic*, June 3, 2020, https://www.the atlantic.com/politics/archive/2020/06/james-mattis-denounces-trump-protests-mili tarization/612640/.

193. Kathryn Dunn Tenpas, James A. McCann, and Emily J. Charnock, "Trump Makes Fewer Public Trips than Recent Presidents. Will that Hurt the Republicans in November?" *Washington Post*, January 17, 2018. See also John Wagner, "Trump and Republicans Bolster Red States, Punish Blue," *Washington Post*, September 25, 2017.

194. Kathryn Dunn Tenpas and James A. McCann, "Compared with Recent Presidents, Trump Does Not Like to Travel—Except When He's Campaigning," *Washington Post*, January 25, 2019. See also Philip Bump, "Trump Has Visited More Than Twice as Many Red Sates as Blue Ones as President," *Washington Post*, May 23, 2019.

195. Jenna Johnson, "Trump's Comfort Zone This Year: Smaller Venues and Rapturous Fans in Places Where He Remains Popular," *Washington Post*, October 22, 2018.

196. Peter Baker, "A President of the People or a President of His People?" *New York Times*, April 16, 2019.

197. Quoted in Robert Costa, Philip Rucker and Ashley Parker, "A 'Pressure Cooker': Trump's Frustration and Fury Rupture Alliances, Threaten Agenda," *Washington Post*, October 9, 2017.

198. Astead W. Herndon and Maggie Astor, "In Criminal Justice Speech, Trump Belittles Obama's Efforts for Black People," *New York Times*, October 25, 2019.

199. Quoted in Michael Tackett, "Some Presidents Felt Trapped in the White House Bubble. Trump Thrives in It." *New York Times*, March 27, 2019.

200. Quoted in Je Concha, "Limbaugh Fumes on Border Wall: 'Trump Gets Nothing and the Democrats Get Everything,'" *The Hill*, December 19, 2018.

201. NPR/PBS *NewsHour* poll, November 28–December 4, 2018.

202. Michael D. Shear, "Trump's Apparent Embrace of Gun Control Measures Stuns Lawmakers," *New York Times*, February 28, 2018.

203. Quoted in Jeremy W. Peters and Maggie Haberman, "After Brief Split, Trump and N.R.A. Appear to Reconcile," *New York Times*, March 2, 2018.

204. Quoted in Josh Dawsey, John Wagner, and Seung Min Kim, "Trump Claims Strong Congressional Support for Strengthening Background Checks for Gun Buys, at Odds with GOP Statements," *Washington Post*, August 9, 2019.

205. Annie Karni and Maggie Haberman, "For Trump, a Time of Indecision," *New York Times*, September 19, 2019.

206. Josh Dawsey, "Trump Abandons Proposing Ideas to Curb Gun Violence after Saying He Would Following Mass Shootings," *Washington Post*, November 1, 2019.

207. Dawsey, "Trump Abandons"; Annie Karni, Maggie Haberman, and Sheila Kaplan, "Trump Retreats from Flavor Ban for E-Cigarettes," *New York Times*, November 17, 2019.

208. Josh Dawsey and Yasmeen Abutaleb, "Trump Lashes Out at HHS Secretary after Briefing Shows Democrats Have Edge on Health Care," *Washington Post*, January 17, 2019.hevron-right.

209. James Hohmann, "Reversals on G-7 and Potentially Syria Show Trump Buckles in the Face of Enough Republican Pressure," *Washington Post*, October 21, 2019.

210. Max Boot, "Trump Doesn't Seem to Grasp that Blue Staters Are Real Americans Too," *Washington Post*, February 17, 2020.

211. Katherine Egan, "How Jared Kushner's Secret Testing Plan 'Went Poof Into Thin Air,'" *Vanity Fair*, June 30, 2020.

212. Mark Smith, *American Business and Political Power: Public Opinion, Elections, and Democracy* (Chicago: University of Chicago Press, 2000); Lawrence R. Jacobs and Theda Skocpol, *Health Care Reform and American Politics*, rev. ed. (New York: Oxford University Press, 2012); Lawrence R. Jacobs and Robert Y. Shapiro, *Politicians Don't Pander: Political Manipulation and the Loss of Democratic Responsiveness* (Chicago: University of Chicago Press, 2000); Darrel West and Burdett Loomis, *The Sound of Money: How Political Interests Get What They Want* (New York: W. W. Norton, 1999).

213. "Exit Polls," CNN.com, http://www.cnn.com/election/2018/exit-polls.

214. Gary C. Jacobson, "Donald Trump and the Future of the American Parties" (paper prepared for delivery at the Annual Meeting of the Midwest Political Science Association, Chicago IL, April 16–19, 2020, 6).

215. *Oxford English Dictionary Online*, s.v. "rule of law," accessed November 30, 2018.

216. Quoted in Richard A. Oppel Jr. "Bowe Bergdahl Avoids Prison for Desertion; Trump Calls Sentence a 'Disgrace,'" *New York Times*, November 3, 2017.

217. Mark Mazzetti, Maggie Haberman, Nicholas Fandos, and Michael S. Schmidt, "Intimidation, Pressure and Humiliation" Inside Trump's Two-Year War on the Investigations Circling Him," *New York Times*, February 19, 2019.

218. See, e.g., Woodward, *Fear*, 270.

219. Donald J. Trump (@realDonaldTrump), "You are witnessing the single greatest WITCH HUNT in American political history - led by some very bad and conflicted people! #MAGA," Twitter, June 15, 2017, 6:57 a.m., https://twitter.com/realdonaldtrump/status/875321478849363968.

220. Donald J. Trump, call to *Fox & Friends*, April 26, 2018.

221. Donald J. Trump (@realDonaldTrump), "Disgraced and discredited Bob Mueller and his whole group of Angry Democrat Thugs spent over 30 hours with the White House Councel [*sic*], only with my approval, for purposes of transparency.

Anybody needing that much time when they know there is no Russian Collusion is just someone . . . looking for trouble. They are enjoying ruining people's lives and REFUSE to look at the real corruption on the Democrat side - the lies, the firings, the deleted Emails and soooo much more! Mueller's Angry Dems are looking to impact the election. They are a National Disgrace!" Twitter, August 20, 2018, 6:28 a.m., https://twitter.com/realDonaldTrump/status/1031503298967363586, and August 20, 2018, 6:38 a.m., https://twitter.com/realdonaldtrump/status/1031505811074412544.

222. Donald J. Trump (@realDonaldTrump), "Just cannot believe a judge would put our country in such peril. If something happens blame him and court system. People pouring in. Bad!" Twitter, February 5, 2017, 2:39 p.m., https://twitter.com/realdonaldtrump/status/828342202174668800.

223. Donald J. Trump (@realDonaldTrump), "Our legal system is broken! '77% of refugees allowed into U.S. since travel reprieve hail from seven suspect countries.' (WT) SO DANGEROUS!" Twitter, February 11, 2017, 6:12 a.m., https://twitter.com/realdonaldtrump/status/830389130311921667.

224. Donald J. Trump (@realDonaldTrump), "Justice Roberts can say what he wants, but the 9th Circuit is a complete & total disaster. It is out of control, has a horrible reputation, is overturned more than any Circuit in the Country, 79%, & is used to get an almost guaranteed result. Judges must not Legislate Security. . . . . . . and Safety at the Border, or anywhere else. They know nothing about it and are making our Country unsafe. Our great Law Enforcement professionals MUST BE ALLOWED TO DO THEIR JOB! If not there will be only bedlam, chaos, injury and death. We want the Constitution as written!" November 22, 2018, 6:21 a.m. and 6:30 a.m., https://twitter.com/realdonaldtrump/status/1065581119242940416, and https://twitter.com/realdonaldtrump/status/1065583286188158976.

225. Sean Sullivan, "Gorsuch Calls Attacks on Federal Judges 'Disheartening' and 'Demoralizing,'" *Washington Post*, March 21, 2017.

226. Adam Liptak, "Chief Justice Defends Judicial Independence after Trump Attacks 'Obama Judge,'" *New York Times*, November 21, 2018.

227. *Department of Homeland Security et al v. Regents of the University of California et al* (2020).

228. Institute for Policy Integrity, "Roundup: Trump-Era Deregulation in the Courts," Institute for Policy Integrity, New York University School of Law, January 22, 2019, policyintegrity.org/deregulation-roundup#fn-1-a.

229. George Washington, "Farewell Address," 1996, https://www.ourdocuments .gov/doc.php?flash=true&doc=15&page=transcript.

230. Jacob E. Cooke, ed., *The Federalist* (Middletown, CT: Wesleyan University Press, 1961), 459.

231. Donald J. Trump, interview with George Stephanopoulos, *20/20,* ABC News, June 13, 2019.

232. Donald J. Trump, interview with George Stephanopoulos, *20/20,* ABC News, June 16, 2019.

233. Peter Baker, "Under Fire, Trump Says He Would 'Absolutely' Report Foreign Campaign Help," *New York Times*, June 14, 2019.

234. See John Bolton, *The Room Where It Happened: A White House Memoir* (New York: Simon and Schuster, 2020), 191, 255, 257, 458–59, 485.

235. Donald J. Trump, interviewed by Steve Doocy on *Fox & Friends*, June 15, 2019.

236. Donald J. Trump (@realDonaldTrump), "This is a horrible and very unfair situation. The real crimes were on the other side, as nothing happens to them. Cannot allow this miscarriage of justice!" Twitter, February 11, 2020, 12:48 a.m., https://twitter.com/realDonaldTrump/status/1227122206783811585.

237. Mitt Romney (@MittRomney), "Unprecedented, historic corruption: an American president commutes the sentence of a person convicted by a jury of lying to shield that very president," Twitter, July 11, 2020, 8:06 a.m., https://twitter.com/MittRomney/status/1281937795616067586.

238. Quoted in Katie Benner, "Barr Says Attacks From Trump Make Work 'Impossible,'" *New York Times*, February 13, 2020.

239. Bolton, *The Room Where It Happened*, 191, 193–94, 458, 485.

240. Pew Research Center poll, January 29–February 13, 2018.

241. Quoted in Julie Hirschfeld Davis and Maggie Haberman, "With 'Spygate,' Trump Shows How He Uses Conspiracy Theories to Erode Trust," *New York Times*, May 28, 2018.

242. Margaret E. Tankard and Elizabeth Levy Paluck, "The Effect of a Supreme Court Decision Regarding Gay Marriage on Social Norms and Personal Attitudes," *Psychological Science* 28, no. 9 (2017): 1334–44.

243. See also *USA Today*/Suffolk University poll, December 11–16, 2018 (registered voters).

244. See, however, ABC News/*Washington Post* poll, January 21–24, 2019.

245. See also Suffolk University poll, October 18–22, 2018.

246. See also Pew Research Center poll, January 9–14, 2019.

247. Pew Research Center poll, January 9–14, 2019.

248. *Washington Post*–Schar School poll, March 26–29, 2019.

249. Fox News poll, May 11–14, 2019.

250. *Washington Post*/ABC News poll, August 26–29, 2018.

251. Quinnipiac University poll, April 26–29, 2019.

252. ABC News/*Washington Post* poll, April 22–25, 2019; Quinnipiac University poll, April 26–29, 2019 (registered voters); NPR/PBS *NewsHour* poll, April 24–29, 2019; *Washington Post*–Schar School poll, March 26–29, 2019; CNN poll, April 25–28, 2019; NBC News/*Wall Street Journal* poll, April 28–May 1, 2019.

253. Washington Post–Schar School poll, March 26–29, 2019.

254. ABC News/*Washington Post* poll, April 22–25, 2019.

255. *Washington Post*–Schar School poll, March 26–29, 2019.

256. Gallup poll, April 17–30, 2019.

257. *Just the News* poll, April 2–5, 2020 (registered voters).

258. Gallup polls, November 11–12, 2014, and December 18–19, 2017.

259. Pew Research Center polls, January 5–8, 2017, February 7–11, 2018, and July 11–15, 2018.

260. Marist College poll, February 5–7, 2018.

261. NPR/PBS *NewsHour* poll, July 19–22, 2018.

262. ABC News/*Washington Post* poll, August 26–29, 2018.

263. NBC News/Wall Street Journal poll, December 14–18, 2019.

264. Pew Research Center poll, March 24–29, 2020.

265. Associated Press poll, February 16–20, 2017.

266. Pew Research Center poll, February 16–March 15, 2017.

267. ABC News/*Washington Post* poll, April 17–20, 2017; Quinnipiac University polls, February 16–21, 2017, and March 16–21, 2017 (both polls of registered voters); Associated Press poll, June 8011, 2017.

268. Associated Press poll, June 8–11, 2017.

269. CNN poll, September 6–9, 2018 (asked of half the sample).

270. Associated Press poll, June 8–11, 2017.

271. NPR/PBS *NewsHour* poll, January 8–10, 2018.

272. McClatchy poll, March 22–27, 2018; NPR/PBS *NewsHour* poll, June 21–25, 2018. In the NPR/PBS *NewsHour* poll, January 8–10, 2018, only 51 percent expressed "confidence" in the courts.

273. Quoted in Peter Baker, "More Than Just a Tweet: Trump's Campaign to Undercut Democracy," *New York Times*, July 31, 2020.

274. Interview with Chris Wallace on *Fox Sunday News*, Fox News, July 19, 2020.

275. Quoted in Baker, "More Than Just a Tweet."

276. Baker, "More Than Just a Tweet."

277. Donald J. Trump (@realDonaldTrump), "RIGGED 2020 ELECTION: MILLIONS OF MAIL-IN BALLOTS WILL BE PRINTED BY FOREIGN COUNTRIES, AND OTHERS. IT WILL BE THE SCANDAL OF OUR TIMES!" Twitter, 6:16 a.m., https://twitter.com/realdonaldtrump/status/1275024974579982336.

278. Donald J. Trump (@realDonaldTrump), "Mail-In Voting, unless changed by the courts, will lead to the most CORRUPT ELECTION in our Nation's History! #RIGGEDELECTION," Twitter, July 21, 2020, 6:41 a.m., https://twitter.com/realdonaldtrump/status/1285540318503407622.

279. Donald J. Trump (@realDonaldTrump), "With Universal Mail-In Voting (not Absentee Voting, which is good), 2020 will be the most INACCURATE & FRAUDULENT Election in history. It will be a great embarrassment to the USA. Delay the Election until people can properly, securely and safely vote???" Twitter, July 30, 2020, 7:46 a.m., https://twitter.com/realdonaldtrump/status/12888181 60389558273.

280. See Donald J. Trump (@realDonaldTrump), "MAIL-IN VOTING WILL LEAD TO MASSIVE FRAUD AND ABUSE. IT WILL ALSO LEAD TO THE

END OF OUR GREAT REPUBLICAN PARTY. WE CAN NEVER LET THIS TRAGEDY BEFALL OUR NATION. BIG MAIL-IN VICTORY IN TEXAS COURT TODAY. CONGRATS!!!" Twitter, May 28, 2020, 8 p.m., https://twitter .com/realdonaldtrump/status/1266172570983940101.

281. CNN poll, April 3–6, 2020; Pew Research Center poll, April 7–12, 2020; Gallup poll, April 14–28, 2020; AP poll, April 16–20, 2020; Suffolk University poll, April 21–25, 2020; Fox News poll, May 17–20, 2020 (registered voters); Quinnipiac University poll, June 11–15, 2020; Fox News poll, July 12–15, 2020,

282. Gallup poll, April 14–28, 2020; AP poll, April 16–20, 2020; ABC News/ *Washington Post* poll, July 12–15, 2020.

283. ABC News/*Washington Post* poll, July 12–15, 2020.

284. "The President Shapes the Public Character of the Nation. Trump's Character Falls Short." *Washington Post*, January 1, 2019.

285. Scott Rasmussen poll, July 19–20, 2019.

Chapter Six

1. George C. Edwards III, *Predicting the Presidency: The Path to Successful Leadership* (Princeton, NJ: Princeton University Press, 2016), chap. 9; Edwards, *The Strategic President: Persuasion and Opportunity in Presidential Leadership* (Princeton, NJ: Princeton University Press, 2009), chaps. 4–5; Edwards, *At the Margins: Presidential Leadership of Congress* (New Haven, CT: Yale University Press, 1989), chaps. 9–10; Jon R. Bond and Richard Fleisher, *The President in the Legislative Arena* (Chicago: University of Chicago Press, 1990), chap. 8; Richard Fleisher, Jon R. Bond, and B. Dan Wood, "Which Presidents Are Uncommonly Successful in Congress?" in *Presidential Leadership: The Vortex of Presidential Power*, ed. Bert Rockman and Richard W. Waterman (New York: Oxford University Press, 2007).

2. Edwards, *Predicting the Presidency*.

3. Edwards, *At the Margins*, chap. 8; Lawrence J. Grossback, David A. M. Peterson, and James A. Stimson, *Mandate Politics* (New York: Cambridge University Press, 2006).

4. George C. Edwards III, Andrew Barrett, and Jeffrey Peake, "The Legislative Impact of Divided Government," *American Journal of Political Science* 41 (April 1997): 545–63.

5. See David W. Rohde, *Parties and Leaders in the Postreform House* (Chicago: University of Chicago Press, 1991); Barbara Sinclair, *Unorthodox Lawmaking: New Legislative Processes in the U.S. Congress*, 5th ed. (Washington DC: CQ Press, 2016).

6. James M. Curry and Frances E. Lee, "Non-Party Government: Bipartisan Lawmaking and Party Power in Congress," *Perspectives on Politics* 17 (March 2019): 47–65.

7. Curry and Lee, "Non-Party Government."

8. Danielle M. Thomsen, *Opting Out of Congress: Partisan Polarization and the Decline of Moderate Candidates* (New York: Cambridge University Press, 2017).

9. See Nolan McCarty, Keith Poole, and Howard Rosenthal, *Polarized America: The Dance of Ideology and Unequal Riches,* 2nd ed. (Cambridge, MA: MIT Press, 2016). See also Gyung-Ho Jeong and Paul J. Quirk, "Division at the Water's Edge: The Polarization of Foreign Policy," *American Politics Research* 47 (January 2019): 58–87.

10. Jeffrey B. Lewis, Keith Poole, Howard Rosenthal, Adam Boche, Aaron Rudkin, and Luke Sonnet, "Voteview: Congressional Roll-Call Votes Database," https://voteview.com/ (accessed July 6, 2019).

11. Bradley Jones, "House Republicans Who Lost Reelection Bids Were More Moderate than Those Who Won," Pew Research Center, December 7, 2018.

12. Mike DeBonis, "House Democrats Explode in Recriminations as Liberals Lash Out at Moderates," *Washington Post,* February 28, 2019.

13. Her retreat came after Vice President Mike Pence gave Pelosi private assurances that the administration would voluntarily abide by some of the restrictions and rules she had sought. Julie Hirschfeld Davis and Emily Cochrane, "House Passes Senate Border Bill in Striking Defeat for Pelosi," *New York Times,* June 27, 2019; Amber Phillips, "What Took Congress So Long to Make a Deal to address the Border Crisis?" *Washington Post,* June 27, 2019; Erica Werner, Mike DeBonis, and Rachael Bade, "House Passes $4.6 Billion Border Bill as Leaders Cave to Moderate Democrats and GOP," *Washington Post,* June 27, 2019; Paul Kane and Rachael Bade, "Backed into a Corner, Pelosi Faces Rebellion from Both Centrists and Liberals," *Washington Post,* June 27, 2019.

14. See, e.g., Gallup poll, September 6–10, 2017; Pew Research Center poll, June 27–July 9, 2017; GW Politics polls, October 17–25, 2018 (registered voters), and December 11–19, 2018 (registered voters).

15. Gallup poll, March 9–29, 2017. See also *HuffPost*/YouGov poll, September 7–9, 2017.

16. Pew Research Center poll, January 10–15, 2018.

17. Pew Research Center poll, January 9–14, 2019.

18. See Laurel Harbridge, Neil Malhotra, and Brian Harrison, "Public Preferences for Bipartisanship in the Policymaking Process," *Legislative Studies Quarterly* 39 (August 2014): 327–55; Laurel Harbridge and Neil Malhotra, "Electoral Incentives and Partisan Conflict in Congress: Evidence from Survey Experiments," *American Journal of Political Science* 55 (July 2011): 494–510.

19. Pew Research Center poll, April 5–May 2, 2016.

20. Pew Research Center poll, November 7–13, 2018.

21. Pew Research Center poll, March 7–14, 2018.

22. Frances E. Lee, *Beyond Ideology: Politics, Principles, and Partisanship in the U.S. Senate* (Chicago: University of Chicago Press, 2009), chap. 4; Francis E. Lee, "Presidents and Party Teams: The Politics of Debt Limits and Executive Oversight, 2001–2013," *Presidential Studies Quarterly* 43 (December 2013): 775–91.

23. Sarah Binder and Mark Spindel, "This Is Why Trump's Legislative Agenda Is Stuck in Neutral," *Washington Post*, April 26, 2017.

24. Robert Costa, "'Hello, Bob': President Trump Called My Cellphone to Say that the Health-Care Bill Was Dead," *Washington Post*, March 24, 2017.

25. Jennifer Steinhauer, "Senate Democrats Sought to Work with Trump. Then He Began Governing," *New York Times*, June 28, 2017.

26. David E. Broockman and Christopher Skovron, "Bias in Perceptions of Public Opinion among Political Elites," *American Political Science Review* 112 (August 2018): 542–63; B. Dan Wood with Soren Jordan, *Party Polarization in America: The War Over Two Social Contracts* (New York: Cambridge University Press, 2017), chap. 8; Gary C. Jacobson, "Partisan Polarization in American Politics," *Presidential Studies Quarterly* 43 (December 2013): 688–708; Geoffrey Kabaservice, *Rule and Ruin: The Downfall of Moderation and the Destruction of the Republican Party, From Eisenhower to the Tea Party* (New York: Oxford University Press, 2012); Thomas E. Mann and Norman J. Ornstein, *It's Even Worse Than It Looks* (New York: Basic Books, 2012); Joseph Daniel Ura and Christopher R. Ellis, "Partisan Moods: Polarization and the Dynamics of Mass Party Preferences," *Journal of Politics* 74 (January 2011): 1–15.

27. Mann and Ornstein, *It's Even Worse than It Looks*, 103.

28. Stephen Wolf, "One Reason Why House Republicans Won't Stand Up to Trump: He Won Easily in Most of Their Districts," *DailyKos*, February 21, 2017, https://www.dailykos.com/stories/2017/2/21/1633754/-One-reason-why-House-Republicans-won-t-stand-up-to-Trump-He-won-easily-in-most-of-their-districts.

29. Philip Bump, "No Matter How Bad It Gets for Him, Here's Why Trump Isn't Getting Impeached this Year," *Washington Post*, July 14, 2017.

30. Pew Research Center poll, September 18–24, 2018. Views on this question were about the same as they were in the April 5–11, 2017, poll.

31. Pew Research Center poll, February 7–12, 2017.

32. YouGov poll, July 15–16, 2017. See also Alexandra Filindra and Laurel Harbridge-Yong, "This Is Why More Republicans in Congress Haven't Criticized Trump," *Washington Post*, August 2, 2017.

33. YouGov poll, August 22–23, 2017.

34. George Washington University Battleground poll, August 13–17, 2017.

35. *HuffPost*/YouGov survey October 24—25, 2017.

36. CNN poll, October 12–15, 2017. See also Larry M. Bartels, "Partisanship in the Trump Era," *Journal of Politics* 80 (October 2018): 1483–94.

37. CNN poll, May 2–5, 2018.

38. Fox News poll of registered voters, August 27–29, 2017.

39. Aaron Blake, "Bob Corker's Poll Numbers Just Plunged among Republicans amid His Trump Feud," *Washington Post*, October 27, 2017.

40. *HuffPost*/YouGov poll, September 7–9, 2017.

41. Paul Kane, "Corker Was Channeling Most Republican Senators. You Wouldn't Know It from Their Silence," *Washington Post*, October 10, 2017.

42. Shu Fu and William G. Howell, "The Behavioral Consequences of Public Appeals: Evidence on Campaign Fundraising from the 2018 Congressional Elections," *Presidential Studies Quarterly* 50 (June 2020): 325–47.

43. Michael D. Shear and Sheryl Gay Stolberg, "As Other Republican Senators Bolt, Lindsey Graham Cozies Up to Trump," *New York Times*, October 26, 2017.

44. Winthrop University poll, February 17–March 12, 2019.

45. David Weigel, "In GOP primaries, Trump loyalty is a Weapon against Conservative Insurgents," *Washington Post*, July 10, 2018.

46. See e.g., Michael Scherer, "Fealty to Trump Has Become the Coin of the Realm for GOP Senate Candidates," *Washington Post*, April 15, 2018; Sean Sullivan, "GOP Candidates Echo Trump on Immigration as President Transforms Party in His Image," *Washington Post*, June 3, 2018.

47. Quoted in Jonathan Martin and Alexander Burns, "Mercurial Trump Rattles Republican Party Ahead of Midterms," *New York Times*, September 8, 2017.

48. David Weigel, "Trump Urges Republicans to Oust Rep. Mark Sanford in Primary," *Washington Post*, June 12, 2018.

49. Jan Zilinsky, "Look at the Kind of District Each Represents, and Their Responses Make More Sense," *Washington Post*, July 20, 2019.

50. Seung Min Kim and Jeff Stein, "With USMCA and Parental Leave, Democrats Say They Won Big Concessions from Trump," *Washington Post*, December 10, 2019.

51. Daniel J. Hopkins, *The Increasingly United States* (Chicago: University of Chicago Press, 2018). See also Joel Sievert and Seth C. McKee, "Nationalization in U.S. Senate and Gubernatorial Elections," *American Politics Research* 47 (September 2019): 1055–80.

52. Gary C. Jacobson, *Presidents & Parties in the Public Mind* (Chicago: University of Chicago Press, 2019), chap. 8.

53. Ashley Parker and Josh Dawsey, " 'I Am on the Ticket': Trump Seeks to Make the Election about Him, Even if Some Don't Want It to Be," *Washington Post*, October 18, 2018; Philip Bump, "Trump: The Election Is a Referendum on Me. Also Trump: Let Me Do an Imitation." *Washington Post*, October 3, 2018; Tessa Berenson, "President Trump Turned the Midterms into a Referendum on Himself," *Time,* November 7, 2018, https://time.com/5446188/donald-trump-midterms-results-reaction/.

54. Alan Abramowitz and Costas Panagopoulos, "Trump on the Trail: Assessing the Impact of Presidential Campaign Visits on Voting Behavior in the 2018 Midterm Elections," *Presidential Studies Quarterly* 50 (September 2020):https://doi.org/10.1111/psq.12664.

55. Pew Research Center poll, November 7–13, 2018. See also Pew Research Center polls, September 18–24, 2018, and June 5–12, 2018.

56. Gary C. Jacobson, "Extreme Referendum: Donald Trump and the 2018 Midterm Elections," *Political Science Quarterly* 134 (March 2019): 9–38.

57. Paul Kane, "House Conservatives Returned to Their Old Ways This Week: Playing Havoc with Spending Legislation," *Washington Post*, December 5, 2017.

58. Matthew N. Green and William Deatherage, "When Reputation Trumps Policy: Party Productivity Brand and the 2017 Tax Cut and Jobs Act," *The Forum* 16 (October 2018): 419–40.

59. Quoted in Paul Kane and John Wagner, "Mattis's Rebuke of Trump Forces Republicans to Choose between Revered Marine and the President," *Washington Post*, June 4, 2020.

60. Donald J. Trump (@realDonaldTrump), "It's very sad that Republicans, even some that were carried over the line on my back, do very little to protect their President," Twitter, July 23, 2017, 3:14 p.m., https://twitter.com/realDonaldTrump /status/889217183930351621.

61. James E. Campbell and Joe A. Sumners, "Presidential Coattails in Senate Elections," *American Political Science Review* 84 (June 1990): 513–24; and George C. Edwards III, *The Public Presidency* (New York: St. Martin's, 1983), 83–93.

62. Nicole Asmussen Mathew, "Dumping Trump and Electoral Bumps: The Causes and Consequences of Republican Officeholders' Endorsement Decisions," *The Forum* 17, no. 2 (2019): 231–55.

63. Andrew J. Clarke and Jeffery A. Jenkins, "Who are President Trump's Allies in the House of Representatives?" *The Forum* 15, no. 3 (2017), 422–23.

64. Gary C. Jacobson and Huchen Liu, "Dealing with Disruption: Congressional Republicans' Responses to Donald Trump's Behavior and Agenda," *Presidential Studies Quarterly* 50 (March 2020): 4–29.

65. Neil Irwin, "Why the Trump Agenda Is Moving Slowly: The Republicans' Wonk Gap," *New York Times*, February 28, 2017.

66. Carl Hulse, "Lisa Murkowski, a Swing Vote on Health Care, Isn't Swayed," *New York Times*, July 26, 2017.

67. James Hohmann, "Teflon Trump Gets Blamed Less by Base for Obamacare Fail than Senate GOP," *Washington Post*, July 19, 2017.

68. Frances Lee, "This Is How Trump Turned the Politics of the Debt Ceiling Upside Down," *Washington Post*, September 10, 2017.

69. Naomi Jagoda, "Conservative Army Bolsters Trump on Tax Cuts," *The Hill*, October 15, 2017.

70. Paul Blumenthal, "Republicans Admit that CEOs and Donors Really Need the Tax Cut Bill to Pass—or Else," *HuffPost*, November 9, 2017.

71. Quoted in Sheryl Gay Stolberg, "Republicans, Entering Homestretch on Tax Cuts, Are Calm and Cooperative," *New York Times*, November 29, 2017.

72. Quotes from Carl Hulse, "For McConnell, Health Care Failure Was a Map to Tax Success," *New York Times*, December 3, 2107.

73. Kelsey Snell, "Some Congressional Republicans Question Tax Plan over Deficit Costs," *Washington Post*, October 2, 2017.

74. Ryan Lizza, "How Republicans Ditched Tax Reform for Tax Cuts," *New Yorker*, September 28, 2017, https://www.newyorker.com/news/ryan-lizza/how-republicans-ditched-tax-reform-for-tax-cuts.

75. Heather Long, "25 GOP Senators Urge Trump to Restart TPP Trade Talks, a Deal He Called a 'Disaster,'" *Washington Post*, February 20, 2018.

76. Long, "25 GOP Senators Urge Trump to Restart TPP Trade Talks, a Deal He Called a 'Disaster.'"

77. Ana Swanson, "Trump Prepares to Formalize Tariffs but Floats Exemptions," *New York Times*, March 7, 2018.

78. Andrew J. Clarke, Jeffery A. Jenkins, Nathan K. Micatka, "How Have Members of Congress Reacted to President Trump's Trade Policy?" *The Forum* 17, no. 4 (2020).

79. ByungKoo Kim and Iain Osgood, "Pro-Trade Blocs in the US Congress," *The Forum* 14, no. 4 (2020).

80. Tory Newmyer, "Free-Trade Republican Lawmakers Mount Revolt against Trump Tariffs," *Washington Post*, June 7, 2018.

81. Nicholas Fandos, "Senate Votes to Reinstate Penalties on ZTE, Setting Up Clash with White House," *New York Times*, June 18, 2018.

82. Paul Kane, "In Flake's War on Trump Tariffs, Judicial Picks Are Caught in the Crossfire," *Washington Post*, June 27, 2018.

83. Jim Tankersley, "Conservative Koch Groups Plan Pro-Trade Blitz, as the Issue Splits Republicans," *New York Times*, June 4, 2018.

84. Marco Rubio (@marcorubio), "I assure you with 100% confidence that #ZTE is a much greater national security threat than steel from Argentina or Europe. #VeryBadDeal," Twitter, June 7, 2018, 9:07 a.m., https://twitter.com/marcorubio /status/1004726433351110656.

85. Glenn Thrush and Thomas Kaplan, "House Farm Bill Collapses Amid Republican Disarray," *New York Times*, May 18, 2018.

86. Mike DeBonis, Sean Sullivan, and John Wagner, "House Republican Leaders Delay Vote on Immigration Bill until Next Week in the Face of Opposition," *Washington Post*, June 21, 2018.

87. Jeffrey B. Lewis et al., "Voteview."

88. "About," RSC [Republican Study Committee], accessed July 25, 2020, https://rsc-johnson.house.gov/about.

89. See, e.g., Tim Alberta, "Defenders of the Faith," *National Journal*, May 25, 2013.

90. Matthew Green, *Legislative Hardball: The House Freedom Caucus and the Power of Threat-Making in Congress* (Cambridge: Cambridge University Press, 2019).

91. Sheryl Gay Stolberg, "Once Outspoken, Paul Ryan Wields His Speaker's Gavel Gingerly," *New York Times*, March 5, 2018.

92. Christopher S. Parker and Matt A. Barreto, *Change They Can't Believe In: The Tea Party and Reactionary Politics in America* (Princeton, NJ: Princeton University Press, 2011); Theda T. Skocpol and Vanessa Williamson, *The Tea Party and the Remaking of Republican Conservatism* (New York: Oxford University Press,

2012), 174, 178; Bryan T. Gervais and Irwin L. Morris, *Reactionary Republicanism: How the Tea Party in the House Paved the Way for Trump's Victory* (New York: Oxford University Press, 2018).

93. DeWayne Lucas and Iva E. Deutchman, "The Ideology of Moderate Republicans in the House," *The Forum* 5, no. 2 (2007): 1–19.

94. Kathryn Pearson, *Party Discipline in the U.S. House of Representatives* (Ann Arbor: University of Michigan Press, 2015).

95. Nolan McCarty, Keith T. Poole, and Howard Rosenthal, *Polarized America: The Dance of Ideology and Unequal Riches* (Cambridge, MA: MIT Press, 2006); Skocpol and Williamson, *The Tea Party and the Remaking of Republican Conservatism*; Ronald B. Rapoport, Meredith Dost, Ani-Rae Lovell, and Walter J. Stone, "Republican Factionalism and Tea Party Activists" (paper presented at the Annual Meeting of the Midwest Political Science Association, Chicago, April 11–14, 2013).

96. Pew Research Center polls, July 17–21, 2013, and November 6–9, 2014.

97. Gallup poll, September 6–10, 2017. See also Pew Research Center poll, September 3–5, 2019.

98. Seth Hill and Gregory Huber, "Representativeness and Motivations of the Contemporary Donorate: Results from Merged Survey and Administrative Records," *Political Behavior* 39 (March 2017): 3–29.

99. Carl Hulse, "Behind New Obamacare Repeal Vote: 'Furious' G.O.P. Donors," *New York Times*, September 22, 2017.

100. Frances E. Lee, "The 115th Congress and Questions of Party Unity in a Polarized Era," *Journal of Politics* 80 (October 2018): 1464–73.

101. Sean Sullivan, Karoun Demirjian and Michael Scherer, "New Volatility Seizes Tense Fight for Control of the Republican Party," *Washington Post*, October 11, 2017.

102. Jeremy W. Peters, "Conservatives Want to Make Mitch McConnell the Symbol of a Toxic Washington," *New York Times*, October 11, 2017.

103. Sarah Binder, "This Is Why Congress Will Have a Hard Time Legalizing DACA," *Washington Post*, September 7, 2017.

104. Steve King (@SteveKingIA), "@RealDonaldTrump If AP is correct, Trump base is blown up, destroyed, irreparable, and disillusioned beyond repair. No promise is credible," Twitter, September 13, 2017, 9:50 p.m., https://twitter.com/Steve KingIA/status/908160999756312576; Laura Ingraham (@IngrahamAngle), "Exactly what @realDonaldTrump campaigned on. Not," Twitter, September 13, 2017, 9:13 p.m., https://twitter.com/IngrahamAngle/status/908151661402750977; Ann Coulter (@AnnCoulter), "At this point, who DOESN'T want Trump impeached?" Twitter, September 14, 2017, 6:05 a.m., https://twitter.com/AnnCoulter/status/9082 85561194078208; Lou Dobbs (@LouDobbs), "Deep State Wins, Huge Loss for #MAGA No Countrvailing WH Force to Globalists Gary Cohn, Dina Powell, Gen. Kelly, Mark Short @POTUS Betrayed," Twitter, September 13, 2017, 11:02 p.m., https://twitter.com/LouDobbs/status/908179237823283201; Robert Costa, "Trump's Diehard Supporters Are Fuming after an Apparent About-face on 'Dreamers,'"

Washington Post, September 14, 2017; Jeremy W. Peters, "Conservatives Recoil at Trump's Accommodation with Democrats over DACA," *New York Times*, September 14, 2017.

105. Quoted in Je Concha, "Limbaugh Fumes on Border Wall: 'Trump Gets Nothing and the Democrats Get Everything,'" *The Hill*, December 19, 2018.

106. Ann Coulter (@AnnCoulter), "Trump proposes amnesty. We voted for Trump and got Jeb!" Twitter, January 19, 2019, 3:18 p.m., https://twitter.com/Ann Coulter/status/1086734750578929664.

107. Amanda Sakuma, "Immigration Hardliners Outraged over Trump's Proposed Shutdown Deal," *Vox*, January 20, 2019, https://www.vox.com/2019/1/20 /18190721/immigration-hardliners-outraged-trump-shutdown-deal; Ann Coulter (@AnnCoulter), "BREAKING: Doctors announce world's first successful spine transplant https://wapo.st/2EAI9vC," Twitter, December 20, 2018, 1:16 p.m., https:// twitter.com/AnnCoulter/status/1075832224312893440.

108. Gary C. Jacobson, "The Triumph of Polarized Partisanship in 2016: Donald Trump's Improbable Victory," *Political Science Quarterly* 132 (Spring 2017), 28.

109. This figure does not include the disputed election in North Carolina's Ninth Congressional District.

110. Skocpol and Williamson, *The Tea Party and the Remaking of Republican Conservatism*; Jeffrey M. Berry and Sarah Sobieraj, *The Outrage Industry: Political Opinion and the New Incivility* (New York: Oxford University Press, 2014), chap. 6.

111. Sarah E. Anderson, Daniel M. Butler, and Laurel Harbridge-Yong, "When Half a Loaf Isn't Better Than No Loaf at All: Gridlock and Legislators' Rejection of Compromise," *The Legislative Scholar* 3 (Spring 2018): 11–12.

112. Jacobson, "The Triumph of Polarized Partisanship in 2016," 28.

113. Sarah Binder, "This Is Why the Republicans Struggle Over Obamacare," *Washington Post*, March 9, 2017.

114. Darrell Issa and Jeff Denham (California) and Will Hurd (Texas).

115. Philip Bump, "Does Nominating More Liberal Candidates Doom Democratic Chances in Texas?" *Washington Post*, March 8, 2018.

116. Jeffrey Lazarus, "These 2 Charts Show Why More Republicans Don't Object to How Trump Fired Comey," *Washington Post*, May 16, 2017.

117. Ryan D. Williamson, "Evaluating Candidate Positioning and Success in the 2018 Midterm Elections," *The Forum* 16, no. 4 (2019): 675–86.

118. Jennifer Steinhauer, "G.O.P. Senators, Pulling Away from Trump, Have 'a Lot Less Fear of Him,'" *New York Times*, May 14, 2017.

119. Sheryl Gay Stolberg, "Jeff Flake, a Fierce Trump Critic, Will Not Seek Re-Election for Senate," *New York Times*, October 24, 2017.

120. Jacobson and Liu, "Dealing with Disruption," 20.

121. Alan I. Abramowitz, *The Disappearing Center: Engaged Citizens, Polarization, and American Democracy* (New Haven, CT: Yale University Press, 2011); Abramowitz, *The Polarized Public: Why American Government is so Dysfunctional* (New York: Pearson, 2012).

122. Christopher McConnell, Yotam Margalit, Neil Malhotra, and Matthew Levendusky, "The Economic Consequences of Partisanship in a Polarized Era," *American Journal of Political Science* 62 (January 2018): 5–18; Seth C. McKee, *Republican Ascendancy in Southern U.S. House Elections* (Boulder, CO: Westview Press, 2010); Charles S. Bullock III, Donna R. Hoffman, and Ronald Keith Gaddie, "The Consolidation of the White Southern Congressional Vote," *Political Research Quarterly* 58 (June 2005): 231–43; M. V. Hood III, Quentin Kidd, and Irwin L. Morris, "Of Byrd[s] and Bumpers: Using Democratic Senators to Analyze Political Change in the South, 1960–1995," *American Journal of Political Science* 43 (April 1999): 465–87; Paul Frymer, "The 1994 Aftershock: Dealignment or Realignment in the South," in *Midterm: The Elections of 1994 in Context*, ed. Philip A. Klinkner (Boulder, CO: Westview Press, 1995), 99–113; Richard Nadeau and Harold W. Stanley, "Class Polarization Among Native Southern Whites, 1952–90," *American Journal of Political Science* 37 (August 1993): 900–19; Martin P. Wattenberg, "The Building of a Republican Regional Base in the South: The Elephant Crosses the Mason-Dixon Line," *Public Opinion Quarterly* 55 (1991): 424–31; Earle Black and Merle Black, *Politics and Society in the South* (Cambridge, MA: Harvard University Press, 1987).

123. Jacobson, "Partisan Polarization in American Politics."

124. Larry M. Bartels, "Partisanship in the Trump Era," *Journal of Politics* 80 (October 2018): 1483–94.

125. ANES 2016, face to face sample. A good review of the data for 2012 can be found in Gary C. Jacobson, "Barack Obama and the Nationalization of Electoral Politics in 2012," *Electoral Studies* 40 (December 2015): 471–81; and Jacobson, "Partisan Polarization in American Politics."

126. Jacobson, "Extreme Referendum."

127. Gary C. Jacobson, "The Effects of the Early Trump Presidency on Public Attitudes toward the Republican Party," *Presidential Studies Quarterly* 48 (September 2018): 404–35; Jacobson, *Presidents & Parties in the Public Mind*.

128. Bump, "Does Nominating More Liberal Candidates?"

129. Jacobson, "The Triumph of Polarized Partisanship in 2016," 28; Steven W. Webster and Alan I. Abramowitz, "The Ideological Foundations of Affective Polarization in the U.S. Electorate," *American Politics Research* 45 (July 2017): 621–47.

130. Geoffrey Skelley, "The House Will Have Just As Many Moderate Democrats as Progressives Next Year," *FiveThirtyEight*, December 20, 2018, https://fivethirty eight.com/features/the-house-will-have-just-as-many-moderate-democrats-as -progressives-next-year/.

131. Jacobson, "Extreme Referendum."

132. Jennifer Steinhauer, "Senate Democrats Sought to Work with Trump. Then He Began Governing," *New York Times*, June 28, 2017; Paul Kane, "Republicans Thought They Could Force 2018 Democrats to Cut Deals, but Trump Keeps Sliding in Polls," *Washington Post*, July 8, 2017.

133. CNN poll, January 14–18, 2018.

134. Jonathan Martin, "Shutdown? It Could Be Forgotten in a Trumpian Flash," *New York Times*, January 19, 2018; David Weigel, Ed O'Keefe, and Jenna Portnoy, "Shutdown Could Hurt Democrats Seeking Reelection in Trump States," *Washington Post*, January 21, 2018.

135. See also Jacobson and Liu, "Dealing with Disruption," 8, 17, 21–22.

136. Lydia Saad, "Trump's Approval Highest in West Virginia, Lowest in Vermont," Gallup Poll, January 30, 2018.

137. Jeffrey M. Jones, "Trump Job Approval 50% or Higher in 17 States in 2018," Gallup Poll, February 22, 2019.

138. Separate NBC News/Marist College poll of Michigan, Pennsylvania, and Wisconsin, August 13–17, 2017.

139. Rema Rahman and John T. Bennett, "GOP Congress Blames White House Chaos for Failures," *Roll Call*, July 28, 2017.

140. Pew Research Center poll, February 7–12, 2017.

141. Gallup Poll.

142. Gary C. Jacobson, "Partisan Polarization in Presidential Support: The Electoral Connection," *Congress and the Presidency* 30 (Spring 2003): 8–11.

143. See, e.g., Marissa Abrajano and Zoltan L. Hajnal, *White Backlash: Immigration, Race, and American Politics* (Princeton, NJ: Princeton University Press, 2015); and "The Parties on the Eve of the 2016 Election," Pew Research Center, September 13, 2016.

144. Francis E. Lee, *Insecure Majorities: Congress and the Perpetual Campaign* (Chicago: University of Chicago Press, 2016).

145. Adam Bonica and Gary W. Cox, "Ideological Extremists in the U.S. Congress: Out of Step but Still in Office," *Quarterly Journal of Political Science* 13 (2018): 207–36.

146. George C. Edwards III and Andrew Barrett, "Presidential Agenda Setting in Congress," in *Polarized Politics: Congress and the President in a Partisan Era*, ed. Jon R. Bond and Richard Fleisher (Washington DC: Congressional Quarterly, 2000).

147. Mike DeBonis and Sean Sullivan, "Trump Wants His Immigration Framework Debated in Senate," *Washington Post*, February 1, 2018.

148. Quoted in David Nakamura and Mike DeBonis, "Trump Administration Assault on Bipartisan Immigration Plan Ensured Its Demise," *Washington Post*, February 17, 2018.

149. Michael Scherer and Josh Dawsey, "Trump Cites as a Negotiating Tool His Policy of Separating Immigrant Children from Their Parents," *Washington Post*, June 15, 2018; James Hohmann, "Trump Team Cannot Gets Its Story Straight on Separating Migrant Families," *Washington Post*, June 18, 2018.

150. Thomas Kaplan and Robert Pear, "End to Health Care Subsidies Puts Congress in a Tight Spot," *New York Times*, October 13, 2017; Peter Baker, "Trump

Adopts Obama Approach While Seeking to Undo a Legacy," *New York Times*, October 13, 2017.

151. Thomas Kaplan and Robert Pear, "End to Health Care Subsidies Puts Congress in a Tight Spot," *New York Times*, October 13, 2017.

Chapter Seven

1. Quoted in Glenn Thrush, "Mitch McConnell, Never a Grandstander, Learns to Play by Trump's Rules," *New York Times*, April 14, 2019.

2. Sean Sullivan, "Can This Marriage Be Saved? Relationship between Trump, Senate GOP Hits New Skids," *Washington Post*, August 1, 2017 (emphasis added).

3. Tim Alberta, *American Carnage: On the Front Lines of the Republican Civil War and the Rise of President Trump* (New York: HarperCollins, 2019), 505–6.

4. "Remarks by President Trump in Cabinet Meeting," October 16, 2017, White House transcript, White House, Washington, D.C.

5. Robert Costa and Amy Goldstein, "Trump Vows 'Insurance for Everybody' in Obamacare Replacement Plan," *Washington Post*, January 15, 2017.

6. Quoted in Robert Pear and Kate Kelly, "Trump Concedes Health Law Overhaul Is 'Unbelievably Complex,'" *New York Times*, February 27, 2018.

7. "Press Briefing by Press Secretary Sarah Sanders," September 5, 2017, White House transcript, White House, Washington, DC.

8. Michael D. Shear, "White House Makes Hard-Line Demands for Any 'Dreamers' Deal," *New York Times*, October 8, 2017.

9. Julie Hirschfeld Davis and Michael D. Shear, *Border Wars: Inside Trump's Assault on Immigration* (New York: Simon and Schuster, 2019), 180–81.

10. Mark Landler and David E. Sanger, "Trump to Force Congress to Act on Iran Nuclear Deal," *New York Times*, October 5, 2017.

11. Michael D. Shear and Sheryl Gay Stolberg, "Conceding to N.R.A., Trump Abandons Brief Gun Control Promise," *New York Times*, March 12, 2018; John Wagner and Seung Min Kim, "'Like a Pinball Machine': Lawmakers Struggle to Negotiate with an Erratic Trump," *Washington Post*, March 4, 2018; Donald J. Trump (@realDonaldTrump), ". . . . On 18 to 21 Age Limits, watching court cases and rulings before acting. States are making this decision. Things are moving rapidly on this, but not much political support (to put it mildly)." Twitter, March 12, 2018, 8:22 a.m., https://twitter.com/realDonaldTrump/status/973187513731944448.

12. Sheryl Gay Stolberg, "Lawmakers Court Trump on Gun Safety, With Some Appealing to His Ego," *New York Times*, September 21, 2019.

13. Sheryl Gay Stolberg, "As Trump Weighs Gun Safety Bills, Barr's Plan Draws Skepticism," *New York Times*, September 18, 2019.

14. Quoted in Carl Hulse, "The Senate: Still Great at Deliberating, but Less So at Legislating," *New York Times*, September 14, 2019.

15. John Wagner and Seung Min Kim, "'Like a Pinball Machine': Lawmakers Struggle to Negotiate with an Erratic Trump," *Washington Post*, March 4, 2018; Mike DeBonis and Paul Kane, "Waiting for Trump, Congress Remains at Loggerheads on Gun Legislation," *Washington Post*, September 10, 2019; Hulse, "The Senate."

16. Robert Costa and David Weigel, "Trump Goes into Dealmaking Mode, Works Behind the Scenes on Health Bill," *Washington Post*, March 9, 2017.

17. Jennifer Steinhauer and Emmarie Huetteman, "Desperate for Presidential Leadership, Republicans Find Little," *New York Times*, February 28, 2017.

18. Peter Baker, "Amid Turmoil from Washington to Wall Street, a Surprisingly Passive President," *New York Times*, February 9, 2018.

19. See also Alberta, *American Carnage*, 401, 420.

20. Sarah Binder and Mark Spindel, "Here Are the 4 Reasons McConnell Couldn't get the Senate to Replace Obamacare—Yet," *Washington Post*, July 18, 2017.

21. Sheryl Gay Stolberg, "After a Chaotic Start, Congress Has Made a Conservative Mark," *New York Times*, December 24, 2017.

22. Robert Pear, "Governors Rally around Health Law Fixes as White House Pushes Repeal," *New York Times*, September 7, 2017.

23. Nicholas Fandos, "McConnell Signals Willingness to Hold Vote on Health Deal if Trump Approves," *New York Times*, October 22, 2017; Tory Newmyer, "McConnell Says Trump Needs to Provide Clarity on Health Care," *Washington Post*, October 22, 2017.

24. Rachael Bade, Josh Dawsey, Seung Min Kim, and John Wagner, "Trump Pressures Wary Republicans to Produce Replacement for Health-Care Law," *Washington Post*, March 27, 2019.

25. Robert Pear and Maggie Haberman, "Trump Retreats on Health Care After McConnell Warns It Won't Happen," *New York Times*, April 2, 2019; John Weaver and Erica Werner, "Trump Abandons Plan for Pre-Election Vote on Health Care after Talking to McConnell," *Washington Post*, April 2, 2019.

26. "2019 Vote Studies: President Support—House," *CQ Magazine*, February 24, 2020.

27. Paul Kane, "Least Deliberative Senate Faces Weighty Task of Holding Trump's Impeachment Trial," *Washington Post*, January 4, 2020.

28. See Yasmeen Abutaleb and Erica Werner, "Trump's Support for Bipartisan Senate Drug Pricing Bill May Not Be Enough to Push It into Law," *Washington Post*, February 18, 2020.

29. See, e.g., Jim Tankersley and Alan Rappeport, "How Republicans Rallied Together to Deliver a Tax Plan," *New York Times*, December 19, 2017; Damian Paletta, Robert Costa, and Philip Rucker, "On Taxes, Trump Is an Eager Salesman— but the Policy Action is on Capitol Hill," *Washington Post*, October 27, 2017.

30. Donald J. Trump (@realDonaldTrump), "There will be NO change to your 401(k). This has always been a great and popular middle class tax break that works,

and it stays!" Twitter, October 23, 2017, 6:42 a.m., https://twitter.com/realDonald
Trump/status/922428118685581313; "I am proud of the Rep. House & Senate for
working so hard on cutting taxes {& reform.} We're getting close! Now, how about
ending the unfair & highly unpopular Indiv Mandate in OCare & reducing taxes
even further? Cut top rate to 35% w/all of the rest going to middle income cuts?"
Twitter, November 13, 2017, 9:06 a.m., https://twitter.com/realDonaldTrump/sta
tus/930089374187950081; Mike DeBonis and Damian Paletta, "Trump Personally
Pushing GOP Leaders To Use Tax Bill To Undermine Obamacare," *Washington
Post*, November 3, 2018.

31. See, e.g., Jim Tankersley and Alan Rappeport, "How Republicans Rallied
Together to Deliver a Tax Plan," *New York Times*, December 19, 2017; Jim Tankersley, "Trump's Red Line Is Holding Up Tax Cuts," *New York Times*, December 1,
2017; Alan Rappeport, "Trump Again Wades Into Tax Debate, Suggesting Repeal
of Obamacare Mandate," *New York Times*, November 13, 2017; Paletta et al., "On
Taxes, Trump Is an Eager Salesman"; Jake Sherman and Anna Palmer, *The Hill
to Die On: The Battle for Congress and the Future of Trump's America* (New York:
Crown, 2019), 150–53.

32. Quoted in Sean Sullivan and Elise Viebeck, "Corker Says White House
Should Stay Out of Tax Debate; Trump Fires Back with Insult," *Washington Post*,
October 24, 2017.

33. Sherman and Palmer, *The Hill to Die On*, 89, 150–51.

34. Sarah Binder, "The House Moved Quickly on a Covid-19 Response Bill.
These 4 Takeaways Explain What's Likely to Happen Next." *Washington Post*,
March 14, 2020.

35. Erica Werner, Josh Dawsey, Seung Min Kim, and Robert Costa, "Trump
Administration, Congress at Odds as They Collide on Coronavirus Economic
Plans," *Washington Post*, March 10, 2020.

36. Michael S. Schmidt and Michael D. Shear, "Trump Says Russia Inquiry
Makes U.S. 'Look Very Bad,'" *New York Times*, December 28, 2017.

37. Glenn Thrush, "Trump's 'Great National Infrastructure Program' Stalled,"
New York Times, July 23, 2017.

38. Ed O'Keefe, "Trump Pushes Back on Chief of Staff Claims that Border
Wall Pledges 'Uninformed,'" *Washington Post*, January 18, 2018. See also Sheryl
Gay Stolberg, "Senators and Trump Inch toward DACA Deal, but a Wall Divides
Them," *New York Times*, January 4, 2018; Ashley Parker, Josh Dawsey, and Ed
O'Keefe, "'Negotiating with Jell-O': How Trump's Shifting Positions Fueled the
Rush to a Shutdown," *Washington Post*, January 20, 2018; Aaron Blake, "Mitch
McConnell's Passive-aggressive Dig at Trump," *Washington Post*, January 17, 2018.

39. Davis and Shear, *Border Wars*, 214–16.

40. Seung Min Kim and Mike DeBonis, "Officials Say Trump Backs GOP Immigration Bills, Despite Comments Opposing Them. One Says Trump Misunderstood Fox News' Question," *Washington Post*, June 15, 2018.

41. Seung Min Kim and Mike DeBonis, "Trump: 'I Certainly Wouldn't Sign' House GOP Immigration Compromise," *Washington Post*, June 15, 2018.

42. Seung Min Kim and Mike DeBonis, "Officials Say Trump Backs GOP Immigration Bills, Despite Comments Opposing Them. One Says Trump Misunderstood Fox News' Question," *Washington Post*, June 15, 2018.

43. Thomas Kaplan and Sheryl Gay Stolberg, "Will He or Won't He? Conflicting Trump Messages Sow Immigration Confusion," *New York Times*, June 15, 2018.

44. Michael D. Shear, Sheryl Gay Stolberg, and Thomas Kaplan, "G.O.P. Moves to End Trump's Family Separation Policy, but Can't Agree How," *New York Times*, June 19, 2018.

45. Amber Phillips, "On Immigration, Trump Is Making Life Absolutely Miserable for Republicans in Congress," *Washington Post*, June 20, 2018.

46. Mike DeBonis, Sean Sullivan, and John Wagner, "House Republican Leaders Delay Vote on Immigration Bill until Next Week in the Face of Opposition," *Washington Post*, June 21, 2018.

47. Phillips, "On Immigration, Trump Is Making Life Absolutely Miserable." See also Davis and Shear, *Border Wars*,. 248–51.

48. Matt Fuller, "Trump Leaves GOP Leaders Out To Dry on Immigration," *HuffPost*, June 22, 2018.

49. Mike DeBonis, Philip Rucker, Seung Min Kim, and John Wagner, "Trump Urges House GOP to Fix Immigration System, Expresses no Strong Preference on Rival Bills amid Uproar over Family Separations," *Washington Post*, June 20, 2018.

50. Mike DeBonis and John Wagner, "House Rejects Immigration Bill Pushed by Trump in Last-Minute Tweet," *Washington Post*, June 27, 2018.

51. Mike DeBonis and Erica Warner, "Republicans Fume after Trump's Latest Immigration Tweet Undermines House Talks," *Washington Post*, June 22, 2018.

52. Rica Werner and Robert Costa, "Republicans Suggest Trump Won't Get All the Wall Money He Wants—but They Are Unclear about What He Wants," *Washington Post*, February 5, 2019.

53. Erica Werner and Seung Min Kim, "GOP in Disarray as Budget Impasse Threatens Shutdown, Deep Cuts—and Default," *Washington Post*, June 15, 2019.

54. Quoted in Jim Tankersley, "Cutting Taxes Is Hard. Trump Is Making It Harder," *New York Times*, October 23, 2017.

55. Quoted in Parker et al., " 'Negotiating with Jell-O.' "

56. John Wagner and Seung Min Kim, " 'Like a Pinball Machine': Lawmakers Struggle to Negotiate with an Erratic Trump," *Washington Post*, March 4, 2018. See also Davis and Shear, *Border Wars*, 182.

57. Donald J. Trump (@realDonaldTrump), "Meeting with 'Chuck and Nancy' today about keeping government open and working. Problem is they want illegal immigrants flooding into our Country unchecked, are weak on Crime and want to substantially RAISE Taxes. I don't see a deal!" Twitter, November 28, 2017, 8:17 a.m., https://twitter.com/realDonaldTrump/status/935513049729028096.

58. Nancy Pelosi (@SpeakerNancy), "@realDonaldTrump now knows that his verbal abuse will no longer be tolerated. His empty chair photo opp showed he's more interested in stunts than in addressing the needs of the American people. Poor Ryan and McConnell relegated to props. Sad!" Twitter, November 28, 2017, 3:28 p.m., https://twitter.com/SpeakerPelosi/status/935621519820062720; Quoted in Thomas Kaplan, "Democrats Pull Out of Trump Meeting as G.O.P. Leaders Hunt for Votes on Tax Bill," *New York Times*, November 28, 2017.

59. Quoted in Paul Kane, "From 'He Likes Us' to 'Sad!': The Rise and Fall of the Trump-Schumer-Pelosi Partnership," *Washington Post*, November 28, 2017.

60. "Remarks by President Trump on Healthcare Vote in the House of Representatives," May 4, 2017, White House transcript, White House, Washington, DC.

61. See, e.g., Thomas Kaplan, Jennifer Steinhauer, and Robert Pear, "Trump, in Zigzag, Calls House Republicans' Health Bill 'Mean,'" *New York Times*, June 13, 2017.

62. Donald J. Trump (@realDonaldTrump), "I suggest that we add more dollars to Healthcare and make it the best anywhere. ObamaCare is dead - the Republicans will do much better!" Twitter, May 28, 2017, 6:57 p.m., https://twitter.com/realDonaldTrump/status/868979531641741313.

63. Damian Paletta and Mike DeBonis, "Trump's Window for Scoring Early Legislative Victories Is Shrinking," *Washington Post*, May 30, 2017.

64. Robert Pear and Thomas Kaplan, "Senate Leaders Try to Appease Members as Support for Health Bill Slips," *New York Times*, June 25, 2017.

65. John Wagner, "Trump: 'I Will Be Very Angry' if GOP Senators Don't Pass a Health-Care Bill," *Washington Post*, July 12, 2017.

66. David Nakamura, "32 Million More Americans Would Be Uninsured by 2026 Under Senate Measure Heading to a Vote Next Week, CBO Project," *Washington Post*, July 19, 2017; Eileen Sullivan and Julie Hirschfeld Davis, "Trump Defends Health Care Bill Over Lunch with G.O.P. Senators," *New York Times*, July 19, 2017.

67. "Remarks by President Trump and Prime Minister Tsipras of Greece in Joint Press Conference," October 17, 2017, White House transcript, White House, Washington, DC; Sean Sullivan and Juliet Eilperin, "Key Senators Reach Bipartisan Health-Care Subsidy Deal, and Trump Expresses Support," *Washington Post*, October 17, 2017.

68. Sean Sullivan, Juliet Eilperin, and Amy Goldstein, Another Last-Ditch Effort to Tackle Obamacare Stalls within Hours of Its Release," *Washington Post*, October 17, 2017.

69. Donald J. Trump (@realDonaldTrump), "I am supportive of Lamar as a person & also of the process, but I can never support bailing out ins co's who have made a fortune w/ O'Care," Twitter, October 18, 2017, 8:41 a.m., https://twitter.com/realDonaldTrump/status/920645935981613057.

70. Juliet Eilperin and Sean Sullivan, "Trump Appears to Back Further Away from Bipartisan Health-Care Push," *Washington Post*, October 18, 2017.

71. Paige Winfield Cunningham, "Trump Is Now the One Holding Up a Health-Care Bill," *Washington Post*, October 25, 2017.

72. Philip Rucker, Sean Sullivan, and Paul Kane, "The Great Dealmaker? Lawmakers Find Trump to Be an Untrustworthy Negotiator," *Washington Post*, October 23, 2017.

73. Donald J. Trump (@realDonaldTrump), "I look forward to working w/ D's + R's in Congress to address immigration reform in a way that puts hardworking citizens of our country 1st," Twitter, September 5, 2017, 3:45 p.m., https://twitter.com/realDonaldTrump/status/905170032229056512; "Congress now has 6 months to legalize DACA (something the Obama Administration was unable to do). If they can't, I will revisit this issue!" Twitter, September 5, 2017, 7:38 p.m., https://twitter.com/realDonaldTrump/status/905228667336499200; Jenna Johnson, "Trump: 'No Second Thoughts' on DACA Decision," *Washington Post*, September 6, 2017.

74. Maggie Haberman and Yamiche Alcindor, "Pelosi and Schumer Say They Have Deal With Trump to Replace DACA," *New York Times*, September 13, 2017; Aaron Blake, "The White House's Nondenial Denials on Its DACA Deal with Democrats," *Washington Post*, September 14, 2017; Eileen Sullivan, "Trump Confirms Support for Law to Protect 'Dreamers,'" *New York Times*, September 14, 2017; Ashley Parker and Robert Costa, "'A New Strategy' for Trump? Democrats Cautious but Encouraged by Fresh Outreach," *Washington Post*, September 13, 2017; Baker and Stolberg, "Trump Reaches Out"; Kelsey Snell, Ashley Parker, and Ed O'Keefe, "White House May Back Off Demand to Pair Border Wall, 'Dreamer' Protections, Trump Aide Says," *Washington Post*, September 12, 2017; Ed O'Keefe and David Nakamura, "Trump, Top Democrats Agree to Work on Deal to Save 'Dreamers' from Deportation," *Washington Post*, September 13, 2017.

75. Elise Viebeck, Ed O'Keefe, and Mike DeBonis, "Ryan Dismisses Potential DACA Deal between Trump and Democrats," *Washington Post*, September 14, 2017; Robert Costa, "Trump's Diehard Supporters Are Fuming after an Apparent About-Face on 'Dreamers,'" *Washington Post*, September 14, 2017.

76. Ed O'Keefe, "Deal or No Deal on DACA? Republicans Say No. Democrats Say Not Yet," *Washington Post*, October 3, 2017.

77. David Nakamura, "Trump Calls for 'Bipartisan' Immigration Deal for 'Dreamers' but Reiterates Demand for Border Wall," *Washington Post*, January 4, 2018; Sheryl Gay Stolberg and Michael Tackett, "White House Immigration Demands Imperil Bipartisan Talks," *New York Times*, January 5, 2018; Michael D. Shear and Eileen Sullivan, "Trump Threatens to Veto Immigration Bills that Don't Meet His Demands," *Washington Post*, February 14, 2018.

78. Donald J. Trump (@realDonaldTrump), "As I made very clear today, our country needs the security of the Wall on the Southern Border, which must be part of any DACA approval," Twitter, January 9, 2018, 6:16 p.m.; Ashley Parker and Philip Rucker, "55 Minutes at the Table: Trump Tries to Negotiate and Prove Stability," *Washington Post*, January 9, 2018; Ed O'Keefe and David Nakamura,

"Trump Offers to 'Take All the Heat' on Immigration, but Also Appears to Contradict Himself," *Washington Post*, January 9, 2018, Davis and Shear, *Border Wars*, 182, 217–19.

79. Parker et al., "'Negotiating with Jell-O'"; Davis and Shear, *Border Wars*, 219.

80. Thomas Kaplan and Sheryl Gay Stolberg, "House Republicans' Hard-Line Immigration Stand Clashes with Trump Overture," *New York Times*, January 10, 2018.

81. Josh Dawsey, "Trump Derides Protections for Immigrants from 'Shithole' Countries," *Washington Post*, January 12, 2018; Davis and Shear, *Border Wars*, 219–23.

82. Quoted in Parker et al., "'Negotiating with Jell-O.'"

83. Quoted in Ed O'Keefe, "Kelly Calls Some of Trump's Campaign Pledges on Immigration, Wall 'Uninformed,' Meeting Attendees Say," *Washington Post*, January 17, 2018; Eileen Sullivan and Maggie Haberman, "Trump Denies Changing His Position on Border Wall," *New York Times*, January 18, 2018; John Wagner, Josh Dawsey, and Robert Costa, "Trump Pushes Back on Chief of Staff Claims that Border Wall Pledges 'Uninformed,'" *Washington Post*, January 18, 2018.

84. Donald J. Trump (@realDonaldTrump), "The Wall is the Wall, it has never changed or evolved from the first day I conceived of it. Parts will be, of necessity, see through and it was never intended to be built in areas where there is natural protection such as mountains, wastelands or tough rivers or water . . . ," Twitter, January 18, 2018, 5:15 a.m., https://twitter.com/realDonaldTrump/status /953948941674078208.

85. Parker et al., "'Negotiating with Jell-O'"; Davis and Shear, *Border Wars*, 229–30.

86. Donald J. Trump (@realDonaldTrump), "Cryin' Chuck Schumer fully understands, especially after his humiliating defeat, that if there is no Wall, there is no DACA. We must have safety and security, together with a strong Military, for our great people!" Twitter, January 23, 2018, 10:07 p.m., https://twitter.com /realDonaldTrump/status/956015565776277510; Sheryl Gay Stolberg and Maggie Haberman, "Border Wall 'Off the Table,' Schumer Says, as Immigration Progress Unravels," *New York Times*, January 23, 2018.

87. Maggie Haberman, Katie Rogers, and Michael D. Shear, "Trump Says He Is Open to a Path to Citizenship for 'Dreamers,'" *New York Times*, January 24, 2018.

88. Michael D. Shear and Sheryl Gay Stolberg, "Trump Immigration Plan Will Demand Tough Concessions from Democrats," *New York Times*, January 25, 2018.

89. Mike DeBonis and Sean Sullivan, "Trump Wants His Immigration Framework Debated in Senate," *Washington Post*, February 1, 2018.

90. Thomas Kaplan and Mark Landler, "'Shut It Down': Trump ThreatensGovernment Shutdown over Border Security," *New York Times*, February 6, 2018;

Mark Landler, "Trump's Latest Surprise: Shutdown Might Be a Good Idea," *New York Times*, February 6, 2018.

91. David Nakamura and Mike DeBonis, "Trump Administration Assault on Bipartisan Immigration Plan Ensured Its Demise," *Washington Post*, February 17, 2018.

92. Seung Min Kim, " 'Trump Blew It': The President Missed His best Chance Yet to Get Funding for His Border Wall," *Washington Post*, March 22, 2018; Mike DeBonis and Josh Dawsey, "Trump Is Open to Short-Term DACA Deal, White House Tells GOP Leaders," *Washington Post*, March 14, 2108.

93. Quoted in Seung Min Kim, " 'Trump Blew It': The President Missed His best Chance Yet to Get Funding for His Border Wall," *Washington Post*, March 22, 2018.

94. Mike DeBonis and Erica Warner, "Republicans Fume after Trump's Latest Immigration Tweet Undermines House Talks," *Washington Post*, June 22, 2018.

95. Mike DeBonis, Sean Sullivan, and John Wagner, "House Republican Leaders Delay Vote on Immigration Bill until Next Week in the Face of Opposition," *Washington Post*, June 21, 2018.

96. Donald J. Trump (@realDonaldTrump), "What is the purpose of the House doing good immigration bills when you need 9 votes by Democrats in the Senate, and the Dems are only looking to Obstruct (which they feel is good for them in the Mid-Terms). Republicans must get rid of the stupid Filibuster Rule-it is killing you!" Twitter, June 28, 2018, 8:08 a.m., https://twitter.com/realDonaldTrump /status/1009785143635206149.

97. Ryan Costello (@RyanCostello), "Wow, this undermines getting undecided GOP members to support the compromise bill," Twitter, June 21, 2018, 8:18 a.m., https://twitter.com/RyanCostello/status/1009787542550573056; Mike DeBonis and John Wagner, "GOP Immigration Bills Backed by Trump Appear Headed for Defeat," *Washington Post*, June 21, 2018; DeBonis et al., "House Republican Leaders Delay Vote."

98. Donald J. Trump (@realDonaldTrump), "Republicans should stop wasting their time on Immigration until after we elect more Senators and Congressmen/ women in November. Dems are just playing games, have no intention of doing anything to solves this decades old problem. We can pass great legislation after the Red Wave!" Twitter, June 22, 2018, 6:06 a.m., https://twitter.com/realDonaldTrump/status /1010116816998490113; DeBonis and Warner, "Republicans Fume."

99. Donald J. Trump (@realDonaldTrump), "HOUSE REPUBLICANS SHOULD PASS THE STRONG BUT FAIR IMMIGRATION BILL, KNOWN AS GOODLATTE II, IN THEIR AFTERNOON VOTE TODAY, EVEN THOUGH THE DEMS WON'T LET IT PASS IN THE SENATE. PASSAGE WILL SHOW THAT WE WANT STRONG BORDERS & SECURITY WHILE THE DEMS WANT OPEN BORDERS = CRIME. WIN!" Twitter, June 27, 2018, 7:39 a.m., https://twitter.com/realDonaldTrump/status/1011952266268545024.

100. Donald J. Trump (@realDonaldTrump), "I never pushed the Republicans in the House to vote for the Immigration Bill, either GOODLATTE 1 or 2, because it could never have gotten enough Democrats as long as there is the 60 vote threshold. I released many prior to the vote knowing we need more Republicans to win in Nov.," Twitter, June 30, 2018, 2:17 p.m., https://twitter.com/realdonaldtrump/status/1013139532290625538.

101. Donald J. Trump (@realDonaldTrump), "Congress - FIX OUR INSANE IMMIGRATION LAWS NOW!" Twitter, July 5, 2018, 9:17 a.m., https://twitter.com/realDonaldTrump/status/1014875894614319104.

102. DeBonis and Warner, "Republicans Fume."

103. David Nakamura and Seung Min Kim, "'He's a Gut Politician': Trump's Go-To Negotiating Tactics Aren't Working in Shutdown Standoff," *Washington Post*, January 9, 2019.

104. Quoted in Julie Hirschfeld Davis, "Trump Threatens Shutdown in Combative Appearance With Democrats," *New York Times*, December 11, 2018

105. Erica Werner, Sean Sullivan, and Seung Min Kim, "Trump's Ultimatum on Border Wall Boxes in Fellow Republicans," *Washington Post*, December 12, 2018.

106. Julie Hirschfeld Davis and Maggie Haberman, "Mercurial Trump Has Made Path Out of Shutdown Much Harder to Find," *New York Times*, January 11, 2019.

107. Julie Hirschfeld Davis and Emily Cochrane, "A Shutdown Looms. Can the G.O.P. Get Lawmakers to Show Up to Vote?" *New York Times*, December 16, 2018.

108. Paul Kane, "Congress Ends with Trump's Fight for Wall, Shutdown and GOP Leaders Hard to Find," *Washington Post*, December 26, 2018.

109. Julie Hirschfeld Davis, "Trump Threatens Shutdown in Combative Appearance With Democrats," *New York Times*, December 11, 2018

110. Quoted in Max Farrand, ed., "CCCLXVII, Jared Sparks: Journal, April 19, 1830," *The Records of the Federal Convention of 1787*, vol. 3, rev. ed. (New Haven, CT: Yale University Press, 1966), 479.

111. Davis and Shear, *Border Wars*, 356–57.

112. Erica Werner, Sean Sullivan, Mike DeBonis, and Seung Min Kim, "Trump Walks out of Shutdown Negotiations after Democrats Reject Wall Money, Calls Meeting 'Total Waste of Time,'" *Washington Post*, January 9, 2019.

113. Emily Cochrane, "White House Signals Retreat on Shutdown Threat," *New York Times*, December 18, 2018.

114. Erica Werner, Damian Paletta, and Mike DeBonis, "Trump Tells Lawmakers He Won't Sign deal to Avert Shutdown, Demands Funds for Border Security," *Washington Post*, December 20, 2018.

115. Alberta, *American Carnage*, 573–74. See also Davis and Shear, *Border Wars*, 351.

116. Donald J. Trump (@realDonaldTrump), "The Democrats, whose votes we need in the Senate, will probably vote against Border Security and the Wall even

though they know it is DESPERATELY NEEDED. If the Dems vote no, there will be a shutdown that will last for a very long time. People don't want Open Borders and Crime!" Twitter, December 21, 2018, 6:24 a.m., https://twitter.com /realdonaldtrump/status/1076090986651099136.

117. Donald J. Trump (@realDonaldTrump), "The Democrats now own the shutdown!" Twitter, December 21, 2018, 9:07 a.m., https://twitter.com/realdonaldtrump /status/1076132028888825857.

118. James Hohmann, "Five Implications of Trump's Oval Office Clash with Pelosi and Schumer over the Border Wall," *Washington Post*, December 12, 2019; Annie Karni and Sheryl Gay Stolberg, "Trump Offers Temporary Protections for 'Dreamers' in Exchange for Wall Funding, *New York Times*, January 19, 2019.

119. "Trump Rejects Potential Shutdown Compromise as He Prepares to Meet Congressional Leaders," *New York Times* News Service, January 2, 2019.

120. Julie Hirschfeld Davis and Michael Tackett, "Trump and Democrats Dig In After Talks to Reopen Government Go Nowhere," *New York Times*, January 2, 2019.

121. Emily Cochrane, "White House Signals Retreat on Shutdown Threat," *New York Times*, December 18, 2018; Michael Tackett and Julie Hirschfeld Davis, "White House Considers Using Storm Aid Funds as a Way to Pay for the Border Wall," *New York Times*, January 10, 2019; Julie Hirschfeld Davis, "Collapse of Two Plans to End Shutdown Propels Urgent Negotiations," *New York Times*, January 24, 2019; John Wagner, Erica Werner, and Josh Dawsey, "Trump Says He Is Not Looking to Declare a National Emergency 'Right Now' for Border Wall, Urges Democrats to Vote Again on Funding," *Washington Post*, January 11, 2019.

122. "Remarks by President Trump on the Government Shutdown," January 25, 2019, White House Transcript, White House, Washington, DC.

123. Seung Min Kim, Erica Werner, and Josh Dawsey, "Trump Threatens Shutdown of 'Months or Even Years' over Border Wall, Says He Could Declare National Emergency to Get It Built," *Washington Post*, January 4, 2019.

124. Nakamura and Kim, "'He's a Gut Politician.'"

125. Lamar Alexander, "Trump Could Reopen the Government and Build a Lasting Legacy All at Once," *Washington Post*, January 2, 2019.

126. Quoted in Davis and Haberman, "Mercurial Trump Has Made Path."

127. Davis and Haberman, "Mercurial Trump Has Made Path"; Davis and Shear, *Border Wars*, 359.

128. Felicia Sonmez, "GOP Senator: Trump Should Be 'Specific and Reliable' like Obama in Border Wall Talks," *Washington Post*, January 2, 2019; Davis and Tackett, "Trump and Democrats Dig In"; "Trump Rejects Potential Shutdown Compromise."

129. Josh Dawsey and Seung Min Kim, "Trump Proves an Enigmatic Negotiator as Government Shutdown Continues with No End in Sight," *Washington Post*, January 3, 2019.

130. Tackett and Davis, "White House Considers Using Storm Aid Funds."

131. Davis and Tackett, "Trump and Democrats Dig In"; Dawsey and Kim, "Trump Proves an Enigmatic Negotiator"; Glenn Thrush, "Mitch McConnell, Never a Grandstander, Learns to Play by Trump's Rules," *New York Times*, April 14, 2019.

132. Quoted in Sheryl Gay Stolberg, "With Deadline Looming, Border Security Talks Face Hurdles in Congress," *New York Times*, January 26, 2019.

133. Philip Rucker, Josh Dawsey, and Seung Min Kim, "Inside Trump's Shutdown Turnaround," *Washington Post*, January 25, 2019.

134. Rucker et al., "Inside Trump's Shutdown Turnaround."

135. "Remarks by President Trump on the Government Shutdown," January 25, 2019, White House transcript, White House, Washington, DC.

136. Ann Coulter (@AnnCoulter), "Good news for George Herbert Walker Bush: As of today, he is no longer the biggest wimp ever to serve as President of the United States," Twitter, January 25, 2019, 1:55 p.m., https://twitter.com/Ann Coulter/status/1088888030901882880.

137. Philip Wegmann, "Either bored or because he was bluffing, Trump blinks on State of the Union," *Washington Examiner*, January 24, 2019.

138. Peter Wehner (@Peter_Wehner), "In the showdown with Nancy Pelosi, Trump's been exposed as pitifully weak, all bluster, a pathetic negotiator. Pelosi rolled him in every way. Egged on by right wingers, the whole thing was buffoonish from start to finish. *This* is how Trump's Art of the Deal works in real life," Twitter, January 25, 2019, 3:52 p.m., https://twitter.com/Peter_Wehner/status /1088917546772938759.

139. Nate Silver, "How President Trump Is Like A Terrible Poker Player," *Five ThirtyEight*, January 28, 2019, https://fivethirtyeight.com/features/how-president -trump-is-like-a-terrible-poker-player/.

140. Emily Cochrane, "Pelosi Says She Will Back a Bipartisan Border Deal, Putting the Onus on Trump," *New York Times*, February 6, 2019.

141. Quoted in Erica Werner, Seung Min Kim, and John Wagner, "Trump Predicts Failure by Congressional Committee Charged with Resolving Border Stalemate," *Washington Post*, January 31, 2019.

142. Donald J. Trump (@realDonaldTrump), "House votes on controversial FISA ACT today. This is the act that may have been used, with the help of the discredited and phony Dossier, to so badly surveil and abuse the Trump Campaign by the previous administration and others?" Twitter, January 11, 2018, 6:33 a.m., https://twitter.com/realdonaldtrump/status/951431836030459905.

143. Eileen Sullivan, Nicholas Fandos, and Charlie Savage, "House Rejects Limits on Surveillance Program After Trump Roils Debate," *New York Times*, January 11, 2018; Ashley Parker, Philip Rucker, and Josh Dawsey, "Trump's 'Ping-Pong' on Surveillance Law Sets Off a 101-Minute Scramble," *Washington Post*, January 11, 2018.

144. Parker et al., "'Negotiating with Jell-O'"; Thomas Kaplan, "Trump Upsets Republican Strategy to Avoid Shutdown," *New York Times*, January 18, 2018; Mike DeBonis, Ed O'Keefe, and Elise Viebeck, "Trump Tweets Create Confusion for Republicans Trying To Avert Government Shutdown," *Washington Post*, January 18, 2018.

145. Quoted in Amber Phillips, "Why Trump's Attempt to Blame Democrats for Ending DACA Is Falling Flat," *Washington Post*, April 2, 2018.

146. Michael D. Shear, "Trump's Apparent Embrace of Gun Control Measures Stuns Lawmakers," *New York Times*, February 28, 2018.

147. Josh Dawsey, John Wagner, and Seung Min Kim, "Trump Claims Strong Congressional Support for Strengthening Background Checks for Gun Buys, at Odds with GOP Statements," *Washington Post*, August 9, 2019.

148. Quoted in Carl Hulse, "Trump's Waffling on Gun Control Confuses Legislative Picture," *New York Times*, August 21, 2019.

149. Quoted in Tom Rogan, "Mick Mulvaney: OK If Tax Reform Increases Deficit," *Washington Examiner*, May 31, 2017.

150. Seung Min Kim, "'No. Did He Do That?' Republicans Chafe at Trump's Trade Policies but Are Reluctant to Confront Him," *Washington Post*, April 19, 2018.

151. Donald J. Trump (@realDonaldTrump), "On the Iraq War Resolution being voted on tomorrow in the House of Representatives [*sic*], we are down to 5000 soldiers, and going down, and I want everyone, Republican and Democrat, to vote their HEART!" Twitter, January 29, 2020, 9:33 a.m., https://twitter.com/realDonald Trump/status/1222543172192129024; "Nancy Pelosi wants Congress to take away authority Presidents use to stand up to other countries and defend AMERICANS. Stand with your Commander in Chiefs!" Twitter, January 29, 2020, 5:59 p.m., https://twitter.com/realDonaldTrump/status/1222670731080863745.

152. Richard E. Neustadt, *Presidential Power: The Politics of Leadership* (New York: Wiley, 1960), 65.

153. Donald J. Trump, with Tony Schwartz, *Trump: The Art of the Deal* (New York: Random House, 1987), 35.

154. Quoted in Philip Rucker, Robert Costa and Ashley Parker, "Who's Afraid of Trump? Not Enough Republicans—at Least for Now," *Washington Post*, June 27, 2017.

155. Mike DeBonis, Robert Costa, and Ed O'Keefe, "GOP Health-Care Bill: House Republican Leaders Abruptly Pull Their Rewrite of the Nation's Health-Care Law," *Washington Post*, March 24, 2917.

156. Sherman and Palmer, *The Hill to Die On*, 50, 165.

157. Robert Costa, Ashley Parker, and Philip Rucker, "The 'Closer'? The Inside Story of How Trump Tried—and Failed—to Make a Deal on Health Care," *Washington Post*, March 24, 2017; Maggie Haberman and Robert Pear, "After Halting Start, Trump Plunges Into Effort to Repeal Health Law," *New York*

Times, March 9, 2017; Glenn Thrush and Maggie Haberman, "Inspiring Little Fear in Senators, Trump Struggles to Sell Health Bill*," New York Times*, July 20, 2017.

158. Sherman and Palmer, *The Hill to Die On*, 84.

159. See, e.g., Edwards, *Predicting the Presidency*, 49–51, 189–94.

160. Costa et al., "The 'Closer'?" But see Sherman and Palmer, *The Hill to Die On*, 169.

161. Costa et al., "The 'Closer'?"; David Weigel, Kelsey Snell, and Robert Costa, "Trump to GOP Critics of Health Care Bill: 'I'm Gonna Come after You,'" *Washington Post*, March 21, 2017. See also Alberta, *American Carnage*, 439.

162. DeBonis et al., "GOP Health-Care Bill"; Julie Hirschfeld Davis, Robert Pear, and Thomas Kaplan, "Trump Tells G.O.P. It's Now or Never, Demanding House Vote on Health Bill," *New York Times,* March 23, 2017.

163. Alberta, *American Carnage*, 440; Sherman and Palmer, *The Hill to Die On*, 85.

164. Sean Sullivan, Robert Costa, and Kelsey Snell, "Trump Joins the Effort to Pass a Health-Care Bill, but another GOP Senator Is Opposed," *Washington Post*, June 23, 2017.

165. Robert Costa and Sean Sullivan, "The Trump-McConnell Bond Is Being Tested. So Is the GOP Agenda," *Washington Post*, June 27, 2017; Sherman and Palmer, *The Hill to Die On*, 143.

166. Glenn Thrush and Jonathan Martin, "On Senate Health Bill, Trump Falters in the Closer's Role," *New York Times*, June 27, 2017; Jonathan Martin and Glenn Thrush, "As Trump's Tactics Fall Short, Pence Takes Lead on Health Care Bill," *New York Times,* June 27, 2017; Rucker et al., "Who's Afraid of Trump?"

167. Matt Flegenheimer, Jonathan Martin, and Jennifer Steinhauer, "Behind Legislative Collapse: An Angry Vow Fizzles for Lack of a Viable Plan," *New York Times*, July 28, 2017.

168. Sean Sullivan, Juliet Eilperin, and Kelsey Snell, "Senate GOP Effort to Unwind the ACA Collapses," *Washington Post*, September 25, 2017.

169. Karoun Demirjian and Philip Rucker, "Trump Calls Senator Investigating His Son's Russia Contacts about . . . Ethanol," *Washington Post*, August 30, 2017.

170. Quoted in Julie Hirschfeld Davis and Jonathan Martin, "At Alabama Rally, Trump Toggles Between Republican Loyalists," *New York Times*, September 22, 2017.

171. Haberman and Pear, "After Halting Start"; Weigel et al., "Trump to GOP Critics of Health Care Bill."

172. Mike DeBonis, "Trump Praises Spending Earmarks, and Capitol Hill Again Erupts in Debate," *Washington Post*, January 9, 2018; Paul Kane, "Trump Embraces Earmarks, but Don't Count on a Similar Hug from GOP Congress," *Washington Post*, January 10, 2018.

173. See, e.g., Davis and Haberman, "Mercurial Trump Has Made Path."

174. Donald J. Trump (@realDonaldTrump), "Tomorrow, the House will vote on a strong Farm Bill, which includes work requirements. We must support our

Nation's great farmers!" Twitter, May 17, 2018, 5:14 p.m., https://twitter.com/real
DonaldTrump/status/997238932311068674.

175. Quoted in Sean Sullivan and Elise Viebeck, "Corker Says White House
Should Stay Out of Tax Debate; Trump Fires Back with Insult," *Washington Post*,
October 24, 2017.

176. Rucker et al., "The Great Dealmaker?"

177. Sherman and Palmer, *The Hill to Die On*, 150–51, 153.

178. Carl Hulse, "For McConnell, Health Care Failure Was a Map to Tax Success," *New York Times*, December 3, 2107.

179. Sherman and Palmer, *The Hill to Die On*, 150–51, 171.

180. Hulse, "For McConnell, Health Care Failure Was a Map to Tax Success";
Mike DeBonis, Erica Werner, and Damian Paletta, "Senate Republican Tax Plan
Clears Hurdle with Help from Two Key GOP Holdouts," *Washington Post*, No-
vember 28, 2017.

181. Paletta et al., "On Taxes, Trump Is an Eager Salesman."

182. Rucker et al., "The Great Dealmaker?"

183. See Kevin Robillard, "Here's The White House Questionnaire for GOP
Candidates Who Want Trump's Backing," *HuffPost*, April 26, 2018.

184. Alan Abramowitz and Costas Panagopoulos, "Trump on the Trail: Assessing the Impact of Presidential Campaign Visits on Voting Behavior in the 2018
Midterm Elections," *Presidential Studies Quarterly* 50 (September 2020): https://
doi.org/10.1111/psq.12664.

185. Philip Bump, "Trump's Late-Election Rallies Weren't the Boon the White
House Insists They Were," *Washington Post*, November 15, 2018.

186. Seung Min Kim, Rachael Bade, and Josh Dawsey, "Trump Opens Up
Camp David as an 'Adult Playground' to Woo GOP Lawmakers during Impeachment," *Washington Post*, November 22, 2019. See also Katie Rogers, "Movie
Nights, Camp David and Cable Messaging: A White House Impeachment Playbook," *New York Times*, December 11, 2109.

187. Donald J. Trump (@realDonaldTrump), "If you want to get money into
the hands of people quickly & efficiently, let them have the full money that they
earned, APPROVE A PAYROLL TAX CUT until the end of the year, December 31. Then you are doing something that is really meaningful. Only that will
make a big difference!" Twitter, March 13, 2020, 7:30 a.m., https://twitter.com/real
DonaldTrump/status/1238442385048305664.

188. Sheryl Gay Stolberg and Jim Tankersley, "Talks Begin on Stimulus Plan as
Trump Plays Down Virus Threat," *New York Times*, March 10, 2020; Erica Wer-
ner, Josh Dawsey, Seung Min Kim, and Robert Costa, "Trump Administration,
Congress at Odds as They Collide on Coronavirus Economic Plans," *Washington
Post*, March 10, 2020; Erica Werner, Mike DeBonis, Paul Kane, and Jeff Stein,
"House Will Vote Friday on Coronavirus Relief Bill, Pelosi Says—with or without
Trump's Backing," *Washington Post*, March 14, 2020; Jim Tankersley and Emily

Cochrane, "House Passes Coronavirus Relief after Democrats Strike Deal with White House," *New York Times*, March 13, 2020; Alan Rappeport, "With Echoes of 2008, Mnuchin and Pelosi Hammer Out a Rescue Deal," *New York Times*, March 13, 2020.

189. Quoted in Ani Ucar, "Ann Coulter Warns Trump: 'You're Dead, Dead, Dead,' If You Don't Build the Border Wall," Vice News, January 16, 2019.

Chapter Eight

1. Bob Woodward and Robert Costa, "Transcript: Donald Trump Interview with Bob Woodward and Robert Costa," *Washington Post*, April 2, 2016.

2. See Christopher Ingraham, "Trump Attacks Republicans on Twitter, but Democrats? Not So Much," *Washington Post*, August 25, 2017.

3. Quoted in Max Farrand, ed., "CCCLXVII, Jared Sparks: Journal, April 19, 1830," *The Records of the Federal Convention of 1787*, vol. 3, rev. ed. (New Haven, CT: Yale University Press, 1966), 479.

4. James M. Curry and Frances E. Lee, "Non-Party Government: Bipartisan Lawmaking and Party Power in Congress," *Perspectives on Politics* 17 (March 2019): 47–65.

5. Curry and Lee, "Non-Party Government."

6. "Trump Attacks McConnell, Ryan over Debt Ceiling," *Politico*, August 24, 2017, https://www.politico.com/story/2017/08/24/trump-mcconnell-paul-ryan-debt-ceiling-241976.

7. Julie Hirschfeld Davis, "Trump Widens Rift with Congress as Critical Showdowns Loom," *New York Times*, August 23, 2017.

8. Philip Ricker and Damian Paletta, "Escalating Feud, Trump Blames McConnell and Ryan for Upcoming 'Mess' on Debt Ceiling," *Washington Post*, August 24, 2017.

9. "Conservatives Mount Opposition to Trump's Deal with Democrats, but Fail to Stop It in the Senate," *Washington Post*, September 7, 2017; Ryan Lizza, "How Democrats Rolled Trump on the Debt Ceiling," *New Yorker*, September 7, 2017; Amber Phillips, "Paul Ryan: A Short-term Debt Ceiling Hike is 'Disgraceful.' Trump: 'Let's Do It.'" *Washington Post*, September 6, 2017.

10. "Press Gaggle by Deputy Press Secretary Lindsay Walters en route Bismarck, ND," *Air Force One*, September 6, 2017.

11. Peter Baker and Sheryl Gay Stolberg, "Energized Trump Sees Bipartisan Path, At Least for Now," *New York Times*, September 7, 2017.

12. Baker and Stolberg, "Energized Trump Sees Bipartisan Path."

13. Frances Lee, "This Is How Trump Turned the Politics of the Debt Ceiling Upside Down," *Washington Post*, September 10, 2017.

14. Ashley Parker and Philip Rucker, "'Trump Betrays Everyone': The President Has a Long Record as an Unpredictable Ally," *Washington Post*, September 9, 2017.

15. Kelsey Snell, "Nancy Pelosi Isn't Apologizing to Democrats for Cutting a Deal with Trump," *Washington Post*, September 8, 2017.

16. Carl Hulse, "McConnell Says Democrats' Glee on Debt Limit Deal Was Premature," *New York Times*, September 11, 2017.

17. Baker and Stolberg, "Energized Trump Sees Bipartisan Path."

18. Jenna Johnson, Mike DeBonis, and David Nakamura, "At Pelosi's Request, Trump Tweets 'No Action' Against DACA Recipients for Six Months," *Washington Post*, September 7, 2017.

19. Peter Baker, "Trump Lashes Out at Congressional Republicans' 'Death Wish,'" *New York Times*, September 8, 2017.

20. Donald J. Trump (@realDonaldTrump), "The approval process for the biggest Tax Cut & Tax Reform package in the history of our country will soon begin. Move fast Congress!" Twitter, September 13, 20176:28 a.m., https://twitter.com/realDonaldTrump/status/907928888587808768.

21. Paul Kane, Ed O'Keefe, and Ashley Parker, "With Little to Lose, Democrats Cautiously Share the Driver's Seat with Trump," *Washington Post*, September 16, 2017.

22. Ashley Parker and Robert Costa, "'A New Strategy' for Trump? Democrats Cautious but Encouraged by Fresh Outreach," *Washington Post*, September 13, 2017.

23. Maggie Haberman, "Trump to Dine Wednesday Night with Congress's Top Democrats," *New York Times*, September 13, 2017; Ed O'Keefe and David Nakamura, "Trump, Top Democrats Agree to Work on Deal to Save 'Dreamers' from Deportation," *Washington Post*, September 13, 2017; Parker and Costa "'A New Strategy' for Trump?"

24. Maggie Haberman and Glenn Thrush, "Why Did Trump Work Again with Democrats? 'He Likes Us,' Schumer Says," *New York Times*, September 14, 2017.

25. John Wagner and Sean Sullivan, "Trump publicly praises Indiana Democrat he recently attacked as 'Sleepin' Joe,'" *Washington Post*, May 30, 2018.

26. Sean Sullivan, "'It's Obscene': GOP Candidate Seethes as Trump Embraces Democratic Senator," *Washington Post*, June 11, 2018.

27. Michael Barbaro, "Trump's New Prom Date: Democrats," *New York Times*, September 8, 2017.

28. Parker and Rucker, "'Trump Betrays Everyone.'"

29. Michael D. Shear, "White House Makes Hard-Line Demands for Any 'Dreamers' Deal," *New York Times*, October 8, 2017; David Nakamura, "Trump Administration Releases Hard-Line Immigration Principles, Threatening Deal on 'Dreamer,'" *Washington Post*, October 8, 2017.

30. Shear, "White House Makes Hard-Line Demands"; Nakamura, "Trump Administration Releases Hard-Line Immigration Principles."

31. Yamiche Alcindor, "After White House Issues Demands, Hopes for an Immigration Deal Dim, *New York Times*, October 9, 2017; Ed O'Keefe and David Nakamura, "If Trump Doesn't Deal on DACA, Some Democrats Threaten a

Government Shutdown," *Washington Post*, October 9, 2017; Ed O'Keefe, "Nancy Pelosi Won't Rule Out Voting Against Spending Bills to Strike DACA Deal," *Washington Post*, October 9, 2017.

32. Donald J. Trump (@realDonaldTrump), "I called Chuck Schumer yesterday to see if the Dems want to do a great HealthCare Bill. ObamaCare is badly broken, big premiums. Who knows!" Twitter, October 7, 2017, 7:17 a.m., https://twitter.com/realDonaldTrump/status/916638685914951680.

33. Mark Landler, "Schumer Says He Rebuffed Another Offer from Trump on Health Care," *New York Times*, October 7, 2017; Philip Rucker, "Trump Says He Called Schumer to Broker Deal with Democrats for 'a Great Health Care Bill,'" *Washington Post*, October 7, 2017.

34. Thomas Kaplan and Robert Pear, "End to Health Care Subsidies Puts Congress in a Tight Spot," *New York Times*, October 13, 2017.

35. Mike DeBonis and Ed O'Keefe, "Trump's Obamacare Attack Heralds New Health-Care Battles on Capitol Hill," *Washington Post*, October 13, 2017.

36. Michael S. Schmidt and Michael D. Shear, "Trump Says Russia Inquiry Makes U.S. 'Look Very Bad,'" *New York Times*, December 28, 2017.

37. Julie Hirschfeld Davis and Binyamin Applebaum, "Trump in Missouri Lays Groundwork for Tax Overhaul but Offers No Details," *New York Times*, August 30, 2017.

38. Donald Trump, "Remarks by President Trump on Tax Reform," White House Press Release, September 6, 2017, White House, Washington, DC.

39. Damian Paletta and Ed O'Keefe, "Trump, Red State Democrats Warily Approach Each Other on Tax Cuts," *Washington Post*, October 16, 2017.

40. Ashley Parker and Ed O'Keefe, "Trump to Host Six Senators from Both Parties for White House Dinner," *Washington Post*, September 11, 2017; Parker and Costa "'A New Strategy' for Trump?"

41. Alan Rappeport, "Trump Goes All in on a Tax Overhaul Whose Details Remain Unwritten," *New York Times*, September 13, 2017; Parker and Costa "'A New Strategy' for Trump?"

42. Michael Tackett, "How Does a Democrat Run for Re-Election in a Trump State? Very Carefully," *New York Times*, October 20, 2017; Julie Hirschfeld Davis and Alan Rappeport, "Trump Proposes the Most Sweeping Tax Overhaul in Decades," *New York Times*, September 27, 2017; John Wagner, "Trump Travels to Indiana to Sell His Tax Plan but Leaves His Usual Zeal at Home," *Washington Post*, September 27, 2017; Damian Paletta, Robert Costa, and Philip Rucker, "On Taxes, Trump Is an Eager Salesman—but the Policy Action is on Capitol Hill," *Washington Post*, October 27, 2017.

43. Tackett, "How Does a Democrat Run for Re-Election?"

44. Paletta and O'Keefe, "Trump, Red State Democrats."

45. Donald J. Trump (@realDonaldTrump), "The Democrats will only vote for Tax Increases. Hopefully, all Senate Republicans will vote for the largest Tax Cuts

in U.S. history," Twitter, October 18,2017, 5:38 a.m., https://twitter.com/realDonald
Trump/status/920599916371693568.

46. John Wagner and Damian Paletta, "Hours after Trashing Democrats on
Taxes, Trump Says He Wants Their Help on a Tax Bill," *Washington Post*, October 18,
2017.

47. Ed O'Keefe, "Democrats to Huddle with White House Officials on Tax
Reform Tuesday," *Washington Post*, November 6, 2017.

48. Jake Sherman and Anna Palmer, *The Hill to Die On: The Battle for Congress and the Future of Trump's America* (New York: Crown, 2019), 152, 163.

49. "Remarks by President Trump in Press Conference after Midterm Elections," White House transcript, November 7, 2018.

50. "Remarks by President Trump in Press Conference after Midterm Elections."

51. Sherman and Palmer, *The Hill to Die On*, 394.

52. Katie Rogers, "Trump Said He Wanted to Work with Democrats on Surprise Medical Bills. Then He Attacked Democrats," *New York Times*, May 9, 2019.

53. Erica Wagner and Damian Paletta, "Trump Scrambles to Salvage NAFTA
Rewrite, Courting Democrats and Trying to Tamp Down GOP Fury," *Washington
Post*, May 1, 2019; Ana Swanson and Emily Cochrane, "Trump's Trade Deal Steals
a Page From Democrats' Playbook," *The New York Times*, December 1, 2019.

54. "Remarks by President Trump on the United States-Mexico-Canada Agreement," October 1, 2018, White House transcript, White House, Washington, DC.

55. Ashley Parker and Josh Dawsey, " 'The Grand Finale': Inside Trump's Push
to Rack Up Political Victories as Impeachment Looms," *Washington Post*, December 14, 2019; Emily Cochrane, Ana Swanson and Jim Tankersley, "How a
Trump Trade Pact Won Over Democrats," *New York Times*, December 19, 2019.

56. Quotes in Parker and Dawsey, " 'The Grand Finale.' "

57. Ana Swanson and Emily Cochrane, "Trump's Trade Deal Steals a Page
from Democrats' Playbook," *The New York Times*, December 1, 2019.

58. Quotes from Seung Min Kim and Jeff Stein, "With USMCA and Parental
Leave, Democrats Say They Won Big Concessions from Trump," *Washington Post*,
Dec. 10, 2019.

59. Cochrane et al., "How a Trump Trade Pact Won Over Democrats."

60. Quoted in Emily Cochrane, "Senate Passes Revised NAFTA, Sending Pact
to Trump's Desk," *New York Times*, January 16, 2020.

61. Donald J. Trump (@realDonaldTrump), "If you want to get money into
the hands of people quickly & efficiently, let them have the full money that they
earned, APPROVE A PAYROLL TAX CUT until the end of the year, December 31. Then you are doing something that is really meaningful. Only that will
make a big difference!" Twitter, March 13, 2020, 7:30 a.m., https://twitter.com/real
DonaldTrump/status/1238442385048305664.

62. "Remarks by President Trump, Vice President Pence, and Members of the
Coronavirus Task Force in Press Briefing," White House transcript, April 8, 2020.

63. Donald J. Trump (@realDonaldTrump), "Crazy 'Nancy Pelosi, you are a weak person. You are a poor leader. You are the reason America hates career politicians, like yourself.' @seanhannity She is totally incompetent & controlled by the Radical Left, a weak and pathetic puppet. Come back to Washington and do your job!" Twitter, April 16, 2020, 8:33 a.m., https://twitter.com/realDonald Trump/status/1250779261595783168; "Nervous Nancy is an inherently 'dumb' person. She wasted all of her time on the Impeachment Hoax. She will be overthrown, either by inside or out, just like her last time as 'Speaker'. Wallace & @FoxNews are on a bad path, watch!" Twitter, April 19, 11:58 a.m., https://twitter.com/real DonaldTrump/status/1251918194639548417.

64. Carl Hulse, "In Stimulus Talks, McConnell Is Outside the Room and in a Tight Spot," *New York Times*, August 5, 2020.

65. Quoted in Erica Werner, Seung Min Kim, and Jeff Stein, "Rocky Rollout for GOP Coronavirus Bill as McConnell Disavows Key White House Ask, Multiple Republicans Revolt," *Washington Post*, July 28, 2020.

66. Quoted in Werner, Kim, and Stein, "Rocky Rollout for GOP Coronavirus Bill."

67. Hulse, "In Stimulus Talks, McConnell Is Outside the Room and in a Tight Spot."

68. Interview with Chris Wallace on *Fox News Sunday*, Fox News, July 19, 2020.

69. Donald J. Trump (@realDonaldTrump), "The Democrats have stated strongly that they won't approve a Payroll Tax Cut (too bad!). It would be great for workers. The Republicans, therefore, didn't want to ask for it. Dems, as usual, are hurting the working men and women of our Country!" Twitter, July 23, 2020, 11:09 a.m., https://twitter.com/realdonaldtrump/status/1286332695023431683.

70. Quoted in Katie Rogers and Emily Cochrane, "'I Just Don't Get It': Republicans Balk at Funding F.B.I. Building in Virus Bill," *New York Times*, July 28, 2020.

71. Quoted in Werner, Kim, and Stein, "Rocky Rollout for GOP Coronavirus Bill."

72. Quoted in Morgan Chalfant, "Trump Says Republicans Criticizing FBI Money Should 'Go Back to School and Learn," *The Hill*, July 29, 2020.

73. Maggie Haberman, Emily Cochrane and Jim Tankersley, "With Jobless Aid Expired, Trump Sidelines Himself in Stimulus Talks," *New York Times*, August 3, 2020.

74. Quoted in Haberman, Cochrane and Tankersley, "With Jobless Aid Expired."

75. "Remarks by President Trump in Press Briefing, Bedminster, NJ," August 8, 2020, White House transcript, White House, Washington, DC.

76. Donald J. Trump, remarks on *Morning Joe*, interviewed by Joe Scarborough, MSNBC, 7:14 a.m., January 26, 2016.

77. Donald J. Trump, remarks at Republican Primary Debate in Miami, Florida, CNN, March 10, 2016, https://www.cnn.com/2016/03/10/politics/republican -debate-transcript-full-text/.

78. See, e.g., Thomas Kaplan, "'Let Obamacare Fail,' Trump Says as G.O.P. Health Bill Collapses," *New York Times*, July 18, 2017; Robert Costa, "'Hello, Bob': President Trump Called My Cellphone to Say that the Health-Care Bill Was Dead," *Washington Post*, March 24, 2017; Maggie Haberman, "In a Call to the *Times*, Trump Blames Democrats for the Failure of the Health Bill," *New York Times*, March 24, 2017.

79. See e.g., Michael D. Shear, "Trump Blames Democrats and 'Some Republicans' for Stalled Agenda," *New York Times*, October 16, 2017.

80. John Wagner and Jenna Johnson, "'Obamacare Is Death': Trump Urges Republicans to Move Ahead with Health-Care Overhaul," *Washington Post*, July 24, 2017.

81. "Remarks by President Trump on Tax Reform," Blue Ash, Ohio, February 5, 2018. See also John Wagner and Sean Sullivan, "Trump Called for Unity—Then Undermined Himself by Attacking Democrats," *Washington Post*, February 6, 2018.

82. Gregory Korte and Eliza Collins, "Flake Condemns Trump for 'Treasonous' Remark: 'Treason Is Not a Punchline, Mr. President,'" *USA Today*, February 6, 2018.

83. "Press Briefing by Press Secretary Sarah Sanders and DOJ Acting Assistant Attorney General of the Criminal Division John Cronan," White House, February 6, 2018.

84. Quoted in Ashley Parker and Philip Rucker, "55 Minutes at the Table: Trump Tries to Negotiate and Prove Stability," *Washington Post*, January 9, 2018.

85. Quoted in Mike DeBonis, "Trump Again Elevates Shutdown Threat, Even as Tensions Ease on Capitol Hill," *Washington Post*, December 6, 2017.

86. David Weigel, "Trump's Joke about Schumer's 'Fake Tears' Sours an Already Complicated Relationship," *Washington Post*, January 30, 2017.

87. Donald J. Trump (@realDonaldTrump), "DACA has been made increasingly difficult by the fact that Cryin' Chuck Schumer took such a beating over the shutdown that he is unable to act on immigration," Twitter, January 26, 2018, 11:16 a.m., https://twitter.com/realDonaldTrump/status/956938973326098432.

88. Quoted in Peter Baker and Michael M. Grynbaum, "Before Expected Call for Unity, Trump Laced into Democrats at Lunch for TV Anchors," *New York Times*, February 5, 2019.

89. Letter from Donald J. Trump to Charles Schumer, April 2, 2020.

90. John Wagner, "Trump Calls Pelosi a 'Nasty, Vindictive, Horrible Person' after She Said She'd Like to See Him in Prison," *Washington Post*, June 7, 2019.

91. Donald J. Trump (@realDonaldTrump), "Nervous Nancy Pelosi is a disgrace to herself and her family for having made such a disgusting statement, especially since I was with foreign leaders overseas. There is no evidence for such a thing to have been said. Nervous Nancy & Dems are getting Zero work done in Congress. . . . ," Twitter, June 7, 2019, 11:57 a.m., https://twitter.com/realDonaldTrump/status/1137040971311353856.

92. Peter Baker, "Under Fire, Trump Says He Would 'Absolutely' Report Foreign Campaign Help," *New York Times*, June 14, 2019.

93. Donald J. Trump (@realDonaldTrump), "Little Adam Schiff, who is desperate to run for higher office, is one of the biggest liars and leakers in Washington, right up there with Comey, Warner, Brennan and Clapper! Adam leaves closed committee hearings to illegally leak confidential information. Must be stopped!" Twitter, February 5, 2018, 6:39 a.m., https://twitter.com/realDonaldTrump/status/960492998734868480.

94. Donald J. Trump (@realDonaldTrump), "How does Da Nang Dick (Blumenthal) serve on the Senate Judiciary Committee when he defrauded the American people about his so called War Hero status in Vietnam, only to later admit, with tears pouring down his face, that he was never in Vietnam. An embarrassment to our Country!" Twitter, January 28, 2019, 8:46 p.m., https://twitter.com/realDonaldTrump/status/1090078588748087296

95. Tackett, "How Does a Democrat Run for Re-Election?"

96. Wagner and Sullivan, "Trump Publicly Praises Indiana Democrat."

97. Donald J. Trump (@realDonaldTrump), "It would show great weakness if Israel allowed Rep. Omar and Rep. Tlaib to visit. They hate Israel & all Jewish people, & there is nothing that can be said or done to change their minds. Minnesota and Michigan will have a hard time putting them back in office. They are a disgrace!" Twitter, August 15, 2019, 8:57 a.m., https://twitter.com/realDonaldTrump/status/1162000480681287683.

98. Julie Hirschfeld Davis, "White House Twitter Account, in Rare Broadside, Attacks 2 Democratic Senators Over ICE," *New York Times*, July 2, 2018.

99. Karen DeYoung, "Trump Says 'It Doesn't Really Matter if Iranian General Posed an Imminent Threat," *Washington Post*, January 13, 2020.

100. Donald J. Trump (@realDonaldTrump), "At some point, and for the good of the country, I predict we will start working with the Democrats in a Bipartisan fashion. Infrastructure would be a perfect place to start. After having foolishly spent $7 trillion in the Middle East, it is time to start rebuilding our country!" Twitter, December 22, 2017, 7:05 a.m., https://twitter.com/realDonaldTrump/status/944192071535153152.

101. Seung Min Kim, "House Democrats Consider How They Would Balance Investigating and Cooperating with Trump," *Washington Post*, October 23, 2018.

102. Seung Min Kim, Josh Dawsey, and Mike DeBonis, "Trump's Bipartisan Infrastructure Plan Already Imperiled as Mulvaney, GOP Lawmakers Object to Cost," *Washington Post*, May 3, 2019.

103. Peter Baker, "Trump Shifts Gears on Infrastructure, Demanding Trade Come First," *New York Times*, May 21, 2019.

104. Peter Baker, Katie Rogers and Emily Cochrane, "Trump Walks Out on Pelosi and Schumer After 3 Minutes," *New York Times*, May 22, 2019; John Wagner, Rachel Bade, and Mike DeBonis, "Trump Abruptly Ends Infrastructure

Meeting with Democrats after Pelosi Says He Is 'Engaged in a Cover-up,'" *Washington Post*, May 22, 2019; Glenn Thrush and Michael Tackett, "Trump and Pelosi Trade Barbs, Both Questioning the Other's Fitness," *New York Times*, May 23, 2019; John Wagner, "Trump Shares Video that Highlights Verbal Stumbles by Pelosi and Questions her Mental Acuity," *Washington Post*, May 24, 2019.

105. "Remarks by President Trump on Supporting America's Farmers and Ranchers," May 23, 2019, White House transcript, White House, Washington, DC; Linsey McPherson, "'For the Good of the Country': Pelosi Hopes Trump Family or Staff Stage an Intervention," *Roll Call*, May 23, 2019.

106. Baker et al., "Trump Walks Out on Pelosi and Schumer after 3 Minutes."

107. Erica Werner, Sean Sullivan, Mike DeBonis, and Seung Min Kim, "Trump Walks out of Shutdown Negotiations after Democrats Reject Wall Money, Calls Meeting 'Total Waste of Time,'" *Washington Post*, January 9, 2019.

108. Katie Rogers, "Inside the Derailed White House Meeting," *New York Times*, October 16, 2019.

109. Donald J. Trump (@realDonaldTrump), "Nervous Nancy's unhinged meltdown!" Twitter, October 16, 2019, 5:29 p.m., https://twitter.com/realDonaldTrump/status/1184597281808498688.

110. Meagan Flynn, "Pelosi Makes Photo Tweeted by Trump Her Twitter Profile Picture," *Washington Post*, October 17, 2019.

111. Donald J. Trump (@realDonaldTrump), ". . . . @FoxNews @BillHemmer The public is watching and seeing for themselves how unfair this process is. Corrupt politicians, Pelosi and Schiff, are trying to take down the Republican Party. It will never happen, we will take back the House!" Twitter, November 1, 2019, 8:52 a.m., https://twitter.com/realDonaldTrump/status/1190265325511757825.

112. "Remarks by President Trump to the Nation," February 6, 2020, White House transcript, White House, Washington, DC.

113. Sheryl Gay Stolberg, "Trump Lashes Out at Manchin, and He Pushes Back," *New York Times*, February 10, 2020.

114. Jennifer Steinhauer, "With Few Wins in Congress, Republicans Agree on Need to Agree," *New York Times*, August 4, 2017.

115. Tim Alberta, *American Carnage: On the Front Lines of the Republican Civil War and the Rise of President Trump* (New York: HarperCollins, 2019), 565.

116. Annie Karni, Trump Signs Landmark Land Conservation Bill," *Washington Post*, August 4, 2020.

117. Donald J. Trump (@realDonaldTrump), "Republicans must stick together!" Twitter, May 9, 2019, 10:58 p.m., https://twitter.com/realDonaldTrump/status/1126697884953370625; "House Republicans should not vote for the BAD DEMOCRAT Disaster Supplemental Bill which hurts our States, Farmers & Border Security. Up for vote tomorrow. We want to do much better than this. All sides keep working and send a good BILL for immediate signing!" Twitter, May 9, 2019, 6:11 p.m., https://twitter.com/realDonaldTrump/status/1126625647214964737.

118. Colby Itkowitz, "Trump Urges Republicans to Vote against Disaster Relief Bill," *Washington Post*, May 10, 2019.

119. Amber Phillips, "President Trump and Mitch McConnell's Reality-Defying Kumbaya at the White House," *Washington Post*, October 16, 2017; Sean Sullivan, "Trump and McConnell Make Nice in Public, but Specter of Bannon Complicates Relationship," *Washington Post*, October 16, 2017; Carl Hulse, "Trump and McConnell See a Way to Make Conservatives Happy," *New York Times*, October 17, 2017; Michael D. Shear and Sheryl Gay Stolberg, "Trump and McConnell Strive for Comity Amid Rising Tensions," *New York Times*, October 16, 2017.

120. David Weigel, Michael Scherer, and Robert Costa, "McConnell Allies Step Up Attacks against Bannon," *Washington Post*, October 25, 2017.

121. John Wagner, "Trump Said He Granted a Disaster Declaration at the Request of North Carolina's Republican Senator. It Came from the State's Democratic Governor." *Washington Post*, September 4, 2019.

122. See, e.g., Seung Min Kim and Josh Dawsey, "'He just Picks Up': Trump and the Lawmakers He Loves to Talk to on the Phone," *Washington Post*, February 19, 2019; Carl Hulse, "For Trump, Staying on the Line Helps Keep the G.O.P. in Line," *New York Times*, July 27, 2019; Sherman and Palmer, *The Hill to Die On*, 48–49.

123. Glenn Thrush, "Mitch McConnell, Never a Grandstander, Learns to Play by Trump's Rules," *New York Times*, April 14, 2019; Kim and Dawsey, "'He just Picks Up'"; Mike DeBonis, Ed O'Keefe, Erica Werner, and Elise Viebeck, "Funding for Government Lapses as Short-Term Spending Bill Stalls in the Senate," *Washington Post*, January 20, 2018; Baker and Stolberg, "Trump Reaches Out to Make More Deals with Congressional Democrats;" Sherman and Palmer, *The Hill to Die On*, 215–16, 224.

124. Sarah Binder, "Dodging the Rules in Trump's Republican Congress," *Journal of Politics* 80 (October 2018): 1454–1463.

125. Mitch McConnell interview with Sean Hannity on *Hannity*, Fox News, December 12, 2019.

126. Max Boot, "The GOP's Declaration of Moral Bankruptcy," *Washington Post*, March 17, 2019.

127. Mike DeBonis, Kelsey Snell, and Robert Costa, "Trump to GOP Critics of Health Care Bill: 'I'm Gonna Come after You,'" *Washington Post*, March 21, 2017.

128. Donald J. Trump (@realDonaldTrump), "Democrats are smiling in D.C. that the Freedom Caucus, with the help of Club For Growth and Heritage, have saved Planned Parenthood & Ocare!" Twitter, March 26, 2017, 7:21 a.m., https://twitter.com/realDonaldTrump/status/845974102619906048.

129. Sean Sullivan, John Wagner, and Amber Phillips, "Trump Shifts Blame for Health-Care Collapse to Far Right," *Washington Post*, March 26, 2017.

130. John Wagner, Mike DeBonis, and Robert Costa, "Trump Threatens Hardliners as Part of Escalating Republican Civil War," *Washington Post*, March 30, 2017; Glenn Thrush, "'We Must Fight Them': Trump Goes After Conservatives of Freedom Caucus," *New York Times*, March 30, 2017.

131. Karen Tumulty, "Trump Struggles Against Some of the Forces that Helped Get Him Elected," *Washington Post*, March 30, 2017; Jonathan Martin and Jennifer Steinhauer, "Trump's Threats against Freedom Caucus Cause Few Shivers of Fear," *New York Times*, March 30, 2017.

132. Philip Rucker, Robert Costa, and Ashley Parker, "Who's Afraid of Trump? Not Enough Republicans—at Least for Now." *Washington Post*, June 27, 2017.

133. Andrew Clarke, "Trump Is Tweeting Threats at the Freedom Caucus. Good Luck with That," *Washington Post*, April 15, 2017.

134. Nicholas Confessore and Alan Rappeport, "Conservative Split over Import Tax Imperils Trump's Overhaul," *New York Times*, April 1, 2017.

135. Paige Winfield Cunningham, "Freedom Caucus Allies Blast GOP Leadership, White House," *Washington Post*, March 31, 2017.

136. Marc Fisher, "Trump's Tools of Persuasion—from Tough Talk to Polite Cajoling," *Washington Post*, June 7, 2017.

137. Glenn Thrush and Maggie Haberman, "Inspiring Little Fear in Senators, Trump Struggles to Sell Health Bill," *New York Times*, July 20, 2017.

138. Thrush and Haberman, "Inspiring Little Fear in Senators"; Sean Sullivan, Kelsey Snell, and David Nakamura, "Trump Threatens Electoral Consequences for Senators Who Oppose Health Bill," *Washington Post*, July 20, 2017; Marina Fang, "Trump Jokes about Fate of Vulnerable GOP Senator During Health Care Talks," *HuffPost*, July 19, 2017.

139. Thrush and Haberman, "Inspiring Little Fear in Senators."

140. Sullivan et al., "Trump Threatens Electoral Consequences."

141. Glenn Thrush and Jonathan Martin, "On Senate Health Bill, Trump Falters in the Closer's Role," *New York Times*, June 27, 2017; Jonathan Martin and Glenn Thrush, "As Trump's Tactics Fall Short, Pence Takes Lead on Health Care Bill," *New York Times*, June 28, 2017.

142. Rucker et al., "Who's Afraid of Trump?"

143. Donald J. Trump (@realDonaldTrump), "Senator @lisamurkowski of the Great State of Alaska really let the Republicans, and our country, down yesterday. Too bad!" Twitter, July 26, 2017, 6:13 a.m., https://twitter.com/realDonaldTrump/status/890168183079960576.

144. Robert Pear, Thomas Kaplan, and Avantika Chilkoti, "Senate Health Care Vote: Disarray Over Narrow Repeal Measure," *New York Times*, July 27, 2017; Juliet Eilperin, Sean Sullivan, and Kelsey Snell, "Senate GOP Leaders Work to Round Up Votes for More Modest Health-Care Overhaul," *Washington Post*, July 27, 2017; Dino Grandoni, "Messing with Murkowski May Not be Illegal, but It Sure Wasn't Very Smart," *Washington Post*, July 28, 2017.

145. Eric Bradner, "Trump's White House Is Recruiting Primary Challengers against Republican Sen. Jeff Flake," *CNN*, July 18, 2017, https://www.cnn.com/2017/07/17/politics/trump-jeff-flake-arizona-primary/index.html.

146. Paul Kane, "Is President Trump Trying to Beat Republican Jeff Flake Next Year? Flake Doesn't Care," *Washington Post*, July 20, 2017.

147. Donald J. Trump (@realDonaldTrump), "The joint statement of former presidential candidates John McCain & Lindsey Graham is wrong - they are sadly weak on immigration. The two . . . ," Twitter, January 29, 2017, 3:45 p.m., https://twitter.com/realDonaldTrump/status/825822320128303110; ". . . Senators should focus their energies on ISIS, illegal immigration and border security instead of always looking to start World War III," Twitter, January 29, 2017, 3:49 p.m., https://twitter.com/realDonaldTrump/status/825823217025691648.

148. "Remarks by the Vice President at the National Governors Association," July 14, 2017, White House transcript, White House, Washington, DC.

149. Robert Costa, Kelsey Snell and Sean Sullivan, "'It's an Insane Process': How Trump and Republicans Failed on Their Health-care Bill," *Washington Post*, July 18, 2017.

150. Alexander Burns and Jonathan Martin, "Trump and McConnell Locked in a Cold War, Threatening the G.O.P. Agenda," *New York Times*, August 22, 2017.

151. Michael D. Shear and Maggie Haberman, "Defiant, Trump Laments Assault on Culture and Revives a Bogus Pershing Story," *New York Times*, August 17, 2017; David Nakamura and Ed O'Keefe, "Deepening GOP Split, Trump Attacks Republican Senators Graham, Flake as 'Publicity-seeking,' 'Toxic,'" *Washington Post*, August 17, 2017. See also Trump's tweet, Donald Trump, (@realDonaldTrump), "Great to see that Dr. Kelli Ward is running against Flake Jeff Flake, who is WEAK on borders, crime and a non-factor in Senate. He's toxic!" Twitter, August 22, 2017, 5:56 a.m., https://twitter.com/realDonaldTrump/status/898136462385979392.

152. John Wagner, "Trump Takes Issue with McConnell's Accusation that He Had 'Excessive Expectations' for Congress," *Washington Post*, August 9, 2017; John Wagner, Ed O'Keefe, and Paul Kane, "Trump Steps Up Attacks on McConnell for Failure on Health-Care Reform," *Washington Post*, August 10, 2017.

153. Burns and Martin, "Trump and McConnell Locked in a Cold War."

154. Donald J. Trump (@realDonaldTrump), "The only problem I have with Mitch McConnell is that, after hearing Repeal & Replace for 7 years, he failed! That should NEVER have happened!" Twitter, August 24, 2017, 8:42 a.m., https://twitter.com/realDonaldTrump/status/900714982823821313; "I requested that Mitch M & Paul R tie the Debt Ceiling legislation into the popular V.A. Bill (which just passed) for easy approval. They . . . ," Twitter, August 24, 2017, 7:19 a.m., https://twitter.com/realDonaldTrump/status/900694112940290049; "didn't do it so now we have a big deal with Dems holding them up (as usual) on Debt Ceiling approval. Could have been so easy—now a mess!" Twitter, August 24, 2017, 7:25 a.m., https://twitter.com/realDonaldTrump/status/900695448465399809.

155. Donald J. Trump (@realDonaldTrump), "Rand Paul, or whoever votes against Hcare Bill, will forever (future political campaigns) be known as 'the Republican who saved ObamaCare.'" Twitter, September 22, 2017, 5:19 a.m., https://twitter.com/realDonaldTrump/status/911173124976193536.

156. Donald J. Trump (@realDonaldTrump), "A few of the many clips of John McCain talking about Repealing & Replacing O'Care. My oh my has he changed-complete turn from years of talk!" Twitter, September 25, 2017, 8:24 p.m.

157. Julie Hirschfeld Davis, "Trump Laces into McCain Over His Opposition to Health Care Bill," *New York Times*, September 23, 2017; Abby Phillip, "Trump Admonishes McCain Over Opposition to Latest Healthcare Push," *Washington Post*, September 23, 2017; John Wagner, "Trump Pins Blame on McCain as Latest GOP Health-Care Bill Sinks," *Washington Post*, September 25.

158. Donald J. Trump (@realDonaldTrump), "John McCain never had any intention of voting for this Bill, which his Governor loves. He campaigned on Repeal & Replace. Let Arizona down!" Twitter, September 23, 2017, 5:42 a.m., https://twitter.com/realdonaldtrump/status/911541328013676544; "Arizona had a 116% increase in ObamaCare premiums last year, with deductibles very high. Chuck Schumer sold John McCain a bill of goods. Sad," Twitter, September 23, 2017, 5:50 a.m., https://twitter.com/realdonaldtrump/status/911543222731706368; "Democrats are laughingly saying that McCain had a 'moment of courage.' Tell that to the people of Arizona who were deceived. 116% increase!" Twitter, September 23, 2017, 5:20 a.m., https://twitter.com/realdonaldtrump/status/911717004222091264; "Large Block Grants to States is a good thing to do. Better control & management. Great for Arizona. McCain let his best friend L.G. down!" Twitter, September 23, 2017, 5:59 a.m., https://twitter.com/realdonaldtrump/status/911545480651378689.

159. Michael D. Shear, "Trump Blames Democrats and 'Some Republicans' for Stalled Agenda," *New York Times*, October 16, 2017.

160. Donald J. Trump (@realDonaldTrump), "Unless the Republican Senators are total quitters, Repeal & Replace is not dead! Demand another vote before voting on any other bill!" Twitter, July 29, 2017, 3:36 p.m., https://twitter.com/realDonaldTrump/status/891397134662193152.

161. Sean Sullivan, "Can This Marriage Be Saved? Relationship between Trump, Senate GOP Hits New Skids," *Washington Post*, August 1, 2017.

162. Sean Sullivan, "GOP Leaders Say It's Time for Senate to Move on from Health Care," *Washington Post*, July 31, 2017; Matt Flegenheimer and Thomas Kaplan, " 'Time to Move On': Senate G.O.P. Flouts Trump After Health Care Defeat," *New York Times*, August 1, 2017.

163. Sullivan, "Can This Marriage Be Saved?"

164. Flegenheimer and Kaplan, " 'Time to Move On'"; Sullivan, "Can This Marriage Be Saved?"

165. Rema Rahman and John T. Bennett, "GOP Congress Blames White House Chaos for Failures," *Roll Call*, July 28, 2017, https://www.rollcall.com/2017/07/28/gop-congress-blames-white-house-chaos-for-failures/.

166. Burns and Martin, "Trump and McConnell Locked in a Cold War."

167. Donald J. Trump (@realDonaldTrump), "Strange statement by Bob Corker considering that he is constantly asking me whether or not he should run again in

'18. Tennessee not happy!" Twitter, August 25, 2017, 7:25 a.m., https://twitter.com /realDonaldTrump/status/901057864516734978.

168. Aaron Blake, "One GOP Senator's Extraordinarily Dim Assessment of the Trump Administration," *Washington Post*, October 4, 2017; Jonathan Martin and Mark Landler, "Bob Corker Says Trump's Recklessness Threatens 'World War III,'" *New York Times*, October 8, 2017; Philip Rucker and Karoun Demirjian, "Corker Calls White House 'an Adult Day Care Center' in Response to Trump's Latest Twitter Tirade," *Washington Post*, October 8, 2017.

169. Donald J. Trump (@realDonaldTrump), "Senator Bob Corker 'begged' me to endorse him for re-election in Tennessee. I said 'NO' and he dropped out (said he could not win without . . . ," Twitter, October 8, 2017, 8:59 a.m., https:// twitter.com/realDonaldTrump/status/917026789188399105.

170. Jonathan Martin and Mark Landler, "Bob Corker Says Trump's Recklessness Threatens 'World War III,'" *New York Times*, October 8, 2017.

171. Donald J. Trump (@realDonaldTrump), "Bob Corker gave us the Iran Deal, & that's about it. We need HealthCare, we need Tax Cuts/Reform, we need people that can get the job done!" Twitter, October 8, 2017, 3:51 p.m., https://twitter .com/realDonaldTrump/status/917130468025348096.

172. Senator Bob Corker (@SenBobCorker), "It's a shame the White House has become an adult day care center. Someone obviously missed their shift this morning," Twitter, October 8, 2017, 10:13 a.m., https://twitter.com/SenBobCorker /status/917045348820049920.

173. Donald J. Trump (@realDonaldTrump), "The Failing @nytimes set Liddle' Bob Corker up by recording his conversation. Was made to sound a fool, and that's what I am dealing with!" Twitter, October 10, 2017, 7:50 a.m., https://twitter .com/realDonaldTrump/status/917734186848579584.

174. Eileen Sullivan, "Corker 'Couldn't Get Elected Dog Catcher,' Trump Says in Renewed Attack," *New York Times*, October 24, 2017; Sean Sullivan and Elise Viebeck, "Corker Says White House Should Stay Out of Tax Debate; Trump Fires Back with Insult," *Washington Post*, October 24, 2017.

175. Donald J. Trump (@realDonaldTrump), "Bob Corker, who helped President O give us the bad Iran Deal & couldn't get elected dog catcher in Tennessee, is now fighting Tax Cuts. . . . ," Twitter, October 24, 2017, 7:13 a.m., https://twitter .com/realDonaldTrump/status/922798321739161600.

176. Senator Bob Corker (@SenBobCorker), "Same untruths from an utterly untruthful president. #AlertTheDaycareStaff," Twitter, October 24, 2017, 7:48 a.m., https://twitter.com/SenBobCorker/status/922807083526914049.

177. Martin and Landler, "Bob Corker Says Trump's Recklessness Threatens 'World War III.'"

178. Sheryl Gay Stolberg, "Jeff Flake, a Fierce Trump Critic, Will Not Seek Re-Election for Senate," *New York Times*, October 24, 2017.

179. Peter Baker and Jonathan Martin, "Trump's Fight with Corker Jeopardizes His Legislative Agenda," *New York Times*, October 9, 2017. See also Sean

Sullivan, "After Trump-Corker Flap, Hill Republicans Choose a Simple Strategy: Avoidance," *Washington Post*, October 9, 2017.

180. Mike DeBonis, Damian Paletta and Elise Viebeck, "Conflict between Trump and Congress Escalates as Difficult Agenda Looms," *Washington Post*, August 23, 2017.

181. Philip Rucker, Sean Sullivan and Mike DeBonis, "Trump Distances Himself from GOP Lawmakers to Avoid Blame if Agenda Stalls," *Washington Post*, August 24, 2017.

182. Sean Sullivan, "Republican Sen. Jeff Flake: 'Our Presidency Has Been Debased,'" *Washington Post*, May 23, 2018.

183. Donald J. Trump (@realDonaldTrump), "How could Jeff Flake, who is setting record low polling numbers in Arizona and was therefore humiliatingly forced out of his own Senate seat without even a fight (and who doesn't have a clue), think about running for office, even a lower one, again? Let's face it, he's a Flake!" Twitter, June 7, 2018, 8:49 a.m., https://twitter.com/realDonaldTrump/status/1004722061808427008.

184. Mitt Romney (@MittRomney), "By all appearances, the President's brazen and unprecedented appeal to China and to Ukraine to investigate Joe Biden is wrong and appalling," Twitter, October 4, 2019, 11:02 a.m., https://twitter.com/MittRomney/status/1180151213993730049; Donald J. Trump (@realDonaldTrump), "Mitt Romney never knew how to win. He is a pompous "ass" who has been fighting me from the beginning, except when he begged me for my endorsement for his Senate run (I gave it to him), and when he begged me to be Secretary of State (I didn't give it to him). He is so bad for R's!" Twitter, October 5, 2019, 9:17 a.m., https://twitter.com/realdonaldtrump/status/1180487139546546182.

185. Donald J. Trump (@realDonaldTrump), "The Never Trumper Republicans, though on respirators with not many left, are in certain ways worse and more dangerous for our Country than the Do Nothing Democrats. Watch out for them, they are human scum!" Twitter, October 23, 2019, 12:48 p.m., https://twitter.com/realDonaldTrump/status/1187063301731209220.

186. Michael D. Shear, Sheryl Gay Stolberg, and Thomas Kaplan, "G.O.P. Moves to End Trump's Family Separation Policy, but Can't Agree How," *New York Times*, June 19, 2018.

187. Sheryl Gay Stolberg and Michael D. Shear, "Senate Rejects Immigration Plans, Leaving Fate of Dreamers Uncertain," *New York Times*, February 15, 2018.

188. Julie Hirschfeld Davis and Michael D. Shear, *Border Wars: Inside Trump's Assault on Immigration* (New York: Simon and Schuster, 2019), 339–40.

189. Quoted in Alberta, *American Carnage*, 489.

190. Donald J. Trump (@realDonaldTrump), "Paul Ryan, the failed V.P. candidate & former Speaker of the House, whose record of achievement was atrocious (except during my first two years as President), ultimately became a long running lame duck failure, leaving his Party in the lurch both as a fundraiser & leader......," Twitter, July 11, 2019, 10:10 p.m., https://twitter.com/realDonaldTrump/status

/1149516400341348354; ". . . . He had the Majority & blew it away with his poor leadership and bad timing. Never knew how to go after the Dems like they go after us. Couldn't get him out of Congress fast enough!" 10:10 p.m., https://twitter.com /realDonaldTrump/status/1149516403075981314.

191. Amber Phillips, " 'Half-Baked Spurious Nationalism': McCain's Most Biting Recent Criticisms of Trump," *Washington Post*, October 17, 2017.

192. Josh Dawsey, "Trump Rejected Plans for a White House Statement Praising McCain," *Washington Post*, August 26, 2018.

193. Jenna Johnson, "Trump's Grand Promises to 'Very, Very Quickly' Repeal Obamacare Run into Reality," *Washington Post*, July 18, 2017.

194. Quoted in Michael D. Shear and Karen Yourish, "Trump Says He Has Signed More Bills Than Any President, Ever. He Hasn't." *New York Times*, July 17, 2017.

195. Jon R. Bond, "Which Presidents Are Uncommonly Successful in Congress? A Trump Update," *Presidential Studies Quarterly* 49 (December 2019): 898–908.

196. "Presidential Support—Trump Divided, Conquered," *CQ Magazine*, February 12, 2018.

197. "CQ Vote Studies: Presidential Support—Trump's Last Hurrah," *CQ Magazine*, February 25, 2019.

198. Frances E. Lee, "The 115th Congress and Questions of Party Unity in a Polarized Era," *Journal of Politics* 80 (October 2018): 1464–73.

199. See, e.g., " 'Dreamers' Can 'Rest Easy,' " Ryan Says, Promising Congressional Action," *Washington Post*, September 6, 2017; Tory Newmyer, "McConnell Says Trump Needs to Provide Clarity on Health Care," *Washington Post*, October 22, 2017; Nicholas Fandos, "McConnell Signals Willingness to Hold Vote on Health Deal if Trump Approves," *New York Times*, October 22, 2017; Sheryl Gay Stolberg, "Senators and Trump Inch Toward DACA Deal, but a Wall Divides Them," *New York Times*, January 4, 2018; Ed O'Keefe, "Trump Pushes Back on Chief of Staff Claims that Border Wall Pledges 'Uninformed,' " *Washington Post*, January 18, 2018; Paul Kane, "Focus Is on an Audience of One—Trump—to Prevail with House GOP," *Washington Post*, January 27, 2018.

200. Drew DeSilver, "A Productivity Scorecard for the 115th Congress: More Laws than Before, but Not More Substance," Pew Research Center, January 25, 2019.

201. See, e.g., Charles Tiefer, "Why Trump's Brutal Fiscal 2017 Budget Is Already Quietly Dead on Arrival in Congress," *Forbes*, March 30, 2017, https:// www.forbes.com/sites/charlestiefer/2017/03/30/why-the-trump-fy2017-brutal -budget-is-already-quietly-dead-on-arrival-at-congress/#b73e18456da5; Leigh Ann Caldwell, "Lawmakers Declare President Trump's Budget Proposal 'Dead on Arrival,' " *NBC News*, May 23, 2017, https://www.nbcnews.com/politics/congress /lawmakers-declare-president-trump-s-budget-proposal-dead-arrival-n763306; Russell Berman, "All the Trump Budget Cuts Congress Will Ignore," *The At-*

lantic, February 12, 2018, https://www.theatlantic.com/politics/archive/2018/02
/trump-budget-congress/553085/.

202. Sean Hannity, *Hannity*, Fox News, February 11, 2019

203. Quoted in Peter Baker and Maggie Haberman, "Trump Puts Best Face on
Border Deal, as Aides Try to Assuage an Angry Right," *New York Times*, February 13, 2019.

204. Donald J. Trump, (@realDonaldTrump), ". . . . If, at a later date, Congress
wants to update the law, I will support those efforts, but today's issue is BORDER
SECURITY and Crime!!! Don't vote with Pelosi!" Twitter, March 14, 2019, 9:13 a.m.,
https://twitter.com/realdonaldtrump/status/1106196591453577217.

205. Emily Cochrane and Glenn Thrush, "Senate Rejects Trump's Border
Emergency Declaration, Setting up First Veto," *New York Times*, March 14, 2019.

206. Donald J. Trump (@realDonaldTrump), "House Republicans should support the TWO YEAR BUDGET AGREEMENT which greatly helps our Military
and our Vets. I am totally with you!" Twitter, July 25, 2019, 8:00 a.m., https://twitter
.com/realdonaldtrump/status/1154375992938549248.

207. Joseph Tanfani, "Senator Warns Trump There Will Be 'Holy Hell to Pay'
If He Fires Sessions," *Los Angeles Times*, July 27, 2017.

208. Karoun Demirjian, "Senators Unveil Two Proposals to Protect Mueller's
Russia Probe," *Washington Post*, August 3, 2017; Steinhauer, "With Few Wins in
Congress, Republicans Agree on Need to Agree."

209. Shear et al., "G.O.P. Moves to End Trump's Family Separation Policy."

210. S. Res. 607, https://www.govtrack.us/congress/bills/115/sres607/text.

211. Ed Mazza, "Republican Senator Asks If Trump Is Recanting His Oath
of Office," *HuffPost*, October 12, 2017, https://www.huffpost.com/entry/ben-sasse
-trump-oath-of-office_n_59dee081e4b0eb18af062f71.

212. Donald J. Trump (@realDonaldTrump), "So interesting to see "Progressive" Democrat Congresswomen, who originally came from countries whose governments are a complete and total catastrophe, the worst, most corrupt and inept
anywhere in the world (if they even have a functioning government at all), now
loudly. . . . . . and viciously telling the people of the United States, the greatest and
most powerful Nation on earth, how our government is to be run. Why don't they
go back and help fix the totally broken and crime infested places from which they
came. Then come back and show us how. . . ." Twitter, July 14, 2019, 7:57 a.m.,
https://twitter.com/realDonaldTrump/status/1150381395078000643.

213. Sarah Binder, "The Republican Senate Just Rebuked Trump Using the
War Powers Act—for the Third Time. That's Remarkable." *Washington Post*, February 14, 2020.

214. Rahman and Bennett, "GOP Congress Blames White House Chaos for
Failures."

215. "Statement by President Donald J. Trump on Signing the 'Countering
America's Adversaries through Sanctions Act,'" White House, August 2, 2017.

216. Damian Paletta, Erica Werner, and Taylor Telford, "GOP Senators Raise Alarms, Criticize Trump as U.S.-China Trade War Heats Up," *Washington Post*, May 14, 2019.

217. Erica Werner, Seung Min Kim, Damian Paletta, and Mary Beth Sheridan, "GOP Lawmakers Warn White House They'll Try to Block Trump's Mexico Tariffs," *Washington Post*, June 4, 2019.

218. Michael D. Shear and Maggie Haberman, "Mexico Agreed to Take Border Actions Months Before Trump Announced Tariff Deal," *New York Times*, June 8, 2019.

219. "How Republican Lawmakers Responded to Trump's Russian Meddling Denial," *New York Times*, July 16, 2018.

220. Will Hurd, "Trump Is Being Manipulated by Putin. What Should We Do?" *New York Times,* July 19, 2018.

221. Amber Phillips, " 'Disgraceful and 'Tragic' John McCain's Excoriation of Trump on Russia, Annotated," *Washington Post*, July 16, 2018.

222. Alex Ward, "House Republicans Are Trying to Block a Vote on the Yemen War," *Vox*, November 13, 2018, https://www.vox.com/policy-and-politics/2018/11/13/18093236/yemen-war-republicans-khanna-vote-rules.

223. https://www.senate.gov/legislative/LIS/roll_call_lists/roll_call_vote_cfm.cfm?congress=116&session=1&vote=00014.

224. Julian E. Barnes and Helene Cooper, "Trump Discussed Pulling U.S. from NATO, Aides Say amid New Concerns Over Russia," *New York Times*, January 14, 2019.

225. Josh Dawsey, Carol Morello, and John Hudson, White House Scraps Plan to Seek Return of Unspent Foreign Aid," *Washington Post*, August 22, 2019.

226. H. Res. 326, https://www.congress.gov/bill/116th-congress/house-resolution/326/text.

227. H. J. Res. 77, https://www.govtrack.us/congress/bills/116/hjres77/text.

228. Aaron Blake, "4 Trump Nominees Have Gone Down in One Week, and He's Got GOP Senators to Blame," *Washington Post*, December 19, 2017.

229. John Gramlich, "Federal Judicial Picks Have Become More Contentious, and Trump's Are No Exception," Pew Research Center, March 7, 2018.

230. Quoted in Emily Cochrane and Nicholas Fandos, "Trading Concessions on Recovery Plan, Negotiators Set Week's End Deadline for a Deal," *New York Times*, August 4, 2020.

Chapter Nine

1. Patrick Caddell, "Initial Working Paper on Political Strategy," December 10, 1976. Quoted in Sidney Blumenthal, *The Permanent Campaign: Inside the World of Elite Political Operatives* (Boston: Beacon Press, 1980), 39. See also 38–42.

2. See, e.g., Sheryl Gay Stolberg and Michael D. Shear, "Senate Rejects Immigration Plans, Leaving Fate of Dreamers Uncertain," *New York Times*, February 15, 2018.

3. William Shakespeare, *King Lear*, 5.2.11, *The Riverside Shakespeare* (Boston: Houghton Mifflin, 1974),

4. "Remarks by President Trump at Turning Point USA's Teen Student Action Summit 2019," July 23, 2019, White House transcript, White House, Washington, DC.

5. "Remarks by President Trump, Vice President Pence, and Member of the Coronavirus Task Force in Press Briefing," April 13, 2020, White House transcript, White House, Washington, DC.

Index